SKIN, KIN AND CLAN

THE DYNAMICS OF SOCIAL CATEGORIES
IN INDIGENOUS AUSTRALIA

SKIN, KIN AND CLAN

THE DYNAMICS OF SOCIAL CATEGORIES IN INDIGENOUS AUSTRALIA

EDITED BY PATRICK MCCONVELL, PIERS KELLY
AND SÉBASTIEN LACRAMPE

PRESS

Published by ANU Press
The Australian National University
Acton ACT 2601, Australia
Email: anupress@anu.edu.au
This title is also available online at press.anu.edu.au

A catalogue record for this book is available from the National Library of Australia

ISBN(s): 9781760461638 (print)
          9781760461645 (eBook)

This title is published under a Creative Commons Attribution-NonCommercial-NoDerivatives 4.0 International (CC BY-NC-ND 4.0).

The full licence terms are available at creativecommons.org/licenses/by-nc-nd/4.0/legalcode

Cover design and layout by ANU Press. Cover image *Gija Kinship* by Shirley Purdie.

This edition © 2018 ANU Press

Contents

List of Figures vii
List of Tables xi
About the Cover xv
Contributors xvii

1. Introduction: Revisiting Aboriginal Social Organisation 1
   Patrick McConvell
2. Evolving Perspectives on Aboriginal Social Organisation:
   From Mutual Misrecognition to the Kinship Renaissance. 21
   Piers Kelly and Patrick McConvell

PART I People and Place

3. Systems in Geography or Geography of Systems?
   Attempts to Represent Spatial Distributions of Australian
   Social Organisation. 43
   Laurent Dousset
4. The Sources of Confusion over Social and Territorial
   Organisation in Western Victoria. 85
   Raymond Madden
5. Disputation, Kinship and Land Tenure in Western
   Arnhem Land 107
   Mark Harvey

PART II Social Categories and Their History

6. Moiety Names in South-Eastern Australia: Distribution
   and Reconstructed History. 139
   Harold Koch, Luise Hercus and Piers Kelly
7. Patriclan Subsets of the Ashburton River District
   in Western Australia 179
   Peter Sutton

8. The Birds and the Bees: The Origins of Sections
    in Queensland 219
    Patrick McConvell

9. Generic Terms for Subsections ('Skins') in Australia:
    Sources and Semantic Networks 271
    Patrick McConvell and Maïa Ponsonnet

10. The Development of Arandic Subsection Names
    in Time and Space 317
    Harold Koch

PART III Kinship Systems

11. Close–Distant: An Essential Dichotomy in Australian Kinship 363
    Tony Jefferies

12. Asymmetrical Distinctions in Waanyi Kinship Terminology 391
    Mary Laughren

13. Genesis of the Trinity: The Convergent Evolution
    of Trirelational Kinterms 431
    Joe Blythe

Index 473

List of Figures

Figure 1: *Maris Pacifici* showing Terra Australis by Abraham Ortelius (33 x 48 cm; scale: 1:40,000,000), Anvers: Imprimerie Plantinienne, 1589. 45

Figure 2: *Cette terre est dite la région Australe* (This land that is called the Australian region) by Guillaume Le Testu, FO XXXV, Le Havre, 1556 46

Figure 3: The distribution of some system types in Australia following the AustKin database 51

Figure 4: Example of a section system (left) of the Ngaatjatjarra group and of a subsection system (right) of the Warlpiri language 52

Figure 5: Mathews's Aboriginal nations according to similar or identical moiety, section or subsection names (thin lines and numbered areas) and identical system types (shaded lines and large areas). 53

Figure 6: Radcliffe-Brown's vision of the 'Kariera tribe' showing 'local groups' (roman numbers) and associated section couples (letters) 60

Figure 7: Davidson's and Radcliffe-Brown's maps of the distribution of social organisation in Aboriginal Australia as summarised by Yengoyan. 62

Figure 8: Berndt and Berndt's map of the distribution and spread of social organisations 66

Figure 9: An approximate extension of the four-section system according to Mathews, Radcliffe-Brown, Berndt and Berndt and AustKin. 66

Figure 10: One of Mulvaney's maps showing ceremonial exchange, ceremonial centres and home localities of ceremonial participants 68

Figure 11: Peterson's drainage basins. 69

Figure 12: Formal representation of the section system. 73

Figure 13: Map generated from the AustKin database of the distribution of section systems 75

Figure 14: Study area 86

Figure 15: Northern Kakadu – Gunbalanya—languages at time of colonisation 109

Figure 16: Gunmogurrgurr names in the northern Kakadu – Gunbalanya area 120

Figure 17: Matharri-Kararrhu moieties, plus Thura-Yura languages. . . 143

Figure 18: Karnic languages; three moiety sets 145

Figure 19: Makwarra-Kilparra moieties; Paakantyi and Lower Murray languages 150

Figure 20: Bunjil-Waang moieties and Kulin languages 156

Figure 21: Howitt's 1904 map of south-eastern Australia 162

Figure 22: Distribution and spread of moiety name sets 168

Figure 23: Map showing the locations of the Ashburton and Gascoyne rivers of Western Australia 181

Figure 24: Sets of section terms in Australia 225

Figure 25: Social category types in Cape York Peninsula 228

Figure 26: Map of the location of Kuku Yalanji and Guugu Yimidhirr 235

Figure 27: Clans of the Tjungundji 244

Figure 28: Maric languages with sound changes affecting section terms 251

Figure 29: Panoan sections 259

Figure 30: Map of distribution of sections and subsections. 274

Figure 31: The first semantic map for {BREATHE} 277

LIST OF FIGURES

Figure 32: Semantic network of {SUBSECTION} (generic term) for the Australian languages surveyed 279

Figure 33: Map of geographical distribution of subsection colexification 280

Figure 34: Position of 'other social categories' in the 'subsection' semantic network 283

Figure 35: Inadequate (top) and supported (bottom) representation of 'subsection/distinctive aspect of the person/person' colexifications. 284

Figure 36: Conceptual explanation for 'subsection/distinctive aspect of the person' colexifications 284

Figure 37: The 'dermis' colexification cluster 285

Figure 38: The 'smell/taste' colexification cluster. 287

Figure 39: The 'body' colexification cluster..................... 289

Figure 40: The 'head' colexification cluster 291

Figure 41: The 'name' colexification cluster 293

Figure 42: The 'country and times' colexification cluster.......... 294

Figure 43: Suggested chain of motivations for 'at times/country' colexifications. 296

Figure 44: The historical spread of subsections and the generic terms 303

Figure 45: Languages of Central Australia 318

Figure 46: Waanyi ascending harmonic generation kin terms 396

Figure 47: Waanyi ascending and descending harmonic generation kin terms 398

Figure 48: Waanyi pattern of wife bestowal 399

Figure 49: Asymmetrical brother-in-law relationship 400

Figure 50: Pattern of wife exchange between cross-cousins 403

Figure 51: Waanyi and Warlpiri grandparent/child terms compared .. 405

Figure 52: Location of Garrwan languages and their immediate neighbours.. 410

Figure 53: The Murrinhpatha trirelational kinterm *yilamarna* 435

Figure 54: An ordinary Bininj Gunwok kinterm anchored to the addressee (left) and a trirelational kinterm anchored to both speaker and addressee (right). The term also encodes the relationship between speaker and addressee 435

Figure 55: Dual propositus trirelational kinterms 436

Figure 56: Trirelational dyadic terms 437

Figure 57: *Kawumamnge*—(literally) 'the female person that he/she (ego's child) refers to as MoMo' 440

Figure 58: The Murrinhpatha trirelational terms all contain an embedded kinterm that is presented as if being uttered by P_2, the son/daughter of P_1 441

Figure 59: The Murrinhpatha kinchart for a male ego (trirelational kinterms are not included).................. 445

Figure 60: The Murrinhpatha kinchart for a female ego (trirelational kinterms are not included).................. 446

Figure 61: Australian languages for which trirelational kinterms have been attested 453

Figure 62: A video still corresponding to Lily's line 46 in Extract 2 —*Bere, kalemamnge tepala murriny nartwardangu*, 'Right, deaf-one "sister", take it away!' 458

List of Tables

Table 1: Kariyarra (Kariera) section terms. 33

Table 2: Warlpiri subsection system 33

Table 3: Coding systems for social categories 73

Table 4: Examples of social category coding 74

Table 5: 'Wotjobaluk Tribe' 94

Table 6: Western Victorian matrimoiety marriage systems as presented in Dawson (1880) and Howitt (1996 [1904]), compared with a typical section system 95

Table 7: Matry terminologies 111

Table 8: Gunbalanya Bininj Gunwok subsection terminology 112

Table 9: Classification of marriages by Gunbalanya Bininj Gunwok speakers. 116

Table 10: Gunmogurrgurr terminology in the languages of the area . . 118

Table 11: Yigurrumu terminology 122

Table 12: Ways of referring to mother's and mother's mother's country 123

Table 13: Analysis of place names. 128

Table 14: Summary of terminological sets 141

Table 15: Analysis of moiety names in Paakantyi and neighbouring languages. 153

Table 16: Moiety naming sets versus linguistic genetic groups 164

xi

Table 17: Language groups of the Ashburton social organisation district 185

Table 18: The subset members' names 186

Table 19: 'Mate' terms in the region recorded by Austin. 187

Table 20: Bates's totems linked to 'phratry' names 190

Table 21: Austin's record of totemic classes. 192

Table 22: Patriclan subsets and sections 193

Table 23: Bates's unpublished data on marriages. 194

Table 24: Extended Bates data 195

Table 25: Bates's field data on permissible 'phratry' marriages. 197

Table 26: Warlpiri subsections 222

Table 27: Kariera sections. 223

Table 28: Warray sections. 223

Table 29: South-east Cape York Peninsula sections. 230

Table 30: Annan River moieties and sections. 236

Table 31: Pragmatic equivalence of Annan River and Queensland General sections according to Roth and Howitt. 236

Table 32: Annan River sections 237

Table 33: Queensland General section terminology 237

Table 34: Hypothesis about the origin of Annan River sections 241

Table 35: Kuinmerburra, also known as Guwinmal 242

Table 36: North-eastern (rainforest) sections 248

Table 37: Hypothesis about the origin of the Queensland General section system from patrimoiety and country interaction. 249

Table 38: Initial dropping in southern Maric section terms 250

Table 39: Different treatment of initial consonants in Maric section terms 251

Table 40: *r > rt. 253

Table 41: Section system of the Lower Arrernte 319

LIST OF TABLES

Table 42: Subsection system of the Central and Eastern Arrernte . . . 320

Table 43: Subsection system of the Warlpiri (adult terms only). 322

Table 44: Subsection system of the Kaytetye
(including junior terms). 322

Table 45: Arrernte section names according to sources 326

Table 46: Additional Arrernte skin names according to sources 327

Table 47: Anmatyerre skin names. 331

Table 48: Kaytetye (and Warumungu feminine) skin names
according to sources. 334

Table 49: Warumungu skin names according to sources 337

Table 50: Warlmanpa skin names. 338

Table 51: Sources of Arandic skin names 341

Table 52: Examples of words in the three lexical strata 343

Table 53: Hypothetic developments of skin names
if borrowed early 344

Table 54: Warlpiri adult skin names as used by the Anmatyerre 344

Table 55: Junior skin names in Warlpiri, Kaytetye and Western
Anmatyerre 348

Table 56: Waanyi terms for relations in FM class. 401

Table 57: Son-in-law *ngakinburrunyi* relationships. 402

Table 58: Waanyi and Warlpiri affinal and non-affinal
terms compared. 407

Table 59: Waanyi and Warlpiri MM terms compared. 407

Table 60: Waanyi and Garrwa harmonic ascending/descending
generation and affinal terms. 408

Table 61: Warluwarric kin terms. 411

Table 62: Tangkic affinal and harmonic FM and MM terms. 415

Table 63: Spousal terms in two Barkly languages 416

Table 64: Marra and Alawa harmonic generation roots. 419

Table 65: The eight attested Murrinhpatha trirelational terms 442

About the Cover

The image used on the front cover of this book is a reproduction of Shirley Purdie's *Gija Kinship*. Below is Shirley's explanation of the painting in Gija, it was recorded, transcribed and translated by editor Patrick McConvell.

In Gija:

Ngagenyel ganggal Nyaajarri-ngel. Ngagenyel gural Nyawurru-ngel. Ngayin Naangariny-ngage. Ngagenyel wigil Nangalangel ...

Translation:

My mother's mother is Nyaajarri skin. My mother is Nyawurru skin. I am Naangari skin. My daughter is Nangala skin ...

In English:

See that's the skin group that name. This my skin group and this is for my dad and auntie family, and this my mother side ...

The editors thank Shirley Purdie and the Warmun Art Centre for allowing them to use it on the cover of Skin, Kin and Clan.

Contributors

Joe Blythe is an interactional linguist specialising in Australian Indigenous languages. He conducts field research on the Murrinhpatha language of the Northern Territory and on the Gija and Jaru languages from northern Western Australia. He is interested in the relationships between linguistic structure and social action, and what these relationships reveal about social cognition and culture. His research interests include gesture, spatial cognition and language evolution. He is particularly interested in social identities and kinship concepts, particularly as instantiated within everyday conversation, and as acquired by children.

Laurent Dousset is Professor of Anthropology at the Advanced School for Studies in the Social Sciences, Paris (EHESS), and is member of Centre for Research and Documentation on Oceania, Marseilles (CREDO). He has been undertaking research in Aboriginal Australia, in particular in the Western Desert area, for over 20 years, with a particular interest in kinship, social organisation, memories on first-contact situations, as well as social transformations. Since 2008, he has also been working in Vanuatu on political organisations and historical transformations. He has published numerous scientific papers and has written or edited several books.

Mark Harvey is an Associate Professor in Linguistics at the University of Newcastle. He has worked with Aboriginal people from Darwin and its hinterland to record linguistic and cultural materials since 1980. Kinship and land tenure are particular research interests. This includes reconstruction of terminological systems and their precolonial patterns of geographical association. The reconstruction and recording of postcolonial history is another significant research focus. This includes consideration of demographic changes and patterns of shift in residential ranges affecting the indigenous populations of Darwin and its hinterland.

Luise Hercus has been recording Aboriginal languages and writing grammars and dictionaries for over half a century, beginning in Victoria and then continuing into far western New South Wales, north-eastern South Australia, and far west Queensland. What has always mattered most to Luise is listening to and recording the old people when they were speaking in their languages about their own country, their stories and traditions, including kinship, and singing traditional songs.

Tony Jefferies is a linguistic anthropologist with a special interest in Australian prehistory. He has worked in native title, mainly in Queensland. His Masters in Philosophy thesis from the University of Queensland concerned the identity and history of the Guwar language of Moreton Island, south-east Queensland. At present, he is in the process of completing his PhD dissertation at The Australian National University, 'The Australian Late Holocene: The case for demic migration, linguo-ethnicity and higher order social organisation'.

Piers Kelly is a linguistic anthropologist at the Max Planck Institute for the Science of Human History in Jena, Germany. His present research explores graphic codes in small-scale communities: their origins, evolution, pragmatic principles and relationships to social organisation. He has previously worked as an etymologist of Aboriginal words in Australian English for the Australian National Dictionary Centre, and as a linguist with the National Commission on Indigenous People, Philippines.

Harold Koch is a linguist (now retired) at The Australian National University. His linguistic research in Central Australia has included descriptive study of the Kaytetye language and analysis of historical developments in Kaytetye and the other Arandic languages. He has also been involved in the documentation of Aboriginal land claims in the region around Kaytetye traditional territory. Another area of research and supervision has been analysing historical records of languages of south-eastern New South Wales. His recent involvement with the AustKin project entails describing the distribution and prehistory of kinship and social category terms over the whole Australian continent.

Mary Laughren received her doctoral degree in 1973 from the University of Nice, France, for a dissertation on Tyebari, a Senufo language of Côte d'Ivoire. From 1975 to 1993, she was employed by the Northern Territory Department of Education to carry out linguistic research in support of school-based bilingual education programs principally in Warlpiri-speaking communities. She joined the linguistics program at the University of Queensland in 1993, continuing her research on Warlpiri language and culture. Since 2000, she has carried out extensive documentation of the Waanyi language and has been engaged with the Waanyi community in language revitalisation projects. Laughren is currently an honorary senior research fellow in the School of Languages and Cultures at the University of Queensland.

Raymond Madden is a Senior Lecturer in Anthropology at La Trobe University, Melbourne, Australia. He has also worked in the native title area, principally in Western Victoria.

Patrick McConvell is a linguistic anthropologist with special interests in kinship and linguistic prehistory. He has taught anthropology at Charles Darwin and Griffith universities, and is now an adjunct associate professor at The Australian National University and Western Sydney University. He has worked with Australian Aboriginal people especially in the north-central region of the Northern Territory, and the Kimberley and Pilbara regions of Western Australia. A recent publication is *Southern Anthropology – A History of Fison and Howitt's Kamilaroi and Kurnai* (Palgrave-MacMillan, 2015) with historian Helen Gardner.

Maïa Ponsonnet holds a PhD from The Australian National University and is currently a Senior Lecturer at the University of Western Australia. She has expertise in Dalabon and other languages of the Gunwinyguan family, as well as in Kriol. Her research deals in particular with the linguistic expression of internal aspects of the person, such as emotions and intellectual states.

Peter Sutton is an author, anthropologist and linguist who has lived and worked with Aboriginal people since 1969. He is a specialist on Cape York Peninsula and also generally in Aboriginal land tenure, and has acted in some 70 land claim legal cases. He has written or edited 16 books on Indigenous languages, visual arts, land tenure, history and policy. His latest books are *The Politics of Suffering: Indigenous Australia and the end of the Liberal Consensus* (2009) and *Iridescence: The Play of Colours* (2015, co-author Michael Snow). His main current project is a biography of Queensland anthropologist Ursula McConnel.

1
Introduction: Revisiting Aboriginal Social Organisation

Patrick McConvell

This volume presents papers written about Aboriginal Australia for the AustKin project. By way of definition, 'kin' refers to kinship terminology and systems, and related matters of marriage and other behaviour; and 'skin' refers to what is also known as 'social categories' and what earlier anthropologists (e.g. Fison & Howitt 1880) called 'social organisation': moieties, sections, subsections and other similar categories. Kinship terms are 'egocentric' in anthropological parlance and skin terms are 'sociocentric'. Different kinship terms are used depending on the ego (propositus) and who is being referred to. Conversely, skin terms are a property of the person being referred to and the category to which he or she belongs—not of their relationship to someone else. However, membership of a skin category does imply a kinship relationship. For example, I was assigned the skin (subsection) name Jampijina by the Gurindji, which means that I am classified as brother (kinship term *papa*) to other people of Jampijina skin, father to Jangala and Nangala, and so on.

Additionally, a 'clan', known as a 'local descent group', is a group rather than a category such as a skin. Namely, it is a group of people who have common rights and interests in property, which may be intellectual property or, importantly, tracts of land. These rights and interests are generally inherited by descent, from fathers and/or mothers and more distant ancestors (although rights can be transmitted in other ways).

By contrast, people of a skin category are not collective owners of anything: for example, the people of the Jampijina subsection do not have common rights and interests in land. However, there are important connections between 'local organisation' (clan) systems, 'social organisation' (skin) systems (Fison & Howitt 1880) and kinship. This volume aims to distinguish between these three systems and to investigate the connections between them.

Those who have studied the kinship and social organisation systems of Indigenous Australians have been equally astounded by their crystalline beauty and frustrated by their impenetrable complexity. Significantly, those impressed by the mathematical elegance of Indigenous kinship and social organisation systems are often viewing them through the prism of social category systems (skins), such as moieties, sections and subsections. Such social categories abstract away from a complex reality to a more idealised pattern. The more complex of these categorisations are unique to Australia (the eight subsections) or nearly so (the four sections). This strengthens the impression that in Australia we are in the presence of something very special, perhaps even primordial.

In this volume, we bring together papers that deal with the phenomena in a less awe-struck frame of mind and look for patterns of relationship and origin in the variation that we see. Nevertheless, what we are witnessing is indeed a monumental achievement in the social realm of a hugely creative group of cultures on the Australian continent. These cultures have been on the move, creating new solutions to problems of social organisation, rather than merely reproducing a template that was established 50,000 years ago. This volume presents the latest findings on Australian Aboriginal kinship systems and explores the extraordinary constellations of kinship terminologies and social category systems across the continent that are unique to Australia. The recent revival of kinship studies has allowed scholars the fresh advantage of technological and methodological innovations in the field. Systematic comparative approaches—inspired by reconstructive methods in historical linguistics—have combined with database-driven analysis to reopen old questions and generate new ones. Within this volume, panoramic modelling of kinship prehistory and diffusions of terms and systems are set alongside detailed investigations of specific models of social organisation.

Today, the study of Australian kinship is far less ambitious in its aims than it was in the nineteenth century, when field research held forth the promise of unifying biological and social sciences, unlocking the enigma of global prehistory and ultimately validating European claims of cultural supremacy (see Chapter 2 for an overview). However, while nineteenth-century scholars foundered in their misguided efforts to reconcile Australian social organisation with the reigning ideologies of the day, the preliminary questions they grappled with remain relevant almost 150 years after they were first posed. The type and distribution of Australian kinship systems, their patterns of diffusion and change over time, and traditional relationships of descent and land tenure are still issues requiring urgent intellectual attention.

The revival of interest in kinship studies, both in Australia and elsewhere, has permitted a reassessment of old questions using new methodological tools. For example, in the AustKin project, linguists and anthropologists are in a position for the first time to address two unresolved questions: How did the unique social category systems found in Aboriginal Australia originate? Further, what has been their relationship with kinship and marriage systems over time?

As Morgan (1997) recognised in 1871, reliable analysis of kinship data can only be performed when the evidence is collected in the language of the informant. He also emphasised the importance of collecting all kinship terms in a given language with a large number of the kin types that constituted their meanings, so that a clear picture of the type of operating kinship system could emerge. This methodological principle was adopted by AustKin, although (as with Fison and Howitt's 1880 correspondents' lists) the kinship term lists available did not always live up to this requirement.

By accurately associating sets of terms with languages, AustKin also opens up the possibility of comparative etymological reconstruction, allowing researchers to deduce whether kinship terms have been inherited from ancestral languages or borrowed from neighbouring groups. Earlier work has clearly shown how important linguistic evidence is to plotting the development and spread of social systems. The gender prefixes in subsection terms of a genderless language such as Warlpiri (masculine Japanangka vs feminine Napanangka) can be explained by tracing the terms to languages far to the north that earlier had gender prefixes of the right form (McConvell 1985). In short, historical changes to systems of social organisation can often be inferred by examining linguistic phylogeny and patterns of diffusion.

While anthropological (ethnological) research on kinship has sometimes been comparative, thus producing synchronic typologies of systems, it has rarely focused on diachronic change and reconstruction. Even the earlier work on transformations by Lévi-Strauss (1969) and the more recent significant work of Godelier et al. (1998) have not tied transformations to times, places and lexical forms. In linguistics, however, there has been a current of research on reconstructing kinship terms and systems (e.g. Blust 1980; Whistler 1980), but not within an Australian context. The aim of the AustKin project has been to apply the comparative method in linguistics to Australian kinship data using systematic querying of databases and to marry the results to anthropological work.

The AustKin II database was the second phase of the AustKin project, which went online in 2013. It is linked to the AustKin I but is able to store, handle and map two additional features of kinship and social organisation: 1) marriage rules, including aspects of prescription, proscription (unmarriageability), preferential and alternative marriages; and 2) category systems such as moieties, semi-moieties, sections and subsections. The aim is to track and visualise how these systems interact with each other over time.

Earlier attempts at typologies of kinship systems often included marriage rules in the definition of kinship systems. This would not be a wise precedent for the AustKin project to follow because we know that sometimes marriage systems do not fit exactly within the kinship terminologies. Due to AustKin's concern with change, we also need to record cases of lack of fit very carefully, as they may represent 'phasing in' of a kinship terminology and marriage system that are not completely harmonious with each other due to time lag or competition between different systems exerting influence on a group. It is important to record marriage rules separately from kinship systems and to compare them as independent factors.

Sections and subsections and their development are topics that have been investigated by two leaders of the AustKin project over the years, including the spread of sections in the Western Desert (Dousset 2005), and the origin and spread of subsections in north central Australia (McConvell 1985, 1997). Sections and subsections are sociocentric divisions, four and eight respectively. Each occurs in separate regions with a little overlap between them. The sections are made up of a set of classificatory or fictive parallel kin of the same or harmonic (+2 or −2) generations. Subsections are divided into two, with those who are classificatory mother's mother (or mother's mother's siblings) and woman's daughter's children to each other separated into a different subsection from siblings and father's father (or father's father's siblings). They are categories that each individual derives from his or her parents; however, the section or subsection term of the child is different from his or her parents. Subsections are unique to Australia, and sections nearly so—there are sections in Panoan-speaking groups in South America.

Unlike kinship terms, which tend to be mostly inherited, subsection terms, and probably most section terms, are diffused (loan words). It seems unlikely that kinship terminologies and social categories (skins) have parallel histories. More complex relationships are being uncovered in this project.

In relation to Australia, there has been a tradition of combining kinship terminology, marriage rules and social categories (sections and subsections) into a unitary 'kinship system' in which these elements are inextricably connected by close functional cohesion. This perception of how Australian systems operate became especially influential due to analyses of section systems by anthropologists exploring componential approaches (e.g. Burling 1962). Often, this neglects the relative independence and differing histories of these elements. More significantly for the project, this approach does not facilitate comparison and the tracing of diachronic interactions of kinship terminology, marriage and social categories that have been identified as major goals.

Beyond these three components, there is also a demographic component: in particular, how marriage patterns relate to the maintenance and transformation of marriage rules, kinship systems and social categories. The possibility of 'bottlenecks' leading to changes in social category systems relates to marriage patterns, general interaction and perhaps population size and density.

A number of writers have proposed hypotheses that relate different social categories to differing ecological conditions (e.g. McKnight 1981; cf. Yengoyan 1976). Ecological determinist hypotheses generally do not work well and are flawed in their synchronic and ahistorical nature—what is needed is an understanding of the movements that drive the diffusion of such systems.

Hypotheses such as those of Keen (1982, 2004) that link polygyny to types of marriage and associated age structure and marriage network flows in different areas of Arnhem Land are more promising. The work done in AustKin I in developing a diachronic dimension for Yolngu kinship in north-east Arnhem Land (McConvell & Keen 2011) can now be merged with the correlational work by Keen to explore the dynamics of how kinship, marriage and demography influence each other over time.

Another wideranging hypothesis to which we pay attention is that of White and Denham (2007), who stated that the functional advantage of kinship systems such as Omaha skewing and social categories such as sections and subsections, lies in their driving force towards exogamy, rescuing small groups from otherwise almost-certain demographic collapse. Simulations could play a role in testing these types of hypotheses.

If the historical reconstruction work in AustKin can find relative or even absolute dates for these institutional changes, we will be able to contribute to a debate that has gone on for some time over whether the society of recent times in Australia is very ancient or if there was a major change, perhaps related to 'intensification' (economic and population growth), identified by archaeologists in the Holocene. It has been argued that this has led to more stable groupings and ethnicities, based on specific types of kinship, marriage and social organisation.

The hypothesis of the origin and spread of subsections now has a secure foundation; however, it still requires more detailed work, which is shown in Chapters 9 and 10. The question of the origin of sections, the older system from which subsections evolved through a merger of two section systems, is still at a more preliminary stage; however, McConvell presents some hypotheses in this volume.

The study of the evolution of Australian kinship systems and their relationship to marriage and social category (skins) systems is not only significant to Australia. Allen (1998) has claimed that the primordial world social organisation was based on a 'tetradic' structure, similar to the sections from which Dravidian-Kariera systems evolved. Hage (2003) has also claimed to have found Kariera systems in protolanguages in many parts of the world.

If the earliest kinship systems we can detect in Australia through our reconstruction methods are Kariera, then this adds some weight to the world primordial (or very early) Dravidian-Kariera hypothesis. However, this is by no means conclusive, as we are likely dealing with protolanguages that are not much more than 5,000 years old. A similar problem of relative short age also besets the idea that Australian sections may be relics of a very early human type of social organisation. It may be that sections are in fact younger than the protolanguages (e.g. Proto-Pama-Nyungan) and this is something AustKin may be able to find out. In order to provide credible answers to these questions, we should not indulge in speculation. There are good linguistic and ethnological methods on hand and these need to be applied systematically.

Further, the question of the relationship between kinship, marriage and other aspects of Indigenous social organisation, such as social categories and descent, is now even more relevant due to native title (see Finlayson et al. 1999; Sutton 2003). For instance, the notion of a body of law and custom belonging to an Indigenous society assumes some common strands that link the different elements. Conversely, it also allows for historical change that may alter the relationship between these elements. The current relevance of the study of kin, skin and clan is highlighted in several chapters in this volume.

The Chapters in This Volume

Evolving Perspectives on Aboriginal Social Organisation: From Mutual Misrecognition to the Kinship Renaissance

In Chapter 2, Piers Kelly and Patrick McConvell provide background on the intellectual history of how Australian Aboriginal social organisation has been perceived by outside observers. Many of the early observers evinced little understanding of or interest in Australian Aboriginal social organisation; however, as European scholars began to adopt social evolutionism, Australia captured imaginations as exemplifying the 'most primitive' forms of social life. The chapter then moves on to the twentieth century when anthropology mainly cast aside evolutionism in favour of synchronic ethnography, led in Australia by Radcliffe-Brown. Structuralist anthropology gave rise to comparative typology, as in the work of Radcliffe-Brown, Lévi-Strauss and Scheffler; however, direct historical or evolutionary models remained rare, only recently re-emerging as part of the 'renaissance of kinship'.

Systems in Geography or Geography of Systems? Attempts to Represent Spatial Distributions of Australian Social Organisation

In Chapter 3, Laurent Dousset proposes that 'social organisation', as defined by Fison and Howitt (1880), of social categories played a significant role alongside 'local organisation', clans and phratries in map-making. 'Social organisation' forms were taken to suggest forms of governance arranged in a historical sequence. Varieties of Australian social organisation are shown on a map generated by AustKin, with moieties, sections, subsections and semi-moieties represented.

The mapping of Australian society is discussed in terms of three periods in the history of the mapping of Indigenous Australia: homogenisation period, organic period and dynamic period. In the homogenisation period, the map of social organisation is one that reflects the history of migration, with more 'modern' tribes progressively imposing themselves onto the sociocultural landscape. In introducing the organic period, Dousset looks at two innovators who departed from the migration-social evolution model in the twentieth century: Davidson, who proposed a geographical approach to social institutions and (naturally) used maps a great deal; and Radcliffe-Brown, who ushered in the structuralist-functionalist rejection of any historical explanations. From his earliest mappings in the Pilbara, Radcliffe-Brown attempted to integrate local and social organisation and gave a geographical basis to sections that was contrary to the reality. The dynamic period in the late twentieth century began with a recognition of the problems of map-making, leading to hesitation about drawing lines on maps and demanding a clear exposition of territoriality in Australia due to land rights and native title cases. At the same time, an awareness of change and the movement of social organisation systems began to appear in maps, hence the name 'dynamic' period.

The Sources of Confusion over Social and Territorial Organisation in Western Victoria

In Chapter 4, Raymond Madden takes a further look at the distinction between 'local' and 'social' organisation that perhaps had not been made clear enough by Fison and Howitt (1880), subsequently leading to some confusion. In the case highlighted by Madden, this confusion has had serious consequences in the native title era, with some people (including

Indigenous Australians) reading the situation as matrilineal inheritance of rights in land—an interpretation that is not justified according to Madden. The chapter's focus is on western Victoria and it homes in on what the early sources on the region, mainly Dawson (1881) and Howitt (1904), had to say about territorial (local) organisation. Dawson (1881) named the local territorial group the 'family', which is ostensibly equivalent to what others have called the 'clan' or 'estate group', recruited primarily by patrifiliation. Howitt (1904) listed three levels of groups associated with hierarchically organised land: 'nations', the cultural blocs of dialect groups; 'tribes', the dialect groups; and 'clans' or 'hordes', the local estate group at the bottom of the hierarchy. The latter two are distinguished by line of descent: 'clan', patrilineal; and 'horde', matrilineal. This formulation turned out to be a major source of confusion, as it was based on whether the area had patrimoieties or matrimoieties.

The second part of the chapter is devoted to change as a result of the colonisation of Victoria in the early nineteenth century. The severe impact on the Indigenous population brought demographic collapse and the concentration of remnants around missions. In turn, this brought about changes in how Aboriginal people thought about their affiliations to land, with the distinct local patrifilial clan identities being replaced by larger conglomerates that were based on cognatic (not lineal) ties. Now, many Aboriginal people in western Victoria believe that their traditional descent and land tenure system was matrilineal, and writers in recent times have also contributed to this perception. It is important in the native title era to understand the history of local and social organisation in the context of colonial history, so that neither the poles of continuity nor destruction of traditional society is unduly emphasised.

Disputation, Kinship and Land Tenure in Western Arnhem Land

In Chapter 5, Mark Harvey moves the scene to the north of Australia. He continues on the topic of land tenure but also addresses the subject of kinship. The theme of interpersonal interaction in the form of disputation and how this affects variation of kinship term usage is also new in this volume.

The chapter begins with the assertion that disputation is more prominent in discussion of marriage than of land tenure. Similar to Madden's discussion in the context of western Victoria, population collapse followed

European incursion in northern Kakadu in the late nineteenth and early twentieth century. According to Berndt and Berndt (1970), disputes between and about marriage partners often hinged on whether they were *gagali* (prescribed marriage partners) or *kanjok* (a broader category of cross-cousins and less favoured as spouses). Another cause of shame and dispute was when a betrothal was not organised early and lapsed, and the cross-cousin relationship instead became one of 'father–daughter'.

Harvey then moves on to land tenure. Apart from language group names at the highest level, the main terminologies are Gunmogurrgurr names and the Yigurumu exclamation referring to areas of land. Harvey links this situation to the lack of public debate about these matters, which is in contrast to the greater public airing of disagreements about kinship and marriage.

In the final section, Harvey reveals evidence, including placenames, that the discontinuous and fragmented nature of estates was in fact an artefact of the colonial history: estates were originally continuous.

Moiety Names in South-Eastern Australia: Distribution and Reconstructed History

In Chapter 6, Harold Koch, Piers Kelly and Luise Hercus deal with the moiety systems of south-eastern Australia, south of the region where section systems were found—although moieties existed in these areas as well. Evidence is carefully sifted through to arrive at accurate descriptions and forms of nomenclature. Further, historical linguistics and ethnology are used to reconstruct the history and etymology of moieties in the region. One conclusion (as other chapters conclude for other social categories) is that moieties spread by cultural diffusion after the time of the protolanguages of subgroups, and not along with the languages as they expanded. Although the authors do not attempt to date these spreads, it is presumed that they must be relatively recent, occurring within the last millennium or two.

Six areas are presented across South Australia, Victoria, the Darling and south-west Queensland, each with its own distinctive pair of moiety terms. Five areas have matrimoieties, with only central Victoria having patrimoieties.

The chapter then reviews earlier attempts at mapping social category naming systems and explores correlations and mismatches within linguistic subgroups. The area around the Darling and Murray rivers is a good candidate for the origin of moiety systems, with the known occurrence of large multiethnic ceremonies in the region presenting as a possible vector of diffusion.

In the final section on etymology of moiety terms, which takes a wider view across eastern Australia, the animal terms that are used in various areas are discussed, with comments made regarding the distinctive features of the two emblematic species, such as body shape, fur versus scales, and habitat. Other aspects that enter into the dichotomies are shade, wind and seasons; however, no overall conclusions about origins are reached.

Patriclan Subsets of the Ashburton River District in Western Australia

In Chapter 7, Peter Sutton discusses 'patriclan subsets', an institution otherwise known as patriphratries, which are named combinations of clans into sets—usually around four. They are quite similar in structure (although not in the form of names) to the patriphratries that are more well known in south-western Australia that have been found as matriphratries in adjacent areas and analysed as semi-moieties due to the reported marriage and filiation rules between them. No such rules have been reported for the Ashburton systems that have been labelled as 'totem classes'. Structurally, they sit somewhere between social categories and local descent groups and would require further study as a possible ancient type of institution. The main source of information on the Ashburton phratries comes from the work of Daisy Bates' fieldnotes (n.d.), which Sutton draws on in this chapter, as well as Radcliffe-Brown's fieldwork and the more recent linguistic work of Austin.

One characteristic of this system that aligns with social categories such as sections is that the named categories are not confined to a single language group but are used over a wide area. Sutton suggests that they are 'counter-territorial', transcending local organisation. They are not exogamous like many non-local matriclans and matriphratries, but do have a tendency towards endogamy.

Sutton compares the phratries of the Ashburton with the *mala* grouping of clans of the north-east Arnhem Land Yolngu, referred to as 'phratries' by Warner (1937), a naming not followed by other anthropologists of the region.

Sutton goes on to discuss marriage and the relationship between phratries and sections. He concludes that 'this system and its associated social etiquette shared several of the key features of universalist kin superclass systems while at the same time being rooted in patrifilial localism'; however, in situating the system as straddling both local and social organisation, he is careful not to imply that this is part of a transition from one to the other.

The Birds and the Bees: The Origin of Sections in Queensland

In Chapter 8, Patrick McConvell looks at sections, the fascinating system of four named sociocentric divisions based on kinship and ideal marriage rules. At its high-water mark, after the full impact of colonial onslaught was felt, sections were in use and transmitted over approximately half the area of Australia. The other major system also expanding in this period was subsections, in the middle of the section distribution in the central north of the continent, with sections to the east, west and south. The focus of the chapter is on how sections could have formed from pre-existing social categories, moieties or phratries. A number of speculative solutions have been proposed, most referring to the fact that a combination of matrimoieties and patrimoieties with some adjustment of marriage could logically produce sections.

The issue for McConvell is whether these suppositions have merit. He examines situations in north Queensland in which there are signs of transitions to sections and finds that evidence of combinations of matrimoieties with patrimoieties is absent. Rather, what seems to have occurred is the interaction of two neighbouring patrimoiety systems, with moiety names referring to two kinds of eagle and bee, in which a modified marriage alliance between the groups led to sections.

One of these nascent section systems (here named 'Queensland General' [QG]) spread across a vast area of interior Queensland with closely similar terms, indicating a rapid and relatively recent spread, probably in the last millennium or two. The distribution of this QG system is similar to that of the Maric subgroup of languages that rapidly spread across interior Queensland in the late Holocene. This tempts an analyst to regard the section system as being carried by the Maric languages, as they split up and spread out, through inheritance. However, linguistic evidence suggests that the section spread did not accompany the breakup of the Maric languages, but rather the sections spread by diffusion after the languages had already expanded, and not from the same origin point or in the same direction.

In north Queensland, tentatively proposed here as the origin area of sections, we cannot use the similarity of forms of terms as a guide to the reconstruction of history of sections as a whole because the forms in different regions are unrelated. This leads us to take a closer look at one of the modes of diffusion of nomenclature identified for south-eastern Australia by Koch et al. (see Chapter 6): 'calquing' or 'loan translation'.

The final part of this chapter takes a broader perspective regarding the question of sections. There is only one system outside of Australia that almost completely matches the Australian system: the Panoan system between the Andes and the Amazon in South America. Not all Panoan-speaking groups have sections but a number of groups have patrimoieties, patriphratries and patriclans that may have played a role in the origin of sections. Linguistic evidence suggests that sections are not old, perhaps one thousand years old or less. The names of sections and moieties are transparently those of animals that have symbolic roles.

Generic Terms for Subsections ('Skins') in Australia: Sources and Semantic Networks

In Chapter 9, Patrick McConvell and Maïa Ponsonnet look at social categories and local organisations that have generic names that are roughly equivalent to 'moiety', 'section', 'subsection', 'clan' and so on. The adoption of other—presumably previous—generic names from other social categories as the term for 'subsection' is one of the points covered in this chapter. However, more significant is the range of terms for subsections drawn from other semantic fields. In the case of *ngurlu*, used for both 'matriclan' and 'subsection' in the Victoria River District of the Northern Territory, this is a word in Gurindji for 'flavour' and it has a range of associated meanings; it is also the term for 'seed' in a number of related languages. Source meanings of generic terms for subsections are split up into several main sets: 1) dermis (skin of body); 2) smell, flavour and associated senses; 3) body; 4) head and associated attributes; 5) name; and 6) time, country and associated senses.

The fact that *dermis* is only found in the languages of the Cobourg Peninsula in western Arnhem Land is part of the evidence that this is the area from which the generic term 'skin' in Pidgin English originated. This is supported by historical evidence from the British early settlements at Port Essington.

Some regions use terms for body or sweat odour for generic subsections. This connection between a person's smell and their essence and identity is a common conceptual link in Australia. 'Body' is also commonly colexified with 'person' but less commonly with 'subsection', and rarely it seems are all three found together represented by one word.

The method of 'semantic mapping', specifically used by Alex François, is utilised in this study to show connections in the other meanings of the terms for 'subsection'. Although semantic maps are not necessarily geographical, the divisions between different meanings of terms for 'subsection' do largely mirror geographical regions. Similarly, semantic maps are not normally used in reconstruction of historical change; however, in this chapter they are harnessed to assist in plotting these changes in conjunction with what we already know about the origin and spread of subsections.

The Development of Arandic Subsection Names in Time and Space

The history of the origin and diffusion of subsections is now firmly grounded in McConvell's (1985) hypothesis, with earlier ideas now generally sidelined as highly speculative and flawed. However, among those who accept the main lines of McConvell's (1985) hypothesis, there are also differences of opinion regarding the detail and chronology based on linguistic evidence. One site of difference has been the historical interpretation of the form of subsection (and section) terms in the Arandic group of languages in Central Australia, which Harold Koch discusses in Chapter 10.

McConvell's (1985) hypothesis proposes that subsections arose from a particular kind of merger of two four-section systems in the region around Katherine (from the west and north) in the Northern Territory that was followed by the diffusion of varieties of the new system to the west, south and east.

McConvell (1985, pp. 6, 10) pointed out that the Set 1 of subsections (A1, B1, C1 and D1) are related in form to the western section terms respectively (A, B, C and D) and that they are also closely similar to the section terms in southern Arandic languages that only have section terms. Koch reviews different hypotheses proposed regarding the historical sequence that might have led to this pattern, including the suggestion that there were two successive spreads from the north: first sections, then subsections. Spencer and Gillen (1969 [1899]) and Elkin (1939–40) reported that the Arrernte said that they had received the subsections from northern groups in recent historical times. Koch's interpretation (which differs from McConvell 1985) is that the addition of gender prefixes *ja-* (masculine) and *na-* (feminine) initially applied to sections, and it was these that spread south first and underwent the full initial syllable dropping that occurs in Arandic (e.g. Japanangka > Penangke). Later, the eight subsections with prefixes diffused south from the group referred to by Spencer and Gillen (1969 [1899]) as 'Ilpirra'—often interpreted as 'Warlpiri', but actually, as Koch shows, 'Anmatyerre'. This scenario, if confirmed, also provides evidence of the previous existence of western sections in the northern savanna belt before the genesis and spread of subsections.

Close–Distant: An Essential Dichotomy in Australian Kinship

Close versus distant relatives is a commonplace expression in European kinship that refers to physical distance, genealogical distance and how frequently and intimately relatives interact. In Chapter 11, Tony Jefferies aims to show that a similar dichotomy is important in the understanding of how Australian Indigenous kinship systems work. According to Jefferies, this has not been fully recognised in the anthropological literature, even though Aboriginal people have been recorded talking about it from the early days of contact, and he argues that it is a central emic concept in their understanding.

The chapter includes an account of various anthropologists who have referred to close–distant in Australia, such as the requirement that a bride be both geographically and genealogically distant from the husband.

In the Western Desert, geographical distance is the key in marriage choices and different terminology is used for close and distant cousins. Dousset (2005) is cited as providing the best description of this, and other ethnographic examples are also presented.

Asymmetrical Distinctions in Waanyi Kin Terminology

The Waanyi language traditionally straddled the Queensland – Northern Territory border to the south of the Gulf of Carpentaria. In Chapter 12, Mary Laughren begins with a detailed description of the meanings and forms of Waanyi kinship terms, explaining when there is a distinction in kinship terms between brother and sister relations and when there is no such gender-based distinction. There are also differences between junior and senior terms in harmonic generations, and instances when one term is applicable for both. These two types of distinctions are called asymmetrical and symmetrical for gender and generation respectively.

This chapter focuses on how these differences in symmetry can be explained. The hypothesis is that asymmetry is related to the marriage alliance and wife bestowal system. However, this is not necessarily a consequence of that type of alliance and bestowal, since the Warlpiri also has this type of system but does not distinguish gender in kinship terms. In relation to generation asymmetry, it is shown in a number of languages in the region that Waanyi patterns conform to an areal type.

One conclusion reached is that 'the marking of both sex and generation-level distinctions in FM and MM class terms is a shared feature of the languages of the southern Gulf of Carpentaria region. Waanyi has borrowed terms from neighbouring southern Warluwarric languages in order to lexify distinctions probably not made in Proto-Garrwan'. The pattern of terms in Waanyi and neighbouring languages reflects areal multilingualism and joint participation in ceremonies and marriage networks.

Genesis of the Trinity: The Convergent Evolution of Trirelational Kinterms

Trirelational kinship terms are a fascinating complexification found in a number of areas of Northern Australia. Since these systems are not usually found by elicitation or superficial fieldwork, they may well have had a wider distribution, but were not discovered before the systems or the languages were lost. On a global scale, they have been recorded in one part of the Amazon; however, the same comments apply: perhaps they were missed elsewhere.

Kinship terms in most languages refer to the relationship between the propositus (anchor or pivot) and the referent. Therefore, if I talk about 'John's father', it is the relationship between John and the referent that fully covers the term 'father'. Whatever relationship exists between 'me', the speaker, and the propositus or referent is not encoded in the kinship term. With a trirelational system it is different: the relationship between me and the propositus and referent is also encoded.

In Chapter 13, Joe Blythe reports not on an established and elaborated system, but a trirelational system in the first throes of birth in the Murrinhpatha language of the Wadeye area of the Northern Territory. The mechanism of its genesis, as far as we can tell, is different from that of other trirelational systems; however, its functional properties are parallel, showing that this is an option that is inherent in the way kinship systems are constituted—but one that is only rarely developed. Blythe applies the notion of 'convergent evolution'—namely, that these trirelational systems arise from similar functional motivations. Whether the common functional motivations he identifies in the need to classify referents in discourse hedged by restrictions and in-group knowledge is sure to be the subject matter of further debate.

The key evidence in this chapter is the lexicalisation of phrases to form trirelational terms and great use is made of historical documentation of this process at an earlier stage, as well as around five hours of transcript of contemporary Murrinhpatha conversation. This provides solid evidence of the interactional pragmatics of kinship and explications by participants.

The next part sets this in the context of historical work on the Murrinhpatha by Stanner (1936) and Falkenberg (1962). This body of work was somewhat unusual compared with the ethnography from that period because it posited a change in progress in the kinship system—a supposition that Blythe reveals as unjustified. However, despite the recording of trirelational terms by Stanner (1936), he did not understand its significance or how it provided an elaboration of kinship that was different from the change he was imagining.

A section follows that cites passages in which participants in conversation use such 'X says TERM to Y' formulas to disambiguate reference and relationships.

One of the conclusions of the chapter is that the emergence of Murrinhpatha trirelational terms is part of a pattern of solutions for usage-based constraints on person reference items. The chapter includes a useful survey and map of trirelational terms across Australia, and a supplement on interaction in discourse.

References

Allen, N 1998, 'The prehistory of Dravidian-type terminologies', in M Godelier et al. (eds), *Transformations of kinship*, Washington DC: Smithsonian, pp. 314–31.

Bates, D n.d., Manuscripts and papers of Daisy Bates (MS 365 and MS 2300), Canberra: National Library of Australia.

Berndt, R & Berndt, C 1970, *Man, land and myth in north Australia: the Gunwinggu people*, Sydney: Ure Smith.

Blust, R 1980, 'Early Austronesian social organization: the evidence of language', *Current Anthropology*, 21(2), pp. 205–47. doi.org/10.1086/202430.

Burling, R 1962, 'A structural restatement of Njamal kinship terminology', *Man*, 62(201), pp. 122–4. doi.org/10.2307/2797628.

Dawson, J 1881, *The Australian Aborigines: the languages and customs of several tribes in the Western District of Victoria, Australia*, Melbourne: George Robertson (Facsimile edition, 1981, Canberra: AIAS).

Dousset, L 2005, *Assimilating identities: social networks and the diffusion of sections*, Sydney: Oceania Publications, Monograph 57.

Elkin, AP 1939–40, 'Kinship in South Australia', *Oceania, 10*, pp. 196–234.

Falkenberg, J 1962, *Kin and totem: group relations of Australian Aborigines in the Port Keats district*, Oslo: Oslo University Press.

Finlayson, J, Rigsby, B & Bek, HJ (eds) 1999, *Connections in native title: genealogies, kinship and groups*, Canberra: Centre for Aboriginal Economic Policy Research, Research Monograph 13.

Fison, L & Howitt, AW 1880, *Kamilaroi and Kurnai*, Melbourne: George Robertson.

Godelier, M, Trautmann, T & Tjon Sie Fat, F (eds) 1998, *Transformations of kinship*, Washington DC: Smithsonian.

Hage, P 2003, 'The ancient Maya kinship system', *Journal of Anthropological Research, 59*(1), pp. 5–21.

Howitt, AW 1904, *The native tribes of south-east Australia*, London: Macmillan & Co. (Facsimile edition, 1996, Canberra: Aboriginal Studies Press).

Keen, I 1982, 'How some Murngin men marry ten wives: the marital implications of matrilateral cross-cousin structures', *Journal of the Royal Anthropological Institute, 17*(4), pp. 620–42.

Keen, I 2004, *Aboriginal economy and society: Australia at the threshold of colonisation*, Melbourne: Oxford University Press.

Lévi-Strauss, C 1969, *The Elementary structures of kinship*, Boston: Beacon Press (translation of Les Structures Élémentaires de la Parenté, 1949).

McConvell, P 1985, 'The origin of subsections in Northern Australia', *Oceania, 56*, pp. 1–33.

McConvell, P 1997, 'Long lost relations: Pama-Nyungan and northern kinship', in P McConvell & N Evans (eds), *Archaeology and linguistics: Aboriginal Australia in global perspective*, Melbourne: Oxford University Press, pp. 207–36.

McConvell, P & Keen, I 2011, 'The transition from Kariera to an asymmetrical system: Cape York Peninsula to north-east Arnhem Land', in D Jones & B Milicic (eds), *Kinship, language and prehistory: Per Hage and the Renaissance in kinship studies*, Salt Lake City: University of Utah Press, pp. 99–132.

McKnight, D 1981, 'Distribution of Australian Aboriginal "marriage classes": environmental and demographic influences', *Man* (n.s.), *16*(1), pp. 75–89.

Morgan, LH 1997, *Systems of consanguinity and affinity of the human family*, Lincoln: University of Nebraska Press. (Smithsonian Institution, vol. 17, 1871.)

Spencer, B & Gillen, FJ 1969 [1899], *The native tribes of Central Australia*, Oosterhout, Netherlands: Anthropological Publications [Reprinted from 1899 edition by Macmillan & Co].

Stanner, WEH 1936, 'Murinbata kinship and totemism', *Oceania*, 7, pp. 186–216.

Sutton, P 2003, *Native title in Australia: an ethnographic perspective*, Cambridge: Cambridge University Press. doi.org/10.1017/CBO97 80511481635.

Warner, WL 1937, *A black civilization: a social study of an Australian tribe*, New York: Harper.

Whistler, K 1980, Proto-Wintun Kin Classification: a case study of reconstruction of a complex semantic system, PhD dissertation, University of California, Berkeley.

White, D & Denham, W 2007, 'The Indigenous marriage paradox', *SASci meeting*, San Antonio.

Yengoyan, A 1976, 'Structure, event and ecology in Aboriginal Australia: a comparative viewpoint', in N Peterson (ed.), *Tribes and boundaries in Australia*, Canberra: Australian Institute of Aboriginal Studies, pp. 121–40.

2

Evolving Perspectives on Aboriginal Social Organisation: From Mutual Misrecognition to the Kinship Renaissance

Piers Kelly and Patrick McConvell

One of the distinguishing features of Australian social organisation is its so-named classificatory system of kinship, whereby a given term may extend to other people, including genealogically distant kin and even strangers. For example, a father's father's brother's son's son may be called 'brother'. By extending the kinship terms through regular principles, everybody in the social universe becomes kin of some kind, an arrangement called 'universal kinship'. So-called skin systems build on classificatory kinship by adding an extra dimension in which a category name is applied to divisions of people, and specific kinship relationships obtain between these social categories. In contrast, kinship terms in Europe are applied only to members of one's immediate family, with fewer terminological distinctions made as genealogical distance increases. The disjunction between these two social models has been a source of misunderstanding ever since outsiders from Europe began visiting and settling on the continent. In this chapter, we plot the history of settler perspectives on Aboriginal social organisation with special attention given to the rise of comparative kinship as an object of scholarly interest in the West. Although Western scholars in the second half of the nineteenth century became increasingly aware of the global diversity of kinship systems, cross-cultural comparisons of kin systems would also give rise to overreaching and wrong-headed theories of unilinear human 'progress'. The misanalysis of ethnographic descriptions from Australia laid the foundations for social evolutionist dogmas; however, as we will show, better documentation and analysis of Australian kinship systems would later help to undermine these same ideologies. The twentieth century saw a round rejection of social evolutionism within kinship studies, eventually leading to new diachronic insights that took into account diffusion and transformation. In turn, the 'new kinship' of the late twentieth century began to recognise the enduring power of kinship to express and define collective Indigenous identities.

Social Evolutionism in Australia

For much of the period of colonial contact, European observers in Australia paid scant attention to Aboriginal social organisation. Many considered Aboriginal sociality in terms of a perceived absence of law and structured relationships. For others, Aboriginal systems of kinship, governance and land tenure were noticed only to the extent that they were perceived to coincide with Western counterparts. The very earliest recorded encounters between Indigenous Australians and visitors reveal attitudes that would persist throughout the period of colonial expansion. After being beached for several months in 1687 and 1688 in the Kimberley, William Dampier barely showed any curiosity about the social dynamics of the local inhabitants, remarking: 'Whether they cohabit one Man to one Woman, or promiscuously, I know not: but they do live in Companies, 20 or 30 Men, Women and Children together' (Dampier 1699 [1688], p. 465). In turn, the locals may well have assumed that the foreign visitors were not fully human, on one occasion fleeing and shouting 'Gurry, Gurry' (Dampier 1699 [1688], p. 469); the term has since been reconstituted as the Bardi word *ngaarri* meaning 'devil' or 'spirit' (Metcalfe 1979, p. 197).

This kind of mutual misrecognition of social roles and organisation continued to play out in the centuries that followed. On a second visit to the Kimberley in 1699, Dampier (1699 [1688]) identified an Indigenous man as a 'chief' and 'a kind of prince or captain'. En route to Australia, Captain James Cook (1821, p. 90) elicited Tahitian words for 'king', 'baron', 'vassal' and 'villain', but would deny any sociality to the people he subsequently encountered in Botany Bay who 'did not appear … to live in societies, but, like other animals, were scattered about along the coast, and in the woods'. As he journeyed north, the appearance of an outrigger canoe at Cape Conway—a technological improvement, in Cook's estimation, on the bark canoes further south—encouraged him to believe 'the people here had made some farther advances beyond mere animal life than those that we had seen before' (Cook 1821, p. 120).

Implicit in these remarks was the emergent progressivist or social evolutionist view that all human societies underwent successive stages of progress from a condition of savagery and barbarism to a state of civilisation, and that innovations in technology corresponded pari passu to advances in social organisation. Progressivist ideologies were to define European attitudes to Indigenous people for the next century, and as long as Australian Aboriginals were seen to lack the presumed advancements of the 'civilised' world, there was little hope of discovering anything of value in their social systems. Indeed, colonisers responded to the imagined deficit in Aboriginal social organisation by following Dampier's impulse and projecting titles onto favoured elders. A succession of 'chiefs' and 'kings' with their attendant 'queens' was proclaimed by local administrators, from King Boongarie 'Supreme Chief of the Sydney Tribe' (d. 1830) to King Jemmy 'last King of the Dabee blacks' (d. 1880) (Smith 1992). Gifted with brass 'king plates' in acknowledgement of their declared rank, the Indigenous monarchs were rarely, if ever, accepted as 'kings' by their own communities, a fact conceded to a greater or lesser extent by settlers (see Lang 1861, p. 337; Troy 1993).

By the second half of the century, a subtle but significant assumption had solidified in progressivist thinking: not only were human societies understood to progress through incremental stages of development, but these stages were universal, unilinear and predictable, even if they evolved at different rates for different communities. Although a deterministic (and Lamarckian) model of social evolution underpinned progressivist thinking in this period, Charles Darwin's *On the Origin of Species* (1859) and *The Descent of Man, and Selection in Relation to Sex* (1871) were to suggest another plausible mechanism, in the form of natural selection, for progressive change over long periods.[1] Significantly, descriptions

---

1   Influenced by social evolutionists such as E. B. Tylor (1878 [1865]), John McLennan (1865) and John Lubbock (1871 [1870]), Darwin would occasionally defer to racialist hierarchies wherein Africans and Aboriginal Australians were situated somewhat in advance of the apes but lower than Caucasians. 'At some future period', Darwin wrote in 1871, 'the civilised races of man will almost certainly exterminate, and replace, the savage races throughout the world. At the same time the anthropomorphous apes … will no doubt be exterminated. The break will then be rendered wider, for it will intervene between man in some more civilised state … than the Caucasian, and some ape as low as a baboon, instead of as at present between the negro or Australian and the gorilla' (Darwin 1871, p. 201).

of 'primitive' communities surviving into the contemporary era were understood as an accurate reflection of European prehistory. Global ethnography now had a new impetus. If, according to the prevailing view, indigenous peoples and cultures were destined to die out or assimilate upon contact with a 'superior' civilisation, the social organisation, languages and technologies of the doomed races needed to be described as a matter of scientific urgency.

Early Documentation and Analysis of Australian Social Categories

Perhaps due to the extraordinary dominance of the social evolutionist discourse in the nineteenth century, observers were slow to document and recognise the complex dynamics of Australian social category systems. However, a handful of settlers deserve acknowledgement for having recorded such systems in the areas they visited. Scott Nind took pains to describe the essential nature of the Nyungar phratries of the Albany region of Western Australia in 1826–29 and reported his findings to the Royal Geographical Society (Nind 1831).[2] Nind listed 'classes' of the Albany area as Erniung, Taa man or Tem, Moncalon, Torndirrup, Obberup, Cambien and Mahnur, and plotted their structural relationship to each other, making him the earliest outsider to both record and comprehend (to some extent) an Australian Indigenous social category system.[3] It is also worth noting that the sailor Captain Barker documented two subsection terms on the Cobourg Peninsula in 1828, but without the kind of understanding Nind displayed of the system involved (see Chapter 9).

By the middle of the century, further examples of Aboriginal social organisation systems in Australia came to the attention of the settler population, and amateur anthropologists put their minds to analysing them, complex and baffling as they were. However, the intricate connections between land, language and kin were not to be easily untangled. The missionary and administrator Edward Stone Parker delivered a lecture in 1854 in which he attempted to plot these complicated relationships,

---

2   With thanks to Peter Sutton for information about Scott Nind.
3   Phratries occupy the middle ground between social categories and descent groups. They descend in a lineal fashion and were probably groupings of clans, so in these respects they resemble descent groups. However, some of them have marriage rules between them, like social categories. The Nyungar phratries have been analysed as semi-moieties, and do not appear to be linked to territories, at least where Nind collected information, placing them closer to the social categories.

as he had observed them in his role as Assistant Protector of Aboriginals in the Port Phillip District. In Parker's account, each Aboriginal family in Victoria had rights to a 'locality': an area of land inherited from father to son. In turn, a group of families that were 'nearly or remotely related to each other' comprised a 'tribe' occupying a given 'district'. Ten or 12 such tribes formed a 'petty nation' whose members inhabited a bounded territory and spoke the same language (Parker 1854, pp. 11–12; see also Chapter 4). Yet, there was nothing in Parker's model to throw light on the dynamics of the posited 'family' itself in terms of marriage rules or kinship terminologies. At the very least, however, his outline provided a precedent for mapping social and linguistic geographies in Australia, even if systems of land tenure remained a blind spot for settlers well into the 1970s and the era of land rights (an enduring legacy of the evolutionist paradigm was the assumption that hunter-gatherers could not own land).[4]

Two years after Parker's address, the missionary William Ridley (1856) published a short paper on the 'Kamilaroi tribe of Australians' that introduced a new and problematic social dimension to Parker's diagram of land, language and family. This concerned a type of system that did not exist in Victoria, but was found in a large part of New South Wales and, as further information was discovered, in large parts of Queensland and Western Australia. Ridley (1856, p. 288) wrote:

> Among many tribes, including those who speak several languages, there are four classes distinguished by their names.
>
> In one family all the sons are called 'ippai' the daughters 'ippātā'. In a second family, all the sons are called 'mŭrrī', the daughters 'mātā'. In a third family, all the sons are called 'kŭbbī', the daughters 'kāpŏtā'. In a fourth family, all the sons are called 'kŭmbō', the daughters 'būtā'.
>
> By some tribes the name 'baiă' is used instead of 'mŭrrī'. The following rules are strictly enforced:
>
> I. An 'ippai' my marry either an 'ippātā' (of another family) or a 'kāpŏtā'.
>
> II. A 'mŭrrī' or 'baiă' may marry only a 'būtā'.
>
> III. A 'kŭbbī' may marry only an 'ippātā'.
>
> IV. A 'kŭmbō' may marry only a 'mātā'.

---

4   Some decades later, Howitt would produce a relatively sophisticated description of local groups in Gippsland (see Fison & Howitt 1880), while Howitt and Fison (1889) developed concepts of local organisation in contradistinction to social organisation in a series of articles in the 1880s.

Evidently, what Ridley had documented was a system of social categories for modelling marriage preference: a system that, importantly, did not need to rely on overarching ideas such as 'tribe' or 'language' at all. Even 'family' in Ridley's usage did not presuppose genealogical proximity, and he switched to other imperfect labels such as 'caste' and 'class' point to the difficulty of finding a suitable semantic fit in English. As is well known, the popular term today is 'skin', and the particular schema involving four named skins (as used by the Kamilaroi and others) is now referred to as a section system, a term later introduced by Radcliffe-Brown in 1913. However, it was Ridley's text and the spreading of the news of sections by Lorimer Fison and A. W. Howitt (1880) that would captivate scholars both in Australia and abroad.

Systematic attention to kinship and social categories in Australia on a wider comparative scale began in the 1860s and continued into the 1880s, coinciding with the era in which progressivist ideology was at the peak of its influence. Social evolutionist theory gave impetus to documentation efforts, especially through the work of Lewis H. Morgan, an American lawyer who organised a massive survey of kinship terminologies across the globe. Although his long kinship questionnaire, or 'schedule', has been criticised for both its reductionism and its unnecessary complexities, it was innovative to the extent that it was to be filled out in the language of the local expert, demanding a close and careful collaboration. Further, mechanisms for detecting inconsistencies were built into the structure of the schedule itself. As McConvell and Gardner (2013, p. 3) put it: 'No other investigation of the period demanded this deep linguistic engagement that confirmed the alterity of the culture under investigation, yet challenged any simplistic analysis of it'.

It was largely from evidence provided in completed and partially completed schedules that Morgan wrote his wideranging work of comparative kinship *Systems of Consanguinity and Affinity of the Human Family* (1871)—the first study of its kind to propose global typologies of social organisation. While Morgan's higher-level analysis of the data in this work betrayed an allegiance to social evolutionism, the main methods and typological work was relatively free of such bias. *Systems of Consanguinity* did not include any data from Australia, but Morgan was confident that he had covered over 80 per cent of the 'human family' and that it was unlikely that anything significantly new would turn up among the 'inferior nations' (Morgan 1871, pp. vii, 467). Nonetheless, he was to include an appendix on Fijian and Tongan kinship, provided by his correspondent in Fiji, the missionary Fison. Extraordinarily, Fison's data showed that the 'inferior' Fijians and Tongans had a Dravidian kinship system, a fact that directly challenged Morgan's hierarchy of global social organisation and ultimately caused the Dravidian type to be demoted to a lower rung of the ladder.

Australians Fison and Howitt were to collaborate with Morgan and follow his methods and theories in the study of Australia and the Pacific. They collected evidence from correspondents in a number of regions in southern Australia during the 1870s, culminating in their influential work *Kamilaroi and Kurnai: Group-Marriage and Relationship, and Marriage by Elopement* (1880). However, the tide of social evolutionist thought, particularly from Europe, left its mark on Fison and Howitt's thinking, even if they were to remain cautious about its grander claims. While Morgan had dismissed the value of Australian kinship evidence in *Systems of Consanguinity*, his subsequent bestseller *Ancient Society* (1877) was to rely heavily on distorted conceptualisations of Kamilaroi kinship and social organisation to sustain a progressivist argument. For Morgan, the inferred phases of 'savagery' and 'barbarism' could each be further subdivided into a notional lower status, middle status and upper status. These tiers amounted to both a value-based hierarchy and diachronic projection, and in Morgan's view the model was so robust that only one case study for each phase was necessary to sustain a complete picture of human prehistory. Even the fact that no societies in the 'lower status of savagery'—presumed to have lacked fire and fishing technologies— had survived into the contemporary era was no impediment, since this phase could be reconstructed from later ones, specifically those occupied by Australian Aboriginals. Progress through each phase was marked, to some extent, by changes in subsistence and technology; however, it was the systems of social organisation, in Morgan's view, that overwhelmingly determined how far a community had advanced towards civilisation. Accordingly, Morgan proposed a scalar model of family structures that corresponded to his phases of human development. Savage society was organised solely by gender and was characterised by the 'consanguine family' involving marriage between genealogical siblings, while the slightly more advanced 'Punaluan family' was defined by group marriage of brothers or genealogically close males to each other's wives. Admission to the phase of barbarism required the adoption of the 'Syndyasmian family' or the non-exclusive pairing of a male and female with equal rights to divorce, while civilisation was eventually reached via the

'Patriarchal family' in which one man had several wives, and ultimately the 'Monogamian family' or 'one man with one woman, with an exclusive cohabitation' (Morgan 1877, p. 28).

Morgan (1877, pp. 48–9) suggested that Indigenous Australians were authentic exemplars of the lowest surviving rung of humanity (the 'middle status of savagery'), and that the Kamilaroi kinship system specifically was 'the most primitive form of society hitherto discovered' representing 'a striking phase of the ancient social history of our race'. Morgan noticed that Kamilaroi totems were matrilineal, while the four 'classes' (i.e. sections) were further subdivided and named by gender. Moreover, according to evidence supplied by the clergyman John Dunmore Lang, a man and a woman who had not met and were from different tribes would address one another as *goleer* (Kamilaroi: *guliirr*, 'spouse') and be accepted as husband and wife, provided they were of the compatible marriageable class. For Morgan, all this corroborated the existence of earlier obsolete kinship systems organised on the basis of gender, 'group marriage' and matrilineal descent.

Challenges to Social Evolutionism

It is worth emphasising that Ridley, whose short ethnographic observations had convinced Morgan of the primitiveness of Aboriginal kinship, was not himself persuaded by the same view. While Morgan regarded sections and related systems to be of scholarly interest only to the extent that they exemplified savagery, Ridley (1855, cited in Lang 1861) reflected that the Kamilaroi section system must have been 'the invention of sagacious and comparatively civilised men'. Later, he was to express the view that Aboriginal kinship represented one of 'two monuments of ancient civilization', the other monument being 'the highly elaborate and symmetrical structure of their language' (cited in Lang 1861, p. 382). Unusual for his time, Ridley's appreciation for the unique 'genius' of Indigenous languages and kinship systems prefigured the more intellectually generous approaches that would come to prominence in the twentieth century.

Morgan's (1877, p. 49) contrary insistence that Kamilaroi kinship was rudimentary and primitive could not be reconciled with what he referred to as its 'bewildering complications', possibly a reference, in part at least, to the totemic marriage rules that applied in addition to the section rules.

Whatever these may have been—and Morgan did not specify—new field research was to raise plenty of difficulties for nineteenth-century models of 'savage' kinship. A key stumbling block was the presumed existence in Australia of 'group marriage', or at least a powerful vestige of it. Holding to the theory that the 'Punaluan family'—in which brothers shared one another's wives—was a necessary stage of human social development, Morgan overgeneralised from reports of 'wife lending', resorted to monosemic interpretations of polysemous terms (assuming, for example, that a marriageable partner was equivalent to an actual 'spouse') and failed to grasp the classificatory aspect of social category systems. 'Under the conjugal system thus brought to light', Morgan (1877, p. 53) wrote, 'one-quarter of all the males are united in marriage with one-quarter of all the females of the Kamilaroi tribes'. Morgan (1880, p. 9) put forward the notion that the primordial marriage divisions were a four-term section system in which each section was naturally divided by gender. In this way, group marriageability became incrementally restricted in its evolution towards an eventual state of 'civilised' monogamy.

Conversely, Ridley was personally well acquainted with the communities in question and gave no credence to the idea of group marriage. As is clear from their private correspondence, Fison and Howitt also rejected this notion, although they did maintain a facade of support for it in *Kamilaroi and Kurnai*. Indeed, much debate in this period between ethnologists (notably the differing opinions of Morgan and Fison) tended to be sterile, based on questionable assumptions for which there was no solid evidence. For instance, Morgan (1872, p. 419) assumed that sections historically preceded moieties and Fison (1872, according to his annotations in Morgan 1872, pp. 424–50) raised the possibility that 'invaders' brought in totems and moieties. On other occasions, Fison and Howitt insisted that sections must have been ancient, dating from the time of humans first occupying and spreading out across Australia (Gardner & McConvell 2015).

These and similar misconceptions stem from an evolutionary perspective on history that fails to account for cultural diffusion. Diffusion was almost certainly the mechanism by which sections spread in the first instance and continued to spread in the nineteenth and twentieth centuries, but the theoretical arsenal available to Australianists at this time could not admit to that possibility. It was not until the turn of the century that diffusion would come to occupy a more central explanatory role, helping to demonstrate the likelihood that moieties existed prior to sections.

The Dravidian structure of Fijian and Tongan kinship terminologies was not the only challenge to Morgan's model that Fison presented. When Fison returned to Australia in 1871, he continued sourcing kinship data for the schedule, further discovering Dravidian and Iroquois type congruences (McConvell & Gardner 2013, p. 6). The 'inferior nations' would prove to be an increasing problem for Morgan's unilinear scheme, and yet Fison was reluctant to dismiss Morgan's model altogether.

Eventually collaborating with Howitt, Fison maintained a regular correspondence with Morgan and went on to co-author a volume on two south-eastern Australian systems with Howitt, published in 1880 as *Kamilaroi and Kurnai* (see Gardner and McConvell 2015 for details of the background to this book and the research that went into it). Morgan, himself, provided an introduction to the work in which he reiterated his theory of group marriage as an early form of primitive social organisation. Nonetheless, in the same volume, Fison attenuated Morgan's strong claim of literal group marriage among the Kamilaroi, while doing his best to salvage the theory as a whole. For Fison, the Kamilaroi section system was only 'theoretically communal' (Fison & Howitt 1880, p. 50), a mere echo of an earlier Punaluan family that was no longer in existence. Of greater interest to Fison were the real-world implications of such hypothetical group marriages in terms of extended relationships between individuals, communities and territories:

> Australian marriage—taking into account, for the present, those tribes only which have the Kamilaroi organization—is something more than the marriage of group to group, within a tribe. It is an arrangement, extending across a continent, which divides many widely-scattered tribes into intermarrying classes, and gives a man of one class marital rights over women of another class in a tribe a thousand miles away, and speaking a language other than his own. It seems to be strong evidence of the common origin of all the Australian tribes among whom it prevails; and it is a striking illustration of how custom remains fixed while language changes. (Fison & Howitt 1880, p. 54)

In other words, the system of 'marital rights', as opposed to outright marriage, transcended—or cut across—the bounded and interlocking groupings plotted by the likes of Parker (1854) for Victoria. Moreover, this universalist model encouraged broader-reaching reconstructions of prehistory that might not be readily achieved via language alone—a methodological insight reached earlier by Morgan (1871, p. 3) in a different context.

As for the account of Kurnai social organisation, contributed by Howitt, this too presented uncomfortable revelations for progressivist theory that the writers struggled to accommodate. For one thing, Howitt observed that the Kurnai did not recognise the Eaglehawk and Crow moiety system of their neighbours, but this was not the only evidence of 'progress'. Howitt wrote:

> The family of the Kŭrnai is a far advance upon that of other Australian tribes; for example, the Kamilaroi. In it has been established a strongly-marked form of the Syndyasmian, or pairing family; there is the power of selection by the woman of her husband, and there is descent through the father, although as yet incompletely recognized … Where we find such a surprising social advance in a tribe which has existed in such isolation, we must, I think, believe that the forces which produced this advance acted from within and not from without. (Fison & Howitt 1880, pp. 234–5)

What follows is a contorted justification for the presumed 'advance' involving speculations about migrations and cultural diffusions.

As descriptions of Australian kinship are more extensive now than they were in the latter half of the nineteenth century, it appears extraordinary that so much hay was made from so little evidence.[5] To justify the ambitious global schema of Morgan, the relatively meagre accounts of Kamilaroi kinship from Ridley and Fison served as a foundation for an entire phase of global human prehistory. Meanwhile, Fison and Howitt's *Kamilaroi and Kurnai* (1880) became wildly influential at an international level, impacting social theorists in anthropology, political science, economics and sociology. It was to be cited in works as disparate as James Frazer's *The Golden Bough* (1911 [1890]), the sociologist William I. Thomas's *Sex and Society* (1907) and Frederick Engels's *The Origin of the Family, Private Property and the State* (1902 [1891]).

The Twentieth Century

The end of the nineteenth century saw different currents arising in the new discipline of anthropology that virtually swept away the once-dominant social evolutionism. Apart from the diffusionism already mentioned, the German historical school had an impact, especially on

---

5   In fact, Fison and Howitt had amassed much more evidence bearing on these questions, but did not use it in *Kamilaroi and Kurnai* (McConvell & Gardner 2016).

the new anthropology in America under Franz Boas. Known as 'historical particularism', the focus was no longer on grand evolutionist schemes but on particular histories of sociocultural institutions in regions. Australia, firmly under the banner of the British Empire and its scholars (apart from the brief aberration in the partnership between Morgan and Fison and Howitt), was drawn into a different style of anthropology: the functionalism of Malinowski and Radcliffe-Brown. This would lead to a more radical departure from not only social evolutionism but also, in practice, nearly all forms of diachronic research, as Radcliffe-Brown's (1952, p. 50) ban on 'conjectural history' extended to almost all forms of historical reconstruction not based on written records.

Conversely, in stepping away from speculation, the new twentieth-century anthropology embraced ethnographic fieldwork with single groups. This too was pioneered in Australia around the turn of the century by another two-man team: Spencer and Gillen. Their detailed description of the Aranda (Arrernte) society in Central Australia (Spencer & Gillen 1899) was hailed throughout the world and inspired major figures such as Émile Durkheim, much as Fison and Howitt had fed the appetites of the social-evolutionists of the previous generation.

Radcliffe-Brown, an Englishman, carried out fieldwork in the Pilbara of Western Australia in 1913, and returned to Australia in 1926 as the inaugural professor of anthropology at the University of Sydney. He left his stamp on the department under A. P. Elkin, and on anthropology in Australia. Radcliffe-Brown was particularly devoted to the study of kinship and social organisation. The school of anthropology that he founded was called 'structural functionalism' and the 'structure' in this formulation alluded to the kinship organisation—the core of society in his view—especially among Australian Aboriginals.

After doing further fieldwork in New South Wales, Radcliffe-Brown published his landmark typology of Australian kinship and social organisation systems, *The Social Organization of Australian Tribes* (1931). Rather than a comprehensive catalogue of all terminologies, the volume listed a number of ideal types, having regard to kinship systems, marriage rules and social categories. While taking account of many minor variations, the main structural types he stressed were Kariera and Aranda. Both these names, and those other types, were the names of Australian ethnic groups or 'tribes'. In this respect, he followed the lead of the American

2. EVOLVING PERSPECTIVES ON ABORIGINAL SOCIAL ORGANISATION

anthropologists who created typologies based on names of ethnic groups, most often those of Native American groups. He did not follow Fison and Howitt in linking Australian kinship patterns to Dravidian.

Radcliffe-Brown's scheme proved effective and it is still generally used today in discussions of social organisation types in Australia. He codified terminology of the field, some of which was very confused for many years, and his standardisation, too, has largely survived. In respect to social categories, he was the first to use the terms 'section' and 'subsection' in his Pilbara work (Radcliffe-Brown 1918, p. 222) and incorporated them into his 1931 work. He also introduced diagrammatic representation and alphanumeric coding of sections and subsections that are still commonly, but not universally, used today (see Tables 1 and 2).

Table 1: Kariyarra (Kariera) section terms.

Code	Terms		Terms	Code
A	Panaka	marry	Purungu	B
	mother/child of		mother/child of	
C	Karimarra	marry	Palyarri	D

Source: AustKin, austkin.net.

Table 2: Warlpiri subsection system.

Code	Terms		Code	Terms
A1m A1f	Japanangka Napanangka	marry	B1m B1f	Jupurrurla Napurrurla
A2m A2f	Jungarrayi Nungarrayi	marry	B2m B2f	Jangala Nangala
C1m C1f	Jakamarra Nakamarra	marry	D1m D1f	Japaljarri Napaljarri
C2m C2f	Jampijinpa Nampijinpa	marry	D2m D2f	Japangardi Napangardi

Source: AustKin, austkin.net.

Ethnographic studies in Australia in the early twentieth century began to paint a more detailed picture of kinship and social organisation. Although Elkin, who took over from Radcliffe-Brown at the University of Sydney, had a background in diffusionist anthropology from his London training, he rarely indulged in hypotheses about prehistoric origins of social institutions. The American Boasian school was not encouraged to pry into Australia. One notable intruder was Daniel Davidson who carried out fieldwork in the Pilbara, not far from where Radcliffe-Brown had worked, and produced *The Chronological Aspects of Certain Australian Institutions as Inferred from Geographical Distribution* (1928)—a topic evidently out of tune with the dominant ahistoricity in Australian anthropology. It dealt prominently with the social categories (e.g. moieties, sections and subsections), reconstructing their history on the basis of their geographical distribution.

The next scholar who brought a revolution in anthropology and thrust Australia back into the spotlight of world attention was Claude Lévi-Strauss, a Frenchman who had done fieldwork in South America. His masterwork was *The Elementary Structures of Kinship*, published in 1949 in French but not translated into English until 1967. The focus was on types of marriage across the world. The 'elementary' forms of the title refer to marriage between specific classificatory relations, such as cross-cousins, forming an alliance between groups. This practice is found in many parts of the world, and in one form or another was ubiquitous among Australian Aboriginals. At the opposite extreme is 'complex' marriage in which an individual can marry anyone as long as they are not of a prohibited degree of closeness considered to constitute incest, such as generally practised in Europe. Australian ethnographic case studies were mined for examples of 'elementary alliance'. Lévi-Strauss distinguished between two types of elementary alliance: restricted and generalised exchange. Restricted is direct or bilateral exchange of cross-cousins; generalised is indirect or asymmetrical, whereby, for instance, a man may only marry one kind of cross-cousin, and in many cases the MBD or matrilateral cross-cousin. Generalised asymmetrical marriage is well known from parts of Asia where 'wife givers' and 'wife takers' are distinguished; however, Lévi-Strauss also pointed it out among the Yolngu (Murngin) in north-east Arnhem Land. This asymmetry is also reflected in the Yolngu kinship terminology whereby the matrilateral cross-cousin or wife *galay* is distinguished from the patrilateral cross-cousin or husband *dhuway*.

Many were entranced by the boldness of Lévi-Strauss's explanatory model. In some ways, it recapitulated evolutionism in placing elementary forms at the beginning followed by transitional forms leading to the complex forms associated with Europe. Others readers were sceptical or downright hostile, mainly reacting to the abstract nature of the schemes and Lévi-Strauss's perceived failure to identify clearly which groups were involved in the 'exchange' or 'alliances'. Anthropologists dedicated to ethnographic rigour such as Les Hiatt, an Australian working in Arnhem Land west of the Yolngu, offered a more detailed picture of how kinship and social and local organisation played out on the ground, whereby groups and alliances were not mechanically driven by set structures, but rather flexible and responsive to local political conditions and agency (Hiatt 1965). Lévi-Strauss replied with a dismissive critique of British-Australian empiricism, which was failing to understand the more abstract structures.

Harold Scheffler returned to the task of an Australia-wide kinship typology after working with Lounsbury's (1964) extensionist 'reduction rules' formalism. This approach provides the ability to make formal generalisations over a wider set of kinship terms in single languages and comparatively across languages. Scheffler's (1978) book on Australian kinship is a work of insight and careful scholarship that amends Radcliffe-Brown's and Elkin's models and reinterprets them in terms of reduction rules and another concept of superclasses.

Post-Structuralism and the Kinship Renaissance

In the 1970s, there was a reaction against structuralism. In kinship studies, this was particularly strong—led by David Schneider (1968) who disavowed the universality of the basic components of kinship in favour of a 'cultural' approach, emphasising the local emic and symbolic. The impact of Schneider and like-minded colleagues was not so much to bring a new theory and method to the anthropology of kinship as to undermine existing methods and in some areas banish the dominant structural approaches, whether those of Lévi-Strauss, Radcliffe-Brown or others, from the academy. In some ways, this was a revival of the antistructuralism of Malinowski (1930), who had complained about 'kinship algebra'. This position found ready allies among students who often found the structuralist approaches too abstract and too divorced from real human interaction. The 'new kinship' and 'relatedness studies' that drew on Schneider also joined forces with the upsurge in gender studies and the general mood that anthropology had been too wedded to models built on Western ideology, such as the emphasis on 'blood ties' and the neglect of other types of relationship that can underly kinship-like relationships. Researchers also expected the rapid transformation of societies to have lasting effects on the applicability of conceptions and networks based on kinship. Today, we realise that exactly the opposite has occurred. Indigenous groups are relying heavily on kinship and social systems for the definition of their collective identities and to emphasise their cultural and historical uniqueness. The renaissance in kinship research during the last 15 years (e.g. Allen et al. 2008; Godelier et al. 1998; Kronenfeld 2009) encompasses both structuralist work and its cultural critique, recognising the surviving strength of kinship systems and exploring their transformations and histories.

This debate, allied to the old arguments concerning the extent to which social phenomena have a biological or cultural basis, rumbles on today (Sahlins 2013). There are hopeful signs that we will not keep repeating this holding pattern, but instead come in to land and think of ways in which culture and biology can be integrated in kinship, which is a prime candidate for such a solution. In Australia, 'new kinship' has been less influential than elsewhere. The effect of the hesitancy around classic kinship in recent times has led to the neglect of solid work in the area rather than the adoption of new paradigms. This volume certainly demonstrates the continuing usefulness of classic approaches, but we are also looking for signs that we are moving on.

References

Allen, N, Callan, H, Dunbar, R & James, W 2008, *Early human kinship: from sex to social reproduction*, London: Wiley-Blackwell. doi.org/10.1002/9781444302714.

Cook, J 1821, *The three voyages of Captain James Cook round the world*, vol. 2, London: Longman, Hurst, Rees, Orme & Brown. doi.org/10.5962/bhl.title.6760.

Dampier, W 1699 [1688], *A new voyage round the world*, vol. 1, London: James Knapton.

Darwin, C 1859, *On the origin of species by means of natural selection, or the preservation of favoured races in the struggle for life*, London: John Murray.

Darwin, C 1871, *The descent of man, and selection in relation to sex*, London: John Murray.

Davidson, DS 1928, *The chronological aspects of certain Australian institutions as inferred from geographical distribution*, Philadelphia: Department of Anthropology, University of Pennsylvania.

Engels, F 1902 [1891], *The origin of the family, private property and the state*, translated by Ernest Untermann, Chicago: Charles H. Kerr & Company.

Fison, L 1872, *Annotated copy of 'Australian kinship'*, c. 1872 [manuscript], held by the National Library of Australia, 3258345.

Fison, L & Howitt, AW 1880, *Kamilaroi and Kurnai: group-marriage and relationship, and marriage by elopement*, Sydney & Melbourne: G. Robertson.

Frazer, JG 1911 [1890], *The golden bough: a study in magic and religion*, vol. 4, London: Macmillan & Co.

Gardner, H & McConvell, P 2015, *Southern anthropology: a history of Fison and Howitt's Kamilaroi and Kurnai*, London: Palgrave Macmillan.

Godelier, M, Trautmann, T & Tjon Sie Fat, F (eds) 1998, *Transformations of kinship*, Washington DC: Smithsonian Institution Press.

Hiatt, LR 1965, *Kinship and conflict: a study of an Aboriginal community in northern Arnhem Land*, Canberra: The Australian National University.

Howitt, AW & Lorimer, F 1889, 'Further notes on the Australian class system', *The Journal of the Anthropological Institute of Great Britain and Ireland*, 18, pp. 31–70. doi.org/10.2307/2842513.

Kronenfeld, D 2009, *Fanti Kinship and the analysis of kinship terminologies*, Champaign: University of Illinois Press.

Lang, JD 1861, *Queensland, Australia: a highly eligible field for emigration, and the future cotton-field of Great Britain*, London: Edward Stanford.

Lévi-Strauss, C 1969 [1967], *The elementary structures of kinship*, Boston: Beacon Press.

Lounsbury, F 1964, 'A formal account of the Crow- and Omaha-type kinship terminologies', in W Goodenough (ed.), *Explorations in cultural anthropology in honor of George Peter Murdock*, New York: McGraw-Hill, pp. 352–93.

Lubbock, J 1871 [1870], *The origin of civilisation and the primitive condition of man: mental and social conditions of savages*, New York: D. Appleton and Company.

Malinowski, B 1930, 'Kinship', *Man*, *30*, pp. 19–29.

McConvell, P & Gardner, H 2013, 'The descent of Morgan in Australia: kinship representation from the Australian colonies', *Structure and Dynamics: eJournal of Anthropological and Related Sciences*, *6*(1), pp. 1–23.

McConvell, P & Gardner, H 2016, 'The unwritten Kamilaroi and Kurnai: unpublished kinship schedules published by Fison and Howitt', in P Austin, H Koch & J Simpson (eds), *Land, language and song: studies in honour of Luise Hercus*, London: Epublishing, pp. 194–208.

McLennan, JF 1865, *Primitive marriage*, Edinburgh: Adam and Charles Black. doi.org/10.5962/bhl.title.50206.

Metcalfe, CD 1979, 'Some aspects of the Bardi language: a non-technical description', in RM Berndt & CH Berndt (eds), *Aborigines of the West: their past and their present*, Perth: University of Western Australia Press, pp. 197–213.

Morgan, LH 1871, *Systems of consanguinity and affinity in the human family*, Washington: Smithsonian Institution.

Morgan, LH 1872, 'Australian Kinship', *Proceedings of the American Academy of Arts and Sciences*, vol. 8, 12 March 1872, meeting no. 642, pp. 412–28.

Morgan, LH 1877, *Ancient society*, Chicago: Charles H. Kerr & Company.

Morgan, LH 1880, 'Prefatory remarks', in L Fison & AW Howitt (eds), *Kamilaroi and Kurnai: group-marriage and relationship, and marriage by elopement*, Sydney & Melbourne: G. Robertson.

Nind, S 1831, 'Description of the natives of King George's sound (Swan River Colony) and adjoining country', *The Journal of the Royal Geographical Society of London*, *1*, pp. 22–51. doi.org/10.2307/1797657.

Parker, ES 1854, 'The Aborigines of Australia', *Lecture delivered in the Mechanics' Hall, Melbourne, before the John Knox Young Men's Association*, 10 May 1854, Melbourne: Hugh McColl.

Radcliffe-Brown, AR 1918, 'Notes on the social organization of Australian tribes, Part 1', *JRAI, 48*, pp. 222–53.

Radcliffe-Brown, AR 1931, *The social organization of Australian tribes*, Melbourne: Macmillan & Co.

Radcliffe-Brown, AR 1952, *Structure and function in primitive society*, London: Cohen & West.

Ridley, W 1856, 'Kamilaroi tribe of Australians and their dialect', *Journal of the Ethnological Society, 4*, pp. 285–93.

Sahlins, M 2013, *What kinship is—and is not*, Chicago: University of Chicago Press.

Scheffler, H 1978, *Australian kin classification*, Cambridge: Cambridge University Press.

Schneider, D 1968, *American kinship: a cultural account*, Englewood Cliffs NJ: Prentice Hall.

Smith, KV 1992, *King Bungaree: a Sydney Aborigine meets the great South Pacific explorers*, Kenthurst, NSW: Kangaroo Press.

Spencer, B & Gillen, F 1899, *The native tribes of Central Australia*, London: Macmillan.

Thomas, WI 1907, *Sex and society: studies in the social psychology of sex*, Chicago and London: University of Chicago Press and T. Fisher Unwin.

Troy, JK 1993, *King plates: a history of Aboriginal gorgets*, Canberra: Aboriginal Studies Press.

Tylor, EB 1878 [1865], *Researches into the early history of mankind and the development of civilization*, Boston: Estes & Lauriat. doi.org/10.1037/12848-000.

PART I
People and Place

3

Systems in Geography or Geography of Systems? Attempts to Represent Spatial Distributions of Australian Social Organisation

Laurent Dousset

> Cartography, we now being to realize, is the product of wider discourses, a form of power-knowledge caught up with the major transformations of world history, created and received by human agents, exploited by elites, to materialize as a world seen through a veil of ideology. (Harley 1991, p. 16)

> It is now generally accepted that maps are social constructions rather than depictions of an objective reality, and insights from recent studies have enlarged and deepened our understanding of cartography. (Etherington 2007, p. 1)

Maps are undoubtedly complex objects that tend to create lives of their own, and in this respect, Australia has always been one of the most fascinating regions. The futurist European maps of the sixteenth and seventeenth centuries depicted a Terra Incognita or Terra Australis (see Figure 1) yet to be 'discovered'. The utopian literature that accompanied the phantasms of a yet-to-be-revealed extraordinary land complemented these maps (e.g. de Foigny 1676). Australia was a reality before it was discovered, not only because of its Indigenous inhabitants but also as an idea in Europe that started with Pythagoras five centuries BCE. It continued to occupy the European mind with Marco Polo's tales and the rich land called Lucac[1] (see Figure 2) that was then thought to be the 'undiscovered' continent, as well as the speculation regarding the location of the biblical Ophir mentioned in the *Books of Kings* and the *Books of Chronicles*, from which the gold for the construction of King Solomon's temple was brought in. The representations of Terra Australis and the maps that depicted the imaginary continent ended up becoming part of the motives for the many expeditions to the Pacific (see Estensen 1998). The graphical representation of Terra Australis in maps as an economically and culturally rich sister of the old European continent became a proof of its existence and an engine for one of the most important changes in human history: the colonisation of the Pacific.

Whatever they represent, maps tend to legitimate and establish the foundations of a particular vision of reality—whether it be observed, reconstructed or entirely imagined. Conversely, once drawn, maps also embody the power to describe things without the need for actual seeing and so become, according to Latour (1987), autonomous actors in the transmission and translation of knowledge. As independent objects, maps end up engendering and replicating a truth that is disconnected from the context and understanding or imagination at their origin. Their capacity to speak through symbols alone, without text and voice, as well as their transportability, limited physical extent and easy reintegration into new frameworks of knowledge production and transmission are likely responsible for their popularity and the fascination they generate.

Through these characteristics, maps stand as objects of authority and power, providing overviews and a vertical perspective, summarising and necessarily stereotyping facts into a single and simplified world (D'Andrade 1992). By revealing some aspects and omitting others, they offer a sense of dominance and an appreciation of the capacity to grasp a sphere that is otherwise too complex and diverse to assimilate. Maps define points and areas; draw boundaries and borders; stress distinctions and similarities, difference and sameness, continuities and discontinuities (or discontinuities through continuities); and create 'land' through the portrayal of a virtual space through the use of criteria that necessarily tend towards generalisation and representativeness. They construct history through selecting certain traces, while consigning others to oblivion (Ricoeur 2000).

---

1   Also spelled 'Locach' or called 'La Joncade' by Le Testu (1556; see also Lestringant 2013).

3. SYSTEMS IN GEOGRAPHY OR GEOGRAPHY OF SYSTEMS?

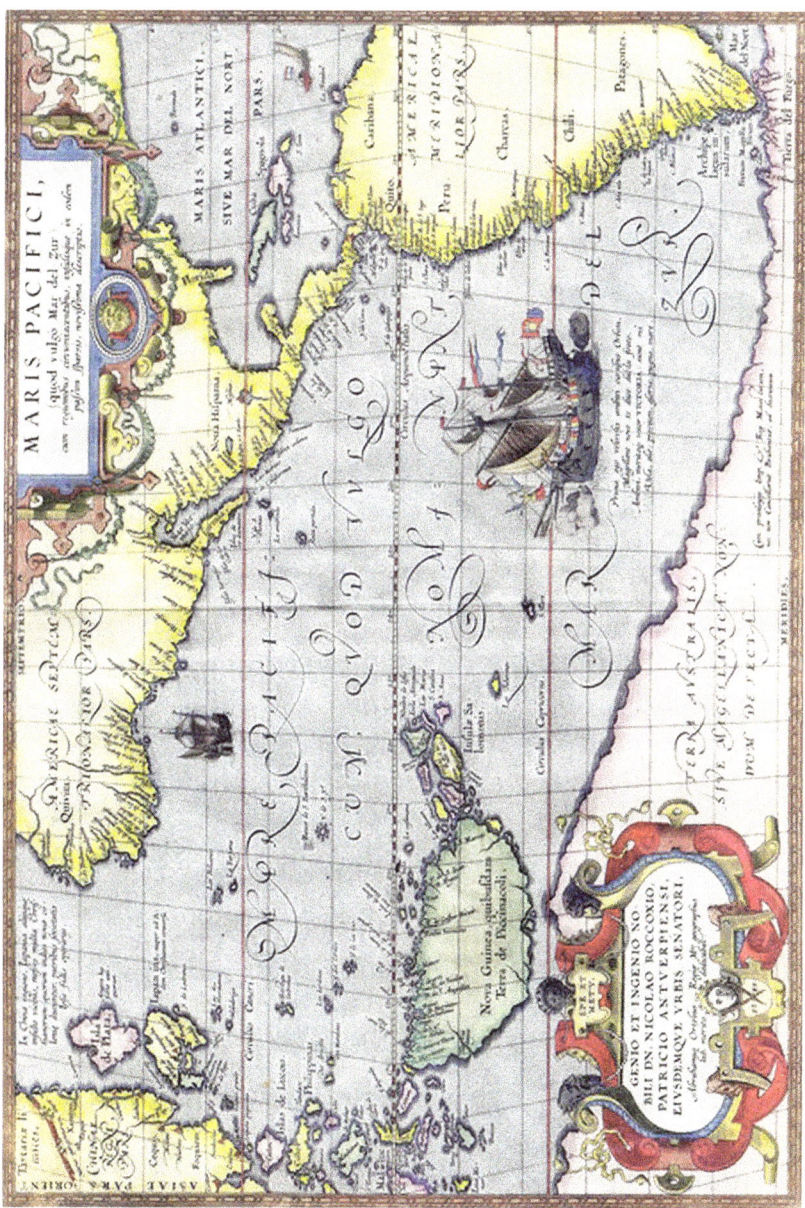

Figure 1: *Maris Pacifici* showing Terra Australis by Abraham Ortelius (33 x 48 cm; scale: 1:40,000,000), Anvers: Imprimerie Plantinienne, 1589.
Source: Wikipedia (2012).

Figure 2: *Cette terre est dite la région Australe* (This land that is called the Australian region) by Guillaume Le Testu, FO XXXV, Le Havre, 1556.
Source: Le Testu (1556).

3. SYSTEMS IN GEOGRAPHY OR GEOGRAPHY OF SYSTEMS?

What has been sketchily summarised regarding the power of maps in general, and maps of Australia in particular, is also valid in the realm of the specific geographic representations developed to draw Indigenous Australian cultures.[2] However, it is also due to this inherent power of maps that:

> Mapping indigenous people across the whole continent of Australia has been riddled with difficulties … The three maps that have set out to do this for the whole of Australia in the late 20th century—by Norman Tindale [1974], Stephen Davis [1993], and David Horton [1996] maps—have been contentious. (Blackburn 2002, p. 134)

These attempts involve an 'Aboriginal territoriality according to non-Aboriginal concepts of boundaries' that is 'fraught with danger' (cf. Sutton 1995; Young 1995). However, it seems that the awareness of the contentious nature of mapping Australian Indigenous cultures is not limited to recent writings. Blackburn did not consider Davidson's (1938) 'ethnic map of Australia', since it is earlier than the period considered by Blackburn in the late twentieth century. Interestingly, Davidson was cautious enough not to draw boundaries around his 'tribes', and simply placed names in a rather geographically neutral space. Was it because Davidson could not do so, or because he did not want to consider territoriality? Was he aware of the inherent difficulties that lines and areas drawn on a map would produce in a colonial context? Or had the intellectual and political environments changed during the second half of the twentieth century, driving researchers such as Tindale (1974) and Horton (1996) to create those maps that Blackburn qualified as contentious?

This chapter attempts to elaborate on the background to these questions, and succinctly articulate the evolution of a style of mapping in which it was Aboriginal social organisation that very early on became the means through which cultural distinctions or similarities, and different historicities more generally, were represented and defined in space. Further, the chapter attempts to place these mapping styles against their general scientific background. I use the expression 'social organisation' as it was shaped and used by Howitt and Fison (1885), meaning a systematic division of a group into a usually even number of categories—such as moieties, sections or subsections—on which marriage regulations are based. Interestingly, in the context of mapping, Howitt (1996 [1904],

---

2   This chapter will not deal with Indigenous modes of representing space. The reader may want to consult Sutton's (1998a, 1998b) two chapters in this realm.

pp. 42–3) distinguished 'social organisation' from what he called 'local organisation', with the latter including geographical groupings called 'clans' in which there is patrilineal descent and 'hordes' in which there is matrilineal descent—which one would think more prone to being mapped.

In some mapping styles, the distinction between social and local organisation was not as clear-cut as Howitt had expressed, which meant that these two domains were sometimes blurred. Moreover, kinship and social organisation in particular were not the only domains of Indigenous society to be mapped. Material culture or ritual characteristics, such as bodily markings during initiations and linguistic classifications, have been frequently represented in space (see Davidson 1936; Mathews 1900; Schmidt 1912) with the aim of reproducing a geographical space reflecting cultural affinities and differences. Of course, 'tribal' distribution has been another object of mapping (see Connelly 1932; Davidson 1936; Mathews 1900; Schmidt 1912). What is particularly interesting about mapping social organisation is that it has been interpreted as a domain that crystallises and typifies Indigenous diversity and similarity, as well as evolution: an opportunity to map time and space simultaneously. Social organisation has often been understood as a marker for change or governance,[3] and as such it has been used to reveal an internal social structure in such a way that it becomes efficient for large-scale comparison—be it within or beyond the Australian scope. In one way or another, maps exposing other cultural characteristics had to reflect or at least overlap to some extent with the distribution of social organisation.

After a brief introduction to Australian social organisation, the chapter suggests three main historical periods—the homogenisation period, the organic period and the dynamic period—in which Australian Indigenous people have been conceptualised within their own homogeneity and diversity through the device of mapping. These periods are not necessarily clearly distinguished from each other and overlap to some extent, essentially operating as a rhetoric device and allowing the typification of certain principles (and scientific ideologies) and characterisation of what I believe to be the evolution of anthropological mapping.

---

3   I do not limit the notion of governance to the question of authority and its legitimisation, but extend it to embrace all that can be considered in shaping the public space, such as obligations of redistribution and rights of access to material and immaterial resources, rules of marriage and circulation of people, as well as systems of land tenure and ritual activity.

For each period, I only mention a few important authors, mostly anthropologists,[4] with no attempt to be exhaustive, but with the aim of discussing the main features and authoritative messages that their maps convey. Maps not only represent 'systems' in space and systems in geography alone, but are also a means to legitimate and illustrate particular epistemologies and their evolution: they become geography or even geometry of systems.

What is Social Organisation?

When anthropologists use the concept of 'social organisation' with respect to Australia in particular, they are not implying a vague idea about the administration of social life in general, but understanding—since Howitt and Fison's (1885) contribution at least—the linguistic and sociological features that are considered specific to, and certainly widespread if not universal in, Aboriginal languages and cultures. The notion of social organisation in Australia reflects linguistic, conceptual and classificatory devices that distribute all members of a group and beyond—and also mythical figures in many languages—into an even number of categories that stand on top of or alongside kinship terminologies or systems of land tenure, and that are interrelated in particular and sometimes complex ways (for an overview and discussion, see Dousset 2011). Australian social organisation has garnered considerable attention, if not fascination, from numerous scholars. To quote one example, Lévi-Strauss (1996 [1973], pp. 41–2) admired the 'crystalline beauty' of the systems that Australian cultures had developed.

There are different types of classificatory devices, and I will summarise the most representative systems without going into too much formal detail. Some of the features of these systems have been used in the AustKin project (see Figure 3) to record and process data, as well as map social categories.

---

4   I do not and cannot deal with archaeology, linguistics, political sciences, demography and, of course, geography itself in this chapter. However, I would suggest that while archaeology and linguistics have to some extent developed their own (although in correspondence with anthropology) means of mapping Australian Indigenous cultures, the other disciplines rely heavily on anthropological mapping.

Systems of social organisation can be divided into two general types. The first type is dualistic in that it opposes two social categories that stand in a direct and identical relationship to each other. The second type could be called indirect dualistic; it still articulates an even number of categories, but these categories do not all stand in an identical relationship to each other. Dualistic systems are moiety systems of which there are two subtypes: matrimoieties and patrimoieties. In these systems, the categories stand in a marriage relationship to each other. Merged alternate generational levels—also called generational moieties—are another system that is of the dualistic type. These are organised around a relationship of filiation, rather than marriage. In particular, patrimoiety and matrimoiety systems are well spread throughout the world and are found in many languages.

Indirect dualistic systems are section, subsection and semi-moiety systems. They are rare on a world scale and generally considered limited to Australia, although some kind of section system seems to be used by groups among Panoan speakers in South America (see Chapter 8; Fleck 2013 cited in McConvell 2013; Hornborg 1993; McConvell 2013). Section or similar systems have also been reported to have existed in ancient China (Cooper 1983; Kryukov 2004) and are in use on the island of Ambrym in Vanuatu (Lane & Lane 1956; Patterson 1976), although the structure of these systems is different from the one found in Australia.

Dualistic systems divide society into two halves that stand in a direct and unique type of relationship to each other. In matrimoiety systems, a person belongs to the same moiety as his or her mother and marries a person of the other moiety, where his or her father came from. In a patrimoiety system, a person belongs to the same moiety as his or her father and marries a person of the other moiety, where his or her mother came from.

Generational moieties are different from the two former systems, as they are not organised by marriage relationships and instead express a relationship of filiation. In this system, a person sits in the same moiety as his or her brothers, sisters and cousins, and grandparents and grandchildren. The other moiety includes a person's fathers and mothers, aunts and uncles, children, nephews and nieces. The relationship between these two moieties is one of filiation (parent–child; child–parent) and not intermarriage, as is the case for the two other moiety systems.

3. SYSTEMS IN GEOGRAPHY OR GEOGRAPHY OF SYSTEMS?

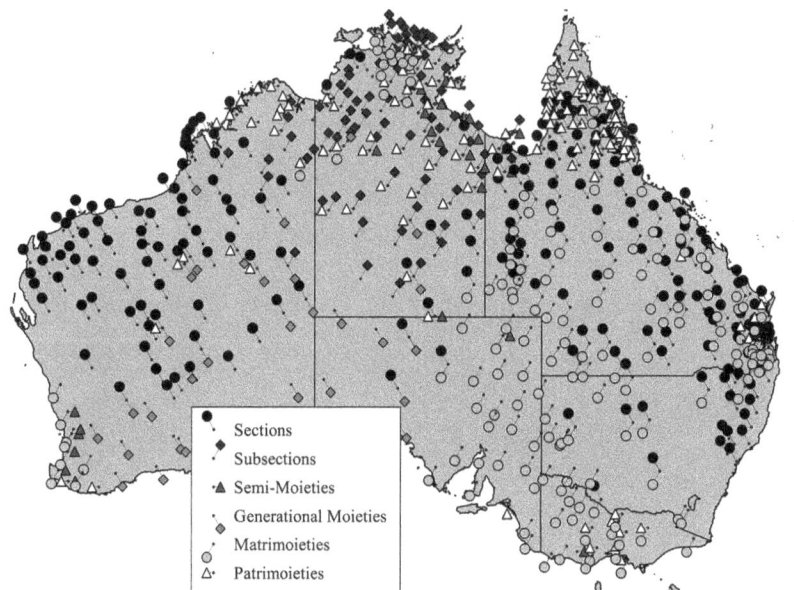

Figure 3: The distribution of some system types in Australia following the AustKin database.

The database has information on 273 sections, 105 subsections, 23 semi-moieties, 154 matrimoieties, 114 patrimoieties and 38 generational moieties. The approximate locations of the languages that know such systems are represented in the map: 172 with sections, 59 with subsections, 17 with semi-moieties, 120 with matrimoieties, 86 with patrimoieties and 29 with generational moieties. A total of 348 languages or dialects, past or present, are documented. One language may use more than one system type. Note that this map does not take into account historical changes or the diffusion of system types, but is a general snapshot of all systems that at any known time in history were or are used by a language.

Source: Author's map built through the AustKin interface, using NaturalEarthData.com open source contour data on QGIS.

Conversely, indirect dualistic systems divide society into more than two categories that stand in various types of relationships to each other, such as marriage, father–child and mother–child. Subsection and semi-moiety systems divide society into eight categories. Some subsection terminologies additionally account for gender differences. Section systems divide society generally into four categories (and some have an additional gender difference).

Three more elements are important to note before we move on to consider the evolution of the mapping of these systems. First, in most, if not all, languages, social categories not only include and classify human beings but also mythological figures or natural species that each sit in one of the available classes. Second, it is well known that social category systems—

sections and subsections, in particular—spread over vast areas of Australia before colonisation (see Dousset 2005; McConvell 1985a, 1996). They are particularly convenient in intertribal and interlanguage encounters and are therefore prone to diffusion because they appear as a simplification, work as a ready-reference index (Fry 1933) and even constitute a lingua franca of kinship. A map displaying the distribution of these systems may thus reveal significant changes from the same map drawn 50 years earlier. Third, social categories have specific Indigenous labels—the moiety names, section names or subsection names themselves—as the examples in Figure 4 illustrate. Therefore, two characteristics have become the object of mapping: the system types themselves and also the Indigenous names that denote the categories within the system.

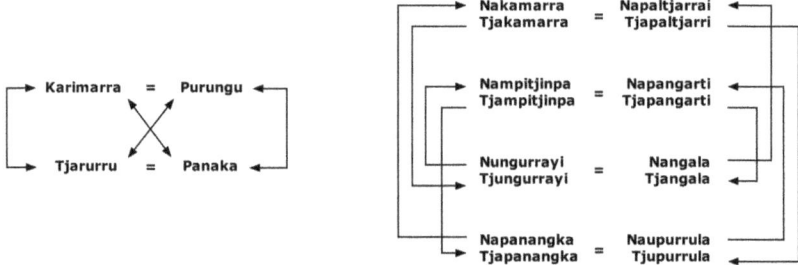

Figure 4: Example of a section system (left) of the Ngaatjatjarra group and of a subsection system (right) of the Warlpiri language.
Equal signs link intermarrying (sub)sections; vertical arrows indicate mother–child relationships; diagonal lines in the section system indicate father–child relationships. For examples of semi-moiety systems, see Maddock (1972); Shapiro (1969).
Source: Author's work.

The Indigenous names given to these categories are usually absolute. This means that the name of the category in which a person stands does not change depending on the speaker. A notable exception is the generational moiety, in which there may be relative and absolute names. This is the case for the Western Desert Ngaatjatjarra people who know both relative and absolute terminologies. The absolute names of these moieties are Tjintultukultul (meaning sun-side) and Ngumpaluru (meaning shade-side). A person is born into one of these two categories. Conversely, the relative names are Nganatarka (meaning 'us, we bone') and Tjanamilytjan (meaning 'them, they flesh') (see Goddard 1992 [1987]). Every person says he or she sits in the Nganatarka moiety, while people from the other moiety are said to stand in the Tjanamilytjan moiety.

Homogenisation: Early Mapping of Aboriginal 'Evolution'

Many of the early attempts to map Australian Indigenous 'nations' or 'tribes' were already based on displaying similarities and distinctions in the domain of social organisation. For example, Mathews's 1900 map (see Figure 5) attempts to group tribes and groups following two criteria: initiation ceremonies that he saw to function as a means of regional and mutual integration and, more importantly, shared 'divisions' (moiety, section and subsection systems and names) (see Blackburn 2002, p. 147).

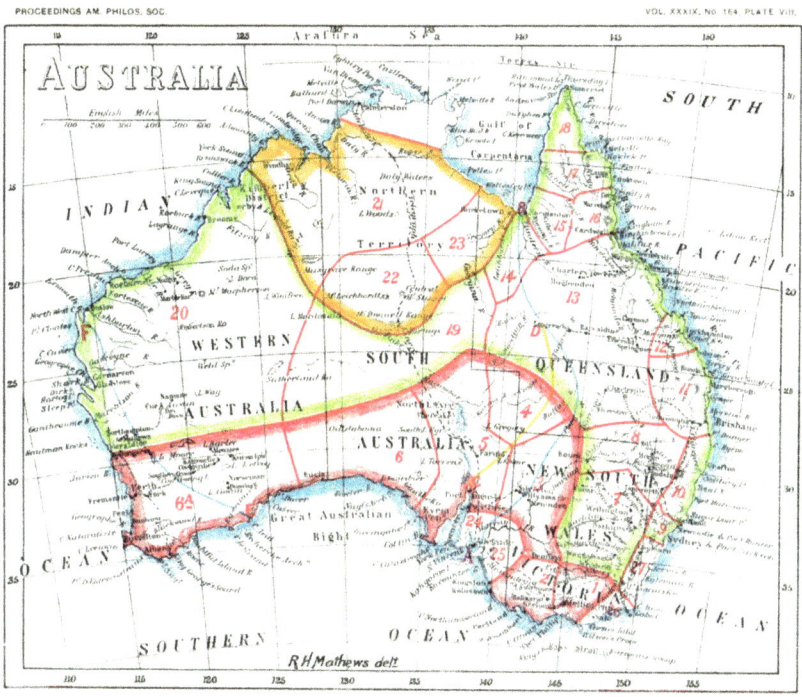

Figure 5: Mathews's Aboriginal nations according to similar or identical moiety, section or subsection names (thin lines and numbered areas) and identical system types (shaded lines and large areas).
Source: Mathews (1900).

SKIN, KIN AND CLAN

The following quotations are extracts from Mathews's own explanations of his map:

> A tribe is divided into sections, which are known by distinguished titles ... The names of these divisions vary in different districts. In a certain tract of country the sections will be known by one set of names, whilst among adjoining tribes a different nomenclature will be employed. Aggregates of tribes holding the same divisional names may, for convenience of reference, be called communities or nations [the thin lines and numbered areas in the map].

> I have prepared a map, showing New South Wales, Queensland, Victoria, South Australia and Western Australia, on which is shown the position of the boundaries of the several nations, each of which is distinguished by a numeral, from 1 to 27. In explaining this map I shall commence with the several nations possessing two divisions [moieties], then those with four divisions [sections], next the tribes with eight divisions [subsections], and lastly a brief reference will be made to those tribes whose marriage laws are of the tooar type [mother-in-law bestowal; areas 24 to 27 in the map]. (Mathews 1900, pp. 574–5).

The shaded lines in the map, dividing Australia into three[5] large areas, represent the grouping of similar system types (as opposed to the fine lines inside these larger areas that represent the grouping of system types and the linguistic proximity of the division names). The southern area reflects the distribution of two division systems (moieties; red in the original colour map); the central area, reaching up to north Queensland in the east, depicts the distribution of the four-division system (sections; green); and the north-central area (numbers 21, 22 and 23) is characteristic of eight divisions (subsections; yellow-orange). Later, we will see that Mathews was not that far off in his representation, and, provided some tolerance is accorded, current anthropologists and linguists accept his general picture (see Figure 8). The strict boundaries that he drew between moiety, section and subsections areas—separated by harsh and thick lines—are significant, and each integrate several 'nations' that themselves are built around the resemblances of the names of these items of social organisation. Moreover, the three types of social organisation systems that function here as the witness of veritable cultural and social boundaries never overlap or crisscross. Instead, they constitute three neatly defined and distinguished geographic areas—and, as we will see, historical layers. Here, the types of

---

5   In fact, there are four areas within the Top End, for which he does not provide any information or classification.

social organisation systems reveal entirely different cultural and historical objects from their ostensible sole purpose of subdividing society into an even number of categories.

Indeed, it is necessary to recall Mathews's ambition in this paper: 'to give a short outline of the probable origin of the native tribes of Australia' (1900, p. 556). He believed that the continent was populated by two waves of migration. The first and most 'primitive' wave is still visible in the south-east, characterised by the existence of the mother-in-law bestowal. 'In some respects', he wrote, 'these people differ in physical type, in weapons, in language and in their ceremonies, from the natives of other parts of Australia, but resemble in several particulars the inhabitants of Tasmania' (1900, p. 560). The second wave of migration is progressive, with tribe after tribe moving into the continent. Mathews believed these migrations and the subsequent competition and warfare among the tribes were the reasons these groups elaborated systems of exchange of women between them in order to settle in new territories and engage in peaceful relationships. Thus, the moiety, section and subsection names all represent the original tribal names of these newly intermarrying groups. The further north we move, the more complex the intertribal alliances become, superimposing themselves onto previously established and simpler intertribal relationships: first between two, then four and finally eight tribes. According to Mathews, the map of social organisation is a map reflecting the history of migration, with more 'modern' tribes progressively imposing themselves onto the sociocultural landscape. The boundaries between systems seem to reflect the geographical reach of waves of new migrations.

Despite the fact that Mathews was a great traveller and had visited many of the Australian regions, as well as read (even though he seldom acknowledged) the existing ethnography, we are faced with a largely evolutionary approach shared by most of his contemporaries: attempts to elaborate maps in which cultural particulars reflect historical chronology, and in which boundaries represent temporal and evolutionary stages. Even though Howitt was a fine ethnographer, scrupulously distinguishing 'facts' from 'theories' (Keen 2000), he had also been tempted by these large-scale and generalising hypotheses, such as when he wrote that 'the division of the people of the tribe into two classes [moieties] is the foundation from which the whole social organisation of the native tribes of Australia has been developed' (Howitt 1996 [1904], p. 89).[6]

---

6 See Howitt (1883, p. 496) where he thought 'that the early state of their society was that of an undivided commune'.

Schmidt (1912, 1919) adopted a similar approach to that of Mathews when he attempted to represent the history of migration and social evolution of Australian Aboriginal tribes and languages through mapping. Similar to Mathews, Schmidt believed that the structure and form of social organisation known by groups attest to cultural and historical affinities. However, Schmidt's approach is a linguistic one. His ambition drove him even further than Mathews in attempting to reconstruct the historical linkages between Australian and Asian languages and cultures. Schmidt identified several large groupings—of which the Tasmanians are the oldest representatives—that reflect waves of migration to the continent. Inspired by Graebner (1906), a geographer and ethnologist who fostered the Kulturkreis theory in Vienna, Schmidt related the age of migration to the complexity of social organisation and placed this within the classification of languages. The older a language and a system, the fewer the social categories used to structure society. Despite the historical approach adopted, Schmidt challenged the evolutionary theory and underlined the importance of migration, diffusion, recombination and transformation. He is one of the first scholars to strongly suggest that sections (what I call indirect dualistic systems) are the result of the encounter and combination of languages with matrimoieties and patrimoieties, or dualistic systems.

However, from the twentieth century onwards, the drive to conflate geography and history has gradually been replaced by the new approaches of the functionalist and structural-functionalist schools of Great Britain. Speculation about the evolution and relative homogeneity of Australian Aboriginal societies gave way to an emphasis on synchronicity and typology, ending in the complete refusal of 'conjectural history' (Radcliffe-Brown 1941).

The Emergence of Integrated Mapping of the Structural-Functionalist Approach

The maps of the early decades of the twentieth century reflect an important change, as well as an inherent contradiction (or dialectic) and emergent imperative. An explicit will emerged to distance this new anthropology from the earlier speculative depictions in which Australian Indigenous cultures were often represented as a rather homogeneous unity. The emergence of fieldwork as a central aspect of the anthropological discipline, with researchers reporting a wide variety of structures and practices, was obviously a main driving factor in this change. The objective was now to represent this newly discovered diversity and complexity of the cultural and social landscape. Davidson's (1928, p. 3) introduction to his thesis is revealing in this respect:[7]

> At first glance one might expect that no great difficulties should be encountered in an attempt to determine the cultural and physical affinities of people characterized by such a fair homogeneity of race and by such a comparatively simple material culture as are the Australians. This notion is soon dispelled, however, when one realizes that in spite of the great deal of attention which has been given to these questions, we still seem to be but little nearer [to] the ultimate objective realization than we were at the offset.

Davidson (1928, pp. 4–5) believed former homogenisations were erroneous and generalisations still difficult because ethnography was insufficient:

> I believe that the time has not yet arrived for an intensive study of Australian culture. Information is still too scarce and that which we have, collected from localities too scattered … I am convinced that many … traits in Australia might have been considered … However, due to the defects in information I have refused to treat them until we have more data at our command.[8]

Conversely, while the need for more ethnographic data and warnings for too-rapid generalisations were expressed, the necessity for typologies became palpable. Indeed, to accommodate the ethnographic diversity in an approach that largely maintained a continental scope, a movement of thought that heavily relied on establishing new homogeneities despite the newly acquired diversity became necessary. Maps that displayed this new diversity-homogeneity dialectic became both central objects of analysis and summaries of general conclusions, and had important impacts for future research.

---

7   While I am not completely convinced Davidson can be considered a structuralist or functionalist, for he is probably closer to the diffusionist approaches, he also values and depicts many features of the functionalist schools: importance of ethnographic data, avoidance of conjectural history, and social institutions seen in embedded and strongly interdependent terms.
8   In another publication, Davidson (1926) argued that it is necessary 'that higher institutional complexities, which are so common and unique in Australia, be reconstructed upon a sounder basis of consideration and less upon theoretical analogies derived from conditions in other regions of the world', clearly distancing himself from the evolutionist and some of the Kulturkreis scholars.

The will to elaborate unifying and comparative perspectives despite the ethnographic diversity probably reached its apotheosis with Elkin, who was a student of Radcliffe-Brown. In his classic *The Australian Aborigines* (1974 [1938]), Elkin expounded typologies of social organisation that in many respects intermingle aspects of Aboriginal culture that are not easily perceived to belong to the same level of social reality. 'Each tribe is subdivided into two or more social groups on the basis of locality, age, sex and unilateral relationship' (Elkin 1974 [1938], p. 112), he wrote when introducing his typologies: local groups are generally patrilineal, patrilocal and exogamous; age grouping and age grades reflect the distribution of authority and respect with regard to age; generation lines reflect the distinct terms and groupings of succeeding generations (today called alternate generational levels or moieties); sex grouping is the 'biological fact of sex difference [that] divides the Aborigines into two groups which for some purpose are mutually dependent' (p. 116); social totemic clans are groups of people related in one line only, through the father or mother, and are usually members of a local group or subdivision of a tribe; moieties divide tribes into halves that are definite social and ceremonial groupings; and sections, subsections and semi-moieties are divisions of 'some tribes into four or eight social groups with their own rules of marriage and descent' (p. 124).

Age, generation, gender, locality, totem and social categories appear on identical levels and in a unified perspective in which the central—that is not to say only—criterion is that of grouping, classification and organisation, preparing the way to reunify a diversity of Aboriginal cultures following rather simplistic distinctions.

Alongside this drive to elaborate criteria that allow the unification of diversity, there emerges another imperative tied to the structural-functionalist school. Social structure reflects social institutions and their mutual interdependence: things that are social are coherent with each other. Essentially, social organisation is seen as a means of distributing people and access, as well as transmission of land, and land tenure systems are seen as the pragmatic and materialistic counterparts of kinship and social organisation, such as sections and subsections. In his famous 1913 paper, Radcliffe-Brown engaged in this dialectic and the elaboration of this imperative: he relied heavily on mapping as a mode of arguing and perpetuating a particular way of thinking about Aboriginal society, its diversity and unity, as well as the mutual and organic integration of social domains.

In this founding paper, Radcliffe-Brown (1913) defined the Kariera as a linguistic and territorial group with a distinct name, a tribe (p. 144) divided into 'local groups' (p. 145)[9] of which membership is 'determined by descent in the male line' (p. 145) and that collectively own the resources of their territory (p. 146). The local group itself is composed of individual families that move independently within the local group territory (p. 147). Members of the local group need to find a spouse in another group: 'in the camp of the local group would be found only men and unmarried women and children who belonged to the group by birth, the married women all belonging by birth to other groups' (p. 147). In a few pages, Radcliffe-Brown constructed an integrated model of social organisation and land tenure that has remained at the centre of many discussions for decades— and is still significant today, in particular in the context of native title (Dousset & Glaskin 2007; Glaskin & Dousset 2011)—in which residence and property are largely coextensive and backed by marriage practice[10] and social organisation. While he thought (in this paper, as well as later papers) this to be a general Australian model, he also established typologies and underlined to a certain extent the existence of diversities based on additional particular marriage rules and what he referred to as 'classes'.

'The Kariera tribe', Radcliffe-Brown (1913, p. 147) wrote, 'is divided into four parts that I shall speak of as *classes*', which constitute the section system. Not surprisingly—as the relationships between the classes need to be compatible with the local group model and kinship terminology— he framed the inherent marriage rules not as prescriptions, but as proscriptions: 'this does not imply that a Banaka [one of the sections] man may marry *any* Burung [another section] woman, but only that he may not marry a woman of any other class' (p. 148). 'The proper person for a man to marry', he later wrote, 'if it be possible, is his own first cousin'; and well before Lévi-Strauss (1967 [1947]), Radcliffe-Brown explained that 'a common custom in this as in most Australian tribes is the exchange of sisters' (p. 156).

---

9   The usage and definition of the notion of 'local group' predates Radcliffe-Brown (1913), of course. McLennan (1970 [1865]) had already used this concept. Interestingly, while Radcliffe-Brown does not quote former definitions in his paper, Howitt and Fison (1885) and more particularly Howitt (1996 [1904], p. 89) had underlined the distinction between 'clan' (as a sociogeographical division) and 'horde': the former being a residential group in a patrilineal system whereby land-using groups and land-owning or land-holding groups are equivalent, and the latter being a residential group whereby landownership is inherited matrilineally (see Chapter 4).
10   Of course, others have discussed these issues before Radcliffe-Brown. But his 1913 paper had in my view the most profound impact on the way the representations of Australian Indigenous cultures were subsequently modelled.

SKIN, KIN AND CLAN

Finally, Radcliffe-Brown (1913, p. 159) eagerly mapped the section system onto his local group model in order to elaborate an integrated and organic view of Aboriginal social organisation and structure (see Figure 6):

> The whole tribe is divided into two couples of classes, Banaka-Palyeri and Karimaera-Burung. Each local group, however, that is, each of the local subdivisions of the tribe, consists of members of one couple only. Thus one local group consists of men and women of the classes Karimera and Burung, while another consists of Banaka and Palyeri men and women. *In the map of the tribe*, underneath the numeral denoting each local group, will be found two letters indicating the couple to which the group belongs. B. P. stands for Banaka-Palyeri, and K. B. for Karimera-Burung. It is thus possible to *realize at a glance the geographical distribution* of the couples. (emphasis added)

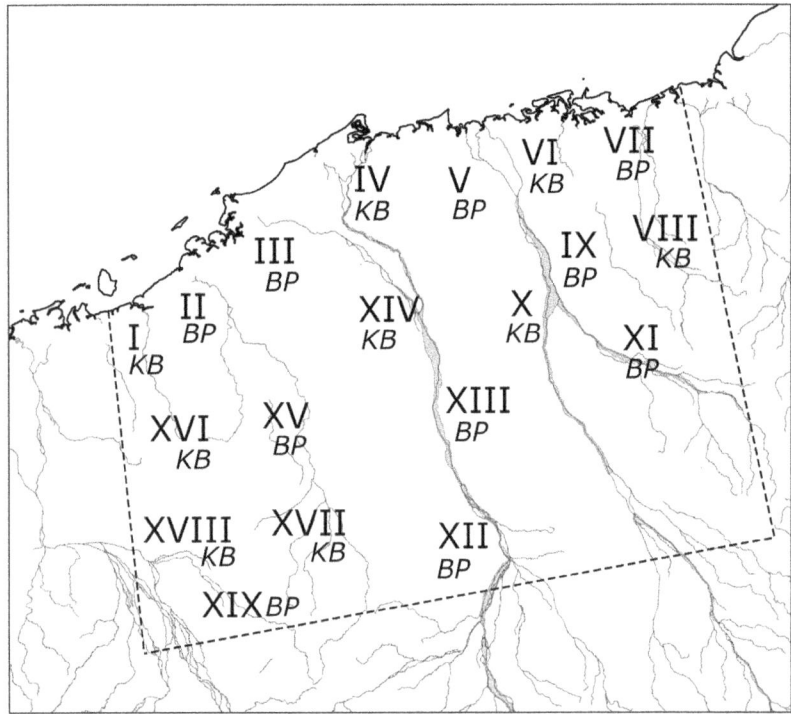

Figure 6: Radcliffe-Brown's vision of the 'Kariera tribe' showing 'local groups' (roman numbers) and associated section couples (letters).
Source: L. Dousset from Radcliffe-Brown's (1913) text and drawing.

Demerath (1966, p. 400) considered Radcliffe-Brown a 'functionalist' in the structural-functionalist school, among those 'guided by an interest in the system as a whole', as opposed to the structuralists of the same school that were interested in 'the analysis of a particular part in the system'. Functionalists ran 'the risk of overestimating system unity' and were 'more concerned with internal process than external change' (Demerath 1966, p. 400). In Radcliffe-Brown's obsession to construct an integrated system, an obvious inconsistency in his geographical depiction of social organisation emerged for at least two reasons, as most researchers who have done fieldwork in Aboriginal Australia would immediately recognise. First, all four sections, and not only two, are simultaneously present in any residential group—be it for formal or pragmatic reasons. For example, if we accept patrilineality to be constitutive of local groups, as Radcliffe-Brown wanted it, then one would supposedly find in any local group a male ego (one section) and his wife (a second section), but also that man's father (a third section) and the latter's wife, ego's mother (a fourth section). However, had Radcliffe-Brown been consistent with his own patrilineal local group model, then he should have depicted father–son section couples and not spouse couples. It could well be that he chose to model the spouse couple in order to comply with his other assertion about sister-exchange, and in order to stress the mutual interdependence of the many local groups through marriage and the circulation of women. Otherwise, his whole concept of the 'Kariera tribe' would have been highly questionable, or at least unstable since it could not reproduce itself with the same distinctions over time. Whatever the reasons, he made certain choices that resulted in the Kariera tribe—or really the Kariera model—becoming one of the ideal types and underlying configuration of any kind of Australian social organisation. In fact, all other 'types' or 'systems' are depicted as derivations or relatives of this basic theme, initiated on an organic integration of social organisation with land tenure and marriage. Mapping these 'types' and 'systems' truly became a system of mapping rather than a mapping of systems.

The Organic Period: From Mapping a Model to Mapping Typologies

Due to this integrated understanding of social structure and institutions, mapping social category systems became a means to both map diversity and homogeneity of Aboriginal culture more generally, provided some explicit (or implicit) typology to group Indigenous tribes into regional and pan-regional subsets (so-called cultural blocks) was articulated. Davidson's (1926, 1928) and Radcliffe-Brown's (1930) maps, differing only a little from each other, are particularly revealing in this respect (see Figure 7).

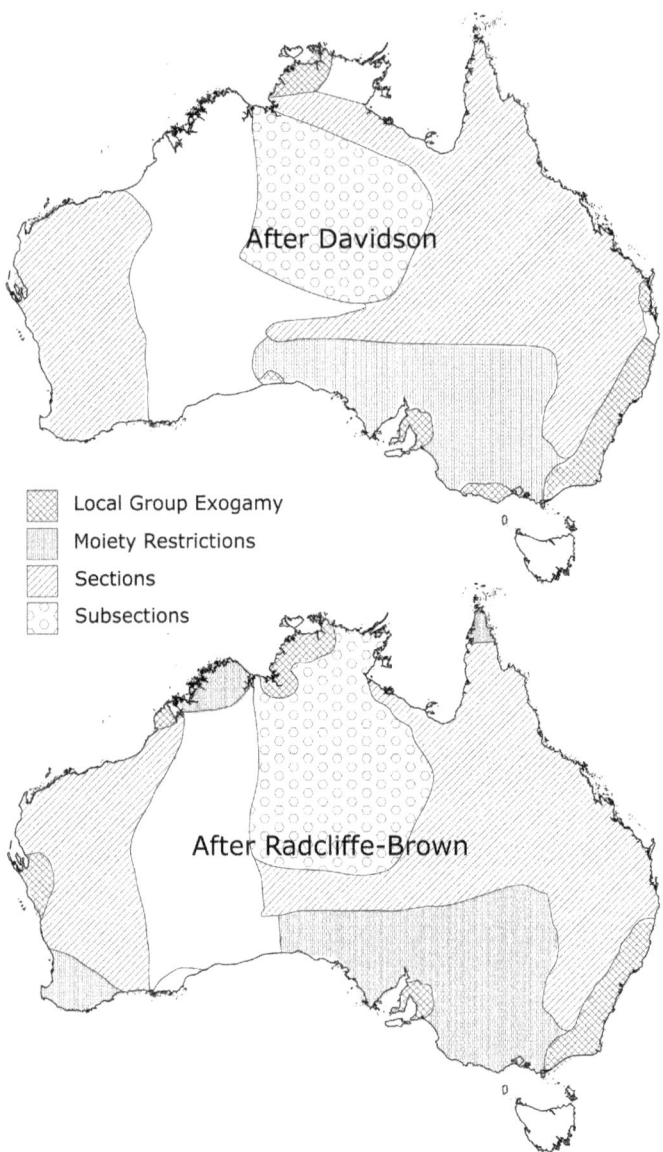

Figure 7: Davidson's and Radcliffe-Brown's maps of the distribution of social organisation in Aboriginal Australia as summarised by Yengoyan.
Source: L. Dousset after Yengoyan (1968b, p. 193).[11]

---

11   It is interesting (and revealing) to note that what Yengoyan labels 'local group exogamy' in his reinterpretation of Davidson's map, Davidson (1926, p. 535) himself simply notes as 'tribes without a class organisation'.

Not surprisingly, these maps display local group exogamy and social category systems. Even though Radcliffe-Brown repeatedly warned against understanding section and subsection systems as regulating marriage, he is in fact unable to distance himself from this view in which social organisation, marriage and land tenure are intrinsically linked, as we have seen in the previous section.

Yengoyan (1968a, 1968b, 1970) went even further, adding population density and size of tribes or linguistic groups to the already integrated view of the distribution of social category systems. He suggested complementing the existing correlation between land tenure and social category systems with an additional materialist foundation (see the critique by McKnight 1981), suggesting that types of social organisation are modes of adaptation to different kinds of environment. This additional factor is related to Birdsell's (1953, 1973) theory, for whom the notion of 'equilibrium' between population size, group size and environmental conditions (in particular, mean annual rainfall [Birdsell 1958]) was intrinsic to hunter-gatherer 'patrilineal-band' societies in general, and Aboriginal Australians in particular. For Birdsell (1973, p. 337), just like Radcliffe-Brown, the patrilineal local group (in contrast to Radcliffe-Brown, Birdsell used the word 'horde') underpins Australian society in general and provides the basis for a possible extension of this Australian model to understand a wider range of hunter-gatherer societies:

> The tribe in Australia possesses special attributes which make it particularly suitable and attractive for the investigation of regularities. Australia is the only continent which at the time of contact was exclusively populated by hunting and collecting peoples. These existed in tribal units, totalling 581 in all, a far greater number than anywhere else in the world. The environmental and cultural factors influencing their structure are better known (Birdsell 1953) than for other populations at a similar economic level. *They are a model for other cellular-structured patrilineal-band types of societies*, both those which have persisted elsewhere into present times and those which are presumed to have been preponderant during the Pleistocene. (emphasis added)

Yengoyan (1968b, p. 194) explained that he aimed to explore 'population size … in terms of its functions and limits on the "ideal" operation of marriage sections', that 'population size is a critical factor in the ideal operation of section systems' (p. 198) and that 'one of the functions of sections and subsections may have been an economic factor in allowing populations to "insure" a vast territorial domain from non-tribal groups'

(p. 199). Thus, Yengoyan was eager to add the economic and ecological components to Radcliffe-Brown's integrated model. Yengoyan's review of the distribution of social organisation has become tangible evidence, largely in the form of maps, of the encounter between the structural-functionalist approach and environmental determinism in Australia.

Mapping Movements and Transformations

The 1960s and 1970s were decades that announced significant changes in the anthropological discipline and approach to Australian Aboriginal cultures. The functionalist and structuralist—and materialist to a lesser degree—schools that had dominated the landscape until then were increasingly accused of constructing metalanguages based on ethnocentric and dogmatic concepts. The interest in practice gradually replaced the focus on structure and systems (Ortner 1984), and investigations moved away from the comparative (geographical or systemic) to embrace local and culturalist emphases.

This shift also became visible in the cartographic elements that new publications produced. Indeed, continental or even regional maps that had objectives other than only approximately situating a group or community became rare, since the focus had turned to particular cultural or social features and practices or minorities. The *Northern Territory Land Rights Act 1976* and *National Native Title Act 1993* reinforced this general tendency, even though the involvement of anthropologists in both these processes relied heavily on rather classic anthropological models. They were also accompanied by the waning of interest (or trepidation) in comparative matters and the obvious interpretation of maps as producers of political and legalistic statements. Most, if not all, maps published after 1976, and even more so after 1993, included a footnote or warning indicating that lines were not really borders, shaded areas were not really surfaces, and these maps could not be used for land rights claims, native title claims or any purpose other than a vague illustration. The inherent power of maps had to be neutralised and disengaged, emptied of the very substance that constituted their essence. They were not supposed to produce simplified worlds anymore, quite the opposite; they were to reveal only the surface of complexities that could not be illustrated, placed into space or even described.

There are of course exceptions to this general trend, such as Berndt and Berndt's (1992 [1964]) and Mulvaney's (1976) maps, and geographical charts produced by linguists or archaeologists. Interestingly, these exceptions depicted elements of change, diffusion, circulation or exchange, stressing either an inherent dynamic or the necessity of shifting the perspective to depict the fragility of boundaries. With the emphasis on the ethnography of detailed local practices and processes, the consciousness for a far more dynamic, but also more localised, Indigenous world emerged—a world in which social change was not solely a consequence of modernity, but something inherent in Aboriginal culture more generally. How to graphically represent transformation, diffusion and exchange became a new challenge for map-keen anthropologists and researchers.

Berndt and Berndt's 1964 map (1992 [1964], p. 55) is an early and, to some extent, premonitory example, as well as being probably one of the best known and most influential examples (see Figure 8). The spatial distribution of social organisation systems that Berndt and Berndt offer is an enriched and nuanced version of previous maps, such as those of Radcliffe-Brown and Davidson. It does not reconsider or even question the foundation of the definition of social organisation, nor the means through which these types contribute to fabricating implicit similarities or differences of Aboriginal life-ways. If we consider the expansion of the section system alone (see Figure 9), we can indeed see that the difference of scope between Radcliffe-Brown's and Berndt and Berndt's maps, and even Mathews's map, is not largely significant.

However, Berndt and Berndt's (1992 [1964]) map (Figure 8) incorporates some considerable differences from previous ones, producing a new kind of aesthetic. There is no drive to fully cover the continent or entire regions with areas particular to specific types of social organisation. Completeness is not necessarily the central ambition. There are empty spaces between rough and suggestive lines and curves, testifying to the confession of a lack of information and acknowledgement of sometimes-fuzzy distinctions and overlaps between typological areas.

Figure 8: Berndt and Berndt's map of the distribution and spread of social organisations.
Source: Berndt and Berndt (1992 [1964], p. 55), reproduced with permission from HarperCollins.

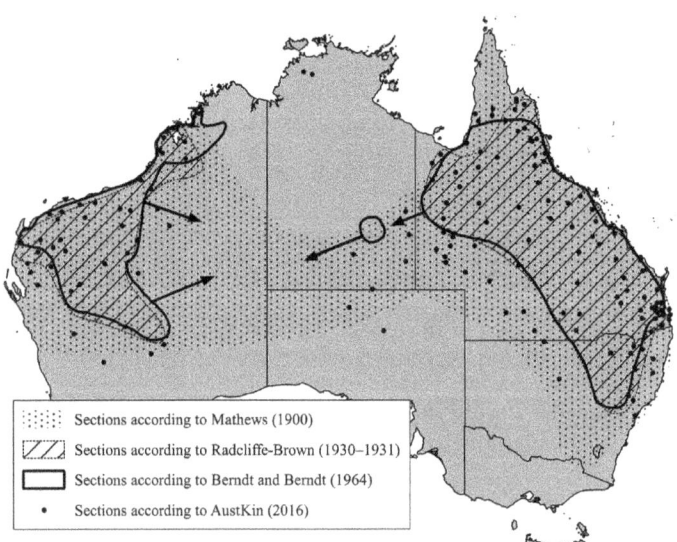

Figure 9: An approximate extension of the four-section system according to Mathews, Radcliffe-Brown, Berndt and Berndt and AustKin.
Source: Compilation by L. Dousset from sources mentioned on map legend.

Berndt and Berndt's (1992 [1964]) map is also distinctive for its addition of more types and subtypes than previous maps had included. The accumulation of knowledge on precise local systems and terminologies, and the identification of a far greater systemic diversity than had emerged from the new anthropological practice are reproduced in Berndt and Berndt's (1992 [1964]) typology and its geographic placement. Most importantly, the map now contained many arrows that crisscross typological areas and is captioned 'Distributional spread of Australian Aboriginal social organisation', rightly pointing to an inherent feature of social organisation. Herein lies the most significant change from any of the other previously discussed approaches and maps. It is often difficult, and in many cases arbitrary to some extent, to identify which areas are characteristic of any system of social organisation; further, the movement, overlap, extension and retraction of such systems in space and time become one of the main characteristics and scientific messages that are produced in this map, as well as others. Maps now reflect the cognition of a world of which the grasp from a static bird's-eye view is becoming increasingly difficult.

Although this chapter principally deals with anthropologists, the maps of archaeologist Derek John Mulvaney (see Figure 10) are an excellent example of this renewed articulation of mapping of Indigenous realities. The presence of identified specific sites and arrows of possible circulation of people, knowledge and particular practices, and absence of tribal or linguistic names and borders or shaded areas, are the core features of a geographical representation that is disengaged from the former typological approaches.

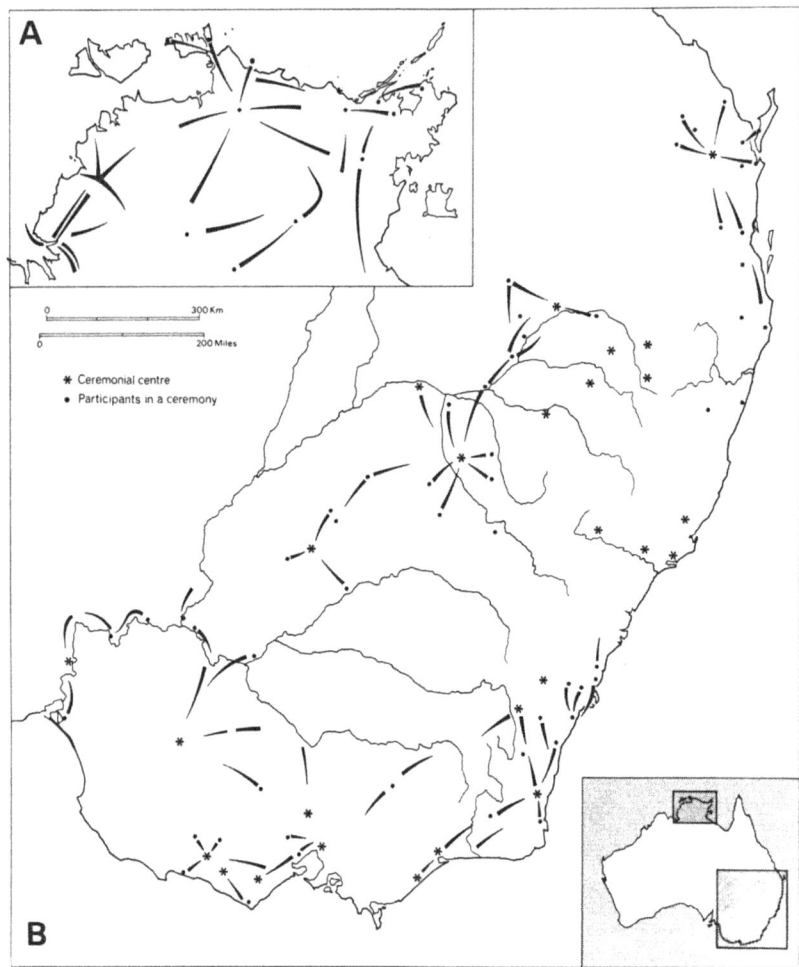

Figure 10: One of Mulvaney's maps showing ceremonial exchange, ceremonial centres and home localities of ceremonial participants.
Source: Mulvaney (1976, p. 76).

Interestingly, Mulvaney's and Nicolas Peterson's chapters, which both reflect this new approach to Aboriginal space, are published in the same volume (Peterson 1976b), alongside contributions by Tindale and Birdsell, even though the latter two are representative figures of the former generation of map-making researchers. In a similar way to Mulvaney, Peterson (1976a) proposed culture areas based on drainage divisions (see Figure 11), and suggested the investigation of affinities, similarities and differences articulated around grand structural features of the landscape rather than cultural typologies. He also acknowledged the existence of movement, exchange and communication between Indigenous groups that increases the complexity of marking cultural or tribal boundaries, as the following explanation testifies:

> The realities of these culture-areas circumscribing populations is open to some independent checking and validation. If the natural boundaries have an historical consequence in tending to restrict communication between the culture-areas, the culture-areas will tend to be endogamous. (Peterson 1976a, p. 67)

Figure 11: Peterson's drainage basins.
Source: Peterson (1976a).

These maps also reflect a change in the understanding of social organisation and its use in comparative or historical approaches. While in previous periods, terminology and system types in particular were seen as characteristics that could be deployed to compare and map Australian cultures more generally, and were understood as strong indicators of historical or social similarities and differences, they are now one of many other elements that contribute to the analysis of social and cultural dynamics—past and present. In this general trend, maps have again become central and explanatory devices—for example, those produced by linguists such as McConvell (1985a, 1985b) or Dousset (2005), both representing possible routes of diffusion of sections or subsections. Freed from being political statements, these maps do not imply boundaries, tribal areas or cultural blocs as such, and they do not reconstruct historical or evolutionary stages that reflect continental-wide schemes. However, they tackle precise and historically situated ethnographic and linguistic data that, represented in space, provide an overview not of Aboriginal culture or general typologies, but of the historical and social dynamics that become visible through the study of social organisation.

Mapping within the AustKin Project

These preliminary conclusions underpin the general framework of the AustKin project, in which many contributors to this volume participated. The general scope—using digital means such as databases, programming and graphical information systems (GIS)—was to elaborate an account as precise as possible of the spatial and temporal distribution of kinship terminologies in the first phase, and of elements of social organisation in the second phase of the project. In this short account of AustKin, I predominantly reflect on the methodologies adopted during the second phase—that is, the study of social organisation. The project is particularly, but not exclusively, interested in the Indigenous terminologies and relationships that these terms express in terms of kin relationships, as well as the possible changes that these terms and relationships underwent in time and space. To avoid, or at least confront the problems of the past, we had to reflect on the precepts to be adopted in three particular domains: nature of information, digital coding of linguistic and systemic characteristics, and means and meanings of spatial representation. While I can only provide a very succinct overview of the thoughts that guided our work, I consider these to have been necessary steps in the course of adopting a critical perspective with regard to the content and nature of mapping.

The Nature of Information

The database system we constructed was made to incorporate data as an 'archival testimony' of something observed (or thought to have been observed) at any particular place and time—not to reflect on whether information was accurate or inaccurate, or true or not. To illustrate with a general example, the expression '*such and such group* has a section system with the following terms' is not something we would take for granted. Instead, the database system would record this information in the following terms: 'a group identified as *such and such* by *such and such author*, recorded at *such and such place and year*, is reported to be using the following terms in what is likely to be *such and such system type*'. Thus, every ethnographic report is treated as a non-exclusive historical record to be included or omitted in any particular context or question that makes use of the data. Moreover, every record is linked to an estimated linguistic entity (based on the official AIATSIS [2017] language list), author, time period and, if possible, geographic place of recording, as well as the reference from which the information was obtained.

Social category terminologies and relationships are interpreted as a historical record of Indigenous cultures, but they are always considered to have been produced in a particular context. This approach allows the integration of several versions of what is supposed to be identical information, such as when more than one researcher works in the same area. Additionally, it provides an opportunity for crosschecking and selective processing of the information that is to be mapped. Further, recording information from various sources on the same language group opens up the possibility of analysis of change over time—whether this change is due to shifting methodologies and scientific backgrounds, or actual sociohistorical and linguistic shifts.

The Digital Coding of Systemic Characteristics

Another important aspect was to code the information in a useful way (allowing for diachronic and comparative analysis), while remaining as neutral as possible. Ridington (1969, pp. 460–1) suggested reading Beaver Indian's kinship system as a two-section system without sections—that is, 'a system with two egocentric conceptual marriage categories that have not crystalized into a sociocentric moiety system because of ecological conditions that favour flexibility in marriage and group affiliation'. This kind of system is probably better termed a 'covert moiety' system, rather than a section system. In particular, it poses the unresolved question of whether covered (not spelled out) systems or categories should be taken into account in descriptions and analysis.

In light of the necessity to formally code data in the AustKin system, the notion of covert characteristics has eventually been adopted as the most neutral and efficient means to representing social category systems. While I am still not convinced that a 'mathematical' or 'formal' feature that has no emic counterpart should be accounted for in an anthropological analysis, the process of decomposing systems of social organisation into covered components enables the elaboration of a model that allows for internal (within the terminological system) and external (between different system types) assessments. Once the existence of covert or logical components is accepted, the various system types can indeed be described in terms of each other.

Let me illustrate this statement through the examination of the section system. It can be read as being built around the combination of a covert (unnamed) or overt (named) matrimoiety system with a covert or overt patrimoiety system. Note here that I use 'moieties' to illustrate sections for the sake of explaining the coding of data only, with no implications on whether these moieties actually exist in a particular language or not. Here, they are a mathematical property of a section system. Each person belongs to one of the four sections, and simultaneously to one of the two patrimoieties and to one of the two matrimoieties. Marriage must take place with someone of the other patrimoiety and of the other matrimoiety of oneself, thus resulting in a section system.

Figure 12 represents the four sections, with each being the combination of a matrimoiety (letters) and a patrimoiety (numbers): A1, A2, B1 and B2. A and B are the two (covered) matrimoieties; 1 and 2 are the two (covered) patrimoieties. Each person is the combination of his or her double moiety affiliation, so that a person in A1 inherits A from his or her mother (matrifiliation) and 1 from his or her father (patrifiliation). As there is an obligation of exogamy from each moiety system, A1 must marry someone from B and someone from 2, and thus find a spouse in B2. A1 is the child of a woman A2 because he or she inherits A from the mother and 1 from the father. A1 and B2 of the same generational level are cross-cousins to each other. The same is true for A2 and B1.

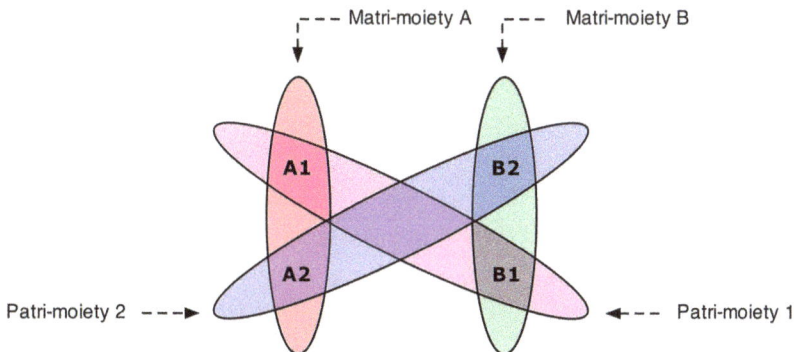

Figure 12: Formal representation of the section system.
(Compare this with the section system of Figure 4.)
Source: Adapted from Dousset (2011, p. 108).

The same principles (using different positions and additional components) can obviously be used to describe patrimoiety and matrimoiety systems, as well as generational moieties, semi-moieties or subsections, resulting in a four-character string that is applicable to all positions in all systems without implying any preliminary and biased interpretation (see Table 3).[12]

Table 3: Coding systems for social categories.

Place in code	Meaning	If irrelevant to describe the system	If relevant, one of the following values is possible	
First position	Gender	0	M	F
Second position	Generation	0	G	H
Third position	Matrifiliation/matrimoiety	0	A	B
Fourth position	Patrifiliation/patrimoiety	0	1 or 3	2 or 4

Source: Author's work.

The 'translation' of the Indigenous terms for each position in their respective systems is coded in Table 4.

---

12   My acknowledgement goes to Tom Honeyman, The Australian National University, who has contributed substantially to the development of this coding.

Table 4: Examples of social category coding.

System type	Possible positions							
Matrimoieties	00A0	00B0						
Patrimoieties	0001	0002						
Generational moieties	0G00	0H00						
Sections	00A1	00B2	00A2	00B1				
Subsections	0GA1	0GB2	0GA2	0GB1	0HA3	0HB4	0HA4	0HB3
Subsections (gendered)	MGA1	FGB2	FGA1	MGB2	MGA2	FGB1	FGA2	etc.

Source: Author's work.

The advantages of this coding are considerable. First, the minimal but necessary amount of information needed to describe a system or terminology is palpable. Second, this coding does not imply significant biases or interpretative constructions, while retaining its capacity for identification and comparison. Third, it is possible to make an informed guess about the type of system encountered even when the terminology reported by the observer is incomplete. Finally, comparative and diachronic analysis of terminologies of identical or multiple system types, as well as terminological permutations, can proceed by comparing the values observed for each component.

The Means and Meaning of Spatial Representation

Despite the previously mentioned precautions, mapping of information remains a complex process, with the selection of accurate coordinates being a key component. Figure 3 perfectly illustrates the difficulties. This map represents several system types recorded by observers at any time of the archival history documented in the AustKin database. For reasons already discussed, these system types have been placed in space as symbols, without inferring any borders, and allowing for the coexistence of several types within one and the same area or language. The coordinates used for each of these languages have been critically constructed by comparing various sources[13] and are believed to be reasonably accurate—at least for the purpose of mapping social organisation. However, Figure 3 also infers that any particular language or group located today was at the same location in 1834, which is the oldest archival source recorded in AustKin

---

13 These sources are Tindale's (1974) maps, the AIATSIS (2017) online mapping system known as AUSTLANG and other local sources used to adjust particular coordinates.

thus far. Essentially, while it is conceivable to map movements of system types in space, and theoretically possible to map movements of languages in space, it is highly difficult to display, on a continental scope, both these movements at the same time. Moreover, it is also very difficult to evaluate if the 'absence' of a system at a time in history and the 'presence' of the same system decades later is a historical change or simply the result of an early incomplete observation.

Figure 13 is another illustration of these complexities. As can be seen, the areas reflecting the distribution of section systems reported before 1930 and the distribution of the systems reported from 1930 onwards do not overlap in large areas. Explanations can be provided for some of these discrepancies. For example, two reasons are given for why section systems are only reported for the periphery of the Western Desert in Western Australia before 1930. First, the bulk of fieldwork in this area only started after the 1930s, and for some areas only after the 1950s. Thus, the information was simply not available earlier. Second, we also know that many groups only recently adopted the section system in this area (Dousset 2005), and after 1930 for the interior regions.

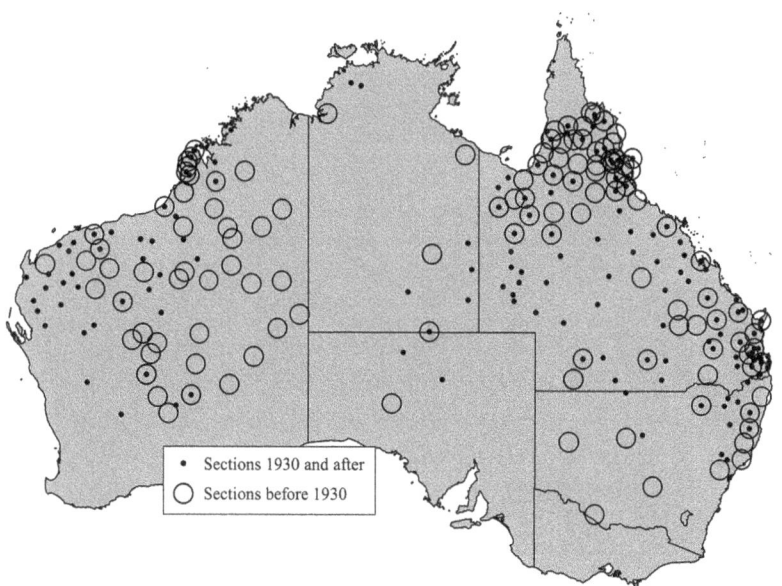

Figure 13: Map generated from the AustKin database of the distribution of section systems.

Small dark circles represent the section systems reported before 1930; large transparent circles represent the section systems reported from 1930 onwards.

Source: Prepared by L. Dousset from various sources.

Explaining the many discrepancies in general terms remains a difficult task. Are the discrepancies due to moving groups, groups adopting new systems (e.g. subsection system) and dropping other systems (e.g. section system), incomplete ethnographies or lack of interest in matters of social organisation, or the diffusion of social category systems? In many cases, the answers to these questions cannot be obtained unless a possible history is reconstructed for each particular location.

Conclusion

This chapter has attempted to outline some general trends that emerged during the evolution of anthropological maps on Aboriginal Australia in the twentieth century. These trends reflect specific but changing conceptions of society in general, and of Aboriginal culture in particular. Due to their inherent capacity to reproduce simplified and transportable worlds, it is not surprising that maps tend to crystallise the most fundamental aspect of the scientific message of the author. Maps are thus the result of particular and necessary partial epistemological approaches. Cartographic representations are built around the feature of certain traces and the oblivion of others. Lines, shades, areas, arrows, colours, points and icons fabricate a visibility that emerges from all that remains invisible. They are interpretative grids, potentially detached from their real-world background of emergence.

The evolution of mapping Aboriginal Australia and social organisation in particular in the anthropological discipline during the twentieth century reflects a departure from the generalist and homogenising attitudes of the former evolutionist approach. Indeed, the evolutionist approach is characterised by rather superficial and incomplete ethnographic data, and for its immense ambitions for continental-wide reconstructions. Social organisation has in this context served as a tool for comparison of culture and society, and is understood as a central and distinctive feature of Australian Aboriginal society.

The structural-functionalist approach that progressively replaced earlier evolutionary speculations from the first decades of the twentieth century onwards changed the scope of the anthropological enterprise—and with it, the nature of mapping. Local cultures and systems were at the centre of investigation, with a considerable increase in the quality and quantity of data. However, the approach remains a holistic one: the social system as a whole had to make sense, and its elements or features had to be mutually tuned and adapted. The necessity for typologies emerged from this second imperative, and it is these typologies—constructing an integrated view of social organisation, land tenure and other social features—that became the central object of mapping.

From the 1960s and 1970s onwards, with the decline of anthropological metadiscourses and the emergence of culturalist and relativist approaches, maps progressively disappeared from publications for at least two reasons: the consciousness of the potential political and legalistic messages conveyed by maps, and a deflection from comparative studies. Thus, researchers that retained regional and continental or historical interests started to produce new forms of maps in which social dynamics, rather than cultural or social areas, became the object of representation. This coincided with the theoretical and ethnographical reconsiderations of the critique on conjectural history that is one of the trademarks of the structural-functionalist school. Provided societies are not considered discrete and integrated systems, linguistic and ethnographic elements may be considered testimonies or indicators of social change, exchange and diffusion. Aboriginal society, in this context, was increasingly seen as inherently dynamic, and maps turned away from featuring borders and instead displayed arrows and shading.

This renewed approach to cultural geography that integrates dynamic and historical spaces is confronted with new technical and epistemological problems: maps now need to be both spatial and chronological, while retaining their portability, power for simplification and explanation, and capacity for replication in new frameworks of knowledge production. These are some of the challenges that we have attempted to address in the AustKin project.

References

AustKin 2017, *The AustKin project*, viewed 31 July 2017, www.austkin.net.

Australian Institute of Aboriginal and Torres Strait Islander Studies (AIATSIS) 2017, *Welcome to AUSTLANG*, viewed 31 July 2017, austlang.aiatsis.gov.au.

Berndt, RM & Berndt, CH 1992 [1964], *The world of the First Australians. Aboriginal traditional life: past and present*, London: Angus & Robertson.

Birdsell, JB 1953, 'Some environmental and cultural factors influencing the structuring of Australian Aboriginal Populations', *The American Naturalist*, 87(834), pp. 171–207. doi.org/10.1086/281776.

Birdsell, JB 1958, 'On population structure in generalized hunting and collecting populations', *Evolution*, 12(2), pp. 189–205. doi.org/10.1111/j.1558-5646.1958.tb02945.x.

Birdsell, JB 1973, 'A basic demographic unit', *Current Anthropology*, 14(4), pp. 337–56. doi.org/10.1086/201347.

Blackburn, K 2002, 'Mapping Aboriginal nations: the "nation" concept of late nineteenth century anthropologist in Australia', *Aboriginal History*, 26, pp. 131–58.

Connelly, JF 1932, 'Distribution of tribes in Western Australia', *Mankind*, 1(5), p. 101.

Cooper, E 1983, 'Ten-section systems, Omaha kinship, and dispersed alliance among the ancient Chinese', *Current Anthropology*, 24(3), pp. 327–40. doi.org/10.1086/203002.

D'Andrade, RG 1992, 'Cognitive anthropology', in T Schwartz, GM White & CA Lutz (eds), *New directions in psychological anthropology*, Cambridge: Cambridge University Press, pp. 47–58.

Davidson, DS 1926, 'The basis of social organization in Australia', *American Anthropologist*, 28(3), pp. 529–48. doi.org/10.1525/aa.1926.28.3.02a00040.

Davidson, DS 1928, *The chronological aspects of certain Australian social institutions as inferred from geographical distribution*, Philadelphia: University of Pennsylvania Press.

Davidson, DS 1936, 'Spearthrower in Australia', *Proceedings of the American Philosophical Society*, 76(4), pp. 445–83.

Davidson, DS 1938, 'An ethnic map of Australia', *Proceedings of the American Philosophical Society*, 79(4), pp. 649–79.

Davis, SL 1993, *Australia's extant and imputed traditional Aboriginal territories (map)*, Melbourne: Melbourne University Press.

de Foigny, Gabriel 1990 [1676], *La terre Australie connue*, Paris: S.T.F.M. & Aux Amateurs de Livres.

Demerath III, NJ 1966, 'Synecdoche and structural-functionalism', *Social Force*, *44*(3), pp. 390–401. doi.org/10.1093/sf/44.3.390.

Dousset, L 2005, *Assimilating identities: social networks and the diffusion of sections*, Sydney: Oceania Publications, Monograph 57.

Dousset, L 2011, *Australian Aboriginal kinship: an introductory handbook with particular emphasis on the Western Desert*, Marseille: Pacific-Credo Publications.

Dousset, L & Glaskin, K 2007, 'Western Desert and native title: how models become myths', *Anthropological Forum*, *17*(2): pp. 127–48. doi.org/10.1080/00664670701438399.

Elkin, AP 1974 [1938], *The Australian Aborigines*, revised edition, London, Sydney: Angus & Robertson Publishers.

Estensen, M 1998, *Discovery: The quest for the great south land*, St Leonards, NSW: Allen & Unwin.

Etherington, N (ed.) 2007, *Mapping colonial conquest: Australia and southern Africa*, Crawley, WA: University of Western Australia Press.

Fry, HK 1933, 'Australian marriage rules', *Sociological Review*, *22*, pp. 258–77. doi.org/10.1111/j.1467-954X.1933.tb01884.x.

Glaskin, K & Dousset, L 2011, 'Asymmetry of recognition: law, society and customary land tenure in Australia', *Pacific Studies*, *34*(2–3), pp. 142–56.

Goddard, C 1992 [1987], *Pitjantjatjara/Yankunytjatjara to English dictionary*, Alice Springs: Institute for Aboriginal Development.

Graebner, F 1906, 'Wanderung und Entwicklung sozialer systeme in Australien', *Globus*, *XC*, pp. 181–6, 207–10, 220–4, 237–41.

Harley, JB 1991, 'The new history of cartography', *UNESCO Courier*, June 1991.

Hornborg, A 1993, 'Panoan marriage sections: a comparative perspective', *Ethnology*, *32*(1), pp. 101–8.

Horton, D 1996, *Aboriginal Australia (map)*, Canberra: AIATSIS, AUSLIG.

Howitt, AW 1883, 'Notes on the Australian class systems', *The Journal of the Anthropological Institute of Great Britain and Ireland*, *12*, pp. 496–512. doi.org/10.2307/2841688.

Howitt, AW 1996 [1904], *The native tribes of south-east Australia*, Canberra, London: Aboriginal Studies Press, Macmillan & Co.

Howitt, AW & Fison, L 1885, 'On the deme and the horde', *Journal of the Anthropological Institute*, *14*, pp. 142–68. doi.org/10.2307/2841853.

Keen, I 2000, 'The anthropologist as geologist: Howitt in colonial Gippsland (review article)', *The Australian Journal of Anthropology*, *11*(1), pp. 78–97. doi.org/10.1111/j.1835-9310.2000.tb00264.x.

Kryukov, M 2004, From ancient Chinese to contemporary mnong-gar, Unpublished manuscript.

Lane, RB & Lane, BS 1956, 'A reinterpretation of the "anomalous" six-section marriage system of Ambrym, New Hebrides', *Southwestern Journal of Anthropology*, *12*, pp. 406–14. doi.org/10.1086/soutjanth.12.4.3629065.

Latour, B 1987, *Science in action: how to follow scientists and engineers through society*, Cambridge: Harvard University Press.

Le Testu, G 1556, *Cosmographie universelle selon les navigateurs tant anciens que modernes*, Le Havre.

Lestringant, F 2013, 'La cosmographie universelle de Guillaume Le Test (1556)', *CFC*, *216*, pp. 91–107.

Lévi-Strauss, C 1967 [1947], *Les structures élémentaires de la parenté*, Paris: Mouton.

Lévi-Strauss, C 1996 [1973], *Anthropologie Structurale II*, Paris: Plon.

Maddock, K 1972, *The Australian Aborigines: a portrait of their society*, Ringwood, Victoria: Penguin Books.

Mathews, RH 1900, 'The origins, organisation and ceremonies of the Australian Aborigines', *Proceedings of the American Philosophical Society, Philadelphia*, *39*(164), pp. 556–78.

McConvell, P 1985a, 'The origin of subsections in northern Australia', *Oceania*, *56*(1), pp. 1–33. doi.org/10.1002/j.1834-4461.1985.tb 02105.x.

McConvell, P 1985b, 'Time perspective in Aboriginal Australian culture: two approaches to the origin of subsections', *Aboriginal History*, *9*(1), pp. 53–80.

McConvell, P 1996, 'Backtracking to Babel: the chronology of Pama-Nyungan expansion in Australia', *Archaeology in Oceania*, *31*(3), pp. 125–44. doi.org/10.1002/j.1834-4453.1996.tb00356.x.

McConvell, P 2013, '"Universal kinship" and "sociocentric kin categories": ancient and human traits?', *Australian Anthropological Society Annual Conference*, November 2013, Canberra: The Australian National University.

McKnight, D 1981, Distribution of Australian Aboriginal 'marriage classes': environmental and demographic influences, *Man* (n.s.), *16*(1), pp. 75–89.

McLennan, JF 1970 [1865], *Primitive marriage: an inquiry into the origin of the form of capture in marriage ceremonies*, Chicago: University of Chicago Press.

Mulvaney, DJ 1976, '"The chain of connection": the material evidence', in N Peterson (ed.), *Tribes and boundaries in Australia*, Canberra: Australian Institute of Aboriginal Studies, pp. 72–94.

Ortner, S 1984, 'Theory in anthropology since the sixties', *Comparative Studies in Society and History*, *26*(1), pp. 126–66. doi.org/10.1017/ S0010417500010811.

Patterson, M 1976, Kinship, marriage and ritual in North Ambrym, PhD thesis, University of Sydney.

Peterson, N 1976a. 'The natural and cultural areas of Aboriginal Australia', in N Peterson (ed.), *Tribes and boundaries in Australia*, Canberra: Australian Institute of Aboriginal Studies, Social Anthropology Series no. 10, pp. 50–71.

Peterson, N (ed.) 1976b, *Tribes and boundaries in Australia*, Canberra: Australian Institute of Aboriginal Studies, Social Anthropology Series no. 10.

Radcliffe-Brown, AR 1913, 'Three tribes of Western Australia', *Journal of the Royal Anthropological Institute of Great Britain and Ireland*, 43, pp. 143–94. doi.org/10.2307/2843166.

Radcliffe-Brown, AR 1930, 'Former numbers and distribution of Australian Aborigines', *Official Yearbook of the Commonwealth of Australia*, 23, pp. 671–96.

Radcliffe-Brown, AR 1941, 'The study of kinship systems', *Journal of the Royal Anthropological Institute*, 71(1–2), pp. 1–18. doi.org/10.2307/2844398.

Ricoeur, P 2000, *La mémoire, l'histoire, l'oubli*, Paris: Seuil.

Ridington, R 1969, 'Kin categories versus kin groups: a two-section system without sections', *Ethnology*, 8(4), pp. 460–7. doi.org/10.2307/3772911.

Schmidt, W 1912, 'Die gliederung der Australischen sprachen', *Anthropos*, 7(1), pp. 230–51.

Schmidt, W 1919, *Die gliederung der Australischen Sprachen: geographische, bibliographische, linguistische Grundzüge der Erforschung der Australischen sprachen*, Wien: Mechitharisten-Buchdrückerei.

Shapiro, W 1969, 'Semi-moiety organisation and mother-in-law bestowal in northeast Arnhem Land', *Man* (n.s), 4(4), pp. 629–40.

Sutton, P 1995, *Country: Aboriginal boundaries and land ownership in Australia*, Canberra: Aboriginal History Monograph 3.

Sutton, P 1998a, 'Aboriginal maps and plans', in D Woodward & GM Lewis (eds), *The history of cartography: cartography in the traditional African, American, Arctic, Australian, and Pacific societies*, vol. 2, book 3, Chicago and London: University of Chicago Press, pp. 387–416.

Sutton, P 1998b, 'Icons of country: topographic representations in classical Aboriginal traditions', in D Woodward & GM Lewis (eds), *The history of cartography: cartography in the traditional African, American, Arctic, Australian, and Pacific societies*, vol. 2, book 3, Chicago and London: University of Chicago Press, pp. 353–86.

Tindale, NB 1974, *Aboriginal tribes of Australia*, Berkeley: University of California Press.

Wikipedia 2012, *File: Ortelius—Maris Pacifici 1589.jpg*, en.wikipedia.org/wiki/File:Ortelius_-_Maris_Pacifici_1589.jpg, accessed 3 February 2014.

Yengoyan, AA 1968a, 'Australian section systems—demographic components and interactional similarities with the !Kung bushmen', *Proceedings of the VIII International Congress of Anthropological and Ethnological Sciences, 3*, pp. 256–60.

Yengoyan, AA 1968b, 'Demographic and ecological influences on Aboriginal Australian marriage sections', in RB Lee & I De Vore (eds), *Man the Hunter*, Chicago: Aldine, pp. 185–190.

Yengoyan, AA 1970, 'Demographic factors in Pitjandjara social organisation', in RM Berndt (ed.), *Australian Aboriginal Anthropology*, Canberra: Australian Institute of Aboriginal Studies, pp. 70–91.

Young, E 1995, 'Aboriginal frontiers and boundaries', in P Sutton, *Country: Aboriginal boundaries and land ownership in Australia*, Canberra: Aboriginal History Monograph 3, pp. 88–92.

4

The Sources of Confusion over Social and Territorial Organisation in Western Victoria

Raymond Madden

Introduction

This chapter looks at the present-day confusion surrounding the relationship between territorial and social organisation in the western Victoria region, and assesses the impact of this confusion on the anthropological modelling of social and territorial changes over time. This chapter also discusses the possible causes and consequences of misrecognition in the written and oral records in relation to the original Aboriginal land tenure in western Victoria. Simply put, the issue that arises is that some contemporary sources suggest that there is matrilineal descent at the local level in the original western Victorian Aboriginal societies. However, there is no credible evidence for matrilineal descent at the local level, but there is credible evidence for patrifilial local estate groups. How did this situation arise? There are a number of published amateur ethnographic and social-geographic accounts of Aboriginal social and territorial organisation in western Victoria that span from the mid-1800s to the early 1900s. Of particular importance are the works of G. A. Robinson (in Clark 1998a–c, 2000), J. Dawson (1881), A. W. Howitt (1996 [1904]), R. B. Smyth (1876), J. Mathew (1911) and R. H. Mathews (1904). While these accounts are useful reconstructive sources, the ethnographic portrait of the contact period in western Victoria remains relatively patchy. Further, there is a complicating factor in the task of reconstruction in that some contemporary reconstructions have misinterpreted key aspects of these early works. For example, the works of Dawson (1881) and Howitt (1996 [1904]) contain information about the matrimoiety social organisation that was found across the region, and the manner in which this information and these systems have been misunderstood has had an impact on the present-day understandings in Aboriginal and research communities of the original territorial and social systems.

Study Area

The study area (see Figure 14) roughly covers the south-western corner and central western area of the state of Victoria. This corresponds with areas commonly referred to as the Western District, south-west Victoria, the Grampians and the southern Wimmera.

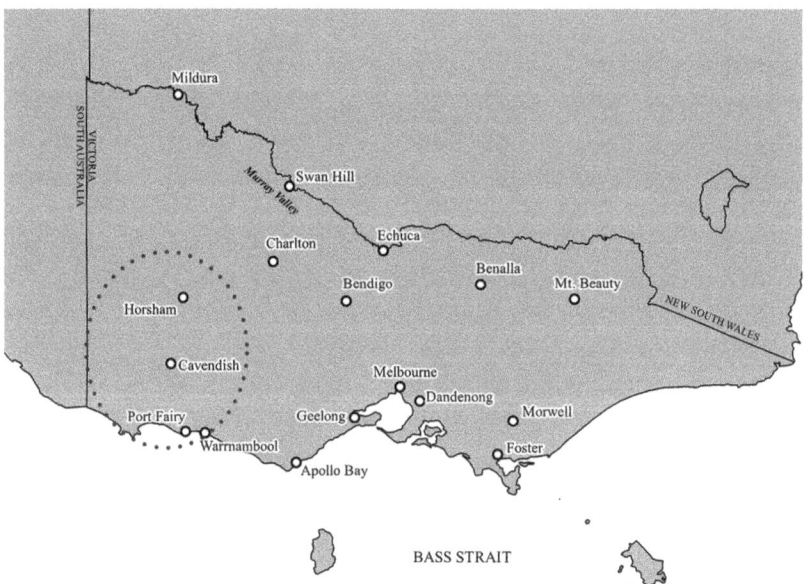

Figure 14: Study area.
Source: Editors' work.

4. THE SOURCES OF CONFUSION OVER SOCIAL AND TERRITORIAL ORGANISATION

Language and Nomenclature

Three macrolanguages were found across the study area. In a small portion of the extreme west of the study area, the Buganditj[1] macrolanguage was present (Blake & Reid 1998, p. 58; Clark 1990, pp. 411–13); however, I will not be dealing with this group in this chapter, other than to note that the information later presented on territorial and social organisation equally applies to the Buganditj as it does to the other groups in the study area. The Maar or 'Warrnambool' macrolanguage was found on the south-west coast and hinterland region (Blake & Reid 1998, p. 58) and includes the dialects of Wullu wurrung, Dhauwurd wurrung, Gai wurrung, Gurngubanud, Big wurrung, Girrae wurrung, Wirngilgnad dalinanong, Djargurd wurrung, Gadubanud (Clark 1990) and Kirrim kirrim wurrung (Dawson n.d.). The Grampians, Wimmera and Mallee regions were covered by the dialects of the large 'western Victorian' macrolanguage (Blake & Reid 1998, p. 58) that includes the dialects of Djab wurrung, Pirtpirt wurrung, Knenknen wurrung, Nundajali, Mardidjali, Jardwadjali, Jagwadjali, Djadjala, Buibadjali, Biwadjali and Wudjubalug (Clark 1990).[2] Original accounts and more recent reconstructions of groups in the study area leave us with a range of nomenclature for the original inhabitants, based on attempts to reconstruct and name differing levels of human organisation (social, territorial, linguistic, geographic and cultural). When referring directly to particular works, I will use the terms as presented in those texts; however, in more general discussion, I will interpolate in order to simplify this nomenclatural landscape. I will refer to the two macrolanguage groups in the study area by reference to the dominant term for 'person' or 'persons'. In the southern section of the study area, the dominant term for person is 'Maar'; in the mid and northern reaches of the study area, the common term for people is 'Guli'. It is the Maar and Guli macrolanguage groups that are the focus of this chapter. The Maar and Guli macrolanguages share a matrimoiety social organisation and the apical totems of this system are referred to in cognate terms: Kuurokeetch and Kappatch for the Maar (Dawson 1881), and Krokitch and Gamutch for the Guli (Howitt 1996 [1904]). For simplicity, in general discussion, I will refer to this overarching social organisation as the Krokitch/Gamutch system (after Howitt 1996 [1904]).

---

1   Alternatively referred to as the Booandik (Stewart 1880), Buganditch (Tindale 1974) or Buandig (Clark 1990).
2   Clark (1990) divided this area into two large related languages that he labelled Jardwadjali and Wergaia; Blake and Reid (1998, p. 58) referred to those areas as the Grampians and Wimmera languages respectively.

Key Early Sources

While there are a number of early ethnohistoric sources for the study area, the questions being posed in this chapter can be worked through adequately with primary reference to two key early sources: Dawson (1881) and Howitt (1996 [1904]). The works of Dawson (1881) and Howitt (1996 [1904]) were in large part an attempt to present a picture of the customs, beliefs and organisation of the Aboriginal population at the point of the arrival of the Europeans. This task was undertaken via the use of Aboriginal informants—usually people who had memories of times before European arrival—and Dawson and Howitt also sought information from other settlers, colonial authorities and mission authorities. In relation to the study area, Dawson (1881, p. iii) and Howitt (1996 [1904], p. x) both had personal contacts with informants from the region and did not need to rely on second-hand accounts.

Dawson (1881)

Dawson lived in the study area from 1844 until his death in 1900. During this time, he formed close and abiding relationships with the local Aboriginal people, such that he was appointed the Local Guardian of Aborigines. He assisted his daughter Isabella in recording the customs and cultures of various Maar and Guli dialect groups with which he came into contact in western Victoria, and they published their research in 1881 in *The Australian Aborigines: The Languages and Customs of Several Tribes in the Western District of Victoria, Australia* (for more on Dawson's life in western Victoria, see Madden 2006, 2010). Dawson's *Australian Aborigines* remains one of the more useful ethnographic records of the first few decades of the post-contact period in western Victoria. Dawson's work assists in clarifying some of the misrepresentations related to social and territorial organisation in the study area. However, it is by no means a comprehensive resolution to all the questions that cohere around this matter, as Dawson's work also contains confusing information that may have contributed to some of the problematic issues being examined in this chapter.

Australian Aborigines is divided into 23 short chapters that cover subjects such as tribes, property, population, marriage and chiefs; matters such as mortuary practices and beliefs, regional meetings and dispute resolution; and broader Indigenous knowledge system information, such as astrological and meteorological knowledge. The work contains a series of tabulated vocabularies in the Chaap wuurong ('broad lip'), Kuurn kopan noot ('small lip') and Peek whuurong ('kelp lip') dialects of south-west Victoria that present lists of general words for each dialect, as well as lists of quadrupeds, birds, reptiles, fishes and crustacea, insects, relationship terms and placenames. Dawson's vocabularies are important in respect to the level of detail they provide on the biosphere and toponymy of the area before colonisation. There is also a section on grammar and sentences, numbers and counting, and a series of short notes—with some in Latin (referring to 'delicate' matters of sexual relations and bodily functions).

Dawson wrote about a number of forms of Aboriginal territorial and social organisation in western Victoria. He described 'families' who held titles to small estates, tribes who were presided over by a chief (Dawson 1881, p. 7), languages into which various tribes were allocated (pp. 2–3) and the 'marriage classes' (pp. 26–37) that occurred across southern parts of the study area. In his writing, Dawson made little of the differences between the larger Maar and Guli language groupings, and he typically wrote about the south-west of Victoria as if it were a large culture bloc.

Howitt (1996 [1904])

Howitt's published writings and manuscript notes cover the latter decades of the nineteenth century and the early part of the twentieth century (1884, 1886, 1888, 1904). His informants were people who had memories of the time when Europeans first arrived in Victoria (or were told of such times by their parents or grandparents). Howitt's work is significant because he personally spoke with Aboriginal people who originated from the northern reaches of the study area (specifically Wotjobaluk, Muckjarawaint and Jupagalk people). Howitt's major work *The Native Tribes of South-East Australia* (1904) is a sprawling tome in excess of 800 pages that collates much of his work across the previous decades and provides information on social, territorial and linguistic organisation across south-east Australia (including the study area). The chapters cover themes such as origins, tribal organisation, social organisation, marriage rules, tribal government and medicine men. This work is thematically typical of the evolutionist-cum-comparative amateur ethnographies that were being produced towards the end of the nineteenth and into the early twentieth century. While Howitt was abundantly aware of the relationship between social and territorial organisation in the original societies of western Victoria, his typology was rather unorthodox. Subsequently, Howitt's work provides some clues as to the possible sources of later confusion regarding local organisation in the study area.

Territorial Organisation

According to Dawson (1881, p. 7), local territory was handed down in a patrifilial fashion (although adoption and birthplace could also confer membership of a local estate group) and each person belonged to the 'tribe' of their father. Dawson's 'tribe' generally corresponds with the contemporary understanding of the dialect group. Dawson (1881, p. 7) compartmentalised his 'tribe' by introducing the concept of the territorial 'family'. This 'family' seems to correspond in large part to the present-day understanding of a small local estate group; for example:

> The territory belongs to the tribe and is divided among its members. Each family has the exclusive right by inheritance to a part of the tribal lands, which is named after its owner; and *his* family and every child born on it must be named after something on the property. (Dawson 1881, p. 7; emphasis added)

Dawson went on to add some confusing detail regarding the distribution of a deceased estate, which will be discussed later in this chapter. While these viri-patrilocal (Dawson 1881, pp. 27, 31) and patrifilial 'families' are associated with particularly well defined tracts of country, they did move off their countries for feasts and ceremonial business associated with seasonally abundant food resources. These feasts have been recorded in a number of sources (Coutts 1981, p. vii; Dawson 1881, pp. 3, 78). However, unsanctioned movement (i.e. trespass) was severely punished, as in other areas of Aboriginal Australia (Dawson 1881, p. 7).

In *The Native Tribes of South-East Australia* (1904, p. 41), Howitt discussed 'tribes' and 'nations':

> I use the word 'tribe' as meaning a number of people who occupy a definite tract of country, who recognise a common relationship and have a common speech or dialects of the same. The tribes-people recognise some common bond which may be their word for 'man', that is, an Aboriginal of Australia … But while individual tribes are thus distinguished from others, there are numerous cases in which the word for 'man' is common to the languages of a considerable number of more or less nearly related tribes, indicating a larger aggregate, for which, in default of a better term, I use the word 'nation'.

Howitt also specified a third level, the 'horde' or 'clan', which is recognisable as a local estate group:

> In order to make clear the definition of the terms I use, the following is given:—
> 1. Nation is used to signify a group of tribes.
> 2. Tribe is used in the sense given at p. 41 [i.e. people who occupy a definite tract of country and recognise a common relationship].
> 3. Horde, the primary geographical division of a tribe having female descent ...
> 4. Clan, the primary geographical division of a tribe with descent in the male line ... (Howitt 1996 [1904], p. 44)

Here, Howitt uses 'horde' to stand for a local group that has a matrimoiety social organisation and 'clan' for a local group that has a patrimoiety social organisation. Similarly to Dawson, this is a complex piece of information that will be discussed later in this chapter. However, what is evident is that in referring to the 'hordes' of the matrimoiety societies (as in the study area), Howitt (1996 [1904], p. 43) was clear that they were patrifilial and the descent he wrote of referred only to social organisation.

Social Organisation

Some early ethnohistoric sources confused or misread information related to social organisation in the study area (see Mathews 1904). For example, while G. A. Robinson was useful in documenting local levels of organisation, he was seemingly unaware of the overlaying social organisation of the people he moved among. In one instance, after recording the details of a man from the 'Cole.ler.cone.deet' (Color gunditj) group, upon whom he had conferred the name 'Pompey', he wrote:

> Cur.er.quite, alias Pompey, conferred by me, country Weeng.burn, at Conenewurt, W. by N. from Kilambete, a 1. Cole.ler.cone.deet, 2. Wen.ne.cood.it.bar. (cited in Clark 2000, p. 69)

'Cur.er.quite' is almost certainly a rendering of 'Kurrokeetch' (after Dawson 1881), one of the matrimoieties found across the study area, and not a 'personal' name that could be seen as an alias for Robinson's conferred name. Still, Dawson and Howitt appreciated the social organisation of the groups that they wrote about. For example, Dawson (1881, p. 26) wrote:

Each person is considered to belong to his father's tribe and cannot marry into it. Besides this division there is another which is made solely for the purposes of preventing marriage between *maternal* relatives. The Aborigines are everywhere [in western Victoria] divided into classes; and everyone is considered to belong to his mother's class, and cannot marry into it in any tribe, as all of the same class are considered brothers and sisters. (emphasis in original)

Dawson's informants told him there were five 'marriage classes' in the southern part of the study area and that they originated from two key ancestors—the 'long-billed cockatoo' (long-billed corella, *Cacatua tenuirostris*) and the 'banksian cockatoo' (red-tailed black cockatoo, *Calyptorhynchus magnificus*):

> The kuukuur minjer, or first great great grandfather, was by descent a kuurokeetch, long-billed cockatoo, but whence he came no one knows. He had for a wife a kappaheear, banksian cockatoo. She is called the kuurappa moel, meaning first great great grandmother. This original pair had sons and daughters, who, of course, belonged to the class of their mother ... As the laws of consanguinity forbade marriages between these it was necessary to introduce wambepan tuuram 'fresh flesh' which could only be obtained by marriage with strangers. The sons got wives from a distance ... and thus the pelican, snake, and quail classes were introduced. (Dawson 1881, p. 27)

> There are five classes in all the tribes of the Western District, and these take their names from certain animals—the long billed cockatoo, kuurokeetch; the pelican, kartpoerapp; the banksian cockatoo, kappatch; the boa snake, Kirtuuk; and the quail, kuunamit. According to their classes the aborigines are distinguished as—
>
> Kuurokeetch, male; kuurokaheeer, female.
> Kartpoerapp, male; kartpoerapp hear, female.
> Kappatch, male; kappaheear, female.
> Kirtuuk, male; kirtuuk hear, female.
> Kuunamit, male; kuunamit hear, female.
>
> Kuurokeetch and kartpoerapp, however, are so related, that they are looked upon as sister classes, and no marriage between them is permitted. It is the same between kappatch and kirtuuk; but as kuunamit is not so related, it can marry into any class but its own. (Dawson 1881, p. 26)

Putting aside the Kuunamit or 'quail' class, these quotations show four non-localised matriclans or matriphratries arranged in 'sister' couplets and operating as a variation of a typical matrimoiety system (see also Howitt

4. THE SOURCES OF CONFUSION OVER SOCIAL AND TERRITORIAL ORGANISATION

1996 [1904], p. 125, who records these same 'sister' couplets in the study area, but not the fifth 'quail' group).[3] While there is no unequivocal evidence to suggest that there are any preferential marriage arrangements between the matriclans of the Kuurokeetch/Kartpoerapp and Kappatch/Kirtuuk moieties, it is tempting to see here the initial stages of a shift from a moiety system to a section system. However, in addition to the origin story, the claim that a typical moiety system underpinned the social organisation of south-west Victoria is supported by the fact that its function was not restricted to regulating marriage, but rather the system was implicated in an ordering of the material, spiritual and cosmological dimensions of life. In this way, all matter and phenomena were said to belong to one moiety or the other. An elegant example of this basic dual structure is given by Dawson (1881, p. ix) when he relayed how his Aboriginal informants described the purple and blue arches of crepuscular light at sunset as 'white cockatoo' and 'black cockatoo' twilight respectively.

Howitt (1996 [1904], pp. 88–9) referred to moieties as 'classes' and saw them as the basic unit of Aboriginal social organisation across Australia. In *The Native Tribes of South-East Australia*, Howitt (1996 [1904], p. 42) stated:

> In all the native tribes of Australia there are geographical divisions of the community determined by locality, and also divisions of the tribe on which the marriage regulations are based. The former are distinguished by certain local names, while the latter are denoted by class names, or totems, and more frequently by both class names and totems.

> In the aggregate of the community these two sets are coterminous, but under female descent no division of the one set is coterminous with the other. That is to say, the people of any given locality are not all of the same class or totem, nor are the people of any one class or totem collected in the same locality.

Here, then, is evidence that Howitt grasped how social organisation overlaid and intermeshed with territorial organisation. He grasped how non-localised matriclans were distributed generally among the patrifilial estate groups and in relation to the study area. This was the point at which Mathews (1904, p. 289) attempted to associate tracts of country with these non-localised social matriclans of the Wimmera, and we will return

---

3   While the 'floating' class of *Kuunamit* or 'quail' might be an anomaly at present, we would do well to heed the advice of Lévi-Strauss (1979, pp. 161–2) on the subject of dual organisation to constantly be on the lookout for a dialectical or third force that complicates apparent simple binaries.

to this point later in a discussion on the work of Clark (1990). In writing about the Guli, who were associated with the mid and northern reaches of the study area, Howitt generally used examples of the Wotjobaluk as indicative of the social organisation of the region. He proposed that the Wotjobaluk matrimoiety system was 'anomalous' due to the fact that some of the 'totems [had] advanced almost to the grade of sub-classes, and they [had] a markedly independent existence' (Howitt 1996 [1904], p. 122). He noted that the system of 'class names, totems, and sub-totems [were] called mir' (Howitt 1996 [1904], p. 122). A quick distillation of Howitt's schema is illustrated in Table 5 (my interpretation of Howitt's labels is indicated in square brackets).

Table 5: 'Wotjobaluk Tribe'.

'Classes' [matrimoiety]	'Totems' [social matriclans]	'Sub-totems' [matrifilial totems]
'Gamutch'	'Jalan—deaf adder' 'Ngungul—the sea' 'Batya-ngal—pelican' 'Wurant—black cockatoo'	[24 totems listed]
'Krokitch'	'Ngaui—the sun' 'Garchuka—galah cockatoo' 'Barewun—a cave' 'Batya-ngal—pelican' 'Moiwilluli—carpet snake' 'Wartwut—the hot wind' 'Munya—a tuber'	[19 totems listed]

Source: Adapted from Howitt (1996 [1904], p. 121).

Howitt (1996 [1904], p. 123) suggested that people were said to 'belong to' or were 'owned' by their 'class' and 'totem', but they 'owned' their 'sub-totem', perhaps hinting at a parent–sibling–child hierarchy in this class–totem–sub-totem arrangement. However, Howitt (1996 [1904], pp. 122–3) also admitted that his data on social organisation were incomplete, especially as they related to the mortuary totems of this system. Nevertheless, he was able to ascertain that each individual after death was also given a mortuary totem based on their living associations. One of Howitt's (1996 [1904], p. 123) informants 'was Krokitch-ngaui. When he died, he would become Wurti-ngaui, which means "behind the sun", or a shadow cast behind the speaker by the sun'.

Further, while Howitt saw the matriclans as having a 'markedly independent existence', he provided no certain data on preferential marriage between the matriclans. As such, despite Howitt's views on this system being 'anomalous' (due to its primary–secondary–tertiary totemic hierarchy), it effectively functioned as a typical matrimoiety system, arranging both the conduct of marriage and all matter and phenomena in a dualistic cosmological order.

In Table 6, the 'equations' formulate the western Victorian matrimoiety marriage systems as presented in Dawson (1880) and Howitt (1996 [1904]), and compare them with a typical section system.

Table 6: Western Victorian matrimoiety marriage systems as presented in Dawson (1880) and Howitt (1996 [1904]), compared with a typical section system.

Howitt's Wotjobaluk matrimoiety system: A (Krokitch); B (Gamutch)	Dawson's matrimoiety system, with its five 'matriphratries': A (Kuurokeetch); B (Kappatch); C (Kartpoerapp); D (Kirtuuk); E (the 'floating' matriclan, Kuunamit)	A typical section system
A = b → B/b a = B → A/a	A/C = b/d → B/b/D/d a/c = B/D → A/a/C/c E = a/b/c/d → A/a/B/b/C/c/D/d e = A/B/C/D → E/e	A/a = B/b → C/c = D/d → A/a

Note: Uppercase is 'male'; lowercase is 'female'; = is 'marriage'; → is 'descent'; / is 'or'.
Source: Adapted from Dawson (1880) and Howitt (1996 [1904]).

To summarise the points on the original forms of organisation, we can state that the study area was predominantly covered by two macrolanguages that, among a range of grammatical and lexical differences, possessed distinct words for 'Aboriginal person(s)'—Maar and Guli. These people were otherwise closely related in social and cultural terms. The macrolanguages were composed of dialect groups that have typically been referred to as 'tribes' in the early literature. Membership of the 'tribe' was patrifilial, and accordingly one got one's language from one's father. The land of the study area was occupied by numerous local estate groups who were patrifilial and viri-patrilocal in organisation. In addition, there were matrimoieties (and/or matriphratries) over the whole of the study area. These matrimoieties were essentially variations of the Krokitch/Gamutch (white cockatoo/black cockatoo) system outlined by Howitt (1996 [1904]).

Colonisation and Social Change

In the intervening years since the violent colonisation of the study area, a number of crucial social changes have occurred in the resident Aboriginal communities, and a quick sketch of these changes will assist in the discussion of present-day confusion around social and territorial organisation. The colonisation of western Victoria has been noted as a particularly violent encounter (Clark 1990, 1995; Critchett 1982, 1990, 1992, 1998). In the first two decades of colonisation, it is estimated that violence, disease and starvation resulted in a population loss of up to 80 per cent in some areas (Clark 1990, p. 53). Correspondingly, there was a loss of language across the area and by July 1880, Dawson (1881, p. 4) was only able to list 14 people who spoke the three local dialects referred to in his text. This population shock and subsequent sedentarisation of the surviving people on missions or reserves also dealt a blow to territorial and social organisation; there were neither the numbers of people nor the freedom of movement to maintain the matrimoieties and original patrifilial estate groups. The surviving local groups quickly began a process of merging and/or collapsing into larger regional territorial domains, as contiguous estate groups were rendered extinct (see Clark 2006). In the decades after the invasive phase of colonisation, the now sedentarised 'mission'-based mobs formed collective identities based on their shared residential attachments and common connections (ancestral and cultural) to the original groups that felt the full force of colonisation. Over time, the old patrifilial estates succeeded into regional cognatic super estates, and there has been a corresponding decline of significance of patrilineal descent and an amplification of cognatic descent. With the loss of moiety systems, there was instead an emphasis on a general rule of family exogamy. This stress on family exogamy fed into an increased depth of descent reckoning, as an effect of education and literacy. Indeed, it is common knowledge that these extended Aboriginal families will have one or more particularly knowledgeable Aunties who can recite genealogies going back as far as seven generations. Finally, over time, there has been a shift towards a more matrifocal family structure (Keen 1988, pp. 12–13), including the increased public status of senior women. These changes are common to many Aboriginal communities that have had a long exposure to colonial forces, and this shift approximates those that have been outlined by Sutton (2003, pp. 206–31) in his discussion of 'post-classical families of polity' and the cognatic shift.

4. THE SOURCES OF CONFUSION OVER SOCIAL AND TERRITORIAL ORGANISATION

Contemporary Issues: Clark (1990)

I have heard Aboriginal people making statements about their ancestral groups that can be paraphrased as: 'we were matrilineal down here in the Western District'. These comments were not necessarily focused on territorial or social organisation specifically, but were general statements about an overarching organisational principal that existed in the past and continues to influence a sense of group and self today. This is as if to say, their communities were, and continue to be, in essence matrilineal. While there is no doubt that a number of factors feed into this contemporary reckoning—such as the tendency towards matrifocal residence and perhaps a general investment in a 'mother earth' philosophy (see Swain 1991)—published sources may have also played a part in the production of this ideology of matrilineality.

In particular, I am referring to social geographer, Ian D. Clark's *Aboriginal Languages and Clans: An Historical Atlas of Western and Central Victoria, 1800–1900* (1990). This text is a significant reconstructive project that has collated and analysed much of the early ethnohistoric records related to the Aboriginal groups of western and central Victoria. Drawing on a wide range of sources, and in particular the information in G. A. Robinson's 1840s journals, Clark undertook the ambitious and worthy task of plotting, as best as he could with the available information, the locations of recorded local estate groups. However, Clark made one consistent anthropological error in relation to the Maar and Guli of the study area, and that was to conclude that western Victorian groups with matrimoieties also had local territorial 'clans' that were matrilineal.[4] Clark (1990, p. 28), who used the term 'clan' for local estate group, said of the Dhauwurd wurrung (south-west Victoria):

> Clan and moiety affiliation was matrilineal and clans were either Krokitch … or Kappatch … However, it is impossible to identify which clans belonged to which moiety because of a lack of detailed information on … marriages.

This statement on local organisation is of course contrary to the data presented in Dawson (1881) and Howitt (1996 [1904]), and this is not an isolated example. In at least five other instances, Clark (1990, pp. 80,

---

4   In one instance, Lydon (2009, p. 41) made this same error in relation to the 'Wergaia' of the northern parts of the study area.

91, 222, 237, 339) suggested that local groups in matrimoiety systems were matrilineal. For example, Clark (1990, p. 80) observed of the '(Ng) Ure gundidj' clan:

> In 1841 this clan had been reduced to one old man ... and his five year old son, who would have belonged to his mother's clan.

Clark also attempted to assign a 'moiety identity' to the clans on the basis that the 'clan head's' moiety affiliation was known (1990, passim). As such, Clark suggested that various localised patriclans belonged to one matrimoiety or another—an obvious misunderstanding of the distinction between social groups and territorial groups, and contrary to Howitt's (1996 [1904], p. 44) information that these two types of organisation, while found together in aggregate at a regional level, were not conterminous at the local level in matrimoiety systems. In attempting to assign the matrimoiety identity of the male head of a local group to the entire local group (all of whom would have belonged to the moiety of their mother(s), except the clan head's actual and fictive bothers), Clark conflated distinct aspects of territorial and social organisation. This is not to say that territoriality and social organisation can be understood in isolation from each other, but rather that such conflations elide the crucial co-constituting duality of organisational structures, and in this case produce a matricentric portrait of descent. Interestingly, Clark documented a related error in one of the early sources: the work of Mathews (1904). In this particular case, it was not a matter of assigning matrimoiety identities to patrifilial estate groups in toto, but rather that Mathews tried to affix locations to a series of non-localised social matriclans (or matriphratries) that belonged to the Krokitch/Gammutch matrimoieties of the Wimmera and Mallee regions. Clark (1990, p. 362) stated that he could not resolve the status of this series of 'clans', as they lacked the usual 'clan' suffixes and he was unable to find any locational data for them. What is obvious here is that Mathews, in an inversion of the error made by Clark, tried to fix social units to particular tracts of local country, and Clark, presumably due to his misreading of local organisation in this area, was left unsure as to what to say in relation to Mathews's data. I would argue that there is no locational data for these groups because they are non-local matriclans.

I hasten to add that these issues do not invalidate Clark's 1990 atlas; it remains a very useful source for working though reconstructions of territory and language in the study area (indeed, alongside Dawson and Howitt, it is one of the first texts I turn to in these matters). Clark's extensive bibliographic section remains one of the most useful research resources available for those interested in the Aboriginal history of central and western Victoria. However, these anthropological errors in the work do require noting, especially since Clark's work is widely read by archaeologists, historians and other researchers, and is also well known in the Aboriginal communities of western Victoria.

Confusion in the Early Sources

While I do not intend to speculate on the precise causes of the anthropological oversights in Clark's work, it is fair to say that the two key ethnohistoric works by Dawson (1881) and Howitt (1996 [1904]) that I have focused on in my sketch of the original systems are themselves confusing and inconsistent. Dawson, in particular, had a range of apparently irresolvable data in his portrait of the original peoples, and I will focus on a few resolvable examples that relate to descent and organisation. Dawson gave an account of the operation of succession to vacant land at the level of the 'family', which I would argue is an instance of a patrifilial estate group. Dawson (1881, p. 7) wrote:

> Should a family die out without leaving 'flesh relatives' of any degree, the chief divides the land among the contiguous families after a lapse of one year from the death of the last survivor … If however there are several claimants, with equal rights to the territory, the chief at once gives an equal share, *irrespective of sex* or age. (emphasis added)

Dawson presented a somewhat unorthodox understanding of landholding in this quotation. The idea that land is apportioned to people 'irrespective of sex' goes against the view presented thus far that local groups in south-west Victoria were ideally patrifilial in the transmission of landholdings. However, we need to take account of the operation of two relevant social norms recorded by him:

> Levirate—where the brother, or nearest male relative, of the deceased estate group owner is obliged to marry his deceased man's wife. (Dawson, 1881, p. 27)

> 1. Viri-patrilocal residence—whereby the female members of the estate group, upon marriage, would move off their father's estate to that of their husband and/or husband's father. (Dawson, 1881, pp. 27, 31)

In considering these norms, we can see that the radically cognatic aspect of the system of succession, as outlined by Dawson, is in fact countered by the underlying patriarchy. In operation, this would essentially reproduce the patrifilial bias that is the norm in local organisation in this region. Due to levirate and viri-patrilocal residence (and the supposedly uniform institution of marriage), the only people left to inherit and inhabit an estate—contested or otherwise—are males.

However, it could still be the case that some women remained in their father's local country after marriage. In these cases, the husband would come to live with the wife on his father-in-law's land. Although the ideal of the viri-patrilocal residence was widespread in Aboriginal Australia, anthropologists working with groups in other parts of Australia found that in practice there was a high incidence of young male affines residing with their in-laws (for an overview, see Hiatt 1966, pp. 81–9; 1996, pp. 23–6; Peterson 1974, 1983). It is possible that this would also have been the case in western Victoria. This means that some women continued to reside in their father's band, which was residentially and economically based on their own patrifilial estate, rather than moving to their husband's father's land and band. While Dawson (1881, p. 7) did not record this type of event, this could have been the source of his 'irrespective of sex or age' comment. However, even if viri-patrilocal residence did operate in western Victoria, it in no way points to a primarily matrilineal landholding system at the local level.

While Howitt's work is clear about the relationship between social and territorial organisation in the study area, some of Howitt's comments, if read in isolation, can be confusing. Howitt (1996 [1904], p. 44) labelled local organisation in an unorthodox manner, using distinct terms for local groups in matrimoiety and patrimoiety societies:

> Horde, the primary geographical division of a tribe having female descent … Clan, the primary geographical division of a tribe with descent in the male line.

It would be easy to read these definitions in isolation and assume that the descent that Howitt spoke of related to the local organisation of 'hordes' and 'clans'. However, it is evident that Howitt was referring to descent as it related to the overarching social organisation that obtains across these hordes and clans. Speaking specifically of matrimoiety societies, Howitt (1996 [1904], p. 43) wrote:

The son is of the *father's horde and tribe*, but of the *mother's totem and class*; of the *local* division to which the father belongs, but of the mother's *social* division. (emphasis added)

These two short examples point to the necessity of rereading early sources in some detail, and to work through the conceptual frames that early amateur ethnographers put in place in order to discern the proper intent of their data. This is not merely a matter of correction of the ethnohistoric and later reconstructive record; rather, it is important to note that these early records and the range of reconstructions that flow from them have the potential to have a wideranging impact in current social and political contexts.

Conclusion

Aboriginal people of the study area have maintained vibrant local oral traditions related to their society, culture and history of survival in the face of ruthless colonial forces (Aboriginal History Programme 1988; Critchett 1998). It is also true that these communities have had a keen interest in the published ethnohistoric and reconstructive accounts of their ancestral groups. The works of Dawson (1881) and Howitt (1996 [1904]) have been reissued as facsimiles in recent decades and, along with Tindale (1974) and Clark (1990), are commonly found in Aboriginal households across the region. While still driven by oral histories, Indigenous knowledge systems are inevitably being influenced by the written record. Moreover, within the last generation, there has been much legal and policy change around cultural heritage and land justice issues, and these texts have all fed into the Aboriginal archaeological, historical, anthropological, legal and governmental views on matters such as territorial boundaries and the composition of traditional owner groups. This has occasioned some contestation over the appropriate labels used to identify Aboriginal groups, and differences of opinion on what 'boundaries' are most appropriately associated with particular groups (which is understandable given the range of linguistic, social and territorial 'boundaries' in the written record).

My concern here is that misreading and misapprehension of original organisational structures makes the task of properly tracking the continuities and changes across the years, and connecting present-day Aboriginal communities to their ancestral structures, much more difficult. (This task is of crucial importance in cultural heritage and native title processes.) The view that 'matrilineality' was the dominant organising principal leads to the suggestion that perhaps less change has taken place than might otherwise have been noted. While in the past, many accounts were overly focused on the 'destruction' of Aboriginal societies (e.g. Rowley 1970), in the present, perhaps we run the risk of continuities being stressed at the expense of the raft of adaptive changes that have occured in order for the Aboriginal communities of the study area to survive—for survive they have. The understandable association between the bias towards matrifocal domestic patterns today and 'matrilineal clans' in the past might have the unintended consequence of eliding the complex duality of the territorial and social organisation of the original groups and underplaying the extent to which Aboriginal groups have rebounded from the violent expropriation of their land at the local level.

References

Aboriginal History Programme 1988, *Memories last forever*, Abbottsford: Aboriginal History Programme.

Blake, B & Reid, J 1998, 'Clasifying Victorian languages', in B Blake (ed.), *Wathurung and the Colac language of southern Victoria*, Canberra: Pacific Linguistics.

Clark, ID 1990, *Aboriginal languages and clans: an historical atlas of western and central Victoria, 1800–1900*, Melbourne: Monash University.

Clark, ID 1995, *Scars in the landscape: a register of massacre sites in western Victoria 1803–1859*, Canberra: Aboriginal Studies Press.

Clark, ID (ed.) 1998a, *The journals of George Augustus Robinson*, vol. 1, Melbourne: Heritage Matters.

Clark, ID (ed.) 1998b, *The journals of George Augustus Robinson*, vol. 3, Melbourne: Heritage Matters.

Clark, ID (ed.) 1998c, *The journals of George Augustus Robinson*, vol. 4, Melbourne: Heritage Matters.

Clark, ID 2000, *The papers of George Augustus Robinson. Vol. 2. Aboriginal vocabularies: south east Australia, 1839–1852*, Clarendon: Heritage Matters.

Clark, ID 2006, 'Land succession and fission in nineteenth-century western Victoria: the case of Knenknenwurrung', *The Australian Journal of Anthropology*, *17*(1), pp. 1–14. doi.org/10.1111/j.1835-9310.2006.tb00044.x.

Coutts, PJF 1981, *Readings in Victorian prehistory. Vol. 2. The Victorian Aboriginals 1800 to 1860*, Victoria: Ministry for Conservation.

Critchett, J 1982, 'A closer look at cultural contact: some evidence from "Yambuk", Western Victoria', *Aboriginal History*, *8*(1), pp. 12–20.

Critchett, J 1990, *A 'distant field of murder': Western District frontiers 1834–1848*, Melbourne: Melbourne University Press.

Critchett, J 1992, *Our land till we die: a history of the Framlingham Aborigines*, Warrnambool: Deakin University Press.

Critchett, J 1998, *Untold stories: memories and lives of Victorian Kooris*, Melbourne: Melbourne University Press.

Dawson, J 1881, *The Australian Aborigines: the languages and customs of several tribes in the Western District of Victoria, Australia*, Melbourne: Robertson.

Dawson, J n.d., *Scrapbook*, MS 11619: La Trobe Library, Melbourne.

Hiatt, L 1966, 'The lost horde', *Oceania*, *37*, pp. 81–92. doi.org/10.1002/j.1834-4461.1966.tb01789.x.

Hiatt, L 1996 *Arguments about Aborigines: Australia and the evolution of social anthropology*, Cambridge: Cambridge University Press

Howitt, AW 1884, 'On some Australian beliefs', *Journal of the Anthropological Institute of Great Britain and Ireland*, *13*, pp. 185–98. doi.org/10.2307/2841724.

Howitt, AW 1886, 'On Australian medicine men', *Journal of the Anthropological Institute of Great Britain and Ireland*, *16*, pp. 23–59. doi.org/10.2307/2841737.

Howitt, AW 1888, 'Further notes on the Australian class systems', *Journal of the Anthropological Institute of Great Britain and Ireland*, *18*, pp. 31–70. doi.org/10.2307/2842513.

Howitt, AW 1996 [1904], *The native tribes of south-east Australia*, Canberra: Aboriginal Studies Press.

Keen, I 1988, 'Introduction', in I Keen (ed.), *Being black: Aboriginal cultures in 'settled' Australia*, Canberra: Aboriginal Studies Press, pp. 1–26.

Lévi-Strauss, C 1979 [1963], *Structural anthropology*, Middlesex: Peregrine Books.

Lydon, J 2009, *Fantastic Dreaming: the archaeology of an Australian Aboriginal mission*, Lanham MD: AltaMira Press.

Madden, R 2006, 'Victoria's Western District', in P Beilharz & T Hogan (eds), *Sociology: place, time and division*, South Melbourne: Oxford University Press, pp. 99–103.

Madden, R 2010, 'James's Dawson's scrapbook: advocacy and antipathy in colonial western Victoria', *La Trobe Journal*, 85(May), pp. 55–69.

Mathew, J 1911, 'The origin, distribution, and social organisation of the inhabitants of Victoria before the advent of Europeans', *The Victorian Historical Magazine*, 1(3), pp. 79–89.

Mathews, RH 1904, 'Ethnological notes on the Aboriginal tribes of New South Wales and Victoria: part 1', *Journal of the Royal Society of New South Wales*, 38, pp. 203–381.

Peterson, N 1974, 'The importance of women in determining the composition of residential groups in Aboriginal Australia', in F Gale (ed.), *Women's role in Aboriginal Australia*, Canberra: Australian Institute of Aboriginal Studies, pp. 9–16.

Peterson, N 1983, 'Rights, residence and process in Australian territorial organization', in N Peterson and M Langton (eds), *Aborigines, land and land rights*, Canberra: Australian Institute of Aboriginal Studies, pp. 134–45.

Rowley, C 1970, *The destruction of Aboriginal society*, Canberra: Australian National University Press.

Smyth, RB 1876, *The Aborigines of Victoria*, Melbourne: John Curry, O'Neil.

Stewart, D 1880, *Aborigines of the Buandik tribe of the south east of South Australia, Introduction*, South Australian Museum Archives AA 307/1.

Sutton, P 2003, *Native title in Australia: an ethnographic perspective*, Cambridge: Cambridge University Press. doi.org/10.1017/CBO 9780511481635.

Swain, T 1991, 'The mother Earth conspiracy: an Australian episode', *Numen*, *38*, pp. 3–26. doi.org/10.2307/3270002.

Tindale, NB 1974, *Aboriginal tribes of Australia*, Berkeley: University of California Press.

5
Disputation, Kinship and Land Tenure in Western Arnhem Land

Mark Harvey

Introduction

This chapter considers the effects of varying levels of disputation on terminologies within the domains of kinship and land tenure. It compares reconstructions of disputation in precolonial Australia with materials on patterns of disputation over the postcolonial period. Precolonially, reconstructions agree that kinship terminologies across Australia were used to frame marriage claims, and involved a high level of disputation (Keen 1982; Merlan 1988). Given the prominence of kinship terminologies in marriage disputes, inconsistencies between and indeterminacies within terminologies were highlighted over time and more likely to be addressed. In contrast, reconstructions agree that land tenure was rarely presented as an overt cause of disputation (Stanner 1979, p. 233; Sutton 1978, pp. 77–8). Therefore, inconsistencies and indeterminacies were less foregrounded and subsequently less likely to be addressed.

Bourdieu (1977, pp. 159–71) drew a distinction, opposing the universe of the discussed, orthodoxy and heterodoxy (opinion), to the universe of the undiscussed—the doxa:

> It is by reference to the universe of opinion that the complementary class is defined, the class of that which is taken for granted, doxa ... The critique which brings the undiscussed into discussion, the unformulated into formulation, has as the condition of its possibility objective crisis, which, in breaking the immediate fit between the subjective structures and the objective structures ... Crisis is a necessary condition for a questioning of doxa but is not in itself a sufficient condition for the production of critical discourse. (pp. 168–9)

In quantitative terms, the opposition is probably better analysed as a continuum from most discussed to least discussed. Precolonially, kinship veered towards the 'discussed' pole of the continuum, as formulation and presentation of opinions on kinship terminologies were a frequent social practice. By contrast, land tenure leaned towards the doxa pole of the continuum, with the formulation and presentation of opinions on land tenure terminologies being an infrequent social practice. I suggest that colonisation constituted an objective crisis that led to changes in the frequency in which opinions on kinship and land tenure were required. This exposed gaps in people's capacities to offer opinions on subjects such as land tenure, and reduced opportunities for the offering of opinions on other subjects such as kinship. As opinions proffered by knowledgeable people are central to analyses of sociality, it is important to consider the factors that affect the offering of opinions. Given that both the precolonial and postcolonial trajectories of kinship and land tenure differ significantly, a comparison of the two will assist in highlighting these relevant factors.

Western Arnhem Land has multiple terminologies in the domains of kinship and land tenure. In addition to egocentric kin terminologies, there are three sociocentric kin terminologies: matry, matrimoiety and subsection. These sociocentric terminologies are further discussed under the section 'Kin Terminologies' in this chapter. There are three terminologies that relate to land tenure: language names, gunmogurrgurr names and yigurrumu exclamations (Berndt & Berndt 1970), which are further discussed under the section 'Land Tenure Terminologies'. Therefore, there is a substantial evidentiary base for examining people's capacities to offer opinions that explain indeterminacies within terminologies, and relationships between terminologies in western Arnhem Land. The data in this chapter are primarily from the northern Kakadu – Gunbalanya area, but some data from adjacent areas are also considered.

Reconstruction in the Northern Kakadu – Gunbalanya Area

In any exercise in reconstruction, it is important to set out the parameters of the database on which the reconstruction is based. As previously mentioned, colonisation is a central parameter in Australia—as in much of the world—and it has had a drastic impact on the northern Kakadu – Gunbalanya area. Figure 15 presents a reconstruction of the associations of the technically distinct languages in the area at the time of colonisation. (For a more detailed analysis of land and language relationships in the northern Kakadu – Gunbalanya area, see Harvey 2002b).

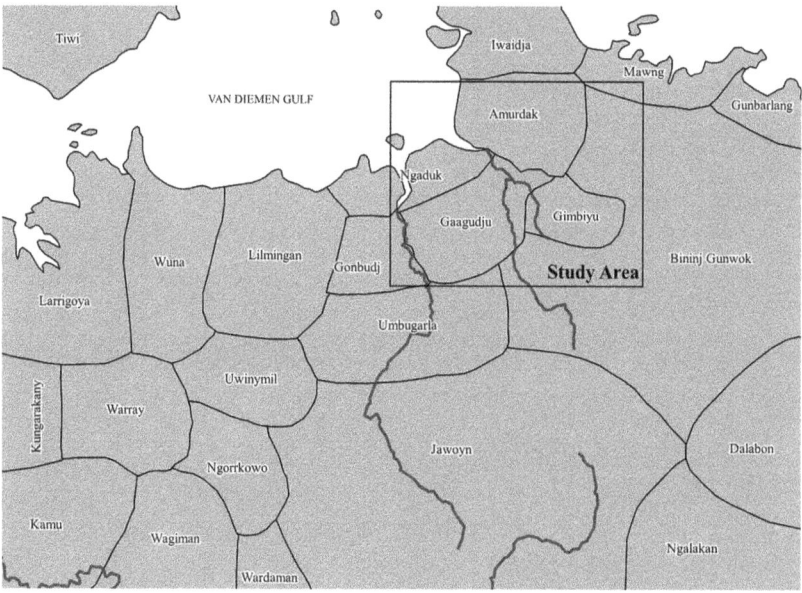

Figure 15: Northern Kakadu – Gunbalanya—languages at time of colonisation.
Source: Author's work.

The most important effect of colonisation was a drastic population collapse. By the 1970s, the Aboriginal population with precolonial connections to the northern Kakadu – Gunbalanya area was approximately 4 per cent of the population that could be reconstructed as having connections to the area at colonisation, with the bulk of the collapse occurring in the period from 1880 to 1920 (Keen 1980, pp. 37–44).

This population collapse had many effects including an extreme reduction in the range of languages acquired by children. Of the languages in the 'study area' shown in Figure 15, only Bininj Gunwok has been acquired as a first language since around 1940. From approximately 1920, it appears that other languages were most frequently used among people who were principally residents further to the west, on the buffalo country (Harvey 2002b, p. 27).

The data presented in this chapter have two principal sources. The first is the extensive research of Berndt and Berndt (1970, p. xiv) at Gunbalanya, which commenced in 1947. The second is the research undertaken in the period from 1970 to 1990 that was associated with the establishment of the Kakadu National Park and related land claims (Keen 1980), and which also includes my own research. Consequently, the great bulk of data were provided by people who were using Bininj Gunwok as their principal daily language; however, there is also some data from people who were using Kriol as their principal daily language. Data from languages other than Bininj Gunwok were provided by people who had not been actively using those languages for some considerable time. Among the other languages, the most extensive data are on Gaagudju. There are limited materials on Amurdak, Giimbiyu and Umbugarla, and there is nothing on Bugurnidja, Gonbudj or Ngombur.

Given this information, the database suggests a greater uniformity in kinship and land tenure practices than was the precolonial situation. The discussion in this chapter is primarily from a Bininj Gunwok perspective, with data from other languages provided where possible.

Kin Terminologies

Only for Bininj Gunwok and Gaagudju are sufficient data available to describe egocentric terminologies. Among Bininj Gunwok speakers, egocentric terminologies vary considerably in their basic structure. In the northern Kakadu – Gunbalanya area, the basic structure is an unusual asymmetric system, with first preference marriage of a man to his actual FZDDD (Harvey 2001, p. 121). The Gaagudju terminology shows the same structure. In addition to the basic terminology used in everyday life, Bininj Gunwok has many other terminologies used in more restricted circumstances.

In addition to egocentric terminologies, three types of sociocentric terminologies are found in this area: matries, matrimoieties and subsections. The patrimoiety terms *duwa* and *yirritja* have also been recorded in the area since the 1940s; however, these terms are clearly postcolonial borrowings from eastern Arnhem Land (Berndt & Berndt 1970, p. 57).

Among the sociocentric terminologies, the matries have the widest geographical range. The principal terms used in the languages of the area are set out in Table 7.

Table 7: Matry terminologies.

Matry	Gaagudju Fem	Gaagudju Masc	Iwaidja	Amurdak	Bininj Gunwok
1	njing-garra-ngaalbu	Ø-yarra-ngaalbu	man-jarri-wuli	warri-yarnkurrk	yarri-yarnkurrk
2	njing-garra-barnaadjinggi ~ njing-garra-barnaadju	Ø-yarra-barnaadjinggi ~ Ø-yarra-barnaadju	man-jarr-wurrkarr	warr-ukarr	yarri-wurrkarr
3	njing-garr-mangiiru	Ø-yarr-mangiiru	man-jarri-wujali	warri-wujali	yarri-burrik
4	njing-garraa-djawa	Ø-yarraa-djawa	man-barlkidj	warri-yarniny	yarri-yarninj
5	djimburruwoodjbu	djimburruwoodjbu	man-jarri-marrangaj	warri-marrangaj	

Source: Author's work.

The matry terminologies are discussed in detail in Harvey and Garde (2015). For current purposes, it should be noted that all the terminologies involve significant linguistic irregularities synchronically, which provides evidence that the matry system is not of recent origin in western Arnhem Land. Only the first four matries were historically found throughout the region. The linguistic evidence suggests that Matry 5 was principally associated with Amurdak and Iwaidja (Harvey & Garde 2015, p. 260). The Gaagudju term *djimburruwoodjbu* means 'white cockatoo', which is one of the principal totems of Matry 5. There is no Bininj Gunwok term for Matry 5 (Berndt & Berndt 1970, p. 65).

The matrimoiety terms in western Arnhem Land are *mardku* and *ngarradjku*. These terms form part of the Bininj Gunwok and Iwaidja lexicons, but did not form part of the Gaagudju lexicon. There is some uncertainty as to whether they formed part of the Amurdak lexicon (Harvey & Garde 2015, p. 238).

Subsection terminologies formed part of the Bininj Gunwok and Iwaidja lexicons. They did not form part of the lexicons of Gaagudju and Umbugarla, which were the languages to the west of Bininj Gunwok. As with the matrimoiety terms, there is some uncertainty as to whether they formed part of the Amurdak lexicon (Harvey & Garde 2015, p. 238). The Gunbalanya Bininj Gunwok terminology, following first preference marriage, is set out in Table 8.

Table 8: Gunbalanya Bininj Gunwok subsection terminology.

ngarradjku matrimoiety			mardku matrimoiety	
A1m	na-ngarridj	=	ngal-wakadj	B1f
A1f	ngal-ngarridj	=	na-wakadj	B1m
A2m	na-burlany	=	ngal-kangila	B2f
A2f	ngal-burlany	=	na-kangila	B2m
C1m	na-wamud	=	ngal-kodjok	D1f
C1f	ngal-wamud	=	na-kodjok	D1m
D1m	na-kamarrang	=	ngal-bangardi	D2f
D1f	ngal-kamarrang	=	na-bangardi	D2m

Source: Author's work.

The extensive set of egocentric and sociocentric terminologies allows for a wide and finely grained range in kin reckonings from the very specific to the very general. There is evidence of overt discussion of principles for mapping between the various levels of generality in reckonings in precolonial times.

Marriage practices are central to Australian kin terminologies—both egocentric and sociocentric. They are also central to the nature of mappings between reckonings at various levels. This follows from the combination of the fact that kin terminologies were understood to be conterminous with the potential social universe, and marriage was positively prescribed to particular classes of kin. Given that every person has a kin classification, if there was a wrong marriage, then this wrong marriage had extended effects for the application of the kin terminology.

By contrast, we may consider a situation in which marriage is positively prescribed to particular classes of kin, but kin terminologies are not understood to be conterminous with the social world. In this situation, a wrong marriage to somebody is not classified as kin would not necessarily have any extended effects on the application of the kin terminology.

The non-kin spouses could simply reclassify each other to the correct kin category, and this reclassification would have no necessary effect on the kin categorisations within their existing kin networks.

Berndt and Berndt (1970) provided detailed data on Gunbalanya Bininj Gunwok marriage preferences. They distinguished a number of gradations in the legitimacy of particular marriage arrangements. Within this set of gradations, they drew an overall distinction between 'legitimate' and 'illegitimate' marriages. The category of 'legitimate marriages' involves two terms: *kakkali* 'spouse' and *kanjok* 'cousin'. Berndt and Berndt did not specifically address the linguistic analysis of these terms, but their analysis proceeded on the basis that the reference sets for *kakkali* and *kanjok* were disjointed. They analysed *kakkali* as 'spouse, first preference spouse' and *kanjok* as 'cousin, second preference spouse'.

Garde (2013, pp. 35–8) provided an alternative analysis of the meanings of *kakkali* and *kanjok*, reporting that when asked about the meanings of the terms *kakkali* and *kanjok*, Bininj Gunwok speakers described their reference sets in terms of a superset–subset relationship. The superset is *kanjok* 'cousin, potential legitimate spouse', and the subset is *kakkali* 'actualized spouse, long-term betrothed, potential legitimate spouse who one has a high degree of claim to'.

As the ensuing discussion will demonstrate, Berndt and Berndt (1970) provided a substantial body of evidence that the achievement of a legitimate marriage often involved the weighing of various competing 'legitimate' claims to potential marriage partners. The usage of the terms *kakkali* and *kanjok* could vary in accordance with the variations in the weighing of competing claims over time. Like Garde, I analyse these variations as reflecting variations in whether a subset term, in this case *kakkali*, can or should be used to appropriately describe an actual or potential spousal relationship at a particular point in time. I do not analyse shifts between *kakkali* and *kanjok* as reflecting shifts between disjointed reference sets.

Berndt and Berndt presented the best-based marriage claim as between people who call one another *kakkali*, and where the husband and mother-in-law classify each other as *na-kurrng* 'son-in-law' and *ngal-kurrng* 'mother-in-law':

> The ideal spouse … is a *gagali* [kakkali], and the ideal mother-in-law from a man's point of view is a *ngalgurng* [ngal-kurrng]. Relatives a man calls by the term *gagali* include MMBDD, FFZSD, FZDDD, and MBDDD. (Berndt & Berndt 1970, p. 94)

Among these relatives, FZDDD is the preferred spouse (Harvey 2001, pp. 121–5). Berndt and Berndt (1970, p. 95) discussed this highest-preference spouse from a woman's perspective:

> Women seem to emphasise the matrilineal 'side' more than men do. In general, we found that they were most likely to cite as an ideal union one in which a woman gives her first daughter to her actual mother' mother's eldest brother's eldest son, as most eligible *nagurng* [na-kurrng]. This trend appeared in ordinary conversations and in comments on actual cases and on myths, and in responses to the question, 'Who is your/their true *nagurng*?' Or in reference to children not yet betrothed, 'Who is your/their mother's true *nagurng*? Where will they look for a wife/husband?'

As the quotation indicates, actual genealogical links between potential spouses favour a marriage claim. Candidates whose relationship to a potential spouse is purely classificatory are less favoured. Nonetheless, marriages with fewer favouring factors, but within the overall *kanjok* 'cousin' class did occur, and were overtly presented as legitimate:

> In second-choice unions they are genealogically related as ganjulg [kanjok]; once they marry they call each other gagali, too, but only as a courtesy term—they are 'not real gagali'. (Berndt & Berndt 1970, pp. 99–100)

Berndt and Berndt (1970, pp. 100–1) presented a range of evidence that showed that actualisation of a less-favoured marriage within the overall *kanjok* 'cousin' class of legitimate spouses did not erase the less-favoured status of these unions:

> *De facto gagali* and *nagurng-ngalgurng* are expected to behave substantially as if their bonds were 'real'—that is, as if they were based on genealogical ties. A man has the usual obligations toward his mother-in-law ... including partial avoidance, but what is uncertain is how far he and she are obliged or entitled to use the special *gungurng* [kun-kurrng] vocabulary in speaking together. It is the only proper medium of conversation in this affinal relationship, but ideally restricted to 'real' *nagurng-ngalgurng*, where the genealogical connection is traceable or implied ... Otherwise, minor departures from the ideal marriage type do not attract much notice in the ordinary way. They are most likely to come to the surface in arguments and quarrels. A husband and wife in such circumstances have a ready-made grievance that each of them can use, even after years of marriage. They can accuse each other of being only *ganjulg* and not real *gagali*, adding (for instance), 'Those [named] are my *gagali*—I should be married to them, not to you!' 'My mother didn't give me to you [or vice

versa]; you're not the right husband [or wife] for me!' Accusations of the same kind are exchanged between son-in-law and mother-in-law too, but mostly indirectly in monologues, or statements addressed to the camp in general without mentioning names.

Berndt and Berndt (1970, p. 100) provided data on variations in the limitation of the *kanjok* class that led into consideration of marriages that were overtly characterised as 'illegitimate' to varying degrees:

> In cross-cousin marriages, the timing of the betrothal is particularly crucial. If such a betrothal is confirmed quite early in a girl's life by relatives, above all by her mother and mother's brother, and preferably at the time of her birth, that in itself legitimizes it for practical purposes, but not to the extent of identifying it with the ideally correct type of marriage. However, if that opportunity lapses and no betrothal is arranged between them, the cross-cousin relationship may change as far as terms are concerned so that the two call each other by the terms for 'father' … and 'daughter' … (The change seems to take place usually before the girl reaches puberty). From that point on, marriage between them is regarded as wrong, but not outrageously so. We recorded a scattering of instances in early marital histories of people who were elderly in 1947, as well as in current unions. Their formal shortcomings were frankly admitted to the extent of labelling them 'wrong', but without the aura of shame and defensiveness that still surrounds 'really wrong' (for example, intra-moiety) unions.

According to information I have gathered, the use of the terms 'father' and 'daughter' is established much earlier than puberty—for actual first cousins, at least. Further, the relationship between actual first cousins using these terms is a highly constrained avoidance relationship, possibly because marriage between them remains a possibility. As such, it is quite different from an actual father–daughter relationship.

It is important to note that the overt classification of these marriages as 'illegitimate' was not limited only to people outside the marriage. The partners in these marriages also overtly classified the marriages as 'illegitimate'. In other words, individual life histories and perspectives were not a factor that affected the overt classification of marriages as 'legitimate' or 'illegitimate'.

The class of 'illegitimate' marriages was itself not uniform, but had subdivisions. Berndt and Berndt (1970, p. 61) provided further information on 'really wrong' intra-moiety unions:

The second Gunwinggu marriage rule is that matrilineal moieties are exogamous ... This ideal has not been seriously challenged. In actuality, there have been a few instances of intra-moiety marriage in recent years. They are conventionally regarded as wrong, but in practice they are tolerated or excused, usually on the grounds that some outside influence is responsible. For example, 'This is Yiwadja custom', or the missionaries have interfered with our rules'.

Berndt and Berndt (1970, p. 64) also provided a further criterion for determining illegitimacy that involves matries:

If moiety exogamy is important to Gunwinggu, semi-moiety exogamy is far more so: it is a 'last-ditch' rule.

They did not discuss whether there were any violations of this rule, and if so, what the responses to such violations might have been. Table 9 summarises the data provided by Berndt and Berndt (1970) on the overt classification of marriages by Bininj Gunwok speakers.

Table 9: Classification of marriages by Gunbalanya Bininj Gunwok speakers.

Marriage between	
kakkali subclass of *kanjok* 'cousin'	First preference marriage. Not overtly criticised.
kanjok not within the *kakkali* subclass	Second preference marriage. Marriage arrangements should follow prototypical timing. Can always be used as a grievance.
'Father and daughter' who were *kanjok*	Overtly categorised as wrong by partners and others. Does not induce 'shame'. Not overtly described as a 'foreign' practice.
Intra-moiety	Overtly categorised as wrong by partners and others. Induces 'shame'. Overtly described as a 'foreign' practice.
Within matry	Described as the most important taboo. No data available on whether violations occurred, and if so what responses violations would have encountered.

Source: Author's work.

The attainment of marriage everywhere in Australia was undoubtedly a complex process, extended in time and involving many individual factors (for a classic account, see Hiatt 1965). Berndt and Berndt (1970, pp. 97–9, 167–73) discussed specific betrothal and marriage processes among Gunbalanya Bininj Gunwok.

However, there is evidence that individual factors were constrained by the overtly discussed norms on marriage. Sutton (2003, pp. 148–151, 246) presented data on marriage actualisation from many areas that were less affected by colonialism. There were no cases in which the percentage of marriages satisfying prescriptive requirements was less than 80 per cent, and the average was 90 per cent.

Given the central importance of marriage attainment to kin terminologies, it is to be expected that overt articulations of norms about marriage would also extend to overt discussion of norms about mappings between reckonings at various levels of the egocentric and sociocentric terminologies.

Discussion of mappings was more likely to arise with finer-grained mappings. By their very nature, larger-scale categorisations and mappings offered fewer opportunities for issues to emerge. In this respect, it is interesting to note that the two larger-scale sociocentric terminologies—matrimoieties and matries—were less flexible in their application than the smallest-scale sociocentric terminology—subsections:

> Moiety and semi-moiety [matry] affiliation is fixed before birth and cannot be changed. Conventionally, this applies to subsection affiliation too, but in actual practice it is more flexible. (Berndt & Berndt 1970, p. 73)

Harvey and Garde (2015, p. 255) discussed variable subsection affiliation in western Arnhem Land. As with marriage attainment, the existence of some flexibility does not demand that there are no norms. In the great majority of cases, subsection usage follows 'straight' usage. People can and do describe departures from standard usage as 'wrong'. Thus, if two people X and Y have the same subsection, then they should not refer to another individual Z with kin terms that differ on the cross versus parallel distinction or the harmonic versus disharmonic generation distinction. If X calls Z by a parallel harmonic term such as 'brother', then Y should not call Z by a cross-term such as 'cousin' or a disharmonic term such as 'father'. If this does occur, then X, Y, Z and other people will all overtly agree that there is something 'wrong' somewhere.

Land Tenure Terminologies

In the period from 1947 to 1990, two name terminologies were used in discussions of land tenure: language name terminologies and a name terminology most commonly known as 'gunmogurrgurr'. The gunmogurrgurr terminology itself has a range of names in the languages of the area (see Table 10).

Table 10: Gunmogurrgurr terminology in the languages of the area.

Amurdak	Iwurrumu
Eastern Bininj Gunwok	gun-nguya
Western Bininj Gunwok	gun-mogurrgurr
Iwadja	nguya, yiwurrumu
Jawoyn	mowurrwurr
Mawng	namanamaj

Source: Author's work.

There is also a third terminology that relates to land. In Bininj Gunwok, this terminology is known as 'yigurrumu'. This name evidently relates to the Amurdak and Iwaja equivalents '(y)iwurrumu' of Bininj Gunwok 'gun-mogurrgurr/gun-nguya'. The yigurrumu terminology did not appear to have been used in discussions of land tenure. Nonetheless, I examine it here, because its lack of usage is in itself a matter of interest.

Language name terminologies were used in discussions of land tenure throughout the region and Australia. As in other regions in Australia, the scale of the area of land to which particular language names were attached could vary greatly. Some areas of land were associated with more than one language name. All cases known to me in the northern Kakadu – Gunbalanya area involved names of significantly different scales. Discussions of land tenure at a more general level tended to use larger-scale language names, while discussions of land tenure at a more specific level tended to use gunmogurrgurr names. The gunmogurrgurr terminology had a more limited geographical range than did the language name terminology. All areas associated with the Bininj Gunwok, Gaagudju and Ngaduk language names were also associated with gunmogurrgurr names at a smaller scale. As we will see in the section 'The Effects of Colonisation on Land Tenure', gunmogurrgurr terminology did not appear to be associated with the areas west of the areas related to Bininj Gunwok, Gaagudju and Ngaduk. It was not found in areas associated with Limilngan, or in areas associated with Bugurnidja, Ngombur and Umbugarla. It is not known whether gunmogurrgurr terminology was found in areas associated with Gonbudj.

Land–language associations were comparatively straightforward in the northern Kakadu – Gunbalanya area. All language names were associated with contiguous sets of sites. No language names were discontinuously associated.[1] For smaller-scale names, there was agreement pertaining to the set of sites associated with that name. This was also the case for most larger-scale names. I encountered only one situation in which there was variation in the geographical extension of a larger-scale language name. This was the term 'Mayali'. Everybody agreed that the area associated with Gundjeihmi was also associated with Mayali. People varied in opinion as to whether areas associated with Kunwinjku were also associated with Mayali.

The gunmogurrgurr terminology had a different internal structuring. Gunmogurrgurr names were commonly associated with discontinuous areas of land. Consequently, some gunmogurrgurr names, such as Mirarr, are associated with large areas, whereas others, such as Manilagarr, were associated with small areas. However, unlike language names, there was no distinction in scale among gunmogurrgurr names.[2] All gunmogurrgurr names were incompatible with one another. It was not possible for a single area of land to be associated with a 'small scale' gunmogurrgurr name and also a 'large scale' gunmogurrgurr name. A particular area of land could only be associated with one gunmogurrgurr name.

Given that two structurally distinct terminologies were used to discuss land ownership, it would be a reasonable hypothesis that reconstructions involving these terminologies should parallel the reconstructions for kin terminologies—that is, there would be evidence to reconstruct the mappings between the two systems and criteria for evaluating the mappings as precolonial topics of overt discussion. However, this is not the case. There is no evidence for the reconstruction of overt discussion on these issues. This can be illustrated by considering the associations of the Mirarr gunmogurrgurr name in the northern Kakadu – Gunbalanya area (see Figure 16). The Mirarr name was associated with six distinct estates and five different language names: Amurdak, Erre, Gaagudju (two distinct areas), Gundjeihmi and Urningangk (Harvey 2002b). With one

---

1   The one apparent exception is discussed in the section 'The Effects of Colonisation on Land Tenure' of this chapter.
2   Berndt and Berndt (1970, p. 55) stated that 'some *gunmugurgur* [gunmogurrgurr] are "bigger" than others and can subsume smaller names in the same large territory. For instance, Djelama is a "big" *gunmugurgur* and Nguluminj is a minor one'. Berndt and Berndt did not provide details on the territorial associations of Djelama and Nguluminj, but they were not associated with the northern Kakadu – Gunbalanya area. They are most probably Kunwinjku names from further to the east of Gunbalanya. Without more information, it is not possible to assess the description that Berndt and Berndt provided. Whatever the details of their associations, it does not alter the fact that in the northern Kakadu – Gunbalanya area gunmogurrgurr names are incompatible with one another.

exception, the conjunction of a language name and a gunmogurrgurr name would suffice to distinguish each estate. This is the case generally throughout western Arnhem Land—the conjunction of a language name and a gunmogurrgurr name commonly distinguishes an estate.

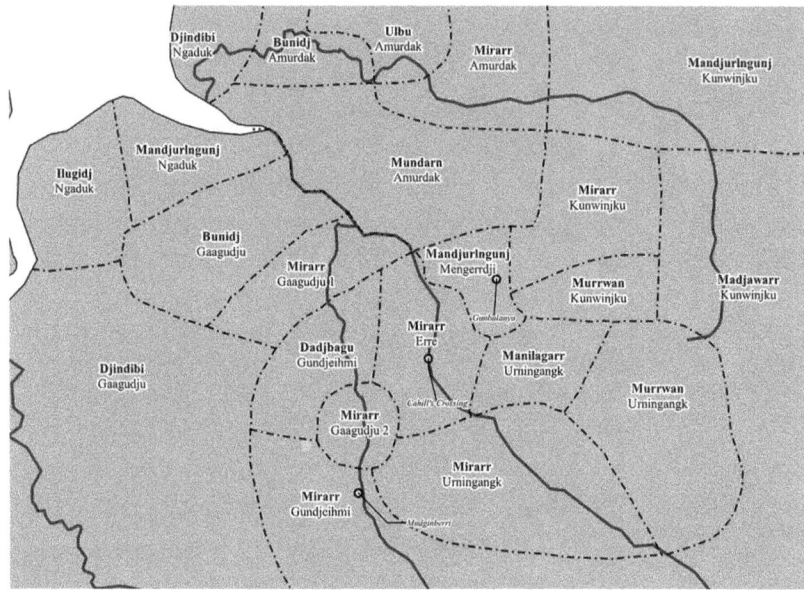

Figure 16: Gunmogurrgurr names in the northern Kakadu – Gunbalanya area.
Source: Harvey (2002, p. xvi).

I discussed land tenure extensively with a range of knowledgeable Indigenous consultants in the period from 1986 to 1989 (five field trips totalling 12 months). All these consultants had been extensively involved with land claims in the period preceding my fieldwork. A discussion about Indigenous land tenure was not an unprecedented activity for any of them, nor was a discussion about areas of land whose ownership was less than straightforward. However, none of these experienced consultants ever conjoined language names and gunmogurrgurr names in such a way as to clearly discriminate one estate from another.

The consultants did not use compound terms such as Mirarr-Amurdak or Mirarr-Gaagudju. They did not produce sentences such as 'This lot Mirarr, they got Amurdak language. That nother lot Mirarr, they got Gaagudju language'. This was even the case when discussions focused specifically on distinguishing different Mirarr estates. There was, in fact, no linguistic evidence that they conceived of language names and gunmogurrgur names as having any kind of mapping relationship.

The same lack of evidence for a mapping relationship is found in the yigurrumu terminology. The yigurrumu terminology differs from the gunmogurrgurr and language terminologies in that its members are not fundamentally referential. Berndt and Berndt (1970, p. 54) provided the following information on yigurrumu:

> Each territory is associated with a named unit of patrilineal descent, the *gunmugurgur* [gunmogurrgurr] … In turn, each of these is linked with another name that is much less widely known. This is the *igurumu* [yigurrumu] or *ngwoia* [gun-nguya][3] (Eastern Gunwinggu), a stylised exclamation that is used also in ritual invocations and therefore sometimes said to be bigger, more important, than the *gunmugurgur* name.

According to the consultants, the yigurrumu names should be cried out when someone sneezed. Keen (pers. comm.) reported that they should be cried out when someone was in danger. The significance of these various usages requires further consideration. However, overall, it is evident that the yigurrumu terminology is an exclamatory, and not a referential, terminology.

Nonetheless, the consultants categorised yigurrumu terms as 'names' and conceived of them as being critically anchored in estates. Therefore, one reasonable hypothesis would be that consultants might refer to yigurrumu names in the context of discourses focusing on clarifying uncertainties about land ownership. This is particularly relevant if yigurrumu names are generally distinctive of specific individual estates.

During the time of my fieldwork from 1986 to 1989, the yigurrumu terminology was less well known than the language name or gunmogurrgurr terminologies. Consequently, I could not obtain complete data on the terminology. The available data are set out in Table 11.

---

3   The 'ngwoia' term used by Berndt and Berndt appears to be the –nguya portion of the word 'gun-nguya'. As discussed, this is the Eastern Bininj Gunwok equivalent of the Western Bininj Gunwok term 'gun-mogurrgurr'. The Berndts' description implies that 'gun-nguya' is the equivalent for both 'gun-mogurrgurr' and 'yigurrumu'. This is not the case; 'gun-nguya' does not include 'yigurrumu' within its reference, and the term 'yigurrumu' is used by Eastern Bininj Gunwok speakers.

Table 11: Yigurrumu terminology.

Gunmogurrgurr	Language	Yigurrumu
Bunidj	Amurdak	Arnbalarr, Imbini
Bunidj	Gaagudju	Mananawangaardi, Galbarraarru, Manabuudja
Djindibi	Amurdak	Marniyalga
Djindibi	Gaagudju	Garlangeebu
MandjurIngunj	Mengerrdji	Magalirra
MandjurIngunj	Ngaduk	(?) Muwarl
Madjawarr	Gunwinjgu	*Djambunu, Nabamgarrk*
Mirarr	Amurdak ? & Gunwinjgu	*Djambunu, Nabamgarrk*
Mirarr	Gaagudju (1 & 2)	*Gamadaagu*
Mirarr	Gundjeyhmi	Ginjmardamba
Manilagarr	Urningangk	Winjbet, Manila
Ulbu	Amurdak	Injgurr, Wadjarra

Source: Author's work.

A couple of cases are highlighted in Table 11 in which yigurrumu names are shared between two estates; otherwise, yigurrumu terms are distinctive of individual estates. Given that yigurrumu terms are not referential, there would be no reason to predict that consultants would use compound terms such as Bunidj-Arnbalarr versus Bunidj-Mananawangaardi. However, it is a reasonable prediction that they might produce sentences such as 'This lot Bunidj, they got Arnbalarr name. That nother lot Bunidj, they got Mananawangaardi name'. Consultants did not do this, and there was no linguistic evidence that they conceived of any systematic mapping relationship between yigurrumu terms and the gunmogurrgurr or language name terminologies.

This lack of evidence for any systematic mapping between the gunmogurrgurr, language name and yigurrumu terminologies was part of a more general lack of evidence for overt discussion over detailed discrimination in land tenure. The lack of precision in discriminating estates from one another is matched by the lack of precision in other important areas, such as the inheritance of land tenure and the nature of relations between clans (the group of owners of an individual estate).

Both gunmogurrgurr and language names were inherited patrifiliatively. They could be inherited from pater and genitor:

Patrilineal descent is the conventional basis of *gunmugurgur* [gunmogurrgurr] membership, but social paternity may affect it. For example, a child may adopt the *gunmugurgur* affiliation of a stepfather who rears him, especially if he is very young when his own father died, or he may later claim dual affiliation from 'both his fathers'. (Berndt & Berndt 1970, pp. 55–7)

However, there is no evidence for any more systematic discussion of either the provision for inheritance from pater or the dual affiliation option.

While primary ownership is inherited patrifiliatively, people also have rights to their mother's estate and other estates. Berndt and Berndt (1970, p. 54) observed that 'other associations are recognised, too: for instance, with a person's mother's country (which is also her father's) and with *her* mother's country'. In Gaagudju, there is a term *guwaaluwa* that means 'mother's country'. This root takes a prefixation to indicate the propositus, such as *ngadj-guwaaluwa* (1sg-mother's country) 'my mother's country'. In Bininj Gunwok, there is a range of terms for 'mother's country' and a term for 'mother's mother's country' (Garde pers. comm.) (see Table 12).

Table 12: Ways of referring to mother's and mother's mother's country.

-bo-garrang	*nga-/birri-bo-garrang*
-water-mother	1sg-/3pl-water-mother
'mother's country'	'my/their mother's country'
karrard-warre-ken	*kakkak-warre-ken*
mother-bad-GEN	MM-bad-GEN
'mother's country'	'grandmother's country'
kun-warddjak/-mirrirn	
IV-warddjak	
'a person whose mother owned the Warddjak/Mirrirn gunmogurrgurr name'	

Source: Author's work.

However, there is no evidence for overt discussion on the more precise delimitation of rights to estates other than the patrifiliative estate. For example, did individuals have inalienable rights of residence and foraging over their mother's country? Keen (1994, p. 125) made the following observation on precisely this point in relation to north-east Arnhem Land:

> In the recent pre-colonial past, conflict among men over the control of country and its resources were probably linked mainly to competition over women and the control of ceremonies, for the non-exclusivity of rights in food resources of country and the flexibility of residence made it unlikely that there were great quarrels over access to those food resources unless major anomalies arose in the relations between the size of groups and country.

An absence of a more precise delimitation is also found when considering relationships among clans, and here we may return to the Mirarr example previously discussed. Does the sharing of the Mirarr name by six clans indicate some kind of systematic relation between these clans? Based on the available evidence, there is no such systematic relationship.

In the period from 1970 to 1990, people commonly described various clans—both those sharing gunmogurrgurr names and those with different gunmogurrgurr names—as 'company'. However, there were no systematic correlations to this 'company' description:

> The majority of these [company] relationships are not corporate, but personal, they are not relationships between clans, but between individual members of clans … The content of [these] company relations varies greatly'. (Levitus 1987, pp. 32–3)

In my own research, responses to questions on an issue such as whether people who shared a gunmogurrgurr name were necessarily co-owners of some kind included 'yes', 'no' and 'yes and no'. For example, when I asked one senior Mirarr estate owner whether the owner of another adjacent Mirarr estate was the same or different to him, he replied, 'Oh different one, but we still same little bit, my cousin'. There was no evidence that the sharing of a gunmogurrgurr name had ever constituted an issue requiring systematic and overt discussion.

The lack of evidence for reconstruction of overt discussions over detailed discrimination in land tenure contrasts strongly with the situation for kin terminologies. As we have seen, there is evidence for the reconstruction of overt discussions over detailed discrimination in kin terminologies, and in the mapping between them.

I suggest that this difference in reconstructions correlates with the significant difference between the two domains in the extent to which they were overtly recognised as motives for disputation. The available data support a reconstruction in which kinship, marriage and sexuality were commonly presented as causes of precolonial disputes:

> Gunwinggu themselves, including women, often cited 'women and corpses' as the outstanding causes of conflict, in mythical or quasi-mythical as well as contemporary situations. Old Mangurug suggested that the reason the Woraidbag are virtually extinct was that 'they were always fighting over women—not over dead men and their killers, but only over women. That's why all of them are dead and their country is empty of people. If we had done the same, we would all be gone now, too'. (Berndt & Berndt 1970, p. 167)[4]

By contrast, there is no evidence that land tenure was commonly presented as an overt cause of disputes. Determining the overall or ultimate causation of disputes is always a fraught exercise. Recognition of differences between overtly presented motives, as opposed to covert and/or inchoate motives, is probably a universal of human cognition. In the case of land tenure, colonisation presents a particular problem. One of the most immediate effects of colonisation was the imposition of Pax Australiana, even in areas where the effects of colonisation were much less. As such, data on disputation from even the earliest periods of colonisation require careful consideration when attempting to reconstruct the precolonial past. The issue of whether land tenure might have been a covert and/or inchoate motive for disputation in precolonial times may not be a resoluble issue.

The opposition in overt presentation of causality between the domains of kinship and land tenure generally appears to hold across Australia. Some analysts present the difference in terms of land tenure not having a causal role. Warner (1964 [1937], pp. 18–19) provided the classic statement of this nature:

> No land can be taken from a clan by an act of war. A clan does not possess its land by strength of arms but by immemorial tradition and as an integral part of the culture. Murngin myth dies hard, and ownership

---

4   It is of interest to note that the Woraidbag (Wardadjbak—which is the Bininj Gunwok term for Amurdak) were not virtually extinct at the time of the Berndts' fieldwork. Up until the late 1960s and early 1970s, there were direct patrifiliates for every known Amurdak estate. However, these patrifiliates were not normally resident in the Gunbalanya area. Despite this lack of residence, all these Amurdak patrifiliates would have been known to significant numbers of people who were long-term residents of Gunbalanya at the time of the Berndts' fieldwork.

of land is in Murngin myth even after the final destruction of a particular clan. It would never occur to a victorious group to annex another's territory, even though the entire male population were destroyed and the dead men's women and children taken by the victors. In the passage of time the clan using it would absorb it into their own territory and the myth would unconsciously change to express this. In the thought of the Murngin, land and water, people and clan are an act of the creator totem and the mythological ancestors, who always announce in myth and ceremony that this is the country of such and such a clan; to expropriate this land as a conscious act would be impossible. Just as the totem, the creator, and the members are a permanent and inextricable part of the culture, so is the clan's ownership of the land.

Hiatt (1965, p. 16) agreed with Warner:

> Disputes over land did not arise, and it was therefore difficult to discover the attitudes of owners towards their estates. I judged that they had an intimate knowledge of their sites and the country included by them but proprietorial interest outside this central core progressively weakened.

Stanner (1979, p. 233) further supported Warner:

> That is not to say there were never occasions on which whole groups were put to the spear, or that there was no lasting bad blood between groups at enmity. It was often so, especially when, by migration or some other cause, neighbour tribes spoke unrelated tongues, or had very distinct customs. But the conquest of land was a great rarity: I do not personally know of a single case. And the war of extermination, with one group bent remorselessly on the complete destruction of the other, as far as I have discovered, was so rare as to be all but unknown.

Sutton (1978, pp. 77–8) presented a slightly different perspective:

> I am not aware of any cases where land has changed hand by acts of war, although I am told that some massacres long ago resulted in clan extinction. I see no reason why this could not happen, however. I do not accept Warner's argument, relating to northeast Arnhem land (1964, pp. 18–19), which says that expropriation of land by acts of war is impossible because tenure is based on mythic charter, and these charters only change unconsciously to express changes of possession. I suggest it would take only a generation or two for mythic charters to be consciously re-written in such cases, and that the memory of massacres would be suppressed just as consciously. It is true, however, that battles were not waged just for the purpose of conquering and settling new lands as has often been the case in other parts of the world.

While Sutton disagreed with Warner as to the potentiality for speed and deliberateness of change in land tenure, he agreed that disputes were not fought over land in and of itself. Keen (2004, p. 266) concurred with Sutton's viewpoint in his presentation of north-east Arnhem Land.

> Yolngu oral history includes some accounts of expansionist individuals who fought for the country and the women of other groups. This kind of aggression was linked to competition between men for marriage to the same women, and hence to polygyny.

Therefore, overall, the reconstruction of a difference in the overt presentation of kinship and land tenure as motives for disputes is well supported by the evidence from across Australia. As discussed, a reconstruction of the full range of causality, including covert and/or inchoate motives, in disputation is a very different matter and not one considered here. Given that land in and of itself was not overtly presented as a cause of disputes, it appears that indeterminacies and inconsistencies in this arena were only rarely forced to the forefront in discourses among Aboriginal people.

The Effects of Colonisation on Land Tenure

The effects of colonisation have been most prominent in relation to land tenure. Land ownership is at the core of colonisation, which fundamentally involves the expropriation of other people's land. The northern Kakadu – Gunbalanya area was one of the areas less affected by colonial expropriation in Australia. Land was not expropriated into private hands, but theoretically remained the property of the Australian government. When the *Land Rights Act* was passed in 1976, the northern Kakadu area became available for claim.

However, the claim process was not straightforward. As previously discussed, although colonisation did not result in effective expropriation of the land, it decimated the populations traditionally associated with the northern Kakadu area. Further, as a result of engagement with colonial economic regimes, the residential ranges of the great majority of people associated with the northern Kakadu area were focused further to the west, closer to Darwin during the period from 1920 to 1970, and possibly even earlier than 1920.

Consequently, by the time the land claim process started in the 1970s, knowledge of land tenure had been attenuated. Even the most knowledgeable people had gaps in their understanding, and the knowledge base of any one individual generally failed to match the knowledge bases of any other individual. The problems of dealing with this attenuation were significantly exacerbated by the fact that there was no recognised or remembered system for overt discourse on indeterminacies in land tenure. Nevertheless, based on research with the most knowledgeable consultants in the 1970s and 1980s, it was possible to reconstruct a relatively coherent overview of land tenure at colonisation (see Figure 16).

However, there is an anomaly in Figure 16. The Mirarr-Gaagudju 2 estate is not contiguous with the other Gaagudju estates. As discussed, language names do not show a discontinuous attachment to the land in this area. In this particular instance, there is evidence that the Gaagudju language name can be reconstructed with contiguous associations. Specifically, there is evidence that the Dadjbagu estate, which is listed as associated with Gundjeyhmi, is historically associated with Gaagudju. The most direct evidence for this comes from a number of placenames in the Dadjbagu estate: Ardaagawa [aḓáakəwa], Garraanggirr [garáaŋgɪr] and Goordawu [góɔḓauu]. The phonetics and phonology of these names are incompatible with Bininj Gunwok (Evans 2003a, pp. 72–105), but perfectly compatible with Gaagudju (Harvey 2002a, pp. 17–92).

Complementing these findings is evidence from placenames that show that the association of Gaagudju with the Mirarr-Gaagudju estate is not of recent origin (see Table 13).

Table 13: Analysis of place names.

Ma-ya-bardeedj=madjiirli	Djaa-yu	Mooyu
3IIIA-PR-?=sand	PR-lie	sore
'The sand, it Xs'	'The sore lies'	

Source: Author's work.

The name *Ma-ya-bardeedj=madjiirli* is a compound, of a rare type with limited productivity (Harvey 2002a, pp. 131–4). The noun *madjiirli* 'sand' is a Class III noun, and *ma-ya-* is the appropriate present tense prefix complex for an intransitive verb with a Class III subject. However, my consultants did not recognise the *bardeedj* constituent. The *Djaa-yu Mooyu* placename is irregular. The noun *mooyu* is a Class III noun, and the regular construction for 'The sore lies' would be *Ma-yaa-yu Mooyu*. It is a recognised principle of internal reconstruction that irregularities that are not themselves the result of horizontal transmission indicate a greater time depth, with the corollary that the greater quantity of irregularity, the greater the time depth (Campbell 2006, p. 230; Crowley & Bowern 2010, p. 125; Ringe 2003, p. 254; Seebold 1975, p. 157).

The evidence from placenames argues that the association of Gundjeyhmi with the Dadjbagu estate is of recent origin. The available evidence on land ownership is congruent with this proposal. In the early twentieth century, eight to nine people in two ostensibly distinct patrilines were primary owners of the Mirarr-Gaagudju 2 estate. There was only one owner for the Dadjbagu estate at this time. A change of ownership involving a change of language affiliation is much more plausible in the situation in which there is a single owner, than in the case of eight to nine owners.

Further, it is not certain that the discontinuity ever had an on-the-ground reality. The anomaly may, in fact, be an artificial effect of colonisation. As discussed, this area was effectively depopulated by 1920. The known histories of owners of the Dadjbagu estate and the Mirarr-Gaagudju 2 estate establish that none of them were normally resident in the northern Kakadu area after 1920, and possibly from an earlier date. If they had been resident, then a more usual process might have taken place. The sole owner of the Dadjbagu estate in the early twentieth century would have changed his primary language affiliation to Gaagudju because the estate was associated with Gaagudju.

The apparent discontinuity in Gaagudju land–language associations is a prototypical example of the indeterminacies and contradictions in geographically based knowledge that often follow the effects of colonisation. This attenuation of geographically based knowledge is not limited to uncertainties pertaining to the associations of particular areas. It also extends to indeterminacies and contradictions concerning the geographical limits of land tenure systems. In this case, the indeterminacies and contradictions involve the extent of the gunmogurrgurr name system. Keen (1980, p. 80) reported evidence that the gunmogurrgurr terminology did not extend to areas associated with Bugurnidja, Ngombur and Umbugarla precolonially:

> I found that people were inconsistent and hesitant in their use of the kunmokurrkurr names Wirlirrku, Marerrmu and (to a lesser extent) Murumburr … People were consistent however in their use of the

language-group names Bukurnidja, Mbukarla and Ngombur. Older people of the Mbukarla and Ngombur language-groups said that really they had no kunmokurrkurr, but the Mayali (Kundjey'mi) people imposed the category on them.

I encountered the same extension of the gunmogurrgurr terminology, although on a more idiosyncratic basis, in work with Nelson Mulurrinj, who in the late 1980s was recognised as a senior landowner in the Cobourg Peninsula area to the north of Amurdak. Nelson had lived for extended periods of time in and around Darwin, and had extensive life history contacts with a range of people whose primary landownership was to areas west of the South Alligator River. During a discussion on clans and clan membership in the Kakadu – Gunbalanya area (which it should be noted was largely in accord with discussions with other consultants), Nelson gave gunmogurrgurr names for people known to him, traditionally associated with the Adelaide and Mary river areas immediately to the west of Kakadu National Park. Not only did Nelson assign these people a gunmogurrgurr name, but the names were also from his area.

I have worked extensively with the traditional owners of the Adelaide and Mary River areas, and there is no evidence for the operation of the gunmogurrgurr name system among them. Indeed, to the contrary, based on discussions with senior Limilngan owner Lena Henry, it appeared that Limilngan owners discussed smaller-scale land tenure primarily in terms of totemic entities. Thus, there was a *madlingi minyayan* 'mature male antilopine wallaroo' country and group of owners. This system of discussing smaller-scale land tenure with a totemic terminology was also found further to the west. It was also used in areas associated with Gulumoerrgin, the language associated with Darwin and its immediate surrounds.

The effects that have been discussed thus far are not structural, and they have not changed the options for discussing land tenure. By contrast, the land claim process has provided an opportunity for the development of a structural change. In this process, compound names consisting of a gunmogurrgurr name and a language name (e.g. Mirarr Erre or Mirarr Gundjeyhmi) were used by European researchers working in the land claim process (Keen 1980). As indicated, these names were used to distinguish estates from one another, as gunmogurrgurr names could not do so on their own. These compound names continue to have some level of usage by people who are frequent users of more formal registers, as in the following Department of the Environment (2013) announcement:

> The Gundjeihmi Aboriginal Council in the Northern Territory will receive $216,000 to document the significant Indigenous heritage sites in Mirarr Gundjeihmi country, to develop management plans and to assist in the transfer of cultural knowledge from local elders to the next generation.

However, compound names are not used by people who are not frequent users of more formal registers. Consider the following statement from the Gundjeihmi Aboriginal Corporation website (2017) for the 'Mirarr Gundjeyhmi' clan.

> Gundjeihmi Aboriginal Corporation is an organisation established, managed and controlled by the Mirarr.

The use of the term 'Gundjeihmi' to describe a corporation of 'Mirarr' owners is obviously predicated on there being some intersection between the two names. However, the two are not conjoined in an individually identifying manner. In the recent past, at least, it was widely understood that there were people who owned the names 'Gundjeihmi' and 'Mirarr' who were not members of the 'Mirarr Gundjeyhmi' clan. In general, it appears that Aboriginal people and others continue to use gunmogurrgurr names alone as identifiers in discussions of land tenure.

However, it should be noted that although people do not use compound terms, such as 'Mirarr Gundjeyhmi', they do recognise the reference of these terms when those terms are used by others. In my own research, I used these compound terms, and all the people I discussed these issues with recognised that 'Mirarr Erre' was distinct from 'Mirarr Gundjeyhmi'. This suggests that, depending on the requirements for precision, compound terms could come to have a more extensive usage. Requirements for precision are in turn likely to be strongly affected by the degree of disputation over land tenure.

The Effects of Colonisation on Kinship

The effects of colonisation on kinship appear to have played out over a longer time frame than its effects on land tenure. The most significant period of change appears to have been the 1960s. Prior to the 1960s, people's daily lives had some significant elements of continuity with the precolonial past. People associated with the northern Kakadu – Gunbalanya worked mostly in the pastoral industry. The majority of people at any particular site were Aboriginal people, and daily residential groupings were small. Most Aboriginal co-residents were longstanding consociates with various kinship links. There was significant movement across country during the annual cycle. Among the people who had become adults by the 1960s, nearly all spoke various Aboriginal languages. They could all describe traditional marriage arrangements, and many described their own participation in such arrangements.

During the 1960s, the employment structure of the pastoral industry changed radically. The great majority of Aboriginal people ceased to work in the industry, and their daily lives became focused in urban areas. In my own research, I did not record any accounts of traditional marriage arrangements after the 1960s. To the west of the Kakadu area, towards Darwin, Kriol became the principal daily language. One immediate consequence of these changes is that many younger people had only limited or no knowledge of more esoteric kinship terminologies, such as trirelational terminologies.

There is another less obvious but more significant effect on kinship terminologies in Kriol. Consider the following entries from the Kriol-English Dictionary (Lee 2007).

> *andi* Usage: Location: F. Variant: anti. n. father's sister, aunt. Usage: Location: BFN. Etym: aunty. SD: B. [Note: some include mother's sister BW and also most skin groups]

> *mami* Synd: mam. *n.* 1) mother; mother's sister; any person in the same skin group as one's mother. Usage: Location: FN. SD: B. [Note: both vocative and reference] 2) mother's cousin. Usage: Location: F. SD: B.

It may be noted that there is variation in how 'mother's sister' is classified. Some speakers classify her as 'mother'. This is the classification in all Aboriginal language terminologies, as these all involve parallel sibling merger. However, some speakers classify her as 'aunt', which in Aboriginal language terminologies only refers to the 'father's sister'. I found this shift towards English classifications to be common among people whose residential ranges were closer to Darwin. I also found that many people accepted both usages, but only actively used the English meaning.

The extent and nature of this shift needs further research, as do the implications for mapping between egocentric and sociocentric terminologies. In this respect, I have found that sociocentric terminologies have very little active usage around Darwin. People born before 1960 usually have a good command of sociocentric terminologies if asked about them, but they do not actively use them. Further research on the knowledge of people born after 1960 is required.

Conclusion

There is evidence that overt discussion of marriages in terms of a fine-grained categorisation of 'rightness' and 'wrongness' can be reconstructed precolonially as a common practice for the northern Kakadu – Gunbalanya area. This overt discussion necessarily entails discussion of the principles for determining the details of kinship terminologies, and overt discussion of the principles for mapping between the various terminologies. In terms of Bourdieu's (1977) analysis, kinship was very much in the universe of the discussed. By contrast, there is no evidence that overt discussion of the details of land ownership terminologies was a common practice, nor any evidence for overt discussion of principles governing mapping between the various terminologies. As such, land tenure lay largely in the universe of the undiscussed.

Colonisation greatly altered both practices and overt discussion patterns. The alterations following from colonisation played out most strongly from the 1960s, as this was the most significant period of postcolonial change. After the 1960s, kinship became a less prominent framing factor for many marriages, and Kriol became the standard daily language for many people. There is evidence of a shift towards English classifications in the Kriol of many people, and it is possible that there are rather variable understandings of Kriol kin terms. As such, it is possible that one effect of colonisation has been to make kinterm usage, and the mapping between various kin terminologies, less specific and detailed than it was precolonially.

Conversely, given that land tenure is one of the prime flashpoints of colonialism, and given the development of 'land rights' in the 1960s and 1970s, people in the period from the 1960s onwards were suddenly faced with more detailed and frequent examination of land tenure than had been the case previously. As people did not have a background in the formulation of opinions on indeterminacies within terminologies, or relationships between terminologies, the development of greater specificity in land tenure has not been speedy. The gunmogurrgurr name and language name compounds provide greater specificity, and although their active usage is largely confined to formal contexts and non-Aboriginal people, Aboriginal people show an immediate passive competence in these compounds. It appears that the future usage of these compounds will depend chiefly on the need for precise opinions in discussions of land tenure.

The need for precise opinions appears to relate most directly to the degree of disputation in the domains covered by particular terminologies. Precolonially, kinship (not land tenure) was the immediate topic of significant disputation. Consequently, offering more precise opinions can be reconstructed as a characteristic of discussions on precolonial kinship terminologies, but not of precolonial land tenure terminologies. Colonisation has to some extent reversed this. Land tenure (not kinship) has been the immediate topic of significant disputation. Consequently, there has been some increase in the offering of more precise opinions on land tenure terminologies, at least in specifically intercultural domains such as the land claim process, whereas kinship terminologies for many Kriol speakers appear to be less precisely defined than those found in Aboriginal languages.

References

Berndt, R & Berndt, C 1970, *Man, land and myth in north Australia: the Gunwinggu people*, Canberra: Aboriginal Studies Press.

Bourdieu, P 1977, *Outline of a theory of practice*, Cambridge: Cambridge University Press. doi.org/10.1017/CBO9780511812507.

Campbell, L 2006, *Historical linguistics: an introduction*, Edinburgh: Edinburgh University Press.

Crowley, T & Bowern, C 2010, *An introduction to historical linguistics*, Oxford: Oxford University Press.

Department of the Environment 2013, *Announcement*, viewed 1 August 2017, www.environment.gov.au/minister/burke/2013/mr20130301.html.

Evans, N 2003a, *Bininj Gunwok: a pan-dialectal grammar of Mayali, Kunwinjku and Kune*, Canberra: Pacific Linguistics.

Evans, N (ed.) 2003b, *The Non-Pama-Nyungan languages of northern Australia: comparative studies in the continent's most linguistically complex region*. Canberra: Pacific Linguistics.

Garde, M 2013, *Culture, interaction and person reference in an Australian language: an ethnography of Bininj Gunwok communication*, Amsterdam & Philadelphia: John Benjamins. doi.org/10.1075/clu.11.

Gundjeihmi Aboriginal Corporation 2017, *GAC*, viewed 1 August 2017, www.mirarr.net/gac.html.

Harvey, M 2001, 'Oenpelli Kunwinjku kinship terminologies and marriage practices', *Oceania*, *72*, pp. 117–42. doi.org/10.1002/j.1834-4461.2001.tb02776.x.

Harvey, M 2002a, *A grammar of Gaagudju*, Berlin & New York: Mouton de Gruyter. doi.org/10.1515/9783110871289.

Harvey, M 2002b, 'Land tenure and naming systems in Aboriginal Australia', *The Australian Journal of Anthropology*, *13*, pp. 23–44. doi.org/10.1111/j.1835-9310.2002.tb00188.x.

Harvey, M & Garde, M 2015, Matries and subsections: bodies and social personae in northern Australia, *Anthropological Linguistics*, *57*, pp. 229–74. doi.org/10.1353/anl.2016.0006.

Hiatt, L 1965, *Kinship and conflict: a study of an Aboriginal community in northern Arnhem Land*, Canberra: Australian National University Press.

Keen, I 1980, *Alligator rivers stage II land claim*, Darwin: Northern Land Council.

Keen, I 1982, 'How some Murngin men get ten wives: the marital implications of matrilateral cross-cousin structures', *Man* (n.s.), *17*, pp. 620–42.

Keen, I 1994, *Knowledge and secrecy in an Aboriginal religion*, Oxford: Clarendon Press.

Keen, I 2004, *Aboriginal economy and society: Australia at the threshold of colonization*, Melbourne: Oxford University Press.

Lee, J 2007, *Kriol-Ingglish dikshenri*, ausil.org/Dictionary/Kriol/index-english/index.htm.

Levitus, R 1987, *Gagudju Association membership*, Report to the Gaagudju Association.

Merlan, F 1988, 'Gender in Aboriginal social life: a review', in R Berndt & R Tonkinson (eds), *Social anthropology and Australian Aboriginal studies*, Canberra: Aboriginal Studies Press, pp. 17–76.

Ringe, D 2003, 'Internal reconstruction', in B Joseph & R Janda (eds), *The handbook of historical linguistics*, Maldon, MA: Blackwell, pp. 244–61. doi.org/10.1002/9780470756393.ch3.

Seebold, E 1975, 'Archaic patterns in the word formation of early Germanic languages', *Transactions of the Philological Society*, 74, pp. 157–72. doi.org/10.1111/j.1467-968X.1975.tb01170.x.

Stanner, WEH 1979, *White man got no dreaming: essays 1938–1973*, Canberra: Australian National University Press.

Sutton, P 1978, *Wik: Aboriginal society, territory and language at Cape Keerweer, Cape York Peninsula*, Brisbane: University of Queensland.

Sutton, P 2003, *Native title in Australia: an ethnographic perspective*, Cambridge: Cambridge University Press. doi.org/10.1017/CBO 9780511481635.

Warner, WL 1964 [1937], *A black civilization: a social study of an Australian tribe*, New York: Harper & Row.

PART II
Social Categories
and Their History

6

Moiety Names in South-Eastern Australia: Distribution and Reconstructed History

Harold Koch, Luise Hercus and Piers Kelly

Introduction

This report[1] forms part of the project 'Skin and kin in Aboriginal Australia: linguistic and historical perspectives on the dynamics of social categories', whose object is to document and map the Australian systems of social category names and reconstruct their prehistory.[2] Social category systems include subsections, sections and moieties. Here, we report on the moiety names in six of the terminological sets found in south-eastern Australia— identified on the basis of (near-)identical names.[3] Typically, these terminological sets extend over a number of different languages, including languages that are not closely related linguo-genetically to one another. Moreover, the terminologies may differ between languages that are closely related to one another. We do not discuss moiety names that co-occur

---

1   We thank Patrick McConvell, Ted Ryan and two anonymous reviewers for their helpful comments on earlier versions of this chapter, but take responsibility for the final content.
2   The project is funded by Australian Research Council grant no. DP120100632; chief investigators Patrick McConvell, Harold Koch, Jane Simpson; and partner investigator Laurent Dousset. See McConvell and Dousset (2012) for a description; the online database can be accessed at www.austkin.net.
3   We use 'system' to refer to kinds of social categorisations (moiety, section and subsection) and 'set' for the terms that occur in languages using the same (or cognate) names in their categorisation system.

with section names in systems of four sections (such as the Queensland General system discussed in Chapter 8) or eight subsections.[4] Thus, we will be primarily discussing six pairs of terms—that is 12 words—plus some minor sets that occur on the fringes of the main ones.

For each of the six sets of terms, plus their variants, we discuss:

- the sources of the information
- the linguistic forms, as spelled in the sources, phonemicised by linguists and spelled in the standardised orthography used by the AustKin project[5]
- the languages in which they occur—the languages as named in the sources, as well as the modern language names[6]
- the linguistic genetic groups[7] that the languages belong to
- the name of the terminology set/type/area as given in the literature
- a map of its distribution[8]
- a comparison of the distribution of the set of moiety terms to that of the genetic subgroup
- whether the moiety names have meanings (other than denoting a social category) in their language.

We then compare our distributions with other summaries in the literature. Using methods from historical linguistics, we offer our reasoning in regard to the historical processes that have led to the distribution of moiety terms across linguo-genetic groups. We argue that cultural borrowing was the main mechanism that spread the terminological sets. We offer indications of the direction of these spreads, which is displayed in Figure 22. Evidence from the etymology of names is sparse, but we suggest that this evidence tends to support an expansion from the Murray–Darling area.

---

4   It is not clear in such cases whether the section names date from before the (sub)section names or were adopted concurrently with or subsequently to the latter.
5   This orthographic system uses voiceless symbols (*p*, *t* and *k*) for stop consonants; digraphs *ng* for the velar nasal; *th*, *nh* and *lh* for laminodentals; *ty*, *ny* and *ly* for palatals; and up to three different symbols for the different kinds of rhotic (*r*-like) sounds: *r* for the English-like glide; *rr* for a tap; *rrh* for a trill that contrasts with the tap; for languages that do not distinguish the latter two, *rr* is used for a sound that can either be a tap or trill.
6   We use the spelling of our sources when reporting their information, otherwise we use the version given in the AustKin database, accessed at austkin.net/index.php?loc=list_languages.
7   All the relevant groupings are subgroups of the Pama-Nyungan family of Australian languages or subgroups of these subgroups (e.g. Central Karnic and Western Kulin).
8   The maps were produced in the first instance by Piers Kelly and revised by Billy McConvell. Boundaries are approximate only and maps are based on information in AUSTLANG, accessed at austlang.aiatsis.gov.au.

The terminological sets we discuss are summarised in Table 14, where we present the terms, our general name for the terminological set and the section of this chapter where each is discussed. It should be stated at the outset that all except the Central Victorian set involve matrimoieties, whereas the Central Victorian terms refer to patrimoieties.[9] The names in Table 14 are ordered insofar as possible to show the pragmatic equivalences (see Chapter 1) across systems, based on the following authorities. *Thiniwa* = *Matharri* follows Howitt (1996 [1904], p. 91) rather than the contradictory indication in Howitt (1996 [1904], p. 138). *Wuthurru* = *Matharri* accords with Howitt (1996 [1904], p. 192). *Wuthurru* = *Thiniwa* follows Elkin's field notes (see section 'The South-West Queensland Set'). *Kilparra* = *Kulparru* is based on Howitt's (1996 [1904], p. 138) statement that 'it seems that Kulpuru is the equivalent of Kilpara, and Tiniwa of Mukwara'. *Kilparra* = *Kurukity* is based on Howitt (1996 [1904], p. 137). Any statements about equivalences between the Central Victorian patrilineal moieties and any of the other matrimoieties are suspect (see subsection 'The *Makwara* and *Kilparra* Set').[10]

Table 14: Summary of terminological sets.

Term	Label	Section
Matharri & Kararrhu	South Australian	The South Australian Set
Thiniwa & Kulparru	Cooper Basin	The Cooper Basin Set
Wuthurru & Parrkatha	South-West Queensland	The South-West Queensland Set
Makwara & Kilparra	Darling River	The Darling River Set
Waang & Bunjil	Central Victorian	The Central Victorian Set
Kamaty/Kapaty & Kurukity	Western Victorian	The Western Victorian Set

Source: Authors' work.

The South Australian Set

One set of moiety terminologies was identified by Howitt (1996 [1904]) as characteristic of the 'Lake Eyre group' of tribes, exemplified by the Dieri [Diyari] of South Australia. Howitt gave the Diyari names as *Matteri* and *Kararu*. We spell the names as *Matharri* and *Kararrhu*, adapting Austin's (1981, p. 10) phonological analysis of the names to the standardised

---

9   Testart (1978) claimed that matrimoieties are prior in all of Australia.
10 For example, Howitt (1996 [1904], p 138): 'In the south-west of Victoria ... Kroki is equal to Bunjil and Kumitch to Waang'.

AustKin orthography. R. H. Mathews (1905, p. 49) called the group characterised by this set of terms the 'Parnkalla nation, whose social divisions are Kirraroo and Matturi'—Parnkalla being the name of a tribe and language in the northern Eyre Peninsula. Elkin (1931, pp. 51, 53) delineated a 'Lakes group' of South Australian tribes and described the distribution of the *Matari* and *Kararu* moiety names as extending from the Wonkamala [Wangkamanha] and Wongkongaru [Wangkangurru] in the north to the Ngaluri [Ngadjuri], Pankala [Parnkalla] and Naua [Nauo] in the south.

Many of the languages spoken by groups that have this set of moiety names belong to the Thura-Yura subgroup of languages, as defined by Simpson and Hercus (2004). There is no question concerning the northern languages: Kuyani, Adnyamathanha (where *Kararrhu* occurs as *Ararrhu*, lacking the initial *k*, as a consequence of a regular sound change in this language), Nukunu[11] and Parnkalla (now normally spelled Banggala). There is some question about how far west this set extends. For the poorly attested Nauo language, once spoken in the southern Eyre Peninsula, no terms are cited in Hercus (1999) or Hercus and Simpson (2001). However, Howitt's 1904 map includes this region within his matrimoiety area, and Elkin (1931, p. 45) included 'Naua' in the *Matari* and *Kararu* groups. Wirangu is the westernmost of the Thura-Yura languages. Hercus (1999, p. 1) stated that 'Wirangu people had the same matrilineal moiety system as their eastern neighbours, with a division into *madhaRi* and *gaRarru*', and cited several kinds of evidence to support this claim. This is consistent with Howitt's (1996 [1904], p. 129) claim: 'The tribes which live on the coast between Eucla and Spencer's Gulf evidently belong to the Lake Eyre group, having the same class names in variations of Matteri and Kararu'. The southern part of the Thura-Yura region presents a different picture. Simpson and Hercus (2004, pp. 181–2) stated: 'All but the southernmost people (Kaurna, Narangga [Narungga] and Ngadjuri[12]) … had a matrilineal moiety system, the main features of which were shared with Karnic people, with moieties, named Mathari and Karraru [*sic*]'.

---

11   The sharp social difference between the Nukunu and their neighbours is highlighted by the fact that as recently as the 1960s, Hercus was told by a Nukunu man that his people regarded the marriage practices of their neighbours as incestuous: 'Those people in the east they were marrying the wrong way, marrying their sisters!' (Hercus 1992a, p. 11).

12   Elkin (1931, p. 53) included in his *Matari-Kararu* group 'Ngaluri', which is identified by Hercus (1992a, p. 24) as Ngalyuri: 'i.e. Ngadjuri'. The presence of moieties is also presupposed by Berndt's (1939, p. 459) comment: 'In the Ngadjuri tribe the curlew was of the *Gararu* moiety; the owl's moiety was unidentified, but was probably the other one, *Matêri*. These moieties were exogamous'.

6. MOIETY NAMES IN SOUTH-EASTERN AUSTRALIA

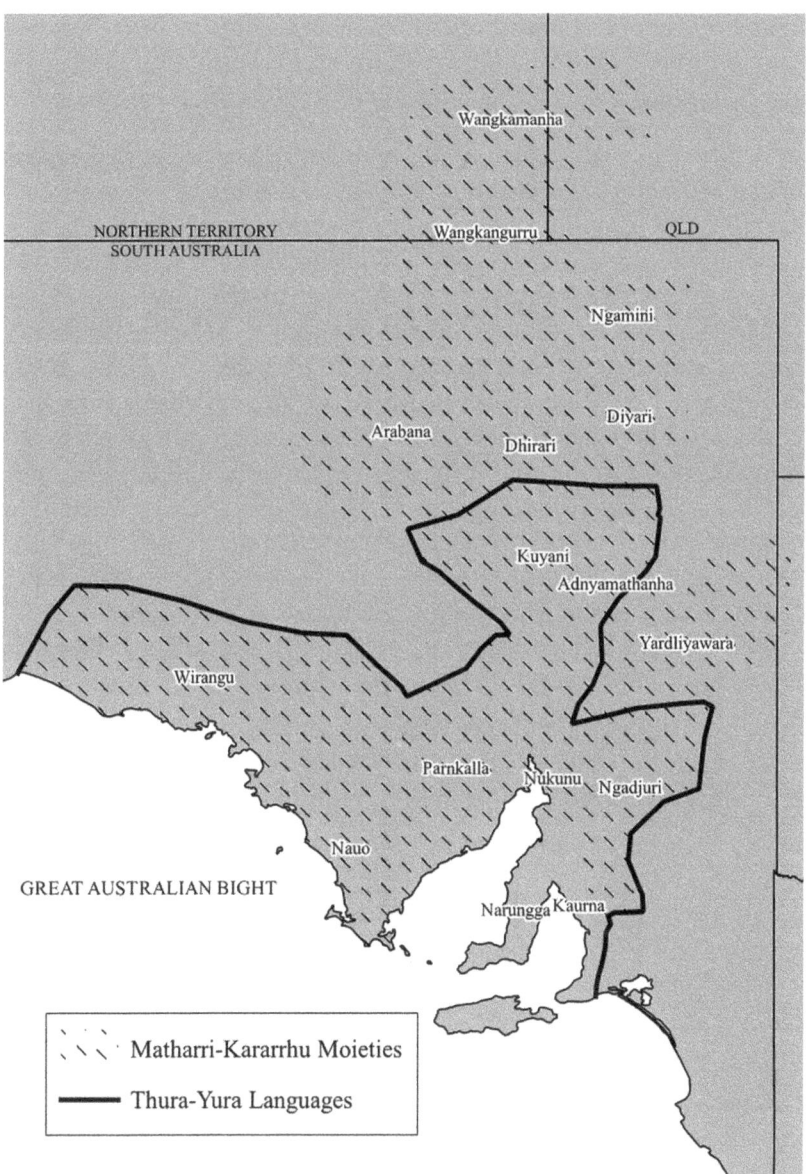

Figure 17: Matharri-Kararrhu moieties, plus Thura-Yura languages.
Source: Authors' work.

Figure 17 indicates the distribution of the *Matharri* and *Kararrhu* moiety names,[13] as well as all the Thura-Yura languages—including the southernmost Kaurna and Narangga, in which these names are not found.

In addition to most, but not all, Thura-Yura languages, these moiety names are found in languages of the Yarli and Karnic subgroups. They occur in Yardliyawarra (according to Hercus's information), which is a member of the small Yarli subgroup and adjacent to Adnyamathanha (of the Thura-Yura group)—with whom its speakers have the closest cultural associations (Hercus & Austin 2004, p. 211).[14] The Karnic languages are a large subgroup (Bowern 2001) located to the north and north-east of the Thura-Yura languages. The Western Karnic languages, Arabana and Wangkangurru, have the *Matharri* and *Kararrhu* terms, plus the adjacent Wonkamala [= Wangkamanha] of Northern Karnic; however, the names are found in only some of the languages usually classified as Central Karnic—namely Diyari, Dhirari [Dhirrari] and Ngamini.[15] The other Central Karnic languages, as well as Northern and Eastern Karnic, have other moiety naming terms—either the Cooper Basin set (see section 'The Cooper Basin Set') or the south-western Queensland set (see section 'The South-West Queensland Set'). Figure 18 shows all the Karnic languages: Karnic languages that have the *Matharri* and *Kararrhu* terminology and those with *Kulpurru* and *Thiniwa*, as well as all languages with *Parrkatha* and *Wuthurru*.

---

13   This area partially overlaps with that of the 'Dieri kinship system', in which the 'mother's mother' term also functions as a sibling term and the 'father's mother' term as 'cross-cousin' (see McConvell 2013, pp. 169–71; Scheffler 1978, pp. 365–84).
14   However, note that Yardliyawarra does not share with Adnyamathanha the absence of initial *k*.
15   Howitt (1996 [1904], p. 95) also included Yaurorka [Yawarrawarrka] in this grouping; however, Mathews and Elkin assigned it to what we are calling the Cooper Basin set (see section 'The Cooper Basin Set'). Breen (2004a, p. 4) alerted us to the fact that Howitt's Yandruwandha and Yawarrawarrka data are not always reliable, sometimes including material that is Diyari or Ngamini.

6. MOIETY NAMES IN SOUTH-EASTERN AUSTRALIA

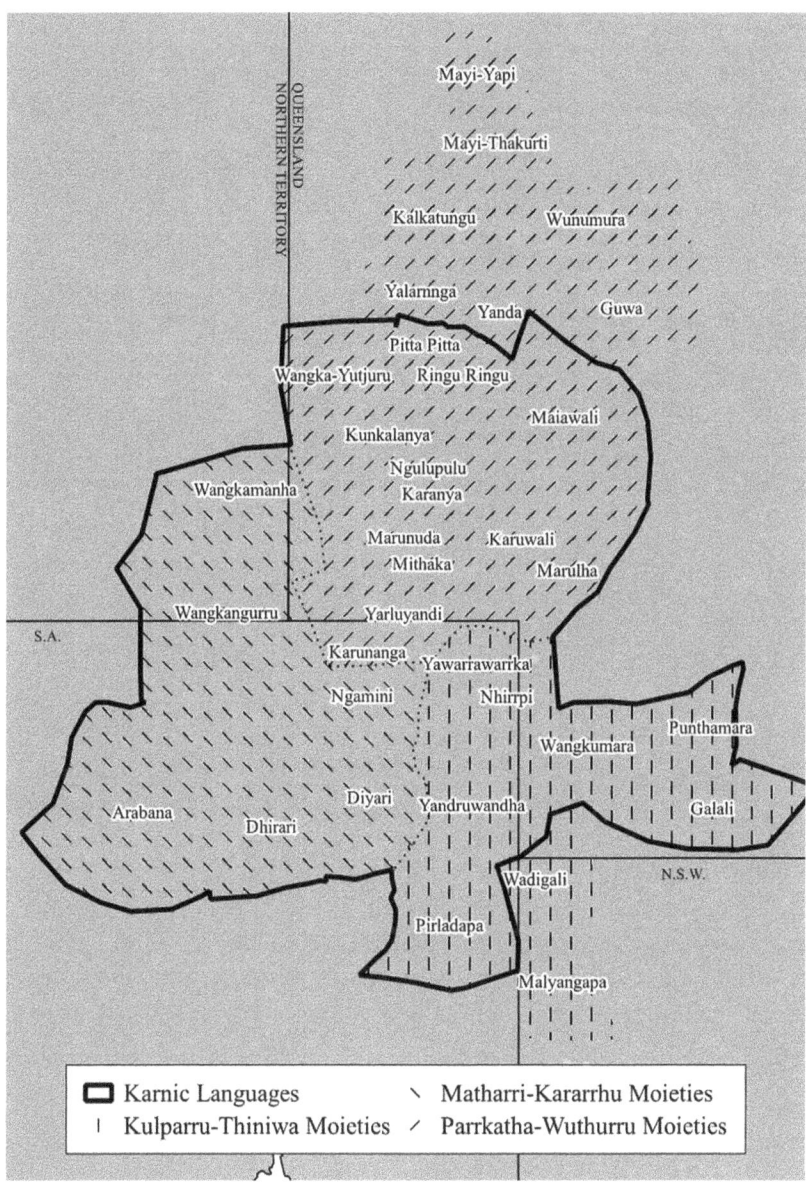

Figure 18: Karnic languages; three moiety sets.
Source: Authors' work.

The Cooper Basin Set

To the east of Diyari, in an area centred on the Cooper Creek, there is another terminological set characterised by the moiety names established in their modern form as *Kulparru* and *Thiniwa* by Wafer and Lissarrague (2008, pp. 423, 428, cf. 458).[16] This echoes R. H. Mathews (1905, p. 51), who called the peoples with these names the 'Wonkamurra nation'; he had earlier called them the 'Yowerawarrika nation' (Mathews 1900, p. 83).[17] The languages with this set of terms include:

- Central Karnic languages from South Australia: Pirladapa[18] (Elkin 1931, p. 53), Yandruwandha (Breen 2004b, p. 22; Elkin 1931, p. 53; Howitt 1996 [1904], pp. 91–2; Mathews 1905, p. 51,), including the Nhirrpi dialect from the hills north of Nappamerri (see Bowern 1999), Yawarrawarrka (Elkin 1931, p. 53; Mathews 1905, p. 51)
- Eastern Karnic languages[19] of Queensland: Wangkumara (Mathews 1905, p. 51; Robertson 1984[20]), Punthamara (Mathews 1905, p. 51), Galali (Mathews 1905, p. 51)
- two of the three Yarli languages: Malyangapa (Elkin 1931, p. 53) and Wadigali (Elkin 1931, p. 53).

Hercus and Austin (2004) noted that people of these two languages shared ceremonies with Wangkumara people and Wadigali also with the Yandruwandha, whereas Yardliyawara people, who spoke the third Yarli language, had ceremonial links with their Adnyamathanha neighbours to the west. We note also that the Central Karnic languages are divided by their moiety terms between the South Australian set, south-west Queensland set and Cooper Creek set. Only the Eastern Karnic group of languages shows consistency with respect to their social category terms.[21] The Karnic languages with *Kulpurru* and *Thiniwa* moiety names can be seen in Figure 18.

---

16   See Chapter 8 for a possible etymological connection between *Kulparru* and the General Queensland section term *Kuparu*.
17   In fact, Mathews used shared moiety or section names as the basis for his recognition of so-called nations.
18   The most authoritative spelling is now *Pilardapa* (e.g. Breen 2004a, p. xvii).
19   See Bowern (2009) on this classification: the status of Galali has been disputed. There has been some doubt about the identification of Punthamara and Galali.
20   Based largely on material elicited by Gavan Breen; names are spelled *Kulpurra* and *Thiniwa*.
21   Wafer and Lissarrague (2008, p. 458) mentioned that in one of his publications, Mathews included Punthamara among the groups that have the most widespread Queensland system of sections.

The South-West Queensland Set

The Karnic languages located north of the Queensland – South Australia border have a different set of moiety names. For Pitta-Pitta and closely related dialects, Roth (1984 [1897], p. 56) gave the matrimoiety names *Ootaroo* and *Pakoota*. The first of these is recognisable as the widespread Queensland term *Wuthurru*. We normalise the second name as *Parrkatha*, following Breen's (1981b, p. 130) phonemicisation of the term in Mayi languages, in spite of Roth's spelling with *oo* in the second syllable for Pitta-Pitta (versus his spelling of *pâ-kŭt-tă* for other languages). Other languages to the north-east share these names, including Guwa, Wunamura, Mayi-Yapi, Mayi-Thakurti and, apparently, Yanda, which Roth (1984 [1897], p. 40) included (as his Yunda) in the Boulia district as a messmate of Pitta-Pitta. To the north, Kalkatungu shares *Ootaroo* but has *Malara* in place of *Parrkatha*; Yalarnnga, between Kalkatungu and Pitta-Pitta, has the moiety name *Wutharru*—the other name, possibly *Malyarra*, cannot be confirmed (Breen & Blake 2007, p. 101). This set of moiety terms exists in a system that also contains four section names.[22]

Among the Northern Karnic languages, we can assume that the same moiety names are also found in Wangka-Yutjuru, which was spoken west of Pitta-Pitta, since Roth (1984 [1897], p. 56) gave *ŭr-tă-roo* and *bŭr-gŭt-tă* as class names among the Roxburgh (Georgina River) blacks. A comparison of Roth's map (1984 [1897], Plate 1) with that of Blake and Breen (1971, before p. 1) places this in Wangka-Yutjuru territory. Elkin (1931, p. 53) reported the Pitta-Pitta moiety names (*Wuturu* and *Parkata* in his spelling) for three further Karnic languages: Ngulupulu (a dialect of Pitta-Pitta according to Blake 1979, p. 184); Yelyuyendi (Yarluyandi);[23] and Marula (Marulta), an alternative name for Mithaka, with which it was a co-dialect (Breen 1971, p. 9). Howitt (1996 [1904], p. 192) had earlier reported the moiety names *Wuturu* and *Parkata* for Ngulubulu, Yelyuyendi and Marula, plus a further Karnic language Karangura (see Hercus 1991). For Karuwali, which is another alternative name for Marulta/Mithaka, Elkin gave moiety names *Wuturu* and *Malura*; the latter appears to be

---

22 For the Pitta-Pitta, these are *Kupuru* and *Wunku* (belonging to the *Wuthurru* moiety), and *Kurrkila* and *Panpari* (belonging to the *Parrkatha* moiety). These section names are shared over a great area of central Queensland (see Chapter 8).

23 From 1965 onward, Luise Hercus found that families of mixed Yarluyandi-Wangkangurru descent were using the Wangkangurru moiety names *Matharri* and *Kararrhu*. The most authoritative spelling is now *Yaluyandi* (e.g. Breen 2004a, p. xvii).

the same term as *Malara*, reported by Roth for Kalkatungu.[24] Elkin did not report section terms for these four Karnic languages. Therefore, we might surmise that in the Northern Karnic languages, the section system is a recent innovation overlaid on an older moiety system. In Figure 18, the Karnic languages with moiety names *Parrkatha* and *Wuthurru* can be compared to all languages with *Parrkatha* and *Wuthurru*. According to Elkin's field notes (seen by Hercus), the *Parrkatha* and *Wuthurru* moieties are pragmatically equivalent to *Kulparru* and *Thiniwa* respectively of the Cooper Basin.[25]

The Darling River Set

The Makwara and Kilparra Set

This had been called the 'Paakantyi system' by Wafer and Lissarrague (2008, p. 420), who spelled the moiety names *Makwara* and *Kilparra*. Earlier Mathews had called this the 'Barkunjee nation' with the terms *Keelparra* and *Mukwarra* (see subsection 'Earlier Mapping of Moieties'). Howitt (1996 [1904], p. 97) referred to peoples with the 'class names … Kilpara and Mukwara' as one of the 'great groups of tribes, having the two-class system'. He included a large number of tribal names, including the 'Itchumundi nation', encompassing the Wilya, Kongait, Bulali and Tongaranka tribes; and the 'Karamundi nation', consisting of the Milpulko, Naualko, Guerno and Barrumbinya tribes, as well as the Barkinji tribe and the Wiimbaio tribe; the latter is an alternative name for the Marawara dialect of Paakantyi. Further peoples mentioned by Elkin (1931, p. 53) as using the *Makwara* and *Kilpara* terms are the Bolali [Bulali], Wilyali and Wilyakali (the last two are alternative versions of the same name). All of these named groups, except the Barrumbinya [Barranbinya], involve people who spoke the Paakantyi language in contemporary terms (Hercus 1982, 1993).[26]

---

24   Breen (1981b, p. 130) gave *maLaRa* for the Mayi language Ngawun (where *L* and *R* represent uncertainty regarding the exact form).
25   We don't know what to make of this comment from Elkin's field notes: 'Police tracker at Birdsville says tribe north of Yelyuyandi = "Mulubulu". The moieties = "Yepari" (= Kararu) & Yeta (= Matari)'. Yelyuyandi and Mulubulu are presumably Yarluyandi and Ngulupulu respectively.
26   Hercus (1982, p. 6) mentioned that the Paakantyi shared the section system with their eastern Wangaaypuwan neighbours, and cited Berndt (1964), who suggested that the sections were 'possibly introduced' (cf. Berndt & Berndt 1981, p. 56)—which we take to refer to a recent adoption.

For Barrumbinya, see Oates (1988a), who called the language Barranbinya, but provided no information on moiety names. Barranbinya is a separate language, perhaps most closely related to Muruwari (on the Culgoa River), which has a four-section system like that of the Central New South Wales languages (Oates 1988b).

As for the southern regions where these moiety names were used, Howitt (1996 [1904], p. 100) stated: 'Tribes having these class names extended up the Murray River as far as the Loddon'. According to his map, these include his Kerinma, Leitchi-Leitchi, Weki-Weki, Wathi-Wathi and Bura-Bura. This apparently includes languages classified in the Lower Murray subgroup (see Horgen 2004)—Kureinji (also known as Kerinma and Keramin and including Yari-Yari), Yitha Yitha, Dadi Dadi (also called Tharti-Tharti)[27] and Yuyu (Wafer & Lissarrague 2008, p. 420)[28]—as well as dialects of the north-west Kulin language: Madhi Madhi, Wadi Wadi, Weki-Weki and Ladji Ladji or Letyi-Letyi (Blake et al. 2011, p. 25).[29] Radcliffe-Brown (1918, pp. 249–50) confirmed the presence of the matrimoieties *Kailpara* and *Mäkwara* (in his spelling) among the Ladji Ladji (his Laitu-laitu) and Dadi Dadi (his Tati-tati).

This set thus overlaps with the whole area of the large Paakantyi language, but also includes the Barranbinya language on its northern fringe, plus some languages of the Lower Murray group, and a small section of the Kulin languages. Figure 19 shows the distribution of the *Makwara* and *Kilparra* terms, the Paakantyi language area, the distribution of the Lower Murray group of languages and the subset of these languages that have the *Makwara* and *Kilparra* moiety names.

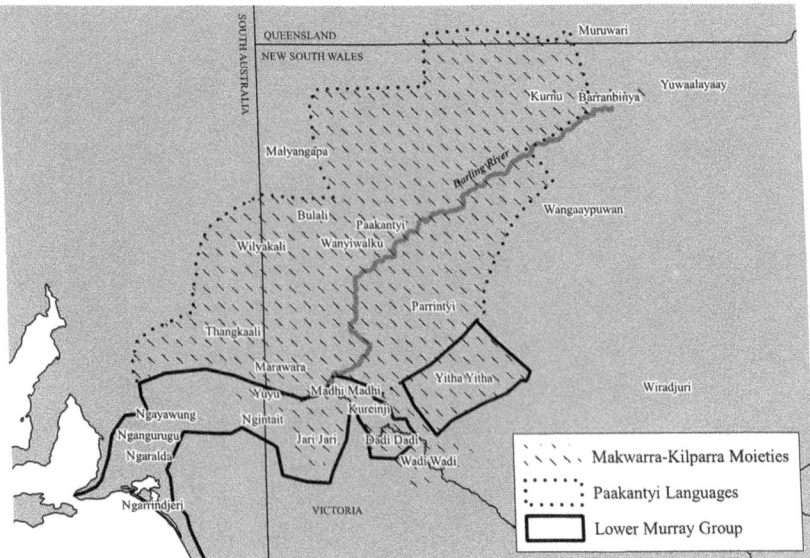

Figure 19: Makwarra-Kilparra moieties; Paakantyi and Lower Murray languages.
Source: Authors' work.

Some of the earliest available references to this set imply that the moiety names have meanings apart from their reference to social categories. Reverend John Bulmer is quoted by Smyth (1878, p. 86) as follows:

> The blacks of the Murray are divided into two classes, the Mak-quarra or eagle, and the Kil-parra or crow. If the man be Mak-quarra, the woman must be Kil-parra. A Mak-quarra could not marry a Mak-quarra nor a Kil-parra a Kil-parra. The children take their caste from the mother, and not from the father.

Fison and Howitt (1880, p. 288) quoted a similar statement from the same man: 'The Wa-imbio [tribe, speaking the Marawara dialect of Paakantyi] are divided into two primary classes, Muquarra (eaglehawk) and Kilparra (crow)'. However, these names are not the ordinary words for 'eaglehawk' and 'crow' respectively, since, according to the Paakantyi dictionary (Hercus 1993), the words for 'eaglehawk' are *pilyara* or *warriku* (in the Kurnu dialect) and 'crow' is *waaku*. Hence, the claim about the meanings of the moiety names being eaglehawk and crow m rather indicate that the two birds were emblematic of the two moie⁻

---

30 Cf. Fison and Howitt's (1880, p. 40) information that for the Mackay ar to Bridgman: 'The symbol of the Yoongaroo division [i.e. moiety] … is the allig: Wootaroo the kangaroo'.

Radcliffe-Brown (1918, p. 249) was told by his Ladji Ladji informant that 'there was a special connection between Kailpara and the emu [note: not the crow] and a similar connection between Mäkwara and the eaglehawk'. The nature of this 'special connection' is not further indicated.

Another possible explanation has been proposed by Wafer and Lissarrague (2008, p. 420):

> In language groups that use the Paakantyi-type moiety system, evidence from a number of groups indicates that the Eaglehawk totem is classed as Makwara (Howitt 1904, pp. 98–100); and, in the one case where Crow is listed as a totem, it is classed as Kilparra (Howitt 1904, p. 100). Thus, it seems fairly clear that the moiety systems of the Darling–lower Murray (Paakantyi-type) and the upper Murray [our Central Victorian system; see subsection 'The Bunjil-Waang Set'] are equated with each other.

However, such social equivalence is not strictly possible, since the eaglehawk–crow system of Central Victoria involves patrilineal moieties, whereas the names of the Darling set denote matrimoieties. Thus, persons classified in the Darling system as 'eaglehawk' share this identity with their mother, while their father must be 'crow'; conversely, in the Central Victorian system, this person's father is also 'eaglehawk', while their mother is 'crow'. Since the two systems only partially overlap, an explanation in terms of the equivalence between different social systems is not tenable.

For the patrilineal eaglehawk and crow system of Central Victoria, see subsection 'The Bunjil-Waang Set'. See also the (somewhat different) matrilineal eaglehawk and crow system of the Alpine languages, described in the section 'The Alpine Area with "Eaglehawk" and "Crow" Moieties'.

Other Two-Term Terminology Sets

Another set of binary classification names is found around the Darling River area—among Paakantyi-speaking peoples, as well as the Malyangapa (of the Yarli linguistic subgroup) to their west and, to their east, the (Ngiyampaa-speaking) Wangaaypuwan and Wiradjuri (of the Central New South Wales linguistic subgroup). The latter two otherwise have a system of four sections that group into two matrimoieties. It is not clear how these alternative names are related, in their meaning and usage, to the standard set of moiety terms. However, we attempt to show below how they may be formally related to one another and the standard terms *Makwara* and *Kilparra*.

Howitt (1996 [1904], p. 106) said of the 'tribes of the Itchumundi nation' (i.e. western Paakantyi) that the names *Mukolo* and *Ngielpuru* 'accompany the class names *Mukwara* and *Kilpara*'. This wording suggests that these are alternative names for the same moiety divisions. The former name recurs among some of the Wiradjuri, who have a system of four sections and whose language belongs to the Central New South Wales subgroup. Howitt (1996 [1904], p. 107) stated that in the Wiradjuri country near Mossgiel, north of the Lachlan River, in addition to the four section names, there are class (i.e. moiety) names *Mukula* (including the *Ipai* and *Kumbo* sections) and *Budthurung*[31] (including the *Murri* and *Kubbi* sections). For the Wongaibon [Wangaaypuwan], north of the Wiradjuri of the Lachlan River, he reported the existence of four sections plus the (matri-)moiety names *Mukumurra* (for the *Murri* and *Kubbi* sections) and *Ngielbumurra* (for the *Ipai* and *Kumbo* sections) (Howitt 1996 [1904], p. 108). Howitt's information on Wangaaypuwan can be compared to that of a later source, Radcliffe-Brown (1923, p. 424), who rendered the moiety names as *Mákaŋära* (or *Mákwaŋära*) and *Kílpuŋära*, attributing his and Howitt's differences between the forms of names to probable 'local differences of dialect'. This does not appear to be an adequate explanation of the facts. Radcliffe-Brown's Wangaaypuwan moiety names match closely the moiety names *Magungera* and *Dilbungera* indicated by Beckett (1967, p. 456) for the Malyangapa to the west of the Paakantyi.[32] To complicate matters further, for the Yuwaalayaay, northern neighbours of the Wangaaypuwan, who also have a system of four section names, the *Gamilaraay, Yuwaalaraay, and Yuwaalayaay dictionary* (Ash et al. 2003, p. 106) reports a social group term *Magula* (that is *Makula* in our spelling system) that contrasts with *Bumbira*.[33] The terms *Magula* and *Bumbira* are also found further north in the Queensland language Bidjara, which also has the moiety names *Wudhurru* and *Yangurru* (Breen 1981a, p. 281).

An analysis of the forms of moiety names in Paakantyi and its neighbours is presented in Table 15 (asterisks represent reconstructed forms). Note that there is evidence for forms with different vowels, such as **muku-* and **maku-*. Howitt's forms suggested a phonemic form *Mukulu* for Itchumundi and Wiradjuri and *Mukumarra* for Wangaaypuwan for one name, and, for the other, *Ngilpurru* for both Itchumundi and

---

31   This term is also given as the name of a totem: 'black duck'.
32   Note that the Cooper Basin terms *Kulparru* and *Thiniwa* were earlier reported for the Malyangapa by Elkin (see section 'The Cooper Basin Set').
33   This information was gained by Ian Sim in the 1950s (John Giacon, pers. comm.).

Wangaaypuwan. In both cases, we have a common stem, *Muku-* versus *Ngilpu-*, followed by a different suffix, *-marra* in Wangaaypuwan and *-lu* or *-rru* (one of which may have been misheard) in Itchumundi. Radcliffe-Brown's and Beckett's names seem to indicate a suffix *-ngarra* (or perhaps *-ngirra*) added to roots *maku-* and *kilpu-*, with the standard Paakantyi forms having an alternative suffix of *-warra* in *Makuwarra* and *-arra* in *Kilparra*, which was perhaps reduced from an earlier *Kilpuwarra*. One should perhaps assume that the forms with *-ngarra* also once occurred in Paakantyi and were borrowed by their neighbours to both the west and the east, with Malyangapa further adapting the word-initial *ki-* of *Kilparra* as *thi*, hence, *Thilpangarra*. Such an adaptation is plausible in the light of the fact that there are no examples of the word-initial *ki-* or *tyi-* in Malyangapa, but plenty of instances of *thi-*, according to the wordlist in Hercus and Austin (2004, pp. 647–54). Interchanges between *ki* and *tyi* are common in Australian languages, and *thi* is the sequence most similar to *tyi*. Therefore, if a word beginning with *ki-* was to be borrowed into a language that lacked initial *ki-* and *tyi-*, *thi-* would be the most obvious replacement. However, there is no clear explanation for the difference between the forms *ngilpu- and *kilpu-, although unexplained interchanges between stops and nasal are known to occur in Australian languages. In summary, these diverse forms used with the moieties seem to be connected historically through a combination of borrowing and adaptation to the resources of the particular languages.

Table 15: Analysis of moiety names in Paakantyi and neighbouring languages.

Language			Suffix
Itchumundi (Howitt)	Mukolo	Ngielpuru	-lu/-rru
Wiradjuri (Howitt)	Mukula		-la
Wangaaypuwan (Howitt)	Mukumurra	Ngielbumurra	-marra
	*muku-	*ngilpu-	
Paakantyi	Makuwarra	Kilparra	-arra
Wangaaypuwan (Radcliffe-Brown)	Mákwaŋära	Kílpuŋära	-ngarra
Malyangapa (Beckett)	Magungera	Dilbungera	-ngarra
Yuwaalayaay (Sim)	Magula		-la
	*maku-	*kilpu-	

Source: Authors' work.

A possible etymology of one of these names can be suggested. A wordlist by Reay (1945, p. 4) gives *Gilpara* 'cold wind, east wind' and *Makwahra* 'rain wind, west wind'. The Paakantyi dictionary does not give a term for cold wind, but it does give a term from the Paaruntyi dialect for 'cold weather', which is *makura* (Hercus 1993, p. 38)—*makurra* in our standardised orthography. This looks like a derivative of the stem **maku-* that we have identified for one of the moiety names. Unfortunately, it is the wrong term, since it was *Kilparra* that was supposedly named from the cold wind. However, this may still reflect the actual etymology if the referents somehow got switched in (their relaying of) Hero Black's explanation in Reay (1945).[34]

The Central Victorian Set

The Bunjil-Waang Set

In a large region of central Victoria, there is a moiety system characterised by the names *Bunjil* (*Puntyil* in our orthography) and *Waang* (*Waa* in some languages), which mean 'eaglehawk' and 'crow' respectively. Howitt (1996 [1904], pp. 126–7) described this population as the 'Kulin nation', after *kulin* 'man' in most the languages (Howitt 1996 [1904], p. 70). Mathews (1898, p. 326) called this system that of the 'Bangarang nation', using a term for [Yorta Yorta speaking] northern groups that was employed by Curr (Furphy 2013). In a rare departure from the norm in south-eastern Australia, these moieties are patrilineal, with the names being inherited from one's father rather than the mother. This claim of Howitt's has been confirmed by later research by Barwick (1984).

Many of the languages with this terminological set belong to the Kulin subgroup and within Kulin to both the east and the West Kulin sub-subgroups. First, there is what Blake (1991) called the Central Victoria language, which is the sole member of the East Kulin subgroup. A second language is the adjacent Wathawurrung, which belongs to the West Kulin subgroup. A third language is most of the Djadjawurrung, the easternmost dialect of the vast Western Victoria language, which also belongs to West Kulin (Blake & Reid 1998, p. 5). However, the westernmost clan of the

---

34   It may be relevant that a hot and cold wind division existed among the Malyangapa, in addition to the regular moiety names (Beckett 1967, p. 457) also in Andyamathanha, and that wind meanings also occurred for generation moieties in the Western Desert (Patrick McConvell, pers. comm.).

Djadjawurrung, Larning Gundidj (Clark's clan 9) according to Clark (1990, p. 162), used the name *Gamadj*, a term that belongs to the Western Victorian set (see section 'The Western Victorian Set').

The accuracy of the moiety names being the names of the eaglehawk and crow is confirmed by linguists: Blake (1991, p. 87) for the Central Victoria language (also called Woiwurrung after one of its dialects) gave *bundjil* 'eaglehawk' and *waang* 'crow'; and Blake et al. (1998, pp. 105, 102) for Wathawurrung gave *bundjil* as one of the words for 'eagle' (original spelling *boondyill*) and *waa* as 'crow'. Howitt (1996 [1904], p. 126) reported that among the Djadjawurrung the name *Bunjil* is replaced by *Wrepil*, which is their term for 'eaglehawk'. The terms *werpil* 'eagle' and *waa* 'crow' are confirmed by Blake's (2011) consolidated account of the Djadjawurrung language. 'Eaglehawk' is also *werpil* elsewhere in the Western Kulin megalanguage—for example, in Wergaia (Hercus 1986, p. 212) and Wadi Wadi (Blake et al. 2011, p. 248).

While the Djadjawurrung, who were linguistically Kulin, 'calqued' one of the moiety names—translating it into their equivalent term—another group used a different strategy. The Bangerang people, which Howitt reported as using the *Bunjil* and *Waang* moiety names, were speakers of the Yorta Yorta language. In this language, according to Bowe and Morey (1999), 'eagle' is *gurranyin* or *wanmirr* and 'crow' is *dangamai* or *wakirr*. We conclude that in Yorta Yorta, moiety names have probably been borrowed from Kulin languages, where they presumably originated. Yorta Yorta does not belong to the Kulin subgroup (eastern or western), but is related closely only to its neighbour Jabulajabula, their Yabula Yabula (Bowe & Morey 1999, pp. 133–6, 275).

One further language shares these moiety names. According to Barwick's (1984, p. 118) clan map, two clans of the Pallanganmiddang [Waywurru] that adjoin the Taungurung (of the Central Victoria language)—the Yowung-illam-balluk around Mount Buffalo and the Warrarakballuk around Wangaratta—are classified as *Bunjil* and *waa* respectively. Barwick (1984, p. 104) quoted Howitt's papers that included in his Kulin nation 'two clans northeast of the Kulin cultural bloc whose speech was utterly different but who had intermarried with Kulin neighbours since pre-contact times'. In this language,[35] 'eaglehawk' is *warrimu* and 'crow' is *berrontha* (Blake & Reid 1999, pp. 24–5). Thus, it appears that (perhaps

---

35 The language is now referred to as Waywurru (Eira 2008).

just part of) the Pallanganmiddang [Waywurru] had adopted the Kulin patrimoiety system along with its names, without translating them into their own language, as the Yorta Yorta had also done. Howitt's information suggested that intermarriage with members of the Central Victoria language group was a mechanism for spreading the moiety names into other languages. As for Howitt's comment that their speech was 'utterly different' from that of the Kulin, this is confirmed by modern linguistic research: the Pallanganmiddang/Waywurru language is not closely related to any other language (Blake & Reid 1998, p. 3).

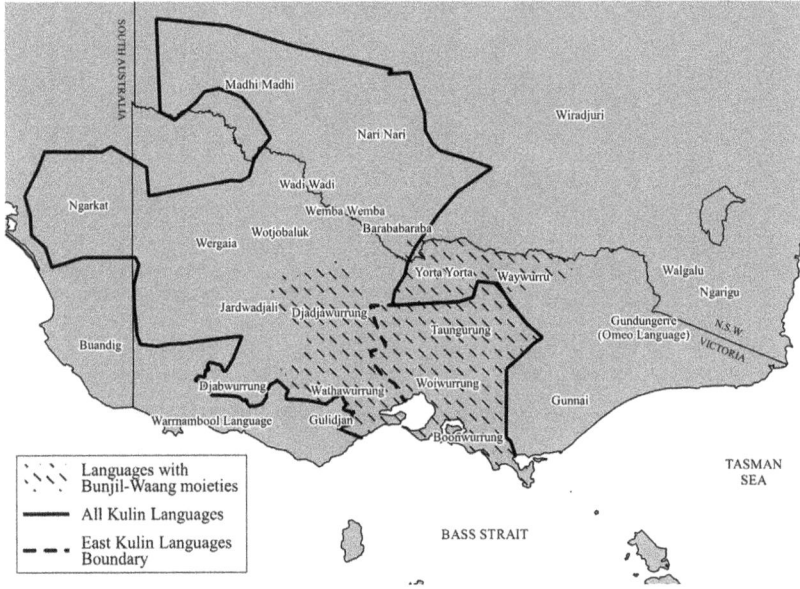

Figure 20: Bunjil-Waang moieties and Kulin languages.
Source: Authors' work.

The relationship between the Bunjil-Waang naming set and the Kulin languages is shown in Figure 20. This map shows the distribution of the Bunjil-Waang set, the extent of the East Kulin language, the furthest extent of all the Kulin languages,[36] as well as surrounding languages that are mentioned in this chapter. The linguistic classification is based on Blake and Reid (1998). Our interpretation of the historical relations between this moiety terminological set and the language groupings yields the following scenario. The moiety system (at least with this set of terms)

---

36 Note that Dadi Dadi, a non-Kulin language, is located within these boundaries (see Figure 19).

is probably later than Proto-Kulin, the ancestor of all the Kulin languages, since the terms are missing from much of West Kulin. It may go back as far as Proto–East Kulin, the relatively undifferentiated ancestor of the central Victoria dialects. Subsequently, the terminological set spread to the adjacent Kulin languages to the west, as well as to the Yorta Yorta in the north-west and to adjacent clans of the Pallinganmiddang/Waywurru to the north-east. While the Djadjawurrung translated the Bunjil terms into their own language, the two northern groups did not substitute their own words but simply adopted the Kulin terms along with their functions of the patrimoiety system.

The Alpine Area with 'Eaglehawk' and 'Crow' Moieties

Howitt suggested that the 'eaglehawk' and 'crow' moieties extended even further east. Howitt (1883, p. 506) ascribed it to 'the Wolgal [Walgalu] tribe, which once inhabited the upper waters of the Hume [i.e. Murray], the Murrumbidjee [Murrumbidgee], and the Tumut rivers'. He also attributed the system to the people of the 'upper waters of the Murray, Murrumbidgee, Snowy, and Tambo Rivers, the Ya-itma-thang, Ngarigo, and Wolgal' (Howitt 1996 [1904], p. 101). These are probably all speakers of dialects of the same language, belonging to the Yuin subgroup of south-eastern New South Wales, known as Walgalu in the Tumut region, Ngarigu in the Monaro area and the Omeo language in Victoria (Koch 2012, p. 140; Wafer & Lissarrague 2008, pp. 106–7): the AIATSIS reference name of this Omeo language is Gundungerre. Here, the moiety names are not the Kulin *Bunjil* and *Waang*, but native names *Malian* 'eaglehawk' and *Umbe* 'crow' in Walgalu, and *Merung* 'eaglehawk' and *Yukembruk* 'crow' in Ngarigu (Howitt 1996 [1904], p. 102). In these languages, there are a number of totems (Howitt lists six to nine for each) subsumed under each of the moiety divisions; these include 'bat' (Walgalu *Nadjanajan* and Ngarigu *Nadjatajan*) under eaglehawk and 'rabbit-rat' *Tchuteba* (in both Walgalu and Ngarigu) under crow.[37] As for the Omeo language, Howitt (1996 [1904], p. 101) stated that the Ya-itma-thang who intermarried with the Ngarigu had among their totems the same

---

37   This bat division is not to be confused with the widespread use (in south-eastern Australia) of the bat as a sex totem for men (see Howitt 1996 [1904], pp. 148–51; Wafer & Lissarrague 2008, pp. 445–7).

Tchuteba 'rabbit-rat' and *Nadjatejan* 'bat', and that these were on opposite sides of the tribe, as manifested in their ball games, in which teams were presumably formed on the basis of moiety membership.[38]

The interpretation of these facts is not clear. One possibility is that the Omeo people had the same system as the Ngarigu and the Walgalu. Another possibility is that they had similar groups of totems, but did not use the overarching eaglehawk and crow names. A possible historical scenario for the Alpine region is that at some point in time, Walgalu and Ngarigu (and perhaps the Omeo people) adopted the Kulin organisation of two moieties headed by eaglehawk and crow and used their own terms rather than borrowing the Kulin names. However, an important difference among the Alpine tribes was that their eaglehawk and crow moieties were matrilineal (Howitt 1996 [1904], p. 197). This fact suggests that their interaction with the Eastern Kulin was much less direct than that of the immediate neighbours of the Eastern Kulin (the Yorta Yorta and Pallanganmiddang/Waywurru), and that they simply borrowed an idea of social organisation, with some of its terminology, and grafted it onto their own system of totems.

One further group that may have had a similar eaglehawk and crow terminology is the Bidawal (also called Bidwell or Birrdhawal) of the south-eastern corner of Victoria. Their language is closely related to the Gunnai of Gippsland. Howitt (1996 [1904], p. 103) mentioned one family of Biduelli (as he called them) with the Ngarigu class name *Yukembruk* 'crow' and a totem *Tchuteba* 'rabbit-rat'—this looks like the Ngarigu system. He noted that another family had the name *Bunjil*, 'apparently connecting the Biduelli with the Mogullum-bitch, a Kulin tribe on Upper Ovens River [in Victoria]'. These names may only have applied to particular families who intermarried with peoples who used the moiety system: the first family involved a man who lived in the Monaro tableland, whose wife was Ngarigu and whose mother was from the Omeo district (Howitt 1996 [1904], p. 80). The fact that individual families not only knew but also used their neighbours' moiety terminology suggests one plausible mechanism by which such a system could have spread from one group to the next.[39]

---

38 Elkin (1964, p. 123) commented that, where ball games were played by moieties, these were part of a ceremonial program, where the facts are better known. This indicates the role of moieties in ceremony.
39 We thank Patrick McConvell for the idea of this as a mechanism of diffusion, and Ted Ryan for the idea that people typically knew their neighbours' system.

The Western Victorian Set

The group with this terminology set was given the label 'Booandik nation' by Mathews (1898, pp. 331–3). The most recent source of data is given by Clark (1990). The matrimoiety names were *Kamaty* or *Kapaty*[40] and *Kurukity*, with feminine versions that took the suffix *-kurrk* (from *kurrk* 'woman'): spelled for instance as *Kamatchgurk* and *Krokitchgurk*. Mathews (1898, p. 333) was told, by Paakantyi people from Balranald, that *Gamadj* and *Grugidj* were pragmatically equivalent to the *Muckwarra* and *Keelparra* of the Paakantyi. This Western Victorian system obtained among several named groups of speakers of the (West Kulin) 'Western Victoria' megalanguage (of Blake & Reid 1998, p. 4), including Wemba Wemba,[41] the Wergaia (called Wotjobaluk in Howitt 1996 [1904], p. 120), Jardwadjali and Djabwurrung. Clark (1990, pp. 91, 237) gave glosses for the moiety names among the Jardwadjali and Djabwurrung: *Gamadj* is said to mean 'black cockatoo' and *Grugidj* 'white cockatoo'.[42] Among the latter two, *Gamadj* [*Kamaty*] has an alternative form *Kaputj* [*Kapaty*]. Consideration of all the sources suggests that the black bird is the Banksian or red-tailed black cockatoo, and the white bird is the long-billed corella.

A similar set of terms is found among what we might call the Bunganditjan languages: Buandig (also known as Bunganditj), the Warrnambool language, and Gulidjan, the Colac language.[43] Fison and Howitt (1880, p. 33) gave the class names of the Mount Gambier (South Australia) tribe [the Bunganditj] as *Kumite* and *Krokī*, with feminine forms *Kumitegor* and *Krokigor*. Blake's (2003a, p. 128) Bunganditj grammar gave *kurukitj* as 'corella'. The speakers of the Warrnambool language,

---

40   The relation between forms with *m* versus *p* is not explained. It is not a regular correspondence between the languages. According to Ted Ryan (pers. comm. 13 November 2016), the *Kapaty* variant may have been used only by people south of the Grampians.
41   Mathews described the group as natives of the Avoca River (1898, p. 333); Mathews also called them Wambawamba (1903, p. 184). Howitt (1996 [1904], p. 138) stated that west of the Avoca River, the Krokitch-Gamutch system was used, in contrast to the Bunjil-Waang system of the Djadjawurrung east of the river.
42   Apart from the exact species of bird that is intended, there is the question of whether these terms are the names of birds in each of the relevant languages or only names of social categories whose emblems are the respective birds.
43   The genetic relationship between Buandig and the Warrnambool language is not certain, and the affiliation of the Colac language is even more doubtful, according to Blake and Reid (1998, pp. 9–12). We nevertheless tentatively group the first two together as a Bunganditjan subgroup. For the location of these languages and those mentioned in the preceding paragraph, see Figure 20.

called the Gournditch-Mara by Howitt (1996 [1904], p. 124), had the names *Kaputch* and *Krokitch*, the feminine form adding the suffix *-yarr*.[44] Each class name had an associated totem and a number of associated sub-totems; *Kaputch* was associated with black cockatoo and *Krokitch* with white cockatoo (Howitt 1996 [1904], p. 124). The glosses can be refined somewhat by the information in Blake's (2003b, pp. 185, 190) Warrnambool grammar, which gave *kapatj* as 'cockatoo, red-tail, black' and *kurukitj* as 'long-billed cockatoo'. Their eastern neighbours, the Gulidjan, likewise had the moiety names *Gabadj* (Black Cockatoo) and *Guragidj* (White Cockatoo) (Clark 1990, p. 222).

The eastern part of the Warrnambool language area seems to have had a pre-moiety system of matri-totems. Howitt (1996 [1904], p. 125) reported that for the natives near Mortlake, Cameron found no class (i.e. moiety) names but four totems: *Krokage* 'white cockatoo, red crest', *Kubitch* 'black cockatoo', *Karperap* 'pelican' and *Kartuk* 'whip snake'. These totems are paired such that 'Karperap is supplementary to Krokage, and Kartuk to Kubitch. Krokage may marry either Kubitch or Kartuk, and Kubitch may marry either Krokage or Karperap, and the children belong to the mother's totem' (Howitt 1996 [1904], p. 125). For the (same) area east of the Gournditch-Mara, Dawson (1981 [1881], p. 26) explained the situation thus: 'Kuurokeetch and Kartpoerapp … are so related, that they are looked upon as sister classes, and no marriage between them is permitted. It is the same between kappatch and kirtuuk; but as kuunamit is not so related, it can marry into any class but its own'. Dawson's wordlist (1981 [1881], p. li) glosses *Kuurakeetch* or *Kuuruukeetch* as 'cockatoo, long-billed' and *kappatch* as 'cockatoo, banksian'.

A possible historical scenario for the south-western Victorian region is that in a system in which totemic groups are ordered into two intermarrying sets (virtual moieties), one totem name could be treated as the lead or dominant totem and then be elevated to the status of a moiety name. As for the particular moiety names, it appears that *kurukity* (in our standardised orthography) is native to the Bunganditjan languages, since it occurs as a bird name in both Buandig and Warrnambool languages. From one or both of these languages, the term must have spread northward to the West Kulin languages, whose term for corella was *katyakarr* (see Dawson 1981 [1881], p. li for Djabwurrung; Hercus 1986,

---

44 We interpret the feminine suffix as *-yarr* rather than the *-iyar* posited by Blake (2003b).

p. 252 for Djadjala [Wergaia] and Wemba Wemba; Hercus 1992b, p. 22 gave the Wemba Wemba and Wergaia forms as *kathəkarr* and *katyekarr* respectively). The name *kapaty* was also given by Dawson as one of the dialectal terms for 'banksian cockatoo' in the Warrnambool language, from which it has apparently spread northward to Djabwurrung (Kulin). The alternative term *kamaty* is found in the remainder of the West Kulin dialects that have this terminology system and in Buandig; therefore, it could have originated in either of these two areas.

The Distribution of Naming Sets

In this section, we survey earlier attempts at mapping the moiety sets that we have discussed. We call attention to the finding that the nomenclature sets do not closely match the linguo-genetic classification of languages. We then provide our interpretation of what the distribution of terms reveals about the history of the systems.

Earlier Mapping of Moieties

Various scholars have attempted to map the distribution of moiety naming sets. Of these, the maps by R. H. Mathews and John Mathew come closest to ours, in giving the moiety names of their sets. However, none of these relate the distribution to language groups as currently understood, except for Dixon (2002, p. 17).

R. H. Mathews's (1898, p. 343) map of Victorian tribes shows his Bangarang, Booandik and Barkunjee (Paakantyi) 'nations', defined largely by their social category organisation. His map of South Australian divisions (Mathews 1900, p. 91) delineates, among others, his 'Parnkalla Nation', 'Yowerawarrika Nation', 'Barkunjee Nation' and the western part of his 'Booandik Nation'.

Howitt's (1996 [1904], facing p. 90)[45] map of south-eastern Australia, reproduced here as Figure 21, indicates the approximate distribution of moiety, section and 'anomalous' class systems. The systems discussed in this paper are represented as 'two classes with female descent' (a large area of South Australia, the south-west corner of Queensland, the Darling River area, the middle Murray, and western Victoria plus south-eastern

---

45 Refer to pp. 832–3 in the 1996 reprint.

South Australia), 'two classes with male descent' (central Victoria) and 'with anomalous class system and female descent' (an area of the far south-west of Victoria that includes the Warrnambool area).

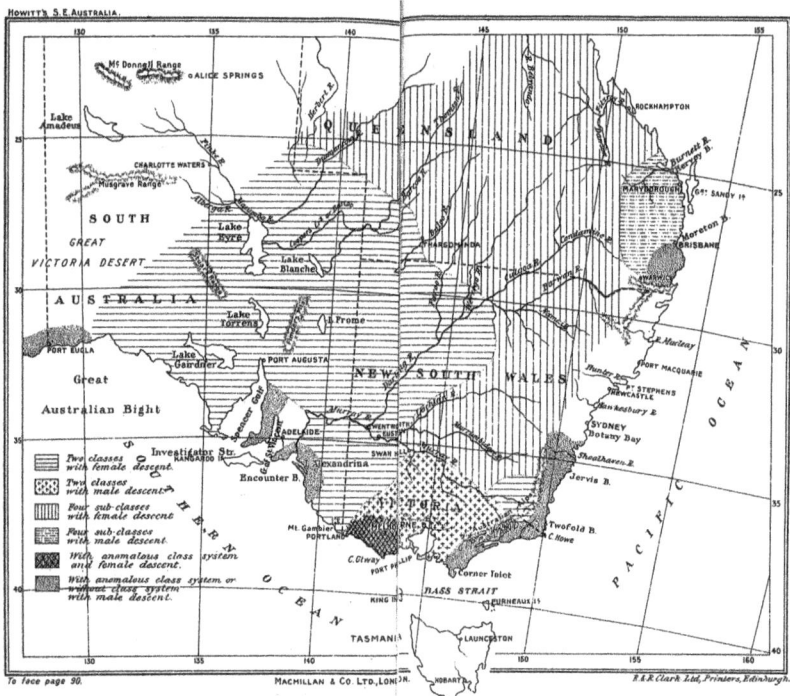

Figure 21: Howitt's 1904 map of south-eastern Australia.
Source: Howitt (1996 [1904]).

John Mathew's (1910, p. 164) map gives the distribution of social category names (his 'phratry names') over most of Queensland, New South Wales and Victoria—South Australia is rather empty. His map gives the *Kilpara-Mŭkwara* system around the Darling River, *Kurokaitch-Kapaitch* in western Victoria, the eaglehawk–crow system of central and eastern Victoria and adjacent parts of New South Wales, and the distribution of the names *Pakoota* and *Wootaroo* in Queensland.

Davidson's (1928, p. 92) map shows where moiety names are present in the whole continent—without any indication of whether these moieties are matrilineal or patrilineal or whether the moiety names coexist with section or subsection terms.

Radcliffe-Brown's (1930–1, between p. 42 and p. 43) map shows the distribution of matrilineal and patrilineal moieties, sections, subsections, semi-moieties, paired sections and areas without moieties or sections. For south-eastern Australia, his map includes a large area involving eastern South Australia, western New South Wales and western Victoria that is marked with matrimoieties, a small area of central Victoria with patrimoieties and an even smaller area in the Alps with matrimoieties.

Berndt and Berndt (1981, p. 55) presented a map displaying 'distributional spread of Australian Aboriginal social organization'. The area we have discussed is included in their A zone, which manifests matrimoieties, with the qualification that sections have been (recently) introduced into Paakantyi; a B zone in central Victoria where patrimoieties are found; and a D^1 zone in far south-western Queensland, where sections have spread.

Dixon's (2002, p. 17) map gives the approximate distribution of moieties, sections and subsections, and the absence of any of these, with admittedly some simplifications and extrapolations. The same map shows his (genetic and areal) classification of languages. One can note a certain degree of correlation of moieties with his linguistic groupings: WA (our Karnic and Yarli subgroups), WB and WC (our Thura-Yura subgroup), V (Paakantyi) and T (our Kulin and Bunganditjan subgroups).

Mismatch of Naming Sets and Linguistic Subgroups

We have documented a mismatch between the distribution of naming sets and that of linguistic subgroups. The results are described in this subsection and interpreted historically in the subsection 'Historical Interpretation of Distribution'. The relations between moiety names and linguo-genetic groups are displayed in Table 16, in which the moiety name sets are given in the columns and the linguistic groupings in the rows. A tick in a cell indicates that the naming set of the top row is manifested in languages of the linguo-genetic group listed in the first column.

Most of the Thura-Yura languages of South Australia have the *Matharri* and *Kararrhu* moiety names, but the moiety system is lacking in the south-eastern part of this subgroup, Kaurna and Narungga. This naming set extends beyond Thura-Yura to include a number of Karnic languages, plus Yardliyawarra in the Yarli subgroup. The 'Cooper Basin set', with names *Kulparru* and *Thiniwa*, covers the languages of the presumed Eastern Karnic sub-subgroup, but also takes in some Central Karnic languages, plus Malyangapa (according to Elkin) and Wadigali of the Yarli subgroup. The

'South-West Queensland set', with moiety names *Parrkatha* (or *Malura*) and *Wuthurru*, is used by speakers of both northern and Central Karnic languages, plus non-Karnic languages to the north (in conjunction with section names). The Darling River set includes the whole Paakantyi language area, plus Barranbinya to the north, and, to the south, several Lower Murray languages and dialects of the Madhi Madhi group of the Western Victoria (West Kulin) language. The Central Victorian set includes the whole of the Central Victoria (East Kulin) language, plus Wathawurrung and Djadjawurrung of the West Kulin sub-subgroup, plus the adjacent but unrelated Yorta Yorta and Pallanganmiddang/Waywurru languages. The Yuin languages in the Alpine area of New South Wales seem to have a related terminology set using their native terms for 'eaglehawk' and 'crow'. Finally, the Western Victorian set takes in most of the Bunganditjan subgroup (but some dialects of the Warrnambool language seem to have a pre-moiety system), as well as much of the West Kulin language area.

Table 16: Moiety naming sets versus linguistic genetic groups.

	SA	Cooper	SWQld	Darling	CentVic	WVic
Thura-Yura	✓					
Karnic	✓	✓	✓			
Yarli	✓	✓				
Paakantyi				✓		
Lower Murray				✓		
Kulin				✓	✓	✓
Bunganditjan						✓
Yotic					✓	
Waveroo					✓	
Yuin					(✓)	

Source: Authors' work.

This mismatch between linguo-genetic groups and social category naming sets has been forcibly noted by Blake et al. (2011, pp. 24–5). Their conclusions are worth quoting in some detail:

> The people of the Mathi group, the neighbouring Murray River and the Paakantyi people to their west and north-west all had a matrilineal moiety system with the two moieties being called *Kilpara* and *Makwara* …
>
> This system … was observed everywhere in **Paakantyi** country from Wentworth to Bourke and into South Australia …

The bulk of the Murray River people [our Lower Murray group] and the bulk of the Kulin people did not have this system, but the people in the far north-west of Victoria and adjacent parts of NSW share it: they formed a very special united group, although they belonged to three different types of languages, Murray River, Kulin and Paakantyi. In other words

> Yitha-Yitha, Tharti-Tharti, Keramin (Kureinyi including also Yari-Yari) and Ngintait (Yuyu)[46] people all shared this Paakantyi system although the rest of the **Murray River** [our Lower Murray] language subgroup did not.
>
> Mathi-Mathi, Letyi-Letyi, and Wati-Wati people all shared this Paakantyi system although other **Kulin** people, like for instance the neighbouring Wemba-Wemba, did not. (boldface in original)

Likewise, Wafer and Lissarrague (2008, p. 420 note 271) commented on Howitt's equating of the *Bunjil* ('eaglehawk') and *Waang* ('crow') moiety names with his 'Kulin nation':

> Evidently this does not apply to the Kulin languages, mentioned above, that use the Kilparra-Makwarra moiety system. Nor does it apply to Perapa-Perapa … which as Howitt himself points out (1904, p. 107), has a section system like that of the Wiradjuri.[47]

Historical Interpretation of Distribution

There are basically two scenarios that can result in the sharing of terms between languages (excluding chance): inheritance from a common ancestor language or acquisition through cultural contact. In the case of common inheritance, the explanation would be that the terms were present in the protolanguage before it diversified into separate dialects and sister languages and that the forms were simply transmitted from generation to generation. Language differentiation proceeds rather slowly, requiring perhaps 500 to 1,000 years for a language to diversify into separate languages—less for the development of distinct but mutually intelligible dialects. This explanation may be valid for two situations described here: Paakantyi and the Central Victorian language are both multi-dialect languages, whose common

---

46   We do not agree with the implied identity of Yuyu and Ngintait, and consider it doubtful that Ngintait had this moiety system. Regarding the Ngintait, Radcliffe-Brown (1918, pp. 247–8) reported: 'I have no exact information about the social organization, but I believe that the tribe had no dual division and was organized into local totemic clans in much the same way as the Nganuruku [Nganguruku] and Yaralde [Ngarrindjeri] tribes'.

47   We do not agree with Wafer and Lissarrague's inference that the very closely related Wemba Wemba also had the section system, since we have shown in the section 'The Western Victorian Set' that it had the Western Victorian set of moiety names.

ancestors Proto-Paakantyi and Proto–East Kulin need not have been very remote in time—perhaps around 1,000 years. In contrast, the Thura-Yura linguo-genetic group is much more diverse, so its common ancestor is likely to have been considerably older. Also, not all of the languages classified as Thura-Yura share the *Matharri-Kararrhu* terminology: in fact, the south-eastern languages lack moiety terms altogether. If we were to posit that the names were inherited from Proto-Thura-Yura, we would have to assume that Kaurna and Narungga had lost the terms (as well as the moiety system)—a proposition that is otherwise unnecessary. We conclude that the terminology has spread subsequent to the differentiation of the Thura-Yura languages (i.e. later than Proto-Thura-Yura[48]), since it is not found in the south-eastern languages of the subgroup. Turning again to the Kulin languages, if one were to project the Bunjil-Waang system back to the Proto-Kulin stage, its presence in the West Kulin languages Wathawurrung and Djadjawurrung would be accounted for (by inheritance), but its absence in other West Kulin languages such as Madhi Madhi and Djabwurrung would be explained as a replacement by terms from the Darling or Bunganditjan system respectively.

The second explanation—acquisition through cultural contact—is clearly required to account for some of the shared terms. There are several mechanisms by which a language could have acquired its moiety names in a situation of cultural borrowing. The terms could simply be borrowed: this is clearly the case for Yorta Yorta and Waywurru (Pallanganmidhang), which have adopted the East Kulin terms *Bunjil* and *Waang*. Another kind of borrowing is called 'calquing' or 'loan translation'. Thus, Djadjawurrung has substituted its equivalent term for 'eaglehawk', *Werpil*. Native terms for 'eaglehawk' and 'crow' have similarly been used in the Alpine region. A third method of cultural borrowing is to adopt the principle of moiety names but supply terms with a different meaning—for example, terms for black and white cockatoo in place of eaglehawk and crow.

Since the distribution of moiety terminologies correlates so poorly with linguo-genetic groups, we conclude that, with the possible exception of Paakantyi and the East Kulin languages, the distribution of terms was formed more recently than the diversification of languages from protolanguages. Hence, the areas in which terms are shared are explained primarily by cultural spread or diffusion rather than by inheritance from common ancestral languages.

---

48   But occurring before the (regular) loss of initial *k* in Adnyamathanha, since the term there is *Ararrhu* rather than *Kararrhu*.

Blake et al. (2011, pp. 25–6) concluded that the matrimoiety terms *Kilpara* and *Makwara* spread from Paakantyi to some Murray River and Madhi Madhi (Kulin) groups in consequence of the fact that the speakers of these languages had come to form a sociocultural bloc.

Direction of Spread

This raises the question of where each set of terms has spread from. Two kinds of evidence can be invoked: the direction of spread points to a place of origin, and the etymology of the forms may conceivably suggest a particular language in which the terms originated. For the South Australian set (shown in Figure 17), we conclude, from the fact that the terms are missing from the south-eastern languages and that they are shared with some Karnic languages around the Lake Eyre basin, that the terms have most likely spread from the (north-)east. This puts their origin close to two other sets—those of the Cooper Basin and the Darling River. The Darling River set is adjacent to both the South Australian and Cooper Basin sets, and so might have influenced the development of both.[49] Further, either or both of the South Australian and Cooper Basin terminological sets could have influenced the South-West Queensland set. The Darling River set was also either adjacent or relatively close, along the Murray River, to the two Victorian nomenclature systems. Moreover, this area is on the boundary between moiety names that are meaningful (the Victorian bird pairs) and without obvious meanings.

In fact, the area around the point at which the Darling and Murray rivers converge would be a good candidate for the locus of the spread of the moiety systems. This was an area of dense populations, involving a number of languages, including some that were not closely related. The people of different groups are reported to have participated in one another's ceremonies—which would have been facilitated by having equivalent moiety groupings.[50] Also of possible relevance is the fact that this region is close to a number of binary classification systems: those involving contrasting birds in Victorian languages, hot versus cold winds in the area west of the Darling and two kinds of bloods east of the Darling.

---

49   Cf. the comment by Blake et al. (2011, p. 25): 'This system [of *Kilpara* and *Makwara* moieties] is closely linked with the matrilineal moiety *Kararru/Matharị* and *Thiniwa/Kulpari* systems of the people to the northwest and north of the Paakantyi in South Australia and adjacent parts of Queensland as described by Elkin (1931) and so the area under discussion forms part of a much larger region of matrilineal moieties'.

50   Clark and Ryan (2009) document from a number of early sources the many disparate groups that occupied the Murray River area between the junctions of the Murrumbidgee and Darling rivers.

If the hints about the possible original meanings of the Darling River names, in terms of hot and cold winds mentioned at the end of the subsection 'Other Two-Term Terminology Sets', reflect reality, this supports the Paakantyi language as being the source of these names. Figure 22 presents a possible scenario for the spread of naming sets.

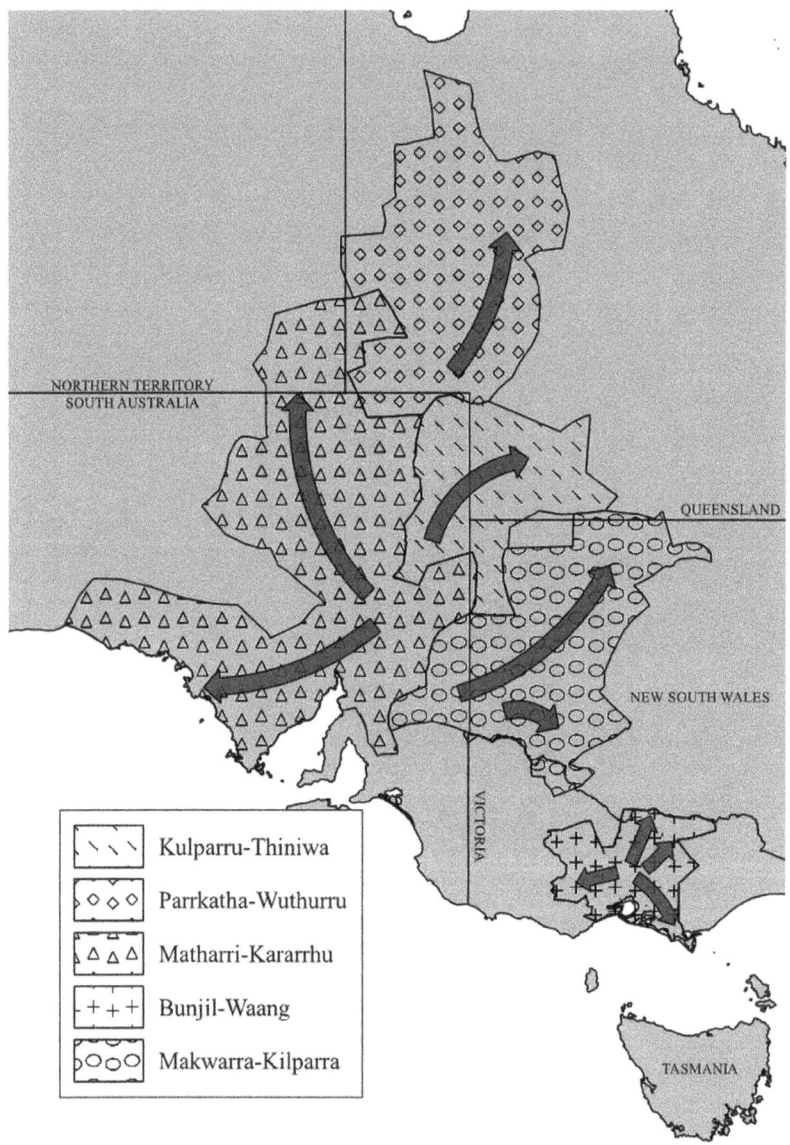

Figure 22: Distribution and spread of moiety name sets.
Source: Authors' work.

Origin of Moiety Systems

Separate from the question of where specific moiety names originated and in what direction they spread is the issue of how moiety systems arose in the first instance. This question is complicated by the fact that a large number of languages to the north and east of the bloc that concerns us had a system of four sections, often along with matrimoiety names (see Figure 21; Chapter 8). It has been assumed that four-section systems are a later development from moiety systems (e.g. Fison & Howitt 1880, p. 37). Hence, it is possible that sets of moiety names existed earlier in languages to the north and east of the Darling River and Cooper Basin, and that the naming sets described above have spread from the north or north-east.

Questions of the origin of moiety systems are further complicated by their widespread distribution in the Australian continent. Besides the areas discussed here, they have been reported in the far south-west of Western Australia, the Kimberley, western and central parts of the Top End and the Cape York Peninsula (Berndt & Berndt 1981, pp. 55–6). Further, many of the regions that now have sections or subsections may have earlier had moiety systems. Hence, it is possible that moieties were created independently in different areas. It is also possible that the names of moieties may have been replaced over time—that is, the most recently attested names were not the only names that were used throughout the history of the system.[51]

The Etymology of Moiety Names

Although we might legitimately assume that the names were once meaningful in the language in which they originated, these origins are now largely inaccessible due to the sparse documentation of vocabularies of these languages, as well as the passage of time, which typically leads to changes in the form and meaning of words. Even within the existing record, it is not always possible to isolate the most relevant languages

---

[51] See, for example, the different reports by Elkin and Beckett concerning the moiety names of the Malyangapa mentioned in the subsection 'Other Two-Term Terminology Sets'. Similarly, the difference between moiety names reported for Gamilaraay around 1900 by Mathews and Howitt—*Dhilbi* and *Kupathin*—and those given by the modern dictionary (Ash et al. 2003)—*Wudhurruu* and *Yanguu* (see Wafer & Lissarrague 2008, p. 453)—probably reflect a replacement during the twentieth century.

and semantic domains. However, some clues can be gained from the kinds of concepts that are used to describe the various systems of dual classification (including moieties) that are found.

Bird names are emblematic of moieties in many parts of Australia—for example, white cockatoo and crow in the south-west (Bates 1985, pp. 74, 192) and in northern Australia (cf. Chapter 8). In our area, we have noted 'eaglehawk' and 'crow' in the East Kulin and Alpine areas and 'corella' and 'black cockatoo' in south-western Victoria. For the Wangaaypuwan, Radcliffe-Brown (1923, p. 425) reported that *kuru* (bandicoot) is the head of the Muämbuän division and the *turu* (brown snake) is the head of the Ṉärawän division.[52] It is possible that a totem name may be promoted or elevated to represent a whole moiety, as suggested at the end of the section 'The Western Victorian Set' (cf. Wiradjuri moiety name *Budthurung*, which is also the name of a totem, 'black duck', as mentioned in subsection 'Other Two-Term Terminology Sets').

Features other than species names that are sometimes used in dual classification systems may have provided a source for moiety names. Opposite physical characteristics of totemic creatures or human beings may be the basis for classification. Features that have been cited include dark versus light complexion for the people of Fowlers Bay (cited in Hercus 1999, p. 1), slender versus heavier/broader features among the Adnyamathanha (Schebeck 1973, p. 24), straight versus wavy hair among the Arrernte (Spencer & Gillen 1927, p. 42), fur versus scales or slow versus quick blood in western New South Wales (Radcliffe-Brown 1923, p. 425).[53]

Further, the location of the camping areas of social groups may be employed in a classification: upper versus lower section of a tree or the light versus dark shade therefrom among the Wangaaypuwan (Radcliffe-Brown 1923, p. 425), or water-dwellers versus land-dwellers among the Arrernte (Carl Strehlow in Spencer & Gillen 1927, p. 41).

---

52   Radcliffe-Brown qualified this statement: 'This is according to the statement of a man of the bandicoot clan, and it is possible that men of other clans might give different statements'. One might infer from this comment that which totem 'heads' one of the two divisions may be subject to competition between social groups and hence liable to variability over time.
53   This fact was used by Mathew (1910) in support of his theory that moieties originated from the amalgamation of two distinct races.

Meteorological contrasts have also been reported as the basis for dual classification: the hot west or north versus the cold east or south wind has been mentioned for Paakantyi (Hercus 1993, p. 32), Malyangapa (Beckett 1967, p. 457) and Adnyamathanha (Schebeck 1973, p. 25). The Kiabara (of south-east Queensland) [Kyabra on modern maps] moieties *Dilebi* and *Cubatine* were associated with floodwater and lightning respectively, according to Howitt (1884, p. 336). These meteorological classifications suggest some etymologies for moiety names. In the subsection 'Other Two-Term Terminology Sets', we proposed a possible etymological link between the moiety name *Makuwarra* (and other terms based on *maku-*) and the Paakantyi (Paaruntyi dialect) term *makurra* for 'cold weather'. The Kiabara information suggests that one could compare the Wangkumara moiety name *Thiniwa* with the term *tyiniwara* 'thunder' in the same language (McDonald & Wurm 1979, p. 108), and speculate whether the moiety name here derives from a meteorological term.

Summary and Conclusions

We have discussed the distribution of six moiety nomenclature terminology sets from south-eastern Australia. We have related the sets of terms to the languages and their genealogical groupings. We have documented the fact that the geographical distribution of naming sets largely fails to match that of linguo-genetic groups. We have taken this as support for a claim that the naming sets have mostly spread subsequent to the diversification of the languages. We have seen some hints concerning the spread of terms through cultural interaction, including intermarriage. We have noted that the moiety name sets are all geographically contiguous to one another and hypothesised that the Darling River is a focal point of these moiety systems and their associated terminology, and hence a candidate for the origin and stimulus for the development of these naming sets in south-eastern Australia. Apart from the transparent naming of moieties in a few languages (mostly in Victoria), the names lack clear etymologies. Nevertheless, we have made some suggestions regarding plausible semantic domains from which the names may have been derived, including bird names, physical features of people and meteorological elements. There is the possibility that some moiety names represent totemic names that have been promoted in a classification hierarchy—as suggested by the western Victorian bird names (see the section 'The Western Victorian Set'). We refrain from speculation on how, where or when moiety systems as a general principle of social organisation originated; and we leave for the future any discussion and evaluation of the various theories that have been proposed since the 1880s. Our study has benefited from, and illustrates the value of, an interdisciplinary approach that combines evidence from anthropology, history, geography and linguistics (both descriptive and historical) to arrive at plausible scenarios to explain the moiety naming systems of south-eastern Australia, which has been a subject of interest since the latter part of the nineteenth century.

References

Ash, A, Giacon, J & Lissarrague, A (eds) 2003, *Gamilaraay, Yuwaalaraay, and Yuwaalayaay dictionary*, Alice Springs, NT: IAD Press.

Austin, P 1981, *A grammar of Diyari, South Australia*, Cambridge: Cambridge University Press.

AustKin 2017, *The AustKin project*, viewed 31 July 2017, www.austkin.net.

Australian Institute of Aboriginal and Torres Strait Islander Studies (AIATSIS) 2017, *Welcome to AUSTLANG*, viewed 31 July 2017, austlang.aiatsis.gov.au.

Barwick, DE 1984, 'Mapping the past: an atlas of Victorian clans 1835–1904', *Aboriginal History*, 8, pp. 100–31.

Barwick, DE 1998, in LE Barwick & RE Barwick (eds), *Rebellion at Coranderrk*, Aboriginal History Monograph 5, Canberra: Aboriginal History Inc.

Bates, D 1985, in I White (ed.) *The native tribes of Western Australia*, Canberra: National Library of Australia.

Beckett, J 1967, 'Marriage, circumcision and avoidance among the Maljangaba of New South Wales', *Mankind*, 6, pp. 456–64. doi.org/10.1111/j.1835-9310.1967.tb01348.x.

Berndt, RM 1939, 'A curlew and owl legend from the Narunga tribe, South Australia', *Oceania*, 10, pp. 456–62. doi.org/10.1002/j.1834-4461.1940.tb00306.x.

Berndt, RM (ed.) 1964, *Australian Aboriginal art*, Sydney: Ure Smith.

Berndt, RM & Berndt CH 1981, *The world of the First Australians*, Revised edition, Sydney: Lansdowne Press.

Blake, BJ 1979, *A Kalkatungu grammar*, Pacific Linguistics B-57, Canberra: The Australian National University.

Blake, BJ 1991, 'Woiwurrung, the Melbourne language', in RMW Dixon & BJ Blake (eds), *Handbook of Australian languages volume 4: the Aboriginal language of Melbourne and other grammatical sketches*, Melbourne: Oxford University Press, pp. 30–122.

Blake, BJ 2003a, *The Bunganditj (Buwandik) language of the Mount Gambier region*, Pacific Linguistics 549, Canberra: The Australian National University.

Blake, BJ 2003b, *The Warrnambool language: a consolidated account of the language of the Warrnambool area of the Western District of Victoria based on nineteenth-century sources*, Pacific Linguistics 544, Canberra: The Australian National University.

Blake, BJ 2011, Dialects of western Kulin, western Victoria: Yartwatjali, Tjapwurrung, Djadjawurrung, Unpublished manuscript, Melbourne: La Trobe University.

Blake, BJ & Breen, JG 1971, *The Pitta-Pitta dialects*, Linguistic Communications 4, Melbourne: Monash University.

Blake, BJ, Clark, I & Krishna-Pillay, SH 1998, 'Wathawurrung: the language of the Geelong–Ballarat area', in BJ Blake (ed.), *Wathawurrung and the Colac language of southern Victoria*, Pacific Linguistics C-147, Canberra: The Australian National University, pp. 59–154.

Blake, BJ, Hercus, L, Morey, S & Ryan, E 2011, *The Mathi group of languages*, Pacific Linguistics 628, Canberra: The Australian National University.

Blake, BJ & Reid, J 1998, 'Classifying Victorian languages', in Barry J. Blake (ed.), *Wathawurrung and the Colac language of southern Victoria*, Pacific Linguistics C-147, Canberra: The Australian National University, pp. 1–58.

Blake, BJ & Reid, J 1999, 'Pallanganmiddang, a language of the upper Murray', *Aboriginal History*, *23*, pp. 15–31.

Bowe, H & Morey, S 1999, *The Yorta Yorta (Bangerang) language of the Murray Goulburn, including Yabula Yabula*, Pacific Linguistics C-154, Canberra: The Australian National University.

Bowern, C 1999, A sketch grammar of Nhirrpi, Unpublished manuscript.

Bowern, C 2001, 'Karnic classification revisited', in J Simpson et al. (eds), *Forty years on: Ken Hale and Australian languages*, Pacific Linguistics 512, Canberra: The Australian National University, pp. 245–61.

Bowern, C 2009, 'Reassessing Karnic: a reply to Breen (2007)', *Australian Journal of Linguistics*, *29*(3), pp. 337–48. doi.org/10.1080/07268600903232733.

Breen, JG 1971, *Aboriginal languages of western Queensland*, Linguistic Communications 5, Melbourne: Monash University, pp. 1–88.

Breen, JG 1981a, 'Margany and Gunya', in RMW Dixon & BJ Blake (eds), *Handbook of Australian languages vol. 2*, Canberra: The Australian National University Press, pp. 274–393. doi.org/10.1075/z.hal2.08bre.

Breen, JG 1981b, *The Mayi languages of the Queensland Gulf Country*, Canberra: Australian Institute of Aboriginal Studies.

Breen, JG 2004a, *Innamincka talk: a grammar of the Innamincka dialect of Yandruwandha with notes on other dialects*, Pacific Linguistics 558, Canberra: The Australian National University.

Breen, JG 2004b, *Innamincka words: Yandruwandha dictionary and stories*, Pacific Linguistics 559, Canberra: The Australian National University.

Breen, JG & Blake, BJ 2007, *The grammar of Yalarnnga: A language of western Queensland*, Pacific Linguistics 584, Canberra: The Australian National University.

Clark, ID 1990, *Aboriginal languages and clans: an historical atlas of western and central Victoria, 1800–1900*, Monash Publications in Geography 37, Melbourne: Department of Geographical and Environmental Sciences, Monash University.

Clark, I & Ryan, E 2009, 'Ladjiladji language area: A reconstruction', *Australian Aboriginal Studies*, *1*, pp. 77–88.

Davidson, DS 1928, *The chronological aspects of certain Australian social institutions: as inferred from geographical distribution*, Philadephia: University of Pennsylvania.

Dawson, J 1981 [1881], *Australian Aborigines: the languages and customs of several tribes of Aborigines in the Western District of Victoria, Australian*, Facisimile edition, Canberra: Australian Institute of Aboriginal Studies.

Dixon, RMW 2002, *The Australian languages: their nature and development*, Cambridge: Cambridge University Press. doi.org/10.1017/CBO9780511486869.

Eira, C 2008, 'Not tigers—sisters! Advances in the interpretation of historical sources for Dhudhuroa and Waywurru', *Aboriginal History*, *32*, pp. 151–64.

Elkin, AP 1931, 'The social organization of South Australian tribes', *Oceania*, 2, pp. 44–73. doi.org/10.1002/j.1834-4461.1931.tb00022.x.

Elkin, AP 1964, *The Australian Aborigines: how to understand them*, 4th edn, Sydney: Angus & Robertson.

Fison, L & Howitt, AW 1880, *Kamilaroi and Kurnai: group-marriage and relationship, and marriage by elopement*, Melbourne: George Robertson.

Furphy, S 2013, *Edward M. Curr and the tide of history*, Canberra: ANU E Press.

Hercus, LA 1982, *The Baagandji language*, Pacific Linguistics B-67, Canberra: The Australian National University.

Hercus, LA 1986, *Victorian languages: a late survey*, Pacific Linguistics B-77, Canberra: The Australian National University.

Hercus, LA 1991, 'Glimpses of the Karangura', *Records of the South Australian Museum*, 25(2), pp. 139–59.

Hercus, LA 1992a, *A Nukunu dictionary*, Canberra: Luise Hercus with the assistance of AIATSIS.

Hercus, LA 1992b, *Wembawemba dictionary*, Canberra: Luise Hercus with the assistance of AIATSIS.

Hercus, LA 1993, *Paakantyi dictionary*, Canberra: Luise Hercus with the assistance of AIATSIS.

Hercus, LA 1999, *A grammar of Wirangu, a language of the west coast of South Australia*, Pacific Linguistics C-150, Canberra: The Australian National University.

Hercus, LA & Austin, P 2004, 'The Yarli languages', in C Bowern & H Koch (eds), *Australian languages: classification and the comparative method*, Amsterdam/Philadelphia: John Benjamins, pp. 207–22, 647–54. doi.org/10.1075/cilt.249.13her.

Hercus, LA & Simpson, J 2001, 'The tragedy of Nauo', in Jane Simpson et al. (eds), *Forty years on: Ken Hale and Australian languages*, Pacific Linguistics 512, Canberra: The Australian National University, pp. 263–90.

Horgen, M 2004, The languages of the lower-Murray, MA thesis, La Trobe University.

Howitt, AW 1883, 'Notes on the Australian class systems', *The Journal of the Anthropological Institute of Great Britain and Ireland*, 12, pp. 496–512. doi.org/10.2307/2841688.

Howitt, AW 1884, 'Remarks on the class systems collected by Mr. Palmer', *The Journal of the Anthropological Institute of Great Britain and Ireland*, 13, pp. 335–46.

Howitt, AW 1996 [1904], *The native tribes of south-east Australia*, Facsimile edition, Canberra: Aboriginal Studies Press.

Koch, H 2012, 'Aboriginal languages and social groups in the Canberra region: interpreting the historical documentation', in B Baker et al. (eds), *Indigenous language and social identity: papers in honour of Michael Walsh*, Pacific Linguistics 626, Canberra: The Australian National University, pp. 123–44.

Mathew, J 1910, 'The origin of the Australian phratries and explanation of some of the phratry names', *The Journal of the Anthropological Institute of Great Britain and Ireland*, 40, pp. 164–70. doi.org/10.2307/2843147.

Mathews, RH 1898, 'The Victorian Aborigines: their initiation ceremonies and divisional systems', *American Anthropologist*, *11*, pp. 325–43. doi.org/10.1525/aa.1898.11.11.02a00000.

Mathews, RH 1900, 'Divisions of the South Australian Aborigines', *Proceedings of the American Philosophical Society*, *39*, pp. 78–91, 93.

Mathews, RH 1903, 'Some Aboriginal languages of Queensland and Victoria', *Proceedings of the American Philosophical Society*, *42*(173), pp. 179–88.

Mathews, RH 1905, 'Ethnological notes on the Aboriginal tribes of Queensland', *Royal Geographical Society of Australasia, Queensland*, *20*, pp. 49–75.

McConvell, P 2013, 'Granny got cross: semantic change of kami "mother's mother" to "father's mother" in Pama-Nyungan', in R Mailhammer (ed.), *Lexical and structural etymology: beyond word histories*, Berlin: de Gruyter Mouton, pp. 147–84. doi.org/10.1515/9781614510581.147.

McConvell, P & Dousset, L 2012, 'Tracking the dynamics of kinship and social category terms with AustKin II', *Proceedings of the EACL 2012 Joint Workshop of LINGVIS & UNCLH*, Avignon, France, 23–24 April 2012, pp. 98–107.

McDonald, M & Wurm, SA 1979, *Basic materials in Waŋkumara (Galali): grammar, sentences and vocabulary*, Pacific Linguistics B-65, Canberra: The Australian National University.

Oates, LF 1988a, *Barranbinya: fragments of a N.S.W. language. Papers in Australian linguistics No. 17*, Pacific Linguistics A-71, Canberra: The Australian National University, pp. 185–204.

Oates, LF 1988b, *The Muruwari language*, Pacific Linguistics C-108, Canberra: The Australian National University.

Radcliffe-Brown, AR 1918, 'Notes on the social organization of Australian tribes. Part 1', *Journal of the Royal Anthropological Institute of Great Britain and Ireland*, *48*, pp. 222–53. doi.org/10.2307/2843422.

Radcliffe-Brown, AR 1923, 'Notes on the social organization of Australian tribes', *Journal of the Royal Anthropological Institute of Great Britain and Ireland*, *53*, pp. 424–46. doi.org/10.2307/2843580.

Radcliffe-Brown, AR 1930–31, *The social organization of Australian tribes*, Oceania Monographs 1, Sydney: University of Sydney.

Reay, M 1945, Bakundji (from Hero Black at Bourke, 1945), Unpublished manuscript, AIATSIS: Canberra.

Robertson, C 1984, Wangkumara grammar and dictionary, Unpublished manuscript, Haymarket: NSW.

Roth, WE 1984 [1897], *Ethnological studies among the north-west-central Queensland Aborigines*, Facsimile edition, The Queensland Aborigines vol. 1, Victoria Park, WA: Hesperian Press.

Schebeck, B 1973, *The Adnjamathanha personal pronoun and the 'Wailpi kinship system'. Papers in Australian linguistics no. 6*, Pacific Linguistics A-36, Canberra: The Australian National University, pp. 1–45.

Scheffler, HW 1978, *Australian kin classification*, Cambridge: Cambridge University Press. doi.org/10.1017/CBO9780511557590.

Simpson, J & Hercus, L 2004, 'Thura-Yura as a subgroup', in C Bowern & H Koch (eds), *Australian languages: classification and the comparative method*, Amsterdam/Philadelphia: John Benjamins, pp. 179–206, 581–645. doi.org/10.1075/cilt.249.12sim.

Smyth, RB 1878, *The aborigines of Victoria: with notes relating to the habits of the natives of other parts of Australia and Tasmania*, Melbourne: Government Printer.

Spencer, B & Gillen, FJ 1927, *The Arunta: a study of a Stone Age people*, 2 vols, London: Macmillan.

Testart, A 1978, *Des classifications dualistes en Australie: Essai sur l'évolution de l'organisation sociale*, Paris: Editions de la Maison des sciences de l'homme et Publications de l'université de Lille III.

Wafer, J & Lissarrague, A 2008, *A handbook of Aboriginal languages of New South Wales and the Australian Capital Territory*, Nambucca Heads, NSW: Muurrbay Aboriginal Language and Cultural Co-operative.

7

Patriclan Subsets of the Ashburton River District in Western Australia

Peter Sutton

Abstract

In the Ashburton River district of Western Australia, individual members of different patrifilial totemic country groups (patriclans) could share a common name that was used in both address and reference for those individuals. This namesake relationship between members of distinct patriclans or descent-based estate-owning groups existed regardless of the linguistic identities of the patriclans concerned and was regional in distribution. This institution had family resemblances to cross-regional identity-sharing systems in other parts of Aboriginal Australia; however, it was unique in its detail. These shared names frequently, but not always, reflected shared patriclan totems. In any case, they structurally yielded subsets of patriclans. In some recorded cases, members of these subsets married each other. These cases may or may not have been post-conquest 'wrong marriages' contracted when the old prescriptive marriage laws were losing force.

Introduction

In this chapter, I discuss certain anthropological and linguistic records from the Ashburton River district of the Pilbara region of Western Australia (see Figure 23). My focus is on several authors' descriptions of subgroupings of descent-based totemic clans—subsets that they variously named 'phratries' (Bates 1913), 'inter-tribal totemic divisions' (Radcliffe-Brown 1931) and 'totem classes' (Austin 1992a–e, 2012). The information left to us regarding these subsets is limited and no longer being socially reproduced. For this reason, we have a small and closed corpus of evidence about them. Their unusual features, though, make it worthwhile for this paper to attempt as comprehensive a description and analysis of them as practicable.

While the evidence for the emotional colour of intra-set relationships among the people concerned is sparse, it does point towards amity—a 'mateship'—based on mutual likeness. The members of these subsets enjoyed a commonality of identity, irrespective of their constituents' linguistic group memberships. These subsets linked people, not only as individuals, but also as members (or perhaps 'representatives' would be closer to classical Aboriginal psychology) of different estate-holding totemic clans both within and across linguistic-territorial boundaries. Although two or more such subsets might have possessed the same linguistic variety, they were not structurally nested subgroups of linguistic groups per se; rather, they were distributed in a mosaic fashion across the landscape—geographically and socially.

They thus formed a superordinate association of women, men and presumably children who were at once both 'same and different'—in the sense of that widespread Aboriginal expression that reflects a philosophical preference for conjoint complementarity rather than monoliths of unity. These patriclan membership subsets formed discontinuous unities of like peoples who differed in other respects. Thus, they were counterterritorial in function, if not intention—that is, one peacemaking role of the patriclan subsets was that within this system, one could find namesakes with linguistic affiliations and home locations far from one's own. In classical Aboriginal Australia generally, namesake relationships are always infused with a positive tone. Shared names often imply shared transcendent substance. That this amity-oriented structural institution formed a mosaic across territorial groups in the present case suggests that the Ashburton system was another example, although unique in detail, of the tendency of Australian societies to codify and formalise social forces that countervailed against the insularity and, at times, aggressive localism typically associated with patrifiliation or patriliny and male political dominance. Balance, not uniformity, was the supreme principle underpinning the valorisation of both kinds of institutions.

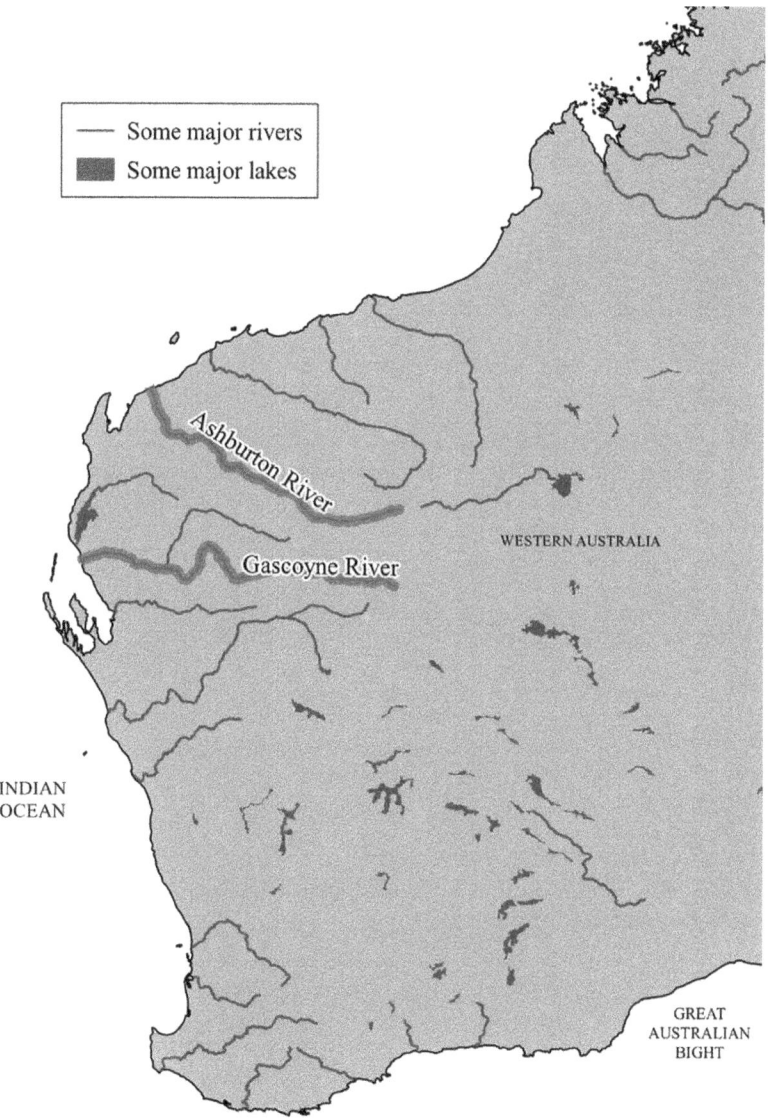

Figure 23: Map showing the locations of the Ashburton and Gascoyne rivers of Western Australia.

Source: Prepared by William McConvell from standard topographic maps of Australia; geodata from Geosciences Australia.

In spite of this distributive function in relation to identity, the Ashburton patriclan subsets were not strictly exogamous. In this sense, their members could not have been culturally constructed as being 'of one blood'. I say this because a structure of a similar kind, widely spread in classical times in much of Australia and still extant in some regions such as the north central Northern Territory, consists of matrilineal totemic clans. Co-members of such descent-based unities were deemed to be of the same 'flavour', 'aroma' or 'meat', which meant there was a ban on sexual relationships between co-totemites, whether within one area or between distantly linked geographical areas. Along with an incest taboo, these matrilineal clans generally combined an ethic of amity between co-members.

Matrilineal social totems identified in these ways include the *dhii* or 'meat' of north Central New South Wales (Ash et al. 2003, p. 61; Mathews 1897, p. 157, 'dheeh'), the *mardu* or 'flavour' of the Lake Eyre region (Hercus 1989, p. 102; Howitt 1904, p. 91, 'murdu') and the *ngurlu* of the north central Northern Territory. *Ngurlu* is used mainly north and north-west from near Newcastle Waters and Beetaloo, and literally means 'taste, flavour' (Gurindji) or 'human scent, smell of a person's sweat' (Djamindjung) (Nash 1982).

The 'Phratries' of North-East Arnhem Land

Religiously linked patrifilial groups in north-east Arnhem Land—the Yolngu region—have some features in common with the Ashburton system. The local missionary and scholar Theodore Webb (1933) referred to these as *mala* (untranslated by him, but generally meaning 'groups') possessing common *rangga* (sacred ceremonies). He implied that the constituents of these *mala* were 'hordes' (patrilineal descent groups; Webb 1933, p. 406). The constituent hordes were not clustered geographically but could be 'as widely separated as Elcho Island on the north coast and Blue Mud Bay on the Gulf of Carpentaria' (Webb 1933, p. 408). On the matter of terminology for such scattered unities, he stated: 'I leave it to be determined whether the term tribe, subtribe, or some other should be applied to these *mala*' (Webb 1933, pp. 408–9).

Lloyd Warner (1958 [1937], pp. 9, 33–5) identified the same sets as 'phratries', an anthropological term from *phratria*, meaning 'brotherhood' in Greek. Each phratry in north-east Arnhem Land belongs to only one of the exogamous patrilineal moieties of the region and has a mythic basis for unity of its members. Its members have similar languages ideologically, but not dialectally. Likewise, there is a doctrine of phratry solidarity that is not borne out in practice, and in two cases, Warner found the phratries 'too nebulous in their composition to give their clan membership'. Warner (1958 [1937], p. 35) regarded the phratries as 'a weak attempt within the culture to create new and larger groups than the clan to control the intra-moiety antagonisms of the clans within it'.

In general, later anthropologists did not settle for Warner's terminology. Ronald Berndt (1955, p. 96) preferred 'parallel descent groups' and referred to 'clans' comprised of linguistic groups that consisted of parallel sets of minimal patrilineal descent groups. Warren Shapiro (1981, pp. 23, 91, 97–8) called Warner's phratries 'totemic unions' and pointed out more of their indeterminateness. Bernhard Schebeck (2001, pp. 46–9) included 'phratry-like names' among his schema of 10 types of collective names in the region but could not find rigid formalisation in their use. Nancy Williams (1986, p. 70) called the relevant entities *manikay mala*. Ian Keen (1994, pp. 65, 75) explicitly rejected 'phratries' and opted for 'groups' (*mala*), given the indeterminacies he described, and the presence of strings of links rather than sets marked by closures. Komei Hosokawa (2003) called Warner's phratries 'clans'.

Despite such differences, the agreed picture for the Yolngu region is one in which identities and sacra may be held in common by people whose local country interests are separated by often considerable distances, people who belong to the same moiety and therefore cannot intermarry, and who may share a common title or group name. The first feature is shared with the Ashburton, while the latter two are not.

The Ashburton District

The Ashburton district is distinctive within the gallery of Australian traditions concerning kin superclasses. Appropriately, Bates (1913, p. 394) commented on 'how interesting the Ashburton tribes are'.

Bates (1913, pp. 393–5) reported the existence of 'certain totem phratries' in a district of Western Australia that she referred to as the Ashburton. She described the Ashburton district as an area running 'from north of Onslow (Ashburton River), towards the Gascoyne River' (Bates 1913, p. 393). It was identified by Bates (1913) as an area in which the Aboriginal people shared a distinctive cluster of key features of social and religious organisation: a four-section system that was subgrouped into two moieties whose members had prescribed ritual roles, the absence of circumcision, localised increase (thalu) ceremonies, a ban on cross-cousin marriages and totemic phratries. She cited no source here other than 'Cornally' and knowledge based on her own fieldwork, which seems to have principally been among the 77 Aboriginal women living at Dorre Island Isolation Hospital in late 1910 and early 1911 (Bates 1966, pp. 97–104; n.d., Notebook 7a: cover sheet). I have used Bates's field materials to flesh out her published description. Bates (1966, pp. 97–104; n.d., Notebook 7a: cover sheet) also acknowledged that her manuscript contained 'part of Cornally's information on marriage laws'.[1]

Radcliffe-Brown (1931, pp. 38–42) acknowledged Bates's 1913 published paper as one of the sources for his own discussion of the Ashburton peoples, whom he denoted as 'Talaindji type' in his taxonomy of Australian social organisation. He had also done fieldwork in the same region in the period from 1910 to 1912 (Radcliffe-Brown 1931, p. 42), and his notes from that work (Radcliffe-Brown n.d.) have been used in this chapter in addition to his published statements. He described the district as being on both sides of the Ashburton River for the lower two-thirds of its length, south to the Gascoyne River (Radcliffe-Brown 1931, p. 38).

Berndt et al. (1979, p. 32 [map], p. 35 [table]) identified a similar Ashburton-centred region of 'traditional social categories and social groups', which he denoted as the 'Central-west coastal and inland' area—subgroup 'E'. Differences between the publication by Berndt et al. (1979) and that of Bates (1913) and Radcliffe-Brown (1931) suggest that Berndt was using his own and/or other unpublished field data as sources in this 1979 essay, which was brief. He did not mention in print the phenomenon that Bates called 'phratries'. Unfortunately, Berndt's field notes remain under a 30-year embargo at the University of Western Australia, and were not made available for this chapter.

---

1   James Cornally, a shepherd, was a resident in the Gascoyne and Ashburton River districts for about 20 years (Biblioteca versila 2015).

7. PATRICLAN SUBSETS OF THE ASHBURTON RIVER DISTRICT IN WESTERN AUSTRALIA

The linguistic-territorial groupings indicated in print as component members of the Ashburton regional social organisational system by Bates (1913), Radcliffe-Brown (1931) and Berndt et al. (1979) are shown in Table 17. I have reordered the groupings to match as many as possible across the rows. Bates (1913) listed only six but added '&c'—implying that perhaps she had recorded more; Radcliffe-Brown (1931, p. 38) listed 11; and Berndt et al. (1979) indicated that there were 18.[2]

Table 17: Language groups of the Ashburton social organisation district.

Bates	Radcliffe-Brown	Berndt et al.
Tallainji	Talaindji	Djalendji
Burduna	Burduna	Buduna
Biniguru	Binigura	Binigura
Baiung	Baiong	Baiyungu
Maia	Maia	Maia
Targari	Targari	Dargari
&c	Noala	Noala
	Tjuroro	Djururu
	Djiwali	Djiwali
	Tenma	
	Warienga	Warianga
		Bandjima[1]
		Inawongga
		Nyanu
		Malgaru
		Yinigudira
		Djungurdia
		Gurama
		Guwari

[1] Radcliffe-Brown placed Pandjima in his 'Kariera Type' subgroup instead.
Source: Bates (1913), Berndt et al. (1979) and Radcliffe-Brown (1931, p. 38).

It is not the aim of this chapter to discuss the differences between these authors in any comprehensive detail; however, it is clear that they agree on a core regional set of six linguistic groups.

---

2   Here, as elsewhere in the chapter, I have retained the original spellings of the Aboriginal words by the source authors.

SKIN, KIN AND CLAN

Additionally, from Bates (1913), Radcliffe-Brown (1931) and Austin (1992a–e, 2012) we may derive a largely parallel record of the names used in address and reference for the members of the patriclan subsets that we are considering (see Table 18).

Table 18: The subset members' names.

Subset		Bates	Radcliffe-Brown	Austin
1	Male	Käjardu (Kagardu)	Kadjardu	Kajartu
	Female	Ngajuri	Ngadjuri	Ngajuri ~ Ngaji
2	Male	Wariara	Wariera	Wariyarra
	Female	Ngogodji	Ngogodji	Ngukuji
3	Male	Waliri (Wadiri)	Waleri	Walirri
	Female	Wilari (Widari)	Wilari	Wilari
4	Male	Yaui(ji)		
	Female	Nyarlu		
5	Male	Wiarrji	Wiardji	Marramalu, Yawiji
	Female	Mambulu	Mambula	Mampulu
6	Male		Wilyaru	Wilyaru
	Female		Ngwolyi	Ngulyi
7	Male	Yirrgun	Yirgu	
	Female	Yirbiji	Yerbidji	
8	Male	Mirdir(ba)	Mirdirba	Murtirr
	Female	Ngalguji	Ngalgudji	Ngalkuji
9	Male		Tambula	
	Female		Murdari	

Source: Austin (1992a–e, 2012), Bates (1913) and Radcliffe-Brown (1931).

Note, though, that individuals were addressed and referred to by the 'totem class names'. Such usage may well have implied a 'totem class' or shared higher order unit; however, but the names were not the names of the totem classes.

The Labelling of the Subsets by Scholars

While Bates (1913, p. 394) referred to 'totem phratries', Radcliffe-Brown (1931, p. 41) referred to the same phenomenon as 'inter-tribal totemic divisions' and avoided the term 'phratry'. It is hardly conceivable that he did so lightly, and, in my opinion, it is a clear rejection of Bates's term. Radcliffe-Brown (1931, p. 41) recorded that Aboriginal people of the region would often refer to their totem as their 'eldest brother'. However, if there was an Indigenous cover term for what Bates called 'phratries', it is unlikely to have been 'brother' or 'sibling', because their members could belong to all four sections—that is, in the correct relationships, they could marry each other. However, it is possible, as suggested by an anonymous reviewer of this chapter, that a 'sibling' identification could be used as a metaphoric cover term.

The cover term in use for Bates's 'phratries' in at least one case is most likely to have meant 'mate' or possibly 'friend' instead. I say this because in her unpublished manuscript (Bates n.d., Notebook 7a p. 98) under the heading 'PHRATRIES', she made a note that had been typed as 'Jadiara = mate, Talainji', followed by a listing of 13 marriages specifying language, section and 'phratry' for each partner and the totem of the male (see Tables 23 and 24). Given that the typist has rendered Payungu waliri as 'wadiri' on the same page, it may be that Bates actually wrote 'Jaliara = mate'. These terms can be compared with the published terms from Austin's (1992a, 1992b, 1992c, 1992e) work (see Table 19).

Table 19: 'Mate' terms in the region recorded by Austin.

Term	Gloss	Language	Source
jali	friend	Jiwarli	Austin 1992e, p. 3
jaliyarra	pair of mates	Jiwarli	Austin 1992e, p. 3
jaligurdi	mate	Thalanyji	Austin 1992a, p. 2
jaligurdi	friend	Payungu	Austin 1992b, p. 2
jali	mate	Tharrgari	Austin 1992c, p. 3

Source: Austin (1992a, 1992b, 1992c, 1992e).

Oddly, Bates (1913) used the term 'phratry' not to refer only to totemic groups, but also to pairs of sections. Hence, the Emu totem 'phratry' of the Burduna tribe was of 'Paljari-Banaka Phratry' (Bates, 1913, p. 394)—with Paljari and Banaka being section terms. As will be discussed, the patriclan subsets were not associated with a single section couple or moiety, as this might have implied.

Acquisition of Membership

Bates (1913) did not explicitly state the rule for acquisition of the 'phratry' totem; however, her list of four examples of possible marriages between members of different 'phratries' shows in all cases that the offspring of such couples belonged to the 'phratry' of the father—not that of the mother. If this was general practice, this would have meant that the rule was one of patrifiliation.

Radcliffe-Brown (1931, pp. 41, 42) was clearer and stated that 'patrilineal clans' of the region were 'grouped together' into 'inter-tribal' totemic divisions, and that 'since the local clan is strictly patrilineal, it follows that the totemic divisions are also patrilineal'. This would imply, although it is not stated, that males in such divisions had the same divisional names as their brothers, sons, fathers, fathers' brothers and so on, while females had the same divisional names as their sisters, brothers' daughters, fathers' sisters and so on.

Distribution

According to Radcliffe-Brown (1931), among the Ashburton-Gascoyne region's nine totemic divisions, only one (Kadjardu/Ngadjuri)[3] was 'found in all the tribes'. The Wilyaru/Ngwolyi division was only found in the southern tribes, while the Yirgu/Yerbidji, Mirdirba/Ngalgudji and Tambula/Murdari divisions were absent in the south—namely among the Maia and Baiong tribes (see Table 18). What he suggested as universal among the Ashburton regional system is the totemic division as a structural and religious entity, not the actual and total set of divisional names or totemic associations per se.

The totemic divisions were scattered across the landscape—both between and within language territories:

> In a list of seventeen local clans of the Baiong tribe, which is probably not complete, there are three Kadjardu clans, seven Waleri, one Wariera, three Wiardji, and three Wilyaru. (Radcliffe-Brown 1931, p. 41)

---

3   The first term is the male name and the second is female for members of the same division.

According to Radcliffe-Brown (1931, p. 42), this interdigitating system of commonly based distinctions that disregarded linguistic unities or differences gave rise to the use of divisional names—and not kin terms—as the predominant form of address between men and women. Gender was marked in the differences between the male and female 'names' that rested on divisional memberships (see Table 18). Austin's (2012, p. 16) later work confirmed both points: 'There are separate terms for male and female members of the totem groups, and the terms are often used to refer to or address people, much in the manner of personal names in English'.

In these three respects—supra-segmentary linkages, eliding of names or kin terms and the principle of amity among those who are akin—the speech etiquette of patriclan subset membership in the Ashburton resembled that of subsection usage in Central and north central Australia. Further, it was quite dissimilar to regions such as Cape York Peninsula where kin terms and clan-based names were among the main norms for address and reference. It was a system bigger and less personalised than putative genealogy, as it was one that flattened the carefully modulated distances and tensions of genealogically based relatedness into a subsection-like pan-regional set of a manageable number of likenesses and differences. It may also have added a rather emotionally light means of disambiguation of interpersonal reference. Such simple conversational functionality is not to be dismissed as a possibility.

Perhaps the most consistently noted and notable element linking members of the various descent-group subsets in the Ashburton case is the addressing of and referring to subset members using distinctive male and female names that reflect subset identity, in preference to the use of kin terms. Ideologically, at least, this was generally in recognition of the totems commonly held among members of the same identity. However, this system was by no means as neat as that would imply. It is the names that are most consistent and the totems less so.

The Totems and Descent Groups

Bates's (1913, p. 394) brief published tabulation of 'phratry' names and totems presented a very simple picture of the relationship between the two. Table 20 retabulates the 'phratry' names and totems for clarity.

Table 20: Bates's totems linked to 'phratry' names.

Totem	Male name	Female name	Tribe	Section couple
Emu	Wariara	Ngogodji	Burduna	Paljari-Banaka
Turkey & Fire	Waliri	Wilari	Burduna	Paljari-Banaka
Kangaroo	Käjardu	Ngajuri	Tallainji	Boorong-Kaimera
Snake	Wiarrji	Mambulu	Tallainji & Burduna	Paljari-Banaka

Source: Adapted from Bates (1913, p. 394).

This indicates that each 'phratry' was associated with one—occasionally two—totems. However, Radcliffe-Brown (1931, p. 41) reported more complexity:

> [The Kadjardu/Ngadjuri division] represents water or moisture, and therefore such things as water birds, frogs, water plants, and grass-seed ... are Kadjardu. Similarly Waleri has for its principle fire and heat, things that are especially associated with hot weather, such as snakes and lizards belong to this division. But for some of the other divisions it has not been possible to discover any simple principle by which things are classified under one or other. Different stars, or portions of the sky, are connected with the totemic divisions.

Indeed, Radcliffe-Brown's unpublished field data (Appendix 1) held the fact that different descent groups whose members shared a common name were identified with widely distinct, if at times semantically related, entities.

In Radcliffe-Brown's (n.d.) field notes, Kadjardu/Ngadjuri was the naming tag for members of clans with the following totems: Yungadji (lizard sp.), Rain, Pandura [Parturra? = Bustard], Galah, Turtle, Bandicoot, Red Ochre, Grass Seed, Kangaroo, Plum Tree, Bony Bream, Honey, Rainbow, Kadjura (mythic snake), Kulyu (edible root), Paljuwara (river sand?), Winter Rain and Thurna (snake). Bates's (1913, p. 324) simple entry of '(Bungurdi) Kangaroo' for this 'phratry' belied—or she had missed—a huge range of variation. The other clans and totems recorded as belonging to the seven 'totemic divisions' by Radcliffe-Brown (n.d.) provide further detail (see Appendix 1).

7. PATRICLAN SUBSETS OF THE ASHBURTON RIVER DISTRICT IN WESTERN AUSTRALIA

However, Radcliffe-Brown (1931, p. 41) was able to state firmly that:

> Any local clan that has rain as its totem belongs to this [Kadjardu] division. Similarly any group that has the fire, sun, and hot weather totem belongs to Waleri (fem. Wilari). The Wariera (fem. Ngogodji) division includes all clans with an emu totem, and all the eaglehawk clans belong to Wiardji (fem. Mambula).

Thus, the correlations between totems and divisions worked best in a one-way direction. All Rain clans were members of the Kadjardu division, but not all Kadjardu division descent groups were Rain clans—a salient point omitted by Radcliffe-Brown (n.d.). He also left aside one apparent exception to the 'all Rain clans are Kadjardu' rule: a 'Warunga' [Warriangga?] tribe's clan of 'Yungo' division was also a Rain clan (see Appendix 1; it could be Kadjardu). Radcliffe-Brown, like many others, apparently liked to see that the loose thrums of the warp and weft of the record were trimmed, and the descriptive picture reduced to something systemically rigorous through a little snipping along the fringes.

The patriclans' totems had corresponding totemic centres at specific sites in the relevant clan estate generally, if not universally (see Appendix 1). These centres were established by mythic beings. Radcliffe-Brown (1931) considered the establishment of the totem centres 'to have been affected by the existence of the inter-tribal divisions'; however, he was coy as to how. He then offered a solo example: 'This Yauardamai (Burduna) or Kardamai (Baiong) seems to be the special culture-hero of the Kadjardu division' (Radcliffe-Brown 1931, pp. 41–2). I suggest that the base evidence in Radcliffe-Brown's (1931) paper is most likely fragmentary, rather than a richness pared down by way of example.

The relevant notes that Radcliffe-Brown took in 1911, tabulated in Appendix 1, are reorganised so that his intertribal totemic divisions are placed first and in alphabetical order.[4]

Table 21 shows Austin's (2012, p. 17) record of totemic classes.

---

4   The raw text material in Appendix 1 was originally keyboarded from Radcliffe-Brown's field notes at the University of Sydney Archives, by Brett Baker, then of the University of Sydney, in 1998. This work was funded by the New South Wales Land Council and the Aboriginal Legal Rights Movement of South Australia in a transcription project organised by myself.

Table 21: Austin's record of totemic classes.

Male name	Female name	Totem	Translation
Walirri	Wilari	Karla	Fire
		Parturra	Bustard
Kajartu	Ngajuri	Yungu	Rain
Wariyarra	Ngukuji	Jankurna	Emu
Marramalu (in Jiwarli & Thiin), Yawiji in Warriyangka & Tharrkari	Mampulu	Warlartu	Eaglehawk
Mirtirr	Ngalkuji	Jiriparri	Echidna
Thampurla	?	Kurrumantu	Goanna

Source: Austin (2015, p. 28).

However, this apparently simple picture is tempered by Austin's (2012, p. 17) comment:

> It appears that the totems listed above for each group are prototypical for the local groups having that totem class name, however, evidence from Radcliffe-Brown's card file suggests that for any given local group there could be many associated totems, not always the one typical of the totem class of the clan.

Marriage, Patriclan Subset and Section Membership

Bates (1913) stated that in the Ashburton, no marriages were permitted 'within the totem phratry', and followed this statement with four examples of 'possible marriages' between 'phratry' members. It is anomalous, then, that in her list of permissible weddings was the pair Wariara (Emu) marrying Wilari (Turkey). Prior to this, Bates had identified Wariara as a male 'phratry' name and Wilari as the equivalent female 'phratry' name—both of which belonged to the Paljari-Banaka section couple (both Burduna tribe in this instance). If there had been a rule of exogamy for these patriclan subgroups, Bates's use of the label 'phratry' for them would be justified. However, exogamy did not apply as a strict rule so much as a common pattern. Further, Bates's assertion that Wilari/Wariara people belonged to the Paljari-Banaka section couple mistakenly implied an alignment between the two sets of categories. In fact, the patriclan subsets and the section terms associated with members of their constituent

7. PATRICLAN SUBSETS OF THE ASHBURTON RIVER DISTRICT IN WESTERN AUSTRALIA

descent groups were not exclusively aligned with each other. Men of all four sections could be named Kadjardu, Waliri, Wiardji, Yauadji and, probably, Yirgu; female equivalents of these are few in the record but can be assumed to also have been applied. Table 22 shows evidence of this.

Table 22: Patriclan subsets and sections.

Subset name	Sections	Source	No. of examples
Kadjardu (m)	Boorong-Kaimera	Radcliffe-Brown	8
Kadjardu (m)	Paljari-Banaka	Radcliffe-Brown	1 + (1?)
Kajardu (m)	Boorong-Kaimera	Bates	1
Waleri (m)	Boorong-Kaimera	Radcliffe-Brown	3
Waliri (m) Wilari (f)	Paljari-Banaka	Bates	1
Wariara (m) Ngogodji (f)	Paljari-Banaka	Bates	1
Wariera (m)	Paljari-Banaka	Radcliffe-Brown	2
Wiardji (m)	Boorong-Kaimera	Radcliffe-Brown	2
Wiardji (m)	Paljari-Banaka	Radcliffe-Brown	1
Wiarrdji (m) Mambulu (f)	Paljari-Banaka	Bates	1
Yanadji (m) Nyalu (f)	Paljari-Banaka	Radcliffe-Brown	1
Yauadji (m)	Boorong-Kaimera	Radcliffe-Brown	2
Yaui (m) Nyarlu (f)	Boorong-Kaimera	Bates	1
Yirgu (m)	Paljari-Banaka	Radcliffe-Brown	2
Yugu? Kadjadu	Boorong-Kaimera	Radcliffe-Brown	1
Yungo ['Rain']	Paljari-Banaka	Radcliffe-Brown	1

Source: Bates (1913) and Radcliffe-Brown (n.d.).

Bates (1913) did not publish her list of 14 female–male relationships, plus a few other people, together with their linguistic group names, section names, 'phratry' memberships and totems. These are my terms as the columns containing these data lacked identifying headers. This list was located in Bates (n.d., Notebook 7a pp. 98–9) and is tabulated in Tables 23 and 24.

Table 23: Bates's unpublished data on marriages.

H lg	H section	H 'phratry'	H totem	W lg	W section	W 'phratry'	W totem
Burduna	Paljari	Wariara	Kajalbu [Emu]	D,argari [sic]	Banaka	Ngogoji	
Bauingu [Baiungu?]	Paljeri	Wariri	Pardura [Bustard]	Burduna	Banaka	Wirdari	
Talainji	Boorong	Kajarda	Bungurdi	–	Kaimera	Ngajuri	
Talainji	Banaka	Kajardu	Bilarra	–	Paljeri	Ngajuri	
Burduna	Kaimera	Mirdirba	Kangaldha [Wild Potato?] and Jiruwari [Echidna]	–	Boorong	Ngalguji	
Talainji	Banaka	Yirrgun	Yeerrgu, roots on buln	–	Paljari	Yirbiji	
Talainji	Paljari	Wiarrji	Warnda or waraueru	Binigura	Banaka	Mambalu	
Burduna	Kaimera	Waliri	Jirdara, iguana	–	Boorong	Wirdari	
Burduna	Kaimera	Yaui	Kaju (snake) and seed	–	Boorong	Nyarlu	
Baiungu	Paljeri	Wadiri	Pardura [Bustard]	–	Banaka	Widari	Pardura [Bustard]
Burduna	Kaimera	Yaui	Kardan etc. seed & kadurdu seed	–	Boorong	Nyardu	
Talainji	Kagardu [sic]	Kagardu	Wong-nguru [Bandicoot]			Ngajuri	Mad, a wilaguru
Burduna	Boorong	Yaui	Madarongu (seed and rain)	–	Kaimera	Nyardu	
Burduna	Kaimera	Mirdir	Jiribardi [Echidna]	–	Boorong	Ngalguji	Jiribardi [Echidna]

Source: Based on Bates (1913), with headers added by Sutton.

7. PATRICLAN SUBSETS OF THE ASHBURTON RIVER DISTRICT IN WESTERN AUSTRALIA

Below this list (Bates n.d., Notebook 7a pp. 98–9) fell an extension (see Table 24).

Table 24: Extended Bates data.

Father and son							
Dargari		Yauiji	Bongana (duck)				
		Nyarlo	Nganmari				
Talainji	Banaka	Kajardu	Baurda	–	Paljeri	Ngajuri	Kardan

Source: Bates n.d., Notebook 7a, pp. 98–9.

It is not entirely clear what this list was meant to represent. However, the heading above the list is as follows:

> PHRATRIES
>
> Nidi and ngallariju relationships, cannot marry. (marginal note) Jadiara = mate, Talainji. (Bates n.d., Notebook 7a p. 98)

Given that the sections of the couples listed by Bates all form impermissible relationships according to the section system, it would seem that this is perhaps a list of actual wrong marriages or a list of imagined wrong marriage possibilities between people who 'cannot marry'. Here, Bates's 'nidi' is most probably the *nyirdi* recorded by Austin as follows: 'wife's parents' (Thalanyji, 1992a, p. 19; Tharrgari, 1992c, p. 15); 'wife's father, daughter's husband' (Payungu, 1992b, p. 27); 'son-in-law, daughter's husband' (Warriyangga, 1992d, p. 14); and 'wife's mother, daughter's husband' (Jiwarli, 1992e, p. 33). Bates's (1913, p. 395) list of Burduna kin terms includes 'Nidi-I—father's sister's son'. I have been unable to identify 'ngallariju'; the 'ngal-' segment suggests a possible first-person dual inclusive pronoun as the stem.

All 14 marriages in Table 23 where the partners' sections are identified are between men and women of the same patriclan subsets, as identified by names—that is, the patriclan subsets shown here are endogamous. This is the opposite of the rule propounded by Bates (1913), who stated that they were exogamous.

The section memberships of the spouses recorded here are also the opposite of the prescriptive marriage rules published by Bates (1913) and Radcliffe-Brown (1931). Bates (1913, p. 393) gave the rule for the Ashburton people as:

Male	Female	Offspring
A. Boorong	= D. Paljari	C. Kaimera
B. Banaka	= C. Kaimera	D. Paljari
C. Kaimera	= B. Banaka	A. Boorong
D. Paljari	= A. Boorong	B. Banaka

[= means marries by rule]

Similarly, Radcliffe-Brown (1931, p. 39) wrote:

Banaka = Kaimera
Burungu = Paljeri

In the 14 marriages recorded by Bates (n.d.) and illustrated in Tables 23 and 24, the relationships are:

Banaka = Paljeri (seven cases)
Boorong = Kaimera (seven cases)

An anonymous reader for this chapter suggested that the marriage evidence gathered by Bates (n.d.) may have been from people who had married wrongly as a result of the massive impact of colonisation, and whose marriages would not have otherwise been representative of precolonial or classical norms or behaviours. However, I would also make the following points. Bates worked anthropologically in Western Australia for 12 years prior to her publication on 'phratries' of the Ashburton (Bates 1913, p. 400)—so, from 1901. The peak of this activity in the Pilbara perhaps occurred in 1911, and the commencement of pastoral and pearling impacts on the region date from the 1860s. Roughly speaking, this impact had begun to take form some 40 years before Bates's records. Anyone aged over 40 who worked with Bates (e.g. at Dorre Island) would have had parents who married before the old system was impacted. Assuming some of these people described their parents to Bates, those descriptions can be expected to reflect precolonial norms. Bates's list of marriages shown in Table 23 are all within patriclan subsets; further, in every case, the sections of the marriage partners are given as a father/child pair. This adds to its appearance of being an artifice emphasising patriclan subset exogamy as a rule. However, this was apparently not the rule because Bates also recorded permissible marriages between members of the same 'phratry'.

Bates (n.d., Notebook 7a p. 99) made a list of permissible marriages between females of particular totems and males of other totems for these same Ashburton people. The intertribal permissible marriages she recorded were presumably given by a woman, as they are all from the

7. PATRICLAN SUBSETS OF THE ASHBURTON RIVER DISTRICT IN WESTERN AUSTRALIA

woman's point of view. Bates did not attempt to associate particular section couples with the totemites, who in this case may be understood as standing for particular patriclans. She also made no record of which totems were associated with which 'phratries'. In Table 25, I have used Bates's and Radcliffe-Brown's data to deduce what these may have been. The numbers in Table 25 correspond to the patriclan subset numbers in Table 18. In instances where I have no data, the entry is marked by '–'. Bates's list was also in Aboriginal language and offered no translations. I have provided translations using Austin's dictionaries of relevant language varieties (various dates) and also alphabetised Bates's material by the first column.

Table 25: Bates's field data on permissible 'phratry' marriages.

Wife's totem	Wife's 'phratry'	Husband's totem	Husband's 'phratry'
Bilana Rain	1	Wor-ngura Bandicoot	1
Bilana Rain	1	Wong-nguru Bandicoot	1
Bungurdi Red Kangaroo	1, 7	Pardura Bustard	3
Jirdara Black Goanna	3	Pardura Bustard	3
Jiribardi Echidna	8	Nganmari	4
Jiriwari cf. Echidna jiribarri	8	Kajalbu Emu	2
Kajalbu Emu	2	Wongana Black Duck	4
Kaju Snake	1, 4, 5	Pardura Bustard	3
Kaju Snake	1, 4, 5	Yirrgu Root	7
Kaju Snake	1, 4, 5	Bilana Cloud	1
Kaju Snake	1, 4, 5	Kajalbu Emu	2
Kardandu [cf. kardan Ranji bush (*Acacia pyrifolia*)]	4	Bauerda Tree [sp?]	-table 2
Kardandu [cf. kardan Ranji bush (*Acacia pyrifolia*)]	4	Nganmari Snake	4
Madaronga [seed type?]	4	Kagalbu [probably kajalbu] Emu	2
Pardura Bustard	3	Bungurdi Red Kangaroo	1, 7
Warrida Eaglehawk	5	Yanga t,adu [*sic*] [thalu?], rain N of Bilbingi	1?
Wong-nguru Bandicoot	1	Nganmari Snake	4
Wong-nguru Bandicoot	1	Bauerda Tree [sp?]	-
Yirrgu Root	7	Wong-nguru Bandicoot	1

Source: Bates (n.d.).

Although somewhat disordered, this evidence again indicates that women and men of the same patriclan subset could, under certain circumstances, marry permissibly. It also makes clear that the invariable patriclan subset endogamy shown in the 14 marriages of Tables 23 and 24 was not a result of a prescriptive rule.

Conclusion

While they were elementally structures that rested on local religious and other rights in estates and totemic descent-group membership, the Ashburton patriclan subsets emphasised pan-territorial and pan-linguistic commonalities and cloaked or elided territorial distinctions. As far as the record allows us to say, they emphasised an emotionally positive pattern of interpersonal address and reference based on this kindred of some among the many. At the same time, the Ashburton patriclan subsets also elided precise reference to the actual inter-kin status, and to differences of seniority versus juniority that otherwise obtained between interlocutors and the people they spoke to or spoke about using the patriclan subset person terms. Unlike many kin terms, the names did not structurally mark senior or junior persons. They were sociocentric rather than egocentric in basis—although the 'groups' they yielded had no proper names that have been recorded. In principle, they were not each identified with only a single father/child section couple. However, they distinguished terminologically between the genders—something one finds often among subsection systems, and at times among section systems, but rarely among the terminologies for sociocentric, geopolitical and religious alliances, including the 'phratries' or wider *mala* of north-east Arnhem Land.

In short, this system and its associated social etiquette shared several of the key features of universalist kin superclass systems, while at the same time being rooted in patrifilial localism.

I make this suggestion, not to advance a theory of evolutionary relationships between such a patriclan subset system and a section system, but merely to imply that some of the common cultural logics and achieved outcomes of ostensibly different social institutions resulted in some of the same ends being accomplished by similar—at times different but cognate—means. The Ashburton patriclan subsets rather look like an experiment in this domain that was shattered by the colonial avalanche, while still on the way to becoming.

Acknowledgements

Those from whom I have learned most about kinship studies due to personal mentoring were the late Kenneth Maddock (Macquarie University lectures 1970); the late Alfred Gell (ANU lectures c. 1975); the late Hal Scheffler (when he was a visiting scholar at the University of Queensland c. 1976); and Bruce Rigsby, my PhD supervisor (1975–78) and long-term interlocutor since.

For the supply of some of the most helpful unpublished information, I also thank Peter Austin, Kingsley Palmer (2007), Dennis Gray (1978) and Patrick McConvell.

References

Ash, A, Giacon, J & Lissarague, A 2003, *Gamilaraay, Yuwaalaraay, & Yuwaalayay dictionary*, Alice Springs: IAD Press.

Austin, P 1992a, *A dictionary of Thalanyji, Western Australia*, Bundoora, Victoria: La Trobe University, Department of Linguistics.

Austin, P 1992b, *A dictionary of Payungu, Western Australia*, Bundoora, Victoria: La Trobe University, Department of Linguistics.

Austin, P 1992c, *A dictionary of Tharrgari, Western Australia*, Bundoora, Victoria: La Trobe University, Department of Linguistics.

Austin, P 1992d, *A dictionary of Warriyangga, Western Australia*, Bundoora, Victoria: La Trobe University, Department of Linguistics.

Austin, P 1992e, *A dictionary of Jiwarli, Western Australia*, Bundoora, Victoria: La Trobe University, Department of Linguistics.

Austin, P 2015, *A Reference Grammar of the Mantharta Languages, Western Australia*. Unpublished draft version 3.7.

Bates, D n.d., Manuscripts and papers of Daisy Bates (MS 365 and MS 2300), Canberra: National Library of Australia.

Bates, D 1913, 'Social organization of some Western Australian tribes', *Report of the Australasian Association for the Advancement of Science*, 15, pp. 387–400.

Bates, D 1966, *The passing of the Aborigines. A lifetime spent among the natives of Australia*, 2nd edition, Melbourne: William Heinemann.

Berndt, RM 1955, '"Murngin" (Wulamba) social organization', *American Anthropologist, 57*, pp. 84–106. doi.org/10.1525/aa.1955.57.1.02a00100.

Berndt, RM, Douglas, W, Kaldor, S & Hallam, SJ 1979, 'The First Australians', in NT Jarvis (ed.), *Western Australia: an atlas of human endeavour 1829–1979*, Perth: Education and Lands and Surveys Departments of Western Australia, pp. 32–7.

Biblioteca versila 2015, viewed 21 October 2017, digital.library.adelaide.edu.au/dspace/handle/2440/88701.

Gray, D 1978, 'Identity' amongst the Carnarvon Reserve mob, MA thesis, University of Western Australia.

Hercus, LA 1989, 'The status of women's cultural knowledge. Aboriginal society in north-east South Australia', in P Brock (ed.), *Women, rites and sites: Aboriginal women's cultural knowledge*, Sydney: Allen & Unwin.

Hosokawa, K 2003, *Yolngumatha ethnographic lexicon: with particular reference to toponyms associated with creation stories and related cultural and environmental terms*, Endangered languages of the Pacific Rim series A1-002, Kyoto: Osaka Gakuin University.

Howitt, AW 1904, *The native tribes of south-east Australia*, London: Macmillan.

Keen, I 1994, *Knowledge and secrecy in an Aboriginal religion*, Oxford: Clarendon Press.

Mathews, RH 1897, 'The totemic divisions of Australian tribes', *Journal of the Royal Society of New South Wales, 31*, pp. 154–76.

Nash, D 1982, 'An etymological note on Warlpiri kurdungurlu', In J Heath, F Merlan & A Rumsey (eds), *Languages of kinship in Aboriginal Australia*, Oceania Linguistic Monographs No. 24, Sydney: University of Sydney, pp. 141–59.

Palmer, K 2007, Jurruru Native Title Application WC00/8 W6007/00, Anthropological Report. Unpublished.

Radcliffe-Brown, AR n.d., Field notes, University of Sydney Archives.

Radcliffe-Brown, AR 1931, *The social organization of Australian tribes*, The 'Oceania' Monographs, No. 1, Melbourne: Macmillan & Co. Limited.

Schebeck, B 2001, *Dialect and social groupings in northeast Arnheim [sic] Land*, Munich: Lincom Europa.

Shapiro, W 1981, *Miwuyt marriage: the cultural anthropology of affinity in northeast Arnhem Land*, Philadelphia: Institute for the Study of Human Issues.

Warner, WL 1958 [1937], *A black civilization: a social study of an Australian tribe*, New York: Harper & Brothers.

Webb, TT 1933, 'Tribal organization in eastern Arnhem Land', *Oceania*, 3, pp. 406–17. doi.org/10.1002/j.1834-4461.1933.tb01675.x.

Williams, NM 1986, *The Yolngu and their land: a system of land tenure and the fight for its recognition*, Canberra: Australian Institute of Aboriginal Studies.

Appendix 1: Radcliffe Brown's 1911 Field Data on Totemic Divisions in the Ashburton District

Divisions	Totems	Sections	Clans	Estates/Places	Lgs
Kadjadu	yungadji lizard		Yirdibura?		Tjuroro
Kadjadu [also:] Waleri? Yagarang	rain		Mangai?		Burduna
Kadjadu	pandura	Burong	Kalgalgara[1]		Tjuroro
Kadjadu	totems: — kobirt, galah; wanguru, bandicoot; bidjura, red ochre; tanbadji (?tarbadja) a tree (plum)	Kai-Bur	Mandari	Territory stretching from Mandarara on the Yannarie R. to Uaroo Station on Rouse Creek. Eastern part of country on beds of Ashburton Series low rocky hills and intervening flats. Western part in granite country. Includes Uaroo and country to west of Rouse Creek.	Talaindji
Kadjardu	rain		Ngalzaramai	NE of Wining?	
Kadjardu	djigura fish		Ma:rdawa:ra[2]		Tjuroro
Kadjardu	djigura fish		Ma:rdawa:ra?		Tjuroro
Kadjardu			Ngarbali		Tjuroro
Kadjardu	tjunguradji honey		Nyirawara?		Tjuroro
Kadjardu	yungadji lizard		Yirdibura		Tjuroro
Kadjardu	rain		Balurda	On Lyndon R?	Burduna
Kadjardu	bungundi (?bungurdi)		Bulara or Kabidjera		Burduna

7. PATRICLAN SUBSETS OF THE ASHBURTON RIVER DISTRICT IN WESTERN AUSTRALIA

Divisions	Totems	Sections	Clans	Estates/Places	Lgs
Kadjardu	bungundi (?bungurdi)		Kabidjera or Bulara		Burduna
Kadjardu	bilana rain		Mangali		Burduna
Kadjardu	kundjarga rain		Wundubaia	Extends from N. side of Minilya R. as far as Mugulu Hill + including Barnabarnong Hill to NW of Wandagu Stn.	Baiong
Kadjardu	bimara rainbow, kadjura a mythical snake, kulyu an edible root, paldjuwara sand (?) ?river sand, waniu wanyu a bush		Walzunmadi[3]		Maia
Kadjardu	bilana[4] rain		Kanmara	At Bibindji, rugged schistose hills with intervening flats; well grassed and with numerous creeks; Uaroo series of Ashburton beds includes Murabandala, Palir creek on road from Uaroo to Towera	Talaindji
Kadjardu	rain above		Tjundalya	Globe still on the Ashburton	Talaindji
Kadjardu	rain		Kunagari	Yannarie Station	Talaindji
Kadjardu	rain		Mandari		Talaindji
Kadjardu	rain		Mindigara	Near Mand's Landing	Talaindji
Kadjardu	rain		Nyagun		Binigura
Kadjardu	bungurdi		Tjalyali		Burduna
Kadjardu	kundjarga = rain		Birgalyiwadu	Level or slightly undulating country with occasional sand hills	Baiong

SKIN, KIN AND CLAN

Divisions	Totems	Sections	Clans	Estates/Places	Lgs
Kadjardu	madjun—turtle; ?winter rain ?Waleri warabidi, red ochre		Warura		Baiong
Kadjardu	rain		Bigalana		Noala
Kadjardu	bilana, rain		Wambun	Level grassy flats with a few sand hills; gum trees	Noala
kadjardu	bilana talu—rain totem		Mangala		Noala
Kadjardu	bilana, rain		Tjaualyaburu	Sand plain with slight sand-hills—of recent origin with corals and shells	Noala
Kadjardu	rain		Yuweri		Noala or Tal.
Kadjardu	bilana—rain		Mangala		Noala
Kadjardu	djigura[5]		Yirda	Talu at Kandang, at a stone near a pool. creek off \pl Ashburton R. below Kurara. Territory includes following pools on Ashburton R. above Hardey Junction—Mazanyi, Midjalmidjala, Yirda, Kandang or Kandangu. — this is in order passing upstream. [Next sentence crossed out:] Beyond Yibidji [\?Yilidji] the next pool is Wirdadji of another local horde which is said to [be] half Binigura half Tjuroro. In the Yirda territory there are also 2 clay-pans Djundalya to the west of the river and Kurara or Kurarda to the east. At Madandji there is a wanamangura (mythical snake). At Kandang is the totem centre of djigura. Ngulyaguru [male]; Wandjaring [male]? he makes ngurawari at Yrrgu.	Binigura

204

7. PATRICLAN SUBSETS OF THE ASHBURTON RIVER DISTRICT IN WESTERN AUSTRALIA

Divisions	Totems	Sections	Clans	Estates/Places	Lgs
Kadjardu	kobirt—galah; wan.guru—bandicoot; bidjura—red ochre; tarbadja—a bush (native plum)		Mandari	Rugged schistose hills and level flats with numerous creeks. Near Yannarie R. the country is of granite formation.	Talaindji
Kadjardu	rain		Mugulu		Burduna
Kadjardu	wandjoain—a bush? a snake? (sulky fellow.)		Wanarainy		Talaindji
Kadjardu	rain	Ban. Palj Marries Bungara, Binguda [local groups]	Wagula	At Bibindji[6] on Cameron's Station	Talaindji
Kadjardu	tintabi	Burong.	Mindangara[7]		Tjuroro
Kadjardu	bungurdi	Int. Amy. ?Walgubadu K.B.[8]	Walyidala	At Walgadazara on Duck Creek includes Nogunmara, Walzainmara, Bilarabuga, Walgadazara	Binigura
Kadjardu	bungurdi	K.B.	Walgubadu		Binigura
Kadjardu	totems rain, at Bibindji; tjintabi	Kai.Bur.	Maianu	At Bibindji; tjintabi; granite hills and grassy flats; Station, Mugeriara (dry country) Maianu; Bilyarbilyarjaga; Bidjura; Bolaru Bangaberi; Maianu; Nanyuthara Stn; Ngamaribila	Talaindji

Divisions	Totems	Sections	Clans	Estates/Places	Lgs
Kadjardu	rain	Kai-Bur.	Bibindji Midari	Small granite rocky hills and flats covered with grass and in places with gum trees. The edge of the coastal plain River running between high banks. Includes Yabangula, Mezering, Darduradji, Bibindji, Ngaralya, Midari. Djibara; Yabungala, Mezering (bilana talu), Darduradji, Bibindji (bilana talu), Daralya, Manadjimandera. Midari rock hole.	Talaindji
Kadjardu	bungurdi — kangaroo	KB	Pidiza	At junction of Henry R + Ashburton R. pools belonging to the group are Irawal, Wambu, Yidiri, Pidiza, Wagurang, Kalgany, Bindaning, Maludji; Irawal; Wambu, Pidiza; [side branch] Wagurang; [main branch] Kalgany; Bindaning; Maludji. Bungurdi talu at Ngurin-ngurin.	Binigura
Kadjardu?	Djigura [Bony Bream]; See Yirda		Kandang?		Binigura
Kadjardu?	rain?		Tubirdji [\? Tubindji]		Noala or Talaindji?
Kadjardu; [in pencil] ?Yirgu	djigura — fish	[in pencil] ngarawari K.B.	Kurara		Binigura
Kaiadu (Ngaiuri) [i.e. Kadjardu (Ngadjuri) M and F terms, same phratry, PS]	thurna — snake		Yulura		Thargari

7. PATRICLAN SUBSETS OF THE ASHBURTON RIVER DISTRICT IN WESTERN AUSTRALIA

Divisions	Totems	Sections	Clans	Estates/Places	Lgs
Mirdir	waila yam see Pindarar Wan.guda? Waleri padura		Wanguda?	On Wan.guda Creek evidently	Burduna
Mirdir?	waila – root		Ngogarbuga	Includes Yulmanidjang. S.W. of Bigali	Burduna
Mirdirba	kangkala		Tjandiyanu		Burduna
Mirdirba	kangalha[9] – root (?kangadha) ?is this really Wariera emu milawizi is Mirdir		Bigali		Burduna
Mirdirba	wailu or kangkala – root		Bugaianu		Burduna
Tambula	wiluru		Pa:da:ri		Tjuroro
Tambula	wiluru		Pa:da:ri?		Tjuroro
Tambula	pirbidjangura snake		Palga[10]		Tjuroro
Tambula	pirbidjangura snake		Palga?		Tjuroro
Tambula	warara		Warara		Tjuroro
Tambula	kalzandira		Wiriura		Tjuroro
Tambula	kalzandira		Wiriura?		Tjuroro
Tambula	punai snake	Kadjawain	Kulangaranu[11]	Kulangaranu is the talu place for punai. There is a tree near to the water-hole which is the head-spring of Budangana Creek.	Tjuroro
Tambulu	wagura crow [scribbled out;] male. tuogane, tagata		Nganyanamuga?		Burduna

SKIN, KIN AND CLAN

Divisions	Totems	Sections	Clans	Estates/Places	Lgs
Wairdji	wabargu—eaglehawk, maiu baby' kadjura—snake? Rainbow? yirabalu—cockatoo		Mo:iurgan		Baiong
Wairera	emu	B.P.	Wadura	On Henry R. between Pidiza and Mumurba (Baiangula)	Binigura?
Waleri	manbi pigeon		Yirigali?		Tjuroro
Waleri	manbi pigeon		Yirigali?		Tjuroro
Waleri	madanma euro, djidara lizard, mungurgura grub (found in sand and clay pans)		Bin.garba		Baiong
Waleri	kala		Yardi		Talaindji
Waleri			Panduzini	Nor N.E. of Wining. Tea-tree Flat—Big lake?	Talaindji
Waleri	kurai		Kuiarai		Burduna
Waleri	mangurgura—grub		Wining		Burduna
Waleri	djarbadi		Bungara?		Burduna
Waleri	pandjuna		Midandjing?		Burduna
Waleri	kala		Malianu	On Yannarie R. above Tjeani	Burduna
Waleri			Mirdalyu ?same as Mumurba		Burduna

7. PATRICLAN SUBSETS OF THE ASHBURTON RIVER DISTRICT IN WESTERN AUSTRALIA

Divisions	Totems	Sections	Clans	Estates/Places	Lgs
Waleri	djambali mirdir [div name?] manandhanu		Mangeri	On Lyndon R	Burduna
Waleri	malu—kangaroo, mogudi—snake; wadowuru—a small mamal ?lizard; mandari—a bush; walyadji—a small mammal (?mouse)		Kulgilya	Country was to S of Minilya R. including Wandadji Hill. Hard plain [—] for Wandadji Hill. Sand ground Abundance of plains kangaroo. Includes Kulgilya, Bulgurdu, Tulbadji, Karamada, Wan.gu, Kulgabulza (clay pan), Kardalgo.	Baiong
Waleri	?tan.gura—frog; ?tangura; minindja centipede kanba = spider		Badjera	Country of low flats flooded during rain	Baiong
Waleri	tjurogo. Varanus sp.		Maia-maia		Baiong
Waleri	kala—fire; djindalba—the sun; padura—bustard		Kwo:ialybadu		Baiong
Waleri	tjurogo, Varanus sp (?same as pandjuna)		Maia-maia		Baiong
Waleri	djidara = lizard		Kardabaia	N of Birgalyiwadu	Baiong
Waleri	kundjalga—a bush		Yalabaia	On coast N of Warura	Baiong
Waleri	yagarang—hot weather; malga—a lizard; ?padura—bustard		Mamurba	(Includes Baiangula); Baiangula horde on Henry River, includes 3 pools, Mamurba (?Mamarba) Baiangula and Mirni (called Minnie Spring) also a claypan Kanberidji or Pundiring and two creeks Madharing and Wan.guda. Mamurba is the totemic centre for yagarnag and ma:lga.	Burduna

SKIN, KIN AND CLAN

Divisions	Totems	Sections	Clans	Estates/Places	Lgs
Waleri	padura — bustard at Wan.guda?; ?yagarang (yanda)		Pindarara (Wan.guda?)	Includes Tjiari, Bindaining, Kuldjan, Ngurawaia, Wan.guda, Pindarara, Pindarangara. Wan.guda is totemic centre of padura.	Burduna
Waleri	kalbany — black opossum; tjudungadji — honey; ?bali — dingo		Mardangu	Kalbany totem centre is at Nanyutara Station. The country included Mardanga rockhole N of Ahburton, Ngadjungarina, Ko:iangulera [or Ko:iangulua?]	Binigura or Talaindji
Waleri	yagarang, ?padura	K.B.	Pididji		Burduna
Waleri	djarbadi	Kai-Bur	Bungarra		Talaindji
Waleri	pandjuna[12]	Kai-Bur	Binguda, Bingudu?		Talaindji
Waleri	manbi [bronze-winged pigeon]	Wurbulain (?section)	Bandima Widani	Widani, a round hill near the Yirigali Creek (Irregully Ck) is the totem centre for manbi	Tjuroro
Waleri manbi		Wurbulain	Yirigali[13]	On Irregully Creek; map of sites: Kulabu, Birikuru, Widani hill manbi talu; Bandima, Bundaringu, Banamita, yagarang is also the talu of this clan	Tjuroro
warara, yam see gen[ealogy]. of Kumbangara horde Kari.			?		Tenma
Warier	kadjalbo emu		Mugubalga		Tjuroro
Warier	kadjalbo emu		Mugubalga?		Tjuroro
Warier	yalibiri emu		Yalgazara		Maia?
Warier	kadjalbi		Nyingulu	Pt. Coates	Talaindji
Wariera	yalibiri emu		Bulazana		Maia

7. PATRICLAN SUBSETS OF THE ASHBURTON RIVER DISTRICT IN WESTERN AUSTRALIA

Divisions	Totems	Sections	Clans	Estates/Places	Lgs
Wariera	emu		Madariri	In De Pledge's country	Talaindji
Wariera	emu		Balidjangu		Binigura
Wariera	kadjalbo emu		Ngaragulhu (Ngaragulzu)	S or S.W. of Bigali	Burduna
Wariera	emu		Bigurgura	Near Nyanyeraddy Station	Burduna
Wariera	kadjalbo — emu		Pirganu	A creek running into Yannarie R. near Tijari Pool	Burduna
Wariera	yalibiri[14]		Wuruwaia	Talu on Lyons R. (near Minmi Creek?) Wuruwaia or Parar near Minmi Creek	Thargari
Wariera	ngalibiri — emu		Ngabariera	Grass flats flooded during rain.	Baiong
Wariera	emu	BP	Pidan	Miran is the totem centre	Binigura
Wariera	emu	see genealogy of Budjurding	Wirumanu	(Batthu — axe)	Talaindji
Wauadji	ngaurara? a sea bird		Kurdalguwadu	East of Yardi Creek	Talaindji
Wiardji	wabargu eaglehawk, yirabalu cockatoo		Wurd.		Baiong
Wiardji	warida		Waridawazara		Burduna
Wiardji	kulyiri		Nguridji?		Burduna
Wiardji	wabargu, eaglehawk; maiu, baby; kadjura, snake (?)		Mo:iurgan	Includes Nyindirbulu	Baiong
Wiardji	wabargu — eaglehawk; yirabalu — cockatoo (or kigili) also kobodju (child)?		Nyingulo:ra	Mand's Landing on coast	Baiong

Divisions	Totems	Sections	Clans	Estates/Places	Lgs
Wiardji	eaglehawk		Wirdinya		Noala
Wiardji	warida — eaglehawk	Ban. Pal.	Widindja		Noala or Talaindji
Wiardji	Kulyiri[15]	K.B.	Mardulu		Binigura
Wiardji	warida[16] — eaglehawk	K.B.	Bululu		Binigura
Wilyari	mulgarda, kala		Nyandu		Maia
Wilyaru	wirgura lizard, ngudjeri spirit, mundjederi, nanaradji mountain devil, tuni snake, nyabaru black ant		Tungari		Maia
Wilyaru	mauari, pandjuna, nyabara, ?kala fire; same as tungari + barubidi		Yiribadi		Maia
Wilyaru	waiuda opossum, maradjongo a small marsupial (opossum?), mardjuru a small mammal (lapostrophus?[17]		Djulaburu	Includes probably Djulaburu,[18] Kuro:ialing, Bugabugara, Kulirbandi, Midalia	Baiong
Wilyaru	wura dingo, tjalbira native cat (?), kundawa a bush		Manduzara		Maia
Wilyaru	totems: tjararu jackass, maradjong animal now extinct (?opossum)		Walgadawara		Maia
Wilyaru	kabalo — dingo wadjari baldjuwara		Minilya		Baiong

7. PATRICLAN SUBSETS OF THE ASHBURTON RIVER DISTRICT IN WESTERN AUSTRALIA

Divisions	Totems	Sections	Clans	Estates/Places	Lgs
Wilyaru	kabalo, dingo (or wura) wadjari; baldjuwara		Minilya	Country includes Muduguru—Buraguri (—Booreeoorilya), level sandy plains with good grass	Baiong
Wilyaru	bari—snake; yindidja, a sp. of marsupial. ?wallaby		Buraura	Country includes Buraura (Boorawoora) Coolkalyu and Yambetharra; country of level sandy plain and low sand hills	Baiong
Wilyaru (Ngolyi)	tjaruru, kalabulzara		Tindinygara		Maia
Yanadji (Nyalu)[19]	nganmari—snake sp.; pardjeda—a mammal; tiredu wild cat; wuzada a bush	Ban. Palj.	Nganyu or Bauarazalu	Barradali Pool of Yannarie R. Bauarazalu = Barradali, Nganyu—Nganyon, Barbandjang—Babbanjung; The talu is (at Bamama?) in the bush some distance E of Yannarie R. other totems tarduradji—fresh water turtle; djalgonung—a red grub; The country includes the following pools on the Yannarie River:—Bauarazalu (Barradali), Nganyu (Nganyon), Barbandjang (Babbajung)	Talaindji
Yargangu	yindidja, wallaby; tarabadja, a bush		Tjaminyu		Noala
Yargangu	yindidja—wallaby?; tarabadja—a bush		Tjaminyu		Noala
Yargangu	madjun—turtle		Windhu	At Mundunu; near Mardu [\? Mardij]. N.E. from Minderoo	Noala
Yargangu	ngurawari—fish; bali—dingo		Djibara		Noala
Yargangu	wongala		Mardi		Noala
Yargangu	wa:gura—crow; tuganu		Walzu	Level grassy flats with gum trees near the river [in blue, 'HI', circled]	Noala
Yargangu?	yagarang—hot weather		Baguraindji	Flat sandy country	Noala

SKIN, KIN AND CLAN

Divisions	Totems	Sections	Clans	Estates/Places	Lgs
Yauadji	ban.ga	Kari.Bur	Wirabara		Warienga
Yauadji[20]	dhodho,[21] dingo	Bur.Kari	Kaguara		Warienga
Yaui	bali dingo		Doyibadu?		Burduna
Yaui	bali—dingo		Kweal		Burduna
Yaui	mogudi[22]—snake		Kalyu		Burduna
Yawaji	wangana—duck? ?wagura—crow		Wilyambari		Thargari
Yirgu	kabardina		Yenigudi	?('belong sea')	Talaindji
Yirgu	bungurdi—kangaroo; djigura—fish; ngurawari—fish	Ban. Pal.	Wuramalu	Granite hills with intervening flats, often stony. River has several large permanent pools incl Ngamanda; The neighbourhood of Globe Hill Station [etc.; many place names omitted here]	Talaindji
Yirgu ?Kadjardu	bungurdi? (emu?) bungurdi?[23]	Ban. Palj.	Warida	East of Nan.gutara	Talaindji (?Binigura)
Yirgu. ?Kadjardu	ngurawari; see yirda.		Yaribidi or Yirgu[24]	talu at Yirgu?	Binigura
Yugu ?Kadjadu	bungundi kangaroo; bandura, magaran dagura badjarang; bandura—bandicoot	Kai-Bur.	Kurdaman	Ngalalangka (hill) talu for bungundi, magaran and dagura. Kundaman (clay-pan) talu for bandura and badjarang. includes claypans Kundaman, Mangalandi, Pindagara. Open flats and granite hills—abundance of kangaroos. includes the hills Walgadazara (Mt. Alexander) and Ngalalangka. granite country	Talaindji
Yungo	rain see gen. War.lx.	Ban.	?		Warunga? [cf. Warriyangga]

7. PATRICLAN SUBSETS OF THE ASHBURTON RIVER DISTRICT IN WESTERN AUSTRALIA

Divisions	Totems	Sections	Clans	Estates/Places	Lgs
—				~~Upstream of Hardey junction: Wirdadji (pool), beyond Yibidji [?Yiidji]~~ [strikethrough original]	~~Half Binigura half Tjurore~~
—	Totems same as Tungari ?same clan, ?totem kurianara a ?seed, ?totem pandjuna		Barubidi		
—	bilungu grub		Tala.		Maia?
—	rain		Kwinywadu		Maia, ?Ingarda
—			Baniazuni		Talaindji
—	ngurawari.?		Kalgalgara	At junction of Hardey – Ashburton	Binigura
—	kadjalbo – emu		Yuramari	On south of Robe River, near Warambu Flat	Noala
—	wongada	B.P.	Wongadamuga		Binigura
—	kadjalbo[25]	Ban.	?	See gen. of Waiamba horde	Targari
—	kurbili, plains kangaroo	Ban. Palj.	Kumbangara		Warienga
—	wandaikura, an edible grub See gen[ealogy] of Kaguara	Bur.	?		Warienga
—	moro, a root	Bur.	Yiridini		Warienga
—	walaindja, wallaby [rock wallaby]	Bur.	Maluwara		Warienga

Divisions	Totems	Sections	Clans	Estates/Places	Lgs
–	tungo (?) tintabi	Burong Kurgabidi [female] Burong. marr. Birgabidi (Tjuroro) Paljeri	?		Djiwali
–	kanma[26], a fish	Kari.	Puanbari		Warienga
–	ngalgu, a root; See gen of Waiamba.	Kari.	?		Warienga
–	kanma, a root; ?same as Puanbari	Kari.Bur	Waiamba		Warienga
–	walardu[27], eaglehawk; See gen of Wirbara horde	Palj.	?		Warienga
–	kurbili, kangaroo [plains kangaroo]	Palj.	Waribungara		Warienga
–	baba rain	Palj.Ban.	Tjiala?[28]	Baba at Tjiala tintabi – grass-seed; at Mindangura bigurda – euro; purnai or punai (?snake) at Kulugaranu	Tjuroro
?	kigili – cockatoo		Bangudja		Binigura
?	emu		Yirbira	Wamaguru [male] Yirbira Mangidi Bularu Kurdilya [these four names linked by a sloping line]	Binigura
?	bungurdi [punggurdi red kangaroo]		?Tjugurgu		Burduna

7. PATRICLAN SUBSETS OF THE ASHBURTON RIVER DISTRICT IN WESTERN AUSTRALIA

[1] This is the Kalgalgare of Palmer (2007): para 186 said to be at the Hardey River junction at a claimants' meeting in 2007.

[2] This is the Marduwara of Palmer (2007): para 186 and cited there as site 51 but on the claim map as site 62.

[3] The character transcribed /z/ here is probably /ʒ/ in the original, as in 'beige' /beyʒ/.

[4] Thalanyji = cloud, thunder (Austin 1992a, p. 22).

[5] Cf. Jiwarli = bony bream (Austin 1992f, p. 5).

[6] See also Kanmara group.

[7] This is the Minangara of Palmer (2007): para 186 and cited there as site 17 but shown on the claim map as site 68.

[8] K.B. = Kaimara-Burong or Karimera-Burung depending on language (see Radcliffe-Brown 1913, p. 159).

[9] Cf. Payungu = wild potato (Austin 1992b, p. 7).

[10] Probably the Palga of Palmer (2007): para 186 where it is given as site 24 and also the Balga(na) of the claim map where it is given as site 2.

[11] This is the Kulangaranu of Palmer (2007): para 186 said to be on the Hardey River upstream from Jila at a claimants' meeting in 2007.

[12] Thalanyji = racehorse goanna (Austin 1992a, p. 21).

[13] This is the Yirigali of Palmer (2007): para 186 in the area of the Irregully Creek of the maps. Not on claim map.

[14] Cf. Yinggarda = emu (Austin 1992d, p. 44).

[15] Cf. = budgerigar, shell parrot in Thalanyji (Austin 1992a, p. 8).

[16] Cf. = wedge-tailed eagle in Thalanyji (Austin 1992a, p. 30).

[17] is on Google but rare; mostly what comes up is — the banded hare-wallaby restricted (in the past) to offshore island Bernier and Dorre.

[18] Same as clan name; may be focal site in that estate.

[19] These are probably the equivalents of Bates's (1913, p. 394) phratry terms 'Yaui' (misprint for Yani?) and 'Nyarlu' (male and female).

[20] Cf. 'yaui', a male totem phratry name (Bates 1913, p. 394).

[21] Warriyangga = dog (Austin 1992e, p. 22).

[22] Cf. = type of snake in Payungu (Austin 1992b, p. 3020).

[23] Thalanyji = red kangaroo (Austin 1992a, p. 24).

[24] I think Yirgu is a phratry term, PS.

[25] Thargari = emu (Austin 1992c, p. 4).

[26] = fish (generic) in Warriyangga (Austin 1992e, p. 4).

[27] = eaglehawk in Warriyangga (Austin 1992e, p. 24).

[28] Probably the name R-B also wrote as Ciala in his genealogies and which is rendered Jila (site 69) in Palmer (2007): para 186 and Jirla (site 57) on the claim map.

8

The Birds and the Bees: The Origins of Sections in Queensland

Patrick McConvell

Introduction

The 'section' type of social categorisation is only found in Indigenous Australia, with one exception in South America that will be discussed briefly in this chapter. The sections are a system of four named divisions in which members of each section have a particular kinship relation to each other section. Corresponding pairs of sections have a relationship of marriage alliance with each other. In the older literature, sections are called 'classes', 'sub-classes' or 'marriage classes'. The section 'How Sections Work' provides a sketch of the functioning of this system; however, the main aim of the chapter is to attempt to ascertain the origins of the section system.

This task begins in the section 'Subsections Arose from Sections' in which the history of the subsection system is analysed. Subsections are only located in the central north of Australia, spread out from an area near the town of Katherine in the Northern Territory. Since subsection systems arose more recently from section systems, their history is more transparent and provides a starting point from which to track the origin of sections. The section 'The Distribution of Section Systems in Australia' describes the geographical distribution of sections that are found surrounding the area of subsections on all sides, in small pockets to the north and south and in very large areas to the east and west. The reason for this pattern is that during their distribution, subsections either diffused to replace previously existing section systems or other forms of social categories. A general idea of the number and location of different section terminologies is also provided.

The section 'Section Systems in Queensland' moves on to our main focus: the section systems in Queensland. There is reason to believe that Queensland may be the area of origin of section systems in Australia more generally, which forms part of the hypothesis being explored. A number of hypotheses have been proposed in regard to how section systems could have originated (including my own hypothesis) and these hypotheses are briefly mentioned. The subsections 'Hypotheses That Sections Arose from the Combination of Different Types of Moiety', 'Hypothesis That Sections Arose from the Combination of the Same Kind of Moiety or Phratry' and 'Sections in the Mapoon Area, North-Western Cape York' propose a new hypothesis that sections arose from the merging of two groups with moieties or phratries of the same lineality (patrilineal in the cases considered here) and the institution of a circulating connubium between them. Once regularised, this type of marriage exchange yielded a section system. Examples of the outcome of such processes are provided for northern Queensland.

In the section 'The Queensland General Section System', the example of a very widespread section system—the 'Queensland General' system contiguous to the other coastal systems discussed in the section 'Section Systems in Queensland'—illustrates how linguistic evidence of form of terms can be crucial in tracing the origin and diffusion of such systems, especially in a case such as this in which the processes are relatively more recent. Of course, it is not possible to trace the development of all section systems in Queensland within the confines of this chapter; however, by addressing one section system in detail—one that was still spreading in the twentieth century—we furnish a preview of how a more complete history can be provided by linking back to the earliest origins of sections.

The section 'Broader Perspectives' looks briefly at these findings from the broader perspectives of: 1) other features in Queensland—language phylogenies and moiety systems; 2) estimates of the age of the Queensland section systems and possible correlates in the archaeological record;

3) preliminary work that David Fleck and I conducted on the section systems among Panoan-speaking groups in South America, and its relevance to the Queensland case; and (4) how these findings may or may not fit in with speculative accounts of 'early human kinship' featuring section-like structures, such as by Nicholas Allen in his tetradic theory. The section 'Conclusions' offers a summary, conclusions and recommendations for further research.

How Sections Work

In a group that has sections, everyone has a section by virtue of being born to parents who have different sections from the child. One's father has a different section from oneself, and so does one's mother. The fourth section is that of one's spouse or potential spouse, and includes one's first cross-cousins. Not only are these basic kin types but all relations also fit into this scheme on the basis of familiar extension rules. For instance, 'father's father' and 'mother's mother' belong to the same section as ego. This illustrates that sections cycle back in every alternate generation—a key property of the system.

If the marriage of the parents is of the first preferred, or 'straight' type, then there will be no question about the assignment of a section term to the children. However, if the marriage is not of this type, then assignment based on the father will be different from that based on the mother. Various principles and strategies are deployed in different groups to settle this question.

The function of sections in determining correct marriage partners has already been mentioned. However, the functions are much broader than this: with a section name, one can be fitted into families of apparent strangers and call them by kinship terms without necessarily knowing their genealogical connections to oneself, or indeed even having any. Thus, many non-Aboriginal and Aboriginal people from areas without sections or subsections can be assigned 'skin' names by Aboriginal people and be incorporated in this way. Thus, the section and subsection systems contribute to broadening the scope of 'universal kinship classification' (Barnard 1978), whereby everyone can call everyone else by a kinship term.

The scope of the section or subsection systems does not terminate when different terms are used. Users of the system are usually entirely familiar with the 'pragmatic equivalence' rules between different terminologies over a wide area (McConvell & McConvell 2015). Therefore, the ambit of the section system is much wider than a single 'society' or language group and operates in a highly extended intercommunal space.

Subsections Arose from Sections

Subsections, or 'skins' as they are colloquially known (for the history of this term, see Chapter 9), are still commonly used across a wide area of the Northern Territory and parts of Western Australia and Queensland. In contrast to sections with four divisions, subsections have eight divisions, based on similar principles to those of sections but with each section divided into two subsections. For instance, while 'father's father' and 'mother's mother' fall into the same section in a section system, they fall into two separate subsections in a subsection system.

The subsection system of the Warlpiri terminology in the Tanami Desert of the Northern Territory is illustrated in Table 26.

Table 26: Warlpiri subsections.

Code	Terms		Code	
A1m A1f	Japanangka Napanangka	Marry	B1m B1f	Jupurrurla Napurrurla
A2m A2f	Jungarrayi Nungarrayi	Marry	B2m B2f	Jangala Nangala
C1m C1f	Jakamarra Nakamarra	Marry	D1m D1f	Japaljarri Napaljarri
C2m C2f	Jampijinpa Nampijinpa	Marry	D2m D2f	Japangardi Napangardi

Source: Author's work.

Further insight into the process that created subsections came from studying the linguistic forms in subsections in comparison to sections (McConvell 1985, 1997). The following was found:

1. The roots in four of (half of) the subsections on the western side of their distribution came from the western section terms—for instance, they were found in the Pilbara.

2. The roots in the other four of (half of) the subsections on the western side of their distribution came from the northern section terms, in an area south of Darwin.

This immediately suggests that the new subsection system arose from a merger of two previous section systems that came from different directions. Further, the two component sets, from the west and north, have a regular relationship to each other. Table 27 shows that the Kariera system, as represented by Radcliffe-Brown (1931), uses the same A–D system as for subsections. Table 28 shows the Warray system of the north, as recorded by Spencer (1914, pp. 53–4). Spelling has been adjusted to modern standards.

Bearing in mind that subsection terms have acquired masculine and feminine prefixes *ja-* and *na-* respectively in their early history (see McConvell 1985), A and C in Kariera are clearly related to subsections A1 and C1 respectively in Warlpiri (and many other systems), and C and D in Warray are clearly related to C2 and D2 in the Warlpiri (and other) subsection systems (note: Warray terms have the normal masculine and feminine prefixes *a-* and *al-* respectively in that language). Terms in other variants of western sections are related to variants of subsection systems; however, brevity does not permit an account of this, nor of McConvell's (1985, 1997) hypothesis about the marriage system that led to the origin of the subsection system.

Table 27: Kariera sections.

Code	Terms		Code	
A	Panaka	Marry	B	Purung
	Mother/child of			Mother/child of
C	Karimarra	Marry	D	Milangka

Source: Radcliffe-Brown (1913, 1931).

Table 28: Warray sections.

Code	Terms		Code	
Am Af	Awinmij Alinmij	Marry	Bm Bf	apularan alpularan
	Mother/child of			Mother/child of
Cm Cf	Ajampij Aljampij	Marry	Dm Df	apangarti alpangarti

Source: Harvey (1986) and Spencer (1914).

The idea that subsections arose from sections is not new. Davidson (1928, pp. 93–4) proposed that:

> The eight-class system represents a development out of the four-class organization.

The linguistic evidence mentioned above is new and conclusive. Those who proposed scenarios for subsection origins have invariably suggested a split in sections internally (e.g. von Brandenstein 1982); however, the linguistic evidence points to the correctness of the merger of two systems through a particular type of marriage exchange.

Davidson (1928, pp. 93–4) went on to say:

> The four classes [sections] have resulted from the foundation of the dual grouping [moieties].

This hypothesis is explored in the next sections.

The Distribution of Section Systems in Australia

Systems of four sections are found across a large part of Australia. We begin in north Queensland—the area of most divergence between the terms in the systems—and work south and west to where the blocks of related terminology are generally larger. The numbered categories indicate terminologies in which the terms are generally linguistically related to each other within the category; the terms are generally not linguistically related between categories.

1. South-western Cape York Peninsula (SWCYP)
2. Central Cape York Peninsula (CCYP)
3. South-eastern Cape York Peninsula (SECYP)
4. Western Queensland (Kalkatungu and Mayi languages) (WQ)
5. Western Kukatj (WK)[1]
6. North-east Queensland (NEQ)[2]

---

[1] McConvell (1985, pp. 14, 23) suggested that these section terms were drawn from the neighbouring subsection terminology.
[2] This set of terms overlaps that of QG in some cases. See the section 'Section Systems in Queensland'.

7. Queensland General (QG)
8. East central Queensland (ECQ)
9. South-east Queensland (SEQ)
10. North-east New South Wales (NENSW)
11. New South Wales General (NSWG)
12. Western (W) (a: WA from Pilbara west, b: eastern branch—E. Arandic; Yarruwinga has C and D terms related to E. Arandic, but A and B are distinct—possibly related to western Queensland terms)
13. North-central (NC) (Warray and Uwinymirr, south of Darwin).

The areas covered by these section sets are shown on Figure 24 and some of the Queensland terminologies will be discussed later in this chapter.

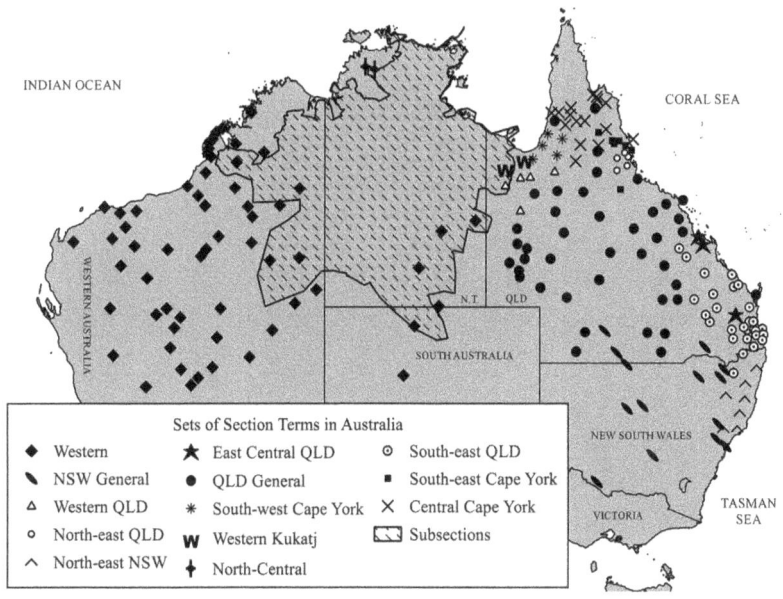

Figure 24: Sets of section terms in Australia.
Source: Prepared by William McConvell from the AustKin database.

I have avoided the use of the term 'cognate' for related terms, as this would imply that the terms descend from a common protolanguage by inheritance. It is fairly clear that many—probably most—section and subsection terms have spread by diffusion as loan words rather than by inheritance. There is a correlation between some of the sets of terms and Pama-Nyungan subgroups, such as between QG and Maric, and south-east Queensland and Waka-Kabic. However, there are problems in assuming that it is inheritance that is the motor of spread rather than diffusion in these cases. First, while the subgroups named have had some historical linguistic work done on them, the work has not been conclusively validated. Second, even if there is isomorphism between the terms in a set and the subgroups, it could still be that the terms are diffused; thus, further investigation of the cognate/loan word status of the terms is needed. This will be further discussed in relation to the QG section system and Maric in particular.

The asymmetry between the east and west in regard to the quantity of divergent section systems has been noted before. Davidson (1928, p. 120) wrote:

> For the entire area of central and western Australia, there are but three different sets of class [section] names ... these occupy a region approximately twice the size of the other twelve. Certainly we may conclude that in the western region the diffusion was comparatively rapid.[3]

Davidson's Map 9 (1928, p. 120; see Figure 7 in Chapter 3) also shows a comparatively higher concentration of different section sets to the east of north Queensland. According to Davidson's geographical distribution theory, this implies that sections were older and diffused more slowly in this area. I now focus specifically on Queensland to ascertain if there is any other evidence that points to the origin and early development of sections in this region.

Section Systems in Queensland

Tracing Connections between Diverse Systems

In the list of sections sets, 1 to 9 are located in Queensland, with 10 and 11 slightly overlapping into Queensland from New South Wales to the south. While most of these will be mentioned in passing, most attention will be paid to sets 6 to 9 in this chapter.

Some of these sets do have some admixture of terms from neighbouring systems, but they are generally self-contained and do not exhibit any clear relationship with other sets in regard to the form of terms. This is

---

3   Davidson's mapping was based on earlier data but the overall picture is substantially correct. The east–west asymmetry is actually even more pronounced, since the central and western terminologies are related rather than separate.

in contrast to subsections in which there are many similarities in forms between different systems. Such a divergence among the section systems suggests that the sections are substantially older than subsections—which we already know, since subsections arose from sections. The diversity of the terminology is greater in the north of Queensland compared with the centre and south, which perhaps suggests a northern origin. However, this is not a foregone conclusion; for instance, McConnel (1939) suggested that at least one of the Cape York Peninsula systems diffused from further south.

The forms of the section terms are generally completely different in the different sets, making the discovery of common original forms an impossible task.[4] However, what is more promising is the idea that there may be a common semantic element in the etymologies of some terms, which can tell us about their origin and diffusion. Non-section meanings are sometimes, but not always (or at least not reliably), reported for sections, and moiety names are nearly always associated with a totemic animal (or more rarely, other natural phenomena). The possibility of section terms being derived from moiety names will be examined next. Evidence shows that some moiety names have the same or similar etymologies—for instance, from bird and bee species, even though they are different in form. It could then be posited that similar meanings of these social category terms diffused between areas, even though the forms of the names of the species are different.

This research into section term origin and diffusion is at the early stages, but there is enough to draw on to begin building hypotheses. I pursue the idea that sections emerged from the interaction of two moiety systems of the same kind in a specific kind of marriage exchange; however, we first need to examine a more popular idea regarding their origin—that sections arose from the interaction of moieties of different kinds.

Hypotheses That Sections Arose from the Combination of Different Types of Moiety

The most common hypothesis about the origin of sections is probably that they arose from the combination of different types of moiety. Three possibilities exist that could all structurally yield a section system:

---

4   There are close similarities between one or two terms in the western Queensland set and the subsections and Arandic sections to the west that suggest a common element, particularly in regard to the term *kangila*.

- patrimoieties and matrimoieties
- patrimoieties and generational moieties
- matrimoieties and generational moieties.

In Queensland, overtly named generational moieties are not known; however, there is an alternative generation equivalence in the kinship systems. The most promising as a combination that could structurally yield a section system is that of the patrimoieties and matrimoieties, as both are known in Queensland, with some areas of close contact or overlap. These are shown in Figure 25.

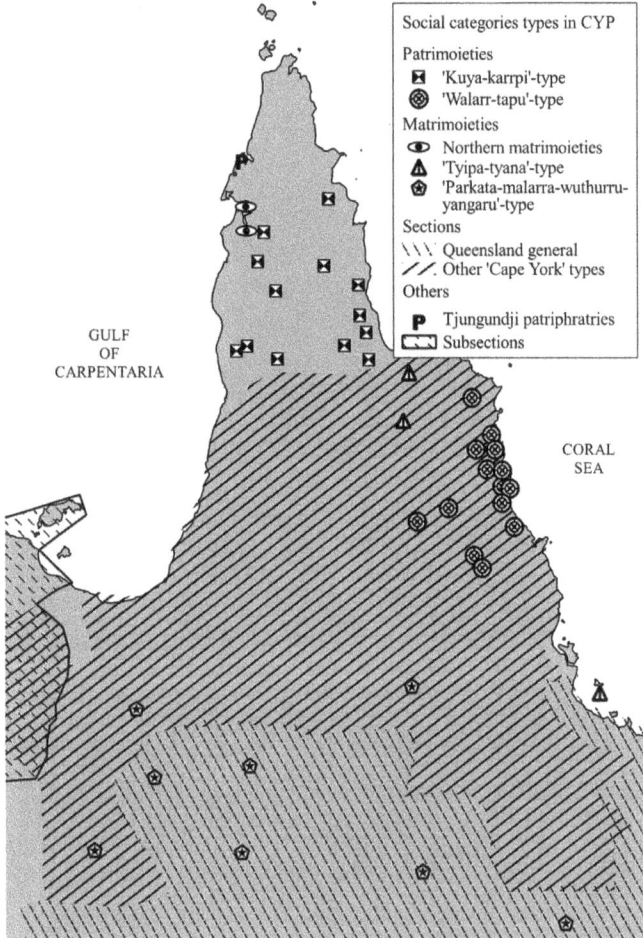

Figure 25: Social category types in Cape York Peninsula.
Source: Prepared by William McConvell from the AustKin database, and information collected from various sources by Patrick McConvell.

These areas would be good candidates for the origin of sections if the hypothesis of section origin from a combination of patrimoieties and matrimoieties was valid. However, there is no clear evidence of the combination of patrimoiety (or patriphratry) terms with matrimoiety terms to form a section system:

1. In the north of Cape York, there are reported areas of matrimoieties in close proximity to named patriphratries (McConnel 1939; Sharp 1939, p. 265). However, there are no known section systems this far north—the most northerly extent of sections is far south of this area.

2. In the north-eastern Cape York, there is an area of patrimoieties with the names of two contrasting bee species, *kuya* and *karrpi*, with a small area of matrimoieties, *tyipa* and *tyana*, just to the south. These areas are adjacent to a region of sections to the west across the Cape York Peninsula; however, there is no telltale evidence of the combination of patrimoiety and matrimoiety terms. One of the closest section systems is that of the south-east Cape York Peninsula (Mbabaram, Dixon 1991; and Djangun, Sharp 1939), which is shown in Table 29. In this instance, one possible term with external relations is D *Karpandji*, which is similar to the regional bee patrimoiety term *karrpi* (*-ntyi* appears to be a suffix in all the terms except B *Worpu*). This connection is considered later in exploring section origin as the meeting up of two patrimoiety systems. *Worpu* (*wurrpu*) is also a bee term in the region and is probably a later importation in north-western groups, replacing the term *Tyilantyi*/*Kilantyi*, cited by Sharp (1939) and Mathews (1899), for more south-eastern groups.[5] D *Kupa-* may be related to the D section (*Kuparu*/*Kupuru*) of the QG system (see section 'The Queensland General Section System').

---

5   For instance, 'hornet, bumblebee' as in Kuku-Yalanji (Herschberger & Herschberger 1986); a related term *wurripa* 'native bee (sugar bag bee) (bigger than watyan, with a beard)' (Tsunoda 2003, p. 115). *Watyan* (Tsunoda 2003, p. 102) is 'smaller than *wurripa* and *kurtya*'. In the closely related language Gugu-Badhun (Sutton 1973, p. 186), there are also three terms for native bee species: *wurripa*, *wathan* and *kurtya*. *Kurtya* is a term related to *kutya* and *kuya*, with a wide distribution in Queensland (see the subsection 'Hypothesis That Sections Arose from the Combination of the Same Kind of Moiety or Phratry'). This suggests that there may be three relevant species in the region; however, there may be factors entering into the emic classification that are not aligned with scientific species such as habitat and nest-type. The fact that there appears to be an alternation between initial *k-* and *ty-* in the older form for this section *kilantyi*/*tyilantyi* reflects a wider sound correspondence in the rainforest and some Maric languages (see the section 'The Queensland General Section System'). If the earlier form is *kila+*, it may be related to the section/subsection root *kangila*/*kela* further west.

3. The same matrimoieties mentioned in (2) are also in contact with another region of patrimoieties to the south named after the two bees, but with different names—*walar* and *dabu*. Again, there is no apparent connection between the matrimoiety terms and the adjacent section terms.

4. South of Cape York Peninsula, on the east coast, there is a further occurrence of the two bees patrimoieties with terms undoubtedly related to those in (2)—*kuya* and *karilba*. There is another widespread matrimoiety system to the west with the terms *wuthurru* and *yangurru* (with no known species translations thus far[6]). There is a gap between the patrimoiety area and the matrimoieties in this case, so it is not surprising that there is no interaction or combination of these systems. However, one of these matrimoiety terms (*wuthurru/wutyurru*) is also a section term around the Queensland rainforest region (north-east Queensland), which will be further investigated in this chapter.

Table 29: South-east Cape York Peninsula sections.

a. Wakura, Tjankun, Waniura, (Um)babaram (Sharp 1939)			
A Kupandji	B Worpu	C Djilandji	D Karpandji
b. Mutju, Ngaikungo, Tjirbal, Mamu, Ngatjan (Sharp 1939)			
A Kupandji	B Djikandji	C Djilandji	D Karpandji
c. Warkeeman (Wakiman) includes Booberam (Mbabaram[1]), Shanganburra (Jangun), Kookoowarra, Mularitchee, Chungki and Koochulburra (Mathews 1899)			
A Koopungie	B Cheekungie	C Kellungie	D Karpungie

[1] Dixon (1991) referred to Mathews on Mbabaram but does not list any section terms in the vocabulary.
Source: Mathews (1899, p. 251) and Sharp (1939, p. 442).

The themes of some of these moiety names, such as the contrasting bees, are considered in the next section.

---

6   *Wuthurru / wutyurru* has been reported as having the meaning 'eagle hawk' in the Warrungu dictionary (Tsunoda 2003, p. 112), but the rest of the entry casts doubt on this. Here, as is commonly found, consultants may give the leading totemic animals when glossing a social category, or the relevant social category when glossing an animal. See also the mention of this term as a matrimoiety in Queensland in Chapter 6.

Hypothesis That Sections Arose from the Combination of the Same Kind of Moiety or Phratry

The origin of subsections has taught us that a new and more complex structure does not necessarily eventuate through a combination of different systems—logical as that may seem in the abstract world of theory. A leap to a new level of complexity can occur because the same or similar kinds of social grouping in a region enter into an interaction that produces the new system. In the case of two systems with sections, the interactions that led to subsections were a kind of regular marital exchange between different groups that originally possessed sections with different terminologies. This hypothesis is based on evidence of the structural positions of the old section terms of the two component groups within the new subsection system.

There is evidence—not as strong as that in the case of subsection origin—that at least some of the major section systems in Queensland arose from a similar combination of two systems of the same kind: patriphratries and patrimoieties. The two systems did not join in an abstract way but through a connubium or regular marriage exchange between two groups who were neighbours. Mathew (1910a; 1910b, p. 140) also suggested that 'the multiplication of classes from two [moieties] to four [sections], and four to eight [subsections] was due to an amalgamation of tribes'.[7]

In regard to subsection origin, it is clear that such a marital exchange and system transformation did not occur in every instance when two groups met up. For subsections specifically, it probably occurred only once—or at most, a handful of times involving mutual influence—in a restricted area west and east of Katherine in the Northern Territory, and diffused from there. In cases in which section systems with different terminologies met up across Australia, nothing as momentous occurred; rather, the neighbouring groups simply arrived at a 'pragmatic equivalence' of section terms and practised a system of the old kind between them, although with intertranslatable terms.

---

7   Mathew's idea of tribal amalgamation lacks evidence, although it is couched in terms of his hypothesis that people resembling 'Dravidians' and 'Veddahs' migrated into north-east Queensland, spread south and 'absorbed the inferior autochthones'. The idea is far-fetched, and even Mathew (1910b, p. 140) was doubtful about it as a hypothesis of section origin. Recent genetic research (Pugach et al. 2013) has bestowed some slight credibility on such ideas of South Indian migration into Australia in the mid-Holocene.

It appears likely that a similar scenario played out in the origin of sections. In most cases whereby moiety and/or phratry systems were in contact, they established pragmatic equivalence (if they were of the same kind—matrilineal or patrilineal). However, in some instances, the regular marriage exchange produced a new system: the section system. At this stage, we cannot be sure if this occurred once in one region, as is proposed for the subsection origin. We examine a region where perhaps a number of such section origins might have occurred. Similar conditions might have provoked the same kind of process in several places. However, it seems most likely that this single or multiple origin of sections took place in Queensland.

One particular idea in respect to the origin of sections that had currency in the late nineteenth century was that they might have arisen from some kind of local descent grouping, such as a clan or phratry (group of clans). This is somewhat similar to, or could be viewed as virtually the same as, the hypothesis that they arose from two neighbouring groups in contact, as in the cases to be considered on the east coast of Queensland. Since sections are not local (tied to places or areas) or co-residential like patriclans or patriphratries, it is hard to imagine how one could have arisen from the other. However, there are possible pathways in Australia that could be investigated, as well as in the Panoan region of South America.

I review the patrimoiety system terminologies of north-east Queensland in the next sub-subsection. In most instances, the moieties were named after species of bees or species of large birds (usually eagles). I move on to a case in sub-subsection 'Roth and Howitt on the Annan River Tribe', in which a section system apparently emerged from the coming together of two such systems in neighbouring groups in an area north of Cairns, as reported by Roth (1904) and Howitt (1904) at the turn of the twentieth century. Another similar process may have also occurred on the Queensland coast, farther south near Mackay, which is also described. In the subsection 'Sections in the Mapoon Area, North-Western Cape York', another possible example of an emergence of sections or section-like groupings on the north-west coast of Cape York Peninsula near Mapoon is analysed.

The Eagles and Bees Patrimoieties in North-East Queensland

In order to understand the origin of sections in this region, it is necessary to understand the patrimoiety systems that preceded sections and the contrasting natural species that provided their names. There are a number of groups with patrimoieties named after a pair of contrasting bee species.

In the north-east Cape York Peninsula, the forms are *Kuya-* and *Karrpa-*.

The form *karrpa-* is replaced by *kapa-* in languages further south, such as the widespread Maric subgroup and neighbouring languages. Terms beginning with *kapa-* are also very widespread in the remainder of coastal Queensland as terms for a honey bee species and a matrimoiety instead of a patrimoiety.[8]

The term *kuya* also has variants *kutya* and *kurtya*, which are probably the older forms before the loss of *r* and lenition *$ty > y$. In some languages, either *karrpa-/kapa-* or *kurrtya-/kutya-/kuya-* are glossed as a native bee in general, rather than a species. However, in some of these cases, this could be a question of the most abundant species in the region providing the generic hypernym (McConvell 2002). In many languages, these two terms name separate species of bee.[9]

For instance, based on fieldwork around Brisbane and on Stradbroke Island, Hockings (1884) identified a form *kaapay* (which he spelled 'karbi') as *Trigona carbonaria*, a small black bee that is now known as *Tetragonula carbonaria*. This form is undoubtedly related to the northern form for the same bee *karrp+* and many other central and southern Queensland forms *kapa+*. This bee was named *T. hockingsi*; however, recent research has failed to find distinctive differences between *T. hockingsi* and *T. carbonaria*. Dollin et al. (1997) noted that 'there is no distinct difference between *T. carbonaria* and *T. hockingsi* in coloration, pilosity or structure'—although there are differences in brood structure.

---

8   Barrett (2005, Appendix E64) reconstructed **kapa* as Proto-Maric 'honey, bee' and this may well be an inheritance, although the possibility of internal diffusion within Maric should not be ruled out. Laffan (2003, p. 105) reconstructed **kapay* 'honey, honey-bee' for Proto-Waka-Kabic and **kapa* for the subgroup Waka.
9   *Kurrtyala/kurrtyala/kuyala* (and possibly the QG section term *kurrkila*) are also associated with (kinds of) eagle, but these seem to be unrelated despite their similarity. See the next section.

The other slightly larger bee with yellowish markings, Hockings was told, was known as *kutya* around Brisbane (which he spelled 'kootchar'). From Hockings's (1884, p. 153) description of the external tube entrance to the nest, this bee was identified in later research as the *Austroplebeia australis*. This form descends from Proto-Wakka-Kabic *kutya 'honey' (Laffan 2003, p. 124) and is related to *kurtya*, *kutya* and *kuya* in northern Queensland.[10]

T. carbonaria and *A. australis* are the two species that name the opposite moieties in northern Queensland. *T. carbonaria* is predominantly found in the inland and *A. australis* is found in the coastal areas (Halcroft et al. 2013; Hockings 1884, p. 153; see Figure 25).

In south-east Cape York Peninsula, the patrimoieties are commonly *Walarr*: *Tapu*. These names are also contrasting bee species. In Kuku Yalanji, *tapu* is a 'small dark bee, nests in trees' (Herschberger & Herschberger 1986), which is probably *T. carbonaria*, and *walarr* is another bee species—perhaps *A. australis*. These bee names form part of the social category system of the neighbouring group speaking a dialect very similar to Kuku-Yalanji—Kuku-Nyungkul—called the 'Annan River Tribe' by Roth (1904) and Howitt (1904).

Roth and Howitt on the Annan River Tribe

While not claiming to have discovered the origin of sections, Howitt (1904) did make some relevant points about the section system among what he calls the 'Annan River Tribe', better known as Kuku Nyungkul, a close affiliate of the Kuku-Yalanji in the Daintree Forest area of south-east Cape York Peninsula. Basic information was supplied to him by Roth (1904). Howitt omitted an important point made by Roth in that the group spoke 'a mixture of Koko-Yerlantchi [Gugu Yalanji, on the south side] and Koko-yimidir [Guugu Yimidhirr, on the north side]'—I return to this point later. Figure 26 is a map of the location of Kuku Yalanji and Guugu Yimidhirr.[11]

---

10 The referent species is likely to be *Austroplebeia australis*.
11 Haviland (1979, p. 29) also recorded that the Annan River people spoke an 'intermediate dialect' with features of both Guugu Yimidhirr and Gugu Yalanji, which was regarded with disdain by more central speakers of these languages; it was called Gugu Buyun 'bad language' in Yalanji and Guugu Yiirrurru 'mumbling talk' in Yimidhirr.

8. THE BIRDS AND THE BEES

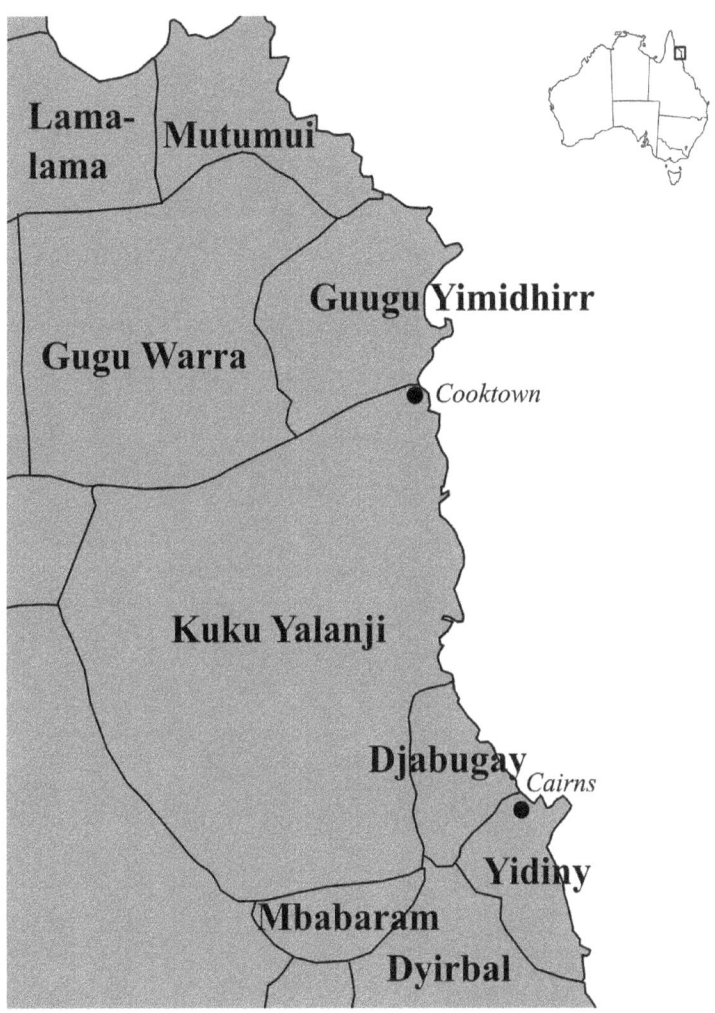

Figure 26: Map of the location of Kuku Yalanji and Guugu Yimidhirr.
Source: Adapted from austkin.net.

Howitt (1904, p. 118) gave the patrimoiety and section terms shown in Table 30. I have added the origin in the two neighbouring languages, Gugu Yimidhirr (GY) in the north and Kuku Yalanji (KY) in the south, which aligns in language provenance with the moiety species names. This is discussed further in the following sections.

Table 30: Annan River moieties and sections.

Patrimoieties		Sections	
Murla a bee	GY	Jorro a bee	GY
		Kutchal saltwater eaglehawk	Not KY
Walar a bee	KY	Walar a bee	KY
		Wandi eaglehawk	KY

Source: Adapted from Howitt (1904).

Roth (1904) stated that the *Walar* bee was identical to the *du-ar* bee of the 'Bloomfield blacks' (KY), and *Murla*, a different species, was the same as the *tabu* (elsewhere spelled *dabu*) of the Bloomfield (KY) and the *jorro* of the McIver River (GY). Roth provided pragmatic equivalences with the QG section system, as is illustrated in Table 31.

Table 31: Pragmatic equivalence of Annan River and Queensland General sections according to Roth and Howitt.[12]

Annan River	Queensland General Sections
Walar	Wungko [Wunku]
Wandi	Kurkilla [Kurrkila]
Jorro	Kupuru [Kuparu]
Kutchal	Banbari [Panpari]

Source: Based on Howitt (1904, p. 140) and Roth (1904).

This set of equivalences implies the following marriage and descent relationships among the Annan River sections (see Table 32) based on the QG system (see Table 33). The arrangement in the tables is not the familiar one used by Radcliffe-Brown (1931) in which the columns are covert matrimoieties AC and BD. Rather C and D have been permuted, so that the columns are the patrimoieties AD and BC (the *Murla* or *Jorro* bee and the *Walar* bee respectively). This change has been made to accommodate the importance of the patrimoieties in the area of north Queensland under discussion here.[13]

---

12 Sharp (1938–9, p. 268) reported: 'Koko Yerlandji (Kuku Yalanji) informants disclaimed a four section system, although Roth (1910, p. 100) ascribes to them an organization of that type; however, since my informants were southern members of the tribe, it is possible that the northern Koko Yerlandji, with whom Roth came in contact, do have sections similar to those of their neighbours to the west and north'.

13 It is worth noting that the C section of QGS has an etymology that may link it to an eagle species, mirroring the species alignment of Annan River C, although not the form.

Table 32: Annan River sections.

Code	Terms		Code	
A	Kutchal (Kurrityal) eagle sp.	Marry	B	Walar bee sp.
	father/child of			father/child of
D	Jorro (Dhurru) bee sp.	Marry	C	Wandi eagle sp.

Source: Based on Roth (1904) and Howitt (1904).

Table 33: Queensland General section terminology.

Code	Terms		Code	
A	Panpari	Marry	B	Wunku
	mother/child of			mother/child of
D	Kuparu	Marry	C	Kurrkila

Source: Author's work.

The covert matrimoieties in the Annan River system (A–C and B–D) align with eagles and bees respectively. The patrimoieties, which are the overt type of moiety in the north-east Queensland region, have an arrangement in which each moiety has a bee species for one section and an eagle species for the other. The patrimoiety names in the region are generally contrasting types of bees, or contrasting types of birds, so Annan River stands out as distinct in this respect.[14]

Howitt (1904, p. 118) remarked:

> This [Annan River] system is peculiar in that the classes [moieties] and subclasses [sections] have *animal names*, and are apparently totems, which as before mentioned, is a *rare occurrence*. In the tribe descent is in the male line, for instance, the children of a man who is, say Murla-Jorro is Murla-Kutchal. (emphasis added)

If we compare this to a relatively recent recording of the Kuku Yalanji lexicon (Herschberger & Herschberger 1986; including some Kuku Nyungkul), the items in the *Walar* (*Walarr*) patrimoiety are present with approximately the same species meanings that were recorded by

---

14 This harmony in the (covert) matrimoiety composition and lack of it in the overt patrimoieties is reminiscent of the study by Alain Testart (1978) in which he showed similar harmony between matrimoieties and the matrilineal totemic group species names of which they were composed, and in contrast the lack of harmony between the totems that belonged to patrimoieties. He proposed a hypothesis that patrimoieties and patrilineal descent replaced matrimoieties and matrilineal descent in various regions of Australia, but that the totemic animals remained attached to the moieties—causing a lack of coherence.

Roth (1904) and Howitt (1904). *Walarr* (which is both a patrimoiety and section term) has these three senses according to the Kuku Yalanji dictionary:

1. Whiskers, beard[15]
2. Name of one of the tribe moieties
3. Type of honey bee almost like the dabu (other moiety), but bigger and nests in trees.

Dabu is defined in the dictionary as a 'small black bee with a light sting' that also nests in trees. None of these bees actually sting, although *T. carbonaria* does defend itself by biting, as observed by Hockings (1884, p. 151).

The *walarr: dabu* patrimoiety division is spread widely across this region and the referents are clearly the two honey bees—identified as *T. carbonaria* and *A. australis* respectively. They are commonly referred to as black and small, versus yellow and larger respectively, and belong to the forest and coastal regions respectively, as opposed to the 'scrub' of the inland. Similar physical and ecological characteristics apply to the bees named *ka(rr)pa-* and *kurtya-/kutya-/kuya-* respectively to the north and south. Whether the species identification is the same in all cases requires further research.

In neighbouring areas, the name of the two patrimoieties is also taken from these two species of bees; however, the linguistic form of the names is different, as will be further discussed.[16]

The other term for a section in the Walarr moiety, *Wandi*, translated to 'eagle-hawk' by Howitt, is glossed in the Kuku-Yalanji dictionary:

> Fish hawk, brown hawk, red-backed sea eagle.
> One of the sacred birds.

Whether these are different species or different English terms for the same species is not clear. 'Red-backed sea eagle' is a common term for the Brahminy Kite (*Haliastur indus*). Howitt's (1904) and Roth's (1904) term 'eagle-hawk' may apply to this bird or a class of large raptors.

---

15 Note that the term *wurripa* in Gugu-Badhun and Warrungu has a referent as a bee 'with a beard'. *Walarr* in Guugu Yimidhirr means 'beard, stubble, moustache' (Haviland 1979, p. 172).

16 Other species also play a role as moiety emblems, based on the Kuku Yalanji dictionary. For instance, the term for 'hornet, paper wasp', *wurrpu,* rendered as *worbu* in earlier sources, is a section term in Mbabaram and Gugu Djangun, not far from Kuku Yalanji and a patrimoiety in groups to the north, where it is said to be a term for a bee species.

8. THE BIRDS AND THE BEES

One striking feature of the arrangement in this moiety is that the moiety term and one component section are the same: *Walarr*. We will return to a discussion of this later. While the terms in the *Walarr* moiety are clearly recognisable as animal species in Kuku Yalanji, the same is not true of the other moiety, as described by Howitt (1904). The section term *Kutchala* [*sic*], said to mean 'salt-water eagle-hawk', is not found in the dictionary, with this or any other meaning. However, there is a very widespread root for wedge-tailed eagle (*Aquila audax*), *kurrityal(a)*, throughout the northern Queensland languages, northern Maric and some languages west of Maric, including Mayi, and penetrating into Arandic (Alpher 2004). A related form for the same bird—mainly *kutyala/kuthala* but with some variation—is found in Yidiny, south of Kuku Yalanji (kuyal[a], Dixon 1991, p. 158), and in southern Maric. The term cited by Howitt (1904) for Kuku Nyungkul— *kutyal* or possibly *kurtyal*—is no doubt a form of this root; whether it means 'wedge-tailed eagle' or 'sea eagle' (*Haliaeetus leucogaster*) in this area is unclear. It seems that this term did not originate as an 'eagle' term in either Kuku Yalanji or Kuku Nyungkul, but was borrowed primarily as a section term from another neighbouring language.[17]

The other two terms in the opposite moiety to *Walarr*—bee terms *Murla* for the moiety and *Jorro* for the other section—are also not native to Kuku Yalanji. As previously mentioned, Roth (1904) also regarded the terms for sections in this moiety as foreign in origin—for instance, *jorro* as belonging to the McIver River, which is Guugu Yimidhirr country. This is undoubtedly Guugu Yimidhirr *dhuru*, glossed as 'native bee species' by Haviland (1979, p. 174)—possibly *A. australis*. *Murla* is Guugu Yimidhirr *mula* 'sugarbag; bee (generic)' (Haviland 1979, p. 174). Alpher (2004) interpreted this as Proto-Paman, but it is variable in meaning in different languages (e.g. 'blood', 'paint' and 'honey').

In more recent times, according to the Kuku-Yalanji dictionary, the other moiety term *Dabu*, which is a bee term, refers to:

1. Small black bee which nests in trees, has a light sting
2. The honey from this bee
3. The name of one of the clan moieties.

---

17 *Kurrityala* is found as the term for wedge-tailed eagle in the neighbouring rainforest languages, as well as more widely in Biri (Terrill 1993, p. 210) and Kongulu (between the Mackenzie River and the lower Dawson where it is an eagle totem name '*kurithulla*'; Howitt 1904, pp. 111–2); and in the form *kutyala* in a number of Maric languages. In Guugu-Yimidhirr, the *gudha* is a 'black bee', probably *T. carbonaria*. This term is related to other widespread bee terms in Queensland but not to eagle terms.

This is most likely *T. carbonaria*.

The section system described by Howitt (1904) may have been a fleeting episode in building such a system, or at least a system that did not last very long. However, it does show how the building blocks of a section system can be put into place in this case and perhaps more generally. Two different ethnic groups with patrimoieties began an interaction and type of exchange. The groups may well have been Gugu Yalanji/Gugu Nyungkul to the south and Gugu Yimidhirr or some subgroup thereof to the north. When we consider the information from Roth (1904) that the group with this system was bilingual in these two languages, it would make sense that the terms in one patrimoiety were drawn from one language and the terms in the other were drawn from the other language.[18]

The origin of the Annan River sections could have eventuated as depicted in Table 34. This is, of course, conjectural, but it is important to put forward a hypothesis to see if further evidence gathered both in this region and elsewhere can support it. Recent names of moieties and sections are used to exemplify the process:

- *Stage I: Separate bee and eagle patrimoieties/patriphratries in neighbouring groups*. It has been noted that in most of the region, the division between moiety names is between two contrasting species of bee or eagle—one associated with the coast and one with the inland. It is assumed that this was also the original arrangement in this part of north Queensland.
- *Stage II: Language group exogamy and pragmatic equivalence of moieties marriage*. In this stage, two neighbouring groups practise patrimoiety exogamy and recognise equivalence of each other's moieties. Marriage continues to be both within and between groups.
- *Stage III: Marriage with other language group and children assigned to equivalent moiety of own language group*. Marriage shifts decisively towards exogamy between language groups, while maintaining moiety exogamy; thus, the preferred marriage is only with a partner of the opposite moiety and other language group. Additionally, patrifiliation places a child of a father in the equivalent moiety of the other language group, in which his father would have normally originated. This sets the stage for the establishment of four sections.

---

18 Elsewhere in northern Australia, one patrimoiety is regarded as 'local' and one as 'foreign', as in the case of Yolngu Dhuwa and Yirritja respectively.

- *Stage IV: Moieties become mixed as to species.* This stage brings the marriage rule in line with practice by making the spouse category the one that is formerly determined by the moiety system of a different language group. This leads to each moiety containing one eagle section and one bee section.
- *Stage V: Development of sections.* The typical structure and functioning of the sections system are achieved.

Table 34: Hypothesis about the origin of Annan River sections.

Stage I: Separate bee and eagle patrimoieties/patriphratries in neighbouring groups				
	'Inland' moiety A		'Coastal' moiety B	
Southern language group 1	*Kurrityal* eagle sp.	marry	*Wandi* eagle sp.	
Northern language group 2	*Dhuru* bee sp. *A. Australis* [Inland, larger yellow]	marry	*Walarr* bee sp. *T. Carbonaria* [Coastal, smaller, black]	
Stage II: Language group exogamy and pragmatic equivalence of moieties marriage				
	'Inland' moiety A		'Coastal' moiety B	
Southern language group 1	*Kurrityal* eagle sp.	marry	*Wandi* eagle sp.	
Northern language group 2	*Dhuru* bee sp. *A. Australis*		*Walarr* bee sp. *T. Carbonaria*	
Stage III: Marriage with other language group and children assigned to equivalent moiety of own language group				
	'Inland' moiety A		'Coastal' moiety B	
Southern language group 1	*Kurrityal* eagle sp.	marry	*Wandi* eagle sp.	Father/child
Northern language group 2	*Dhuru* bee sp. *A. Australis*		*Walarr* bee sp. *T. Carbonaria*	
Stage IV: Moieties become mixed as to species				
	'Inland' moiety A		'Coastal' moiety B	
Southern language group 1	*Kurrityal* eagle sp.	marry	*Wandi* eagle sp.	Father/child
Northern language group 2	*Dhuru* bee sp. *A. Australis*		*Walarr* bee sp. *T. Carbonaria*	

Stage V: Development of sections			
	Patrimoiety A/D		Patrimoiety B/C
	A *Kutchal* (*Kurrityal*) eagle sp.	marry	B *Walar* bee sp.
	father/child of		father/child of
	D *Jorro* (*Dhuru*) bee sp.	marry	C *Wandi* eagle sp.

Source: Author's work.

Origin around Mackay on the Queensland Central Coast

Another section system that shows signs of having developed from the interaction of two patrimoiety systems is that of Guwinmal, reported as Kuinmurbera by Roth (1898). This terminology differs from others that we have mentioned so far in Queensland and has a restricted range on the central coast. The section system is set out in Table 35 (presented in the same way as Table 34), aligning the patrimoieties in columns rather than matrimoieties, but retaining Radcliffe-Brown's (1931) coding. Note that *-an* is a version of a common feminine suffix in the region (*-kan*).

Table 35: Kuinmerburra, also known as Guwinmal.

Am	*Karilburra*	Bm	*Koorpal*
Af	*Karilburran*	Bf	*Koorpalan*
Dm	*Kooealla*	Cm	*Moonal*
Df	*Kooeallan*	Cf	*Moonalan*

Source: Mathews (1898, p. 333).

D *kuyala* is close to the northern Queensland bee moiety term *kuya-*, which has been previously mentioned.[19] The complementary section term in the same patrimoiety *karilpurra* has a resemblance to the rainforest A section *karrpawuru* (see the section 'The Queensland General Section System') and to north Queensland and more widespread terms for moieties and honey bee contrasting with the *kuya* moiety/species. *Kurpa-* is a widespread section and matrimoiety root, and the section term *kupuru* in the QG section system will be discussed. Less familiar is the term *munal*, which was recorded by Roth (1898) as *mannal* (*manal*).

---

19   It also has a resemblance to the form of the eagle moiety term found in Yidiny kuyala; however, the latter is restricted to this language and probably the result of a local and isolated lenition *ty > y. Roth (1898) also recorded at Rockhampton and Yeppoon the section terms *koo-da-la*; *koor-pal*; *ka-ral-be-ra*; *mun-nal*, with *kuthala* rather than the lenited *kuyala*—the latter attributed to the Torilla, Pine Mountain, dialect. Roth aligned this to the QG term *koorkkilla* (*kurrkila*); see the next section.

Sections in the Mapoon Area, North-Western Cape York

In Australia, Roth (1910) was a champion of the idea that sections might have arisen from local groupings such as clans, and claimed that 'sections' around Mapoon in Cape York were local groupings. Mathews (1900) also made a similar claim. As Thomson (1934, pp. 222–6) explained, the authors' information came from Reverend N. Hey and it contained a number of errors. The ethnography and linguistic analysis of Roth and Mathews has also been questioned by Crowley (1981).

It seems doubtful that the marriage and descent patterns between the four named groups identified were truly section-like. Thomson (1934, p. 224) stated that 'sections' were not found among the group, who he labelled 'Tjungundji', in question. However, there are 'four groups with names derived directly from the cardinal points of the compass … to one of which each of the clans belong … according to its geographical position in relation to each other'. To this extent, Thomson agreed with Roth (1910) in that these groupings, which should properly be called patriphratries, were 'named after separate localities', although the actual names in Thomson's account diverge from those of Roth and Mathews.[20]

Thomson (1934) mapped the nine clans of the Tjungundji, as shown in Figure 27.

Unfortunately, the distribution of the clans across the patriphratries is not recorded on the map or elsewhere in the article. Thomson (1934) noted that both the patriclans and the patriphratries were exogamous. Further, according to Roth (1910, p. 104), by the time he recorded them, these patriphratries were functioning as sections—that is to say, there was not only exogamy but a positive preference for marriage with a particular other phratry, and a rule of filiation not to the father's phratry but to another phratry.

---

20   Sharp (1939) endorsed Thomson's (1934) account on the basis of his independent investigation in the region. Thomson interpreted the earlier writers as mistaken, but this is not necessarily the case. Three of the four names of the phratries are clan names (Thomson 1934, p. 225); however, it is quite possible that a clan name might be used for a higher taxonomic level, alongside a geographical nomenclature (Thomson 1934, p. 222).

SKIN, KIN AND CLAN

Figure 27: Clans of the Tjungundji.
Source: Thomson (1934, p. 220).

The hypothetical transition could have been the same kind as that diagrammed in Table 34 for Annan River, except that patriphratries were the initial building blocks. Overt moieties are not known to have been present in this area and may not have been strictly necessary to trigger the process that led to sections.[21] Descent is within the male's phratry—that is, children inherit their father's phratry and country initially; however, this could have had marriage and filiation rules added that might have yielded something like a section system.[22]

---

21   There is evidence that patriphratries were a form of organisation prior to sections in other parts of the country; see Chapter 7 for the case of Western Australia.
22   This is of course hypothetical, as the existence of section-like operations in the Mapoon area is denied by reliable investigators some 35 years after its first observation. Shapiro (1967, p. 466) proposed that among the Tjungundji, as described by Sharp and Thomson, 'it seems quite possible that these four groups [phratries] are semi-moieties'. The term 'semi-moiety' is not to be read here in its usual meaning (and criticised by Shapiro) as an overlay on subsection organisation, but rather as localised patriphratries with specific marriage prescriptions between them.

Thomson (1934) acknowledged that there were four patriphratries, but contended that they were named by the four points of the compass. Unfortunately, he did not state which patriclans (shown in Figure 27) belonged to which of the phratries, or if there were any marriage rules, along with clan and phratry exogamy. As well as challenging the findings of Mathews (1900) and Roth (1910) that phratries operated like sections, Thomson also questioned the names that they published for the phratries, since they were either clan or territory names. This is not a devastating criticism, since it is quite possible for a component clan name, or territory name, to act as a name for the whole phratry.

Summary

This section has discussed several section systems that show signs of having developed from the interaction of two patrimoiety or patriphratry systems in two neighbouring territories and language groups, including marriage between different countries and the affiliation of a child to its mother's territory. This gave rise to section systems. With the exception of the far northern Tjungundji/Ngerrikudi system around Mapoon, these share a common element of having moiety totems based on two species of honey bee and two species of eagle. These became the source of names for a number of section systems in the region.

The Queensland General Section System

The Spread of a Section System in the Queensland Interior

Having explored the probable origin of some section systems in northern and central coastal Queensland, we now turn to a section terminology in the interior, which we call the QG section system. We have already encountered this system as Roth recorded the pragmatic equivalence of it with the Annan River system (see Tables 32 and 33). The QG section system is the most widespread system in Queensland, covering a very large area of interior Queensland, and stretches from just south of Cape York Peninsula in the north to close to the New South Wales border in the south, and close to the east coast in places to far western Queensland.

Although the terminologies in this system are similar to each other, there are differences that can be analysed to help us further understand the history of the system and how it may relate to other systems.

There is an approximate coincidence of this area and the spread of the Pama-Nyungan subgroup of languages known as Maric—after the common word for 'person' *mari* (Barrett 2005; Beale 1975). However, I avoid calling this set of sections 'Maric' because that could imply that the sections were inherited along with the languages. As noted, social categories such as sections are usually diffused rather than inherited. In this case, it might be that the section system spread with the languages; however, this needs to be investigated empirically before judgements are made. Thus far, the evidence seems to point to the sections not spreading with the languages.

The QG section system terminology is represented in Table 33. These forms are found with little variation over the whole of area of this set.[23]

Changes in the Forms of Queensland General Section Terms and Their Implications

Survey

There are variations in form in some languages that have a bearing on the origin of the terminology and its subsequent diffusion. Those to be discussed include:

- a change from *k* to *ty* preceding *i*—affecting the form *Kurrkila*, producing *Kurrtyila* in Biri
- a substitution of initial *p* for initial *k* in the southern Maric D term *Kanpari*, yielding *Panpari* elsewhere
- the dropping of initial consonants (linked to the previous point), especially *k*, in various languages in the south and west and to some extent further north in the QG section system area

---

23 At the current stage of research, it does seem likely that the code letters do represent pragmatic equivalence with the western sections and between all members of the QG section system (McConvell & McConvell 2015). Mathews (1905, p. 53) gave an example of the lack of pragmatic equivalence between Muruwari sections and Ngiyambaa/Wayilwan, and there are other examples such as this in NSW and Queensland in systems other than QG—but apparently not those with the QG terminology.

8. THE BIRDS AND THE BEES

- the loss of an additional initial syllable *thu-* in the C term *thuwunku* in part of southern Maric, yielding *wunku* elsewhere.
- the fortition of the glide *r* to the retroflex stop *rt* in southern Maric—for example, producing *marti* from *mari* 'person'. This does not affect the section term *panpari/kanpari*.

From these sound changes and other evidence adduced, it is proposed that the QG terminology system originated in the south of the Maric area, and from there spread east and north. It is also probable that the Maric subgroup of languages spread in the opposite direction from the north-east. The relationship of these two events will be briefly reviewed in the next section.

Kurrkila and Kurrtyila

Barrett (2005, p. 27) wrote of sound correspondences in Maric:

> The sequence gi—rare initially and non-existent intervocalically—has become dyi in the eastern dialects [Biri], an example of a common assimilation of the stop to the following front vowel.

As an example, Barrett (2005, Appendix 2 E42) gave **pikirri* 'dream', reconstructed as Proto-Maric and found in southern languages; it is also found in Biri as *pithi* and other Biri dialects Baradha and Yambina as *pityiri*. Another example from Barrett (2005, Appendix 2) is A90 **makirra* 'clay, paint', reflected as *matyirra* in Biri and neighbouring dialect Wiri. Gugu-Badhun and Warrungu in the north retain the form *makirra*.[24]

This is the preferred explanation of the correspondence between the section term *Kurrkila* in most Maric languages and *Kurrtyila* in Biri, and implies, following Barrett's reconstruction of **k* in this environment, that *Kurrkila* is the original form.

There is a possible alternative explanation of this variation that is rejected here. There is a regular sound change in a number of north Queensland rainforest languages whereby a *ty* before *i* becomes *k*—that is, the reverse of the above change in Biri. Examples include 'liver' *kipa* in Girramay, Nyawaygi and Wargamay, which is otherwise very widespread as *tyipa* in north Queensland and other Pama-Nyungan languages as far away as

---

24 E02 **piki* 'lips' apparently does not undergo this palatalisation, although there is a probable cognate *piyi* in Wiri.

Victoria (Alpher 2004).[25] Another example is 'mother's father' *ngaki* in the rainforest languages, which is otherwise very widespread as *ngatyi* and usually reconstructed as Proto-Pama-Nyungan (McConvell 1997, 2013).

The section term *Kurrkila* is found in the rainforest languages that exhibit this change such as Nyawaygi and Wargamay. These languages do not consistently have the QG terminology but *kurrkila* occurs as B in all three examples given in Table 36. Dyirbal only has this term shared with the QG section system, but the other terms are from the local north-east system. Nyawaygi additionally has C *wunku* shared with the QG section system. Wargamay has only one of the north-east terms left—A replaced by *wutyurru*, which is not a section term of the QG section system but a matrimoiety term mainly associated with the QG section system. This anomaly, which is also found in Warrungu and Gugu-Badhun, is discussed further below.

Table 36: North-eastern (rainforest) sections.

Dyirbal	A *karrpawuru*	B *kurrkila*	C *tyikunkarra*	D *kurkurru*
Nyawaygi	A *kapawuu*	B *kurrkila*	C *wunku*	D *kurkurru*
Wargamay	A *wutyurru*	B *kurrkila*	C *wunku*	D *kurkurru*

Source: Dixon (1972, p. 31; 1981, p. 513; 1983, p. 5).

If the hypothesis that sections began from interactions of two sets of patrimoieties in neighbouring groups is correct, we might expect to find evidence that the other terms in the QG section system were moieties with original totemic animal meanings. No solid evidence of this kind has emerged thus far,[26] and may be hard to find due to the time depth of the events and limited amount of data on the languages in the relevant area. We continue here to plot the spread of the QG section system and return later to the broader question of the origin of sections in Queensland.

---

25 Alpher (pers. comm.) suggested that the Proto-Pama-Nyungan form should be **kipa* rather than **tyipa*. **K > ty* in the environment of a following front vowel would certainly be more common and 'less marked' on a world typological scale; however, the reverse appears to have occurred here. The form *kipa* 'liver' is also found in Dharumbal (Holmer 1983; Terrill 2002, p. 58) but although this is some distance south from the North Queensland rainforest, in Rockhampton, it does not necessarily support a reconstruction of **kipa* to *pPNy*. Another possibility is a linguo-genetic link between the rainforest languages and Dharumbal. Terrill (1998, p. 87; 2002, p. 15) saw Dharumbal as dissimilar to Biri to the north and Waka to the south. There are other examples of *k* corresponding to a laminal before *i*—such as *kira* 'teeth' (*kirra*?; Terrill 2002, p. 101) whereby *thirra* and *yirra* are much more common throughout Pama-Nyungan and *tyirra* is found alongside *yirra* in Biri (Alpher 2004).
26 Holmer (1983, pp. 339, 374) reported what appeared to be a patrimoiety system among the Biri with the terms *wunku: kangurru*. The first of these is also a section term in the QG section system.

Based on linguistic evidence, it seems probable that the QG section terms *panpari/kanpari* and *wunku/thuwunku* originated among the southern languages of the Maric subgroup—not necessarily as far from the north as they are now—assuming a spread of languages. Speculatively, these two could have been southern patrimoiety terms, and *kupuru* and *kurrkila* the northern moieties (as illustrated in Table 37), who entered into marriage exchange with them; however, there is no direct evidence of this. One might point to the presence of *kurrkila* in the rainforest languages with different section terms as (albeit weak) evidence of a potential northern origin for the term.

Table 37: Hypothesis about the origin of the Queensland General section system from patrimoiety and country interaction.

Patrimoieties	A/D	B/C
North	A *kupuru*	B *kurrkila*
South	D *kanpari/panpari*	C *thuwunku/wunku*

Source: Author's work.

An alternative hypothesis is that these QG section system terms might not have come from patrimoieties, but perhaps matrimoieties, will be discussed later in this chapter.

Initial K/P Alternation in South-Western Maric

A striking variation in section terms is the frequency of D *panpari* in the northern and central Maric areas and *kanpari* in southern Maric (Bidyara and Margany/Gunya). This is not a common type of sound change in any of the languages.[27] However, although it is not apparently very common in the limited vocabularies that we have available for Maric, it does seem to have some regularity in general vocabulary.[28]

For instance, Breen (1973) cited the term *kapu+* (*gabu*, *gabugadhi* and *gabuwadhi*) meaning 'later' in Bidyara; however, other sources have *papu* in the same meaning in south-western dialects:

- *babo* (C) W. R. Conn in Curr 1887 Upper Warrego and Paroo Rivers
- *babo* (P) L. M. Playfair in Curr 1887 the Upper Paroo ['by and by']
- *bobo* (H) L. M. Playfair in Curr 1887 the Upper Paroo ['by and by'].

---

27 Where it does occur, the solution is usually to seek a reconstruction in some intermediate sound such as *kw* in Indo-European, which yields *p* in some languages and *k* in others. There is no evidence for this kind of solution in this case.
28 Thank you to Tony Jefferies for giving me access to his compilation of Maric vocabularies.

Obviously, it would be beneficial to find more examples such as this, as well as external cognates of forms that would decide which of the initial consonants is the original. Fitzgerald (1997, p. 162) cited a form *kalypu* in Bagandji 'by and by, later', which could be a cognate of *kapu* in Maric. While Fitzgerald mentioned lenition of *ly* to *y* before peripheral consonants in another language, there is no cogent justification for loss of *ly* that I am aware of. If this were firmed up, or parallel examples found, this would strengthen the case for the direction initial $*k > p$ in some southern Maric dialects. Other considerations discussed in the next section do point strongly in this direction.

Initial K-Dropping

This initial k/p alternation in south-western Maric seems to be connected with the widely acknowledged process of loss of initial *k* in several Maric dialects creating initial vowels. Barrett (2005, p. 21) cited this change in Yandyibara, south of Blackall between the upper Bulloo and Barcoo rivers; however, it actually exists in a number of languages in south-central Maric. In this case, there are intermediate forms of the same root (*apu*+) with no initial consonant:

- aboouthy (S) ['by and by']
- aboo (B) ['by and by'].

There is evidence for the direction of this change being $*k > p$. In a list of 90 items collected by Jefferies (2010), 19 alternate #*k* and #zero in different dialects; some have #*w*; and none alternate #*p* and #zero.

In some languages on the southern edge of Maric such as Gunggari,[29] which is illustrated in Table 38, but also in the west with Guwamu, the initial dropping affects all the section terms except *wunku*. However, if we accept the proposal that the original form of D was *kanpari*, then this pattern follows the more restricted results of dropping of initial *k* only.

Table 38: Initial dropping in southern Maric section terms.

A *Upurr* [upur?] < *kupuru	B *Urrkila* < *kurrkila
C *Wungku* [wunku?] < *wunku	D *Anpirr* [anpir?] < *kanpari

Source: Jefferies (2010).

---

29 These forms displaying an awareness of initial k-dropping are cited by Fison and Howitt (1880, pp. 39–40; see also Gardner & McConvell 2015, p. 163) from a language named Unghi (Ungkayi), which is undoubtedly a form of Gunggari with initial *k* lost and $*r > y$.

In Wakelbura, which may be either Miyan or Yagalingu (Wafer & Lissarrague 2008, p. 421, fn 276), south of Biri but north of Bidjara, there is a different pattern with B and D retaining initial consonants, but A losing the initial *k* (see Table 39).

Table 39: Different treatment of initial consonants in Maric section terms.

A *Upu* < **kupuru*	B *Kurrkila* < **kurrkila*
C *Wunku* < **wunku*	D *Panpayi* < **kanpari*

Source: Author's work.

In accordance with our reasoning, *panpari* is a later form diffusing from the south to the north after the change $*k > p$ had applied; $*k > p$ feeds on $*k > \emptyset$. Kurrkila does not undergo $*k > \emptyset$, as it is presumably a later innovation and initial dropping had ceased in the area by this time.

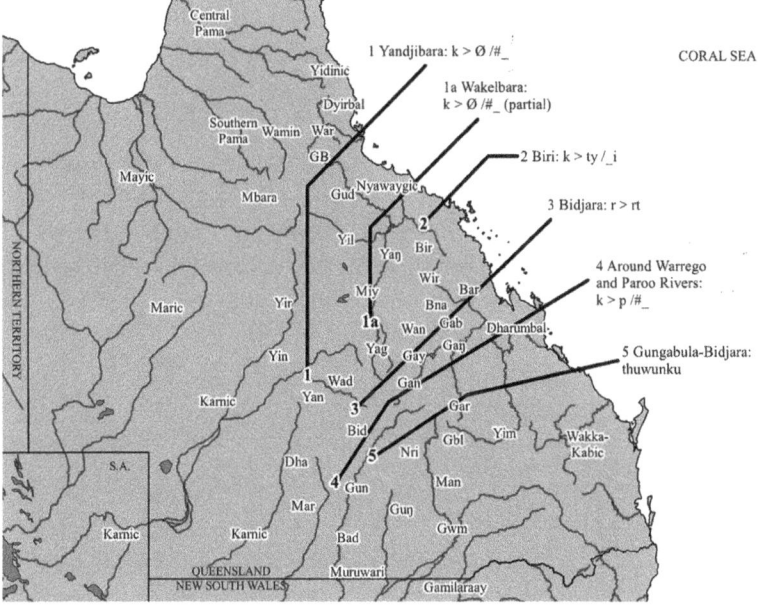

Figure 28: Maric languages with sound changes affecting section terms.
Source: Adapted by William McConvell from Barrett (2005), with location of sound changes by Patrick McConvell.

Thuwunku/Wunku

The term *wunku* is very widespread in QG/Maric; however, in a few languages in the south, the related term has an initial syllable—written *du-* or *d-* (Bidjara and Gungabula respectively; Breen 1972) in sources, perhaps to be interpreted as *thu-*. Since there are no known prefixes in these languages, the form with three syllables is likely to be earlier. The presence of the form *thwunku* in one language is witness to a weakening of the initial syllable and probable shift of stress to the second, heralding the loss of the first syllable.

A hypothesis about the origin of the form *thuwunku* is presented below. The source of the section term *thuwunku* (which becomes *wunku* in most Maric languages) is obscure. Perhaps the closest match is the rainforest section term *tyikun*, which is augmented by an element/suffix *–karra*. It could be suggested that the *–ku* in *thuwun-ku* is a suffix, and that there is lenition of *k > w* in the former second consonant that becomes the initial after dropping the initial syllable. Initial *k > w* in the environment of following *u* is known in southern and central Maric, but there is just one example of *k > w* in the second consonant (medial) position in Barrett's (2005) vocabulary list.[30] Further, the fact that the nearest related form of the older form *thuwunku* in southern Maric languages is far removed to the north-east in another subgroup of languages just outside the Maric border needs to be explained. One might have to look at a scenario in which *tyikun* was widespread in earlier times, but was replaced in the south by tyuwun, then *tyuwunku* and then *wunku*, which diffused across Maric with the QG section system, leaving only a few instances in the rainforest.[31]

---

30   Barrett (2005, Appendix) B01 **kutyala > wutyala* 'bandicoot'; Proto-Maric B13 p-M **kutha > wutha* 'nose'; and **kakuparra > kawuparra* 'kookaburra' in Biri dialects only.

31   An alternative etymology of *thuwunku* could be from the 'shade' moiety *Dunggu* among the Muruwari and neighbouring groups. Roth regarded this as equivalent to the 'blood' moiety *Muggulu* (*Makulu*, alternative *Makula* in Yuwalalaay; Sim 1998). This has the advantage of referring to groups adjacent to the south-western end of Maric, the proposed location of the origin of the QG section system, rather than adjacent to the north-east of Maric; however, the details of 'blood' and 'shade' moieties and the word *dunggu* are unclear—the latter does not appear in the Muruwari vocabulary in Oates (1988).

*r > rt in Southern Maric

This sound change of fortition is well attested in many examples and appears to be regular (Terrill 1993, pp. 129–32). Examples can be found in Table 40.

The direction of change is evidently *r > rt, since the forms with r are solidly supported as reconstructions in wider protolanguages—for example, *mara 'hand', *kakara 'moon' in Proto-Pama-Nyungan, yuri 'kangaroo > meat' and *puri 'fire' Proto-Paman (Alpher 2004).

Table 40: *r > rt.

	Bidyara	Biri
Man	mardi	mari
	Also, Margany-Gunya Alpher (2004), cited from Breen	
Hand	marda	mara *mara PPNy
Meat	yurdi	yuri
	Also, Margany-Gunya Alpher (2004), cited from Breen	
Moon	gagarda	gagara

Source: Based on Barrett (2005) and Jefferies (2010).

In this particular case, it is interesting to note that the sound change did not occur in the QG section terms. Two terms meet the conditions for its application: *kupuru* and *kanpari/panpari*; however, neither **kupurtu* nor **kanparti/panparti* are found in any language.

The significance of this lies in linguistic stratigraphy. If fortition of r is a regular change, as we can infer, and section terms were present in the area at the time when it was operating, then this change would have happened to the sections. As it did not occur, the conclusion can be drawn that the section terms were not in the southern Maric area when the change occurred. This is potentially useful in the search for the chronology of section spread. However, there is currently no item in the lists of words available that is affected by r fortition or susceptible to the change (but has not undergone it), whose referent is datable by history or archaeology. However, this is not to say that no such data exist or could be explored in future.

The most important lesson from this information is that the Maric language subgroup spread independently of, and earlier than, the QG section system. While some of the general vocabulary would have been later loan words from other languages, the bulk would have been inherited from the Maric protolanguage. In the course of this expansion, some such inherited words changed form in different branches, such as through the fortition of *r* discussed in this section. Words that had entered the language at the Proto-Maric stage or during early spread and diversification of the subgroup would have undergone this change. However, since the section terms did not undergo this change, they must have entered the relevant languages after the change had stopped operating.

The Linguistic Prehistory of Maric and Its Relation to Queensland General Section System Diffusion

The Queensland General Section System and the Maric Subgroup of Languages

Writers have arrived at different conclusions about the origin and path of spread of the Maric languages. Dixon (2002, pp. 682–3) placed the origin on the central Queensland coast near Mackay, moving first in two advances north and west, then finally south, and adduced a Karringbool legend to support a coastal origin. This hypothesis is based on the highest lexical similarity of Maric with northern coastal languages, which I have been calling the rainforest languages (Dixon's H, Herbert River; and Jc, Proserpine—Ngaro and Giya). This implies a longer contact between early Maric and these languages.

Barrett (2005, pp. 112–3) challenged this hypothesis and instead proposed that the early Maric moved towards the coast near Mackay, separating into two groups of related coastal languages in the rainforest and Dharumbal/Waka-Kabic, which was followed by a southward expansion from the interior homeland around the Burdekin River (the border of the east and north internal Maric subgroups).

As already shown, the QG section terms (or at least two of them) originated from languages that are present today in the very south on the periphery of the Maric subgroup. Diffusion of the sections must have taken a northern direction from there to occupy a large zone. However, both hypotheses regarding the language subgroup spread point to a northern origin (albeit differing in detail) and a subsequent relatively recent southern expansion. Evidence cited in the last section shows that the language spread occurred before the sections diffused north.

It may be then that the source of the QG section terms should be sought on the southern borders of Maric. The terms in northern New South Wales and south-east Queensland (Waka-Kabic) do not appear for the most part to be related to the QG section system terms in their form—although as has been noted, semantic calques (or animal totems) could be involved, rather than borrowing of sound forms of words.

A Possible Role of Southern Matrimoieties in Queensland General Section Origin

One of the matrimoiety terms in the 'Wangkumarra' system (Eastern Karnic, far north-western NSW, and adjacent to Queensland and South Australia) is *kulparra*—plausibly connected and pragmatically equivalent to *kilparra*, a matrimoiety term of western NSW (Mathews 1905, p. 50; Wafer & Lissarrague 2008; see Chapter 6) and encroaching slightly into Queensland, with a hint at least that these terms may have originated in a term for 'emu'.[32] These terms may be related to the QG A section term *kupuru* (variant *kuparu*) and perhaps the Kuwinmal B section term *kurpal*. This implies that the QG section system was built at least partially from matrimoieties, contrary to the model of interaction of patrimoieties leading to section origin in north-east of Queensland. More research is needed on these matters.

Summary

This section has demonstrated how linguistic evidence can show where section terms originated and the direction in which they spread. Somewhat surprisingly, in the case of the QG system, the answer seems to be from the south, close to the New South Wales border. Unlike in the previous

---

32 Breen (pers. comm. to Wafer & Lissarrague 2008, p. 420). Barrett (2005, Appendix) reconstructed *kulparri 'emu' for Proto-Maric, although many of the reflexes are *kulpari*, which indicates that the proto-form may have had a glide *r*. Kilparra and Mukwara to the west of Maric are said to mean 'eaglehawk' and 'crow', but there is some confusion about which is which in different sources. Mathew (1910b) denied that he heard anyone giving animal meanings to these terms, stating that they were merely equivalent moieties to those in the region (Victoria and South Australia) where the moiety terms are literally the words for 'eagle' and 'crow' (see also Chapter 6).

section, the evidence for a particular mechanism of section origin from a combination of patrimoieties or patriphratries did not amount to much—at least as far as we know.

More generally, the pattern being observed here is not only that language expansion and section diffusion are independent processes, but also that one follows the other and can occur in an opposite direction across approximately the same territory associated mainly within the group of closely related languages/dialects known as Maric. It would be instructive to find out if this kind of pattern—in which a language expands and then at the margin of expansion a new cultural feature is contacted and spreads back as an innovation through the country through which the language initially spread—is known elsewhere.

Broader Perspectives

Sections and Moieties

Their Relative Independence

While anthropological treatments of sections and Aboriginal testimony by and large treat sections and moieties as being part of one system—the former being halves of the latter—the sets of terms for each do not always go together. For instance, while the QG section system discussed in the last section tends to be found in conjunction with a moiety system made up of the pair of terms *wuthurru*: *yangurru* (and some variants, especially of the latter), this set of moiety terms has a wider distribution than the QG section system, extending further north-west and east than the section sets. The two kinds of terminology appear to have diffused to a great extent independently and probably at different periods.

However, the question that most concerns us is the extent to which moiety terms entered into the origin of sections. The case of the north-eastern sections examined in the section 'Section Systems in Queensland' does point to patrimoieties and their terms being involved in section origin through amalgamation of two local groups (perhaps language groups)—each with two pairs of patrimoieties participating in a particular kind of marriage exchange and filiation. The patrimoieties in this area are also notable for having a fairly transparent association with two types of moiety totems: bees and eagles; and in some cases amounting to use of two contrasting species terms as the names of the moieties.

8. THE BIRDS AND THE BEES

Moieties elsewhere in Queensland are less clearly associated with a pair of natural species; further, there is no real evidence of this in many instances, nor has it been proven that this was the case in the distant past.

The Queensland General Matrimoiety System

This is the situation with the widespread moiety system *wuthurru: yangurru* (and variants)[33] that occupies a wide zone of the interior of Queensland— similar to the region of the QG section system, but not necessarily closely connected with the section system historically.

Clearly, the QG moiety system is different from the north-eastern case in other ways as well. It is a matrimoiety system, as compared with the patrimoieties of the north-east. Another contrasting feature is that there is very little evidence of the involvement of moieties in the origin of the QG sections unlike in the north-east. The term *wutyurru* (a variant of *wuthurru*), generally a matrimoiety term, does turn up as a section term in a handful of languages in the north-east (Wargamay among the rainforest languages, and Warrungu, a northern Maric language). A preliminary hypothesis would propose that this term was imported into the local section system to replace the A section term *karrpawuru* (rainforest) or *kupuru* (QG) in an ad hoc way and does not go back to an early stage of section origin itself.

However, older connections do exist between the linguistic forms and meanings of moieties and sections, which enable us to begin sketching the origins of the section systems in at least some parts of Queensland.

Some Historical Links between the Moieties and Sections

It has already been mentioned that two of the roots of moiety terms occur as both patrimoieties in the north-east and matrimoieties in the south-east (Waka-Kabic). It was proposed that these reflect totemic associations with two species of bees. The issue of how matrilineal institutions were replaced by patrilineal institutions (or vice versa) has been one that has provoked many scholars of an evolutionist or diffusionist (and usually speculative) turn of mind to spill much ink—I do not intend to add to that pool at this point. This shall be tackled in another publication,

---

33   Mathew (1910a) claimed to have discovered a meaning for *wuthurru/wutyurru* 'crow', which is said to contrast with opposite moiety terms such as *yangurru*, which are said to mean 'white cockatoo'. The data and supposed sound correspondences on which this is based have no validity and should be dismissed.

building on evidence and more solid work on Australia (such as by Testart 1978) without the baggage of grand theories. For now, I simply note that the linguistic connections mentioned briefly here do suggest that there has been a change in lineality of moieties in Queensland that will have to be taken into consideration in any full account of the origin of sections, and similar patches of patrimoieties amid matrimoieties are found in Victoria (see Chapter 6) and Western Australia.

The two moiety terms that are shared between the north-east and south-east of Queensland are *karrpi(ya[n])* and *kuya(n)*. The term *karrp+* is also found as a section term in far southern C and one of the rainforest languages: K in Gugu Djangun and Mbabaram, and K in Dyirbal. In Gugu Djangun and Mbabaram, *-ntyi* appears to be a suffix, which occurs with three of the four other section terms. One of these (A) is *kupantyi*, so the root is likely to be *kupa-*, which is related to the QG section term *kupuru/kuparu*.

These phenomena do not constitute an argument for a cross-cutting of patrimoieties and matrimoieties as the trigger of section origin—the earlier hypothesis that has been rejected here and replaced by the amalgamation of patrimoieties from two neighbouring countries in a new marriage exchange and filiation system. The fact that terms that refer to matrimoieties from another part of the country occasionally became section terms in an already-established section system is not an argument for the hypothesis that sections arose from a combination of matrimoieties and patrimoieties. However, it is possible that a process essentially parallel to that, based on patrimoieties, happened elsewhere—based on matrimoieties. This could have been the origin of the QG section system and other section systems in southern Queensland and New South Wales; however, analysis of those processes will have to await another publication.

Sections in South America

While subsections are an institution unique to Australia, sections are not. There are a number of other examples in different parts of the world that are disputable; however, the section systems in the Panoan family of languages around the meeting of the borders of Brazil, Bolivia and Peru can be counted as a clear example of sections.

8. THE BIRDS AND THE BEES

A description and discussion of the Panoan section system appeared 20 years ago in the English-language anthropological literature (Hornborg 1993; Kensinger 1995), and there are some publications in Spanish and Portuguese. David Fleck (2013), a linguist/biologist who lives in the Panoan area, has also published relevant material on this topic.

The picture in different Panoan groups is complex and includes major changes in the history of the groups—both before and after colonisation. A few groups have, and have had for a long time, sections in the sense of having four named social categories, with two in each patrimoiety; of these, Kashinawa (Casinanahua) is probably the best known. Figure 29 shows a map by Fleck (2013, p. 8) with my rough overlays. There are marriage rules that require a person to marry a certain other category in the opposite moiety, and filiation rules that place their children in the other section in their own moiety.

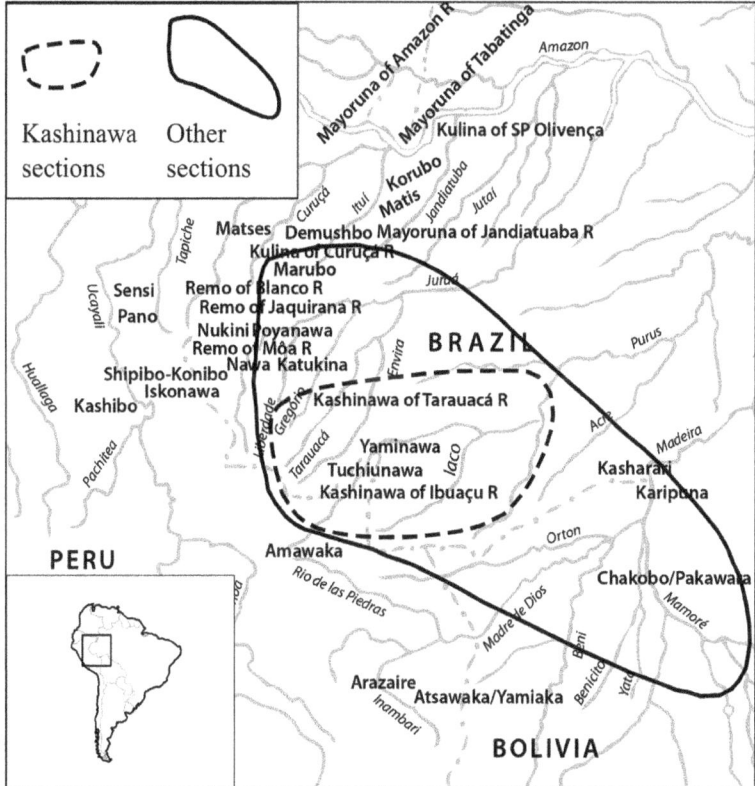

Figure 29: Panoan sections.
Source: Adapted from Fleck (2013).

This is very similar to Australian sections. The section and moiety names are animal names, which is not so much the case in Australia, for sections at least, although historical enquiry can determine a 'totemic' animal origin of the name in some cases. Not all Panoan groups have sections—some have patrimoieties, or residential or non-residential clan groups, and often the same or similar names are applied to different social groups or categories in different language groups. We have noted a little of this in Australia, in which a matrimoiety term has been used for a section in another place.

One point emerges clearly from the Panoan sections in comparison with Australian sections. Unlike in some areas of Australia, there are no matrilineal moieties, phratries or clans in any of the Panoan areas, so it is highly unlikely that the hypothesis of sections emerging from an overlap of patrilineal and matrilineal institutions would have any justification in this instance. This supports the position adopted that this is not a plausible hypothesis in relation to Australia, where there are matrilineal institutions in some regions.

Further, there is evidence that Panoan sections may have arisen from amalgamation of patrimoieties and local clans or clan-like village groupings in processes that are familiar in South American ethnology, that are often referred to as a type of 'ethnogenesis' (Hornborg & Eriksen 2011). This seems to parallel the process that was proposed for northern Queensland in 'Section Systems in Queensland'.

Fleck (pers. comm.) was not certain whether sections could be reconstructed to Proto-Panoan, and I share his doubts. Panoan is not a very old family and is estimated to be between 1,000 and 2,000 years in age, although these calculations were done before the outlier Mayoruna was taken into consideration (Fleck 2013, p. 21). While the linguistic comparative method may not be the best way of conceptualising the development of such social category systems, there are other indications that the systems and terminologies of Panoan sections are relatively recent, which will be described elsewhere. While no doubt older than Panoan sections, Australian sections are also relatively recent—originating in the last few thousand years of the late Holocene. The implications of this are addressed in the next section.

Sections and 'Tetradic Society'

Sections were a fashionable topic in the late nineteenth and early twentieth centuries after they were discovered in eastern Australia by Ridley (1856 reported in Fison & Howitt 1880) and studied in Western Australia by Radcliffe-Brown (1913). The first cohort of enthusiasts stoked the fires of various evolutionist theories of the time; however, Radcliffe-Brown chose to explain the system in terms of structural functionalism.

For a time, sections almost disappeared from the world stage in anthropology; however, in the last decades, the topic has re-emerged from the shadows, largely due to the work of Nicholas Allen. He was an early leader in what appears now to be a significant trend in contemporary anthropology: attempting to reconstruct early human society and family. Echoes of the nineteenth-century social evolutionists can be heard quite clearly in the content of their theories and methods, which are often speculative.

In a series of articles and chapters, Allen (1986) proposed that the 'primal' form of human society was 'tetradic'—a system of four sociocentric divisions consisting of a cross-cutting of exogamous lineal and endogamous generational moieties. Fison and Howitt (1880, endorsed by Morgan) also saw the section system as the primordial human family system. Allen sketched the changes ('rupturing of equations') that produced the later kinship systems from this foundation. His offerings were surprisingly well received by social anthropologists considering how they had almost all eschewed 'conjectural history' for nearly a century following the dictates of Radcliffe-Brown.

The 'tetradic society' has a remarkable resemblance to the section systems of Australia, and Godelier sees Allen's inspiration in this. However, Allen (2008, pp. 108–9) has recently denied this and claimed that the tetradic society concept has nothing to do with Australian sections:

> Godelier (2004) … thinks that the congruence of egocentric and sociocentric in tetradic systems is unrealistic. This is partly because of certain historical claims by Australianists.

The 'historical claims by Australianists' would appear to be an oblique reference to my own work and that of Dousset. Allen (2008, p. 109) added:

Although tetradic theory uses some Australianist analytical vocabulary, Australian data are not essential to it. If all Aboriginals had been wiped out by epidemics or genocide before the advent of ethnographers, one or other tetradic structure would still be the simplest way to organise a society where everyone is related to everyone else. It is a matter of logic.

The issue here is evidence—not 'logic' alone. If the Australian section system 'happens to be' the same as the primal society based on Allen's thought experiment, then what is the relationship between the two? The most obvious hypothesis would be that the Australian section system is in some way a remnant 'survival' of this supposed proto-human 'tetradic' system.

However, there is evidence to support the idea that Australian sections are not 60,000 years old as Allen claimed the tetradic system to be, but less than 6,000 years old, and probably more likely 3,000 years old, diffusing through that period up to the twentieth century. The Australian (and Panoan) section systems were a product of a revolution brought about by interaction of moieties of the same kind in neighbouring groups that were in the process of some kind of merger instituting a new system of marriage and filiation. They were not—in Australia, let alone the world—the primordial system.

Conclusion

The origin of sections should not be approached by placing this origin at the dawn of human society and reproducing the speculative histories of the old social evolutionists or their modern counterparts. We should put aside the aversion social anthropology has had to studying social dynamics and prehistory and harness the tools we need to generate hypotheses that can be tested with data.

This chapter began with the example of the research into the origin of subsections—the successor in the sequence of sociocentric categories to sections. This was successful in producing a concrete hypothesis that has largely been accepted, but which has also generated alternative interpretations with continued productive debate.

Sections are a more difficult proposition. They are older, more diverse and complex, and not all systems could be analysed in this one chapter. The two main elements addressed were:

a. a group of section systems found in the north-east of Queensland
b. a widespread system with little internal variation in interior Queensland—here called the Queensland General section system.

A common element in (a) was the background of patrimoieties, whose names related to names of totemic animals—species of eagles or bees. It was demonstrated that the section systems that arose in this region were composed of what had been patrimoieties of this type—two each from two neighbouring groups that had undergone a kind of amalgamation, adding group country exogamy to moiety exogamy, and a rule of filiation to a parent from the other country.

In the case of (b), detailed linguistic analysis was necessary to establish that the origin of sections was not in the same area as (a) to the north of the QG section system, but in the south-west of the QG section system—that is, at the extreme south of its distribution. One of the oddities that emerged is that this section system did not spread along with the language subgroup with which it is mainly associated, north to south; but rather in the opposite direction, south to north.

This reinforces an important point: institutional origins and spreads that may look at first sight to be closely and functionally related may be relatively independent, and have their own histories and periods of growth and spread. This necessitates detailed and careful study of these histories. The role of historical linguistics—both of inheritance and diffusion—has been a key focus in this chapter; however, many other disciplines can and should be brought into this kind of enquiry in the long term.

For instance, questions can be raised about why sections emerged and spread as they did, as well as why languages also spread, and the relationship between the two processes. Language spread can occur when a group enters an area where the previous population has dwindled due to scarcity of resources; however, the situation has changed enough to attract the new group in. In Australian prehistory, this kind of sequence can be dominated by factors of climate, or a group battling with scarcity moving in on a group better provided with resources. Climate change can be the background for either of these scenarios.

If we direct our attention to the Maric languages of interior Queensland, it can be seen that they are very similar to each other, suggesting an age from first dispersal of not much more than 1,000 years. It may not be a coincidence that in eastern and Central Australia, there was a wet spell around 700 to 1000–1150 AD, followed by a transition and a particularly dry spell around 1200–1500 AD (Vance et al. 2013; Williams et al. 2010). Williams et al. (2010) claimed that the Aboriginal population increased in this period. A hypothesis could be that Proto-Maric spread from a north-east homeland beginning around 700–800 AD to take advantage of burgeoning resources in the inland in several stages over the next few hundred years—perhaps as deterioration of climatic conditions drove them further on.

According to the hypothesis regarding the origin of the QG section system, it was only created when Maric speakers reached the southern area, which we might estimate as being around 1200–1300 AD. After that, the QG section system diffused back through the Maric area, and this would have been a rapid diffusion because it would certainly have been in place throughout the area well before the arrival of white invaders in the nineteenth century.

Several aspects of this modelling could be incorrect, causing the chronology to be off to some degree—but it is not completely unreasonable. If it is correct, or slightly inaccurate, it shows just how recent the development and spread of at least some of the section systems in Australia are. Certainly, some of the other section systems in Queensland would be older, especially those in north Queensland—only some of which we have examined here. This is a matter for further research; however, my guess is that the oldest would only be a few thousand years old.

The other questions to tackle here are not only why the QG section systems spread back so rapidly across the Maric languages, but also why it followed the boundaries of Maric so well (not perfectly, but still a close fit) when it did spread back. One might think that in its diffusion from the south, the QG section systems could well occupy an entirely different set of areas, both inside and outside Maric. Was it that there existed an internal coherence and dense social network among the Maric languages/dialects, which at the time would have been mutually intelligible, having just separated from each other a few hundred years previously at most? After the new system was created, it spread rapidly and effectively in this environment; what's more, it reinforced the long-distance kin-like ties that sections provide.

References

Allen, N 1986, 'Tetradic Theory: an approach to kinship', *JRAI*, *17*, pp. 87–109. [Reprinted in R Parkin & L Stone (eds) 2004, *Kinship and family: an anthropological reader*, Oxford: Blackwell, pp. 221–36.]

Allen, N 2008, 'Tetradic theory and the origin of human kinship systems', in NJ Allen, H Callan, R Dunbar & W James (eds), Early human kinship: from sex to social reproduction, Oxford: Blackwell, pp. 96–112. doi.org/10.1002/9781444302714.ch5.

Alpher, B 2004, 'Pama-Nyungan: phonological reconstruction and status as a phylogenetic group', in C Bowern & H Koch (eds), *Australian languages: classification and the comparative method*, Amsterdam: John Benjamins, pp. 93–126, Appendix 'Pama-Nyungan Etyma' pp. 387–570. doi.org/10.1075/cilt.249.09alp.

Barnard, A 1978, 'Universal systems of kin categorization', *African Studies*, *37*, pp. 69–81. doi.org/10.1080/00020187808707509.

Barrett, B 2005, Historical reconstruction of the Maric languages of ventral Queensland, Masters thesis, The Australian National University.

Beale, A 1975, The Maric languages, BA honours thesis, The Australian National University.

Breen, GJ 1972, Unpublished fieldnotes Bidyara and Gungabula, 2011, AIATSIS MS159.

Breen, GJ 1973, *Bidyara and Gungabula grammar and vocabulary*, Monash University, Linguistic Communications 8.

Crowley, T 1981, 'The Mpakwithi dialect of Anguthimri', in RMW Dixon & BJ Blake (eds), *Handbook of Australian languages 2*, Amsterdam: John Benjamins B.V., pp. 146–94. doi.org/10.1075/z.hal2.07cro.

Davidson, DS 1928, *The chronological aspects of certain Australian social institutions as inferred from geographical distribution*, Philadelphia: University of Pennsylvania.

Dixon, RMW 1972, *The Dyirbal language of North Queensland*, Cambridge: Cambridge University Press. doi.org/10.1017/CBO 9781139084987.

Dixon, RMW 1981, 'Wargamay', in RMW Dixon & B Blake (eds), *Handbook of Australian languages 2*, Amsterdam: John Benjamins, pp. 1–144. doi.org/10.1075/z.hal2.06dix.

Dixon, RMW 1983, 'Nyawaygi', in RMW Dixon & B Blake (eds), *Handbook of Australian languages 3*, Amsterdam: John Benjamins, pp. 430–525.

Dixon, RMW 1991, 'Mbabaram', in RMW Dixon & B Blake (eds), *Handbook of Australian languages 4*, Amsterdam: John Benjamins.

Dixon, RMW 2002, *Australian languages: their nature and development*, Cambridge: Cambridge University Press. doi.org/10.1017/CBO 9780511486869.

Dollin, A, Dollin, L & Sakagami, S 1997, 'Australian stingless bees of the genus Trigona', *Invertebrate Taxonomy*, *11*, pp. 861–96. doi.org/10.1071/IT96020.

Fison, L & Howitt, AW 1880, *Kamilaroi and Kurnai: group-marriage and relationship, and marriage by elopement: drawn chiefly from the usage of the Australian Aborigines: also the Kurnai tribe, their customs in peace and war*, Melbourne: G. Robertson.

Fitzgerald, S 1997, 'A preliminary analysis of the laminal lateral in Pama-Nyungan languages', in D Tryon & M Walsh (eds) *Boundary rider: essays in honour of Geoffrey O'Grady*, Canberra: Pacific Linguistics C-136, pp. 155–74.

Fleck, D 2013, *Panoan languages and linguistics*, Washington DC: American Museum of Natural History Anthropological Papers 99.

Gardner, H & McConvell, P 2015, *Southern anthropology: a history of Fison and Howitt's Kamilaroi and Kurnai*, London: Palgrave and Macmillan. doi.org/10.1057/9781137463814.

Godelier, M 2004, *Métamorphoses de la parenté*. London: Verso (Champs, trans. 'The Metamorphoses of Kinship').

Halcroft, M, Spooner-Hart, R & Dollin, A 2013, 'Australian stingless bees', in P Vis, S Pedro & D Rouben (eds), *Pot honey: a legacy of stingless bees*, New York: Springer, pp. 35–72. doi.org/10.1007/978-1-4614-4960-7_3.

Harvey, M 1986, Ngoni Waray Amungal-yang: the Waray language from Adelaide River, MA thesis, The Australian National University.

Haviland, J 1979, 'Guugu Yimdhirr', in RMW Dixon & BJ Blake (eds) *Handbook of Australian languages 1*, Canberra: Australian National University Press, pp. 27–181.

Herschberger, HD & Herschberger, R 1986, *Kuku-Yalanji dictionary*, Darwin: SIL-AAB Work Papers B 7.

Hockings, HJ 1884, 'Notes on two Australian species of Trigona', *Transactions of the Royal Entomological Society of London*, 32(1), pp. 149–57.

Holmer, N 1983, *Linguistic survey of south-eastern Queensland*, Canberra: Pacific Linguistics D-54.

Hornborg, A 1993, 'Panoan marriage sections: a comparative perspective', *Ethnology*, 32(1). doi.org/10.2307/3773548.

Hornborg, A & Eriksen, L 2011, 'An attempt to understand Panoan ethnogenesis in relation to long-term patterns and transformations of regional interaction in western Amazonia', in A Hornborg & J Hill (eds), *Ethnicity in ancient Amazonia: reconstructing past identities from archaeology, linguistics, and ethnohistory*, University Press of Colorado, pp. 129–54.

Howitt, AW 1904, *The native tribes of south-east Australia*, London: Macmillan & Co.

Jefferies, T 2010, Notes on Maric languages, Unpublished manuscript.

Kensinger, K 1995, *How real people ought to live: the Cashinahua of eastern Peru long grove*, Illinois: Waveland Press.

Laffan, K 2003, Reconstruction of the Wakka-Kabic languages of south-east Queensland, BA honours thesis, The Australian National University.

Mathew, J 1910a, 'The origin of the Australian phratries and explanation of some of the phratry names', *JRAI*, 40, pp. 164–70. doi.org/10.2307/2843147.

Mathew, J 1910b, *Two representative tribes of Queensland, with an enquiry concerning the origin of the Australian race*, London: T. Fisher Unwin.

Mathews, RH 1898, 'Divisions of Queensland Aborigines', *Proceedings of the American Philosophical Society*, *37*(158), pp. 327–36.

Mathews, RH 1899, 'Divisions of some Aboriginal tribes, Queensland', *Journal of the Royal Society of New South Wales*, *33*, pp. 108–14.

Mathews, RH 1900, 'Group names and initiation ceremonies', *Journal of the Royal Society of New South Wales*, *33*, Appendix divisions of some north Queensland tribes, pp. 250–381.

Mathews, RH 1905, 'Ethnological notes on the Aboriginal tribes of Queensland', *Transactions of the Royal Geographical Society of Australasia, Queensland*, *20*, pp. 49–75.

McConnel, U 1939, 'Social organization of the tribes of Cape York Peninsula, North Queensland', Oceania, *10*(1), pp. 54–72. doi.org/10.1002/j.1834-4461.1939.tb00256.x.

McConvell, P 1985, 'The origin of subsections in northern Australia', *Oceania*, *56*, pp. 1–33. doi.org/10.1002/j.1834-4461.1985.tb02105.x.

McConvell, P 1997, 'Long-lost relations: Pama-Nyungan and northern kinship', in P McConvell & N Evans (eds), *Archaeology and linguistics: Aboriginal Australia in global perpsective*, Melbourne: Oxford University Press, pp. 207–36.

McConvell, P 2002, *Semantic change*, Lecture/presentation in Australian comparative linguistics course, The Australian National University.

McConvell, P 2013, 'Proto-Pama-Nyungan kinship and the AustKin project: reconstructing proto-terms for "mother's father" and their transformations', in P McConvell, I Keen & R Hendery (eds), *Kinship systems: change and reconstruction*, Salt Lake City: University of Utah Press, pp. 192–216.

McConvell, P & McConvell, W 2015, 'Mapping pragmatic equivalence of sections and subsections across Australia', Paper presented to the Australian Languages Workshop, Kioloa, March; and CHAGS conference, Vienna, September.

Oates, L 1988, *The Muruwari language*, Canberra: Pacific Linguistics C-108.

Pugach, I, Delfin, F, Gunnarsdottir, E, Kayser, M & Stoneking, M 2013, 'Genome-wide data substantiate Holocene gene flow from India to Australia', *PNAS*, *110*(5), pp. 1803–8. doi.org/10.1073/pnas.1211927110.

Radcliffe-Brown, AR 1913, 'Three tribes of Western Australia', *JRAI*, *43*, pp. 143–94.

Radcliffe-Brown, AR 1931, 'The social organization of Australian tribes', *Oceania*, *1*, pp. 1–4 [reprinted as Oceania Monographs 1]. doi.org/10.1002/j.1834-4461.1931.tb00015.x.

Ridley, W 1856, 'On the Kamilaroi tribe of Australians and their dialect', *Journal of the Ethnological Society of London*, *4*, 285–93.

Roth, W 1898, 'The Aborigines of the Rockhampton and surrounding coast-districts', in WE Roth (1898–1903), *Reports to the commissioner of police and others, on Queensland Aboriginal peoples 1898–1903*, FILM 0714 SL Qld.

Roth, W 1904, 'Letter to Howitt', in Howitt collection held at AIATSIS, Canberra. Ms 69, Box 5, Folder 3, Paper 4.

Roth, W 1910, 'North Queensland ethnography', *Bulletin no. 18. Social and individual nomenclature. Records of the Australian Museum*, pp. 79–106. doi.org/10.3853/j.0067-1975.8.1910.936.

Shapiro, W 1967, 'Semi-moiety organization: some moot points in the literature', *Mankind*, *6*(10), pp. 465–7. doi.org/10.1111/j.1835-9310.1967.tb01349.x.

Sharp, RL 1939, 'Tribes and totemism in north-east Australia', *Oceania*, *9*(3–4), pp. 254–76, 439–61.

Sim, I 1998, *Yuwaalayaay, the language of the Narran River*, Walgett, NSW: Walgett High School.

Spencer, B 1914, *Native tribes of the Northern Territory of Australia*, London: Macmillan & Co.

Sutton, P 1973, Gugu-Badhun and its neighbours: a linguistic salvage study, MA thesis, Macquarie University, Sydney.

Terrill, A 1993, Biri: a salvage study of a Queensland language, BA honours thesis, The Australian National University.

Terrill, A 1998, *Biri*, München: Lincom Europa.

Terrill, A 2002, *Dharumbal: the language of Rockhampton, Australia*, Canberrra: Pacific Linguistics.

Testart, A 1978, *Des classifications dualistes en Australie: essai sur l'évolution de l'organisation sociale*, Paris et Lille: Maison des Sciences de l'Homme & Lille III. doi.org/10.4000/books.editionsmsh.5757.

Thomson, D 1934, 'Notes on a Hero Cult from the Gulf of Carpentaria, North Queensland', *JRAIGB&I*, 64, pp. 217–35. doi.org/10.2307/2843808.

Tsunoda, T 2003, *A provisional Warrungu dictionary*, University of Tokyo, Department of Asian and Pacific Linguistics.

Vance, TR, van Ommen, TD, Curran, MAJ, Plummer, CT & Moy, AD 2013, 'A millennial proxy record of ENSO and eastern Australian rainfall from the law dome ice core, east Antarctica', *Journal of Climate*, 26, pp. 710–25. doi.org/10.1175/JCLI-D-12-00003.1.

von Brandenstein, CG 1982, *Names and substance in the Australian subsection system*, Chicago: University of Chicago Press.

Wafer, J & Lissarrague, A 2008, *A handbook of Aboriginal languages of New South Wales and the Australian Capital Territory*, Nambucca Heads, NSW: Muurbay Aboriginal Language & Culture Cooperative.

Williams, A, Ulm, S, Goodwin, ID & Smith, M 2010, 'Hunter-gatherer response to late Holocene climatic variability in northern and central Australia', *Journal of Quaternary Science*, 25(6), pp. 831–8. doi.org/10.1002/jqs.1416.

9
Generic Terms for Subsections ('Skins') in Australia: Sources and Semantic Networks

Patrick McConvell and Maïa Ponsonnet

Introduction

This chapter examines the generic terms for subsections in Australia—that is, the general terms that are applied to them as an institution in various Aboriginal languages. These Aboriginal language terms are roughly parallel to 'subsection' in academic English or 'skin' in more vernacular and Aboriginal English. As will be argued later, 'skin' is actually a loan translation from one of these Indigenous terms in one part of the country; however, generic terms have a variety of sources in different areas. The generic terms usually originate from words with different meanings, such as body parts or emanations like sweat and smell, and may also have been terms for other social categories, such as 'totemic' clans, before being applied to subsections. The polysemy of the generic term for 'skin' with these source meanings may continue in the current language. For example, in Dalabon, the term for subsection is *malk*, which also means 'weather/season'; thus, one can ask, 'What is your *malk*?', or 'What is your subsection (weather/season)?'

We are not concerned with specific terms for individual subsections in different languages, which have a different history unrelated to the history of the generic terms (McConvell 1985a) and which are being explored in-depth in the AustKin II ('Skin and Kin') project and in chapters in this book (McConvell & Dousset 2012). We also do not go deeply into the generic terms for other social categories, such as sections and totems. In Australia, social groups such as phratries or clans are often associated with things in the world that represent them emblematically. For instance, matriphratries on Croker Island are represented by sun, fire, rock and pandanus. In many places, totems are animals such as species of mammals, reptiles, birds and bees. There are semantic connections between these totems and the generic terms for subsections, which we outline, but this topic will be explored more fully on a different occasion.

In the Dalabon corpus of the second author, the generic term for subsections was used mainly to discuss relationships between spouses or potential spouses, especially when the adequacy of a given relationship was being questioned. Thus, the existence of a generic term facilitates explicit judgements on the conformity of behaviours with rules of kinship, and accentuates the binding power of this social structure. The existence of such terms is therefore socially significant, and the way they are used deserves in-depth study from the point of view of anthropological linguistics. However, this is not the task we devote ourselves to in this chapter; instead, we focus on issues of lexical and typological semantics related to word forms used as generic labels for subsections. Further data on usage would certainly assist in the analysis of semantic shift, since usage provides the bridging contexts that determine semantic change. However, collecting data on usage for 45 languages was not possible in the context of this preliminary research; thus, the question of usage is open to further research.

We have assembled generic terms for most subsection systems and their other meanings (where available). We show here that there are semantic connections between generic terms across the area where subsections are found and beyond, and we represent this on a semantic map. A semantic map (François 2008; Haspelmath 2003) is not a geographical map, but one that shows where polysemous words have put more than one sense together (such as those that have a sense like 'subsection' and a sense like 'body'). In this case, we extend the function of a semantic map to demonstrate that it also corresponds closely to the geographical map. Polysemies (or 'colexifications' in François's terminology, which we follow) occupy discrete areas on the map, either because of inheritance of the colexification in a language family or subgroup, or diffusion of the colexification. This allows us to trace the history of these semantic associations, which also relates to the layering of different social category systems as they diffuse over time.

There have been claims that there is a fundamental conceptual unity in many or all of the subsection and section systems, related to supposed differences in bodily or mental characteristics of members of these different social categories (e.g. von Brandenstein 1982); however, this hypothesis has been challenged (McConvell 1985b). Here, we study the colexifications of generic terms for subsections of around 45 languages (including some dialect varieties). We make an inventory of the domains to which they relate etymologically, and assess whether these domains concentrate mostly on bodily or mental characteristics, as previously hypothesised.

Subsections

Subsections are a system of eight sociocentric categories. All people who recognise each other as being in the same world of kin—which may extend far beyond a language group and even beyond the confines of Indigenous people—have a 'subsection' or 'skin' name. This is normally determined by the 'skin' of their parents. The 'skin' name is different from the skin of either parent but the parents' skin identities determine that of the child. Each of the eight categories has a particular kinship relationship with a person (an Ego). This means that when a person with a particular identity meets someone, even a stranger, they can immediately call each other by an appropriate kinship term, based on kinship links—known or supposed. For instance, if you meet someone with the same skin name, that person is your 'brother' or 'sister', their mother is your 'mother' and so on. There is also one skin (or sometimes two) that is 'straight' for any Ego—meaning that they are a legitimate marriage partner. (For more details of the system, see Chapters 1 and 3.)

In contrast, sections only have four terms. Each section represents a combination of the kinship types in two subsections. For instance, in a section system, one's own section contains people who are 'mother's mother' to Ego, as well as those who are 'brother' and 'sister'. In the most widespread type of subsection system (which we shall call 'classic'), 'mother's mother' is in a different subsection from 'sister'.

Linguistic investigation has revealed that the subsection system grew out of the meeting of two section systems, from the west and from the north. These two systems engaged in a particular type of marriage circulation that brought the new and more complex system into being, around the Katherine area of the Northern Territory (McConvell 1985a). From there, the new subsection system spread west into the Kimberley, south into Central Australia, north-east into Arnhem Land and east along the Gulf of Carpentaria and through the Barkly Tableland into the westernmost part of Queensland.

Around the periphery of this area of subsection expansion are other areas of sections—in Western Australia, parts of Central Australia (see Chapter 10) and very large areas of Queensland and New South Wales (see Figure 30; for the possible origin of sections in Queensland, see Chapter 8). In at least some of the areas where subsections are located, there were sections at some previous period[1] that have now disappeared. In other areas where subsections are found, there were and are still other social category systems, such as matrilineal totemic clans and phratries. The adoption of generic terms for such categories to refer to subsections is part of the story that we will unfold here.

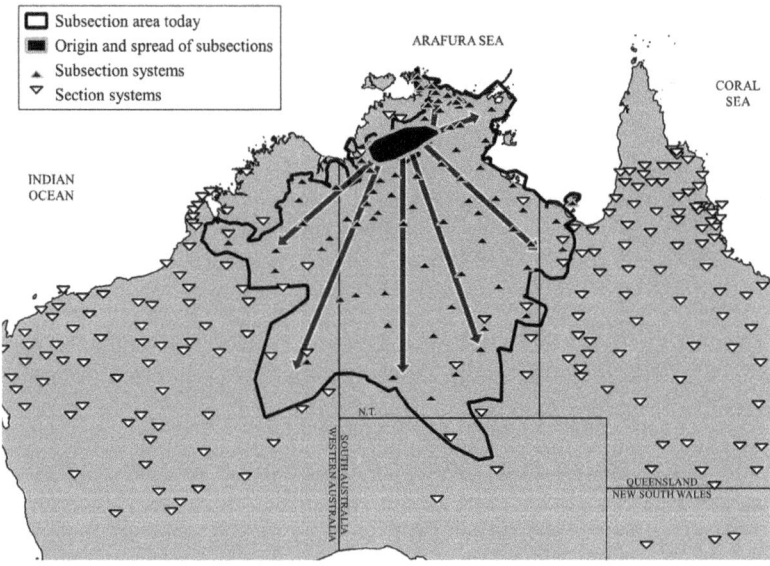

Figure 30: Map of distribution of sections and subsections.
Source: William McConvell.

---

1   McConvell (1996, 1997) estimated that the origin and beginning of subsection diffusion took place around 1,500 years ago. Harvey (2008) implied a date several thousand years earlier by reconstructing subsection terms to Proto-Mirndi. Mirndi is a very old family judging by the low number of lexical cognates. While both these hypotheses are tentative and more work is needed, we favour a date nearer to McConvell's and are doubtful about the Proto-Mirndi reconstruction. Absolute chronology is not part of the current exercise, but this chapter contributes evidence to relative chronology of subsection spread, which may be converted to absolute chronology by calibrating linguistic changes to archaeological dates (cf. McConvell & Smith 2003).

Methods

The terms for subsections (and a few sections) were assembled into a spreadsheet showing:

- their language
- the generic term for subsection in the language
- 'strict' colexifications, i.e. other senses of the subsection term
- 'loose' colexifications, i.e. senses to which a word relates etymologically
- other terms possibly related in form (whether cognate or borrowed)
- the source (e.g. dictionary, ethnography or pers. comm.)
- notes.

Some of this information was also entered into the AustKin II online database. So far, there are data for around 45 languages (including some dialect varieties), with at least 37 distinct colexifications (of course, these figures are indicative, since neither language delimitations nor sense delimitations are entirely discrete). This sample is large enough to identify patterns and articulate hypotheses that will be discussed later on. However, there are many instances in which we have no data or inadequate data on generic terms for subsection for the languages that have subsections. No data might mean that there was no generic term or that it was not recorded; where a term had been recorded but without a colexified sense, it might have been that there was no polysemy or that it was not recorded.

In almost all languages for which we have data, the generic term for subsection colexifies or loosely colexifies another meaning—that is, the generic term also has another sense in the same language or in a neighbouring language. There were a few exceptions to this general observation:

- There are a few languages that have no generic term for subsection.
- There are a few languages that have a vague term—for example, 'something'.
- There are a few languages that use 'kind' including suffixes—for example, 'What kind are you?' means 'What subsection are you?'
- In a number of languages, the term for subsection is the same as that for another social category. For instance, in the Victoria River District and western Arnhem Land, the colexification is between 'matriphratry'

and 'subsection'. At least one family (Bunuban—two languages) has a term that only colexifies another social category—patrimoiety—and does not have a more concrete colexification or etymology of which we are certain.

- A few languages have a term for subsection that is not obviously a word for something else in the same language nor, as far as we have discovered, relates etymologically to such a word in another language, which suggests a further remote etymology. This is a rare occurrence and only two examples have been found so far—both in the same language Wanyi: *nginyngi* (Mary Laughren [pers. comm.] incorrectly recorded this as *nini* in an earlier source) and *kuku*. It is possible in this case that there could be other connections that have not yet come to light.[2]

We have constructed a 'semantic map' using the methods of François (2008). We refer the reader to this publication, the review by McConvell and Ponsonnet (2013) and Haspelmath (2003) for more comprehensive discussions of semantic maps and associated methods.[3] We began with the sense 'subsection' as a 'pivot' or starting point and then traced a network in which the meanings that constituted plausible semantic extensions of one another, represented by individual cells, were located spatially closer to each other. This process, as we have used it, is not based on a standard way of analysing semantic composition or semantic distance, but rather based on subjective judgement and our knowledge of polysemies and semantic extensions in Australian languages. Of course, this reliance on intuition is not satisfactory. Thus, the organisation of the cells on the map is tested against actual colexifications, whereby a line is drawn to connect two senses when these senses are colexified by at least one language. If two senses have been placed adjacent to each other but are not found to be colexified in any language, then the map is 'falsified' and subsequently reorganised.

---

2   Subsections in eastern Mirndi languages have suffixes -*nginytya* (masculine) and -*nginytyu* (feminine) (e.g. Jingulu: Pensalfini 2003, pp. 12–3). It is possible that the -*nginy* here is related to the Garrwa-Wanyi word for generic 'subsection' and the Jingulu word for 'seed' *nginytyu*. The Mirndi languages have masculine and feminine genders; however, -*tya* and -*tyu* are not the regular forms of the gender suffixes, nor do they relate to the gender suffixes in Wakaya, a neighbouring Pama-Nyungan language (-*u* [masc.] and -*i* [fem.]). However, the eastern Mirndi suffix -*nginytyu* is also homophonous with the word for 'seed' in Jingulu.

3   Cf. Evans (1992a), Evans and Wilkins (2001) and Jurafsky (1996) for examples of graphic representations of semantic networks. Schapper, San Roque and Hendery (2016) presented colexifications of 'tree', 'firewood' and 'fire' in Australian and Papuan languages projected on to geographical maps.

In the corpus used by François (2008), some languages colexified 'breathe' with certain senses, and other languages did so with other senses again, with partial overlap across languages. The patterns of colexification found across languages can be summarised in the form of a semantic map taken from François (2008, p. 185) and reproduced in Figure 31. This is a simplified initial network with the pivot 'breathe', bringing in evidence from a number of languages in various language families from different parts of the world. The links between adjacent items reflect semantic proximity in synchrony and do not claim to represent diachronic relations. However, each link could, and many do, have a counterpart in diachronic change.[4]

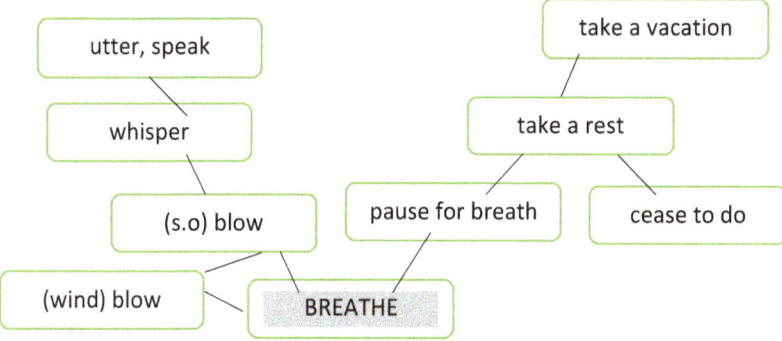

Figure 31: The first semantic map for {BREATHE}.
Source: After François (2008, p. 185).

In practice, it was sometimes impossible to find alternative connections when the map had been 'falsified'. In some cases, a 'step' in the chain of semantic associations might be 'missing'—that is, it was not represented in our corpus. An example of this would be as if no language colexified 'pause for breath' and 'take a rest' in Figure 31. Some would colexify 'breathe' and 'pause for breath', and some 'breathe' and 'take a rest', but none would display the whole chain as represented in Figure 31—perhaps because some languages in which the word for 'breathe' also means 'take a break' have lost the sense 'pause for breath'. In our case, such 'missing' colexifications may result from gaps in our data. Alternatively, the missing senses might be absent in synchrony, but could have existed historically and disappeared—'washed away' by history. François's method explicitly

---

4 Whether these are all potentially bidirectional or some only unidirectional is not investigated, nor is the issue of whether all such changes pass through a 'bridging' polysemy as in the hypothesis of Evans and Wilkins (2000). See also McConvell (2013, p. 195) on the hypothesis for kinship terms.

sets historical concerns aside; however, our purposes are slightly different. Therefore, when a conceptually attractive connection between two senses is missing from the data, and no alternative conceptual association seems plausible, cells representing the senses in question are linked with a dotted line, indicating that the association between the two senses is hypothetical.

This method is heuristic, based on meanings or senses of words available in sources, without an explicit semantic theory or decompositional practice as a foundation. We do not concern ourselves initially with whether a sense of a word is contextually determined or an entirely separate meaning. Such considerations may come into play after an entire semantic map is assembled, as a kind of 'bootstrapping' method. In our approach, we go beyond the typological semantic map to a geographical map of the spatial distribution of colexifications, and then add the historical dimension to the geographical map.

The Maps

Semantic Map of the 'Subsection' Network

Using the method previously mentioned, we constructed a semantic map of the network of colexifications involved with the generic term for subsection. Initially, this was completed without reference to geographical distribution. We identified nine main trends of colexification in the data and a few other minor ones (they are listed here in the order of presentation adopted in this section):

1. other social categories
2. dermis
3. smell, flavour and associated senses
4. body
5. head and associated attributes
6. name ('what are you called?')
7. time, country and associated senses
8. shadow (uncertain)
9. country, times and associated senses.

9. GENERIC TERMS FOR SUBSECTIONS ('SKINS') IN AUSTRALIA

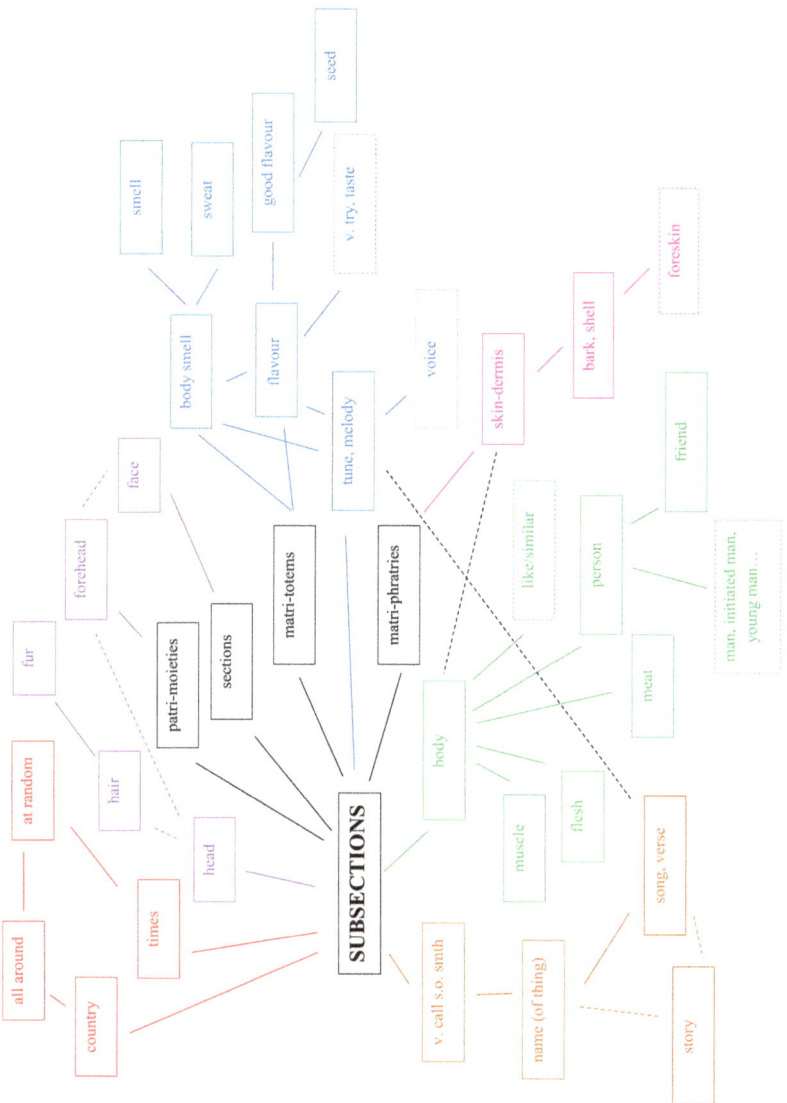

Figure 32: Semantic network of {SUBSECTION} (generic term) for the Australian languages surveyed.
Source: Authors' work.

Cells represent units of sense strictly colexified with the pivot 'subsection' (i.e. other senses of the words that mean subsection). Dotted cells represent units of sense loosely colexified with the pivot (i.e. with some historical relationship to the pivot). Lines between cells indicate that the two senses are actually colexified (i.e. that there is a word with these two senses) in at least one language. Dotted lines between cells indicate that we have hypothesised that the senses in question may be colexified in a language that is not included in the sample, or may have been colexified in the past.

Geography

To some extent, the different colexifications of subsections map on to discrete and continuous geographical regions. Therefore, the semantic clusters identified on the semantic map also cluster geographically. The match is not perfect, but the mismatch effect may be amplified by the fact that we do not have information for all languages in which subsections were used, and some languages in the same regions do not have the subsection system. As a result, the geographical map has 'gaps' (see Figure 33). Nevertheless, for most clusters, the geographical trends are relatively clear. In the following paragraphs, we discuss the clusters and their areal distribution.

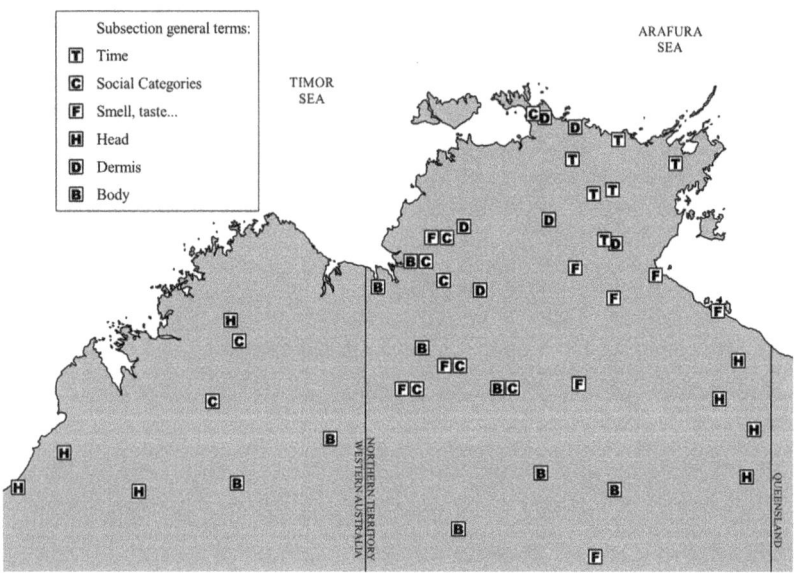

Figure 33: Map of geographical distribution of subsection colexification.
Source: William McConvell.

In the following section, we present each of the semantic clusters highlighted on the maps. We discuss our hypotheses regarding their semantic extensions and motivations, as well as their geographical distribution.

It appears immediately that the colexifications of the terms for 'subsection' mostly relate to the person and personal identity. The semantic range of these colexifications recalls the semantic network of Australian words for 'person' that was studied by Evans and Wilkins (2001). This work demonstrated the close semantic association between physical and social aspects of the person—an association also at play in the semantic network around generic terms for subsection (which partly overlaps the one for 'person'). In the following subsections, we discuss the motivations and articulate hypotheses for these colexifications.

In the first cluster of colexifications, subsection is colexified with other social categories. We hypothesise that a large number of other colexifications of generic terms for subsections could have gone 'through' the 'subsection/other social category' colexification. This hypothesis is represented on the semantic map (see Figure 32) by the fact that it is often necessary to go 'through' a 'social category' cell in order to reach the cells in other clusters. This aspect of the structure of the map results from the fact that for several clusters, there exists at least one language in which a tripartite colexification of the type 'subsection/other social category/member of the cluster' can be observed. In addition, many of these colexifications occur near the region where subsections originated as an institution, and several of them involve totemic social groups, such as groups emblematically represented by an animal. This hypothesis has consequences for mechanisms of semantic extension, as well as for the history of subsections (see the section 'History'). Further, colexifications involving distinctive aspects of the person such as 'dermis' may perhaps also relate to distinctive aspects of the totem (see section 'Physical Characteristics of Totem Animals').

The following sections discuss the other clusters. Colexifications involving distinctive aspects of the person such as the skin, smell and body are grouped together. This section opens with a discussion of the nature of chains of semantic associations leading to 'subsection/distinctive aspects of the person' colexifications. There are two plausible scenarios: first, these colexifications relate to distinctive features of the members of a social category (see the section 'Direct Associations between Social Categories and

Physical and Mental Characteristics'); second, these colexifications relate to distinctive features of the totem animal linked to the subsection or a previous social category system in the region in question (see the section 'Physical Characteristics of Totem Animals'). It may also be that in some places, there is a trinity of links between person characteristics, totem characteristics and social category. In this section, distinctive aspects of the person clusters are discussed one by one: 'dermis', 'smell and flavour', 'body', 'head', 'name' and, very briefly, 'shadow'. 'Country and times' present a cluster involving colexifications that are not distinctive aspects of the person.

Other Social Categories

These are colexifications with terms for other social groups such as matrimoieties and patrimoieties, as in the languages of the Victoria River District, whereby the word *ngurlu* means both 'subsection' and 'matri-totem categories' (among other senses). These colexifications have been discussed by Evans and Wilkins (2001) and their motivation is straightforward. Subsections are relatively recent social categories. When they appeared, they had to be named. In such a situation, extending the meaning of a pre-existing social category to cover the sense 'subsection' is a natural process.[5] The social category colexifications and the other colexifications described in the following paragraphs are not mutually exclusive. Rather, as evident in Figure 34, for three of the most extensive clusters of colexifications identified (namely the 'dermis', 'smell and flavour' and, to a minor extent, 'head' cluster), at least one element of the cluster takes part in a threefold colexification of the type 'subsections/other social category/element of the cluster'. In addition, these colexifications with social categories occur in languages located near the region where the subsections system originated (see the section 'Subsections' and McConvell 1985a). It is thus possible to hypothesise that a significant number of colexifications of subsections—namely the ones in the 'dermis' and 'smell and flavour' clusters, and possibly some in the 'head' cluster—derive from initial colexifications of subsections with another social category.

---

5   Sections (the fourfold division) predated and were replaced by subsections in at least part of the area now occupied by subsections. This transition needs more research, and while there are a few clear examples whereby subsections replaced sections in the twentieth century (Western Kimberley, eastern Gulf of Carpentaria and Arandic in Central Australia), it is not patently clear that the generic term for 'section' was taken over by subsections.

9. GENERIC TERMS FOR SUBSECTIONS ('SKINS') IN AUSTRALIA

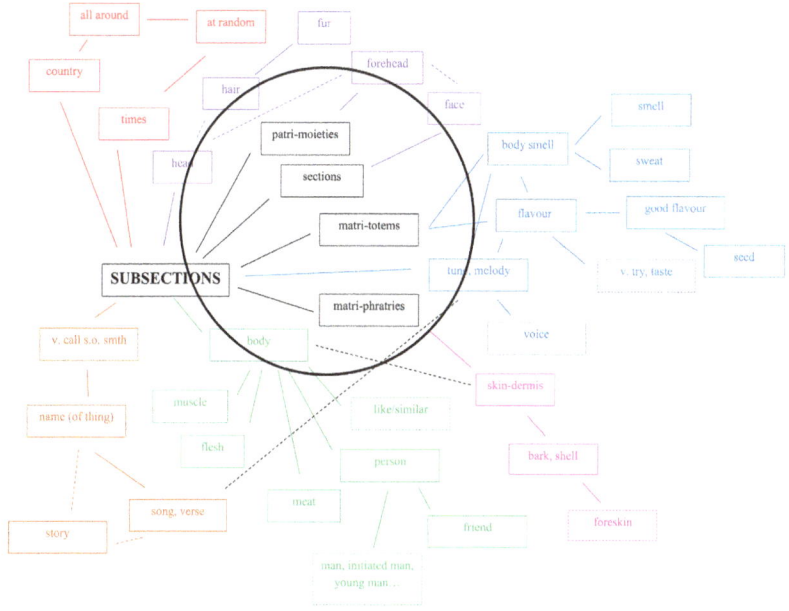

Figure 34: Position of 'other social categories' in the 'subsection' semantic network.
Source: Authors' work.

Distinctive Aspects of the Person

A large proportion of the colexifications of subsections have to do with the body and other aspects of the person that are all distinctive features likely to reveal and represent a person's identity: dermis, smell, voice, flesh, and body parts such as head, face and forehead (see Figure 32). These semantic associations between aspects of the body and subsection categories confirm Evans and Wilkins's (2001, p. 496) observation that '"body", "person" and "social identity" are intimately linked in semantic associations'. The concept of person may appear to constitute a natural conceptual 'bridge' between the notion of social category and physical appearance. This suggests that words for 'person' colexify with subsection, and also with 'body' and various aspects of the person (such as body, dermis and smell). If this is the case, a large number of languages should display threefold polysemies of the type 'person/subsection/distinctive aspect of the person'. However, as pointed out by Evans and Wilkins (2001, p. 505), such threefold colexifications are rare. Instead, we find many twofold colexifications of the type 'subsection/distinctive aspect of the person'. Hence, the representations in Figure 35 are incorrect, because

283

subsections and features of the person should connect directly, as they do on the map of the general network in Figure 32 and in the adequate representation in Figure 36.

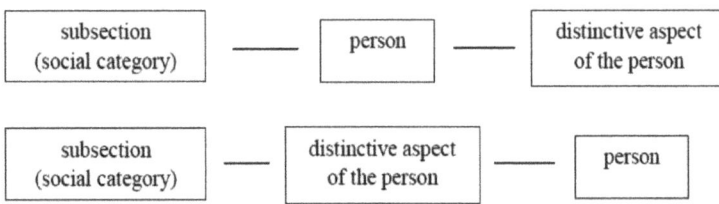

Figure 35: Inadequate (top) and supported (bottom) representation of 'subsection/distinctive aspect of the person/person' colexifications.
Source: Authors' work.

Evans and Wilkins's explanation for the frequent colexifications between social categories (which include subsections) and various aspects of the person is that speakers associate these concepts spontaneously. In their framework—which we endorse—colexifications (or polysemies in their terms) are evidence of conceptual association (see also Evans & Wilkins 2000; Sweetser 1990). More specifically, the conceptual association between social categories and aspects of the person is metonymic, with a distinctive aspect of members standing for the set.[6] In the section 'Direct Associations between Social Categories and Physical and Mental Characteristics', we discuss an alternative hypothesis—namely, that the metonymy associates the group label with distinctive aspects of the animal totem that represents a group, rather than distinctive aspects of members of the group. This hypothesis is attractive but not well supported by the data currently available.

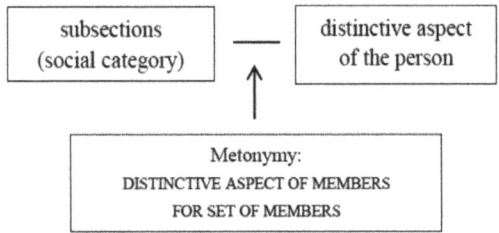

Figure 36: Conceptual explanation for 'subsection/distinctive aspect of the person' colexifications.
Source: Authors' work.

---

6   This metonymy may be further analysed as 'distinctive feature for member plus member for set'.

9. GENERIC TERMS FOR SUBSECTIONS ('SKINS') IN AUSTRALIA

In the following sections, we discuss each of the 'distinctive aspects of the person' clusters in more detail, starting with the most widespread and semantically consistent clusters ('dermis', 'smell and flavour' and 'body'), before moving on to clusters that display less consistency ('head'), are less widespread ('name') or for which the data are evanescent ('shadow').

Dermis

Colexifications with 'dermis' or related senses are found for instance in Iwaidja (Croker Island) where *-ngurlhi* means 'subsection' and 'dermis'. The Iwaidja *-ngurlhi* displays a threefold colexification of the type 'subsection/totemic social category/dermis' and, more specifically, 'subsection/matri-phratries/dermis' (with matriphratries being a totemic social category). It is therefore plausible that the 'subsection/dermis' colexification was mediated by the 'subsection/matriphratries' and the 'matriphratries/dermis' colexifications.

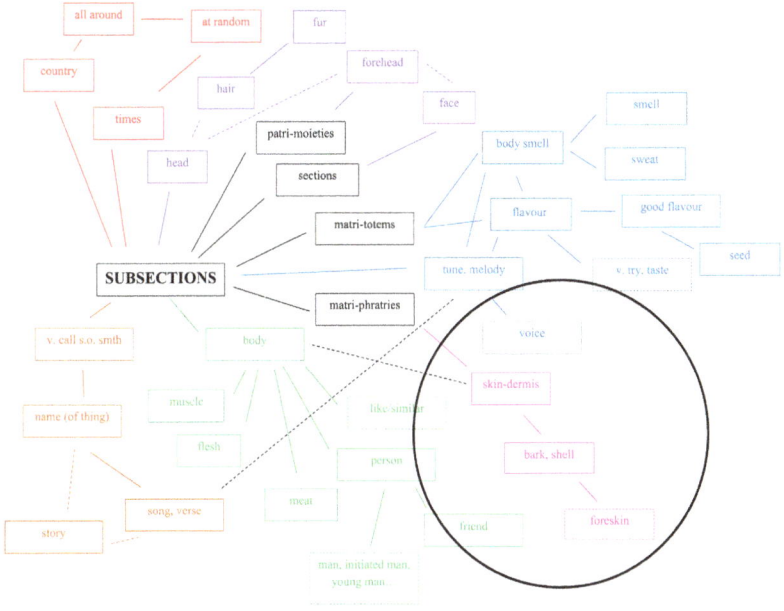

Figure 37: The 'dermis' colexification cluster.
Source: Authors' work.

Apart from dermis, the main colexification in this cluster is other types of outer covering in the natural world, such as bark and shell. This results from a standard polysemy between dermis, bark and shell, which is found in many Australian languages. A link between 'dermis' and 'body'

285

as a whole seems plausible. Although the 'dermis/body' colexification is not attested in the sample, it is found in other languages in the world, including a few Australian languages (Western Desert languages; Wilkins 1996, pp. 285–7). This may create a link with the body cluster.[7]

As previously explained, the 'subsection/dermis' colexification is also exemplified in Kriol, Pidgin and Aboriginal English, and mainstream English. The section '"Skin" Enters English' discusses our best hypothesis in respect to where this colexification was borrowed into these 'new' languages. Geographically, the distribution of this colexification is apparently continuous, extending between the Victoria River District (Wardaman) and the Cobourg Peninsula (Iwaijan languages), via the western Arnhem Land (central Gunwinyguan languages).

Smell and Flavour

Colexifications with 'smell' or related senses are represented by blue dots on the geographic map (see Figure 38). This colexification is well instantiated in Yanyuwa (towards the eastern edge of the subsection area, on the Gulf of Carpentaria) where *ngalki* means 'scent, odour, perfume, taste', as well as 'subsection' (and other related senses). 'Smell' colexifications prominently involve the notion of 'sweat smell' or distinctive body odour, as well as the notion of 'flavour'. In some languages, the same word also means 'odour' or 'scent' in general, and 'odour' and 'flavour' are colexified in some.

Kirton and Timothy's (1977) discussion of the senses of *ngalki*, the Yanyuwa term for subsections, offers some clues to understanding this colexification. The word means 'smell, voice, tune, subsection', and the authors argued for a monosemous interpretation of the cluster, with 'essence' as a common core. This formulation may be improved if we replace 'essence' by 'distinctive aspect/property'. Kirton and Timothy (1977) listed the following senses for the Yanyuwa word *ngalki*: subsections for humans and some other animates, the sweat of armpit for humans, the smell or taste of food, the perfume of a flower and the tune of a song (a further extension is found in the neighbouring Marra language, where the reduplicated form *ngalkingalki* means 'subsection' and 'voice'—another distinctive aspect of the person). While it is clear

---

7   This colexification is found in Papuan or Papuan-influenced Pacific indigenous languages including Pacific pidgin—for example, Takia (Austronesian) *tini*; Waskia (Papuan) *kumik* 'his/her/its body, skin, bark, surface' (Ross 2007, p. 121) and Tok Pisin *skin* 'skin, body, shell'.

how the term 'essence' relates to this list, it also seems that each of its items are 'distinctive features' or 'distinctive aspects' of the thing in question. Among Aboriginal groups, humans' armpit sweat (i.e. flavour–smell) is distinctive of one's identity. For instance, someone visiting an important site should put their hands under their armpit to collect sweat and lay their hand somewhere (e.g. on a rock), in order to signal their presence to the spirits. Hence, body smell is a token for identity and a distinctive aspect of the person. Since the nature of 'essence' is unclear, and its relation to distinctive features a matter of unresolved philosophical debate, it seems preferable to avoid this gloss, and replace it with 'distinctive feature' or 'distinctive aspect'.

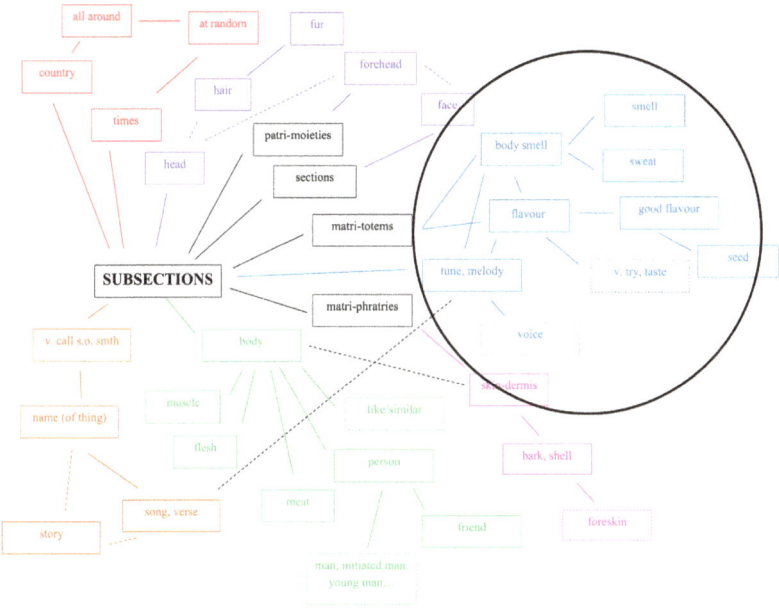

Figure 38: The 'smell/taste' colexification cluster.
Source: Authors' work.

In eastern Ngumpin languages, the form encapsulating the 'subsection/matri-totem/flavour' colexification is *ngurlu*. This word is found throughout the Victoria River District in Ngumpin languages, meaning primarily matrilineal totemic clans, and secondarily subsections, probably indicating that the name was transferred from the former to the latter institution when subsections diffused into this area. It is also used in some neighbouring Non-Pama-Nyungan languages to the north for both institutions, where both forms of social category are recognised. It is used among groups, for subsections only, where matrilineal clans are not used, such as in the north-east Kimberley (Jarragan languages).[8]

The 'flavour and smell' cluster has further ramifications. At least one of the 'flavour' words in eastern Ngumpin, *ngurlu*, has a number of less expected colexifications, such as 'attractive' and 'seed'. Presumably, the first of these has something in common with expressions like 'good taste' (an attested extension of 'taste') and 'tasty' when applied in contexts unrelated to food, whereas 'seeds' are the edible and tasty parts of cereal grasses that were a staple in this area. In Jingulu, the term for subsection is colexified with a nominal *manyku*—probably related to the verb *manyk-* 'try, taste', with the 'smell' sense absent. Interestingly, the suffix used with masculine subsection terms in Jingulu is homophonic with, and perhaps etymologically related to, the Jingulu word for 'seed' *nginju*. This recalls the 'subsection/seed' colexification encapsulated by *ngurlu* in eastern Ngumpin.

The 'flavour and smell' cluster of colexifications with subsection is geographically widespread. It is found across a number of Non-Pama-Nyungan families in the western Gulf of Carpentaria, Barkly Tableland and some of the Arandic languages of Central Australia. Due to a lack of data on generic names of subsections for some languages, it is not certain that this is a continuous distribution, but this has not been ruled out. The Arandic languages have a closely similar set of senses to the one found in Yanyuwa (the set of 'distinctive features' discussed above). These languages colexify 'smell' and 'taste', as well as 'subsection' and 'section', so this could be an areal feature, despite the distance involved. Anmatyerr *arreyn/arreytn* (eastern) and *arreny* (western) also colexify 'subsection' with 'song, verse, tune' (reminiscent of the Yanyuwa association with 'tune'), albeit with a different word. There is no Arandic word with a threefold colexification 'subsection/smell, flavour/tune'.

---

8   There is a superficial similarity between the form *ngurlu* 'seed, flavour, matrilineal totem, subsection', which appears to have been inherited first in the Ngumpin-Yapa subgroup of Pama-Nyungan, and the terms for matrilineal 'totem, subsection' in Iwaidjan (*ngurlhi, ngiri*) in which the colexification is with 'skin, bark'. The Kunwinyku/Mayali form *kurlah* 'skin' could be related to Iwaidjan *ngurlhi*, since the third singular possessed form in Iwaidja is *kurlhi*.

Body

Our data do not feature any threefold 'subsection/other social category/body' colexifications, but include a threefold 'subsection/body/person' colexification (see Figure 39). The words that mean 'subsection' and 'body' can also mean 'meat, flesh' and 'muscle'. In some readings, the latter is synonymous with 'flesh', but also has a distinct meaning of a bulge of muscle, viewed externally and as a more localised instantiation of that 'calf-muscle' and 'calf' in general in Jaru (Wrigley 1992, p. 16). Another sense in the cluster related to 'body' is the property attribute of a person or animal in good condition as opposed to too thin—also an expected extension of 'body' (Evans & Wilkins 2001, p. 504).

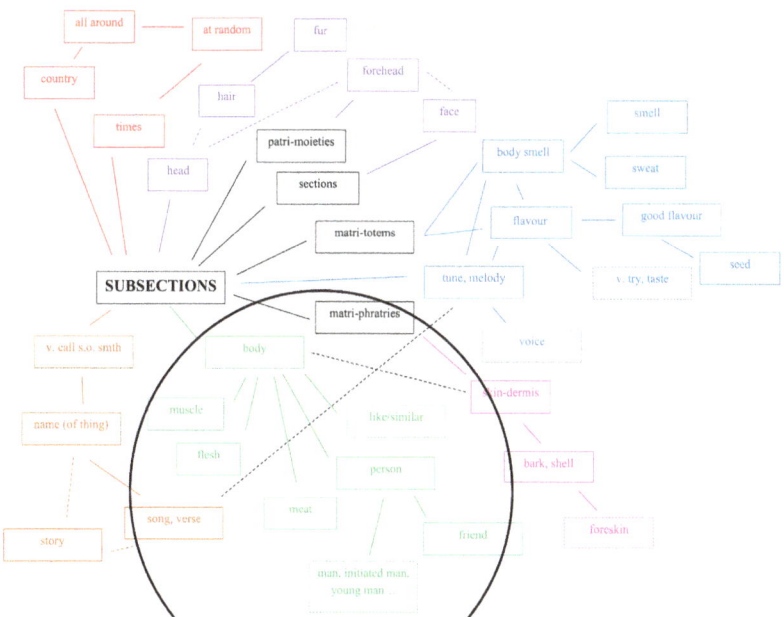

Figure 39: The 'body' colexification cluster.
Source: Authors' work.

The cluster also includes the sense 'person'. The body/person colexification is quite widespread in a number of Australian language groups, especially in Central Australia and in languages to the north-west. This colexification has been explored by Evans and Wilkins (2001) and is found in languages in different parts of the world, including English 'somebody'. In the area of Australia we are focusing on, strict colexification of person and body is found in parts of the Western Desert—for instance, *yarnangu/arnangu* in the southern Western Desert. In spite of the frequency of the twofold 'body/person' colexification, our language set contains only one example of a triple colexification 'subsection/body/person' (*tyerrtye* in Arrernte). There is also only one case of loose colexification, with the 'person' word *puntu*. Evans and Wilkins (2001, p. 499) reported that *puntu* means 'subsection' in Warlpiri, where it also means 'friend, companion'. *Puntu* means 'person' and 'body' respectively in some other languages, but not in Warlpiri.[9]

The 'like, similar' meaning of 'body' is also cross-linguistically common and is found in the Daly area (*nginipunh*, Murrinhpatha). It is classed as 'loose', since the form meaning 'like, similar' is no longer a noun, but has become grammaticalised as a suffix. Thus, the relationship with the homophonous noun meaning 'subsection' and 'body' is etymological. Another word that colexifies 'body' and 'subsection' in the northern Victoria River District Ngumpin languages, *mayi*, is found in another Ngumpin language Wanyjirra (Chikako Senge pers. comm.), some distance away, as a 'like, similar' suffix.

In terms of geographical distribution, the 'subsection/body' colexification is found to the west of the subsection distribution, mainly in Ngumpin languages (Pama-Nyungan), but also in Murrinhpatha, a neighbouring Non-Pama-Nyungan language to the north. This colexification is exemplified by a range of diverse forms. In Ngarinyman and Mudburra, in eastern Ngumpin (Pama-Nyungan) in the Victoria River District, the form that colexifies 'subsection' and 'body' is *mayi*. In the northern neighbouring western Mirndi languages, the form *mayi* means 'body', but not 'subsection'. In western Ngumpin, the same 'body/subsection' colexification is found. In Jaru, the term *buya* meaning 'body', 'flesh' and 'muscle' is used for 'subsection' (Wrigley 1992, p. 16), and in Walmajarri the term *ngilyki* 'flesh' also means 'subsection' (Richards & Hudson 1990, p. 190). In Gajirrabeng, a northern Jarragan language in the east Kimberley, the term for subsection is not the same as 'body' but is derived from it, albeit by a morphological process that is not fully understood. In this instance, the 'body' word (*juwugeng*) is also colexified with 'person'—a kind of polysemy known elsewhere.

---

9   Whether this results from some kind of constraint or is accidental is not clear. See the next section for further historical interpretation.

Head

Another cluster of colexifications, represented by purple dots on the map (see Figure 40), concerns body parts around the head. This includes 'head', 'face', 'forehead' and 'hair' (and 'fur' as an extension of words meaning 'hair'). This colexification is found, for instance, in Ungarinyin (Kimberley) where *amalarr* means both 'subsection' and 'forehead' (as well as 'moiety'). The head and its attributes, especially the face, are also very distinctive of individual identity (Evans & Wilkins 2001; Ponsonnet 2009). A particularity of this cluster is that it is geographically discontinuous. Colexifications involving face and forehead are found in the north-west of the subsection area, and are actually more frequent for sections than subsections; colexifications involving the head and hair are found in the south-east of the subsection area, around the middle of the Gulf of Carpentaria on the Queensland coast.

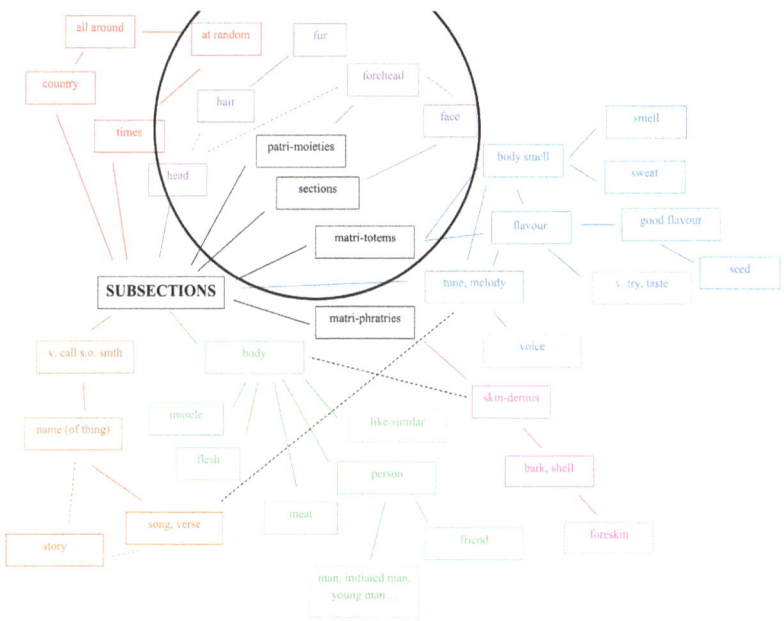

Figure 40: The 'head' colexification cluster.
Source: Authors' work.

Threefold colexifications involving 'subsection/other social category/ attribute of the head' are found with 'forehead' and 'patri-moieties' and with 'face' and 'sections' at the eastern edge of the subsection area. Terms for 'face, forehead' (*miparr*, *ngumpa*) are used for sections in the Marrngu languages of the south-western Kimberley and eastern Pilbara.

In Ungarinyin, a Worrorran language in the central Kimberley where subsections are only marginally used, the colexification of 'forehead' with generic patrilineal moiety has been extended to subsections.

'Head' and 'hair' are found as colexifications of 'subsection' on the opposite side of the subsection area, in the extreme east of the expansion of subsections in the Tangkic family of languages on the Gulf of Carpentaria coast and islands. 'Head' and 'hair' are occasionally found colexified in Australian languages, but not in Tangkic (at least not in recent times) where there are two separate items that are both colexified with 'subsection'. The colexification of 'hair/fur' and '(sub)section' is found far south in lower Arrernte. For concepts of types of hair in relation to social categories, see the section 'History'. Threefold colexifications involving 'subsection/other social category/head or hair' are absent in our data. Hence, head-related colexifications (with hair [fur], face and forehead) are recurrent in the data, but are scattered on each side of the continent, and thus form a less consistent cluster.

Name

Colexifications with 'name' and related senses are represented by orange dots on the map (see Figure 41), and occur only in a few languages at the extreme south of the subsection area. This small cluster relates to a more literal way of expressing the function of subsection terms. Some languages do not have a colexification of the same kind that we have been discussing—that is, based on a noun. To enquire about someone's subsection, one asks, 'What are you called?' or 'What is your name?' These expressions are vague and do not specifically refer to subsections. However, forms derived from 'calling by name' have become specific to talking about subsections and sections as in western Arrernte and Anmatyerr. Again, a name is obviously a distinctive aspect of the person; however, this time, the colexification does not result from metonymies involving aspects of the person, but simply from a pragmatic bridging context in which the more generic concept of name is used to enquire about the more specific category of subsection. In Anmatyerre, the form *arreyn/arreytn* (eastern) and *arreny* (western) colexify 'subsection', 'name' and 'song, verse or tune'. This recalls the sense of 'tune' colexified with 'smell and flavour' by the word *ngalki* in Yanyuwa, much farther to the north-east. Again, songs usually relate to social categories and personal identity and may be treated as tokens of identity.

9. GENERIC TERMS FOR SUBSECTIONS ('SKINS') IN AUSTRALIA

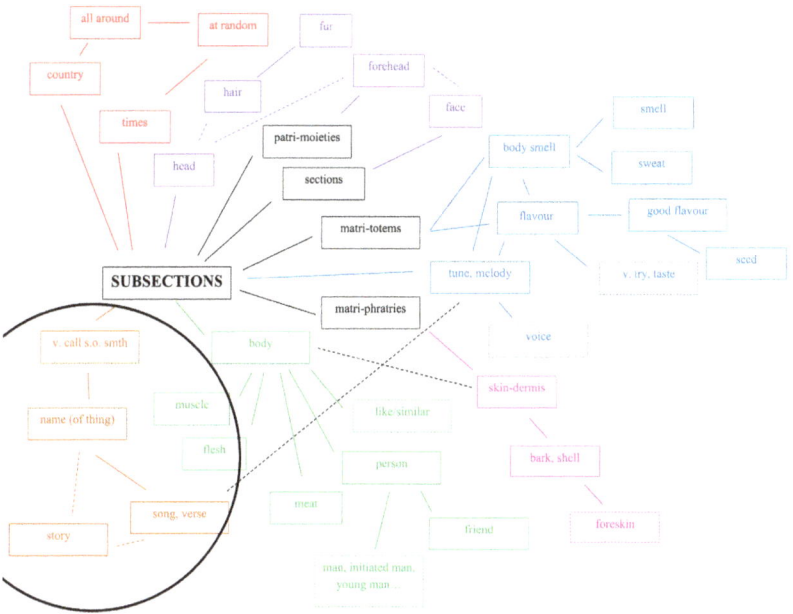

Figure 41: The 'name' colexification cluster.
Source: Authors' work.

Shadow

In the Bunuban languages, the term for subsection, *kuru*, is also extended from patrilineal moieties. It is possibly related to the word for 'shadow, shade' *kururru*, but the derivational mechanism is unclear.[10] Semantically, there is often colexification in Australian languages between 'shadow' and 'reflection, image', which is plausibly related to the identity aspect of social category membership. There are other connections between social categories and types of shade in other regions—for instance, in the Western Desert and northern New South Wales/southern Queensland.

Country and Times

This cluster of colexifications is represented by red dots on the geographic map (see Figure 42). It occurs in a discrete region to the east of the Top End, in central and eastern Arnhem Land, adjacent to the area where 'dermis'

---

10   In Jaru and eastern Walmajarri *kurukuru* is 'black'—the etymology could be 'like shadow (dark)'. *Kuru* is 'eye' in Western Desert language and there are cognates in a number of western Pama-Nyungan languages with sound changes pointing to the relatively great age of the root (McConvell & Laughren 2004). Since 'eye', 'face' and 'forehead' are commonly colexified, it is possible that the Bunuban subsection generic is a 'loose' (historical) colexification of the 'head' set.

colexifications are found. For example, in Dalabon (Gunwinyguan, Arnhem Land), the noun *malk* means both 'subsection' and 'weather, season'. This set of colexifications is rather different from the others and its internal semantic connections are puzzling. In various Gunwinyguan languages (Arnhem Land) and in the neighbouring Burrarra, the form *malk* is found to colexify 'subsection' and the senses 'at times', 'all around', 'at random', 'weather/season' and 'country' (however, no language has all colexifications). In addition, among the Gunwinyguan languages, Kuninjku uses the form *kurn* for subsection, which is cognate with Dalabon *kurnh*, meaning 'place', for instance.

In some Bininj Gun-wok dialects, the form *malk* also means 'liver'. However, 'liver' is *marlk* in Dalabon, with a retroflex lateral. In addition, neither the sense 'liver' nor any closely related sense (e.g. abdominal part) are colexified with 'subsection' anywhere else. The presence of the retroflex and the absence of attested semantic associations suggest that the colexification of 'subsection' and 'liver' in Bininj Gun-wok results from homonymy.

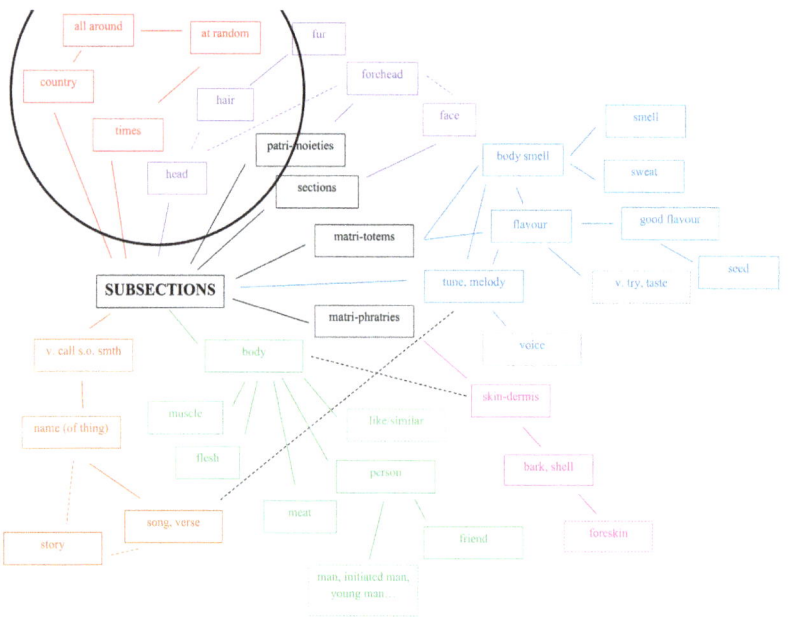

Figure 42: The 'country and times' colexification cluster.
Source: Authors' work.

It is not impossible that the colexification between 'subsection' and 'at times', 'all around', 'at random', 'weather/season' and 'country' also results from homonymy. Indeed, in Yolngu, 'subsection' is *maalk* and 'at times' is *malk*. Since the Gunwinyguan languages do not use a vowel length distinction, the Yolngu *maalk* could have been borrowed as *malk* from neighbouring Non-Pama-Nyungan languages, resulting in homonymy with another lexeme *malk*, meaning 'at times'. However, the existence of an independent (loose) colexification of 'subsection' and 'country', with the Kuninjku *kurn* (cognate with Dalabon *kurnh*, 'place'), suggests that the conceptual association, even if it resulted from homonymy originally, would have been reanalysed as a polysemy at some point.

In spite of this possibility that the colexification between 'subsection' and 'at times', 'all around', 'at random', 'weather/season' and 'country' may result from homonymy, it is also worth considering the hypothesis that it is inherently a polysemy. The conceptual associations between these senses are puzzling, but not implausible. Apart from 'subsection', the most widespread sense of *malk*, and thus its probable oldest known sense, is 'at times'. Several paths of semantic associations between this sense and the others—'at random', 'all around', 'weather/season' and 'country'—seem plausible.

Saulwick's (2003) Rembarrnga dictionary indicates a bridging context in which the adverb *malk* could mean 'at times', 'at random' and 'all around': *malk* is used to describe someone 'shooting at random in the air'. Shooting at random is likely to involve shooting several times and all around. This would explain how the older meaning 'at times' could extend to 'all around'. In Dalabon, *malk* is used in compounds meaning 'look all around' (*malk-nan*, *nan* 'see/look'), which suggests an extension to 'country'. It is typically the country that one looks at when 'looking around'; therefore, this Dalabon compound also offers a bridging context for the extension from the sense 'all around' to the sense 'country'. The association with 'weather/season' or 'season' may relate to the fact that these are also descriptions of the environment or surroundings.

These semantic associations can also be presented from a different angle. The connection between country or place and time has been reported by Evans (1992a). For instance, an association between 'country' and 'times' (as in 'a number of times') is suggested by the Warlpiri word *ngurra*, which means a camp (i.e. a place, that can further extend to 'country'), but also a night spent at a given camp, where places correspond to successive stopovers along an itinerary (Musharbash 2008, p. 34). The Gurindji cognate is used in expressions such as *ngurra kujarra* 'two camps, two nights', in which place and time units are conceptually merged. The sense 'all around' could also derive from the same concept of cyclic itinerary (a series of 'camps' or stopovers along a journey). In addition, the notion of stopovers on a cyclic itinerary could also explain the extension 'weather/season'. With this scenario of semantic extension, the sense 'subsection' could also relate to the 'stages of a cycle' (this time, a cycle of successive generations), similar to 'weather/season'. While this scenario is not implausible, it is highly speculative and there is little evidence to support it. The previous scenario (based on contexts such as 'to look all around' and 'to shoot at random') is better supported by actual bridging contexts in Rembarrnga and Dalabon.

In the scenario presented in Figure 43, whereby 'at times' connects to 'country' via 'at random' and 'all around', it is not entirely obvious how this colexification set relates conceptually to 'subsection'. A possible link may be via the notion of totemic site (place and country). Bininj Gun-wok dialects have *malng*, meaning 'clan spirit which returns to a deceased's country after death', which could plausibly be cognate with *malk*, and could therefore support this conceptual path. While the *k* > *ŋ* sound change is not straightforward and not clearly attested among the Gunwinyguan family, it is rendered more plausible by an environment in which the word occurs frequently in the Bininj Gun-wok dialect Kune (which is very close to Dalabon, both geographically and linguistically). As Kune has obligatory suffixes on some nominal subclasses (Evans 2003; Ponsonnet in prep.), the default form of the word *malng* in this dialect is *malng-no*. In this default environment, the first consonant of the suffix explains the shift to a nasal as backwards assimilation. Seen as a reference to personal totemic birth site, the 'subsection/country' colexification reconnects with the aspect of the person or totem clusters.

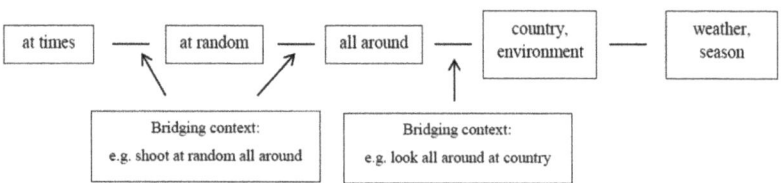

Figure 43: Suggested chain of motivations for 'at times/country' colexifications.
Source: Authors' work.

Another puzzling feature in this cluster is that in Ngalakgan, the form *malk* is also reported to colexify the sense 'dermis', linking the 'country/times' cluster to the 'dermis' cluster. Conceptual associations between 'dermis' and the 'at times' cluster ('all around', 'at random', 'weather/season' and 'country') are relatively loose.[11] Since in varieties of Kriol or Aboriginal English, the form *skin* is broadly used for both 'subsection' and 'dermis', it is not impossible that speakers have imposed 'dermis' back translations on words for subsections that did not originally mean 'dermis' (in fact, such back translations from 'subsection' to 'dermis' are confirmed for Arrernte).

Generic Terms and Ethnotheories of the Body and Personal Identity

Direct Associations between Social Categories and Physical and Mental Characteristics

A number of concepts that are used as generic terms for subsections also play a part in Aboriginal ethnotheories of social categories that include subsections. For instance, the concept 'dermis' came into English as the word *skin*, meaning subsection. In some places, the colour of people's skins (dermis) is supposed by local Aboriginal people to be associated with certain subsections. Similarly, 'hair' is used as a generic term for subsection in the east and south of subsection distribution, and in some places the type of hair (straight/curly) is said to be associated with subsections. It should be noted that Aboriginal people do not, so far as is known, make a conscious association between generic terms and these ethnophysiological ideologies, nor is there any good fit between the languages that have particular generic terms and particular ideologies. For instance, it is not reported that people say, 'We call subsection "dermis" because it reflects differences in our skin colour'.

---

11   It was suggested to us that the dermis is 'all around' the body. However, this is not very convincing, especially since in Ngalagkan, only the sense 'at times' is reported, not 'all around', which is probably derived from 'at times'. Also, the 'dermis' is 'all around' the body in a way that does not match occurrences of this sense in the cluster in which 'all around' refers to the whole environment rather than a thin envelope.

One researcher who made a great deal of such associations and other associations related to characteristics of body shape and mental disposition is von Brandenstein. After initially developing his approach with sections, he later moved on to write a book about subsections. The work by von Brandenstein (1982) was received with great scepticism by most, but praised by some. McConvell's (1985b) review article is highly critical of von Brandenstein's methods and results. One of von Brandenstein's (1982, p. 5) methodological principles proposed that:

> If a superstructure of the highest philosophical order is found to have existed in one Australian region and to have ruled a particular sociocultural practice there, it must also be involved in other regions where similar or identical sociocultural practices can be observed.

He continued on to suggest that the Dreaming ensured absence of change, and was wrongly interpreted by people using European notions of change, such as Testart (1978). The idea that high-order philosophical superstructure 'rules' practice is highly dubious. Leaving this aside, there is also the notion that the existence of a practice in one place implies that a superstructure or ideology found in that place 'is involved' in another place where the practice is also found, even if there is no evidence for the existence of the ideology. This is an absurd method that leads to the invention of all kinds of non-existent explanations.

A list was collected by von Brandenstein (1982, p. 6, see pp. 150–1 for notes and references) of what we are calling 'generic terms' for subsections and other social divisions, and their semantic associations. This list overlaps significantly with what we have already presented. It includes the following:

- flesh or meat
- body
- skin
- head
- forehead or face
- hair
- eyes
- side
- liver or temper
- colour

- taste
- scent (armpit sweat)
- voice
- identifying essence
- half
- run or section
- mate or friend
- namesake.

The list is a mixture of generic terms for moieties, sections and subsections, and may also include totemic clans, with no apparent attempt to make historical or geographical sense of the distribution. The prime reference for 'taste' is Yanyula *ngalgi* (*ngalki*, Yanyuwa, Gulf of Carpentaria; Kirton & Timothy 1977), which is also rendered as 'identifying essence' ('distinctive feature' in our terms). This is linked to an addendum discussing *ngurlu* 'matri-totems', 'flavour', 'seed' and 'good taste' (eastern Ngumpin, Victoria River District), which is apparently proposed as being related linguistically to *ngalgi*. Our preferred interpretation is that the colexification might have spread widely and subsequently been 'borrowed', but it is unlikely that the forms are cognates. The addendum contains a great deal of misleading information. The Dalabon subsection generic, citing Maddock (1969, pp. 37, 53), is said to be both dermis and liver/temper. According to our analysis, the latter is a confusion between the word *malk* and *marlk*.

Despite von Brandenstein's (1982) strictures on history, he did propose a hypothesis on the origin of subsections by way of adding a 'side set' of terms related to attributes of body and temperament to the previous sets in the section system. There does not seem to be any attempt in this book to link these attributes to the generic terms of sections or subsections. The history that von Brandenstein proposed is highly abstract and detached from the realities of the world and society. McConvell's (1985a) concrete and original hypothesis regarding the origin and diffusion of subsections also did not take into account the generic terms as part of the story. In his critique of von Brandenstein, McConvell (1985b, pp. 56–9) emphasised that beliefs about traits attributed to sections and subsections are not universally present in the areas where the social categories exist, and are not equally important nor consistent across different areas. However, the fact remains that there are a handful of generic names that are found for these systems that, although diverse, have certain similarities and perhaps relate to ethnophysiological and ethnopsychological aspects of the person. We have started the task of reconstructing the diffusion or inheritance of generic names and examining how this fits with the diffusion of the specific social category terminologies themselves. A further stage would be to match the history and geography of the ethnogenetic systems to the generic terminologies.

The core of the generic social category terms in their more concrete meanings seems to point to characteristics that identify individuals. The term 'individual essence' has been used; however, this might be adding a literal 'essentialist' slant and 'distinctive aspects'—including the dermis, smell and flavour, body, head and its attributes and name— might be preferred. As pointed out by Evans and Wilkins (2001), it is no coincidence that some of these senses have also come to mean 'person' in Australia and elsewhere. Aspects of the body that are particularly liable to being used for generic social category terms are those that are most apparent and specific to individuals. There is a semantic unity to these various complexes despite the fact that they have their own histories, and it makes sense to suggest that these colexifications reflect speakers' conceptual associations between distinctive aspects of the person and social category. From this perspective, it is interesting to note that von Brandenstein's (1982) theory is not entirely at odds with Evans and Wilkins's (2001) suggestions in relation to the Australian concept of 'person', as von Brandenstein's postulated beliefs are also related to the same fundamental attributes that identify individuals. Our preliminary study of the semantic network of the generic term for 'subsection' partly confirms Evans and Wilkins's (2001) suggestions.

Physical Characteristics of Totem Animals

Another hypothesis proposed to explain the colexification of 'subsection' with senses that denote aspects of the person is that colexifications may result from an association of social categories with aspects of totemic figures, such as the animals for which totems or 'dreamings' are identified, rather than with distinctive aspects of the person. Thus, this hypothesis is different from the one that von Brandenstein (1982) proposed. While there are associations between sections and aspects of personal identity for sections in some areas, this is very rare for subsections.

The two scenarios—one involving conceptual association of social categories with distinctive aspects of its members, and the other relying upon distinctive aspects of the totem independent of aspects of the members—are not exclusive of each other. The former may apply for colexifications in some languages, and the latter with others. As previously mentioned, the scenario involving aspects of the totem rather than aspects of the person is not yet unambiguously supported by the data that we currently have in hand. Nevertheless, this scenario has one interesting advantage over the other: it is in line with the near-complete absence of folk theories that attribute distinctive physical features to people according to their subsection.

This hypothesis is further supported by the fact that some of the social categories in question—in particular, matri-totems in the Victoria River District and matriphratries among Iwaidja speakers—are associated with totemic emblems. Across the continent, totems are often animals, which may be referred to metonymically using some of their most salient features. Most Australian languages have a colexification of 'meat' and 'animal'; thus, in areas in which social categories such as totems or sections are called 'meat' in Aboriginal English and a 'meat' term in a local language, this can also be translated as 'animal'. In some areas where totems are animals, restrictions may be placed on the consumption of that particular animal. The cultural salience of totem consumption may justify metonymies whereby one's totem is designated as one's 'meat' or 'flavour'. For example, in Kayardild, the word *wuranda* colexifies the senses 'food', 'meat, flesh', 'totem' and 'kind' (Evans 1992b).

At this stage, the actual nature of totems in regions where 'subsection/totemic social category' colexification is known to occur does not support this hypothesis particularly well. Our data feature several threefold colexifications involving subsections, totemic social groups and flavour or smell. We find 'subsection/semi-moieties/flavour–smell' in Yanyuwa, but also, close to the region where subsections originated, Ngan'gi (Daly family) has 'subsection/matri-totem/flavour–smell'. A bit further south, in eastern Ngumpin languages (which do not colexify flavour and smell), the colexification set includes flavour, but not smell ('subsection/matri-totem/flavour'). Thus, the aspect-of-totem scenario, whereby 'subsection/aspect of person' colexifications obtain via metonymies involving aspects of the totem (here, flavour, naturally extending to smell by virtue of a widespread monosemy) and not of the person, is a plausible explanation for the colexifications in this cluster.

In the case of Yanyuwa, it would seem that the generic term for subsection could apply both to the distinctive aspects of persons and those of totems. Based on Kirton and Timothy (1977), it appears that flavour and smell are core senses of the word *ngalki* (other distinctive features such as the melody for a tune being marginal). 'Flavour/smell' colexifications are common in Australian languages and probably correspond to a single concept in languages in which they apply. As previously explained, body smell is a token for human's identity (and for some animals). Further, *ngalki* also refers to the flavour(–smell) of an animal when it is eaten, and this could apply to an animal totem. Another sense of *ngalki*, 'tune of a song', may easily relate to totemic features, given that many local songs are totemic songs (i.e. they recount the journeys and adventures of ancestral beings). However, none of these social categories involve totemic figures; therefore, the aspect-of-totem scenario is less plausible for this cluster.

History

The Diffusion of Subsections and Subsection Generic Terms

As already mentioned, the relationship of different senses of lexical items is not purely synchronic but can involve change from one meaning to another, with an intermediate stage of polysemy/colexification. This stage is either discoverable in other languages as synchronic, or plausibly reconstructed by identifying one or several 'bridging contexts' in which sense 'A' is ambiguous with sense 'B'.

These kinds of hypothesised historical change can be traced by anthropological modelling and from linguistic studies—particularly of the changes in individual subsection terms and their relationships with earlier systems such as sections (McConvell 1985a, 1997). The development of different generic terms for subsections can provide evidence that feeds into the hypotheses regarding the historical origin and spread of subsections (Evans & Wilkins 2000).

The diffusion of subsections is known from historical distribution. However, evidence about the spread and change of subsections also constrains and moulds what we might conclude about the history of generic terms. Figure 44 is a rough map that shows the broad outline of the diffusion of subsections overlaid on the map of generic terms for subsections (see Figure 32). The remainder of this section briefly explains the history of subsections and how it fits within the history of generic terms, including how generic terms may add to our understanding of subsection diffusion. The section '"Skin" enters English' is a case study of a particular development in which the 'subsection/dermis' colexification spread to western Arnhem Land and incorporated into Aboriginal English, before spreading widely as the term 'skin'.

The subsection system is found in the central north of Australia. It does not extend to the north Kimberley or the central Top End of the Northern Territory around Darwin and the Tiwi Islands. The system was reported in the Daly River region in the mid-twentieth century (subsequently abandoned) and in eastern Arnhem Land, but it is clear from historical data that the system had only spread into these regions within the last 100 years. Subsections also recently spread into Central Australia, replacing the section system (see Chapter 10).

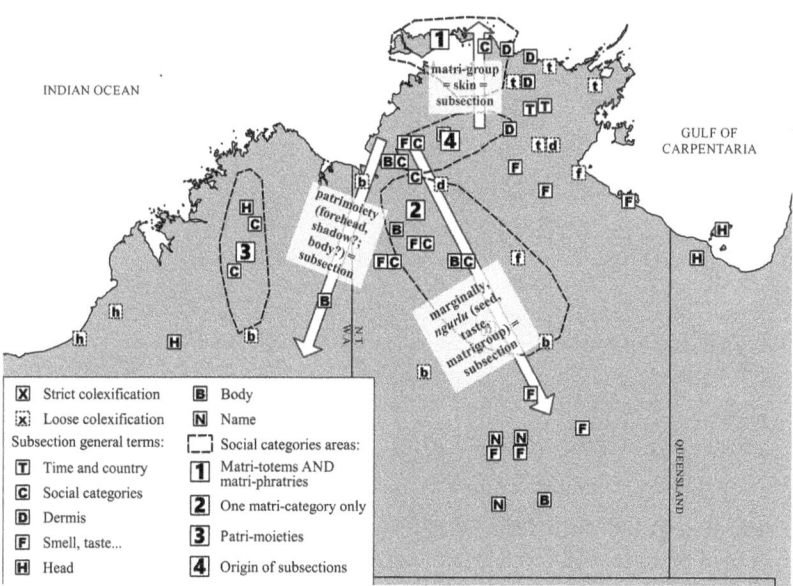

Figure 44: The historical spread of subsections and the generic terms.
Source: William McConvell.

The subsection system emerged in the area around Katherine in the Northern Territory and diffused from there in several directions, replacing or adding to previous social category systems. This general hypothesis is supported by persuasive linguistic evidence (McConvell 1985a, 1997).

While others (e.g. Harvey 2008; Chapter 10) have offered modifications of detail, this general hypothesis has not been strongly challenged. The hypothesis also includes a modelling of how the subsection system derived from the meeting up and interaction of two section systems—one from the west and one from the north. According to the hypothesis, this involved a particular kind of circular connubium (asymmetrical marriage between groups). We will not go into the details of this reconstructed history, but it does provide a background as to how we might view the distribution and history of the generic terms for subsections.

There were at least four main early pulses of diffusion (McConvell 1985a):

1. south-west through the east and central Kimberley
2. south into Central Australia
3. south-east to the Barkly Tableland and Gulf of Carpentaria
4. north-east into central western Arnhem Land.

All of these diffusions occurred in stages and had later extensions—including extensions within the last century—further into parts of eastern Arnhem Land and north-eastern Western Desert, as well as north into Daly River. In the next part, we comment on the generic terms for subsections that are related to each of these major diffusions.

South-West Diffusion

Two of the three Jarragan languages in the east Kimberley do not have generic terms for subsections but use a suffix for 'kind' (*-nge-*) on interrogatives relating to subsections and on the subsection term itself (e.g. *jangala-ngeny* 'Jangala kind'). The northernmost Jarragan language Gajirrabeng has a word for subsections derived from 'body' *joowoondeng*, and also uses the term *ngoorloong*, which is borrowed from eastern Ngumpin *ngurlu*. Since the latter has as its primary meaning 'matriclan' to the east, and matriclans are not part of the Jarragan culture, it is probably a relatively recent loan from the east in the meaning 'subsection'. However, the 'body' colexification does relate to others in the immediate area (northern east Ngumpin *mayi* and Daly River). 'Body' also continues to the south in the Kimberley with Jaru and Walmajarri. Therefore, it seems likely that the 'body' colexification had its origin in northern-eastern Ngumpin and spread with the south-west diffusion. The apparent absence of this colexification in two languages in the middle of this spread remains to be explained.

In the west Kimberley, Nyulnyulan languages sections related to those of the Pilbara are reported from the early to mid-twentieth century, although their role in social organisation was marginal. The generic terms for 'section' in the Pilbara and adjacent Western Desert also meant 'face' in the local languages (e.g. Nyangumarta *ngumpa,* Karajarri *miparr*), but 'face' for subsection is not reported in the west Kimberley. The term 'forehead' (*amalarr*) is used for generic subsection in the central Kimberley in the southern Worrorran language Ngarinyin, where subsection use was marginally encroaching, and 'forehead' and 'face' are commonly colexified. The origin of this is not necessarily the same as for the 'section/face' colexification in the Pilbara, since 'forehead' is a term for patrimoiety, an important institution in the central Kimberley, and it appears that as subsections moved out to the edge of their distribution, their generic names were equated with the locally important pre-existent social category. The same colexification 'subsection/patrimoiety' occurred in the Bunuban languages south of Worrorran; however, the term was not a 'forehead/face' term. In fact, the generic term for subsections in this language family (*kuru*) is not immediately interpretable. It could be related to 'shadow' (*kururru*) or perhaps the common word for 'eye' (*kuru*), which is commonly colexified with 'face'.

Southern Diffusion

According to McConvell (1985a), the southern diffusion of subsections started in western Mirndi (Jaminjungan) and neighbouring languages. It probably spread quite soon into the eastern Ngumpin languages to the south. Across this area, apart from the north where 'body' (*mayi*) is used, the only generic term for subsections, *ngurlu*, is also the term for matrilineal clan, another important institution that probably existed in the region before subsections originated and spread. In fact, *ngurlu* is not a particularly common designation for generic subsections in this area, and some people claim there is really no term for generic subsection. This is reminiscent of the apparent absence of a true term for generic subsection in western neighbours Miriwung and Kija, in the east Kimberley. Going further south to the Warlpiri, the term *puntu* for generic subsection, also meaning 'friend' or 'relative', also seems to be unique. The root is etymologically related to words for 'person' in other languages and from there to the meaning 'body'; however, this history is not retained in the Warlpiri meaning.[12]

South of Warlpiri, subsections spread into Arandic languages (see Chapter 10). The northern languages have colexification with 'body smell', and this is extended to 'tune' and other senses in some cases. This links to the 'smell/taste' cluster in languages further north, which is discussed in the subsection 'South-Eastern Diffusion'. In southern Arandic, the colexification is with 'hair', which could be linked to the same colexification in the central Gulf of Carpentaria. These are probably generic terms for sections that have been shifted to subsections.

In the Victoria River District, apart from *ngurlu* with an origin in 'seed', there is another element that may come from 'seed': the suffixes *-nginytyu/-nginytya*, on subsection terms in Jingulu—the first of which is a word for 'seed' in Jingulu. This suggests that there may have been a wider area in which 'seed' was matriclan and later transferred to subsection, with the 'flavour' meaning a later development.[13]

South-Eastern Diffusion

The subsection terms of south central Arnhem Land are quite divergent from the western ones, and both the southern and eastern pulses into the country of the Gulf of Carpentaria add further divergences, probably indicating an early split in terms. The generic terms for subsection in the south-east diffusion are generally part of the 'smell/taste' cluster; however, at the eastern limits of subsections, we enter the 'hair/head' zone, probably transferred from terms for 'section'.

---

12 *Puntu* is probably a loan word from Western Desert with a meaning shift, narrowing from 'person' (earlier < body), or it could be inheritance with meaning shift. *Pinti* is 'skin' in Warlpiri. This could be < *puntu* as *u* > *i* is a known sound change (e.g. *puntaru* > *pintaru* 'quail') but could be a separate item altogether. Warumungu *punttu* is definitely subsection, with no strict colexification in that language, but there is a verb *punttu-ji-na* 'get used to', which seems related to the 'relation, companion' sense in Warlpiri.
13 Alpher (2004) listed many cognates of the form *ngurlu* or *ngulu* in Pama-Nyungan with the meaning 'forehead' and/or 'face', including *urle* in Arrernte (with regular initial dropping). Kaytetye, a divergent northern Arandic language, has another cognate *erlwe* 'eye' = 'seed'. The 'eye/seed' polysemy is well known in Australia and elsewhere (Brown & Witkowski 1981, 1983), as is 'eye/face' and 'forehead/face'.

North-Eastern Diffusion

The western branch of the north-east diffusion in Iwaidjan, western Gunwinyguan, and Wardaman is characterised by the 'dermis' colexification of subsection. This is familiar to us through the Aboriginal English use of 'skin' for subsection (also, *skin* < Eng. 'skin' in Kriol), which we argue in the next section had its origin in Iwaidjan. For some languages, there is some risk that reports of 'skin' generic terms for 'subsection' might have resulted from back translation by informants inspired by Aboriginal English, Pidgin or Kriol. However, this was generally not the case.

In eastern Gunwinyguan and other languages in central Arnhem Land, the term *malk* is used for subsection and this term itself diffuses east into other languages including Yolngu Matha (*maalk*), along with diffusion of the subsection terms themselves up to the mid-twentieth century. The term is very different in meaning from other clusters that we have encountered and apparently polysemous in multiple ways. One of the leading senses is 'country', but this does not seem to relate to any pre-existing social category system, as far as can be determined. The most likely social categories that have relationships with areas of country are patrimoieties and semi-moieties.

There is an area in south-eastern Arnhem Land where the subsection diffusion never reached. This is in an area where there are semi-moieties. Semi-moieties operated in conjunction with subsections elsewhere—for instance, further south-east along the Gulf.

Another area to which subsections diffused in the last century is the Daly River/Port Keats (Wadeye) region—although subsections are no longer in use there. In this area, generic subsection terms were adopted from matrilineal totemic clans that were called 'body smell' (various terms).

Overall Historical Explanation of Generic Subsection Terms Pattern

Close to the subsections origin area on the western side, there are some examples of 'body/flesh' generics extending south-west; however, there is an area where either generics as such are missing or the term for matriclan (also polysemous with 'seed'), a pre-existing social category system, has taken over. One possibility is that the 'body/flesh' generic was the earliest throughout the area and then the matriclan generic was adopted. The fact that this term was used for two different social categories may have weakened it in the meaning 'subsection'.

On the eastern side of the origin area in north-central Arnhem Land, 'skin' is the most common subsection generic. Its semantic relation to 'body' on the western side of the origin area may be relevant here; however, the 'body/dermis' colexification is not found in northern Australia unlike many Pacific areas. South-east of the 'skin' area is the central Arnhem Land region in which *malk* is the prime generic term for subsection, with a set of meanings around 'country'. The term subsequently spread east in the nineteenth and twentieth centuries.

Outside this central area of diffusion, encounters with other pre-existing social category systems probably determined the choice of generic terms for subsections. To the south-east, there is a large arc from the western Gulf of Carpentaria to northern Central Australia in which 'smell/taste' dominates. Beyond that in the eastern Gulf and southern Arandic, 'hair/head' is the favoured cluster, probably reflecting generic terms for the earlier sections in that area at the limits of subsection spread.

'Skin' Enters English

As previously noted, there is an area in north-western Arnhem Land in which the colexification of subsection is 'skin'. This area also overlaps the area of matrilineal clans that were also called by the local word for 'skin (dermis)' in at least one language—Iwaidja. This is the source of the word 'skin' in Pidgin English, then Kriol (*skin*) and Aboriginal English and then partially in Australian English more generally.

There was a British presence on the Cobourg Peninsula from the mid-nineteenth century, with a military settlement at Port Essington in the 1840s. There were Aboriginal people visiting and living at this settlement in this period and Pidgin English, based on New South Wales Pidgin, was being used as a lingua franca.[14] As early as 1828, Captain Barker recorded forms of subsection terms on Cobourg Peninsula, namely *Nagary* and

---

14   Initial communications were in Macassan Pidgin or Malay but within a short time of the settlement being established, and certainly by the late 1840s, an English-based Pidgin was the main language of communication between the whites and local Aborigines (Harris 1985, pp. 165–6).

Nakila at Raffles Bay. These are similar to recent forms used in Marrgu/Iwaidja *Na-ngarrij* and *Na-angila*. In 1847, Confalionieri, a shipwrecked Catholic priest, recorded the subsection term *Nagoyo* in Garig at Port Essington.[15] This is evidence that subsections were in use in the region from early in the nineteenth century.

In 1895–1905, Joe Cooper, a white buffalo hunter, had camps on Melville Island among the Tiwi and on Cobourg Peninsula working with Iwaidjan speakers. In 1905, he took a party of Iwaidjan speakers to work with him on Melville Island and they stayed until 1914. Cooper married an Iwaidjan woman and had children including a son Reuben, who set up a sawmill on the Cobourg Peninsula. Cooper was visited by the anthropologist Baldwin Spencer in 1910 and 1912. Spencer collected details of the social organisation of the Iwaidjan groups, the Tiwi and others. The information gathered included subsections and matrilineal social categories. The Iwaidjan groups had subsections, matriclans and matriphratries, while the Tiwi had matrilineal categories and no subsections. Spencer and Gillen (1904) recorded the Pidgin term 'skin (dermis)' being used for matriphratries among the Tiwi, and for both matriphratries and subsections among the Iwaidjan speakers.

Spencer did not record the generic subsection or matriphratry terms among Iwaidjan groups, but it is, and has been for a long time, the term for 'dermis' in the local language (*-ngurlhi*). However, he did record the generic term for matriphratries among the Tiwi, *pukui*, which translates as 'sun'—a completely different colexification from any of the other social category terms that we have found in northern Australia. Spencer and Gillen (1912) noted the use of the term 'skin (dermis)' for this category in English among the Tiwi by the first decade of the twentieth century:

> The members of groups that are *amandinni* are supposed to belong to the same 'skin', or *pukui*, and may not intermarry.

The origin of the term 'skin' among the Tiwi can certainly be ruled out because they did not use a term for 'skin' generically for any social category, and they do not have subsections, which is the prime referent of 'skin' in general usage. The two groups of languages that did use a term for dermis as the generic term for subsections and matriphratries were

---

15   The current term is *Na-wuyuk* but this is the form *Na-kuyuk*. This indicates that the sound change of medial lenition *$*k > w$* took place after 1847 (cf. Evans 1997, p. 257). Confalionieri glossed this as 'father' but this is clearly a mistake, as he did not understand subsections.

Iwaidjan in the Cobourg Peninsula and some central Gunwinyguan languages in Arnhem Land, adjacent to the Cobourg Peninsula. Of these, the Iwaidjan languages are most likely to be the source of transfer of the term 'skin' to Pidgin English, based on the model of local language colexification. There was white settlement from the mid-nineteenth century and intensive interaction between the Iwaidjan, Tiwi and other Aboriginal groups and Joe Cooper on the Cobourg and Melville Island at the end of the nineteenth and early twentieth centuries, with attestation of use of the Pidgin term in the latter period. Since this is the earliest report of use of the term 'skin' for social categories, and there is a colexification of 'dermis' and 'subsection/matriphratry' precisely in the area of the Cobourg Peninsula Iwaidjan languages, we propose that this was the origin of the term. From around the turn of the century, the term 'skin' spread in Pidgin, Aboriginal English and general parlance through the Northern Territory, and into other areas such as the Pilbara and Queensland where it was used to mean other social categories such as sections and moieties (Sharp 1939, p. 442), even though dermis is not the local term in the languages of any of these areas.

This polysemy of the local language words among northern Gunwinyguan groups is likely to have been borrowed from Iwaidjan neighbours, as it only affects a restricted area close to Iwaidjan, and other western and eastern Gunwingjuan languages have different colexifications. The association of matrilineal social categories with dermis may be ancestral in the Iwaidjan family, although it was extended to subsections much later, perhaps in the last 200–300 years.

The Gunwinyguan groups that used the 'dermis' colexification in their traditional languages are less likely to have been the source of the Pidgin/English term. In his account of his stay with Paddy Cahill at Oenpelli on the east Alligator River in 1911, Spencer (1928) took down a lot of ethnographic information. He clearly stated that subsections were not in use among the Kakadu or other groups resident in that area, and there is no mention of the term for 'dermis' being used (see Mulvaney 2004). There was less interaction with the white settlement in the late nineteenth century in the mainland areas with the dermis colexification, so it is less likely to have started in that period. However, this would have been fertile ground for initial expansions of the Pidgin/English *skin* generic term.

Conclusions

This chapter has described the terms used to refer to subsections generically throughout the ambit of that system of social categories in northern and Central Australia. One of these generic terms has come into Aboriginal English and English more generally: *skin*. Terms for 'dermis' were not generally used in traditional Indigenous languages for subsection. However, we propose that polysemy (colexification) between 'dermis' and 'social category', including 'subsection', was present in the Iwaidjan family of languages and some Gunwinyguan neighbours, and then spread into Pidgin around the Cobourg Peninsula during early contact with the British settlement on the Cobourg Peninsula in the mid-nineteenth century, and thence more widely into Aboriginal English and Kriol.

Apart from 'dermis', some other 'body' terms colexify 'subsection' more widely—a prime example being 'body' itself. 'Body' commonly colexifies 'person', and in a couple of cases 'person' or a derivative is the word for subsection. Items related to 'head', such as 'face' and 'hair', are also generic terms for subsection in some areas. These express a distinctive feature of a personal identity. In addition, there is a link to another cluster of generic terms for subsection, 'smell/taste', through the important indicator of personal identity in most Australian cultures 'body/sweat smell', which is colexified with other descriptors of individual identity of cultural elements such as 'tune'. The 'taste' meaning is related etymologically to 'seed' in the Victoria River District and Barkly Tableland. A different cluster is found in central Arnhem Land that is linked to concepts like 'country'—perhaps again through personal identity; however, further research is required.

This chapter has analysed polysemies using knowledge and methods from various disciplines, considering linguistic facts that have included semantic analysis along with historical and geographical linguistic comparisons, cultural practices and social history. Combining disciplines highlights semantic correlations and historical developments that could not have been unveiled otherwise. From the point of view of linguistic methodology, this chapter was the opportunity to use and test a type of 'semantic map' originally developed by François (2008). In this particular instance, the semantic map, which links together colexifications, fits together very neatly with the geographical distributions of the different clusters. The history of the origin and diffusion of subsections is quite well known as it is relatively recent and has been investigated via linguistic means. The chapter includes a first attempt to link this historical expansion to the history of spread of the colexification clusters of subsection generic terms. One of the features of this development has been that colexifications of other earlier social categories such as matriphratries and patrimoieties were taken over by the new subsections as they diffused into these areas.

References

Alpher, B 2004, 'Pama-Nyungan: Phonological reconstruction and status as a phylogenetic group', in C Bowern & H Koch (eds), *Australian languages: classification and the comparative method*, Amsterdam: John Benjamins, pp. 93–126, 187–570, 681–6. doi.org/10.1075/cilt.249.09alp.

Brown, C & Witkowski, S 1981, 'Symbolism and cognition', *American Ethnologist*, *8*(3), pp. 596–615. doi.org/10.1525/ae.1981.8.3.02a00110.

Brown, C & Witkowski, S 1983, 'Polysemy, lexical change and cultural importance', *Man*, *18*, pp. 72–89. doi.org/10.2307/2801765.

Evans, N 1992a, 'Multiple semiotic systems, hyperpolysemy, and the reconstruction of semantic change in Australian languages', in G Kellerman & M Morrissey (eds), *Diachrony within synchrony*, Bern: Peter Lang Verlag, pp. 475–508.

Evans, N 1992b, *Kayardild dictionary and thesaurus: a vocabulary of the language of the Bentinck Islanders, north-west Queensland*, Parkville: University of Melbourne.

Evans, N 1997, 'Macassan loans and linguistic stratification in western Arnhem Land', in P McConvell & N Evans (eds), *Archaeology and linguistics: Aboriginal Australia in global perspective*, Melbourne: Oxford University Press, pp. 237–260.

Evans, N 2003, *Bininj Gun-Wok: a pan-dialectal grammar of Mayali, Kunwinjku and Kune*, Canberra: Pacific Linguistics.

Evans, N & Wilkins, D 2000, 'In the mind's ear: the semantic extensions of perception verbs in Australian languages', *Language*, *76*(3), pp. 546–92. doi.org/10.2307/417135.

Evans, N & Wilkins, D 2001, 'The complete person: networking the physical and the social', in J Simpson, D Nash, M Laughren, P Austin & B Alpher (eds), *Forty years on: Ken Hale and Australian languages*, Canberra: Pacific Linguistics, pp. 493–521.

François, A 2008, 'Semantic maps and the typology of colexification: intertwining polysemous networks across languages', in M Vanhove (ed.), *From polysemy to semantic change*, Amsterdam/Philadelphia: John Benjamins, pp. 163–215. doi.org/10.1075/slcs.106.09fra.

Harris, J 1985, 'Contact languages at the Northern Territory British military settlements 1814–1849', *Aboriginal History*, 9, pp. 148–69.

Harvey, M 2008, *Proto-Mirndi: a discontinuous language family in Northern Australia*, Canberra: Pacific Linguistics.

Haspelmath, M 2003, 'The geometry of grammatical meaning: semantic maps and cross-lingusitic comparison', in M Tomasello (ed.), *The new psychology of language*, vol. 2, Mahwah: Lawrence Erlbaum, pp. 211–43.

Jurafsky, D 1996, 'Universal tendencies in the semantics of the diminutive', *Language*, 72(3), pp. 533–78. doi.org/10.2307/416278.

Kirton, JF & Timothy, N 1977, 'Yanyuwa concepts relating to "skin"', *Oceania*, 47(4), pp. 320–2. doi.org/10.1002/j.1834-4461.1977.tb01302.x.

Maddock, K 1969, The Jabuduruwa: a study of the structure of rite and myth in an Australian Aboriginal religious cult on the Beswick Reserve, Northern Territory, PhD thesis, University of Sydney.

McConvell, P 1985a, 'The origin of subsections in Northern Australia', *Oceania*, 56(1), pp. 1–33. doi.org/10.1002/j.1834-4461.1985.tb02105.x.

McConvell, P 1985b, 'Time perspective in Aboriginal Australian culture', *Aboriginal History*, 9, pp. 53–80.

McConvell, P 1996, 'Backtracking to Babel: the chronology of Pama-Nyungan expansion in Australia', *Archeology in Oceania*, 31, pp. 125–44. doi.org/10.1002/j.1834-4453.1996.tb00356.x.

McConvell, P 1997, 'Long lost relations: Pama-Nyungan and northern kinship', in P McConvell & N Evans (eds), *Archeology and linguistics: Aboriginal Australia in global perspective*, Melbourne: Oxford University Press, pp. 207–36.

McConvell, P 2013, 'Proto-Pama-Nyungan kinship and the AustKin project: reconstructing proto-terms for "mother's father" and their transformations', in P McConvell, I Keen & R Hendery (eds), *Kinship systems: change and reconstruction*, Salt Lake City: University of Utah Press, pp. 190–214.

McConvell, P & Dousset, L 2012, 'Tracking the dynamics of kinship and social category terms with AustKin II', *Proceedings of the EACL 2012 Joint Workshop of LINGVIS & UNCLH*, Avignon, France, pp. 98–107.

McConvell, P & Laughren, M 2004, 'Ngumpin-Yapa subgroup', in H Koch & C Bowern (eds), *Australian languages: classification and the comparative method*, Amsterdam: Benjamins, pp. 151–78. doi.org/10.1075/cilt.249.11mcc.

McConvell, P & Ponsonnet, M 2013, 'Review of *From polysemy to semantic change* (Vanhove 2008)', *Journal of Language Contact*, 6(1), pp. 180–96. doi.org/10.1163/19552629-006001004.

McConvell, P & Smith, M 2003, 'Millers and mullers: the archaeolinguistic stratigraphy of seed-grinding in Central Australia', in H Andersen (ed.), *Language contacts in prehistory: studies in stratigraphy*, Amsterdam: John Benjamins, pp. 177–200. doi.org/10.1075/cilt.239.14mcc.

Mulvaney, J 2004, *Paddy Cahill of Oenpelli*, Canberra: Aboriginal Studies Press.

Musharbash, Y (ed.) 2008, *Yuendumu everyday: contemporary life in a remote Aboriginal settlement*, Canberra: Aboriginal Studies Press.

Pensalfini, R 2003, *A grammar of Jingulu: an Aboriginal language of the Northern Territory*, Canberra: Pacific Linguistics.

Ponsonnet, M 2009, 'Aspects of the semantics of intellectual subjectivity in Dalabon (south-western Arnhem Land)', *Australian Aboriginal Studies*, 1, pp. 16–28.

Ponsonnet, M in prep., *Nominal subclasses in Dalabon (south western Arnhem Land)*.

Richards, E & Hudson, J 1990, *Walmajarri-English dictionary*, Darwin: SIL.

Ross, M 2007, 'Calquing and metatypy', *Journal of Language Contact, 1*, pp. 116–43. doi.org/10.1163/000000007792548341.

Saulwick, A 2003, A *first dictionary of Rembarrnga*, Maningrida: Bawinanga Aboriginal Corporation, Maningrida Arts and Culture.

Schapper, A, San Roque, L & Hendery, R 2016, 'Tree, firewood, and fire in the languages of Sahul', in M Koptjevskaya-Tamm & P Juvonen (eds), *Lexico-typological approaches to semantic shift and motivation pattern*, Berlin: De Gruyter.

Sharp, LR 1939, 'Tribes and totemism in north-east Australia', *Oceania*, *9*(3–4), pp. 254–65, 439–61. doi.org/10.1002/j.1834-4461.1939.tb00232.x.

Spencer, B 1928, *Wanderings in wild Australia*, London: Macmillan & Co.

Spencer, B & Gillen, FJ 1904, *The northern tribes of Central Australia*, London: Macmillan & Co.

Spencer, B & Gillen, FJ 1912, *Across Australia*, London: Macmillan & Co.

Sweetser, E 1990, *From etymology to pragmatics: metaphorical and cultural aspects of semantic structure*, Cambridge: Cambridge University Press. doi.org/10.1017/CBO9780511620904.

Testart, A 1978, *Des classifications dualistes en Australie*, Paris/Lille: Maison des Sciences de l'Homme/Lille III.

von Brandenstein, CG 1982, *Names and substance in the Australian subsection system*, Chicago: University of Chicago Press. doi.org/10.4000/books.editionsmsh.5757.

Wilkins, D 1996, 'Natural tendencies of semantic change and the search for cognates', in M Durie & M Ross (eds), *The comparative method reviewed: regularity and irregularity in language change*, Oxford: Oxford University Press, pp. 264–304.

Wrigley, M 1992, *Jaru dictionary*, Draft edition, June, Halls Creek: Kimberley Language Reseource Centre.

10

The Development of Arandic Subsection Names in Time and Space

Harold Koch

Introduction

This chapter builds on the findings of McConvell (1985, 1996) regarding the spread of subsection terms in north central Australia.[1] It explores the timing and direction of the spread of section and subsection terms into the Arandic subgroup of languages in finer detail, and takes into consideration historical evidence from early sources such as Gillen's correspondence (Mulvaney et al. 1997). The chapter pays particular attention to issues of phonological change within the Arandic languages (Koch 1997b) and principles of adaptation of loan words between these languages and Warlpiri, as outlined in Koch (1997a, 2014). New proposals include the replacement of terms during the course of history and the positing of some intermediate terms that are not directly attested. Attention is paid to the history of the documentation of the systems, as well as native traditions regarding their origins.

---

[1] I am grateful to Patrick McConvell and two anonymous referees for helpful feedback.

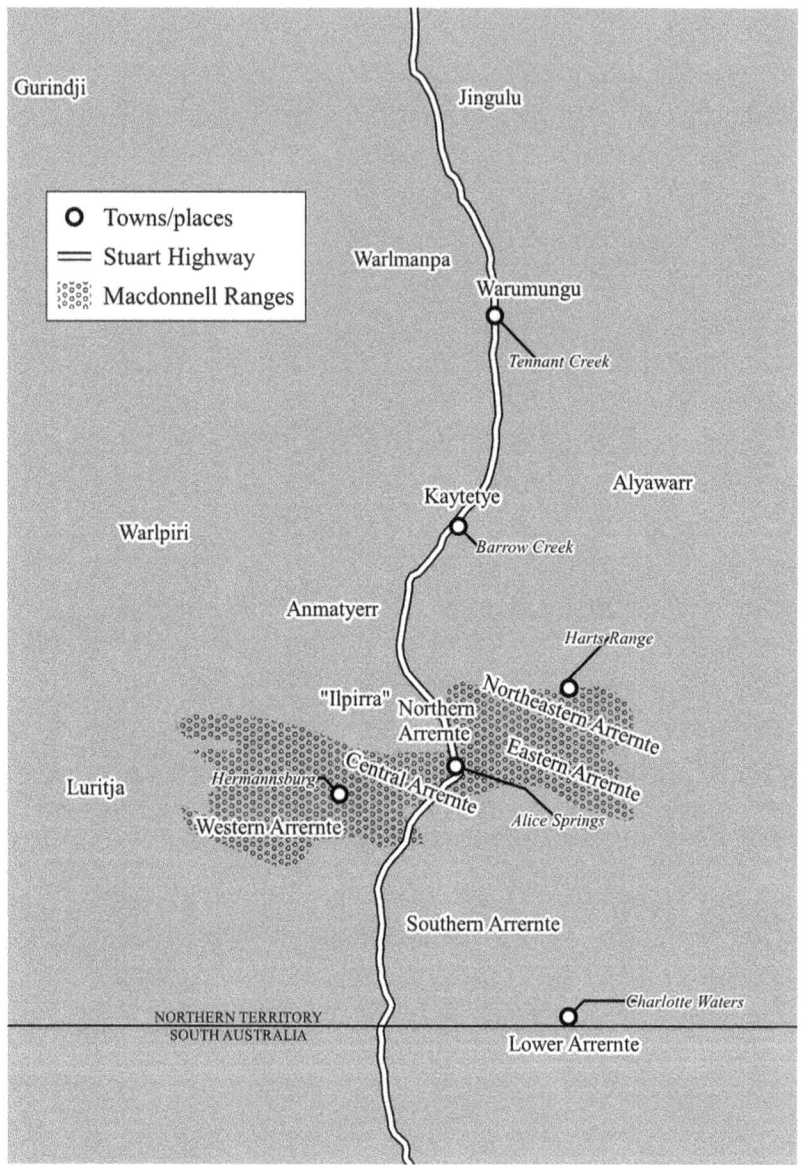

Figure 45: Languages of Central Australia.
Source: Author's work.

10. THE DEVELOPMENT OF ARANDIC SUBSECTION NAMES IN TIME AND SPACE

Overview of Systems of the Arandic Peoples and Their Neighbours

The Arandic languages all include a system of social category terms that are called, in the terminology introduced by Radcliffe-Brown (1918, 1930–31), sections and subsections—also popularly referred to as 'skins'. The southernmost Arandic group, the Lower Arrernte, have a system of four sections, as shown in Table 41, in which the sections have been given letter codes according to Radcliffe-Brown's practice, but are displayed in an arrangement that follows Spencer and Gillen (1927, p. 445; 1969a [1899], p. 72; cf. 1969b [1904], p. 90).[2] The sections are arranged into patrimoieties (P and Q), such that a member of each patrimoiety marries a member of the opposite patrimoiety (marriage relations are indicated by the = sign), and a man's child belongs to the same patrimoiety as (but a different section from) their father. The father–child relations are indicated by means of the vertical lines; thus, A's child belongs to section D, and D's child belongs to section A. Mother–child relations are not directly indicated in this display, but can be computed through the mother's partner—thus, the child of a female *Penangke* (A) is traced through her *Perrurle* (B) partner and belongs to the *Kemarre* (C) section. AC and BD constitute matrimoieties, although these are not directly displayed. Further, A and B belong to one generation level and C and D to another. These generation levels include people related as siblings, spouses, grandparents and grandchildren; each generation level consists of members of sets of alternate generations.

Table 41: Section system of the Lower Arrernte.

		P		Q		
→	A	Penangke	=	Perrurle	B	←
|						|
→	D	Peltharre	=	Kemarre	C	←

Source: Spencer and Gillen (1927, p. 445).

The eight-term subsection system is illustrated in Table 42, with the skin terms of the Central and Eastern Arrernte (Henderson & Dobson 1994, p. 41). In a subsection system, each section is divided into two subsections (e.g. A1 and A2). There are four patricouples: A1 + D2, A2 + D1, B1

---

2   The spelling has been adapted to the system used for Central and Eastern Arrernte.

+ C1 and B2 + C2. Patrimoieties and generational levels are the same as the four-section system. The eight-term subsection system makes an overt terminological distinction within a section between first and second cross-cousins. Thus, a person in the *Penangke* (A1) subsection will find their second cousin (e.g. a man's mother's mother's brother's daughter's daughter) in the *Perrurle* (B1) subsection, but their first cross-cousin (e.g. a man's mother's brother's daughter or father's sister's daughter) in the *Angale* (A2) subsection. The preferred marriage partner is a second cousin, although a classificatory (but not actual) first cousin may be a second-choice partner. Thus, a *Penangke*'s preferred wife is *Perrurle*, as shown by the = sign. In instances in which children result from a marriage other than the preferred one signalled in the table (e.g. in the case of a *Penangke* father and an *Angale* mother), the child may take the skin appropriate to the mother (i.e. *Peltharre*) or the father (i.e. *Pengarte*), or use both (e.g. *Peltharre-Pengarte*), perhaps according to the context.

Table 42: Subsection system of the Central and Eastern Arrernte.

			Patrimoiety P		Patrimoiety Q			
→		A1	Penangke	=	Perrurle	B1	←	
	→	A2	Kngwarreye	=	Angale	B2		←
	→	D1	Peltharre	=	Kemarre	C1	←	
→		D2	Pengarte	=	Ampetyane	C2		←

Source: Henderson and Dobson (1994, p. 43).

Moieties are not named; nevertheless, patrimoieties are recognised terminologically in two ways. First, non-singular pronouns in some dialects of Arrernte (as well as in Anmatyerre, Alyawarr and Kaytetye) are marked for differences of social category. Thus, in North-eastern Arrernte, 'we two' is *ilanthe* if its referents belong to different patrimoieties (e.g. 'I and my spouse' or 'I and my mother'), *ilake* if the term refers to 'me and my father' or 'me and my brother's child' and *ilerne* for 'me and my brother or sister' or 'me and my father's father'. The last two forms show that a further distinction is made between generation levels if the referents of the pronoun are within the same patrimoiety. The second linguistic reflex of the patrimoiety division is the fact that there are egocentric terms that distinguish 'people in my patrimoiety' from 'people in the other patrimoiety'. The term for the former is *ilakakeye*, based on the first-person dual pronoun *ilake*, which means 'I and my father', or *anwakerrakeye*, based on the first-person plural pronoun, which means

'I and my father plus others (all members of the set belonging to different generational levels of the same patrimoiety)'. The term that designates 'other patrimoiety' is *alakakeye* (based on the third-person dual pronoun *alake*, which means 'they two related as a person and their father'), or *malyanweke*, which may be etymologically akin to 'our in-laws' (*anweke* being the dative form of the historic first-person plural pronoun). Apart from these linguistic reflexes, the patrimoiety distinction plays a certain role in social behaviour: members of the two patrimoieties were observed by Spencer and Gillen to camp separately (see Spencer & Gillen 1927, p. 229, figure 69) and to play complementary roles in ceremonial rituals.[3]

Spencer and Gillen (1927, pp. 41–2) reported on several Indigenous theories concerning the nature of patrimoieties. The [Central and Northern][4] Arrernte refer to the members of the AD and BC moieties as *mberga oknirra* [*akngerre*] 'big men' and *mberga tungwa* 'little men' respectively, with *mberga* denoting the human body—that is large-bodied versus small-bodied. People of the AD moiety are further distinguished as having straight hair, while BC members are said to have wavy hair. Spencer and Gillen claimed there is no anatomical difference to support either of these distinctions; the results of an examination of hair samples by Dr O. W. Tiegs (Spencer's University of Melbourne colleague) are described in Spencer and Gillen (1927, pp. 597–9 Appendix E: Hair Structure). They also mentioned Carl Strehlow's statement that the [Western] Arrernte formerly used the terms *kwatjarinja* [*kwatyarenye*] 'water-dwellers' and *alarinja* [*ahelharenye*] 'land-dwellers' to designate the AD and BC moieties respectively.

The two generational levels, similar to the patrimoieties, are not named, but there is a term *nyurrpe* that means 'belonging to the opposite generational level'. Thus, for a person in the A or B sections, all members of the C and D sections are *nyurrpe*, and vice versa. The combinations A + B and C + D are sometimes referred to as generational moieties.

Groups to the north of the Arandic groups, including the Warlpiri, Warlmanpa and Warumungu, have an eight-subsection system like that of the northern Arandic groups. However, there are two principal differences. Each subsection term in the non-Arandic languages distinguishes

---

3   'The existence of the two primary divisions is very evident during the performance of such ceremonies as the Engwura' (Spencer & Gillen 1927, p. 41).
4   Modern spellings of Spencer and Gillen's Arrernte terms are given in square parentheses where these are known.

SKIN, KIN AND CLAN

the gender of its members. Terms for males begin with *j* (equivalent to the *ty* of Arandic orthographies), while terms for females begin with *n*. The Warlpiri terms are given in Table 43, using the same arrangement as Table 42.[5]

Table 43: Subsection system of the Warlpiri (adult terms only).

A1	Japanangka	Jupurrurla	B1
	Napanangka	Napurrurla	
A2	Jungarrayi	Jangala	B2
	Nungarrayi	Nangala	
D1	Japaljarri	Jakamarra	C1
	Napaljarri	Nakamarra	
D2	Japangardi	Jampijinpa	C2
	Napangardi	Nampijinpa	

Source: Meggitt (1962, p. 165); Laughren (1982, p. 76).

A second characteristic of the northern systems is that they include separate junior terms, which also make a distinction of gender. Thus, there are four terms for each subsection: a pair of masculine and feminine adult terms and a pair of corresponding gendered junior terms. The north-western Arandic languages Anmatyerre and Kaytetye share the gendered junior terms of their western neighbours, but only have normal Arandic (with a few exceptions in Kaytetye) gender-neutral terms for their adult terms. The complete Kaytetye system is presented in Table 44, where each cell gives the adult name, the junior male name and the junior female name.[6]

Table 44: Subsection system of the Kaytetye (including junior terms).

			Patrimoiety P		Patrimoiety Q		
→		A1	Apenangke	B1	Pwerle	←	
			Tyaname		Tywerlame		
			Ngamane		Ngamperle		
	→	A2	Kngwarreye	B2	Thangale		←
			Tywekertaye		Tyangkarle		
			Ngapete		Ngangkale		
	→	D1	Kapetye	C1	Akemarre	←	
			Tyapalye		Tyakarre		
			Ngalyerre		Watyale		

---

5   For the terms and structure of Warlpiri skin names, see Laughren (1982).
6   See Turpin and Ross (2012, pp. 809–10) for the forms. The junior terms are used for children. Since the second half of the twentieth century, when the use of surnames became common, junior skin names have often been used as surnames by people who otherwise lacked a surname, and these names have continued in use through adulthood.

		Patrimoiety P		Patrimoiety Q	
→	D2	Apengarte Tyapeyarte Ngampeyarte	C2	Ampetyane Tyamperlke Mpetyakwerte	←

Source: Turpin and Ross (2012, pp. 809–10).

The remainder of this chapter will be devoted to describing what is known about the history of the Arandic systems. We address questions of when, where and in what manner the terminology of the Arandic languages developed.

Historical Explanations in the Literature

The historical scenario regarding Arandic skins that has been presented in previous scholarship includes the following points:

1. All Arandic terms are assumed, on the basis of their formal similarities, to have been borrowed from languages to the north(west).
2. Geographically, the southern and eastern varieties have only four terms, but the remaining groups each have eight terms.
3. The four-term system is interpreted as the earlier system. It is assumed that there were two successive spreadings of terms from the north.
4. There is historical evidence that some of the Arandic groups adopted the eight-term system only in the 1880s, receiving this system from their northern neighbours.
5. The formal differences between the Arandic terms and those of their neighbours—in particular, differences involving the initial consonant (C) and vowel (V) of the names—need to be accounted for with respect to the relative chronology of the Arandic sound changes and the borrowing of these terms.

Spencer and Gillen, in particular, have emphasised the fourth point (which will be further explored in the sub-subsection 'Central Arrernte'):

> The division into eight has been adopted (or rather the names for the four new divisions have been), in recent times by the Arunta tribe from the Ilpirra tribe which adjoins the former on the north, and the use of them is, at the present time, spreading southwards. (Spencer & Gillen 1969a [1899], p. 72)

> The names derived, so the natives say, from the Ilpirra, a strong tribe living to the north of the Arunta, have gradually spread southwards. (Spencer & Gillen 1927, p. 42)

> In regard to … the introduction of eight, instead of four class names, we know, as a matter of fact, that this change has actually entered the Arunta from the north and at the present moment is spreading southwards. (Spencer & Gillen 1969b [1904], p. 20)

Elkin (1939–40, pp. 199–200) drew out the inferences listed in points 2 and 3:

> In the northern parts of the Aranda tribe, as Spencer and Gillen point out (*The Arunta*, Vol. I, p. 44), each of the four sections was divided into two parts, and the old name was retained for one part or subsection … The new terms, like the old four, came from the north and north-west, as a comparison with the subsection terms of the Loritja and Warramunga make clear … The Aranda told Spencer and Gillen that they had received the system from the north. Apparently they had adopted the section system first, and later the subsection system.

McConvell (1985; 1996, pp. 130–2) presented a scenario for the spread of sections and subsections to the Arandic languages. The section terms derive ultimately from the Pilbara region, but spread eastwards as far as the Victoria River District, where Jaminjungan languages were spoken. There, they acquired gender prefixes *ja-* [*tya-*] masculine and *na-* feminine, then diffused southward through the Warlpiri to Arandic, perhaps 800–500 years ago. These terms were subject to the first phase of Arandic sound changes, which deleted the first consonant and the following vowel—for example, changing **Tyapanangka* to **Penangke*. Later, perhaps around 500 years ago, in the Victoria River area, an eight-term subsection developed out of the combination of a south-western and north-eastern (from the perspective of the Northern Territory) section system and spread south by the same route as earlier sections. These additional terms were subject to a different phonological change in Arandic, which deleted the original consonant but not the following vowel—for example, **Tyapangarti* became **Apengarte*. This second borrowing took place around 1850, according to the account given in Spencer and Gillen (1969a [1899], p. 72). The processes by which the terms were modified in the Arandic languages will be explored further in the section 'Borrowing, Sound Change and Relative Chronology'.

The following discussion will examine the historical aspects of skin names in greater detail, paying attention to the early documentary sources, relations between five different Arandic groups (Lower Arrernte, Central and Western Arrernte, Anmatyerre, Alyawarr and Kaytetye) and relations with three external groups (Warlpiri, Warumungu and Warlmanpa). I highlight terminological differences between Arandic groups and include separate discussions on the origin of skin terms in each. I also revisit the issue of how the borrowing of terms interacts with the historical sound changes and discuss some of the possible mechanisms of adoption of subsections, based on local traditions. Finally, I make some inferences about the absolute dates for the adoption of the terms. Reconciliation of the information in the old sources will have to await another occasion.

Survey of Arandic Groups

Lower Arrernte

The Arandic section names were first documented in 1875. In that year, the stationmaster Christopher Giles supplied Taplin with the following information concerning the Aboriginal people in the vicinity of the Charlotte Waters Telegraph Station, whose tribal name was reported as Antakerrinya and whose language was said to be Arrinda (Giles 1879, pp. 89, 91).[7] There were four 'class-names', spelled: *Paroola/Parroola*, *Panúngka/Poonungka*, *Booltára* and *Koomurra*. Essentially, the same terms were reported over the next two decades for other areas where Arrernte was spoken, including Alice Springs and Hermannsburg Mission. Table 45 gives the terms as spelled in various sources, as well as their representation in modern orthography.[8] Giles (1879) is the earliest source on Lower Arrernte. Schulze's (1891) terms are taken from the first missionary report on the subsection system among the Western Arrernte (see the

---

7   Cf. Gillen's comment in a letter dated 29 January 1903 that 'the Southern Arunta often speak of themselves as Antikirunya' (Mulvaney et al. 1997, p. 434)—that is, Antekerrenye, which means 'southern'. In the twentieth century, the term 'Antakarinya' became established as the name of a group of speakers of Western Desert dialects in the area west of Lake Eyre. This situation is apparently indicated already in Gillen's letter of 30 July 1897: 'There is a tribe up the Albinga [Alberga] and spreading away to the Musgraves who call themselves the Antikerinya and speak the Luritcha [Western Desert] tongue' (Mulvaney et al. 1997, p. 178).
8   In addition to the usual problems that non-linguists had in spelling words in Australian languages (variability of voiced and voiceless consonants like *b* and *p*, the ambiguity of English *u* [e.g. in *put* versus *putt*] and failure to signal two different kinds of *r*-sound), Arandic languages include a central vowel spelled *e* and pronounced something like the *e* of English *the*, which was perceived in many different ways.

sub-subsection 'Western Arrernte'). Stirling's (1896) terms are from his report on the Horn Scientific Expedition to Central Australia and is not specific as to which subgroup of the Arrernte it applies to. Gillen's (1896) terms are also from the report on the Horn Expedition; it can be taken to reflect the central dialect of Arrernte spoken at Alice Springs, where Gillen was the telegraph stationmaster. Spencer and Gillen's (1969a [1899], p. 69) terms reflect later research by Gillen in association with Spencer, mainly concerning the same Central Arrernte group. Mathews's (1899) terms represent data supplied by a correspondent and relate to the Eastern Arrernte of Harts Range and Arltunga. Strehlow's (n.d.) data are from his unpublished dictionary compiled in 1909 and represent the Western Arrernte of Hermannsburg Mission. Breen's (2000) terms denote the forms given in the dictionary of Western Arrernte. Finally, Henderson and Dobson's (1994, p. 41) terms represent the four-term system that is still in effect in the modern north-eastern dialect of Arrernte.

Table 45: Arrernte section names according to sources.

	A	B	C	D
Giles 1879	*Panúngka/ Poonungka*	*Paroola/ Parroola*	*Koomurra*	*Booltára*
Schulze 1891	*Bunanka*	*Purula*	*Gomara*	*Beltara*
Stirling 1896	*Panunga*	*Purula*	*Kumarra*	*Pultarra/ Pultharra*
Gillen 1896	*Panunga*	*Purula*	*Kumarra*	*Pultarra*
Spencer & Gillen 1899	*Panunga*	*Purula*	*Kumara*	*Bulthara*
Mathews 1899	*Panungka*	*Parulla*	*Koomara*	*Bultara*
Strehlow n.d.	*Pananka*	*Purula*	*Kamara*	*Paltara*
Breen 2000	*Penangke*	*Pwerrerle*	*Kemarre*	*Peltharre*
Henderson & Dobson 1994	*Penangke*	*Perrurle*	*Kemarre*	*Peltharre*

Source: Breen (2000), Giles (1879), Gillen (1896), Henderson and Dobson (1994, p. 41), Mathews (1899), Schulze (1891), Spencer and Gillen (1899), Stirling (1896) and Strehlow (n.d.).

Arrernte

Western Arrernte

The first reports of an eight-term subsection system came from missionaries associated with the Hermannsburg Mission in Western Arrernte territory. Schulze (1891, pp. 223–7) included a section on the 'eight-class system', which spelled out which groups could intermarry and what skin their offspring belonged to (see Table 45 for Schulze's spelling of the traditional four names and Table 46 for the four new terms). The eight-term system allows 'under certain circumstances' (Schulze 1891, p. 224) for an alternative marriage between A1 and B2 (and generally between the 1 and 2 members of each section), in terms of Table 42. Schulze claimed that the child's subsection is always determined by that of its father. Schulze's system has the children of a male *Penangke* (A1 in Table 42) in the *Peltharre* subsection and those of a *Kngwarreye* in *Pengarte*—which does not agree with the modern system or that described by Spencer and Gillen (1969a [1899], p. 70) for Central Arrernte; however, it would be accurate if the skin of the child is determined by that of the mother and if some of the marrying pairs were of the alternative type.

In Stirling's (1896, p. 47) discussion of the Arrernte section system, he reported that he was unable to find confirmation of Schulze's system and noted that another Hermannsburg missionary, Reverend H. Kempe, in writing to Howitt, 'admit[ted] only the four classes here mentioned'—in the same tribe that Schulze described. Stirling (1896, p. 48) reported that Schulze's four supplementary names 'were perfectly well recognised by the natives, and were stated to be the corresponding or equivalent names of the four divisions in other neighbouring tribes, though what these tribes were I could not gather further than that a northerly habitat was vaguely indicated'.

An eight-term system was also given in Strehlow's (n.d.) dictionary of Western Arrernte, by Spencer and Gillen (1969a [1899]) for Central Arrernte and by Mathews (1899) for Eastern Arrernte. Table 46 gives the second set of skin names that were provided by various authorities.

Table 46: Additional Arrernte skin names according to sources.

	A2	B2	C2	D2
Schulze 1891	*Knuraia*	*Ngala*	*Mbutjana*	*Pungata*
Spencer & Gillen 1899	*Uknaria*	*Ungalla*	*Umbitchana*	*Appungerta*
Mathews 1899	*Knurraia*	*Ngala*	*Mbutjana*	*Pungata*
Strehlow n.d.	*Knuraia*	*Ngala*	*Mbitjana*	*Bangata*
Breen 2000	*Kngwarreye*	*Ngale*	*Mpetyane*	*Pengarte*
Henderson & Dobson 1994	*Kngwarraye*	*Angale*	*Ampetyane*	*Pengarte*

Source: Breen (2000), Henderson and Dobson (1994, p. 42), Mathews (1899, p. 72), Schulze (1891), Spencer and Gillen (1899, p. 72) and Strehlow (n.d.).

Central Arrernte

Gillen (1896, pp. 162–3) reported the same four class names that were in use among the Lower Arrernte for the 'McDonnell Range tribe'. However, it is apparent that the situation had already somewhat altered by the time the report was published. In a letter to Spencer on 31 January 1896, Gillen reported that the eight-class system was adopted by the Arrernte during the preceding 15 years (i.e. from 1880) and that the system and its terms were taken over from their northern neighbours, whom he called the Chitchica:

> The 8 classes of which the missionaries spoke is the class system of the Chitchica which I was surprised to find is rapidly being adopted throughout the McDonnell Ranges. The blacks tell me that they first began to adopt it some fifteen years ago … and that during the last two or three years it has almost come into general use. Questioned as to why they should adopt the system of another tribe, my old alaartunja says, 'That one very good him makeum walk straight'. The blacks about the Mission district [Hermannsburg] *and Eastern McDonnells* who mix a great deal with the Chitchica were the first to adopt the system—If you compare my Arunta table of relationships with the Eight Class system you will see at a glance how it simplifies matters. (Mulvaney et al. 1997, p. 96)

This important statement needs to be deconstructed if we are to discern which group was the source of the names and which subgroup of the Arrernte was the first to adopt them. In this scenario, the source is given as the Chitchica. In a later letter (14 July 1896), Gillen corrected the term Chitchica: 'This should be "Ilpira", not Chitchica which means foreigners generally, it is from the "Ilpira" that these people have bagged the 8 classes' (Mulvaney et al. 1997, p. 130). This correction was repeated several times in subsequent letters to Spencer (Mulvaney et al. 1997, pp. 110–11, 130, 169). However, we still need to ask: who were the Ilpira? It is clear from a careful reading of Spencer and Gillen that their Ilpira or Ilpirra did not denote the (eastern) Warlpiri, as did the term Arlpere in modern Arrernte,[9]

---

9   The glossary compiled by David Wilkins and Alison Petch and included in Mulvaney et al. (1997, pp. 487–533) incorrectly makes this misleading identification as well, when it glosses Ilpirra as Warlpiri, adding the comment: 'Ilpira or Ilpirra particularly refers to a division of the Warlpiri on the Anmatyerre side' (Mulvaney et al. 1997, p. 505). Meggitt (1962, p. 168) also took the 'Ilpirra tribe' of Spencer and Gillen (1969a [1899], p. 90) as referring to the 'south-eastern Walbiri'. McConvell (1985, p. 6) likewise assumed that this denoted the Warlpiri: 'Spencer and Gillen (1927) tell us that the Aranda originally had a section system and that the four extra terms (A2, B2, C2, D2) were borrowed, from the Warlpiri to the north, not long beforehand'.

10. THE DEVELOPMENT OF ARANDIC SUBSECTION NAMES IN TIME AND SPACE

but rather the Anmatyerre.[10] Gillen commented in a letter dated 29 January 1903: 'The Ilpira and Unmatjira are really one tribe and at anyrate [*sic*] the Arunta always apply the term Ilpira to them' (Mulvaney et al. 1997, p. 343); and later on 1 February 1903: 'It's a funny thing that we never heard the term Unmatjira amongst the Arunta who always speak of them as Atchichika "foreigners" or "strangers"' (Mulvaney et al. 1997, p. 435). They did not encounter the name Unmatjira [Anmatyerre] until they met representatives of the more northern part of this tribe while at Barrow Creek in June 1901; the first mention in Gillen's diary is in the entry for 17 June (Gillen 1968, p. 126). The referent of the name Ilpirra has obviously changed during the twentieth century; but a close association between the Anmatyerre and the Warlpiri apparently persisted.[11]

Which subgroup of the Arrernte was the first to adopt the extra terms? The answer to this question depends on how one is to interpret the words in italics in the quotation from Gillen's letter: '*and Eastern McDonnells*'. The editors of Gillen's letters informed us that 'editorial insertions are always in italics' (Mulvaney et al. 1997, p. viii). However, I do not see any basis for this insertion. Without it, Gillen denoted the Arrernte at Hermannsburg Mission as the first adopters of the new system. In a letter dated 7 November 1895, he had already described the 'Mission station' as a place 'where the Looritcha, Arunta and Chichica intermingle' (Mulvaney et al. 1997, p. 88). Thus, it appears that soon after the founding of the mission in 1877, the Western Arrernte, began to use the subsection system of their northern neighbours, the Anmatyerre, some of whom spent time at Hermannsburg. Other Arrernte along the MacDonnell Ranges also took up the use of this system during the course of the next 15 years, with the result that its use became established in the Alice Springs area by 1895. This history accounts for the fact that the skin names belonging to the second set given by Spencer and Gillen for the Arrernte are identical to those given for their Ilpirra (i.e. the Anmatyerre).

---

10   For example, a display of the relative locations of the Arunta, Ilpirra, Illeowra [Alyawarr] and Kytiche [Kaytetye] in Gillen's letter of 25 April 1896 (Mulvaney et al. 1997, p. 112) places the Ilpira to the north-west of the Arunta, west of the Illeowra and southwest of the Kytiche, which accurately represents the location of the group that has been called Anmatyerre—cf. the map in Strehlow (1947), where the name Unmatjera is attached to the whole area that is designated Ilpirra on Spencer and Gillen's maps (e.g. Spencer & Gillen 1927, p. 5).

11   Strehlow (1947, p. 52) reported that the Northern Arrernte asserted the purity of their language versus that of other Arandic groups: 'The Western Aranda and the Southern Aranda are both half-Loritja; our neighbours, the Unmatjera, are half-Ilpara'. Meggitt (1962, p. 40) reported that the Warlpiri regarded the 'Yanmadjari' as 'half-Walbiri and one people with us'.

Southern Arrernte

The Southern Arrernte are (linguistically) a subgroup of the Western Arrernte. The eight-term system was apparently introduced to the Southern Arrernte some time after it was received by the Western Arrernte—perhaps during the early part of the twentieth century, judging from the following account in Strehlow (1947, p. 72):

> In contrast to their Northern and Western tribesmen whose groups were each divided into eight classes, the Southern Aranda had their marriages regulated by a four-class system only; and the Southern men stuck to their own traditions tenaciously. On my visit to Horseshoe Bend in 1933 I found there two old Southern men who addressed one another as 'brother', though they ostensibly belonged to two different classes. When I asked them how they could use this appellation when they were separated by reason of their differing classes, they replied that, in the old days, they had both belonged to the same marriage class. Their own group, however, had become almost extinct long since; and strangers who had the eight-class system had come in from the Northern groups and from bordering Loritja [Western Desert] territories. The two old Southern men had been put into different classes by these newcomers, since one of them had married a wife who came from an eight-class group; and the marriage had now been 'legalized' according to the ideas of the strangers. They finished their explanation with some very scathing remarks about the Northern Aranda who had had the presumption of attempting to force their own system upon old Southern territory, where men had lived orderly lives under the four-class system as far back as memory and tradition could reach.
>
> The four-class system is the better of the two for us Southerners; we cannot understand the eight-class system. It is mad and purposeless, and only fit for such crazy men as the Northern Aranda are; *we* did not inherit such stupid traditions from *our* fathers.

From the modern Southern Arrernte wordlist (Swan & Cousen 1993), one can infer that the eight-term system has persisted—although the wordlist only lists five of the expected terms: *Penangke* and *Kemarre* from set 1, and *Ngale*, *Mpetyane* and *Pengarte* from set 2.

Anmatyerre

As previously mentioned, Spencer and Gillen's Ilpira/Ilpirra and Unmatjira both correspond to the modern Anmatyerre group. Table 47 presents the skin names given for Ilpirra by Spencer and Gillen (1969a [1899], p. 90), Unmatjira by Gillen (1968, p. 151), Central Anmatyerre and Eastern Anmatyerre by Green (2010, p. 743), and Iliaura [Alyawarr] by Spencer and Gillen (1969a [1899], p. 90). Comparing the forms, we note that the final vowel, which is spelled with an *a* by Spencer and Gillen and with an *e* in modern orthographies of E/C Arrernte and Kaytetye, is omitted in the modern orthography of Anmatyerre (and Alyawarr). In her orthography, Green (2010, p. 744) also omitted initial vowels, while noting that 'many words in Arandic languages may be pronounced either with or without the initial *a* vowel'. A systematic phonetic difference is that modern Central Anmatyerre lacks the prestopped nasals found in other Arandic varieties: this accounts for the absence of the *k* in *Ngwarray*. The only substantive difference between Gillen's Unmatjira and both Spencer and Gillen's Ilpirra and modern Central Anmatyerre is that the former has a form *Thungalla* for B2; this must be identified with the *Thangale* characteristic of Anmatyerre's north-eastern neighbour Kaytetye. We can assume that around the year 1900, some subgroups of the Anmatyerre, as well as a subgroup of the Alyawarr, had adopted the Kaytetye term in place of *Angale*, but subsequently dropped *Thangale* in favour of the more widespread *Angale*. The other aberrant forms, shown in boldface in Table 47, are D1 *Petyarre* and B1 *Pwerle*, which are shared with Alyawarr. The 'Iliaura' forms are further discussed in the next section.

Table 47: Anmatyerre skin names.

	Ilpirra (Spencer & Gillen)	Unmatjira (Gillen)	Central Anmatyerre (Green)	Eastern Anmatyerre (Green)	Iliaura (Spencer & Gillen)
A1	Panunga	Panunga	Penangk	Penangk	Apanunga
A2	Uknaria	Uknaria	Ngwarray	Kngwarray/ Ngwarray	Uknaria
D1	Bulthara	Bulthara	Peltharr	**Petyarr**	Appitchara
D2	Appungerta	Appungerta	Pengart	Pengart	Appungerta
B1	Purula	Purula	Pwerrerle	**Pwerl**	Upilla
B2	Ungalla	*Thungalla*	Ngal	Ngal	Thungalla
C1	Kumara	Kumara	Kemarr	Kemarr	Akumara
C2	Umbitchana	Umbitchana	Mpetyan	Mpetyan	Umbitchana

Source: Gillen (1968, p. 151), Green (2010, p. 743) and Spencer and Gillen (1969a [1899], p. 90).

Alyawarr

The Alyawarr, in the north-eastern part of Arandic territory, have a system of four section names rather than eight subsection terms. It might be assumed that these should be the same four original terms that are found among the Lower Arrernte. However, there are four facts that contradict this expectation, each of which requires a historical explanation.

1. The A term is not the expected *(A)penangke* from the first set, but *Kngwarreye* (i.e. A2 from the second set).
2. Alyawarr's B term is not the *Perrurle* of E/C Arrernte or the *Pwerrerle* of Central Anmatyerre, but *Pwerle* (or *Apwerle*), like the *Pwerle* of Kaytetye.
3. Alyawarr's D term is not *Peltharre*, but an isolated form *Apetyarre*.
4. Spencer and Gillen (1969a [1899], p. 90) gave for their 'Iliaura' tribe an eight-member subsection system.

I suggest the following explanations. For the first issue, I propose that a subgroup of the Alyawarr was in close contact with neighbours (Anmatyerre and/or Kaytetye) who had the subsection system. From the Alyawarr viewpoint, the system of their western neighbours had two terms that were equivalent to each of their own; therefore, they could regard them as synonyms. At some point, they substituted the alternate term *Kngwarreye* for their earlier *Apenangke*.[12] This innovation was then copied by all Alyawarr who had a four-term system. This probably happened before the eastward migration of some Alyawarr to Lake Nash in far west Queensland, which took place between 1925 and c. 1935, according to Yallop (1969, p. 192). This scenario assumes that Alyawarr once had the A term *Apenangke*. The second problem is easily solved by assuming that the Alyawarr obtained their B term via Kaytetye, which also has *Pwerle*, or possibly from Warumungu, where the form was *Juppurlu*. For the D term *(A)petyarre*, I likewise propose a borrowing from Kaytetye, since this language provides a bridge to its ultimate source in Warlmanpa, as explained in the next section. The fourth question, concerning Spencer and Gillen's eight-term Alyawarr group, can be resolved by positing that at least one group that once identified as Alyawarr had indeed adopted the subsection system, but that they subsequently changed their affiliation to Eastern Anmatyerre. In a letter dated 29 January 1903, Gillen commented:

---

12   For a possible parallel, cf. southern Nyangumarta, where the section name Panaka was substituted with Jangarla by some people due to a death (Sharp 2004, p. 20).

'They [the Ilpira and Unmatjira] are also so mixed up with the Illiaura that is difficult to tell where one ends and the other begins' (Mulvaney et al. 1997, p. 434). The forms quoted by Spencer and Gillen (1969a [1899], p. 90) for the modern Eastern Anmatyerre are almost identical to those given by Green (2010, p. 743)—see Table 47. The only significant difference is that Spencer and Gillen's B2 form, like Gillen's Anmatyerre, is *Thangale*, which seems to have been borrowed from Kaytetye. Thus, Spencer and Gillen's Anmatyerre and Iliaura data demonstrate that there were local variants of the skin system within the larger groups of Arandic peoples.

Kaytetye

The first systematic recording of the 'Kytiche' (as Gillen called them) subsection names was done by Gillen at the end of 1895, according to his letters to Spencer (Mulvaney et al. 1997, pp. 96, 113). There is evidence that the Kaytetye already had the eight-subsection system by 1874: the names of the alleged perpetrators of the 1874 attack on the Barrow Creek Telegraph Station, given in Vallee (2006, p. 113), are recognisable as subsection names belonging to the second set of skin names: *Conarie* [*Kngwarreye*], *Apogita* [*Apengarte*], *Umpijamma* [*Ampetyane*] and *Songalla* [*Thangale*].[13]

The junior subsection names, which Kaytetye and some of the Anmatyerre share with Warlpiri, and which distinguish gender (unlike the main terms), were already in place by 1901. This can be concluded from the fact that Gillen's diary (1968, pp. 163–4; cf. Mulvaney et al. 1997, pp. 341–2) of his and Spencer's 1901 fieldwork at Barrow Creek names two children by their junior names: a boy *Tchanama* [*Tyaname*] and a girl *Nun-galla* [*Ngangkarle*].[14]

Even before Gillen's study, Howitt and Fison (1889, p. 44) published a set of eight names, with male and female terms, obtained through Allan Giles of Tennant Creek.[15] These are said to be the names of 'Waramunga'; in reality, the masculine terms are Kaytetye and the feminine terms are

---

13 Gillen (1968, pp. 144, 168) identified a *Thungalla* [*Thangale*] man named Arabinya-urungwinya (cf. p. 120) as having been implicated in this attack.
14 For a detailed study of junior skin names, see Koch and Simpson (forthcoming).
15 The same data and analysis are given in a letter from Fison to Howitt, dated 14 July 1884.

Warumungu.[16] Mathews (1899, p. 77) published a similar list, purporting to be the male and female terms for the 'Warramonga'. These along with Spencer and Gillen's (1969a [1899], p. 90) published 'Kaitish' list are given in Table 48. The final terms in each cell of Table 48 are the modern Kaytetye terms (in the 'masculine' column) from the dictionary (Turpin & Ross 2012)[17] and the modern Warumungu female terms (in the 'feminine' column) from Simpson (2002).

Table 48: Kaytetye (and Warumungu feminine) skin names according to sources.

	Source	Masculine	Feminine
A1	Howitt & Fison 1889 Mathews 1899 Spencer & Gillen 1899 Turpin & Ross 2012 / Simpson 2002	*Apononga* *Aponunga* *Apanunga* *Penangke*	*Napononga* *Napanunga* *Napanunga* *Nappanangka*
A2	Howitt & Fison Mathews Spencer & Gillen Turpin & Ross	*Ungerai* *Ungary* *Uknaria* *Kngwarraye*	*Namajili* *Namagillie* *Namigilli* *Namikili*
D1	Howitt & Fison Mathews Spencer & Gillen Turpin & Ross / Simpson	*Kabaji* *Kabajee* *Kabidgi* *Kapetye*	*Kabaji* *Nalcharrie* *Naltjeri* *Naljarri*
D2	Howitt & Fison Mathews Spencer & Gillen Turpin & Ross / Simpson	*Apongardi* *Apungata* *Appungerta* *Pengarte*	*Napongardi* *Napungartie* *Napungerta* *Nappangarti*
B1	Howitt & Fison Mathews Spencer & Gillen Turpin & Ross / Simpson	*Opala* *Opalla* *Purula* *Pwerle*	*Narila* *Naralu* *Naralu* *Narrurlu*
B2	Howitt & Fison Mathews Spencer & Gillen Turpin & Ross / Simpson	*Tungeli* *Tungulli* *Thungalla* *Thangale*	*Nungeli* *Nungalli* *Nungalla* *Nangali*
C1	Howitt & Fison Mathews Spencer & Gillen Turpin & Ross / Simpson	*Akamara* *Akamarra* *Akomara* *Kemarre*	*Nakamara* *Nakomara* *Nakomara*

---

16 However, the D1 term *Kapaji* is used for the feminine as well as the masculine instead of the expected *Naljarri*, and the C2 feminine *Tampajona* is the Warumungu masculine form.

17 Note that the dictionary standardises the spelling of all Kaytetye skin names with an initial consonant; this can be compared to Table 44, which includes the initial vowel that was typically pronounced in the 1970s.

	Source	Masculine	Feminine
C2	Howitt & Fison	Ampajona	Tampajona
	Mathews	Ampajona	Lambein
	Spencer & Gillen	Umbitchana	Nambin
	Turpin & Ross / Simpson	Mpetyane	Nampin

Source: Howitt and Fison (1889), Mathews (1899), Spencer and Gillen (1899), Simpson (2002) and Turpin and Ross (2012).

Three features of the Kaytetye set require explanation. First, the B1 term is *Pwerle* rather than the *P(w)errurle* expected on the basis of Arrernte and Anmatyerre.[18] This is easily accounted for by assuming that it was borrowed not from Warlpiri *Jupurrurla* but from Warumungu or Warlmanpa *Jup(p)urla*, which in common with a few other northern neighbours has lost the third syllable (see McConvell 1985, pp. 4–5).

Second, the B2 form *Thangale* includes an initial consonant, unlike *(A)ngale* of other Arandic languages. It has apparently been borrowed from Warlpiri *Jangala* or Warumungu *Jangali* without the normal initial truncation (see the section 'Arandic Phonology, Sound Change and Borrowing Patterns'). Spencer and Gillen's phonetic rendition of the name indicates that the initial consonant was pronounced as a dental (see Table 49). A possible motivation for this special treatment is that this name is a syllable shorter than the other names (except *Juppurla*).[19]

The third exception is D1 *Kapetye*, which differs from both Arrernte and Anmatyerre *Peltharre* and from Alyawarr *Apetyarre*. Like *Thangale*, this name always begins with a consonant and consists of only three syllables instead of the four of most of the Kaytetye skin names (if the optional initial vowel is counted). A possible source is the Warlmanpa term *Japaja*, which likewise is a syllable shorter than expected (see the subsection 'Warlmanpa'). The initial consonant *k* is unexpected, but otherwise it could be analysed as an adapted copy of Warlmanpa *Japaja*. A D1 form *Kappiji* is attested in Spencer and Gillen's Warumungu alongside *Jappaljarri* (see Table 49); however, the vowels are more easily explained if the direction of borrowing was from Warlmanpa to Kaytetye

---

18 Spencer and Gillen (1969a [1899]) is the only source that gives *Purula* for B1. This seems to be an Arrernte term that could be used in place of *Pwerle*. Later, Spencer and Gillen (1969b [1904], p. 98) stated that, in comparison to Arunta, Ilpirra and Iliaura, 'in the Kaitish and Unmatjera, Bulthara is replaced by Kabbadji and Purula by Opila'. *Opila* would represent **uperle*, later pronounced as *Pwerle*.
19 It is not impossible that Thangale may be a reborrowing or updating that replaced an earlier **Angale*.

and thence to some subgroups of the Warumungu.[20] Kaytetye *Kapetye* may have replaced an older form **Apetyarre*, if, as we suggested, Alyawarr borrowed its form from Kaytetye. I suggest that this putative form would have been the normal outcome of borrowing from an earlier (and unattested) Warlmanpa form **Japajjarri* (with a double stop consonant) that developed via **Japatjarri* from the original **Japaljarri* (attested in Warlpiri). The lateral *l* became a stop *t* before another consonant in a number of other words in Warlmanpa.

Neighbouring Languages

This section gives the skin names in the neighbouring languages from which the Arandic languages have borrowed their terms. The Warlpiri terms were given in Table 43.

Warumungu

Table 49 presents the forms of the skin names given for 'Warramunga' by Spencer and Gillen (1969a [1899], p. 91) and Gillen (1968, p. 179), 'Warramunga, Walpari, and Wulmala' by Spencer and Gillen (1969b [1904], p. 100), as well as the modern representations by Simpson (2002, p. 30). Regarding spelling, note that a) *tj*, *ch* and *dg* are alternative ways of spelling the palatal sound; b) *th* (with a dental articulation) is the most typical pronunciation of the laminal stop in the old sources; c) the laminal stop (whether pronounced as dental or palatal) is represented by *j* in the modern orthography; and d) the modern analysis recognises distinctive long consonants spelled with *pp* and *kk*. The only substantive difference between the sources is in D1: during their stay with the Warumungu at Tennant Creek in 1901, Spencer and Gillen encountered both the terms *Kabidgi* and *Tjapeltjeri* for D1. The latter is given in their 1904 publication, but the former in the table of Gillen's diary, which also mentions *Chapalcharrie* (e.g. Gillen 1968, p. 178). *Tjapeltjeri* is the same as Warlpiri *Japaljarri* and *Kabidgi* is identical to *Kapetye* of the Kaytetye. It seems that both terms were in use—perhaps within different subgroups of the Warumungu. The main differences between Warumungu and Warlpiri masculine terms are a) the variant D1 *Kappiji* (as it would be spelled in the modern orthography) in place of *Japaljarri*;

---

20 I assume the (somewhat centralised) allophone of Warlmanpa /a/ was interpreted in Kaytetye as its central vowel /e/, which was then pronounced as [i] before the palatal *ty* and then copied by Warumungu as /i/.

10. THE DEVELOPMENT OF ARANDIC SUBSECTION NAMES IN TIME AND SPACE

b) the shorter form *Juppurla* for B1 versus Warlpiri *Jupurrurla*; and c) the shorter form *Jampin*[21] for D2 versus Warlpiri *Jampijinpa*. The last form probably originated as **Jampijin* and results from the lenition of the *j* to *y* and subsequent reduction of *iyi* to *i*. Note that there is no evidence for the final *pa* syllable that occurs in Warlpiri; it is known that *pa* was a late addition to Warlpiri words that otherwise ended in a consonant (Hale 1973, pp. 452–5).

Table 49: Warumungu skin names according to sources.

	Source	Masculine	Feminine
A1	Spencer & Gillen 1899 Gillen 1968 Spencer & Gillen 1904 Simpson 2002	Thapanunga Thapanunga Thapanunga Jappanangka	Napanunga Napanunga Napanunga Nappanangka
A2	Spencer & Gillen 1899 Gillen 1968 Spencer & Gillen 1904 Simpson 2002	Chunguri Chunguri Tjunguri Jungarrayi	Namagili Namagillie Namigilli Namikili
D1	Spencer & Gillen 1899 Gillen 1968 Spencer & Gillen 1904 Simpson 2002	**Kabidgi** **Kabidgi** Tjapeltjeri Jappaljarri	Nalchari Nalcharrie Naltjeri Naljarri
D2	Spencer & Gillen 1899 Gillen 1968 Spencer & Gillen 1904 Simpson 2002	Thapungerta Thapungartie Thapungarti Jappangarti	Napungerta Napungartie Napungerta Nappangarti
B1	Spencer & Gillen 1899 Gillen 1968 Spencer & Gillen 1904 Simpson 2002	**Chupilla** **Chupilla** Tjupila **Juppurla**	Naralu Naralu Naralu Narrurlu
B2	Spencer & Gillen 1899 Gillen 1968 Spencer & Gillen 1904 Simpson 2002	Thungalli Thungalli Thungalla Jangali	Nungalli Nungalli Nungalla Nangali
C1	Spencer & Gillen 1899 Gillen 1968 Spencer & Gillen 1904 Simpson 2002	Thakomara Thakomara Thakomara Jakkamarra	Nakomara Nakomara Nakomara Nakkamarra
C2	Spencer & Gillen 1899 Gillen 1968 Spencer & Gillen 1904 Simpson 2002	Chambein Chambein Tjambin Jampin	Lambein Lambein Nambin Nampin

Source: Gillen (1968, p. 179), Simpson (2002, p. 30) and Spencer and Gillen (1899, p. 91; 1904, p. 100).

---

21 The form *Lambein* seems to be an error; the text of Gillen's (1968, p. 230) diary gives *Nambein* instead, which agrees with the form given in their second volume.

Warlmanpa

While based at Tennant Creek in 1901, Spencer and Gillen also met with people belonging to the 'Wolmalla Tribe ... which occupies a tract of country adjoining the Warramunga south western boundary' (Gillen 1968, p. 251). They are said to be intermarried with the Warumungu and to share their system of organisation. Spencer and Gillen witnessed their ceremonies associated with a site called Tchalyirpa [Jalyirrpa], whose owners appeared to belong to the Kabidgi and Chunguri classes (Gillen 1968, p. 254). This group can be identified with the Warlmanpa of the Kanturrpa estate (Aboriginal Land Commissioner 1991, p. 19).[22] Spencer and Gillen (1969b [1904], p. 100) gave a unified listing of skin names for 'Warramunga, Walpari, and Wulmala' (see Table 49). They also met some members of the 'Walpari Tribe', described as adjoining the western border of the Warumungu and extending a long way to the south and west (Gillen 1968, p. 251), whose 'totemic system etc. is on all fours with the Warramunga' (p. 258). Spencer and Gillen (1969a [1899], p. 91) had earlier published a skin name list attributed to the 'Walpari tribe', which must have been obtained before the 1901 trip, presumably through Gillen's contacts with the Tennant Creek Telegraph Station. A comparison of this list with the modern Warlmanpa terms recorded by Nash (1979) shows that they are virtually identical (see Table 50); in fact: 'their equivalence with the modern Warlmanpa terms (as opposed to modern Warlpiri subsection names) is part of the evidence that Spencer and Gillen's "Walpari" at Tennant Creek were probably speakers of Warlmanpa' (Nash 2015).

Table 50: Warlmanpa skin names.

	Source	Masculine	Feminine
A1	Spencer & Gillen 1899 Nash 1979	*Chapanunga* *Japanangka*	*Napanunga* *Napanangka*
A2	Spencer & Gillen Nash	*Chunguri* *Jungurra*	*Namilpa* *Namurlpa*
D1	Spencer & Gillen Nash	*Chapatcha* *Japaja*	*Napatcha* *Napaja*
D2	Spencer & Gillen Nash	*Chapungarta* *Japangarti*	*Napungarta* *Napangarti*

---

22 'There seemed to be a consensus that the site Jalyirrpa belongs to Kanturrpa: it lies just beyond the western limits of Warumungu country, where Warlpiri and Warumungu people are to some extent mixed' (Aboriginal Land Commissioner 1991). Cf. the comment (p. 26): 'Kanturrpa is the name of a group of Warlmanpa or Warlpiri people'.

10. THE DEVELOPMENT OF ARANDIC SUBSECTION NAMES IN TIME AND SPACE

Source		Masculine	Feminine
B1	Spencer & Gillen Nash	Chupilla Jupula	Napula Napula
B2	Spencer & Gillen Nash	Chungalla Jangala	Nungalla Nangala
C1	Spencer & Gillen Nash	Chakuma Jakama	Nakuma Nakama
C2	Spencer & Gillen Nash	Champechinpa Jampijinpa	Nambechinpa Nampijinpa

Source: Nash (1979) and Spencer and Gillen (1899, p. 91).

Comparison of Forms between the Northern Languages

The forms of the skin names in the three northern languages are sufficiently similar (with the exceptions noted in the next paragraph) to point to a common original set of terms that were borrowed into each of these languages. Nevertheless, the few differences between the languages help to identify the sources of the Arandic terms. The Warlpiri terms are considered closest to the original form (cf. McConvell 1985, p. 4): the only changes they have undergone are the replacement of *rt* by *rd* (a retroflex flap) in D2 *Japangardi* and the addition of *pa* to the end of C2 **Jampijin*. The last change is shared with Warlmanpa, whereas Warumungu preserve a form with final *n*. Warlmanpa and Warumungu both have shorter forms for B1, *Jupula* and *Juppurla* respectively, that lack the third syllable of Warlpiri *Jupurrurla*. Three Warlmanpa terms lack the fourth syllable found in the other languages: *Jungurra(yi)*, *Jakama(rra)* and *Japa(l)ja(rri)*. Further, D1 *Japaja* lacks the *l* of *Japaljarri*; I assume that this reflects a sound change whereby a lateral sound became a stop before another stop, as in *jitpitpi* 'Eucalyptus setosa' versus Warlpiri *jilpilpi*, *purtku* 'warm' versus Warlpiri *purlku*, and *jurtatja* 'members of wife's patriline' versus Warlpiri *jurdalja*. An inherited *Japaljarri* would have become *Japatjarri*, which we must assume simplified to *Japajarri*. This form would be the basis for the loan word *Apetyarre* found in Alyawarr and hypothesised to have been once present in Kaytetye. The dropping of the final syllable of *Japajarri/Napajarri*, *Jakamarra/Nakamarra*, and *Jungurrayi* would have taken place after *Japajarri* was borrowed in Kaytetye (as *Apetyarre*).

The feminine forms in the northern languages generally correspond to the masculine forms, albeit with initial *n* in place of the *j* of the masculine terms—with the following exceptions: a) for B1, the vowels of the first syllable differ for Warlpiri *Napurrurla* versus *Jupurrurla*, Warumungu *Narrurlu* versus *Juppurla* and Warlmanpa *Napula* versus *Jupula*; b) for D1, Warumungu *Naljarri* shows a shortened form versus *Jappaljarri*, and is radically unlike the alternative Warumungu form *Kappiji*; and c) for A2, Warumungu and Warlmanpa have feminine forms *Namikili* and *Namurlpa* that do not match the respective masculines *Jungarrayi* and *Jungurra*.

Different Sources for Different Arandic Languages

All Anmatyerre forms can be explained in terms of a Warlpiri source, provided that D1 was borrowed before *pa* became fixed on *Jampijinpa*. The B1 form of Kaytetye and Alyawarr, whose earliest Arandic form would have been **uperle*, must come from Warumungu (or possibly Warlmanpa, which lacks the retroflexed *rl*); further, the Arandic form must be based on the masculine *Jupurlu*, since the feminine form, with a different vowel in the first syllable, would rather have yielded **Arrwerle*. The Alyawarr C form *Apetyarre* can be traced to a Warlmanpa **Japatjarri*, resulting from an earlier *Japaljarri* and preceding the more recent *Japaja*. It is assumed that this form was transmitted by the intervening Kaytetye, where an earlier **Apetyarre* was later replaced by *Kapetye*. Note that the *j* from the middle of **Japajarri* was copied as Alyawarr *ty*, whereas the form of *Japaljarri* copied by Anmatyerre resulted in Arandic *th* (in **Apeltharre*). The Kaytetye D1 form *Kapetye* is interpreted as an updated version of **Apetyarre*—reborrowed or remodelled after Warlmanpa shortened its **Japatjarri* to *Japaja*. It is not known why the word-initial *j* was adapted as *k* for this term rather than being truncated as in the other terms, except for *Thangale*. It is hypothesised that *Kappiji* was borrowed from Kaytetye into some subgroups of the Warumungu. Finally, the B2 form *Thangale* of Katyetye, recorded also for Spencer and Gillen's 'Unmatjira' and 'Iliaura', could have been borrowed from *Jangala* in any of the three languages; preference can possibly be given to Warumungu as the source, on the basis that Spencer and Gillen more frequently rendered initial *j* as *th* (rather than *tj* or *ch*) before the vowel /a/ for this language—presumably because they heard the Warumungu laminal stop as more dental than palatal in articulation. It is possible that Kaytetye *Thangale* represents an updating of an earlier **Angale*, which is the presumed earliest form in the other Arandic languages.[23] Table 51 summarises the possible sources of the

---

23   An alternative scenario in which Kaytetye only borrowed the term *Thangale* later than the rest of the set 2 terms hardly seems realistic.

Arandic skin names, each of which is given in its presumed earliest form, including initial vowels that were subsequently lost in some dialects. The languages and their abbreviations are Lower Arrernte (LA); (Western, Central and Eastern) Arrernte (Ar), Anmatyerre (An), Kaytetye (K), Alyawarr (Al), Warlpiri (Wlp), Warlmanpa (Wmp) and Warumungu (Wru). The section 'Borrowing, Sound Change and Relative Chronology' describes the phonology of the Arandic forms in more detail.

Table 51: Sources of Arandic skin names.

	Source language	Form		LA	Ar/An	K	Al
A1	Wlp/Wmp/Wru	Japanangka	Apenangke	√	√	√	
A2	Wlp/Wmp/Wru	Jungarrayi	Kngwarreye		√	√	√
B1	Wlp	Jupurrurla	Uperrurle	√	√		
B1	Wmp/Wru	Jupurla	Uperle			√	√
B2	Wlp/Wmp/Wru	Jangala	Angale		√		
B2	Wlp, Wmp, Wru	Jangala	Thangale			√	
C1	Wlp/Wmp/Wru	Jakamarra	Akemarre	√	√	√	√
C2	Wlp/Wmp	Jampijin*	Ampetyane		√	√	
D1	Wlp/Wru	Japaljarri	Apeltharre	√	√		
D1	Wmp	Japajarri	Apetyarre				√
D1	Wmp	Japaji	Kapetye			√	
D2	Wlp/Wmp/Wru	Japangardi	Apengarte		√	√	

Source: Author's work.

Borrowing, Sound Change and Relative Chronology

Arandic Phonology, Sound Change and Borrowing Patterns

The Arandic languages differ in their phonology from the norms found in the languages to the north and west from which they have presumably obtained their skin names. While words in other languages typically begin with a consonant, Arandic words may begin with a vowel.

While other languages use only the vowels *a*, *i* and *u*, Arandic languages make sparing use of *i* and *u* but heavily use a central vowel (as in English *the*) that is spelled *e*. Arandic languages also have a set of rounded consonants, spelled *Cw* (where *C* is a consonant); *e* after a rounded consonant sounds like *u* in other languages.

The distinctive phonological structure of the Arandic languages results from a series of phonological changes (or sound changes) that occurred during the history of these languages. These changes are described and justified in Koch (1997b) and summarised in Koch (2004). Koch (2007) added a few details about how Kaytetye and the rest of the Arandic languages developed differently with respect to words beginning with *Cya-*, *Cyu-* and *wi-* (where *Cy* stands for any palatal consonant). If the skin names were borrowed into the Arandic languages, as everyone agrees they were, the question arises as to when this borrowing occurred relative to the distinctive Arandic sound changes—in particular: 'initial dropping'. The relevance of these changes to the borrowing of skin names was highlighted by McConvell (1985, p. 6).

As a consequence of the Arandic sound changes and later borrowing patterns, we can distinguish three chronological phases of Arandic languages, which have resulted in three separate strata of Arandic vocabulary. Examples are shown in Table 52 (here, as elsewhere, * marks forms that are unattested but reconstructed). These lexical sets have different characteristics with regard to the treatment of (non-final) vowels and initial consonants. In all three sets, final vowels are always *e* (= shwa).[24] Word-internal vowels are treated differently: in stratum I, all vowels except those in the first syllable are changed to *e*; in strata II and III, non-final vowels largely preserve their quality—*i* is copied as *e*, *a* as *a* but as *e* in the second syllable of four-syllable words (where it reflects a higher allophone in the source language), and *u* as either *u* or *we*, which is interpreted as a rounded variant of *e* that is conditioned by rounding on the preceding consonant. The initial consonant is deleted in all words of strata I and II, but is retained in stratum III. I have interpreted vocabulary in stratum II as the result of a borrowing pattern that copies vowels (except final ones) faithfully but truncates the initial consonant (Koch 1997a, 2014). This pattern was facilitated by the existence of many pairs of words

---

24 In the analysis by Breen and Pensalfini (1999), they argued that the final vowel is absent from the phonological representation of words. This analysis is reflected in the orthographies of Alyawarr and Anmatyerre, where final vowels are not written.

that displayed this same pattern—some being old inherited cognates but others resulting from the Warlpiri borrowing of Arandic vowel-initial words and adding an initial consonant (*y*, *w* or *ng*) to fit them to Warlpiri phonotactics, which requires an initial consonant (see Koch 2014).

Table 52: Examples of words in the three lexical strata.

		Source	Outcome	Gloss
I	Inherited words that have undergone sound change	kaparli ngumparna kurrparu kayirra pankulV	aperle *umperne *urrpere ayerre[re] ankele	father's mother wife's brother magpie north cousin
II	Loan words adapted with truncation	jurdalja kangkuru mingkurlpa marliyarra	urtaltye angkwere (i)ngkwerlpe arleyarre	wife's mother elder sister native tobacco initiate
III	Loan words adapted without truncation	majardi japirnpa janyungu kajalarra marrrapirnti wanapari	matyarte tyapernpe tyanywenge katyelarre marrrepernte wanapare	pubic tassel boil, sore tobacco fruit pick nose-bone dingo

Source: Koch (2014).

Skin Names and Lexical Strata

I have claimed that the Arandic skin names of both sets 1 and 2 belong to stratum II—that is, their lack of an initial consonant is explicable by the pattern of borrowing with truncation (Koch 2014). However, the junior skin names of Anmatyerre and Kaytetye belong to stratum III and represent loan words that follow a more recent pattern of adaptation that does not involve consonant truncation (see subsection 'Late Borrowing of Junior Skin Names').

McConvell's solution basically posits that skin names were borrowed before the Arandic sound change that deleted initial consonants ceased to operate—which would place them in my stratum I. Table 53 shows the expected fate of the set 1 skin names if they had been borrowed before the operation of *all* presumed Arandic sound changes: these are set alongside the Warlpiri originals and the attested Arandic forms. Note that in this hypothetical stratum I scenario, all the vowels except those in the first syllable would become *e*. Further, the *ngk* cluster would lose its stop (see Koch 1997b). However, the actual vowel adaptation patterns are identical to those of stratum III, which are clearly loan words postdating the sound changes, and to stratum II, which we claim also represent adapted loan words postdating the sound changes. The (adult) skin names clearly do not belong to stratum III, since they do not preserve the initial consonant. If they belonged to stratum III, they would look like the forms in the rightmost column of Table 53. We know this from the fact that the Anmatyerre dictionary (Green 2010) gives the Warlpiri names as they are used by Anmatyerre people today. Table 54 gives the Anmatyerre versions of the masculine and feminine Warlpiri (adult) skin names. (Note that the Anmatyerre spelling system does not represent final vowels.)

Table 53: Hypothetic developments of skin names if borrowed early.

	Warlpiri source	Hypothetical Arandic I	Actual Arandic	Arandic III
A1	Japanangka	Apenenge	Apanangke	Tyapenangke
C1	Jakamarra	Akemerre	Akemarre	Tyakemarre
D1	Japaljarri	Apeltherre	Apeltharre	Tyapeltyarre
B1	Jupurrurla	Uperrerle	Uperrurle?	Tyweperrerle

Source: Author's work.

Table 54: Warlpiri adult skin names as used by the Anmatyerre.

	Warlpiri	Anmatyerre (stratum III)
A1	Japanangka Napanangka	Tyapenangk Napenangk
A2	Jungarrayi Nungarrayi	Tywengarray Nwengarray
B1	Jupurrurla Napurrurla	Tyweperrerl Napwerrerl
B2	Jangala Nangala	Tyangal Nangal
C1	Jakamarra Nakemarr	Tyakemarr Nakemarr
C2	Jampijinpa Nampijinpa	Tyampetyenp Nampetyenp
D1	Japaljarri Napaljarri	Tyapeltyarr Napeltyarr
D2	Japangardi Napangardi	Tyapengart Napengart

Source: Green (2010).

McConvell claimed that two pieces of evidence indicate that sets 1 and 2 entered the Arandic languages in separate chronological phases. McConvell (1985, p. 23; 1996, p. 131) cited the different treatment of Warlpiri *j* in the earlier borrowed *Peltharre* (from *Japaljarri*) and the more recently adopted *Mpetyane* (from **Jampijin*) as evidence for chronologically different sound changes. However, this difference can be interpreted as the consequence of the fact that the Warlpiri laminal consonant *j* corresponds to two separate Arandic consonants—a lamino-dental *th* and a lamino-palatal *ty*. Warlpiri *j* had a palatal allophone before the *i* of **Jampijin*, which was naturally reproduced as *ty* in the Arandic languages, while the normal allophone that occurred before *a* in *Japaljarri* was reproduced as the dental *th*. There is no need to assume different chronological strata. Further, the penultimate vowel of Arandic *(a)mpetyane* versus Warlpiri *Jampijinpa* needs explaining. I have made the following suggestions: the Warlpiri source was **Jampijin* (before the final syllable *pa* became a fixed part of the stem); the final vowel was added because it was required by Arandic phonotactics; and a form borrowed and adapted as **ampetyene* had its third vowel altered to *a* to fit the pattern of other skin names, which had a vowel pattern *a-e-a-e* (Koch 2014).

A stronger argument for making a chronological distinction between sets 1 and 2 is made by McConvell from the differential treatment of initial vowels in the skin names. He observed that in Spencer and Gillen's list of Arrernte and 'Ilpirra' [= Anmatyerre] skin names, all the set 2 terms begin with a vowel but those of set 1 with a consonant. While recognising that this is no longer the situation in current Arandic languages,[25] he concluded that 'the earlier transcription seems too systematic to be an error on Spencer and Gillen's part' (McConvell 1985, p. 23). However, it is not clear that this difference is phonologically significant for two reasons. First, the skin name lists given by other scholars do not differentiate between sets 1 and 2. It can be seen from Table 46 that forms quoted by Schulze, Strehlow and the modern Western Arrernte dictionary—all reflecting Western Arrernte—and Mathews's Harts Range Arrernte all involve initial consonants in set 2, as well as set 1 terms. Further, initial vowels are found in set 1 skin names in Kaytetye and Spencer and Gillen's Iliaura (see Table 47); hence, a solution that might conceivably work for Arrernte will not account for all Arandic languages. A second reason to

---

25 Although McConvell (1985, p. 23) stated that 'no Aranda subsection terms have the initial vowel in the commonly used forms today', initial vowels are used in Wilkins's (1989, p. 35) B2 *Angale* and in Henderson and Dobson's (1994) B2 *Angale* and C2 *Ampetyane* (see Table 46).

doubt the significance of initial vowels in the skin names comes from the well-known variability of initial vowels in Arandic languages. Stirling (1896, p. 10) already commented on the uncertainty of whether final and initial vowels were present in Arrernte words. Green (2010, p. 744) noted that 'many words in Arandic languages may be pronounced either with or without the initial *a* vowel'. Wilkins (1989, pp. 81–2), for the Mparntwe (Alice Springs) dialect of Arrernte, agonised over the proper representation of the large number of words that might be pronounced either with an initial consonant or with an initial vowel *a*. Breen (2001, p. 65) described the 'comparative absence of initial vowels, especially /a/' from Western Arrernte. Thus, it seems to me that the skin names of sets 1 and 2 were all borrowed into Anmatyerre with an initial vowel, which was variably pronounced, and when further borrowed into Western Arrernte, the vowel was characteristically omitted—as well as in Lower Arrernte, which would have received the terms via Western Arrernte. I suggest that Spencer and Gillen did not so much make an error as simply standardise variable forms in a way that could imply a patterned distinction.[26]

McConvell's (1985, pp. 6, 23; 1996, p. 130–2) discussion of Arandic skin names posited two separate borrowing strata for sets 1 and 2, with both preceding a stratum (our III) that does not involve consonant deletion. However, both of these earlier strata are assumed to involve the historical Arandic sound changes of 'initial dropping'—the first deleting the beginning consonant and vowel (changing *Japanangka* to *Penangke*) and the second deleting only the first consonant (changing *Japangardi* to *Apengarte*). According to McConvell's conception (clarified by personal communication of 31 August 2014), the set 1 forms were borrowed, then underwent the sound change #C_1 > Ø (deletion of first consonant of the word) and then the change #V_1 > Ø (deletion of first vowel of the word). At a later stage, set 2 forms were borrowed and underwent the change #C_1 > Ø, but not #V_1 > Ø. This scenario requires the persistence of the first sound change—that the 'sound change of initial dropping … was still operative up until the mid-nineteenth century' (McConvell 1996, p. 130)—but not that of the second change. In my view, this solution raises problems

---

26 I imagine a scenario as follows. Gillen (who had worked at telegraph stations in Lower Arrernte and then Central Arrernte territory) first learned the four section names from the Lower Arrernte, who omitted the initial vowel. When he later became familiar with the Central Arrernte terms, which had a variable vowel, he assumed they were the same as the forms he already knew from Lower Arrernte. He first learned of the second set of terms from the Anmatyerre, who characteristically pronounced the initial vowel. Then, when he realised the same terms were also being used among the Central Arrernte, he assumed they were vowel-initial like the Anmatyerre forms, although they were in fact variable.

of both relative chronology—consonant deletion applies both before and after vowel deletion—and the duration of a sound change.[27] How can a sound change persist after it has altered all the candidate phonemes? The only input to the change would be words borrowed after the change first operated. At best, the 'change' would exist merely as a constraint, motivated by the absence of word-initial consonants. However, why would it continue after the deletion of initial vowels again allowed words to begin with a consonant (i.e. after *Apenangke* had changed to *Penangke*)? It seems to me that the only way the persistence of such a sound change can be interpreted is in terms of the adaptation of loan words, so that their resulting form is like that resulting from the original sound change. This makes McConvell's solution for set 2 skin names equivalent to mine. One can then ask whether set 1 skin names could not have been treated the same way, and been borrowed after the consonant-deletion change had already taken place—that is, in my stratum II.

Thus, according to my interpretation, the chronology of borrowing and sound changes is as follows. After the major Arandic sound changes had taken place (in stratum I), there was a pattern of borrowing (from Warlpiri and other languages with initial consonants) that involved the truncation of the first consonant (stratum II). In Western Arrernte, in particular, there was a subsequent change that eliminated the resulting initial vowel, especially if it was *a*. At some time, around or before the mid-nineteenth century, a second set of skin names was borrowed by Anmatyerre and Kaytetye; these were also adapted by the deletion of the first consonant (still according to stratum II processes). When passed on to western and Central Arrernte, these new terms were treated just like the pre-existing set 1 skin names, which involved dropping the first vowel, at least in Western Arrernte. Consequently, Warlpiri *Japangardi*, which was borrowed into Anmatyerre as *Apengarte*, was further adapted as *Pengarte*, and so on.

Late Borrowing of Junior Skin Names

There were some skin names that were borrowed according to the recent pattern of Arandic borrowing, which preserved intact the initial consonant (our stratum III). These are the junior skin names found in Kaytetye and western dialects of Anmatyerre. Formally, the junior terms are almost

---

27 Recent theoretical work on sound change suggests that their period of operation is typically of rather short duration (e.g. Janda & Joseph 2003).

identical to their Warlpiri counterparts—allowing for the differences in phoneme systems and orthographies.[28] Their formal similarity can be seen in Table 55, which presents the male and female terms of Warlpiri, Kaytetye and Western Anmatyerre (the latter is based on Green 1998, p. 105; 2010). Obviously, the junior terms are later borrowings than the adult terms.[29]

Table 55: Junior skin names in Warlpiri, Kaytetye and Western Anmatyerre.

		M	F
A1	Wlp Kay WAnm	Janama Tyaname Tyanam	Ngamana, Nangka Ngamane Ngaman
A2	Wlp Kay WAnm	Jukurdayi Tywekertaye Tywekertay	Ngapita, Ngampukulu Ngapete Ngapet, Ngampekwerl
B1	Wlp Kay WAnm	Jurlama, Jupurru Tywerlame Tywerlam, Tyweperr	Ngampurla, Ngapurru Ngamperle Ngamp(w)erl, Napwerr
B2	Wlp Kay WAnm	Jangkarli Tyangkarle Tyangkarl	Ngangkala, Nangali Ngangkale Ngangkal, Nangaley
C1	Wlp Kay WAnm	Jakarra Tyakarre Tyakarr	Wajala, Nakakutu, Nakarra Watyale Watyal, Nakakwet, Nakarr
C2	Wlp Kay WAnm	Jampirlka, Jampit Tyamperlke Tyamperlk	Ngampijakurdu, Nampit Mpetyakwerte Mpetyakwert, Ngampin
D1	Wlp Kay WAnm	Japalya Tyapalye Tyapaly	Ngalyirri Ngalyerre Ngalyerr
D2	Wlp Kay WAnm	Japayardi, Jangari Tyapeyarte Tyapeyart, Tyapart[1]	Ngampayardi, Ngampeyarte, Ngampeyart, Ngampart

Source: Laughren (1982, p. 76); Turpin and Ross (2012, pp. 809–10); Green (2010, p. 744).
[1] *Tyapart* versus *Tyapeyart* and *Ngampart* versus *Ngampeyart* reflect language-internal reduction of the sequence *eya*.

---

28 These names are identical to adult names found in languages further to the north, such as Gurindji and Jingulu.
29 Meggitt (1962, p. 165) implied that the Warlpiri junior terms were used only among the eastern Warlpiri then living at Philip Creek, and suggested, improbably, that these were 'probably borrowed from the Yanmadjari [Anmatyerre] tribe'.

In addition to the junior skin names, there are two examples of the retention of initial consonants in adult skin names. The B2 form *Thangale*, comparable to Warlpiri *Jangala*, is found in Kaytetye, as well as in Spencer and Gillen's Anmatyerre and Alyawarr. This may represent a late updating of an earlier **Angale*—for which I cannot offer any motivation. Likewise, the Kaytetye D1 term *Kapetye* may represent an updating of an earlier **Apetyarre* (which is found in Alyawarr) under the influence of Warlmanpa **Japaji*—with an unexplained substitution of *k* for initial *j*.

Social Aspects of the Adoption of New Social Categories

Native Traditions on the Origin of Skins

Spencer and Gillen attempted to obtain Indigenous accounts of the origin of the social categories. As might be expected, Aboriginal people gave explanations in terms of the activities of Dreaming characters. For example, Gillen's diary for 3 July 1901 records a Kaytetye tradition[30] according to which the Moon man Arilpa [*Arelpe*] assigned marriage classes to people:

> Men of all classes visited Arilpa who furnished each man with a wife of the proper class and explained to them the awful enormity of marriage outside of the proper class … It was from the great Arilpa that the Kaitish people—so says the tradition—learnt the proper class into which each of the 8 divisions was to intermarry. (Gillen 1968, p. 154)[31]

Such accounts did not satisfy Spencer and Gillen's quest for historical answers:

> How on earth this class system arose in these Central Tribes is a mystery into which we have probed deeply without a shade of success. The blacks do not appear to have any tradition as to its origin. (Gillen 1968, p. 155)

> We have been quite unable to discover the meaning of these names in any of the central tribes, or to obtain the slightest clue as to their origin, which must date very far back. (Spencer & Gillen 1969b [1904], p. 98)

---

30 For a similar Warumungu tradition, see Spencer and Gillen (1969b [1904], p. 429).
31 See Spencer and Gillen (1969b [1904], p. 412) for another version of this story. The Moon man is associated with a place called Karla karlu. I believe this refers to a site around the Devils Marbles, on the boundary between the Kaytetye and Warumungu lands. This is consistent with the likely northern source of skin names borrowed into Kaytetye. Another Kaytetye myth about the Moon man, given in Koch (1993, pp. 4–10), also has the Moon man coming from the north, from Warumungu country.

Some of the myths involved the mention of the skin names of participants. While Anmatyerre, Kaytetye and Warumungu stories mention the subsections of the Dreamings, it appears that the Arrernte myths presented in Spencer and Gillen (1927, 1969a [1899]) only attribute the four section names to Dreamings. This may be significant, given that Kaytetye and Anmatyerre had the eight-term system earlier than did the Arrernte; the Arrernte adoption of the second set of names was probably too recent for these names to have become fully integrated into their mythology.

Spencer and Gillen claimed to discern four or five chronological layers of the Dreamtime from Arrernte accounts. This is best summarised in Spencer and Gillen (1927, p. 322). In the first period, the supernatural Dreamings formed human beings, each of whom implicitly belonged to the particular totem (plant or animal) out of which they were formed. In the next stage, Ullagubbera [*alekapere*] (little hawk) men introduced the use of circumcision by means of stone knives (instead of firesticks) and assigned the four section names, but without respect to any marriage regulations. Achilpa [*atyelpe*] (wild cat) men then introduced the rite of subincision and the more advanced *engwura* [*angkwerre*] initiation ceremony. Later, a number of people of the Emu clan first introduced marriage regulations whereby *Penangke* must marry *Perrurle* and *Peltharre* must marry *Kemarre*, but allowing that a person could marry someone classified as either *anua* [*anewe*] or *unkulla* [*ankele*]—that is, second or first cross-cousin. A subsequent reform followed an assembly of a number of groups of Emu people, held at Urliipma and then at Apaura, both in the southern part of the territory of the Ilpirra [Anmatyerre], north of the MacDonnell Ranges. Here, it was decided that marriage was to be restricted to people related as *anua* [*anewe*]. After an *engwura* [*angkwerre*] ceremony was performed, 'the people stood up, each man with his wife or wives behind him, and those who were wrongly united were separated, and the women were allotted to their proper *Anua* [*anewe*] men' (Spencer & Gillen 1927, p. 321). Spencer and Gillen (1927, p. 323; 1969a [1899], p. 422) further commented:

> It is not without interest to note that, according to tradition, the emu men who introduced the division of the sections now in use live away to the north, because the adoption of the distinctive names for the eight groups thus created is at the present time taking place in the Arunta tribe, and, as a matter of actual fact, these eight names did originate in the north, and gradually spread southwards through the tribe.

I would add that the meetings described in the final stage may reflect actual memories of the kind of social consultative processes that took place when the Arrernte adopted the eight-term subsection system, around 1880, from their Northern Anmatyerre neighbours.

Another mythological tradition reflects the split of sections into subsections. This story suggests that subsections might at first have been considered by some to be merely alternative names for the pre-existing section names. It also may also indicate that the introduction of subsections did not always result from harmonious consultations. In 1901, Spencer and Gillen recorded from the Warumungu a story about two ant women (so-called because they fed on the eggs of the ant Echilpa):

> [The two ant women] quarrelled about their class names. One suggested that they should both be Naralu [*Narrurlu*, i.e. B1] the other objected and said she intended to be Nungalli [*Nangali*, i.e. B2] the upshot of the little difference was that they fought until they died. They bled profusely … and the blood may be seen at the present day in the form of some huge red stones at Unbiria where the fight took place. (Gillen 1968, p. 202)[32]

The introduction of sections must have complicated traditions about the Dreamings that were associated with particular sacred sites. This may be reflected in stories that attribute two Dreaming persons to a particular sacred site. Spencer and Gillen recorded a tradition concerning the Kaytetye site Anira [*Arnerre*] in which a euro man Arininga [*Areynenge* 'euro'] emerged in the Dreamtime:

> At sunset he slept, and when the sun arose he split into two, one of whom was a Purula[33] and the other a Kumara [*kemarre*] (i.e. father and son). At sunset the two joined together to form a Purula, who went down into the waterhole out of which at sunrise he emerged and divided into two again. After this they remained separate. (Gillen 1968, p. 147; Spencer & Gillen 1969b [1904], p. 158, cf. p. 418)

This bifurcation was undoubtedly motivated by the fact that this site was linked to the *Pwerle* and *Kemarre* patricouple after the introduction of section names (and later subsections). The splitting of the Dreaming would have allowed a pre-existing personage to be equally associated with both of the relevant names.

---

32 See Spencer and Gillen (1969b [1904], p. 423) for another version of this story.
33 Spencer and Gillen here use the Arrernte form of the skin name in place of the normal Kaytetye *Pwerle*.

Possible Implementation of the Subsection System

We have no direct evidence of how the adoption of the subsections proceeded socially. Nevertheless, some ideas can be proffered on the basis of how this took place elsewhere, as well as from the native traditions. It is likely that not all members of a group adopted subsection names at the same time, but that the adoption of the new system had a certain duration, as argued by Dousset (2005, p. 79) in relation to the adoption of the section system by the Western Desert peoples. The first adopters were presumably people married to members of other groups who already used subsection names. It is possible that group decisions at major get-togethers played a role in promoting the adoption of the system in whole groups, along the lines of Spencer and Gillen's account of the assembly of the Emu people mentioned in the subsection 'Native Traditions on the Origin of Skins'. It is also possible that some members of the group, who perhaps did not participate in such decision-making forums, felt they were being coerced into accepting the new system—as suggested by Strehlow's account of the two Southern Arrernte men (see sub-subsection 'Southern Arrernte'). Spencer and Gillen's mythological account of the two Warumungu women who fought over their subsection names (see subsection 'Native Traditions on the Origin of Skins') may also point to a resistance to the new system of nomenclature. Strehlow's story also indicates the relevance of marriage between four-term and eight-term people (rather than arbitrary splitting of sections) as a factor in promoting the new terms. Gillen's letter (see sub-subsection 'Central Arrernte'), in which he stated that 'the blacks about the Mission district ... who mix a great deal with the Chitchica were the first to adopt the system', points to the role of post-contact settlements in facilitating contact, which presumably involved intermarriage, between groups that had formerly used the four- versus eight-term system. It is likely that some confusion obtained for a time after the adoption of the new system. This may partially account for the disparity between Schulze and Spencer and Gillen (see sub-subsection 'Western Arrernte'). Schulze's system involves the simple joining of the original four terms and their filiations with the new set of terms—that is, it continues *Penangke-Peltharre* as a patrifilial pair rather than switching it to *Penangke-Pengarte* beside *Kngwaraye-Peltharre*.

10. THE DEVELOPMENT OF ARANDIC SUBSECTION NAMES IN TIME AND SPACE

Towards an Absolute Chronology

On the basis of the formal similarity of Warlpiri terms to those of other languages to their north(west) and evidence for the rapid adoption of similar systems elsewhere, Meggitt (1962, p. 168) concluded that:

> The diffusion of subsections in the central desert followed hard on the spread of sections. It is probable that the Walbiri received the section system no more than a century ago [i.e. c. 1860] and subsections 20 or 30 years later [i.e. 1880–1890].

These dates are too recent, as noted by McConvell (1996, p. 131). The subsection system was spreading to Arrernte from the Anmatyerre around 1880. The Anmatyerre and Kaytetye must have had this system somewhat earlier. Kaytetye already had set 2 terms in the early 1870s. The differences in mythology between Kaytetye and Anmatyerre vs Arrernte suggest that the former would have had the subsection system at least a generation earlier than the Arrernte. This would take us back to the first half of the nineteenth century at the latest. There is really no way of knowing how long the Kaytetye and Anmatyerre (or the Warumungu, Warlmanpa and Warlpiri) had the section system before they adopted the subsection system. However, the fact that sets 1 and 2 are treated similarly as loan words indicates that the Arandic languages received the set 1 terms after the major Arandic sound changes had taken place. Unfortunately, we have no way of knowing the date of these sound changes.

Summary and Conclusions

We have considerably refined the picture of how section and in particular subsections were adopted into the Arandic languages. It has been important not to treat the Arandic languages as a single unit but to distinguish between the various Arandic groups and subgroups—both in terms of the skin names used and the date and direction of their adoption of extra skin names.

We have seen that even separate language groups are not uniform with respect to their skin terms. We have mentioned an Alyawarr subgroup with eight terms instead of the normal four. We have noted a subgroup of the Anmatyerre with *Thangale* in place of *Angale*, and observed that some subgroups of the Warumungu used *Kappiji* in place of *Jappaljarri*.

In terms of the direction of spread, the previously accepted northern origin of the terms has been confirmed. However, we have also found that there were two prongs to the southward expansion of the subsection terms: a western wave that took forms from Warlpiri into Anmatyerre and thence into Arrernte, and an eastern wave that involved the transfer from Warumungu and/or Warlmanpa into Kaytetye and thence into Alyawarr.

Our reconstruction of the history of skin names has posited intermediate stages that included forms that are not directly attested (* marks unattested forms). The main replacements we have posited are 1) Alyawarr has replaced the A term *Apenangke with the A2 Kngwarreye of its neighbours; 2) Kaytetye has replaced a hypothetical D1 form *Apetyarre (preserved in Alyawarr) with Kapetye; 3) in Warlmanpa, the original D1 *Japaljarri became *Japatjarri as a result of sound change, then was later shortened to Japaja; and 4) some of the Warumungu replaced their Jappaljarri with Kappiji, borrowed from Kaytetye, but later abandoned this form in favour of the original Jappaljarri.

We have addressed the issue raised by McConvell regarding the timing of the adoption of skin names relative to the Arandic sound changes of initial deletion. We have claimed that both the original four section terms and the second set of four subsection names were borrowed after the Arandic sound changes affecting the beginning of words, and have explained the absence of initial consonants in the Arandic forms in terms of initial truncation that is characteristic of a pattern of adapting loan words from languages that have preserved their initial consonants. It was only in this sense that 'initial-dropping remained a productive rule in Arandic phonology', as claimed by McConvell (1985, p. 6). We have shown that, in contrast to this adaptation of both the first and second sets of (adult) skin names, the junior skin names of Kaytetye and Anmatyerre followed a more recent pattern of borrowing that does not apply this truncation adaptation.

We have established some dates at which the eight-term system was being adopted and other dates before which the systems must have been adopted. The original set of four section names had spread as far as the southernmost variety, Lower Arrernte, by 1875. The four terms of the second set were already present among the Kaytetye by 1874. They must have been in Anmatyerre by this time as well, since they were spreading from Anmatyerre into Arrernte during the 1880s. One member of the second set was borrowed from either Anmatyerre or Kaytetye into Alyawarr before the eastward expansion to Lake Nash in the 1920s and 1930s. Meanwhile, the junior subsection terms were in Kaytetye by 1901.

References

Aboriginal Land Commissioner 1991, *Aboriginal Land Rights (Northern Territory) Act 1976, McLaren Creek Land Claim: Report No. 32: Findings, recommendation and report of the Aboriginal Land Commissioner, Mr Justice Olney to the Minister for Aboriginal Affairs and to the Administrator of the Northern Territory*, Canberra: Australian Government Publishing Service.

Breen, G (ed.) 2000, *Introductory dictionary of western Arrernte*, Alice Springs: IAD Press.

Breen, G 2001, 'The wonders of Arandic phonology', in J Simpson et al. (eds), *Forty years on: Ken Hale and Australian languages*, Pacific Linguistics 512, Canberra: The Australian National University, pp. 45–69.

Breen, G & Pensalfini, R 1999, 'Arrernte: a language with no syllable onsets', *Linguistic Inquiry*, 30, pp. 1–25. doi.org/10.1162/002438999553940.

Dousset, L 2005, *Assimilating identities: social networks and the diffusion of sections*, Oceania Monographs 57, Sydney: University of Sydney.

Elkin, AP 1939–40, 'Kinship in South Australia', *Oceania*, 10, pp. 196–234. doi.org/10.1002/j.1834-4461.1939.tb00276.x.

Giles, C 1879, 'The "Antakerrinya" tribe, Central Australia', in G Taplin (ed.), *The folklore, manner, customs, and languages of the South Australian Aborigines*, Adelaide: Government, pp. 89–92.

Gillen, FJ 1896, 'Notes on some manners and customs of the Aborigines of the McDonnell Ranges belonging to the Arunta tribe', in B Spencer (ed.), *Report on the work of the horn scientific expedition to Central Australia vol. part IV: anthropology*, London: Dulau & Co., pp. 161–86.

Gillen, FJ 1968, *Gillen's diary: the camp jottings of F. J. Gillen on the Spencer and Gillen expedition across Australia 1901–1902*, Adelaide: Libraries Board of South Australia.

Green, J 1998, Kin and country: aspects of the use of kinterms in Arandic languages, MA thesis, University of Melbourne.

Green, J 2010, *Central and eastern Anmatyerr to English dictionary*, Alice Springs: IAD Press.

Hale, K 1973, 'Deep-surface canonical disparities in relation to analysis and change', in TA Sebeok (ed.), *Current trends in linguistics, volume 11: diachronic, areal, and typological linguistics*, The Hague: Mouton, pp. 401–58.

Henderson, J & Dobson, V (comp.) 1994, *Eastern and central Arrernte to English dictionary*, Alice Springs: IAD Press.

Howitt, AW & Fison, L 1889, 'Further notes on the Australian class systems', *Journal of the Anthropological Institute of Great Britain and Ireland*, 18, pp. 31–70. doi.org/10.2307/2842513.

Janda, RD & Joseph, BD 2003, 'Reconsidering the canons of sound-change: towards a "Big Bang" theory', in BJ Blake & K Burridge (eds), *Historical linguistics 2001: selected papers from the 15th International Conference on Historical Linguistics, Melbourne, 13–17 August 2001*, Amsterdam/Philadelphia: John Benjamins, pp. 205–19.

Koch, G (ed.) 1993, *Kaytetye country: an Aboriginal history of the Barrow Creek area*, Alice Springs: Institute for Aboriginal Development.

Koch, H 1997a, 'Comparative linguistics and Australian prehistory', in P McConvell & N Evans (eds), *Archaeology and linguistics: Aboriginal Australia in global perspective*, Melbourne: Oxford University Press, pp. 27–43.

Koch, H 1997b, 'Pama-Nyungan reflexes in the Arandic languages', in D Tryon & M Walsh (eds), *Boundary rider: essays in honour of Geoffrey O'Grady*, Pacific Linguistics C-136, Canberra: The Australian National University, pp. 271–302.

Koch, H 2004, 'The Arandic subgroup of Australian languages', in C Bowern & H Koch (eds), *Australian languages: classification and the comparative method*, Current Issues in Linguistic Theory 249, Amsterdam: John Benjamins, pp. 127–50, 575–80. doi.org/10.1075/cilt.249.10koc.

Koch, H 2007, 'Divergent regularity in word-initial truncation in the Arandic languages', in D Eades, J Lynch & J Siegel (eds), *Language description, history and development: linguistic indulgence in memory of Terry Crowley*, Creole Language Library 30, Amsterdam: John Benjamins, pp. 267–80. doi.org/10.1075/cll.30.27koc.

Koch, H 2014, 'Loanwords between the Arandic languages and their western neighbours: principles of identification and phonological adaptation' [available online], in L Gawne & J Vaughan (eds), *Selected papers from the 44th conference of the Australian Linguistic Society, 2013*, Melbourne: University of Melbourne, pp. 311–34, viewed 7 August 2017, minerva-access.unimelb.edu.au/handle/11343/40970.

Koch, H & Simpson, J forthcoming, 'Junior skin names in Central Australia: function and origin', in P Monaghan, M Walsh & R Lucas (eds), *Peter Sutton: Ethnographer and contrarian*, Wakefield Press.

Laughren, M 1982, 'Warlpiri kinship structure', in J Heath, F Merlan & A Rumsey (eds), *Languages of kinship in Aboriginal Australia*, Oceania Linguistic Monographs 24, Sydney: University of Sydney, pp. 72–85.

Mathews, RH 1899, 'Divisions of north Australian tribes', *Proceedings of the American Philosophical Society*, 38(159), pp. 75–9.

McConvell, P 1985, 'The origin of subsections in northern Australia', *Oceania*, 56, pp. 1–33. doi.org/10.1002/j.1834-4461.1985.tb02105.x.

McConvell, P 1996, 'Backtracking to Babel: the chronology of Pama-Nyungan expansion in Australia', *Archaeology in Oceania, 31*, pp. 125–44. doi.org/10.1002/j.1834-4453.1996.tb00356.x.

Meggitt, MJ 1962, *Desert people: a study of the Walbiri Aborigines of Central Australia*, Sydney: Angus & Robertson.

Mulvaney, J, Morphy, H & Petch, A (eds) 1997, *'My dear Spencer': the letters of F. J. Gillen to Baldwin Spencer*, Melbourne: Hyland House.

Nash, D 1979, Preliminary vocabulary of the Warlmanpa language, Unpublished manuscript, Cambridge, Mass.: Massachusetts Institute of Technology.

Nash, D 2015, *Warlmanpa subsections*, accessed 7 August, www.anu.edu.au/linguistics/nash/aust/wpa/kinship.html.

Radcliffe-Brown, AR 1918, 'Notes on the social organization of Australian tribes', *Journal of the Royal Anthropological Institute of Great Britain and Ireland*, 48, pp. 222–53. doi.org/10.2307/2843422.

Radcliffe-Brown, AR 1930–31, 'The social organization of Australian tribes', *Oceania*, 1(1), pp. 34–65; 1(4), pp. 444–56.

Schulze, L 1891, 'The Aborigines of the upper and middle Finke River: their habits and customs, with introductory notes on the physical and natural-history feature of the country', *Transactions of the Royal Society of South Australia*, 14(1), pp. 210–46.

Sharp, JC 2004, *Nyangumarta: a language of the Pilbara region of Western Australia*, Pacific Linguistics 556, Canberra: The Australian National University.

Simpson, J 2002, *A learner's guide to Warumungu*, Alice Springs: IAD Press.

Spencer, B & Gillen, FJ 1927, *The Arunta: a study of a Stone Age People*, 2 vols, London: Macmillan [Facsimile edition 2011, Virginia, Northern Territory: David M. Welch].

Spencer, B & Gillen, FJ 1969a [1899], *The native tribes of Central Australia*, Oosterhout, Netherlands: Anthropological Publications [Reprinted from 1899 edition by Macmillan & Co].

Spencer, B & Gillen, FJ 1969b [1904], *The northern tribes of Central Australia*, Oosterhout, Netherlands: Anthropological Publications [Reprinted from 1904 edition by Macmillan & Co].

Stirling, EC 1896, 'Part IV—Anthropology', in B Spencer (ed.), *Report on the work of the Horn Scientific Expedition to Central Australia*, London: Dulau & Co.; Melbourne: Melville, Mullen and Slade, pp. 1–157.

Strehlow, C n.d., Aranda–Loritja–English dictionary, Unpublished manuscript, Australian Institute of Aboriginal and Torres Strait Islander Studies, Canberra.

Strehlow, TGH 1947, *Aranda traditions*, Melbourne University Press [Reprinted 1968, New York: Johnson Reprint Corporation].

Swan, C & Cousen, M 1993, *A learner's wordlist of Pertame*, Alice Springs: Institute for Aboriginal Development.

Turpin, M & Ross, A 2012, *Kaytetye to English dictionary*, Alice Springs: IAD Press.

Vallee, P 2006, *God, guns and government on the Central Australian frontier*, Canberra: Restoration.

Wilkins, D 1989, Mparntwe Arrernte: studies in the structure and semantics of grammar, PhD thesis, The Australian National University.

Yallop, CL 1969, 'The Aljawara and their territory', *Oceania*, *39*(3), pp. 187–97. doi.org/10.1002/j.1834-4461.1969.tb01005.x.

PART III
Kinship Systems

11
Close–Distant: An Essential Dichotomy in Australian Kinship

Tony Jefferies

Abstract

This chapter looks at the evidence for the close–distant dichotomy in the kinship systems of Australian Aboriginal societies. The close–distant dichotomy operates on two levels. It is the distinction familiar to Westerners from their own culture between close and distant relatives: those we have frequent contact with as opposed to those we know about but rarely, or never, see. In Aboriginal societies, there is a further distinction: those with whom we share our quotidian existence, and those who live at some physical distance, with whom we feel a social and cultural commonality, but also a decided sense of difference. This chapter gathers a substantial body of evidence to indicate that distance, both physical and genealogical, is a conception intrinsic to the Indigenous understanding of the function and purpose of kinship systems. Having done so, it explores the implications of the close–distant dichotomy for the understanding of pre-European Aboriginal societies in general—in other words: if the dichotomy is a key factor in how Indigenes structure their society, what does it say about the limits and integrity of the societies that employ that kinship system?

Introduction

Kinship is synonymous with anthropology. Morgan's (1871) *Systems of Consanguinity and Affinity of the Human Family* is one of the founding documents of the discipline. It also has an immediate connection to Australia: one of the first fieldworkers to assist Morgan in gathering his data was Lorimer Fison, who, later joined by A. W. Howitt, began the task of investigating the kinship systems of Australian Indigenes. Since then, Australian kinship has often been at the forefront of anthropology's theoretical investigation of its meaning and significance, most notably in the work of Lévi-Strauss (1969). Australian kinship has provided case material for expositions on many innovative approaches to the study of kinship structure and logic, such as Scheffler's (1978) application of extensionist theory to Australian systems. In short, in the study of Australian kinship, there can be traced a veritable history of kinship study taken as a whole, either as evidence in the advancement of new theories or by the application of theory developed from societies elsewhere in the world to Australian societies (e.g. Meggitt's 1962 use of 'descent theory' in respect to the Warlpiri; see Kuper 2005). All of these approaches can be said to share a common characteristic: they are theories developed by anthropologists who have then applied them to their Australian subject matter. This chapter seeks a different approach: it will examine the evidence for a particular theoretical model that appears not to have had its origins in anthropological theorisation, but is emic, intrinsically Indigenous, the presence of which in ethnography can be attributed solely to having been observed in, or elicited from, Aboriginal informants.

I am aware of only one study of Australian kinship that has recognised the centrality of the close–distant dichotomy in Aboriginal kinship: D. H. Turner's (1980) *Australian Aboriginal Social Organization*. As will be demonstrated, the close–distant dichotomy in the Indigenous conceptualisation of kinship was observed from the outset of the study of Australian societies, and its recurrence in ethnographic description since has been a persistent motif. This chapter seeks to examine explanations for this ubiquity. The first task is to determine whether the dichotomy is a genuine Indigenous conception. The chapter is to discover if the dichotomy is universal in Aboriginal kinship, if it has the same degree of significance in all systems, and if the role it plays in kinship systems is identical or varies from system to system.

If, as is contended, the close–distant dichotomy is an Indigenous conception, then we need to find the value of this for interpretation: should we assume the dichotomy is interesting, but ultimately irrelevant to the understanding of kinship systems? Or do we conclude that the Indigenous view ought to be privileged, not only because it is the Indigenous view, but also because it provides otherwise unobtainable insight into the nature of the kinship-structured society? My sympathies lie with the latter proposition, as expressed by Needham (1962, p. 259) in his comments on the difficulties he and his colleagues experienced in trying to understand the Wikmunkan system of Cape York:

> The source of all our analytical difficulties may be traced to a single factor, namely, a failure to apprehend Wikmunkan social life through the categories and connecting ideas of the peoples themselves. Instead, their social organization was conceived and described in terms of the concern for genealogical connection which is habitual to a European observer but which is fundamentally mistaken in understanding a society of this kind.

While understanding the Indigenous reasoning behind kinship structure may provide a corrective for the mistaken notion that a society's kinship can alone be understood by the application of Western analytical concepts, the social implications of Indigenous reckoning still remain. To suppose that the close–distant dichotomy was employed by its practitioners with a consciousness of its wider anthropological implications, questions regarding the physical and social limits that kinship structure imposes, the integrity or homogeneity that a kinship system implies for a society, historical development, and so on, are unlikely. If, as surmised, the close–distant kin dichotomy was a ubiquitous feature of Aboriginal societies across their distribution, then an institution of this significance ought to reflect these broader implications. The chapter concludes with a brief exploration of the questions that this dichotomy raises for a wider understanding of Aboriginal social organisation.

The Close–Distant Dichotomy: A Short History

The first, most central question, whether or not the dichotomy is a genuinely Indigenous idea, is not easy to answer. Some anthropologists have claimed outright that it has no role in the systems they have studies. At least one authority, Turner (1980, p. viii), claimed universality for the principle. In any event, its recurrence in ethnographies from the discipline's beginnings, even in those that programmatically adhere to conventional forms of analysis, requires explanation. In most cases, the role of the close–distant dichotomy falls into somewhat of an ambivalent category. It is spelled out in very few ethnographies as a means through which people themselves understand and construct their relationships. And yet, it is not, like descent or affinal theory, a well-discussed and commented upon part of the anthropological lexicon of kinship. It is fair to say that the dichotomy usually appears by default, as a ubiquitous recourse for explanation, often with the explicit or inferred understanding that it has been derived from informants. It has rarely been discussed as a principle as such.[1] Textually, this ambivalence expresses itself in the frequent use of inverted commas around the words 'close' and 'distant' (see Turner 1980, p. viii). Again, it is difficult to know whether this is because the anthropologist has heard it expressed in these words from their informant, or whether it is an acknowledgement of its unorthodoxy in scholastic usage. However, it is clear that from the outset of professional anthropology, it is a distinction that has been observed and recorded in the field. Radcliffe-Brown (1930, pp. 2, 236), for example, described the process of betrothal in the Kumbaingeri system as follows:

> Marriage is prohibited with one's own mother's brother's daughter, or father's sister's daughter. A man marries a woman who belongs to the same section and generation as his mother's brother's daughter, and who is, according to the terminology, a relative of the same kind. *But she must come from another part of the country, and must not be closely related to him.* The normal procedure was described to me as follows. A woman who is 'father's sister' to a boy, possibly his own father's sister, would look out for a wife for him. Finding a woman who was her 'sister', but not closely related to herself or her nephew, she would induce the latter to promise her daughter in marriage to the boy. From this moment this woman becomes the boy's mother-in-law, and he must avoid her. It is, therefore, preferable that he should never have met her before the arrangement is made [empahsis original].

Elkin (1937–38), like Radcliffe-Brown, made rare, yet specific, references to the close–distant dichotomy. I have found only one occasion in which Elkin generalised the ubiquity and force of the distinction in Aboriginal kinship:

---

1 An exception is Radcliffe-Brown (1930, pp. 438–9), of whom Turner (1980, p. ix–x) commented: 'The theoretical implications of the concepts "close" and "far-away" were anticipated but never fully explored by Radcliffe-Brown'.

> The tendency amongst the Australian Aborigines is to select the mother-in-law rather than the wife, and to seek her as far away as possible both in geographical position and relationship, on account of the avoidance associated with her and her parents. This is even noticeable among many tribes in which second-cousin marriage is permissible, with the result that this marriage tends to be rare … by seeking a more distant wife's mother than own father's sister, father's mother is not drawn into the relationship of wife's mother's mother.[2] (Elkin 1937–38, p. 432)

In several instances, Elkin provided good evidence that the dichotomy was acquired firsthand from his informants. For example, in quizzing his Arabana informants on the workings of their system, Elkin (1937–38, p. 441) encountered the following response: 'When first speaking to them I received the impression that a man could marry his cross-cousin, but when they realized that the woman concerned was the daughter of one's own mother's brother or own father's sister, they protested in decided terms that such a marriage was impossible'. The reason for this misunderstanding, in the informant's terms, is later made clear:

> With regard to mother's mother's brother's daughter's daughter, my informants stated that she might be either *bilya*, the term which is also applied to mother's brother's daughter and with whom marriage is prohibited, or *nupa*, wife; but when they realized that I meant own second cousin, some hesitated and even denied the possibility of such marriage, saying that such a woman was too close, 'all one relation' and that she came from a man's own *kadini*, mother's mother's brother. (Elkin 1937–38, p. 443)

From this, Elkin (1937–38, pp. 442–3) drew the following conclusion in respect to Arabana affinal relationships: 'A man may marry a woman called *nupa*, the daughter of a "distant" *kagaga* and *ngauwili*, mother's brother and father's sister, who are distinguished from own mother's brother and father's sister by being called *kagaga taru* and *ngauwili yambua*'.

Elkin (1938–39, p. 45) provided several examples throughout his *Oceania* series 'Kinship in South Australia' of the way in which the close–distant dichotomy melded in with other aspects of kinship and social organisation. For example, the Wilyakali have 'special terms' to distinguish 'own' from

---

2   There is much that could be teased out of Elkin's work on the distance dichotomy; however, space does not permit such an excursion here. Elkin's interpretation of the motivation for distant affinal relationships in this passage—that Male Ego seeks a distant mother-in-law for the sake of obviating rigorous avoidance strictures with close kin—is, in my view, an insufficient explanation for the dichotomy.

distant kin. There are several instances of how the distance distinction overrides or negates totemic relationships: 'As far as kinship rules went, this marriage was quite in order, but a far distant social totemic relationship was found to exist between them, "which make them brother and sister". The kindred, however, decided that, as this relationship was a far distant one, it could be ignored' (Elkin 1938–39, p. 52). Additionally, there are case studies, particularly of Western Desert (Aluridja) informants, that highlight the application of the close–distant dichotomy in the calculation of relationships with individuals, otherwise strangers, upon their entering the 'close' community. The possibility that Western Desert culture provides a somewhat distorted perception of the importance of the close–distant dichotomy to Australian kinship, by virtue of the special physical conditions that apply, will be returned to later (see Elkin 1932, pp. 304–5 quoted in Turner 1980, p. ix, in respect to the Karadjeri).

In a very different environment, Stanner (1936–37) examined the kinship of the Murinbata of the coastal tropics, specifically the evolution of their system as it adjusted to the eight-subsection system introduced from the Djamindjung to their south. Like Elkin, Stanner (1936–37, pp. 197–8) had recourse to distance in the determination of kin terms, particularly those with direct application to marriage: 'Marriage with own cross-cousins was prohibited. These marriages were effectively prevented by extending the terms for mother (*kale*) and mother's brother (*kaka*) to one's own cross-cousins, but not to the children of more distant mother's brothers and father's sisters. One's own cross-cousins were "little *kale*" and "little *kaka*"'. This distance-based distinction was still effective some 40 years later when Falkenberg and Falkenberg (1981, p. 175) resumed Stanner's work on Murinbata kinship: 'A man should not marry a *pugali* who is the daughter of *kaka ngoitnan* in his mother's local clan, but only a *pugali* who is the daughter of *kaka ngoitnan* "from far away", i.e. from another local clan. Further, a man should not marry a *pugali* who is the daughter of *bip:i ngoitnan* from his own local clan, but only a *pugali* who is the daughter of *bip:i ngoitnan* "from far away"'; and 'A Murinbata does not distinguish terminologically between those *pugali* whom he cannot marry and those who are eligible as his wives, but when such a distinction is desirable or necessary he will refer to the former as *pugali* and to the latter as *pugali pugali*, i.e. *pugali* "from far away", who are the children of *kaka ngoitnan* and *bip:i ngoitnan* from alien clans' (Falkenberg & Falkenberg 1981, p. 178).

Similarly, Hiatt (1965, p. 78), however working with the Gidjingali of the Blythe River of Arnhem Land, another well-endowed tropical environment, acknowledged the role of the dichotomy, without arriving at any understanding of its basis:

> The only men with rights to their wives were those married to the six women in class A. I have distinguished class B from the others because giving a man his FZD was a recognised subsidiary to orthodox bestowal. In distinguishing close from distant relationships I have assigned marriages to classes C or D if, as well as having the appropriate classificatory relationship, the partners are linked as cognates (MFZDD, MBD, &c.). This corresponds roughly with a distinction *made by the natives themselves*, who spoke of 'close' and 'distant' connections but did not apply any strict criterion.

Generally speaking, the relationship between genealogical distance and spatial distance is ambiguous. Radcliffe-Brown (1930, pp. 438–9) commented: 'When natives speak of "distant" relatives they combine in the one conception both genealogical remoteness and geographical distance'. For the anthropologist, therefore, getting the balance right in the implication of distance is not always easy. Turner (1980, p. viii) drew attention to the fact that expressions of kinship distance in English— 'close', 'far-away', 'near', 'distant' and so on—are 'strictly genealogical' and 'may have unfortunate implications for our understanding if we translate them directly'. One could argue the term 'classificatory' comes into use as a corollary for distance—that is, the determination of distant kin relationships is founded on an abstract (and sometimes variable) structure of quasi-genealogical relationships (McConnel 1933–4, p. 350; Sutton 1978, p. 199). Conversely, 'close' kin have a greater claim to a biological relationship (although this too, as the evidence suggests, is hardly a fixed principle), while with kinfolk who are 'distant', the possibility of a genealogical relationship based on biology diminishes, and relationships are not genealogical but 'classificatory'.[3] This is a distinction that in one form or another goes back to the earliest ethnographic work in Australia.

---

3   This distinction hardly applies to anthropologists without exception. For example, Hiatt (1965) made use of expressions such as 'close classificatory' and 'distant classificatory' relatives throughout his work, without making clear on what basis the distinction was made (for examples of the former, see Hiatt 1965, pp. 96–8). Barnes (1965, p. viii) alluded to Hiatt's failure to define this distinction (which, notwithstanding, recurs frequently throughout his work) in his foreword: 'Most descriptions of Aboriginal marriage arrangements, and of involvement in quarrels and fights, are in terms of ties of "close" or "distant" kinship of one kind or another. The reader is usually left in the dark about the exact meaning of "close" and "distant", if one exists'.

Howitt (1904, p. 161), for example, contrasted one's 'own' children from one's 'tribal' children, where 'tribal' is a synonym for 'classificatory' (see Radcliffe-Brown 1913, p. 158). In Stanner (1936–37, p. 199), we see the ready potential for substitution of the terms 'distant' and 'classificatory':

> The term *pugali* has been taken over from the Djamindjung to denote those cross-cousins who could not have been married under the former Murinbata system, and may still not be married under the altered system. Distant cross-cousins referred to as 'half *pugali*' whose subsections are appropriate, may be married, but they are then called by the normal Murinbata term for wife (*purima*). This was the term formerly applied only to classificatory mother's brother's daughters and father's sister's daughters ... It is worth noting that the children of female *pugali* are being called *wakal nginar*, a term formed by the suffixation of *nginar* (mother-in-law) to the ordinary bisexual term for child (*wakal*). The *wakal nginar* is distinguished from the *pipi nginar*, who is the classificatory father's sister (*pipi*). Both these women give their daughters to a man.[4]

Similar to the correlation of distant kin with classificatory kin is the equation by both Stanner and Falkenberg of distant kin with 'different hordes', 'alien local clans' and similar expressions, as well as specific references to entities such as the 'mother's clan'. It is a reasonable inference that no matter how attenuated the role of physical distance becomes in the determination of kinship relationships beyond one's patrigroup, the close–distant principle remains equally effective. Turner (1980, p. ix) quoted R. M. and C. H. Berndt (1970, p. 87) on the Gunwinggu, for whom 'even though genealogical proximity is significant' in reckoning 'closeness', 'it can be offset by other factors. One is territorial affiliation. Two men from the same or adjacent small territories or cluster of named sites are "brothers" even if no genealogical links can be traced. Each is "close father" to the other's sons, and may be acknowledged as "closest father" if no "father" from a common grandparent is living ... The fact of being neighbours is important in itself, but mythical and ritual connections are even more so'. The parameter of distance in these more closely knit coastal societies is not absolute; there is no determinative relation between distance and the desirability of alliance, and, in fact, the opposite tendency may apply—the desire for alliance with immediate neighbours. In these

---

4 Stanner (1935–36, pp. 443–4) made a similar, and perhaps more telling, distinction in respect to Djamindjung kinship: 'Classificatory mother's brother's daughters and father's sister's daughters may be married, and marriages seem to be allowed with distant mother's mother's brother's son's daughters, distant classificatory sisters, and distant classificatory mothers'.

more densely populated areas, the desire for broad interrelationships is balanced by the desire to preserve the strength of a core group that is both genealogically and spatially proximate.

McConnel's (1933–34) work on the Wik-Mungkan of Cape York drew very similar conclusions to that of Stanner, as we perhaps might expect from people of two reasonably similar environments. Like Stanner (1935–36, 1936–37) and Falkenberg and Falkenberg (1981), the use of the terms 'close' and 'distant' appears throughout:

> It often happens that *muka* [FeB] and *kala* [MyB] in the mother's clan may be married to *pinya* [FyZ] from more distant clans than the father's; also, that *pinya* in the father's clan may be married to *muka* and *kala* in more distant clans than the mother's. A distant *pinya* is not compelled to give her daughter to her husband's sister's son—nor is a *muka* from a distant clan entitled to insist upon the marriage of his son with his wife's brother's daughter. The element of choice enters into the situation. (McConnel 1933–34, p. 341)

The 'element of choice' McConnel referred to is the scale of desirability in the contract of affinal relationships already commented on in Stanner's and Falkenberg's analyses of the Murinbata, and by the Berndts in respect to the Gunwinggu. While spatially distant relationships are sought after for certain reasons, so too is the maintenance or extension of relationships with clans with whom connection already exists. McConnel (1933–34, p. 341) concluded that:

> A *pinya* from a distant clan may wish her daughter to marry back into 'company' clans in her own locality with which her clan has older connections and more urgent obligations. She may, however, prefer her daughter to marry her husband's sister's son, since she must live in her husband's locality, and would like to keep her daughter near her. In this case she will 'promise' her daughter to her sister's son.

As a consequence, a local group will be composed of women who have married in whose 'common *kattha* [M] may hail from a number of different clans near and far' (McConnel 1933–34, pp. 330–1). This results in the local clan being able to exercise a number of options in the alliances it wishes to contract with other clans—both 'close' and 'distant' (which are, of course, relative determinations) (McConnel 1939–40, pp. 448–9). Similarly, Sutton (1978, p. 106) observed in the coastal Wik groups that marital partners were usually preferred with kin on the 'closer' end of the physical distance scale:

The preferred marriage is that between classificatory (non-actual) cross-cousins of the type MBD = FZeS whose clan estates are in close proximity. I will later show that there is a tendency for marriages to form regional clusters which may be defined by two major parameters, the inland/coastal distinction and ritual group membership.

This 'preference for marriage with near neighbours' was the result of a strong political tendency among the coastal Wik:

Local endogamy is politically motivated. It binds the local groups of an area into mutual support when threatened from outside on any scale, and reduces conflict at the local level. This is a conscious policy and stated quite clearly and often by my informants … The social bond between affines of a locality make for military strength. It is often mentioned in descriptions of fighting that one group were *munhtha-mooerinhthjanha*, a compound term denoting a set of cross-cousins. (Sutton 1978, p. 130)

Among the Wik, the desire to acquire kin at a distance was correspondingly weaker. However, as with the inland Wik-Mungkan, alliances with distant kin could still be contracted if a political advantage or ambition was served (Sutton 1978, pp. 83–4), and, as with inlanders, marriage contracted at distance appeared more often to involve the direct exchange of 'sisters' (see McConnel 1939–40, pp. 451–3). With coastal Wik, 'for demographic reasons those kin who are more distant genealogically tend also to be those kin who come from more distant places and from groups who are politically disjunct from those of ego' (Sutton 1978, p. 199).

The role played by physical distance can be seen to vary considerably between coastal peoples (or, at least, it might be assumed, among peoples with relatively high levels of population density) and those where this is less the case. In *Australian Aboriginal Social Organization*, Turner (1980, p. 7) identified a contrasting tendency between societies whose application of the distance dichotomy was to achieve close or progressively more distant relationships 'between the benefits of patri-group endogamy or of ever-expanding "patri-group family" exogamy and their associated "brotherhood" types', and sought to raise this distinction to a general principle. It is a dichotomy he explored by comparison between, at the endogamous extreme, the Kaiadilt of Bentinck Island and the Warnungmanggala of Groote Eylandt, both in the Gulf of Carpentaria, and at the other, exogamous pole, the Yaralde of coastal South Australia. While 'exogamy outside one's own and male ancestors' "patri-group families … would not create such close ties within the patri-group as endogamy [it] would achieve the widest possible range of organic-like relations and most comprehensive network of mechanical ties with the larger society"' (Turner 1980, p. xi). Conversely, less expansive alliances 'are thereby able to achieve a degree of solidarity between a number of patri-groups through intermarriage within a relatively small circle … The security achieved, though not covering as many contingencies as under the Yaralde system nor allowing for as intimate a knowledge and as efficient an exploitation of the local area as, theoretically, under endogamy, nevertheless would be considerable within the collective estates of a small number of groups whose members engaged in constant intercourse and exchange and thus, as a collective, formed a geographically continuous population' (Turner 1980, p. 7).

The Western Desert

The coastal Wik, and other densely populated societies, perhaps represent one extreme of a scale of distance reckoning that extends at the other end to the Western Desert peoples, for whom alliance at physical distance was a premium. No doubt this contrast was predicated by the different environmental and political conditions that animated these societies. As Western Desert life was physically uncertain and critically variable, connection over distance was imperative (see Smith 2013, pp. 296–98, 329–30). However, this was more than simply a matter of survival, as the historically rapid expansion of the Western Desert people across their vast distribution must surely have been facilitated by their ability to readily (if not periodically) coalesce and operate as a collective when necessary (see Elkin 1939–40, p. 203; McConvell 1996; Myers 1986, pp. 155–6, 159). For coastal dwellers such as the Wik, where one's own and adjacent countries provided the greater part of the necessities of life, relationships at distance were far less pressing. Diametrically opposite political necessities also applied; the extension of influence might be desirable in the desert, but defence of one's own well-endowed country through strong local connections was the overriding concern for coastal peoples.

For the unique circumstances of their environment, Western Desert kinship provides a forum for some of the chief issues that arise from the close–distant dichotomy: its Indigenous origin and the relationship between genealogical and physical distance, and the social context of the dichotomy. From the outset, ethnographers have recorded the close–distant dichotomy in Western Desert society. Sackett (1976, p. 139) recapitulated the discipline's state of knowledge up until his fieldwork:

> Aborigines throughout the Western Desert state the prescribed rule of marriage is to a cross-cousin 'a little bit far away' (Berndt & Berndt 1945, p. 151; 1964, pp. 70–4; Fry 1950, p. 290; Yengoyan 1970a, p. 85), making a system which has been termed a variant of the Kariera practice. As Radcliffe-Brown (1931, p. 439) and Piddington (1970, p. 342) note, the distance implicit in this rule is conceptualized in genealogical as well as spatial terms. In other words, ego must not marry a relative from his own local group or an actual cross-cousin from another country. In all likelihood, a spatially close cross-cousin would also be an actual MBD/FZD, though the converse need not be true.

Numerous sources have since made clear that the close–distant dichotomy is the guiding principle in the determination of kin relationships for the Western Desert people, one that has emerged from within the culture itself. Myers (1986, p. 175) recorded the following:

> Distance is the key, as one young Papunya man made clear in explaining why he could not marry a girl he admired from his own settlement. They were, he said, 'from one *ngurra*'. In the Pintupi view, they were 'too close' (*ngamutja* 'from nearby'), and one's spouse must be 'from far away' (*tiwatja*).

Although not kin terms, this specific terminology is used to differentiate close and distant kin takes us one step closer to the idea that the distance is at the centre of Western Desert kinship structure. Myers (1986, p. 195) stated outright that kin categories were also based on a physical interpretation of the close–distant dichotomy:

> In deciding how to classify individuals in kin terms, Pintupi regularly make a distinction between 'close' and 'distant' kin that has an important impact on classification. This distinction effectively makes locality another criterion of the kinship system. The isomorphic relationship between being 'close' and being 'family' is explicit. 'Close' (*ngamu*) refers to geographical or spatial proximity, contrasting with 'distant' (*tiwa, warnma*) or 'far away'.

Sackett (1976, p. 142) documented that distance is not simply a criterion of affinal alliance or other kin relationship, but is integral to Western Desert kinship terminology—that is, it is encoded in kin terminology itself:

In addition to forming a closed system of relationship and behaviour, kinship determined marriage. It should be recalled that among the Kariera a man married a woman who he called by the term applied to an actual MBD (Radcliffe-Brown 1930, p. 48). In the Western Desert this rule was not applicable, for actual cross-cousins were kept terminologically distinct from more distant MBD/FZD (*njuba*) and called *djudju/malyanj* or *yinganji* (Tonkinson 1966, pp. 111–12). Likewise, male cross-cousins— the brothers of *yinganji*—were termed differently from their more distant counterparts. Occasionally they were addressed as *gudja/maljanj*, the same as siblings and parallel cousins, but most usually as *wadjira* or *djamidi*, meaning close cross-cousin of the same sex. The brothers of *njuba*— distant MBD/FZD—were called *yungguri*, *maridji*, or *magunjdja*.

It can hardly be argued that physical distance is not a primary consideration, and, in my view, *the* primary consideration upon which the structure of the Western Desert kinship system is built. Nevertheless, the issue that inevitably occurs in kinship description emerges—namely, the relationship between genealogical distance and physical distance, or, as has already been broached, whether the distinction between 'close' and 'distant' is a corollary of consanguineal and classificatory genealogical categorisation. The implication that arises from the latter possibility is that if distant kin are classificatory kin, that is, are only kin by virtue of adherence to an all-embracing and coherent kinship system that has only a relatively small and limited biological component, then there is every probability that the philosophical underpinning of the system is not genealogy but physical distance. In other words, genealogy as analogy becomes the means by which social relationships are enumerated. Most anthropologists (perhaps with the exception of Needham) have seen genealogical distance (for which, henceforth, the reader should interpret, unless otherwise specified, as biological genealogy) as integral to the interpretation of the close–distant dichotomy, even if this is seen as concurrent with physical distance. Dousset (2003, p. 53) provided the best description of the interrelationship between these two measures of distance in kinship in the Western Desert:

> Sanctioned marriages among the Ngaatjatjarra are between cross cousins or between persons of the cross-cousin category two generations removed, such as classificatory MF or SS for female Ego, and a classificatory FM or DD for male Ego. Another jural marriage prescription is that marriage partners have to be 'distant', distance being measured in both genealogical and spatial terms. Genealogically speaking, a cousin has to be at least of the third degree to be a potential spouse. As genealogical memory does

usually not exceed two generations, this means that the couple should not be able to trace a connecting genealogical link through their parents or grandparents. Spatially, wife and husband have distant geographical origins, with widely separated places of conception and birth, have not been prolonged co-residents prior to marriage, and are not associated with identical sites of significance. Hence, a bilateral cross-cousin prescription and a proximity proscription are operating. This is also reflected in people's discourse, where geographic closeness is conflated with genealogical closeness, and where 'coming from the same country' is considered creating identical 'consanguineal' ties as being the common offspring of parents or grandparents. In terms of marriage descriptions and obligations as pronounced by indigenous people themselves, and in terms of modelling these descriptions, affiliation to land and genealogical structure cannot be disconnected. The genealogical aspect in the choice of spouses is described in terms of an obligation, hence a prescription, while the spatial part is pronounced as an interdiction, hence a proscription. Moreover, only about 2 per cent of marriages do not conform to these prescriptive and proscriptive rules.

It is clear from Dousset's account that neither the genealogical nor spatial determinant acts separate to the other, that calculation of relationship depends on both. As Elkin's verbatim report of the logic employed by his informant to arrive at an acceptable social compromise indicates, neither was an absolute, but perhaps existed more on a scale of social acceptability, with a large grey area of special circumstances and factors that could be tolerated if not too much was at stake:

> Another woman who came to the camp was related to R__ as *malan* (younger sister). Her mother was own sister to his mother, and so was *ngurndju* (mother) to him. Moreover, as her husband was *kamaru* (mother's brother) to R__, their marriage was from R__'s point of view a 'brother-sister' union. I was given to understand also that their marriage was a 'little bit' wrong because they both came from one 'country' (Oparina way), and had not observed the rule of local exogamy— an exceptional occurrence. If, however, R__'s *kamaru* had belonged to a different 'country' from that of his mother's sister, all would have been in order, even though it would still have been a 'brother-sister' marriage. Of course such 'brother' and 'sister' may be distant cross-cousins, seeing that a mother's brother's female cross-cousin is his 'sister', Ego's mother. (Elkin 1939–40, p. 218)

The question becomes one of sociocentric underpinning of the ideals that underlie Western Desert calculations as to the permissible, as distinct from the intolerable, and, deeper still, understanding why these principles exist in Western Desert social reckoning. Myers (1986, p. 175) dismissed one assumption for the Western Desert that is usually relevant to Aboriginal intergroup relationships: 'Marriage constitutes one means of reproducing relatedness among individuals in a region'—that is, 'the Pintupi prescription that spouses should come "from one country" cannot be reduced to the sociocentric formulation of marriage into a different band or descent group'.

Along with the extraordinary freedom that Western Desert people possessed in making personal arrangements outside their immediate circle (although, of course, these were not devoid of social and political considerations) came what appeared to be a consciousness of the Western Desert people and culture as a whole. In his consideration of what constituted the Australian 'tribe', Berndt (1959, p. 92) concluded of the Western Desert that 'we might legitimately assume that there is a common awareness of belonging to a cultural and linguistic unit, over and above the smaller groups signified by these names, even though the actual span of the wider unit is not specified'. Berndt (1959, pp. 90–1, 103) described this Western Desert unity as a 'social or cultural bloc' with 'no strict boundaries' and within which 'movements were relatively frequent', with limitations on the breadth of the individual's or local group's involvement in the whole being imposed by distance: 'People are accustomed to moving over a fairly large stretch of country, this was *not* by any means a matter of covering the whole cultural bloc' (see Turner 1980, p. 9).

Sackett (1976, p. 142) noted that 'Western Desert kinship formed a closed system, with ego related to all other persons in his social universe by actual or classificatory linkages'. He drew the conclusion that this was a 'total system', in which marriage based alliances were open-ended, such that 'an alliance established between two groups by marriage could not be renewed or re-established for at least three generations' (Sackett 1976, p. 146). Again, while physical restrictions meant the system could not have operated to produce social inculcation across its distribution, it was nonetheless a system predicated on the idea of a whole society, and not simply as an extension of the local group—a point that Myers (1986, p. 10) also made: 'The Pintupi assert [that] they are all family'. As Myers (1986, p. 190) explained: 'Each part, each local "unit", can be produced only through cooperation of the larger structure. The organization of ceremony, requiring participation of others from far away, provides one way of constituting Pintupi society as a whole'. The role kinship plays in the organisation of this society is as 'a structure that articulates the society not as a coordinated ordering of distinctive local groups, but as a set of related categories'.

The extent to which Western Desert people can be said to constitute 'a society' is debatable; most scholars of the Western Desert people would, I think, agree with Dousset (pers. comm., 24 April 2014): 'I personally don't think the entire Western Desert constitutes a society, but many societies'. This introduces another debate that will briefly be returned to in the conclusion, which is the role of kinship in the Western Desert people's recent expansion into and across the Western Desert (see Dousset 2003; Hercus 1994, pp. 21–2; Holcombe 2004; McConvell 1996, 2001, p. 162; Myers 1986; Smith 2013, pp. 333–4; Strehlow 1947, pp. 61–2; Vincent 2011). In addition, there is a perception in anthropology, based on the vast expanse of its distribution and sparseness of its population density, and the divergent character of many of its social institutions, that Western Desert society represents a separate case among Aboriginal societies, or, at least, it is seen as an extremity in Aboriginal social organisation. Even in a world of harsh conditions, the Western Desert stands out as ranking among the absolute harshest. It is logical, therefore, to conclude that because Western Desert people were so thinly spread across a hostile environment, they had no option but to accentuate the physical distance calculus of their kin relationships. Nonetheless, social relationships designed not only to hold a society together and ensure its survival, but also to allow it to prosper in these conditions are characteristic of desert peoples generally (in respect to the Warlpiri, see Meggitt 1962, pp. 1, 49; Smith 2013, pp. 269–73). Western Desert kinship may represent an extreme manifestation of the close–distant dichotomy; however, it is one that features in Australian desert and arid societies more generally.

Turner's (1974) Study of Groote Eylandt Kinship

At the other end of the distance scale, we find coastal societies for whom environmental conditions for the hunter-gatherer are at their most conducive, and, as a consequence, population densities at their highest. The evidence for the close–distant dichotomy in coastal peoples such as the Wik and Murinbata has already been examined, but two studies, in my view, have especial significance in the investigation of kinship distance in these societies. I refer to Turner's (1974) *Tradition and Transformation: A Study of Aborigines in the Groote Eylandt Area, Northern Australia* and Rumsey's (1981) 'Kinship and context among the Ngarinyin'. Turner (1974, p. 16) made it apparent that distance is a crucial consideration in the reckoning of Wanungamagalyuagba kin relations:

> It was found that knowledge of the terms used by an ego to refer to the two parents was not by itself enough for either I or an Aboriginal to work out what their children should be called. It was necessary to know, in addition, how each of the parents stood in relation to an ego in terms of whether they were his 'close' (*augudangwa*) or 'far-away' (*auwilyagara*) relatives. On discovering that 'close' and 'far away' were factors taken into account by ego in this decision process, informants were asked whether the relatives they had named in response were considered 'close' or 'far-away'.

However, this was to prove a considerably different reckoning of distance than in, say, the Western Desert—both in its internal set of positive and negative conditioners, and because of the very different social structure to which it was applied. For the most part, Turner's in-depth study concerns the four 'hordes' or local groups inhabiting Bickerton Island, a small island in the Gulf of Carpentaria between the mainland coast and the larger nearby Groote Eylandt (the study extends to include the larger orbit of Bickerton social life, taking in the mainland and Groote peoples). The Bickerton system has none of the freewheeling capacity to form marital alliances (either personally or structurally), as does the Western Desert system. Nonetheless, closer inspection reveals some similar kinship principles. While the Western Desert system excludes affinal alliance between kin known to share a common grandparent (which is pragmatically equated with common country), as does the Bickerton system. Like the Western Desert, consanguinity between the individual and their society was a matter of calculation: '"closeness" and "far-awayness" were reckoned in degrees' (Turner 1974, p. 16):

> Thus, members of Bickerton local groups consider each other 'close' relatives, even though one person may not actually have had a consanguineal relative in another's local group within genealogical memory. The relative is considered 'close', however, because of an implied correspondence based on the belief that the Bickerton local groups intermarried in the distant past. Such a relative is considered less 'close' than one who has had an actual male or female ancestor located in one's own local group. Here, the nearer this ancestor is to that ego's own generation level, the 'closer' he considers the relative. On the other hand, a person belonging to a Wanindiliyuagwa or Nunggubuyu local group [i.e. of Groote Eylandt

or the mainland respectively] is always considered 'far-away', unless he has a consanguine in an ego's local group in living memory, or unless he is a local group mythically linked to that ego's. (Turner 1974, p. 39)

The set of ideal relationships between the four Bickerton groups is mandated in the Nambirrirma myth: 'The Wuramarba call the Wanungwadararbalangwa *naningya* [MMBDS] and *dadingya* [MMBDD]; Wuramara call the Wanungwadararbalangwa *nabera* [ZS] and *dabera* [ZD]', and so on [all from the male propositus] (Turner 1974, p. 24 table 6). Thus, because 'an ego's "sons" are called *nanugwa* and a *nanugwa's* "mother" is called *dadingya*; it is found that ego must call his own spouse *dadingya*. Knowing that Wuramarba calls Wanungwadararbalangwa *dadingya*, it can be concluded that Wurumarba's spouse is from this local group'. In total then, 'he [ego] calls the members of each local group by a different set of terms' (Turner 1974, p. 26).[5] Turner (1974, pp. 34–5) described the structural linkage between these groups as follows:

> Aborigines see people as manifesting a substance and essence which is derived in part from their affiliation with a patrilineal local group through their father and in part from their affiliation with groups of their other consanguines. It is these interrelations that are, finally, the critical factors in their classification of kin … it is the fact that a particular individual belongs to a particular local group, say A, had a father (also A) born from a woman whose local group was B, and was himself born from a woman whose local group was C, who in turn was born from a woman whose group was D. This sociological-genealogical arrangement will be referred to as the 'local group family' and includes a person's linkage to his own local group (through his father and father's father), as well as to his father's mother's patrilineal local group, his mother's, and his mother's mother's.

Genealogical reckoning for the Wanungamagalyuagba, unlike Western Desert society, is much more restricted and targeted, and can be seen as prescriptive rather than prohibitive. While Western Desert kinship does have its regional and residential subgroups, these are not determinative of relationship to anything like the degree found on Groote Eylandt and Bickerton Island. The Wanungamagalyuagba system is a relationship

---

5   This is very much like the Murinbata system, as described by Falkenberg and Falkenberg (1981, pp. 143–5), in which, similarly, the four 'patrilineal descent lines' that comprise Murinbata society are each composed of different, generationally skewed, terms that distinguish them from Ego's own 'close' 'patrilineal' group. Hiatt's (1965, pp. 44–46, 50) tentative (to use his term 'hypothetical') reconstruction of Gidjingali kinship in terms of the interrelationship between four patrilineal groups, and his description of the interaction of 'communities' points to much of the same sort of relationship (see Hiatt 1965, pp. 25–6, 33).

of the individual's *group,* not the individual, to Bickerton Island's society as a whole. Turner (1974, p. 3) reported: 'It is the identification of men with their respective countries which seems to be at the basis of Wanungamagalyuagba social organisation, and indeed, the organization of all Aborigines in the Groote Eylandt area'. Personal identity is always given in terms of one's country. Kin relationship is determined by a raft of factors that indicate proximity to the local group:

> A 'close' relative is anyone who has or can be deduced to have had a consanguineal relative in an ego's own local group. The nearer the relative is to an ego's own generation level and the more similar his 'local group family' is to that of an ego's, the 'closer' an ego will consider the 'close' relative in question. 'Closeness' is thus reckoned in terms of a certain type of correspondence between 'local group families'. (Turner 1974, p. 38)

The Wanungamagalyuagba system is much more locally group-centric in its orientation than Western Desert groups at the other end of the scale—despite the fact that a central tenet of both systems is the prohibition of marriage within one's group, axiomatic with one's country. Desirable marriage for the Wanungamagalyuagba is seen as avoiding closeness, outright in respect to one's own group, but also to any woman 'whose forebears have recently formed some kind of marital alliance with the man's local group' (Turner 1974, pp. 39–44). The most desirable marriage partner will be that who is 'really the most distant from him in terms of the relationship between her consanguines and people in his own local group'. However, 'the most distant woman will still be one in a local group whose members exchanged women with, or took women from, an ego's local group two generations ago' (Turner 1974, p. 58). The reality is somewhat more ambiguous with the Bickerton Island groups, as is probably the case with coastal peoples generally (see Hiatt 1965, pp. 71–84):

> Suppose the object were to prevent a man from marrying, first, someone in his own local group, second, someone in a group mythically linked to his, and third, someone outside these local groups whose consanguines were in his own local group, or in a local group linked to his. Under these circumstances and setting aside the intra-moiety prohibition for the moment it would be expected that ideally the woman he defined as 'ideal wife'—always called dadingya—would be most distant in these terms … dadingya, however, would not be 'farthest-away' in strictly local group terms … Now relatives designated other than dadingya (e.g. denda, maminyamandja) may have consanguines in local groups only linked to an ego's and be more desirable as wives from a 'farthest-away' point of view. Regardless of this … informants said that the ideal marriage would still be

> with a dadingya whose father's mother was actually in one's own local group as in the 'only-four-local group' situation. This indicates a definite preference for a woman in a local group into which one's father's father married and to which he gave his diyaba/dadiyamandja ('sisters') in return as wives. In other words, the maintenance of an exchange relationship between ego's and another local group in alternate generations is preferred to acquiring a still 'farther-away' woman in local group terms. (Turner 1974, p. 92)

Unlike in the Western Desert, whereby acquisition of a 'distant' wife is good in unconditional terms, the object in the Wanungamagalyuagba case is the strengthening, or reinvigoration, of specified intergroup relations over time:

> Marriage is then preferred with a *relatively* 'close' woman within the four [patrilineal local groups]. This ideological framework would seem to be a means of extending relationships outward to any number of alien groups yet of maintaining solidarity within a limited circle though encouraging 'sister'-exchange between two groups in *alternate* generations, primarily on the level of the local group but occasionally on that of four more inclusive units (the complexes). This arrangement is formalised by the combination of two complexes into 'somewhat "brother"-like groupings' to form one exogamous moiety, but the links so-formed are not sufficiently strong to permit 'sister'-exchange on a local group basis in consecutive generations. (Turner 1974, p. 98)

To summarise, the close–distant dichotomy among the Wanungamagalyuagba (and probably among coastal peoples generally) is not an open-ended desirability for 'distant' relationship, but a compromise between 'closeness' and 'distance': distant enough to be exogamous in respect of the local group and its recent attachments, but close enough to conform to a previous history of reciprocal interrelationship. This form of distance implies spatial distance—that is, the interrelationship of different groups and their countries; and genealogical distance, whereby certain genealogical relationships are prohibited on the grounds of being too recently enacted (e.g. an alliance between members of the same generation), while others, at the requisite temporal distance (two generations apart), are encouraged. As Turner (1974, p. 102) described it, what is required in 'an ideal wife' is one 'who is relatively distant, sociologically'. For Turner, 'this system may be seen as a compromise between the need for continually extending alliances over a wide range through obtaining wives from groups with no previous relationship to one's own local group, and the need for stability and solidarity within a restricted circle of groups—in the interest of survival'.

Rumsey's (1981) 'Kinship and Context among the Ngarinyin'

Rumsey's (1981) study of the kinship system of the Ngarinyin of the Kimberley region of Western Australia proceeded from a different perspective, with ostensibly different concerns; nevertheless, it has significant relevance for the close–distant dichotomy. In the Ngarinyin system, there is 'the tendency for all persons within a single agnatic line to be called by the same kinterm'. In ego's patriline, the usual Australian generational distinction is made: 'Father (G + 1) and son (G −1) are called by the same term (*idje*), whereas father's father (G + 2) and son's son (G − 2) get called by the same terms as elder brother and younger brother (G + 0) respectively' (p. 181). However, this is not the case in patrilines other than ego's; for example, 'if a man of one local clan or group be my "uncle", *kandingi* (MB), then every man in it, irrespective of age, is my "uncle": and every woman is classified as my "mother", *ngadji*, being sister to *kangingi*' (Elkin 1964, pp. 106–7 quoted in Rumsey 1981, p. 182). Therefore, we have what might be described as an instance of 'extended skewing', well beyond, for example, that of the mother's brother/mother's brother's son conflation that is associated with Omaha skewing. Rumsey (1981, p. 182) qualified the application of this systematisation: 'The Ngarinyin do not (at present anyway) think of or express relationships *exclusively* in those terms'. The close–distant dichotomy overlays this identification, operating in much the same terms as we have encountered in the studies already examined:

> Marriage norms were expressed both positively and negatively: marrying within one's moiety was traditionally punishable by death; marriages into the opposite moiety varied in degrees of correctness, depending on spouse's kin class, and within each class, on socio-spatial-cum-genealogical 'distance' (distant relatives always being more highly valued for marriage than close ones). For a man these degrees ranged from 'highly prescribed' in the case of distant 'father's mother' (a class which also included FMBD, FMBSD, etc.), down to 'highly proscribed' in the case of a close relative of the 'mother' class. (Rumsey 1981, p. 183)

Much the same rubric of relationship applies: notional (or classificatory) degrees of 'consanguinity' are tolerated, provided the person in question is at far enough spatial remove. Rumsey's analysis of the Ngarinyin system draws these two threads together. Whereas we might think of the term 'mother' (*ngaji*) as the archetypically closest, and hence most proscribed, term of relationship, in its classificatory or distant aspect it implies the opposite: 'The term *ngaji*, which in most contexts means "my (classificatory) mother", was here being used as a cover term for "women of the opposite moiety", mother being an especially salient exemplar of that class' (Rumsey 1981, pp. 183–4). As such, it articulates a class for which a priori the investigation of affinal alliance is possible. Rumsey (1981, p. 184), investigating the context of these merged terminologies, uncovered further implications:

> *Maanggarra* belongs to an interesting set of Ungarinyin terms, each of which refers to the set of clan estates associated with all of ego's kinsmen of a given class. In the case of *maanggarra*, the relevant class is *garndingi*, and just when *maanggarra* is the topic of discourse, *garndingi* can be used to cover the entire range of kintypes which Elkin's informants assigned to it, namely all the men of mother's agnatic line, regardless of generation level. The reason for this is not difficult to discern: since clan membership is, in practice, determined by patrifiliation, all the members of any agnatic line—including those consisting of ego's MF, MB, MBS, etc.—belong to the same clan. Hence in the discussion of *maanggarra*, the distinction normally implemented by the alternate-generation terms, *garndingi* and *mamingi*, becomes irrelevant, just as distinctions among alter-moiety female kin classes becomes irrelevant when the topic at hand was moiety exogamy.

At the outset of his discussion, Rumsey (1981, p. 181) referred to the 'unusual' status that anthropology had accorded the Ngarinyin kinship system in the past; Radcliffe-Brown (1930), Elkin (1931–32) and Scheffler (1978) are all noted as having regarded the Ngarinyin system as one that 'differs significantly' (Scheffler 1978, p. 417) from Australian norms. This, I believe, is not so, and hidden in the terminologies of eastern Australia collected by Fison, Howitt and others are many indications that a similar distinction is encoded between kinship reckoned among 'close' kin and separately in respect to 'distant' kin. This is a distinction that was observed as far back as Radcliffe-Brown (1930, p. 446): 'Outside the circle of his immediate relatives he tends to classify other persons according to the hordes to which they belong. There are certain collective terms of relationship which the individual applies to different hordes. This tendency to treat their horde as a unit is ... a determining factor of some importance in the Australian systems'. As Rumsey (1981, pp. 184–5) concluded in respect to the Ngarinyin system: '[There is] a high degree of correspondence between the generation-merging usage of the terms *garndingi* [MB] and *ngaji* [M], and contexts wherein the topic of discussion is interclan relations rather than intraclan or interpersonal ones … marriage … is in large measure conceived of as an interclan transaction'. Rumsey (1981, p. 185–6) only commented on the use of 'vocative terms' (e.g. 'my father' and 'my mother') in respect to close kin—terms that 'are not nearly as apt to be used over "widened" ranges of kintypes as are the "referential" terms'. It is my belief that many as yet poorly studied Australian kinship systems have a distinction, both in terminology and structure based on the close–distant dichotomy, that is integral to them.

Conclusion

This brief and necessarily selective review of the close–distant dichotomy in the literature of Australian kinship has sought to address three key areas: 1) the pervasiveness of the dichotomy; 2) whether or not it is a genuine product of Indigenous thought; and 3) whether it is a matter of sentiment—of ideal—or whether distance is a determinative instrument in the structure (and, therefore, the terminology) of kinship.

The first point is not conclusive: although many of the prime authorities on Australian kinship have recognised close–distant dichotomy; equally, other authors make no mention of it at all. One factor in favour of the possibility that it represents a commonality in Australian kinship is its recorded presence in systems from various and diverse parts of the continent. Variance in application of the dichotomy in relation to distance and different standards of desirability, argues for an evolution that has gone hand in hand with the development of kin systems to fit historical and environmental circumstances.

The supposition that the close–distant dichotomy is an Indigenous conception is more certain. To my own knowledge, the dichotomy appears nowhere else in anthropology so frequently as it does in Australia. Nor can it be said to have a history of theoretical development within the discipline compared with descent theory or affinal theory. In most cases, it appears as though the anthropologist had been alerted to its importance by his or her informants, or observed it directly in action. There are, of course, numerous instances in which documentation of the dichotomy is noted directly from the informants, as quotation or case histories. In my view, there can be very little doubt that the close–distant dichotomy is a kinship principle through which Aboriginal people understand their own society and its interrelationships.

The last question—is the close-distant dichotomy structural (that is, not simply an ideal Aboriginal society's cherish and strive towards, but actually encoded in structure)—is the least resolved of the three. Further work is necessary to demonstrate how the close–distant reckoning works in a kinship system, although many of the works cited in this chapter provide a good indication. I believe that enough has been shown in the sources reviewed to indicate the likelihood that kinship systems are founded on distance and that distance has a determinative role in the articulation of structure and terminology.

Some mention might be made of extensionist theory (otherwise, rewrite rule analysis, cf. Read 2001, pp. 243–4). Advocates of extensionist theory may argue that the close–distant dichotomy has already been well dealt with in the surmise that 'fathers' must inevitably extend from 'a father', the biological father, and so on, and that the dichotomy is structurally implied in Indigenous terminology to begin with. One only has to draw attention to Rumsey's (1981) Ngarinyin example of 'mothers' who end up representing anything but the biological mother—in fact, one could say, the social antithesis of the biological mother (i.e. those who provide the key to those one is able to marry). Again, this question can hardly be given the breadth of consideration it deserves; however, it is significant that a champion of extensionist theory such as Shapiro (1979, p. 56) used the following example in discerning the difference between a 'full' father and 'partial' father:

> Now consider that the adjectives *dangang* ('full') and *marrkangga* ('partial') can be used to modify any relationship term in this language—say, *bapa* ('father'). It is *ipso facto* clear that a 'full father' is not only different from a 'partial father'; he is *more* of a 'father' as well. And this is precisely the sort of subclassification that interests Scheffler. Who then is a 'full' father? When I first heard these adjectives used to modify relationship terms, I assumed that a 'full' member of any category is simply the occupant of that category who is genealogically closest to Ego. This assumption, I think, stemmed from a general ethnocentricism, as well as from rarer parochialism that pervades the culture of kinship buffs. Thus I was certain that a 'full' father is none other than one's real, true, genuine and (above all) socially presumed father. But I was wrong. The Miwuyt [i.e. Yolngu] subcategory 'full father' does indeed include one's genitor, but it embraces others as well—specifically, any 'father' who is a member of one's genitor's (and one's own) ritual lodge. All other 'fathers' are 'partial fathers'. Analogous notions apply to the subclassification of other Miwuyt categories.

In respect to Shapiro's Yolngu example, at least, any tangible distinction between focal 'fathers' and extended 'fathers' (or any other relative) is based on the close–distant dichotomy that has been the subject of this chapter. Unlike extensionist theory, which is based purely on the application of logic, the close–distant dichotomy can be shown to be well founded in Indigenous thought and practical application. In my view, two related deductions follow: extensionist theory ends up becoming so all-embracing as to be effectively meaningless; and kinship structure has to do with the society, not the family, and biological designations as foci or anything else are irrelevant. In other words, analogy has become confused with aetiology. The implications of the close–distant dichotomy are indeed large and attempts to answer them will have to await a further forum.

References

Barnes, J 1965, 'Foreword', in L Hiatt (ed.), *Kinship and conflict: a study of an Aboriginal community in northern Arnhem Land*, Canberra: Australian National University Press, pp. vii–xi.

Berndt, RM 1959, 'The concept of "the tribe" in the Western Desert of Australia', *Oceania*, *30*, pp. 88–106. doi.org/10.1002/j.1834-4461.1959.tb00213.x.

Berndt, RM & Berndt, CH 1970, *Man, land and myth in North Australia: the Gunwinggu People*, Sydney: Ure Smith.

Dousset, L 2003, 'On the misinterpretation of the Aluridja Kinship system type (Australian Western Desert)', *Social Anthropology*, *11*(1), pp. 43–61. doi.org/10.1111/j.1469-8676.2003.tb00071.x.

Elkin, AP 1931–32, 'The social organization of South Australian tribes', *Oceania*, *2*, pp. 44–73. doi.org/10.1002/j.1834-4461.1931.tb00022.x.

Elkin, AP 1937–38, 'Kinship in South Australia', *Oceania*, *8*, pp. 419–25. doi.org/10.1002/j.1834-4461.1938.tb00434.x.

Elkin, AP 1938–39, 'Kinship in South Australia', *Oceania*, *9*, pp. 41–78. doi.org/10.1002/j.1834-4461.1938.tb00216.x.

Elkin, AP 1939–40, 'Kinship in South Australia', *Oceania*, *10*, pp. 196–234. doi.org/10.1002/j.1834-4461.1939.tb00276.x.

Falkenberg, A & Falkenberg, J 1981, *The affinal relationship system*, Oslo: Universitetsforlaget.

Hercus, L 1994, *A grammar of the Arabana-Wangkangurru language, Lake Eyre Basin, South Australia*, Pacific Linguistics Series C. No. 128, Canberra: Department of Linguistics, Research School of Pacific Studies, The Australian National University.

Hiatt, L 1965, *Kinship and conflict: a study of an Aboriginal community in northern Arnhem Land*, Canberra: Australian National University Press.

Holcombe, S 2004, 'The politico-historical construction of the Pintupi Luritja and the concept of tribe', *Oceania*, 74(4), pp. 257–75. doi.org/10.1002/j.1834-4461.2004.tb02854.x.

Howitt, AW 1904, *The native tribes of south-east Australia*, London: Macmillan & Co.

Kuper, A 2005, *The reinvention of primitive society*, London: Routledge.

Lévi-Strauss, C 1969, *The elementary structures of kinship*, Boston: Beacon Press.

McConnel, U 1933–34, '"The Wik-Munkan and allied tribes of Cape York Peninsula, N.Q.". Part III—kinship and marriage', *Oceania*, 4, pp. 310–67. doi.org/10.1002/j.1834-4461.1934.tb00113.x.

McConnel, U 1939–40, 'Social organization of the tribes of Cape York Peninsula', *Oceania, 10*, pp. 434–55. doi.org/10.1002/j.1834-4461.1940.tb00305.x.

McConvell, P 1996, 'Backtracking to Babel: the chronology of Pama-Nyungan expansion in Australia', *Archaeology in Oceania, 31*, pp. 125–44. doi.org/10.1002/j.1834-4453.1996.tb00356.x.

McConvell, P 2001, 'Language shift and language spread among hunter-gatherers', in C Panter-Brick, RH Layton & P Rowley-Conwy (eds), *Hunter-gatherers: an interdisciplinary perspective*, Cambridge: Cambridge University Press, pp. 144–67.

Meggitt, M 1962, *Desert people*, Chicago: University of Chicago Press.

Morgan, LH 1871, *Systems of consanguinity and affinity in the human family*, Washington: Smithsonian Institution.

Myers, FR 1986, *Pintupi country, Pintupi self*, Canberra: Australian Institute of Aboriginal Studies.

Needham, R 1962, 'Genealogy and category in Wikmunkan society', *Ethnology*, *1*(2), pp. 223–64. doi.org/10.2307/3772877.

Radcliffe-Brown, AR 1913, 'Three tribes of Western Australia', *Journal of the Royal Anthropological Institute*, *43*, pp. 143–94.

Radcliffe-Brown, AR 1930, 'The social organization of Australian tribes: Part I', *Oceania*, *1*(1), pp. 34–63. doi.org/10.1002/j.1834-4461.1930.tb00003.x.

Read, DW 2001, 'Formal analysis of kinship terminologies and its relationship to what constitutes kinship', *Anthropological Theory*, *1*(2), pp. 239–67. doi.org/10.1177/146349960100100205.

Rumsey, A 1981, 'Kinship and context among the Ngarinyin', *Oceania*, *51*, pp. 181–92. doi.org/10.1002/j.1834-4461.1981.tb01448.x.

Sackett, L 1976, 'Indirect exchange in a symmetrical system: marriage alliance in the Western Desert of Australia', *Ethnology*, *15*(2), pp. 135–49. doi.org/10.2307/3773325.

Scheffler, HW 1978, *Australian kin classification*, Cambridge: Cambridge University Press. doi.org/10.1017/CBO9780511557590.

Shapiro, W 1979, *Social organization in Aboriginal Australia*, Canberra: Australian National University Press.

Smith, M 2013, *The archaeology of Australia's deserts*, Cambridge: Cambridge University Press. doi.org/10.1017/CBO9781139023016.

Stanner, WEH 1935–36, 'A note on Djamindjung kinship and totemism', *Oceania*, *6*, pp. 441–51. doi.org/10.1002/j.1834-4461.1936.tb00204.x.

Stanner, WEH 1936–37, 'Murinbata kinship and totemism', *Oceania*, *7*, pp. 186–216. doi.org/10.1002/j.1834-4461.1936.tb00451.x.

Strehlow, TGH 1947, *Aranda traditions*, Melbourne University Press [Reprinted 1968, New York: Johnson Reprint Corporation].

Sutton, P 1978, Wik: Aboriginal society, territory and language at Cape Keerweer, Cape York Peninsula, Australia, PhD thesis, University of Queensland.

Turner, DH 1974, *Tradition and transformation: a study of Aborigines in the Groote Eylandt area, northern Australia*, Australian Aboriginal Studies No. 53, Canberra: Australian Institute of Aboriginal Studies.

Turner, DH 1980, *Australian Aboriginal social organization*, Atlantic Highlands, NJ: Humanities Press International.

Vincent, E 2011, 'The everyday effects of native title: attending to Indigenous self-accounts', *Australian Anthropological Society conference paper*, Brisbane.

12
Asymmetrical Distinctions in Waanyi Kinship Terminology[1]

Mary Laughren

Introduction

Background

Waanyi[2] kinship terms map onto an 'Arandic' system with distinct encoding of the four logical combinations of maternal and paternal relations in the ascending harmonic ('grandparent') generation:

---

1 Without the generous collaboration of the late Mr Roy Seccin Kamarrangi, who valiantly attempted to teach me Waanyi between 2000 and 2005, this study would not have begun. I also acknowledge the assistance received from the late Mr Eric King Balyarrinyi and his companions at the Doomadgee nursing home. I am indebted to Gavan Breen, who shared his Waanyi field notes and insights with me, and to John Dymock, who gave me copies of his vast corpus of Waanyi vocabulary. Thank you to the two anonymous reviewers, whose input to the development of this chapter was substantial, and to Barry Alpher, who provided invaluable feedback on an earlier draft. Errors of fact or interpretation remain my responsibility. The research on Waanyi was supported by a number of small ARC grants through the University of Queensland and the Waanyi Nation Aboriginal Corporation.
2 Waanyi was traditionally spoken in land watered by the upper branches of the Nicholson River and its tributaries, which straddles the Queensland–Northern Territory border to the south of the Gulf of Carpentaria (see Tindale 1974; Trigger 1982). The most closely related language is Garrwa (Breen 2003; Mushin 2012), spoken to the immediate north of Waanyi. The Garrwa-Waanyi language block lies between the northern and southern branches of the Warluwarric language group (Blake 1988, 1990) and is bordered on the east by the Tangkic language Yukulta, also called Ganggalida, (Keen 1983; Nancarrow et al. 2014), which Seccin referred to as Nyangka. To the west of Waanyi, languages belonging to the Barkly language family were spoken (Harvey 2008). The Waanyi data presented herein are drawn principally from my 2000–2005 recordings of the late Mr Roy Seccin

FF (*kangku*), FM (*ngawiji/ngabuji*), MM (*kukudi/kuku*) and MF (*mimi*).[3] Unlike comparable systems such as the Warlpiri (Laughren 1982), Waanyi lexifies the male/female distinction for the maternal parents of ego's parents (FM and MM); the term designating a parent's mother and her sisters differs from the one designating her brothers. For the FM relationship, *ngawiji* (FM[Z]) is formally distinguished from *ngabuji* (FMB); for the MM relation, *kukudi* (MM[Z]) is distinguished from *kuku* (MMB). The kin identified as the paternal parents of ego's parents are referred to by terms that apply to both male and female members of these sibling sets: *kangku* denotes any member of the FF set (FF, FFB and FFZ), while *mimi* denotes any member of the MF set (MF, MFB and MFZ).[4] The sex distinctions encoded by the terms for members of ego's FM and MM sibling sets in the speech of the late Mr Roy Seccin reflect those for the spousal relation, which is a special case of the FM relationship: *nawi* 'husband (H) or husband's (senior) brother (HsB)' and *mangkarri* 'wife (W) or wife's sister (WZ)'. Waanyi also distinguishes 'wife' from 'wife's brother (WB)' (*kayikayi*), which is further distinguished from a man's sister's husband (*nabinabi*).[5] Sex is also lexically distinguished in the senior sibling relationship (members of the same subsection as FF kin): *bawa* (senior) 'brother' and *balala* or *maju* 'senior sister'. It is not distinguished in the junior sibling terms *dawirri* or *kakulu*.[6] Sex is also marked in ascending disharmonic relations: father or father's brother versus father's sister; mother and mother's sister versus mother's brother; and mother's male versus female cross-cousins (MMBS/D). However, no gender distinction is marked for father's cross-cousins (FMBS/D), who belong to

---

Kamarrangi and my 2007–2008 recordings of the late Mr Eric King Balyarrinyi, and supplemented by Elwyn Flint's 1964 recordings of Waanyi speakers at Doomadgee, Gavan Breen's field notes and transcriptions of recordings made with several Waanyi speakers in the 1960s and 1970s, work by Charles Osborne (1966) based on his own fieldwork, and John Dymock who recorded Waanyi language over a lengthy period between the 1960s and mid-1990s.

3   Abbreviations for kin relations are F = father, FF = father's father, M = mother, MF = mother's father, FM = father's mother, MM = mother's mother, S = son, D = daughter, H = husband, W = wife, B = brother and Z = sister. F and M are also used to designate more abstract paternal and maternal relationships respectively. Parentheses are used to indicate possible inclusion in the denotation of a term (e.g. H(B) is to be read as 'husband or husband's brother'). A forward slash between symbols indicates 'or' as in B/Z meaning 'brother or sister'. The symbols 's' and 'j' are used to indicate 'senior' versus 'junior' kin relations (e.g. sB 'senior brother' versus jB 'junior brother'). Appendices 2 and 3 display the Waanyi kintrems, non-affinal and affinal, respectively.

4   *Mimi* also denotes the child of *ego*'s father's sister (FZS/D), as well as MF(Z/B) and BDS/D.

5   The distinction between H(B) (*nawi*) and HZ is probably encoded as well, but I have not recorded a term for the latter relationship, and have not found it recorded in other sources.

6   The term *dawirri* has been recorded as either 'junior brother' or 'junior sister' by Breen, Osborne and Dymock, in addition to *kakulu* recorded by Dymock (1993). Both terms are found in the Seccin corpus. Breen, Flint and Osborne record *balala* 'elder sister', both *balala* and *maju* are recorded by Dymock (1993), while only *maju* (also the Garrwa term) is in the Seccin corpus.

the same subsection as Ego's maternal child (ZS/D). Sex distinctions are only encoded in the descending disharmonic generation kin terms for the children of ego's female cross-cousins (MBDS/D)—members of the same subsection as (MMBS/D).

All 'grandparent' terms may be used reciprocally as 'grandchild' terms, although there are additional specific 'grandchild' terms.[7] In the Seccin corpus, the MM relation *kuku/kukudi* (ascending) contrasts with the descending *ngurrali* (ZDS/D). There is also a more general 'grandchild' term *murimuri* that is sometimes used in place of the corresponding 'ascending' term.[8]

Waanyi kinship terms are listed for reference in Appendices 2 and 3.

Aims

In this chapter, I explore possible explanations as to why these patterns of asymmetrical distinctions in the encoding of both sex and generation level are found within the set of harmonic generation kin terms. First, I outline the salience of these distinctions with respect to the marriage alliance and wife-bestowal system, in which a daughter is bestowed by her father on his upper generation male relative, who is the son of the bestower's MM, and by her mother on the son of her MMB. Thus, sons-in-law for both men and women are children of kin in their MM class. Such a system involves wife exchange between male cross-cousins (*maku*) (MBS) of each other's

---

7 The neighbouring and closely related Garrwa language encodes the ascending versus descending, as well as the more general senior versus junior distinction (e.g. aunt/niece and mother-in-law/daughter-in-law) by the addition of a suffix *-nya* to designate the descending/junior term (Mushin 2012, pp. 47–8). Breen also recorded this usage for Waanyi (GB-Tape571-IG and GB-Tape572-IG), as did Osborne and Dymock, but not Flint. I did not record a productive systematic use of this suffix and will not discuss it in this chapter.

8 Breen recorded *murimuri* as the descending (grandchild) counterpart of *kangku* (FF) only. In the Seccin corpus, it is sometimes used as a reciprocal for both *kangku* (FF) and *kuku* (MMB). Mushin (2012, p. 48) recorded Garrwa *murimuri* as the grandchild counterpart of *kangku* (FF), *kukuli/kukudi* (MM) and *mimi* (MF), even though these forms also occur with the 'junior/descending' suffix *-nya*. Interestingly, Garrwa *kangku-nya* does not denote a descending FF relationship, but rather the FFZ relationship (see discussion of the Wambaya feminine suffix *-nya* in the subsection 'Barkly Languages and Other Non-Pama-Nyungan Neighbours'). Thus, *murimuri* seems to designate descending harmonic kin relations *not* in the class of ego's FM (from which a spouse is drawn)—that is, *ngawuji*. This would seem to correspond to the wider uses of *kangku* recorded for Garrwa by Mushin (2012, p. 48) as a 'grand-uncle' term. The stem *muri* is recorded in the non-Pama-Nyungan Marra spoken north of Yanyula along the western coast of the Gulf of Carpentaria for both ascending and descending members of either sex of *ego*'s FF set; the reduplicated form *murimuri* is a vocative form (Heath 1981, p. 115), which is compatible with its use in Garrwa and Waanyi as a grandchild-referring term, as well as the form most likely to be borrowed.

sister's daughter's daughter (*ngurrali*)—a descending MM kinswoman.[9] A further impetus towards the lexical encoding of the sex of *ego*'s parents' maternal parent (and members of their sibling class) is the lexical marking of a sex contrast in the spousal terms, as well as in affinal terms, denoting siblings of a spouse.[10] Second, I show that the Waanyi pattern of marking sex contrasts is not the necessary consequence of a Waanyi-type marriage alliance and wife-bestowal system, since the Warlpiri language does not make these distinctions, despite the Warlpiri system of marriage alliance and wife bestowal being equivalent to the Waanyi one. However, key generation levels are marked in both languages. Third, by comparing the Waanyi harmonic ascending and descending kin terminology with that of neighbouring languages—starting with closely related Garrwa followed by languages of the Warluwarric, Tangkic and Barkly groups—I show that the Waanyi lexical pattern conforms to a wider regional one. I explore the sources and indications of direction of borrowing of Waanyi terms that encode both sex and generation level contrasts within the asymmetrical pattern of linguistically encoded contrasts in harmonic generation terms. On the basis of a further comparison with the slightly more distant Marra and Alawa, I suggest that the regional pattern that is found in the Gulf area may have emerged from a series of innovations that were motivated by changes in the system of wife and brother-in-law bestowal.

Organisation of Chapter

Following the introductory material, relevant elements of the Waanyi kinship system and terminology are set out in the section 'Waanyi Kin Terms' that show how the affinal relation terms mesh with the system of kin relation terms, based on maternal and paternal lines of ascent and descent. In the section 'Two Arandic Systems Compared: Waanyi and Warlpiri', the Waanyi terminology is compared with the Warlpiri. Although both groups have the same underlying system of kin relations and systems of marriage bestowal and exchange, Warlpiri kin terms do not encode the sex distinctions marked in Waanyi FM, MM and spousal terms. In the section 'Waanyi and Neighbouring Languages', Waanyi terms are compared with those expressing the same relations in languages

---

9   I recorded *makungu* as female cross-cousin. Breen and Osborne recorded *makungu* as 'cousin' (not distinguishing sex).

10 The practice in some kinship studies of excluding 'spousal' relations from affinal (in-law) relations does not reflect the denotation of kin terms in the Australian context, since the morpheme for 'spouse' typically also applies to the spouse's (same sex) sibling. I include 'spousal' terms in the class of 'affinal' terms.

of the groups that are the immediate neighbours of Waanyi—starting with Garrwa, the language most closely related to Waanyi, forming with it the Garrwan group (or family) (O'Grady, Voegelin & Voegelin 1966) and extending to languages of the Warluwarric, Tangkic and Barkly groups. Relevant data from the non-Pama-Nyungan Marra and Alawa languages spoken to the north-west of the Garrwan languages and their immediate neighbours are examined. Similarities and differences in the lexical patterns in these languages are explored, revealing cognates and borrowing patterns. The major findings of an analysis of the distribution of forms and lexical patterns across the languages surveyed are presented in the section 'Conclusions'.

Waanyi Kin Terms

Like other Australian kinship vocabularies, each term can denote a wider set of kin than do kinship terms in modern Indo-European languages. Australian kinship systems are classificatory, in that all persons are included in a relationship class that (potentially) contains members consanguineally (or by adoption) related to Ego (see Scheffler [1978] for relevant discussion). The system of kin relation terms is based on combinations of the two basic relationships: maternal and paternal (Laughren 1982, 2001). Further distinctions may be lexically marked with respect to ascending versus descending relationships, sex, seniority within sibling sets in the harmonic (Ego's and Ego's grandparents and grandchildren) and disharmonic (Ego's parents and Ego's children) generation moieties. However, apart from the maternal/paternal distinction and the harmonic/disharmonic distinction, other distinctions such as sex and seniority are not encoded for all kin categories.[11]

Affinal relationships are grafted onto this same system, as they are entered into with a subset of kin restricted by marriage 'laws' and conventions, as well as established or negotiated systems of wife exchange and wife bestowal between particular family groups. Some affinal relationships are marked by special terms that are substituted for the more general non-affinal terms; others remain unmarked.[12]

---

11   Primogeniture plays a crucial role in determining seniority in *ego*'s generation as an inherited feature from the grandparent generation via the parent generation.
12   Only the most favoured or 'first choice' marriage pattern is described herein. Less restrictive spousal alliances between members of the same generation moiety, such as between a man and his classificatory MBD or ZSD, or his MMBSD or ZDD, are also entered into.

SKIN, KIN AND CLAN

Waanyi Harmonic Generation Kin Terms

The terms that distinguish kin in the ascending harmonic (grandparent) generation from Ego are shown in Figure 46.[13] Paternal relations (marked by a solid line) are distinguished from maternal relations (marked by a broken line). Terms for Ego's 'mother' and 'father' are also shown.

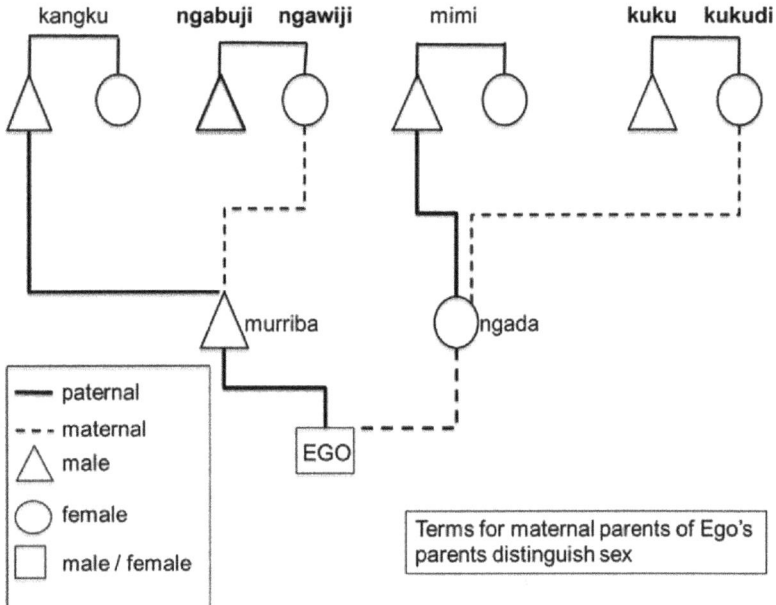

Figure 46: Waanyi ascending harmonic generation kin terms.
Source: Author's work.

Only the terms denoting ego's parents' maternal parent sibling sets distinguish male from female members. The male members of the FM set are called *ngabuji*, a phonologically more conservative cognate containing the stop /b/ of *ngawiji*, with the lenited glide /w/, which denotes the female members. Given the widespread existence of the /b/ form (e.g. *ngabuji*, *ngabuju* and other variants) with same or related meanings in many languages of northern Australia extending west of Waanyi, this form is likely to have entered Waanyi later than the /w/ form.[14] The terms for

---

13   The kin terms shown in each of the figures can be used by Ego to refer to any member of the designated set or class; thus, each triangle, circle or rectangle should be interpreted as representing a sibling set, as well as any member of that set.
14   Waanyi shows evidence of an historic lenition of /b/ to /w/ in intervocalic position in pre-Waanyi—for example, *bawa* 'elder brother' < **baba*, or *nawi* 'husband' <**nabi* (cf. *nabinabi* 'brother-in-law').

396

MMB and MM(Z) are related in a different way; they share the same root, *kuku*, but the female term has the historical kin suffix *-di* (written *-rdi* or *-rti* in other languages), which is widely distributed across Australian languages.[15] *Kukudi* is the only Waanyi kinterm that unambiguously contains this suffix that is not productive in either Waanyi or Garrwa.[16] It has been borrowed into Waanyi as a monomorphemic word to mark the sex distinction between MM(Z) and MMB in the same way that *ngabuji* has been borrowed to distinguish FMB from FM(Z).[17]

This chapter explores the motivation for lexically marking the sex distinction in these two sets of ascending harmonic relations, the maternal parents of ego's parents (FM and MM), as opposed to the other two sets, made up of individuals that are paternally related to ego's parents (FF and MF). While harmonic terms do not generally encode the ascending (grandparent) versus descending (grandchild) distinction, such a distinction is marked in the MM set, since a specific 'descending' term *ngurrali* contrasts with the more general *kuku*/*kukudi* pair, as shown in Figure 47[18]—this is the second anomaly to be examined. This lexicalised distinction between grand-uncle (MMB) and grand-nephew/niece (ZDS/D) was explained to me by Roy Seccin in referring to his sister's daughter's son: 'Like I call him *ngurrali*, he call me *kuku*' (Roy Seccin Kamarrangi, 04Tape6, 2002). As symbolised by the square shapes in Figure 47, the descending term applies to either male or female referents. Figure 47 also shows that while paternal children *jawaji* (man's or brother's children) are distinguished from maternal children *jabulu* (woman's or sister's children), the sex of these children is not distinguished by these terms.

---

15 See Nash (1992) for a comparative study of this morpheme that was reprised by McConvell (2008). This suffix has not been found to denote 'female' or mark feminine gender, but rather marks a first-person (speaker) propositus where productive, as in Marra (Heath 1981).
16 Waanyi and Garrwa *kadidi* MB may also contain this suffix—although it may also reflect stem final syllable reduplication.
17 The typical Australian contrast between alveolar and post-alveolar consonant sounds is highly restricted in Waanyi (Breen 2003); sounds symbolised by *d*, *l* and *n* are usually pronounced with a post-alveolar articulation.
18 Other sources record *kukulinya*, and not *ngurrali*, as the descending term. A reviewer pointed out that neither Osborne nor Breen recorded *kuku* as MMB; however, Breen (Ivy George, tape no. 569, side 1) recorded *kujawuja* as MMB, in contrast with MM *kukudi* or *kukuli*, which are both terms that were also recorded by Flint and reproduced in the Seccin corpus. Whether the MMB term is *kuku* or *kujawuja*, in lexical contrast with MM *kukudi*, remains to be explained. Osborne (1966) recorded *kujawaja* as 'grandfather' without further specifying, while Dymock (1993) listed *kujawuja* as FF, along with *kangku*.

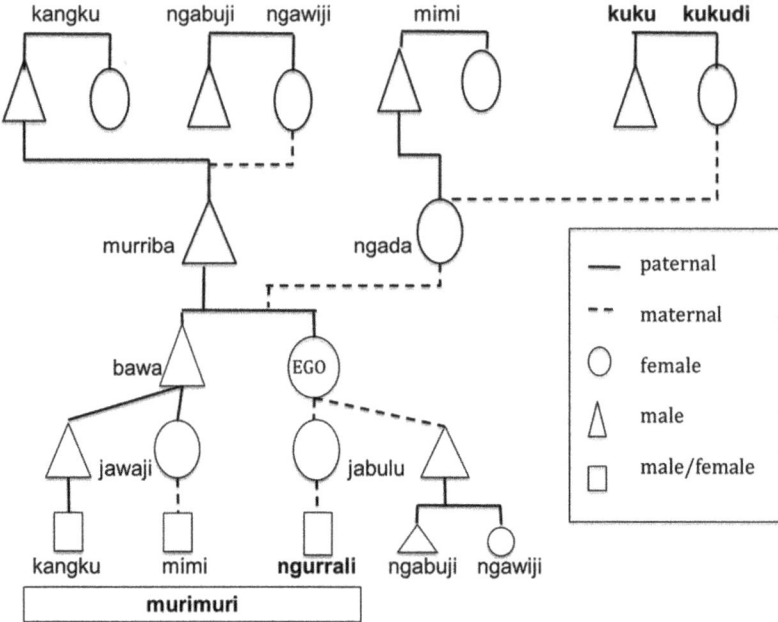

Figure 47: Waanyi ascending and descending harmonic generation kin terms.
Source: Author's work.

We now address the question of the possible motivation for these somewhat anomalous distinctions in terms of the overall system of kin relationships: why is the sex distinction limited to Ego's parents' maternal parents, and why is the ascending/descending relationship lexically marked with distinct terms that only denote kin in an MM relationship? Is there anything that makes these particular relationships special, or that distinguishes them from the others in terms of social roles? The first line of enquiry I explore is the role that these relationships play in wife bestowal and exchange, and the way that affinal relationships and terminology intermesh with non-affinal relationships and terminology in Waanyi.

From a woman's point of view, as shown in Figure 48, her *nawi* 'husband' belongs to the male set of FM *ngabuji* kin, while from a man's point of view, it is his sister's husband *nabinabi* who belongs to the ascending *ngabuji* set, as shown in Figure 49.[19]

---

19 In the neighbouring Tangkic language Yukulta, *nabinabi* is 'wife's brother' (Keen 1983, p. 291), while in the northern Warluwarric language Yanyula, it is recorded as 'sister's husband' (Bradley 1992, p. 509).

12. ASYMMETRICAL DISTINCTIONS IN WAANYI KINSHIP TERMINOLOGY

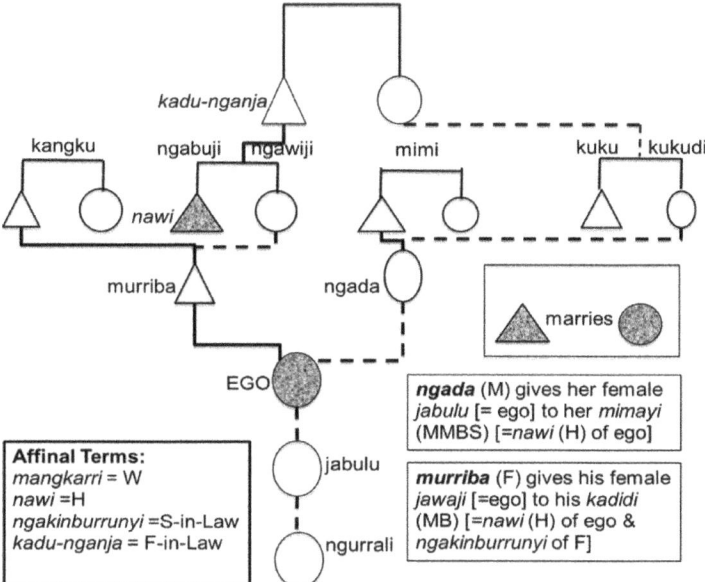

Figure 48: Waanyi pattern of wife bestowal.[20]
Source: Author's work.

It follows then that a man's *mangkarri* 'wife' and *kayikayi* 'wife's brother' belong to the descending set of FM *ngawiji/ngabuji* kin. Thus, the sex distinction in the spousal terms—*nawi* (H[B]) versus *mangkarri* (W[Z])—is reflected in the non-affinal terms that refer to the larger kin sets: *ngabuji* (male) versus *ngawiji* (female).

Figure 49 shows how a man's father-in-law (*kadu-nganja*) belongs to the class of his sister's son (*jabulu*), while his (senior) brother-in-law (*nabinabi*), who is his sister's husband, belongs to the set of his ascending *ngabuji* (FM).[21] His wife (*mangkarri*) and her brother (man's [junior] brother-in-law called *kayikayi*) belong to the set of his descending female *ngawiji* and male *ngabuji* respectively.[22] While Figure 48 shows how a woman marries a member of the set of her father's mother's brother, a man should not marry a woman whom his father calls *ngada* 'mother', as indicated by the barred circle in Figure 49.

---

20   In Figures 48 and 49, the affinal terms are in italics, while the non-affinal terms are in plain typeface.
21   The term *kadu-nganja*, the Garrwan 'father-in-law' term, is mentioned in the footnote on *mimayi* in Table 57.
22   *Kayikayi* (written in Alawa and Marra as *gaygay*) is quite widely distributed as a 'brother-in-law' or 'spouse' term in languages spoken in the south-west Gulf of Carpentaria region.

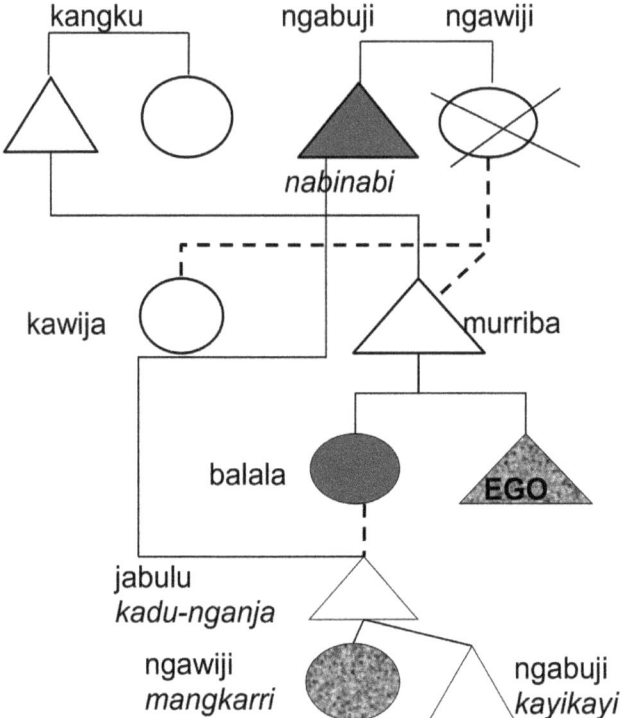

Figure 49: Asymmetrical brother-in-law relationship.
Source: Author's work.

The data in Figures 48 and 49 show that affinal terms encode more semantic distinctions than do non-affinal harmonic generation terms. While terms such as *nawi* (H) and *mangkarri* (W) encode sex distinctions, as do their non-affinal counterparts *ngabuji* (FMB) and *ngawiji* (FM[Z]), the former pair also encode the ascending/descending distinction through their respective correspondence with the brother-in-law terms that distinguish *nawi*, ascending members of the *ngabuji* set, from *kayikayi*, (descending) members of the *ngabuji* class. Again, the distinction between *mangkarri* 'wife' and *kayikayi* 'wife's brother' mirrors the sex distinction between *ngawiji* and *ngabuji*, and both contrast with the ascending generation terms, *nawi* 'husband' and *nabinabi* '(man's) sister's husband'. These contrasts are summarised in Table 56.[23]

---

23   A reviewer pointed out that *ngabuji* is not recorded by either Breen or Osborne. I could only find a term for father's mother and none for father's mother's brother in these works, so the absence of *ngabuji* does not entail that this term is a recent borrowing into Waanyi, since it was not elicited. Both terms were recorded by Trigger (1982, p. 26).

Table 56: Waanyi terms for relations in FM class.

	AFFINAL TERMS		NON-AFFINAL TERMS	
	Male	Female	Male	female
ascending	*nawi* H(eB) *nabinabi* ZH(B)	? HZ	*ngabuji* FMB/ZSS	*ngawiji* FM(Z)/ZSD
descending	*kayikayi* HjB/WB	*mangkarri* W(Z)		

Source: Author's work.

Considering the lexical pattern discussed above, it is possible that the gender distinction in the FM non-affinal terms followed the introduction of affinal terms marking gender distinctions. *Ngawiji* may have narrowed its meaning to designate female-only members of the FM class when the male term *ngabuji* was introduced. We return to this question in the section 'Waanyi and Neighbouring Languages'.

As shown in Figures 46–48, the other grandparent relation, whose male and female members are called by distinct but related terms, is the MM relationship, which plays a key role in wife bestowal. As already mentioned, a person (male or female) bestows their female *jabulu* 'maternal child' on their *mimayi* 'son-in-law', who is the male *paternal* child of a member of their MM class (i.e. of their mother's mother's brother [= *kuku*]). As for their female *jawaji* 'paternal child', she is bestowed on their *kadidi* 'mother's brother', who is the *maternal* child (MMS) of a member of their MM class (i.e. the son of their *kukudi*).[24] Thus, we see that the MM (*kuku/kukudi*) relation plays a key role in wife bestowal. A man bestows his daughter on the son of his female *kukudi*, while a woman bestows her daughter on the son of her (male) *kuku*.[25] While the relationship between a man and his son-in-law (= *kadidi* 'uncle') remains within the same matrimoiety and does not call for strict avoidance behaviour, a woman is in the opposite matrimoiety to her son-in-law (= *mimayi*)—a relationship that is marked by elaborate avoidance conventions. Thus, the lexical marking of the contrast between male and female members of one's MM

---

24   Waanyi has a range of terms for MB including *kamburru* 'senior uncle' and *kabubu* 'junior uncle', as well as *kadidi*. The conditions that determine the use of *kadidi*, as opposed to the other two terms, are uncertain.

25   Trigger (1982, pp. 26–7) recorded Waanyi *gugudi* MM(Z) contrasting with *kangku* (MMB) and FF(B/Z). Mushin (2012, p. 48) recorded a similar distribution of terms for Garrwa. The transitive relationship verb *kuku-mba* 'be MM(B/Z) to' is built on the stem *kuku* that is unmarked for sex. Irrespective of the term used to distinguish MMB from MM(Z), what is salient to this discussion is the fact that the sex distinction is lexified for nouns.

class would seem well motivated from a functional or social perspective, since their paternal children are potential sons-in-law and mothers-in-law. These relationships are summarised in Table 57.

Table 57: Son-in-law *ngakinburrunyi* relationships.[26]

AFFINAL	NON-AFFINAL	
ngakinburrunyi 'son-in-law' of **man**	child of *kukudi* = *kadidi*	same matrimoiety, non-taboo
ngakinburrunyi 'son-in-law' of **woman**	child of *kuku* = *mimayi*[1]	other matrimoiety, taboo 'poison cousin'

Source: Author's work.

[1] *Mimayi* has the same meaning in the Barkly language Wambaya (Nordlinger 1998, p. 287). In Alawa (Sharpe 2001, p. 72) and Marra (Heath 1981, p. 119), *-mimay* is an affinal 'spouse' root, which may host a gender affix. Breen recorded *kuwana-nganja* 'daughter/son-in-law' (also cited for Garrwa by Mushin on the basis of Trigger's field notes) and *mandawala-nganja* 'father-in-law' of the female speaker. Osborne and Flint only recorded *kadu-nganja* 'father-in-law' — the term used by Seccin.

I now turn to the other anomaly shown in Figures 46 and 47, whereby it is only in the MM grandparent class that the ascending/descending distinction is specifically marked by lexically distinct terms in Seccin's speech. What is distinctive about the MM grandparent–grandchild distinction that might motivate the lexical marking of this distinction?

Another aspect of wife bestowal is the practice of wife exchange between men who are cross-cousins, and thus members of opposite patrimoieties and matrimoieties, who call each other *maku* or *mimi*. These men 'exchange' their female *ngurrali* (ZDD) as marriage partners; these women call their MMB *kuku*. Thus, we see that the asymmetry between ascending and descending members of the MM set is socially marked as a relationship between wife giver and wife receiver. This pattern of wife exchange is mediated by mother-in-law bestowal: a man bestows his sister's daughter (*jabulu*) as mother-in-law (*ngunyarri*) of his cross-cousin (*mimi/maku*), who belongs to the same superset as his mother's father (*mimi*). His own child is a potential son-in-law/mother-in-law of his *ngurrali*.

The key relationships involved in this practice of wife exchange are shown in Figure 50.

---

26   The literal meaning of *ngaki-n-burru-nyi* is 'one towards me/mine' (*ngaki* is first-person dative pronoun). The suffix *-nyi* is frequently used on kin terms in Breen's Waanyi recordings—seemingly marking a vocative or citation usage. Mushin (2012, p. 49) cited *burrunyi* as a S/D-in-law term.

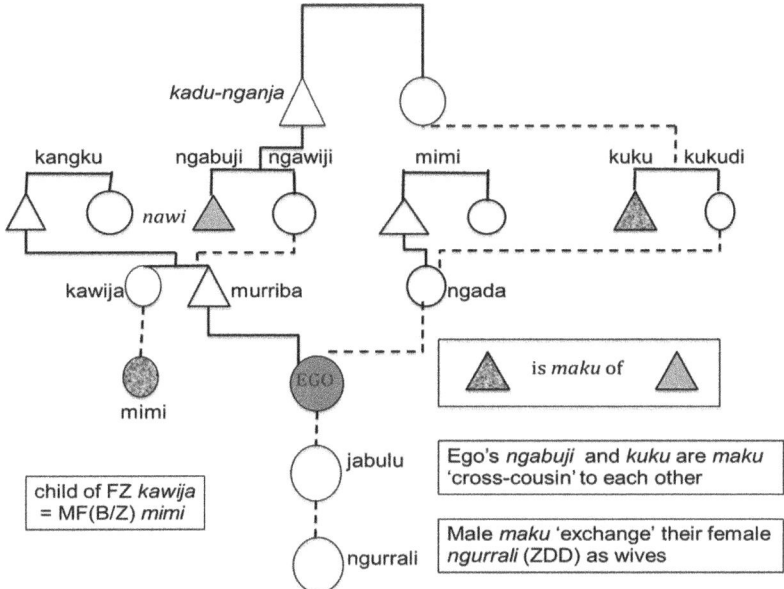

Figure 50: Pattern of wife exchange between cross-cousins.
Source: Author's work.

Figure 50 shows how the *nawi* (H) of female Ego belongs to the class of her *ngabuji* (FMB)—the *maku* ('cross-cousin') of ego's *kuku(di)* (MM[B/Z]).[27] This *kuku* would refer to Ego as his *ngurrali*. Ego's *kuku* is married to Ego's *mimi*, who is the child of Ego's *kawija* (FZ) and the *ngurrali* (ZDD) of Ego's *nawi* (H). The mother-in-law exchange illustrated in Figure 50 involves ego's M (*ngada*) and ego's FZ (*kawija*).

Summary

What we've shown so far is that the anomalous marking of sex and ascending/descending distinctions in Ego's 'grandparent/child' generation correlates with distinctive roles in the traditional practice of wife bestowal and exchange. A woman's husband is drawn from the set of her male ascending FM kin, her *ngabuji,* while conversely a man marries a wife from his descending FM kin, his *ngawiji*. The gender distinction encoded in these non-affinal terms mirrors the gender distinction encoded in the corresponding affinal terms, *nawi* H(eB) and *mangkarri* W(Z). The gender distinction in the MM terms *kuku* and *kukudi* marks the

---

27   Flint also recorded *mimi* as both MF and MBS, but *makungu* as MBD.

salience of this relationship in the system of wife bestowal involving cross-cousins. The marking of the descending MM category by the term *ngurrali*, which contrasts with the ascending terms *kuku* and *kukudi*, also correlates with the distinctive roles of wife bestower (*kuku*) and bestowed (*ngurrali*) within this pattern of wife exchange. The terms that specify a 'female' member of the FM and MM grandparent relationships apply to the maternal parent of ego's father-in-law and mother-in-law—these relationships being highly taboo in traditional Waanyi society. A man's father-in-law is the son of his wife's *ngawiji*, while his mother-in-law is the daughter of his wife's *kukudi*, as shown in Figure 50, where 'wife' is *ego*. However, as will be seen in the next section, there is no necessary relationship between this marriage pattern and the lexical pattern found in Waanyi ascending and descending harmonic terms.

Two Arandic Systems Compared: Waanyi and Warlpiri

Waanyi and Warlpiri[28] kinship systems are virtually identical with respect to their systems of marriage alliance, wife bestowal and exchange. However, an examination of Warlpiri grandparent/child terms reveals that the lexical marking of gender distinctions in ascending harmonic generation terms for the maternal parents of ego's parents found in Waanyi is not a necessary concomitant of this system of wife bestowal and exchange. However, I argue that these lexical contrasts are not random, but reflect key social distinctions at the core of the shared system of affinal kin relationships.

Warlpiri Ascending/Descending Harmonic Generation Kin Terms

No gender distinction is lexified in the Warlpiri nomenclature for harmonic ascending and descending non-affinal kin terms. As in Waanyi, identical terms are used for both ascending (grandparent) and descending (grandchild) sets. However, we find the same anomalous pattern as seen

---

28   Warlpiri is a Pama-Nyungan language of the Ngumpin-Yapa group (McConvell & Laughren 2004) spoken in an area over 1,000 km to the south-west of the Waanyi-speaking area. These languages were traditionally separated by the non-Pama-Nyungan Barkly languages and the Pama-Nyungan languages of the Warluwarric, Arandic and Warumungu groups. See Figure 52.

12. ASYMMETRICAL DISTINCTIONS IN WAANYI KINSHIP TERMINOLOGY

in Waanyi with respect to the MM set. The ascending MM term *jaja* may be replaced by a specifically descending generation term *mirntirdi*.[29] Additionally, the ascending and descending FM relations may be distinguished by the use of *yapirliyi* (derived from Arandic *aperl plus the first-person propositive suffix *-ey*) for the descending term in opposition with the unmarked term *yaparla* (*ngapuju* is used in place of *yaparla* or *yaparliyi* in north-western or Lajamanu Warlpiri).[30]

Waanyi and Warlpiri Compared

A comparison of relevant Waanyi and Warlpiri kin terms is shown in Figure 51.

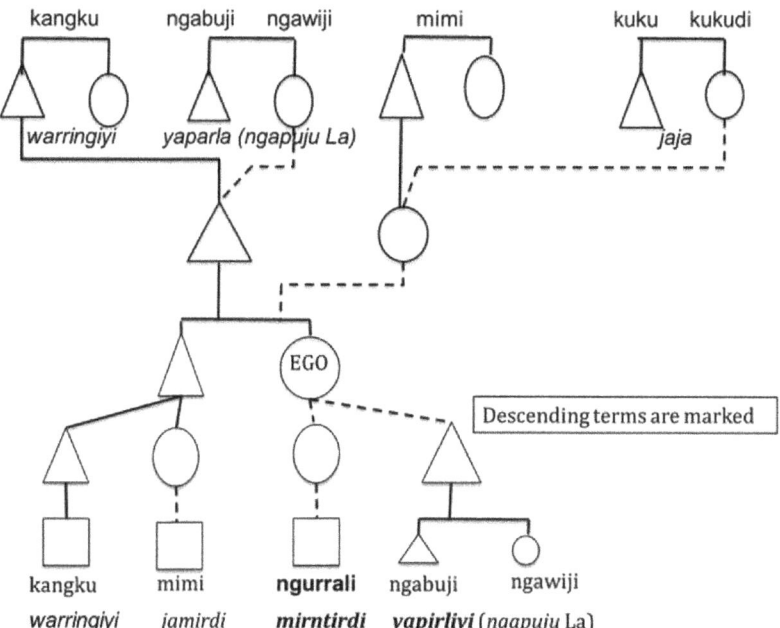

Figure 51: Waanyi and Warlpiri grandparent/child terms compared.[31]
Source: Author's work.

---

29 This term may be cognate with Wakaya *mintara* (Spencer, cited in Breen 2000c).
30 The terms *ngapuju* and *yapirli* are used to designate the spousal relationship between specific ascending and descending disharmonic kin respectively: *ngapuju* refers to the spouse of speaker's father or mother, or father's brother or sister (but not of mother's brother), while *yapirli* refers to the spousal relation between female speaker's brother's son and his wife (speaker's MBSD). Warlpiri *ngapuju* is clearly cognate with both Waanyi *ngabuji* and *ngawiji*.
31 In Figure 51, the Waanyi terms are written in plain typeface above their Warlpiri counterpart in italics. Terms that are specifically 'descending' are in bold face.

Another relevant way in which Warlpiri kin terminology differs from Waanyi is in the use of the same term to refer to both husband and wife (i.e. *kali*), with the special dyadic suffix *-nja* denoting a husband and wife pair.[32] Thus, the Warlpiri spouse term fails to encode either the sex or the generation level contrast between husband and wife. Recall that Waanyi distinguishes wife (*mangkarri*) from husband (*nawi*). As mentioned in the section 'Waanyi Kin Terms', this distinction may well have served as a trigger of sorts for making a distinction between male and female members of one's FM set from which marriage partners are drawn.

The marriage pattern shown in Figures 48 to 50 in which a woman marries up into the set of her FM while a man marries down to a ZSD was reflected in the asymmetrical brother-in-law terms in Waanyi, as shown in Figure 49. Despite the lack of differentiation in the spousal terms, Warlpiri has an identical pattern of brother-in-law terms, distinguishing a descending generation wife's brother *karntiya* from an ascending generation sister's husband *ngumparna* (*kalyakana* in eastern Warlpiri).[33]

Summary

A comparison of Waanyi and Warlpiri FM terms reveals a number of differences in the marking of the male–female distinction in terms relating to members of Ego's FM set, as shown in Table 58. Waanyi marks both sex and seniority distinctions in its affinal terms, but only sex in its non-affinal FM terms. Warlpiri marks seniority in both affinal and non-affinal terms; however, the marking of seniority is restricted to the brother-in-law of man terms in affinal terms. The sex distinction is confined to the brother-in-law/sister-in-law distinction in that a man refers to male siblings of his wife or sister's husband by distinct terms from that used by a woman to refer to the female siblings of her husband or of her brother's wife (i.e. *mantirri*).

---

32   *Kali* is likely to be an old Pama-Nyungan term for 'spouse' or 'father's mother', since cognates are found in languages as geographically distant as Warlpiri, Yolngu (*kali* 'wife' in Yan-nhangu) and the Maric language Kangulu (*kali-njila* 'father's mother' recorded by Sharpe 1967).

33   Both the Warlpiri senior and junior brother-in-law terms are cognate with related terms in non-Pama-Nyungan languages spoken in the southern Gulf of Carpentaria region: *karndiya* 'wife' in Yukulta, containing the Proto-Tangkic root **karndi* 'wife' (see Table 62); *ngumbarna* non-lenited stem of dyadic brother-in-law terms, related to non-dyadic *wumbarna*, in Marra (Heath 1981, pp. 111, 119).

Table 58: Waanyi and Warlpiri affinal and non-affinal terms compared.

	AFFINAL TERMS				NON-AFFINAL TERMS			
	H(B)	W(Z)	Man's ZH	WB	FMB	FM(Z)	ZSS	ZSD
Waanyi	nawi	mangkarri	nabinabi	kayikayi	ngabuji	ngawiji	ngabuji	ngawiji
Warlpiri	kali		ngumparna/ kalyakana	karntiya	yaparla/ngapuju		yapirliyi	

Source: Author's work.

As shown in the comparison of Waanyi and Warlpiri MM terms in Table 59, both languages can mark the ascending/descending generation distinction, but again only Waanyi marks the sex distinction, which is restricted to the ascending generation terms.

Table 59: Waanyi and Warlpiri MM terms compared.

	MMB	MM(Z)	ZDS/D
Waanyi	kuku	kukudi	ngurrali
Warlpiri	jaja		mirntirdi

Source: Author's work.

In the section 'Waanyi Kin Terms', I argued that the pattern of lexically marked distinctions in the Waanyi grandparent/child relationships is not random, but motivated by the system of wife exchange and bestowal. This comparison with the Warlpiri pattern of corresponding affinal and non-affinal terms shows that the pattern of sex-marking found in the Waanyi terms is not a necessary linguistic response to this system of marriage relations. In the next section, I consider the influence of language contact on Waanyi, and the implied social interaction within the Gulf region, which is one of the most linguistically diverse regions in Australia.

Waanyi and Neighbouring Languages

In this section, semantically related kin terms in the language groups neighbouring Waanyi are surveyed to see if the Waanyi lexical pattern is a generalised feature of languages spoken in the southern area of the Gulf of Carpentaria, and also to detect if there are clues as to probable patterns of lexical innovation in Waanyi and their sources. If the Waanyi pattern, as opposed to the Warlpiri pattern, is shared in this area, then the question remains as to the motivation for these asymmetrical patterns of lexical markedness. The existence of these distinctions in Waanyi may be seen as an adaptation to a regional pattern. If so, what motivated this lexical pattern and its spread, and how did it proceed?

Waanyi and Garrwa Compared

The language most closely related to Waanyi is Garrwa, forming a Garrwan group, in which we find a similar pattern to the Waanyi one, as shown in Table 60.[34] Breen (2003) distinguished two varieties of Garrwa: eastern and western. The Garrwa data cited in this section are western Garrwa—taken mainly from Mushin (2012).[35]

Table 60: Waanyi and Garrwa harmonic ascending/descending generation and affinal terms.

		Waanyi	Garrwa[1]	Shared Garrwan
Affinal	H(B)	nawi	nawu/kayikayi	nawi/u
	HZ/BW	?	manjikarra	
	W(Z)	mangkarri	mani/ngabuji	
	mZH	nabinabi	?	
	WB	kayikayi	nganawarra	
Non-affinal	FMB	ngabuji	ngabuji/kangku	
	FM(Z)	ngawiji	ngawuji/ngabuji	ngawiji/ngawuji
	MMB	kuku/kujawuja	kangku	kuku-
	MM(Z)	kukuli/kukudi	kukuli/kukudi	

Source: Author's work.

[1] Bradley (1992) recorded Yanyula *nganawarra* 'brother-in-law' (mZH) and *manjikarra* 'sister-in-law' (wBW). Garrwa *kayikayi* is used only as an address form (Mushin 2012, p. 49). Mushin (2012, p. 48) recorded *ngawuji* as FM only, *ngabuji* as both FM and FMB and also *kangku* as FMB (as well as FF). Breen (n.d.) recorded only *ngawiji* FM in both Waanyi and Garrwa. Breen (n.d.) recorded Garrwa *kukuli* MM and *kukudi* DD. The grandparent/child terms listed by Mushin (2012, p. 48) indicate a terminological system in flux in which the sex distinction has been extended to all ascending terms by extending the use of

---

34   The classification of Garrwan as Pama-Nyungan (see Harvey 2009) or non-Pama-Nyungan (see Blake 1988, 1990; O'Grady, Voegelin & Voegelin 1966) is disputed. O'Grady (1979) placed Proto-Garrwan as a sister to Proto–'nuclear' Pama-Nyungan, while Proto-Tangkic was a sister of Proto-Garrwan-Nuclear Pama-Nyungan. See Evans (2003) for a discussion of this 'offshoot' model of genetic relationships descending from a proto-Australian node.
35   Breen (2003, p. 457) cited both *mani* and *mangkarri* as Waanyi terms for 'wife', and distinguished eastern Garrwa *mangkarri* from western Garrwa *mani*. In Roy Seccin's Waanyi speech, and also from Eric King, I recorded only *mangkarri* 'wife'. Flint, Dymock and Osborne recorded only *mangkarri* 'wife'. Osborne also glossed *mangkarri* as 'spouse' and 'husband'—although he also recorded *nawi* 'husband'.

relational stems—for example, *kangku* FF, FMB and MMB, *kukudi* and *kangku-nya* FFZ, *ngawuji* FM *mimi* MF(B/Z) of man but *bujarra* MFZ of woman. This last term is also MyZ in both Garrwa and Waanyi.

The distinction between husband and wife is lexically marked in both Garrwa and Waanyi: the Garrwa 'husband' term *nawu* is cognate with Waanyi *nawi* 'husband', while the 'wife' terms differ. The Garrwa alternative 'husband' term *kayikayi* denotes WB in Waanyi.[36] Unlike in Waanyi, the Garrwa upper harmonic generation terms do not distinguish between male and female. The female-referring Waanyi FM term *ngawiji* is cognate with Garrwa *ngawuji*. Both Garrwa MM(B/Z) terms *kukudi* and *kukuli* are also recorded in Waanyi by Breen and in the Seccin corpus; only *kukudi* is recorded by Osborne, as are the two other grandparent terms *mimi* MF and *kangku* FF. In Garrwa, the distinction between ascending and descending harmonic kin is marked by adding a 'descending' suffix *-nya* to the corresponding ascending term; thus, *kukudi-nya* or *kukuli-nya* corresponds semantically to Waanyi *ngurrali* in the Seccin corpus.[37] As will be seen in the next section, some of the Waanyi terms that are not found in Garrwa may have had their origins in southern Warluwarric languages bordering Waanyi but not Garrwa territory.

Comparison with Warluwarric Languages[38]

The relationship between the Garrwan and Warluwarric languages is quite intimate in the sense that the Garrwan homeland extends from the northern and southern upstream branches of the Nicholson River in north-western Queensland to west of the Robinson River in the Northern Territory (see Figure 52), and thus separates the northern Warluwarric language Yanyula, spoken in the Borroloola area and on the adjacent Sir Edward Pellew Islands in the southern Gulf of Carpentaria, from the southern Warluwarric languages (see Blake 1990; Brammall 1991; Carew 1993). Waanyi's southern border is defined by the northern border of the Warluwarric languages Yinjirlanji and Wakaya. The documentation of Yinjirlanji is particularly poor.

---

36   In the Seccin corpus, *kayikayi* is also used to refer to husband's junior brother.
37   This suffix is also found in Breen's Waanyi data and both *kukulinya* and *ngawujinya* are recorded by Dymock (1993) as grandchild terms.
38   Breen (2004) referred to this group of languages as *Ngarna* languages, since they all share an innovative first-person singular nominative pronoun *ngarna*. However, this innovation seems to be shared with many western Pama-Nyungan languages that retain it as the first-person enclitic *-rna*. Hence, I have chosen to retain the earlier group name used by O'Grady, Voegelin and Voegelin (1966), drawn from the name of one of the languages of this group.

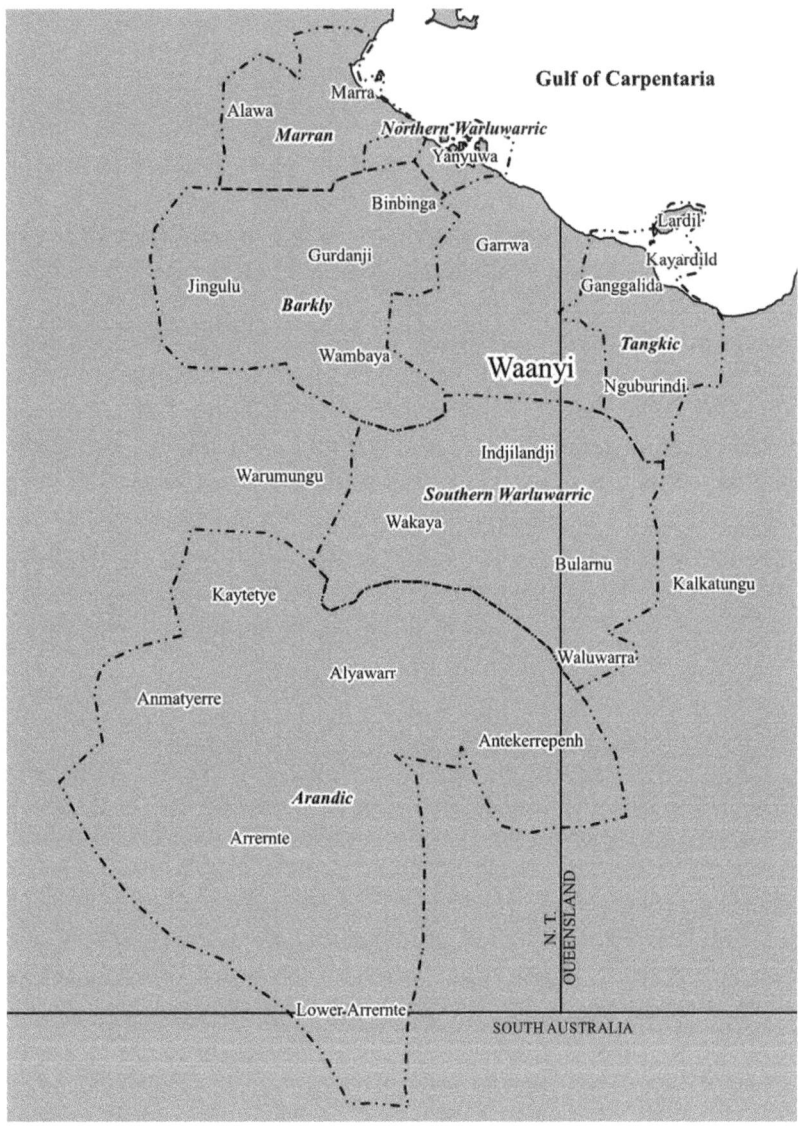

Figure 52: Location of Garrwan languages and their immediate neighbours.
Source: Editors' work.

As shown in Table 61, Waanyi *mangkarri* 'wife' is identical to the reconstructible Proto–southern Warluwarric term for 'wife', corresponding to Yanyula *mangkayi* 'woman's son's child' (ZSS/D), based on the data compiled by Breen (2000a–d). Proto–southern Warluwarric **mangkarri* has undergone well-documented sound changes in daughter languages, such as the loss of the nasal /ng/ in Bularnu and Warluwarra, with the compensatory tensing and devoicing of the following homorganic stop in Warluwarra (Breen 2004), in which this term is glossed as both 'sister-in-law' and 'spouse', as opposed to *ngutjana* 'wife'. It is likely that Waanyi borrowed *mangkarri* from Warluwarric to distinguish 'wife' (ZSD) from 'husband' (FMB).[39] There are gaps in the data on the southern Warluwarric languages because of the conditions under which these languages were recorded. In the northern language Yanyula, there is a clear pattern in both affinal and non-affinal terms in which the sex distinction is not lexicalised in the stems. However, sibling seniority is marked: *-yalanji* 'spouse of senior sibling' and *-miyangki* 'spouse of junior sibling'.[40] While no Yinjirlanji 'wife' term has been recorded, the other southern languages formally distinguish 'wife' from 'husband' in the manner of the neighbouring Garrwan languages.

Table 61: Warluwarric kin terms.

	Northern	Southern			
	Yanyula[1]	Yinji-rlanji	Wakaya	Bularnu	Warluwarra
Affinal					
W(Z)	*-wangu kayikayi*		*mengkarr*	*magarri/ magarradha*	*makarri/ ngutjana*
H	*-yalanji -miyangki*	*yila*	*yili(nhath)*	*nganadha*	*dhawarra*
Non-affinal					
FM(B/Z)	*ngabuji*	*babi*	*jinkirdi* (m) *bubabi* (f)	*Yabara*	*bawa(ra)*
ZSS/D	*mangkayi*				
MM	*kuku* (m) *kukurdi* (f)	*yabi*	*jinkirdi* (m) *yiberi* (f)		*wapa*
ZDS/D	*wukuku*		*jinkirdi* (m) *yiberi* (f) *ngurrarl(tu)*	*gudhaninya*[2]	

Source: Author's work.

[1] While the Yanyula terms *ngabuju* and *mangkayi* mark the ascending/descending distinction in the harmonic generation, their Warlpiri cognates mark this same distinction but in the disharmonic generation. *Ngapuju* denotes the spousal relationship between F and M, or FZ and FFMB; whereas *mangka.n-* denotes the spousal relationship between man's D and his MB, or woman's S and her DSD 'daughter-in-law'.
[2] Bularnu *gudha* in *gudhaninya* is possibly cognate with *kuja* in *kujawuja*.

---

39   In both Waanyi and Garrwa, there is other evidence of lexical borrowing of non-kin words including verbs that correspond with Proto-Warluwarric forms reconstructed by Breen (2004), such as verbs ending in *-nja* (e.g. *karrinja* 'stand', *luwanja* 'spin' and *nanganja* 'get').
40   Mushin (2012, p. 49) cited *miyangi* as WZ/HB in Garrwa; Heath (1981, p. 120) cited Marra *-miyangkay* stem for man's younger brother's wife and woman's husband's elder brother.

Terms for 'husband' in Warluwarric languages vary. Like the Garrwan languages, three of the southern Warluwarric languages have a contrasting male and female spouse term, whereas the northern Warluwarric language Yanyula has a single 'spouse' stem, which is differentiated for male or female by the addition of gender-marking prefixes in the manner of some neighbouring non-Pama-Nyungan languages (Bradley 1992).[41] It is possible that this (Warlpiri-like) pattern in which male spouse is not lexically distinguished from female spouse may have been the original Warluwarric pattern, with the distinct male (as opposed to female) spouse terms being an innovation in each of the southern Warluwarric languages with the adoption of the lexical pattern and perhaps vocabulary from a neighbouring language. If the Yanyula meaning of *mangkayi* as descending member of the FM class is original, then it is not surprising to see *mangkarri* 'wife' in southern languages, given that a wife is drawn from this 'descending' FM set, as shown in Figure 46. The 'spouse' term that may derive from Proto-Warluwarric, due to its presence in both northern and southern languages, is **yala ~ *yila*, with reflexes *-yala(nji)*, *yila* and *yili*.

The resemblance between the Waanyi descending MM set term *ngurrali*, shown in Figure 48 and discussed in the section 'Waanyi Kin Terms', and the Wakaya *ngurrarl* in Table 61 is obvious.[42] Thus, Warluwarric languages appear to provide the source for at least two of the Waanyi terms under discussion: *mangkarri* (W) and *ngurrali* (ZDS/D).

It is not possible to reconstruct a Proto-Warluwarric FM term. The form **babi* that McConvell (2008, p. 323) proposed as the Proto-Pama-Nyungan FM term is found in two members of the southern Warluwarric branch: Yinjirlanji and Wakaya.[43] Given its widespread distribution in languages to the immediate east and south of the area under consideration, including in the Tangkic languages (to be discussed in the subsection 'Tangkic Languages'), its presence may be due to borrowing. In Wakaya, the only Warluwarric language for which distinct FM(Z) and FMB terms have been recorded, it is the term containing *babi* (*bubabi*) that designates the female member of the set. The northern Warluwarric language Yanyula has an FM term that matches the Waanyi male FMB form

---

41 Wakaya marks gender distinctions by suffixation.
42 Words ending in a lateral or rhotic consonant borrowed into Waanyi are typically augmented by final vowel /i/.
43 Following Carew (1993), Breen (2004, p. 226) grouped Yinjirlanji and Wakaya in the Ngarru branch of southern Ngarna (our Warluwarric), as opposed to Bularnu and Warluwarra.

ngabuji—a term not found in other Warluwarric languages. In Yanyula, unlike Waanyi, this form does not encode the sex of referent. It is unlikely that Yanyula borrowed this word from Waanyi or vice versa, given that these languages are not immediate neighbours, being separated by Garrwa. Either language could have borrowed this word from another source, such as a Barkly language (to be discussed in the subsection 'Barkly Languages and Other Non-Pama-Nyungan Neighbours').

Interestingly, the MM term cannot be reconstructed in either southern or Proto-Warluwarric. There is only evidence of a distinct descending generation term in Wakaya. A southern Warluwarric term **yVbVrV* may be the source of the Wakaya *yiberi* MM, as well as the Bularnu *yabara* FM, and may be related to Yinjirlanji *yabi*. The Warluwarra and Bularnu terms for the MM relationship appear to be distinct innovations, as are the Yanyula terms that are identical in form and meaning to the corresponding Waanyi terms (i.e. *kuku* MMB and *kukurdi* MM[Z]). Yanyula also has a distinctive, but related, descending generation term *wukuku* that follows a pattern of word formation that is quite common in north-west Queensland and southern Gulf languages, whereby the final CV of a kinterm is reduplicated to derive a related term, such as a grandchild term from a grandparent form or a special vocative or nominative form—for example, Kalkutungu FM *papi* > *papipi*, MM *muju* > *mujuju*, MF *jaji* > *jajiji* and FF *ngaja* > *ngajaji* (Blake 1979, pp. 81–2). Given that the Proto-Warluwarric word initial /k/, continued as such in southern languages, corresponds with /w/ in Yanyula (Brammall 1991; Carew 1993), it seems likely that this 'descending' form *wukuku* derives from an earlier **kukuku* form. The 'ascending' /k/ initial forms *kuku* and *kukurdi* must be later innovations in Yanyula from a non-Warluwarric source. This source may be a Garrwan language, since one finds Garrwa *kukuku* glossed as a dyadic MM term: '"MM and DS/D" (a maternal grandmother and her grandchild)' (Mushin 2012), in addition to *kukudi* and *kukuli*; however, other languages in contact with Yanyula are also possible sources.[44]

---

44 Other examples of this pattern of partial reduplication in Garrwan languages are G. *bababa-nya* 'younger B/Z' (cf. *baba* 'elder B/Z') and W. *kabubu* 'junior MB'.

Tangkic Languages

The Tangkic languages spoken to the north and east of Waanyi (and Garrwa) also distinguish wife from husband, as shown in Table 62. Unlike the Warluwarric languages that are classified as Pama-Nyungan, the Tangkic languages are classified as non-Pama-Nyungan, although they have many Pama-Nyungan features (Evans 1995).

Although 'wife' in all three languages can be derived from a common Tangkic source, as shown in Table 62, 'husband' cannot, since the Lardil *yukarr* differs from the form common to the southern Tangkic Yukulta and Kayardild (Evans 1995, p. 12).[45] The Tangkic ascending FM term **babi*, whose reflexes in two southern Warluwarric languages were discussed in the section 'Comparison with Warluwarric Languages', differs from the descending (ZSS/D) terms. However, all three Tangkic languages show the same form-meaning pattern, apart from the lack of sex distinction in Lardil in the descending MM term *manyin,* akin to the Waanyi and Warlpiri pattern. Unlike Waanyi, but like Garrwa and Yanyula, all members of Ego's ascending FM group are referred to by a single term that does not distinguish male from female members. Again, unlike Waanyi, the distinction between ascending and descending generation FM kin *is* marked, without encoding a sex distinction. As mentioned in the previous section, two southern Warluwarric languages have reflexes of Tangkic **babi* as their FM form.[46] This form differs from the Garrwan FM *ngawiji*, but is widespread in Pama-Nyungan languages, including those of the Kalkutungu (Blake 1979) and Maric groups (Alpher 2014) spoken to the south-east in Paman and Wik languages (Hale 1976a–c).[47] The ascending MM term is also distinct from the descending MM terms in all three of these Tangkic languages, although the descending form in the southern languages is distinct from the northern Lardil form. As previously noted, while the southern languages distinguish the sex of the descending MM class members by unrelated forms, this distinction is not made in Lardil.

---

45 Tangkic **karndi* may be cognate with Warlpiri *karnta* 'woman'; certainly, the Yukulta nominative form *karndiya* with the case-marking suffix *-ya* has been borrowed unanalysed into Warlpiri as 'wife's brother' or as a term designating either a girl or boyfriend.

46 The absence of *babi* as a grandparent/child term in either of the non-Pama-Nyungan Marra-Alawa or Barkly languages closest to the Garrwan and Tangkic-speaking areas suggests the presence of a lexical boundary in this area, marked by the presence or absence of a reflex of **babi* as the FM term, which does not align with the Pama-Nyungan/non-Pama-Nyungan boundary.

47 Hale (1976a, 1976b) seemed to have mistakenly reconstructed Paman **papi* as MF, although the supporting language forms are glossed FM (Alpher, pers. comm. July 2014).

Table 62: Tangkic affinal and harmonic FM and MM terms.

	AFFINAL		NON-AFFINAL				
	H	W	FM	ZSS/D	MM	ZDS	ZDD
Yukulta	dirrkurli	karndi-ya	babiju	ngarrmanda(thu)	ngarriju	malunginta	kirrkunku
Kayardild	dirrkuli; dunda H(B), WB	karndi W(Z/B), HZ	babiju karndi	-ngarrmanda	ngarriju	malunginta	kirrkunku
Lardil	yukarr	kernde	babe	Nginngin	nyerre	manyin	
Tangkic		*karndi	*babi-	*ngarr-	*nyarri		

Source: Author's work.

A comparison of the Tangkic forms with Waanyi forms in Table 62 reveals no formal resemblance between them, and hence there is no evidence of either common descent or borrowing of these kin terms between these language groups, despite other evidence of borrowing between Waanyi and Yukulta that goes beyond the scope of this study. However, the lexical patterns of these languages converge with respect to which semantic distinctions are formally marked.

The fact that southern Warluwarric *mangkarri* and Tangkic *karndi-* W(Z) also have reflexes as affinal terms in the geographically distant Warlpiri language suggests that they may descend from terms that did not specify gender but rather the junior or descending spousal relationship ZSS/D, as with Yanyula *mangkayi*, which would apply to wife and wife's siblings. The use of Kayardild *karndi* as a general FM set term also points to the fact that a potential wife is drawn from this set. The variation in 'husband' terms within both the southern Warluwarric and Tangkic languages suggests independent innovations of specific 'husband' terms—either by narrowing the meaning of an original 'spouse' term or the introduction of a male-referring term.

Barkly Languages and Other Non-Pama-Nyungan Neighbours

The Barkly languages form a group of non-Pama-Nyungan languages spoken to the immediate west and south of the Garrwan group (see Harvey 2008). These languages have a gender-marking system marked by suffixation on nouns, which serves to distinguish male and female members of a relational set. In Table 63, data from two of the better documented of these languages are presented. The Wambaya data are from Nordlinger (1998) and the Jingulu data from Pensalfini (2011). Wambaya was spoken in an area to the immediate west of Waanyi country, whereas Jingulu was spoken further west, separated from Wambaya by another Barkly language, Ngarnka.

Table 63: Spousal terms in two Barkly languages.

	Wambaya	Jingulu
Affinal		
H	*gari* (H, ZH)	*ngambiya*
W	*gari-nya* (W, HZ) *munggujbili-nya*	*ngambiyi-rni* *kabi-rni* *nayu-rni*
Non-Affinal		
FM(B/Z)	*ngabuji* (m) *ngayiji-nya* (f)	*ngabuja* (m) *ngabuji-rni* (f)
ZSS/D	*ngaji-mi-ji* (m) *ngaji-mi-nya* (f)	
MM(B/Z)	*gugu* (m) *gugu-nya* (f) *gugu-rda* (f)	*kuka* (m) *kuku-rni* (f)
ZDS/D	*gugu-mi-ji* (m) *gugu-mi-nya* (f)	*kaminjarra* (m) *kaminjirri-rni* (f) ZDS/D & BDS/D

Source: Author's work.

[1] Based on Pensalfini (2011), the distinction between the ascending and descending MM relation in Jingulu is marked by distinct stems, as opposed to the FM relation in which this distinction is not lexicalised. However, the descending term applies to both the descending FM and MF relations.

As the data in Table 63 show, the stem of the female term is mostly, but not in all cases, the same as that of the male term. For example, in both languages, husband is formally distinguished from wife by means of gender suffixes on a common stem—*gari* in Wambaya and *ngambiyV* in Jingulu—which marks the affinal relationship between spouses and their siblings, such that Wambaya *gari-nya* denotes any female member in the scope of this relationship (e.g. W, WZ and HZ), while the unaffixed term denotes any male member (i.e. H, HB or ZH). As in Waanyi and Garrwa, these Barkly languages formally distinguish male from female spouse and their siblings, but they do so by means of gender marking rather than distinct stems.[48] However, the presence in Jingulu of 'wife' terms *kabi-rni* and *nayu-rni* bearing the feminine *-rni* suffix without an attested use of their stem in a corresponding 'husband' term raises the possibility that these stems derive from historic 'spouse' or non-affinal FM terms. This seems especially likely in the case of *nayu*, which bears a close phonological resemblance to the Garrwan 'husband' term **nawi/u* (see Table 60).

Like Waanyi and Garrwa, these Barkly languages also distinguish the affinal 'spousal' terms from the non-affinal FM and ZSS/D terms that between them designate the superset (or subsection) of which a spouse is a member. While the more westerly Jingulu does not formally distinguish ascending from descending FM kin, Wambaya does by augmenting the stem by the suffix *-mi* to which the gender suffix is attached. The Wambaya ascending FM terms not only distinguish male from female members by means of gender affixation, but also have distinct (if cognate) stems. The male form is identical to the Waanyi FMB and Yanyula FMB/Z term *ngabuji*, while the FM(Z) stem *ngayiji* is almost identical to the Waanyi and Garrwa *ngawiji*.[49] It is not possible to know at what stage this word entered Wambaya—it might have entered the language from Garrwan as *ngawiji*, undergoing just the change from /w/ to /y/. If we were to reconstruct the ultimate ancestor of this word, it would be in the form **ngabu-ju* in a language in which the final syllable functioned as a suffix (see McConvell 2008 for a discussion of kin suffixes including *-ju ~ -thu* in Australian languages). The fact that the various cognate forms that occur in Garrwan and Barkly languages, as well as in Yanyula, have analysed the original suffix as part of the stem, suggests that these terms were borrowed into these languages—although, in two stages. We argued in the section 'Waanyi Kin Terms' that the lenited form (with medial /w/) in Garrwan languages must predate the entry of the non-lenited *ngabuji* form. However, in the case of Wambaya, it is more likely that the lenited form entered this language from a Garrwan language in order to mark the male/female distinction with distinct stems (in addition to the feminine suffix), given its absence from Jingulu. Unlike in the Garrwan languages, there is no evidence in Wambaya for historical lenition of intervocalic stops to glides.

---

48 The Warluwarric languages, Wakaya and Yanyula, also have formal gender systems including a masculine/feminine contrast.
49 The correspondence between Garrwan *w* and Barkly *y* is observed in both the spouse term (*nawi/u* versus *nayu*) and the Wambaya FM(Z) term (*ngawiji* versus *ngayiji*).

The other interesting difference between Wambaya and Jingulu is that the former encodes the ascending/descending contrast in the FM set with distinct stems in addition to a 'descending' suffix -*mi*-, while this distinction is unmarked in Jingulu. While the Wambaya affinal 'spousal' terms are unrelated formally to the FM-ZSS/D terms, the two sets of corresponding Jingulu terms may be related; however, showing this to be, or not be, the case takes us beyond the scope of this chapter.

Turning now to the Barkly MM-ZDS/D terms, we find the same stem as in the corresponding Garrwan and Yanyula terms—namely, *kuku*.[50] The distinction between male and female terms is marked by affixation, as is the ascending/descending contrast in Wambaya only. We recall that the distinction between male and female MM class members in both Waanyi and Yanyula is marked by a suffix—written -*rdi* in Yanyula and -*di* in Waanyi (whereby there is no contrast between alveolar and retroflex stops). However, this suffix is not active in either language.[51] The female form *kuku(r)di* has been borrowed into these languages as an unanalysed form contrasting with the root form *kuku*. Nordlinger (1998, p. 69) documented alternative feminine suffixes, -*nya* or -*rda*, on three of the Wambaya grandparent terms, including FM and MM terms.[52] We might speculate that both Waanyi and Yanyula incorporated their contrasting MM forms from a Barkly language closely related to Wambaya, in which the female affix was -*rdi*, rather than -*rda*.[53]

It is also possible that Yanyula borrowed the contrasting *kuku* and *kuku(r)di* from a non-Pama-Nyungan source, given its absence from the southern Warluwarric languages. This said, the presence of *wukuku* in Yanyula (see Table 61), with the descending generation MM meaning, suggests pre-Yanyula **kuku* MM, unless it can be shown that *wukuku* has been borrowed into Yanyula. An alternative source of the -(*r*)*di* suffix is from neighbouring Marra, which affixes -*rdi* (~-*ri*) to certain kin stems,

---

50 The use of 'g' in the Wambaya orthography does not indicate a different sound, since there is no voicing contrast in these languages; therefore, the Wambaya 'g' corresponds to Jingulu 'k' (also the symbol used in the writing conventions of the other languages under consideration).
51 The suffix -*rdi* is found on kin terms over a wide area without having a female or feminine-marking function (McConvell 2008; Nash 1992). It seems to contrast with other sets of original kin suffixes such as -*ju*/-*thu*, seen on the Tangkic MM and FM terms in Table 62.
52 These variants were also recorded for the term for mother's sister.
53 Other Barkly languages such as Kurdanji and Binbinka were spoken in the area to the north of Wambaya, bordering on Yanyula and Garrwa countries. The documentation of these languages is too fragmentary to allow us to know if -*rdi* marked feminine in either of these languages. Nordlinger (1998, p. 68) noted that Wambaya -*rdi* is the non-absolutive suffix form on kin terms referring to males—for example, *gari* 'husband' (absolutive) and *gari-rdi* 'husband' (non-absolutive).

including some harmonic terms to signal a first-person propositus reading (e.g. *muri-rdi* 'my FF(B)/BSS'), while the prefix *n-* marks feminine gender. However, while *gugu* is the MM(B/Z) stem in Marra vocative forms, alternating with *kaka,* Heath (1981, pp. 115–17) did not record it bearing the *-rdi* suffix in its first-person propositus form. Neither a Barkly language (on the basis of our limited data) nor a Marra origin accounts for the presence of *kukurdi* in Yanyula and Waanyi as the marked feminine term contrasting with *kuku*. Alawa and Marra affinal and non-affinal harmonic roots are listed in Table 64.[54]

Table 64: Marra and Alawa harmonic generation roots.[55]

	AFFINAL		NON-AFFINAL			
	H/W	WB/ZH	FM	MF	MM	FF
Marra	mimay/maygurla	wumbarna (senior) mimi (junior)	mimi	bija(ja)	kuku/kaka kangkurl (ZDS/D)	muri
Alawa	mimay	kaykay	jabjab, kardikardi (FM/MF)		kuku(ku) wujarra (ZDS/D)	kangku muri (BSS/D)

Source: Author's work.

While Marra, like the Garrwan and other languages surveyed herein, distinguishes FM from MF, Alawa does not. However, *mimi*, which is both FM and WjB in Marra, denotes MF in Garrwan languages, whereby it also applies to FZS/D and MBS cross-cousins. The Marra distinction between *mimi* FM and *bija* MF may reflect an innovation from a system such as the Alawa one that does not mark this distinction. This innovation may have been motivated by a change in marriage patterns in which this distinction was salient. In a first cross-cousin marriage in which a mother-in-law and father-in-law are drawn from the sets containing ego's FZ and MB respectively, the spouse is from the set that contains both MF and FM, as in a four-section system, and equivalence between a 'spouse' and 'cross-cousin' term is to be expected. However, the equivalence between the

---

54 *Kuku* as a MM term is not limited to non-PN languages; it is also attested in PN languages including those in the Maric group (see Breen 1973 for Bidyara-Gungubula descending generation examples: *gugunyundila* DD and *gugundyila* DS). It is also possible that the *kuku* root in Warlpiri *kukurnu* 'junior B' is cognate with *kuku* 'MM/DD/S' in the languages discussed herein.

55 Both languages have additional terms that denote the kin classes in Table 63, which sets out a simplified list privileging terms cognate with those found in Garrwan languages. Heath's (1981, pp. 96–129) documentation of Marra kin terms and associated morphology showed considerable complexity with stems varying as a function of the value of the propositus suffix and the discourse use. For ease of comparison, I have transcribed 'g' in cited sources by 'k'.

Marra *mimi* FM and WB, as distinct from *bija* MF, reflects a second cross-cousin marriage, as in the vocabulary of the other languages considered.[56] Traces of a transition from one type of marriage to another is also seen in the use of *mimay* as the H/W term in both Marra and Alawa, whereas *mimayi* applies to a spouse's MB, which includes a woman's son-in-law in Waanyi. The change in the system of wife bestowal can be modelled as the move from the direct bestowal of a man's daughter as spouse of his sister's son to an indirect exchange between cross-cousins of sister's daughters as mother-in-law, as previously discussed. Within such a marriage system, the role of MM(B) plays a crucial role, which motivates the linguistic expression of the socially relevant distinction between MM(B/Z) and other grandparent relations and may account for the spread of a distinct MM term such as *kuku*, which has crossed a number of genetic linguistic boundaries in the Gulf area. The association of *kangku/kangkurl* with both MM and FF also points to a previous 'section-like' system in which these relational categories were subsumed into a single class. *Mimayi* is not the only term that denotes a harmonic generation relation in Alawa, but a disharmonic one in Garrwan. The Alawa MF/FM term *kardikardi* has the same form as the Garrwan ZS/D term written *kadikadi*.[57] Conversely, the disharmonic Alawa *ngabuji* HF has the same form as the harmonic Garrwan FM.

Conclusions

Explored herein are the possible motivations and sources for the rather irregular or anomalous pattern of marking of sex distinctions and generation levels in Waanyi harmonic ascending/descending kin terms. I have argued that these lexical contrasts are not random but reflect key social distinctions at the core of the system of affinal kin relationships and the way in which these affinal relationships intersect with the classificatory non-affinal kinship terminology. While the distinctions encoded in the kin terms discussed correspond to very salient distinctions in terms of traditional marriage alliances and wife-bestowal practices, a comparison with a more western Pama-Nyungan language, namely Warlpiri, shows

---

56   Marra *bija* MF may be cognate with the initial two syllables in Waanyi *bujarra* MBD 'cousin-mother' (Trigger 1982, p. 24), as well as F/MjZ (Seccin corpus) contrasting with *mimi* FZS/D and *maka(ngu)* MBS/D. Mushin (2012, p. 48) recorded *bujarra* as MFZ, MjZ and FjBW.
57   Heath (1981, p. 117) recorded disharmonic *gardigardi* 'mother's senior sister' alternating with stem *-jamul*.

that the Waanyi lexical pattern that formally distinguished the sex of members of the FM and MM classes cannot be solely attributed to these features of social organisation. However, the existence of a marked term for descending members of the MM class in both Waanyi (*ngurrali*) and Warlpiri (*mirntirdi*) would indicate that this distinction is in fact more salient than the sex distinction. This generational distinction in MM class terms is also found in other Gulf languages, including the Tangkic, (some) Warluwarric and Barkly languages, as well as in Marra and Alawa.

The question was then raised as to whether the existence, in Waanyi, of spousal terms that distinguish both generation level and sex might not trigger, or at least reinforce, the marking of sex distinctions in FM non-affinal terms—that is, *ngabuji* male member of FM class and *ngawiji* female member of FM class. Recall *nawi* 'husband' = male member of FM class in upper harmonic generation to spouse, while *mangkarri* 'wife' = female member of FM class in lower harmonic generation to spouse. In comparing Waanyi and Garrwa, we also noted the distinct ways in which generation level is marked in these languages. While in Waanyi, the lexical marking of the ascending/descending contrast in harmonic generation terms is limited to the MM class (abstracting away from the use of *murimuri* as a more general descending generation term), Garrwa employs the suffix *-nya* to mark descending generation terms, as part of a more general distinction between senior and junior members of a related pair. There is also evidence that this suffix also operated in Waanyi.

Casting the net more widely, it was found that languages of four distinct groups—Garrwan, Warluwarric, Tangkic and Barkly—share a lexical pattern that involves a formal distinction between affinal spousal terms and non-affinal FM terms, as well as a distinction between male and female spousal terms. However, the marking of a male/female distinction in non-affinal terms is less common in those languages lacking formal gender-marking affixation. In Tangkic languages, while the ascending/descending contrast is marked in both FM and MM classes, the sex distinction is marked on the descending MM terms only in the southern Tangkic languages Kayardild and Yukulta that are spoken in close proximity to the Garrwan languages (see Table 62).

What is quite striking in comparing Tangkic and Garrwan non-affinal terms is the lack of cognate terms for the relationships under discussion, despite their geographical adjacency. However, at least two Garrwan affinal terms are cognate with Tangkic ones: Waanyi senior brother-in-law term *nabinabi* 'ZH' is identical to the Yukulta junior brother-in-law WB term (and the Yanyula ZB term); and Waanyi affinal 'father-in-law' term *kadu-nganja* equates with the Tangkic **kardu* ZS/D as a non-affinal term, and as 'father-in-law' when used as an affinal term. Recall that a father-in-law is drawn from the superset containing one's sister's children. A comparison of Warluwarric and Garrwan terms indicates a greater number of Warluwarric terms shared with Waanyi than with Garrwa. These Waanyi terms of probable Warluwarric origin reinforced, if they did not initiate, the expression of the sex distinction in the spousal terms—*mangkarri* 'wife' contrasting with the inherited Garrwan spousal term *nawi*/*u* 'husband'. Borrowing allowed the marking of the ascending/descending contrast in the MM set: *kuku*/*kukudi* versus *ngurrali* (< Wakaya *ngurrarl*) in the Seccin corpus. It was also noticed that FM terms in two southern Warluwarric languages appear to be cognate with the Tangkic term **babi*—further indications of possible contact induced borrowing between members of these language groups. Conversely, the shared Barkly and Garrwan FM and MM terms are quite distinct from either the Tangkic or southern Warluwarric ones. The Yanyula FM and MM terms, which are quite distinct from those in the southern Warluwarric languages, possibly resulted from borrowing from their non-Pama-Nyungan neighbours, following the separation of the northern and southern Warluwarric languages. However, the presence of the descending MM term *wukuku* with a lenited initial consonant suggests the possibility that a pre-Yanyula MM term **kuku* was shared with the Barkly, Garrwan and other non-Pama-Nyungan languages. This scenario raises the possibility that the southern Warluwarric languages replaced *kuku* with terms that were borrowed from other languages or through extending the meaning of items from their own lexicons, which would account for the diversity of MM terms in these languages. A similar scenario might also explain the distribution of FM terms in southern Warluwarric languages, which distinguishes Yinjirlanji and Wakaya from Bularnu and Warluwarra.

The Barkly languages are typologically quite distinct from the Garrwan and Tangkic languages in terms of having a highly transparent and morphologically active system of gender marking. Thus, contrasting masculine and feminine kin word forms with shared roots is used to express the sex distinction, as seen most clearly in the Jingulu data (Table 63). This contrasts with the use of distinct male- and female-referring lexical roots in the other languages. However, Wambaya, spoken in the immediate vicinity of Waanyi, marks the sex contrast for FM ascending kin by distinct lexical roots that are almost identical with the Waanyi forms, as well as the addition of the feminine suffix to the female-referring stem. Like the Tangkic languages (Table 62), Wambaya, but not Jingulu, also marks the ascending/descending FM generation contrast with distinct stems, as well as with a special descending generation suffix *-mi* to which the gender suffix is attached. However, Jingulu does not mark the generational contrast. Recall that western Garrwa, and some dialects of Waanyi, also mark the descending generation with a suffix *-nya*.

The pattern that emerges is the marking of both sex and generation level distinctions in FM and MM class terms as a shared feature of the languages of the southern Gulf of Carpentaria region; further, more lexically marked distinctions are made towards the eastern end of this region, especially in the southern Tangkic languages. Waanyi has borrowed terms from neighbouring southern Warluwarric languages in order to encode distinctions that were probably not made in Proto-Garrwan. These include *mangkarri* 'W(Z)' and *ngurrali* 'ZDS/D', as well as incorporating, along with Yanyula, a female MM form *kukudi*, possibly derived from a neighbouring non-Pama-Nyungan language, as opposed to the unmarked *kuku* MMB. Although Barkly languages formally distinguish all male from female kin because of their gender-marking system, it is all the more notable that the marking of the sex contrast is confined in Waanyi to the MM and FM classes and not to the other 'grandparent' classes, despite the similarity of stem forms for the FF form *kangku* across Barkly, Garrwan and Tangkic languages.[58]

It is also notable that Waanyi and Garrwa share their FM and MM terms with the Barkly languages and Yanyula, rather than with southern Warluwarric or Tangkic languages. While Tangkic and some southern Warluwarric appear to share cognates of the FM term < *babi, there are no shared grandparent terms between Garrwan and Tangkic languages, despite the fact that these languages share a border on the eastern side of the Garrwan group. This suggests that the Garrwan-speaking peoples may have origins originally extending to the south and west of the area they occupied at European contact, rather than to the north-east of this area.

---

58 The Garrwan MF term *mimi* is shared with the Warluwarric languages, but not with the Barkly or Tangkic languages. However, it is found in Marra as both a non-affinal FM term (Heath 1981, pp. 118–19) and the affinal brother-in-law term.

Finally, the 'anomalies' in the Waanyi terms for ascending and descending harmonic generation terms reflect a shared system of marriage alliance and wife bestowal in a context of social and linguistic interaction between the peoples of the southern Gulf of Carpentaria region, leading to the 'adjustments' in kin terminologies seen in the Waanyi examples discussed. This contact was marked by multilingualism, as well as shared ceremonies and wife exchange across language groups. A more extensive comparison of kin terminologies across these languages, and a closer study of linguistic changes, both semantic and phonological, within groups, might permit the establishment of a relative time line to the borrowing and a surer evidenced directionality of the borrowing that has taken place since these language groups have been in such close contact.[59] A brief comparison with the lexicalisation pattern in affinal and non-affinal harmonic generation terms in the Marra and Alawa languages that are not spoken in immediate contact with the Garrwan-speaking area has led to the speculation that the lexical anomalies found in Waanyi and neighbouring languages reflect the change from a first cross-cousin marriage to a second cross-cousin marriage system involving mother-in-law exchange, in which the FM and MF classes have distinct roles. In FM and MM classes, Ego's parents' maternal parents have the complementary roles of wife receiver (FM) and wife bestower (MM), while within the MM class the distinction between wife bestower (MM[B]) and bestowed (ZDD) is also lexically marked.

References

Alpher, B 2014, *Proto-Pama-Nyungan etyma list*, Microsoft Word document file, accessed 6 August 2014.

Blake, B 1979, *A Kalkatungu grammar*, Pacific Linguistics B-5, Canberra: The Australian National University.

Blake, B 1988, 'Redefining Pama-Nyungan: towards the prehistory of Australian languages', in N Evans & S Johnson (eds), *Aboriginal Linguistics I*, Armidale, NSW: University of New England, pp. 1–90.

---

59 Another aspect of the kin terminologies within these languages is the lexical marking of the senior/junior sibling relationship not only in the set of Ego's siblings, which is almost universal in Australian languages, but also in Ego's F and M sets. Again, this seems to be a phenomenon with its origins in the east, so that marking these distinctions in Garrwan languages has also involved borrowing kin terms from neighbouring languages, including Warluwarric.

Blake, B 1990, 'Languages of the Queensland/Northern territory border: updating the classification', in P Austin, RMW Dixon, T Dutton & I White (eds), *Language and history: essays in honour of Luise A. Hercus*, Pacific Linguistics C-116, Canberra: The Australian National University, pp. 49–66.

Bradley, J 1992, *Yanyuwa wuka: language from Yanyuwa country. Ms 240p*, St Lucia, Qld: The University of Queensland.

Brammall, D 1991, A comparative grammar of Warluwaric, BA (honours) thesis in linguistics, The Australian National University.

Breen, GJ n.d., Unpublished Waanyi field notes shared with Laughren.

Breen, GJ 1973, *Bidyara and Gungabula: grammar and vocabulary*, Linguistic communications 8, Melbourne: Monash University.

Breen, GJ 2000a, *Grammar and dictionary of Bularnu*, Alice Springs, NT: Ms. Institute for Aboriginal development.

Breen, GJ 2000b, *Grammar and dictionary of Warluwarra*, Alice Springs, NT: Ms. Institute for Aboriginal development.

Breen, GJ 2000c, *Grammar and dictionary of Wakaya*, Alice Springs, NT: Ms. Institute for Aboriginal development.

Breen, GJ 2000d, *Injilanji vocabulary and grammar notes*, Alice Springs, NT: Ms. Institute for Aboriginal development.

Breen, GJ 2003, 'Wanyi and Garrwa comparative data', in N Evans (ed.), *The non-Pama-Nyungan languages of northern Australia: comparative studies of the continent's most linguistically complex region*, Pacific linguistics 552 / Studies in language change, Canberra: The Australian National University, pp. 425–62.

Breen, GJ 2004, 'Evolution of the verb conjugations in the Ngarna languages', in C Bowern & H Koch (eds), *Australian languages: classification and the comparative method*, Amsterdam: John Benjamins, pp. 223–240. doi.org/10.1075/cilt.249.14bre.

Carew, M 1993, Proto-Warluwarric phonology, BA (honours) thesis in linguistics, University of Melbourne.

Dymock, J 1993, 'Something deep and rich: Indigenous and post contact environment and heritage materials relevant to the Lawn Hill/Riversleigh district of Queensland', *Report prepared for Department of Environment and Heritage Queensland*, August 1993.

Evans, N 1995, *A grammar of Kayardild*, New York: Mouton de Gruyter. doi.org/10.1515/9783110873733.

Evans, N 2003, 'Introduction: comparative non-Pama-Nyungan and Australian historical linguistics', in N Evans (ed.), *The non-Pama-Nyungan languages of northern Australia: comparative studies of the continent's most linguistically complex region*, Pacific linguistics 552 / Studies in language change, Canberra: The Australian National University, pp. 3–25.

Flint, E 1964, Audio recordings of Waanyi language made at Doomadgee Qld as part of the Queensland Speech Survey of Aboriginal English. Canberra: Australian Institute of Aboriginal and Torres Strait Islander Studies (Audio collection: QSS_01, Accession No. 005928–006071).

Hale, K 1976a, 'Phonological developments in particular northern Paman languages', in P Sutton (ed.), *Languages of Cape York*, Canberra: Australian Institute of Aboriginal Studies, pp. 7–40.

Hale, K 1976b, 'Phonological developments in a northern Paman language: *Uradhi*', in P Sutton (ed.), *Languages of Cape York*, Canberra: Australian Institute of Aboriginal Studies, pp. 41–9.

Hale, K 1976c, '*Wik* reflections of Middle Paman phonology', in P Sutton (ed.), *Languages of Cape York*, Canberra: Australian Institute of Aboriginal Studies, pp. 50–60.

Harvey, M 2008, *Proto Mirndi: a discontinuous language family in northern Australia*, Pacific linguistics 593, Canberra: The Australian National University.

Harvey, M 2009, 'The genetic status of Garrwan', *Australian Journal of Linguistics*, 29(2), pp. 195–244. doi.org/10.1080/07268600902823102.

Heath, J 1981, *Basic materials in Mara: grammar, texts and dictionary*, Pacific linguistics C-60, Canberra: The Australian National University.

Keen, S 1983, 'Yukulta', in RMW Dixon & BJ Blake (eds), *Handbook of Australian languages*, vol. 3, Canberra: The Australian National University, pp. 191–226.

Laughren, M 1982, 'Warlpiri kinship structure', in J Heath, F Merlan & A Rumsey (eds), *Languages of kinship in Aboriginal Australia*, Oceania linguistic monographs no. 24, Sydney: University of Sydney, pp. 72–85.

Laughren, M 2001, 'What Warlpiri "avoidance" registers do with grammar', in J Simpson, D Nash, M Laughren, P Austin & B Alpher (eds), *Forty years on: Ken Hale and Australian languages*, Pacific linguistics 512, Canberra: The Australian National University, pp. 199–225.

McConvell, P 2008, 'Grand-daddy morphs: the importance of suffixes in reconstructing Pama-Nyungan kinship', in C Bowern, B Evans & L Miceli (eds), *Morphology and language history: in honour of Harold Koch*, Current issues in linguistic theory 298, Amsterdam/Philadelphia: John Benjamins, pp. 313–27. doi.org/10.1075/cilt.298.27mcc.

McConvell, P & Laughren, M 2004, 'The Ngumpin-Yapa subgroup', in C Bowern & H Koch (eds), *Australian languages: classification and the comparative method*, Amsterdam: John Benjamins, pp. 151–77. doi.org/10.1075/cilt.249.11mcc.

Mushin, I 2012, *A grammar of (western) Garrwa*, Pacific linguistics 637, Berlin: Walter de Gruyter Mouton. doi.org/10.1515/9781614512417.

Nancarrow, C et al. (comp.) 2014, *Ganggalida dictionary and thesaurus: a vocabulary of the Yugulda language of the Ganggalida people, north-west Queensland*, Cairns, Qld: Gangalidda and Garawa Native Title Aboriginal Corporation, c/o the Carpentaria Land Council.

Nash, D 1992, 'An Australian kinship affix *-rti*', in N Evans & C Goddard (eds), Memorial volume for Steve Johnson, *Australian Journal of Linguistics*, 12(1), pp. 123–44. doi.org/10.1080/07268609208599473.

Nordlinger, R 1998, *A grammar of Wambaya, Northern Territory (Australia)*, Pacific linguistics C-140, Canberra: The Australian National University.

O'Grady, G 1979, 'Preliminaries to a proto Nuclear Pama-Nyungan stem list', in SA Wurm (ed.), *Australian linguistic studies*, Pacific Linguistics Series C-54, Canberra: The Australian National University, pp. 107–39.

O'Grady, G, Voegelin, C & Voegelin, F 1966, 'Languages of the world: Indo-Pacific fascicle six', *Anthropological Linguistics, 8*(2), pp. 1–197.

Osborne, C 1966, *A tentative description of the Wanyi language. Ms. 58p*, Canberra: Australian Institute of Aboriginal and Torres Strait Islander Studies (Manuscript collection: PMS1360).

Pensalfini, R 2011, *Jingulu texts and dictionary*, Pacific linguistics 536, Canberra: The Australian National University.

Scheffler, H 1978, *Australian kin classification*, Cambridge: Cambridge University Press. doi.org/10.1017/CBO9780511557590.

Sharpe, M 1967, *Language elicitation and discussion from Woorabinda, Qld*, Canberra: Australian Institute of Aboriginal and Torres Strait Islander Studies (Audio collection: SHARPE_M10 - 01062).

Sharpe, M 2001, *Alawa nanggaya nindanya yalanu rugalarra: Alawa-Kriol-English dictionary* (longer edition), Adelaide: Caitlin Press.

Tindale, N 1974, *Aboriginal tribes of Australia*, Berkeley/Los Angeles: University of California Press, and Canberra: The Australian National University Press.

Trigger, D 1982, *Nicholson River (Waanyi-Garrawa) land claim*, Darwin: Northern Land Council (map prepared by J Dymock and D Trigger), p. 134.

12. ASYMMETRICAL DISTINCTIONS IN WAANYI KINSHIP TERMINOLOGY

Appendix 1: Waanyi Non-Affinal Kin Terms Cited in This Chapter

Ascending harmonic		Descending harmonic		Ascending disharmonic		Descending disharmonic		Same generation	
FF(B/Z)	kangku	BSS/D	kangku, murimuri	F	murriba	BS/D	jawaji	sB	bawa
FM(Z)	ngawiji	ZSD	ngawiji	FZ	kawija			sZ	balala/maju
FMB	ngabuji	ZSS	ngabuji	MB	kadidi, kabubu	ZS/D	jabulu	jB/Z	dawirri/kakulu
MF(B/Z)	mimi	FZS/D	mimi, murimuri	M	ngada			MBS/D	mimi, maku(ngu)
MM(Z)	kukudi	ZDS/D	ngurrali; murimuri	MMBS	mimayi	ZDSS	mimayi	FZS/D	mimi
MMB	kuku			MMBD	ngunyarri	ZDSD	ngunyarri		

Appendix 2: Waanyi Affinal Kin Terms

Harmonic		Disharmonic	
H(sB)	nawi	HF/WF	kadu-nganja
W(Z)	mangkarri	MMBD; MBDD; H/WM	ngunyarri
Man's ZH	nabinabi	MMBS; MBDS; ZDH	mimayi
WB; HjB	kayikayi	DH	ngakinburrunyi

13

Genesis of the Trinity: The Convergent Evolution of Trirelational Kinterms

Joe Blythe

Introduction

While ordinary kinterms encode kinship relations between pairs of individuals, trirelational kinterms are semantically dense expressions that encode kinship relations between three individuals. Several times, these terms have emerged independently on the Australian continent. This emergence is explained as a convergent evolutionary process driven by interactional preferences that shape the design and use of person reference items in conversation. The case in point is the pragmatically motivated lexicalisation of trirelational kinterms in Murrinhpatha.

Trirelational kinterms, also known as triangular (Evans, Johnson & Kohler 1992; Garde 2002; Heath 1982), triadic (Alpher 1991; Garde 2013, 2014), ternary (Green 1998; McGregor 1996) and shared (McConvell 1982; O'Grady & Mooney 1973) kinterms, are typologically unusual among the world's languages. These complex items are not unique to Australia and have also been attested in the Brazilian Amazon (Lea 2004) and Patagonia (Evans, Golluscio & Mellico 2010). However, why they have flourished so prolifically in Australian languages has been somewhat of an enigma. While occasionally, related forms point to shared inheritance and/or lexical diffusion in a handful of cases—for example, Pintupi,

Warlpiri and Gurindji (McConvell 1982, p. 100; 1991) and western Arrernte, Alyawarr and eastern Anmatyerr (Green 1998, pp. 41–5)—the scattered distribution of these terms across different language families suggests multiple independent innovations.

In biology, convergent evolution is the process whereby similar ecological pressures yield similar adaptations in lineages that are unrelated or distantly related. The resultant organisms share similar morphological or behavioural adaptations that suit the ecological conditions they inhabit, despite having potentially different sources. As a result of parallel selective pressures driving convergent structuration within the language domain, I here assume an overarching theory of generalised evolution that subsumes biological evolution, cultural evolution, evolution of concepts and evolution of language (e.g. Croft 2000; Hull 1990; Levinson 2006).

In this chapter, I further an argument presented in Blythe (2013) that many of the unusual kin-based lexical and morphological phenomena identified in Australian languages have emerged as a result of roughly analogous cultural practices and preferences guiding the selection of person reference items in face-to-face conversation. Consequently, approximately equivalent structures have emerged through evolutionary convergence. Australia is a continent characterised by extensive classificatory kinship and widespread taboos that impose limits on the use of personal names. Classificatory kinship and naming taboos jointly exert selective pressures that have seen a variety of highly specialised kin-based referential expressions emerge in languages that are only distantly related. Blythe (2013) presented a case study in pragmatically motivated grammaticalisation of kin-based morphosyntax in Murrinhpatha (kin-based pronouns), as evidenced by diachronic reanalysis and interactional linguistics. The implication of that study is that analogous constraints on language use are behind the convergent evolution of similar kin-based pronoun paradigms across the Australian continent. In this chapter, I argue that the lexicalisation of trirelational kinterms in Australian languages is also driven by analogous constraints on reference, and facilitated by the existence of similar all-encompassing kin-based frameworks that provide circuitous pathways by which interlocutors can comply with those constraints. The second Murrinhpatha case study demonstrates one route by which circuitous reference formulations can become lexically frozen as trirelational structures.[1]

---

1   In Blythe (2010, p. 451), I stated that trirelational kinterms were unattested in Murrinhpatha. At that stage, I did not realise that these infrequently used complex kinterms were trirelational.

In describing the lexicalisation process, I reappraise early ethnographic reports into Murrinhpatha kinship to determine if previously attested kinship terminology has persisted into the twenty-first century; and if so, what can be gleaned about its appearance or non-appearance in a corpus of informal Murrinhpatha conversation (Blythe, n.d.). The larger corpus includes more than 60 hours of unprompted face-to-face conversations conducted by male and female speakers of all ages. Of this, four hours have been transcribed and annotated thus far. Most recordings are high-definition video filmed with a wide-angle lens. I set up the recordings and then extracted myself from the scene as the conversations commenced. Some parts of transcripts are included in this chapter and Appendix 4 provides a guide to transcription conventions.

A corpus of spontaneous conversation is invaluable in illuminating the interactional pragmatics of kinship terminology, such as the differential epistemic leveraging of ego versus altercentric kinterm reckoning (Blythe 2010). Additionally, the unsolicited explication of genealogical relations in informal conversation provides an authentic Indigenous metalanguage of kinship, rather than the sorts of purpose-driven metalanguage that emerge within elicitation contexts. Further, when kinterms alleged from earlier sources fail to surface in conversational corpora, an investigation can be instigated into whether the use of the alleged forms has waned, or whether the forms were provided so as to satisfy a particular line of ethnographic questioning. Despite these benefits, complete reliance on conversational corpora for information on low-frequency items is impractical. Studying conversation is an extremely useful addition to the fieldworker's toolkit and augments conventional ethnographic methods (including elicitation), but it does not replace them.[2]

All kinterms are deictic expressions that express a relationship between individuals or groups of individuals. Regular kinterms, or 'binary' kinterms (McGregor 1996, 2012), are two-place predicates. They express the relationship between a referent (the person being spoken about)

---

2   Although I might appear to privilege conversational corpora in the study of kinship, I wish to point out that the investigation undertaken here has demanded extensive elicitation of both kinship semantics and kinterm usage. Kinterms were collected from ethnographic sources, working lexicon files, conversational transcripts and field notes. Most transcripts have been interlinearised (a process that demands extensive elicitation). Kinterms attested in conversation were crosschecked against elicited genealogies and genealogies were used to generate and crosscheck kincharts. Figures 59 and 60 represent my current understanding of a kinship system that is almost certainly evolving, but not in the manner suggested by earlier ethnographers (see below). I thank an anonymous reviewer for suggesting these methodological clarifications.

and a propositus or anchor (the person[s] to whom the referent is being related). Thus, in the expression 'your mother', the kinterm 'mother' is grammatically anchored to the addressee by the possessive pronoun 'your'. Essentially, 'mother', in this instance, has an overt second-person propositus. Kinterms can also be covertly anchored. Normally, a covert propositus is pragmatically recoverable through conventionalised connotation. Thus, if a man speaking to his wife uses the term 'mum', his wife will probably infer the term as being used for reference to *his own* mother, and not hers, and that a first-person propositus is being implied. If he then uses the same term 'mum' when addressing his child, those present will infer that the term is probably being used for reference to his wife, the child's mother, and that a second-person propositus is being implied. If he then uses the term 'mum' when addressing his brother, the brother will probably infer a covert first-person inclusive propositus (i.e. *our* mother).

Trirelational kinterms are semantically dense referential items that express relationships between three individuals (i.e. they are three-place predicates). The Murrinhpatha trirelational term *yilamarna* expresses the relationship between a man and his brother. Unlike the ordinary brother term (*ngathan*), *yilamarna* also expresses the relationships between the man and his child (*wakal*) and between the child and the brother (*yile*, see Figure 53). The relationships between all three individuals are encoded. As most trirelational terms are anchored in two places, they effectively have two propositi. Thus, if the triad encompasses the speaker, the addressee and the referent, then we have the speaker as propositus and the addressee as propositus. Figure 54 compares a regular Bininj Gunwok term to an approximately equivalent trirelational term. The regular kinterm *nakurrng* (Figure 54, left) is overtly anchored to the addressee with the possessive pronoun *ke*, meaning 'your MoMoBrSo' (Garde 2002, p. 157). If the individual referred to previously is the nephew of a male speaker, the trirelational term *ke nakurrng* can also be used (Figure 54, right). Thus, the term would mean the person who is your MoMoBrSo and my ZiSo, given that you are my DaCh (Garde 2002, p. 422). In this case, the relationship of the referent to the speaker (*kangkinj*, mZiSo) and of the addressee to the speaker (*mamamh*, DaCh) are inferable because the now-fronted free pronoun *ke* appears in a more prominent position. Trirelational terms are more specific than their regular counterparts because they have more restrictive denotata. They can be used effectively for reference to only a subset of the individuals that could potentially be referred to with the regular kinterms.

13. GENESIS OF THE TRINITY

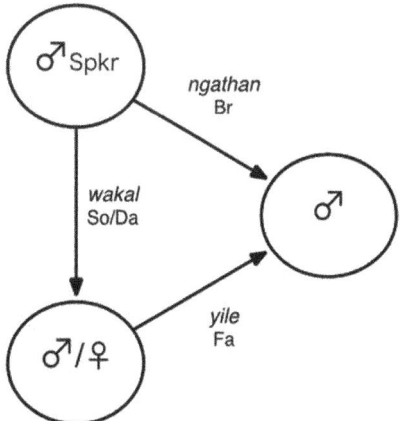

Figure 53: The Murrinhpatha trirelational kinterm *yilamarna*.
Source: Author's work.

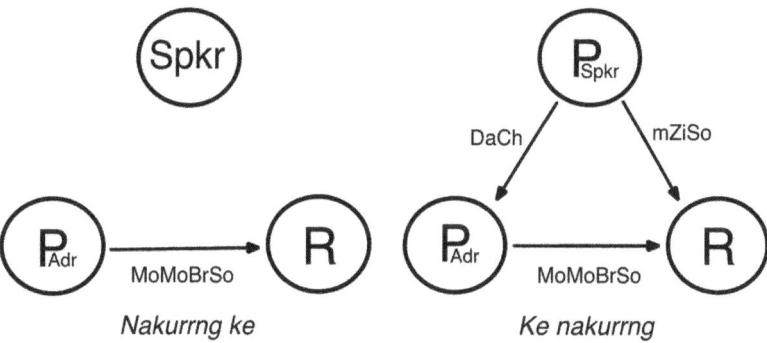

Figure 54: An ordinary Bininj Gunwok kinterm anchored to the addressee (left) and a trirelational kinterm anchored to both speaker and addressee (right). The term also encodes the relationship between speaker and addressee.
Source: Author's work.

Within the literature, there is considerable variation in how researchers describe the mapping of the participant roles pertaining to speech events onto the triad of individuals semantically implicated by trirelational kinterms. This is partly due to usage conventions specific to the language in question and partly due to structural variation within the semantics of the terms. A number of authors have described trirelational kinterms as encoding relationships between speaker, addressee and a(n) (external, third person) referent. Thus, McGregor (1996, p. 219) described Gooniyandi's 'ternary monadic' terms as having an Ego (always the speaker), a Propositus (usually the addressee) and a Referent. Merlan (1989) described Jawoyn's Yenderr terms similarly, but captured this configuration using the term Speaker, rather than Ego. The Murrinhpatha terms do not map as consistently onto participant roles. When used for reference to a third person, they are normally anchored to the speaker and are further anchored externally—*not* to the addressee. They can also be used as vocatives, whereby the referent is the addressee. They are then anchored both to the speaker and externally.[3]

The cross-linguistic similarity emerges when the triad of expressed individuals is decoupled from participant roles. Trirelational terms can then be grouped into two basic types. The most common type is that with two propositi and a single referent (see Figure 55)—terms are used to speak about a particular individual, but in a way that explicates (or implicates) the genealogical connection to two other individuals, who may or may not be participants in the actual speech event. The Murrinhpatha terms are of this type.

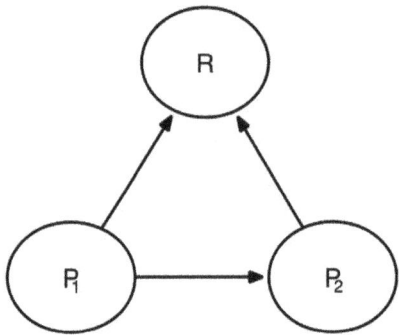

Figure 55: Dual propositus trirelational kinterms.
Source: Author's work.

Less common are the trirelational variants of dyadic kinterms.[4] These are terms used for reference to a pair of related individuals that are anchored in various ways to a single propositus (as in Figure 56). In Gooniyandi, there are five contrastive terms used for husband-and-wife dyads. Each dyad

---

3   An interactional analysis of one of these terms used vocatively in conversation is included as a supplement to this chapter.
4   Dyadic morphemes (Evans 2003; Merlan & Heath 1982) are specialised dual affixes to kinterms that mark that a pair of individuals are related in the manner of the relationship expressed in the base kinterm. For example, if the Gooniyandi term dyadic suffix *-langi* is attached to *goornda* (male cross-cousin), then the term *goornda-langi* would denote a pair of cousins (McGregor 1996, pp. 219–21).

relates to the speaker in different ways. For example, the term *marralangi* denotes a husband-and-wife pair, one of whom is the speaker's opposite-sex sibling or cross-cousin (McGregor 1996, p. 228). The term *woordoolangi* denotes a husband-and-wife pair, one of whom is the speaker's same-sex sibling or cross-cousin (McGregor 1996, p. 228). Similar trirelational dyads exist in Banyjima (Dench 1980), Nyangumarta (O'Grady & Mooney 1973), Gurindji (McConvell 1982) and the Mapundungun language of Patagonia (Evans, Golluscio & Mellico 2010).

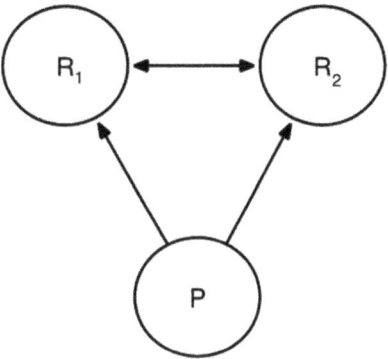

Figure 56: Trirelational dyadic terms.
Source: Author's work.

In some respects, this demarcation of types is something of a hair-splitting exercise, because, as McGregor (1996, p. 226) pointed out, dyadic kinterms have an inherent propositus that so happens to be one of the referents. In which case, whether the triad being expressed is conveyed with two propositi or two referents is really a question of the prominence being given to the individuals captured within the triad—thus, it has more to do with the pragmatics of tokens than the semantics of types. In which case, if it is predominantly an individual being spoken about, then the first model would better apply. If a pair is being spoken about, then the second model would better apply.

In the following sections, I examine the semantics of the Murrinhpatha trirelational kinterms and their usage. Strangely, the terms are not necessarily used for a triad of genuine individuals. The additional semantic resources of these terms allow reference to a 'nameless' person to be triangulated through a third (perhaps imaginary) individual, which means dealing with a structural ambiguity within the larger Murrinhpatha kinship system. Four of the trirelational kinterms provide structural solutions to pragmatic problems in that they plug functional holes in the array of regular kinterms. In turn, this has allowed another four structurally similar terms to enter the larger kinship lexicon, even though these are not required to fill similar pragmatic holes. The fact that Murrinhpatha forms are only used for kin for whom there are some form of name avoidance is evidence pointing to their evolutionary history.

In the concluding section, I survey the range and usage of trirelational kinterms in other Australian languages and find evidence to support a theory of convergent evolutionary origins springing from person referencing performed within contexts of personal name avoidance. Being lexically compact and semantically precise forms that are not names, trirelational kinterms have evolved to satisfy preferences for minimality, recognisability and circumspection about cultural protocols. As similar interactional conditions apply across the continent, recurrent structures emerge that satisfy what amount to analogous design constraints. The explanation proposed for these multiple innovations is well known in evolutionary biology, but has seldom been invoked in diachronic linguistics.

Trirelational Kinterms in Murrinhpatha

Murrinhpatha is a polysynthetic head-marking language spoken in the coastal region bounded by the Moyle and Fitzmaurice rivers, predominantly in Wadeye and surrounding communities. Prior to the establishment of a Catholic mission in 1935 on Murrinhpatha land, the region had no permanent European population. As the mission became better established, speakers of Marri Tjevin, Marri Amu, Magati Ke, Marri Ngarr and Jaminjung took up residence and began using Murrinhpatha for daily communication. The use of these neighbouring languages has waned drastically, while Murrinhpatha has emerged as the regional lingua franca.

In 1935, the anthropologist W. E. H. Stanner travelled with a group of missionaries to Murrinhpatha country to establish the first mission in the Moyle and Fitzmaurice rivers' region. Four years later, the mission was relocated to Port Keats, which is now the community of Wadeye. Although he did not fully grasp their semantic complexity, Stanner (1937, pp. 314–15) remarked upon a group of morphologically complex 'circumlocutory' terms that 'make references to or about a person even more indirect by tracing the relationship through an earlier generation'. These circumlocutory terms are only used for kin for whom there is some degree of name avoidance. The Murrinhpatha observe strong name avoidance between actual sons- and mothers-in-law, poison cousins (MoMoBrCh/MoBrDaCh/FaZiDaCh) and opposite-sex siblings. Between same-sex siblings, names can be used for third-person reference, but are seldom used for address—instead nicknames such as *tepala* ('deaf one') are greatly preferred. Names of recently deceased persons are avoided by the entire community, while names of the distantly deceased are avoided by close relatives for considerably longer and sometimes indefinitely.

The trirelational term that a man uses for reference to his WiMo or MoMoBrDa is *kawumamnge*. This term is transparently composed of a kinterm procliticised to a verb (see Box 1). All Murrinhpatha trirelational terms are composed in this fashion—at least historically.

Box 1: Transcript—incipient trirelational term for 'wife's mother' formed with 'say'.

```
kawumamnge
kawu=mam                    -nge
MoMo=3SG.SB.8say/do.NFUT-3SG.F.IO
"'kawu', he/she says/said to her"
```

Source: Author's work.

Kawu is a grandparent term (MoMo), whereas the verb *mamnge* is normally used to report prior speech directed to a female addressee: 'he/she says/said [it] to her'. In explicating the term, a female consultant stated that if her son-in-law was to refer to her using the term *Kawumamngeka, mamka kardu wakalwa, wakal ngarra nukunuya*, '[in saying] "*kawumamnge*", the child talks, his own child'. The term literally means 'the female person that he/she calls MoMo', whereby 'he/she' should be understood as the man's *wakal* (So/Da). Figure 57 shows that the relationship between the child and the referent (MoMo/wDaCh) is overtly expressed. The man's child as the person addressing the referent is covertly expressed (inferable). Since two sides of the triangle are clearly understood, the third relationship (WiMo/MoMoBrDa) can also be inferred.

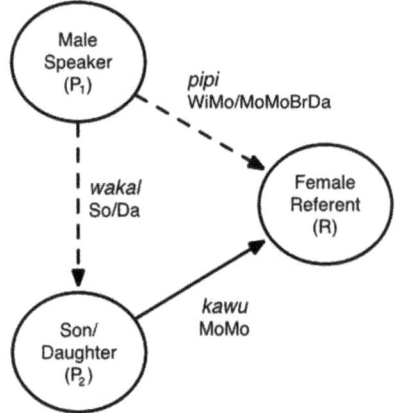

Figure 57: *Kawumamnge*—(literally) 'the female person that he/she (ego's child) refers to as MoMo'.
Source: Author's work.

In the scenario depicted in Figure 57, the mother-in-law is the referent (R), the speaker is a propositus (P_1), and the son/daughter is both the propositus for the embedded term *kawu* and a second propositus (P_2) for the trirelational term. In Murrinhpatha, eight trirelational terms have been attested—all of which are used in situations in which some form of name avoidance is appropriate. The terms are formulaic (see Figure 58) in that all contain an embedded kinterm for whom no avoidance would be expected (i.e. the relationship between P_2 and R is 'in the clear'; see Figure 58). In each of these terms, the relationship between P_1 and P_2 is invariant as 'son/daughter'.[5] As P_2 is always the direct progeny of P_1, only the avoidance relationship (P_1–R) needs to be inferred. Where the Murrinhpatha trirelational terms perhaps differ from other systems is that an actual son or daughter needn't exist. Essentially, the terms make an indirect reference to R by triangulating through P_2, which is possibly an imaginary descendent of P_1.

---

5   For this reason, P_1, the person to whom these Murrinhpatha trirelational terms are anchored, is equivalent to (but not synonymous with) Ego. Although these infrequently used terms have only ever been volunteered with the speaker as P_1 (Ego), elicitation tests suggest that it is theoretically possible to have P_1 as the addressee. As such, P_2 would be the addressee's son or daughter.

13. GENESIS OF THE TRINITY

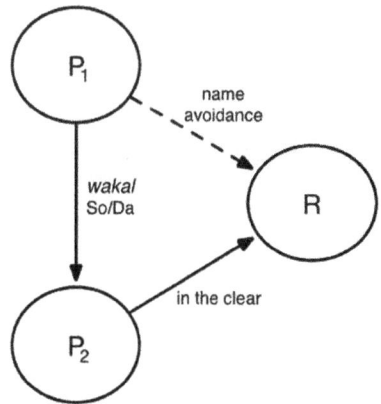

Figure 58: The Murrinhpatha trirelational terms all contain an embedded kinterm that is presented as if being uttered by P_2, the son/daughter of P_1.
Source: Author's work.

Although less intense than the avoidance between a man and his mother-in-law, a woman also avoids the name of her husband's mother. The trirelational term that a woman uses for her HuMo (or MoMoBrDa) is *mangkamamnge*—literally, 'he/she calls her *mangka*' (see Box 2). Pragmatically, the term can be understood as 'the woman that my child calls *mangka* (FaMo), who I shouldn't mention by name on account of her being my HuMo (or MoMoBrDa)'.

> **Box 2: Transcript—incipient trirelational term for 'husband's mother' formed with 'say'.**
>
> ```
> mangkamamnge
> mangka=mam              -nge
> FaMo   =3SG.SB.8say/do.NFUT-3SG.F.IO
> "He/she calls her mangka"
> ```
>
> Source: Author's work.

Table 65 lists the eight attested Murrinhpatha trirelational kinterms.[6] They are all lexicalised clauses that include an embedded kinterm. There are four terms for spouse's parents and four terms for siblings, depending

---

6   Language consultants volunteered roughly half of these terms when particular individuals were mentioned in transcription and elicitation sessions. The rest of the paradigm was fleshed out through targeted elicitation. The list appears to be exhaustive. Other avoided kin types predicted to yield trirelational kinterms (e.g. a woman's daughter's husband) were not forthcoming (although in the case of wDaHu, a phrasal circumlocution was provided). Although only one term has emerged unsolicited in the four-hour annotated conversational corpus (*kalemamnge*, 1 token), I expect the larger collection contains further tokens.

on the gender of P_1 and the gender of the referent. The terms used for reference to a female all contain the framing speech verb *mamnge*. As third singular subjects of verbs are unmarked for gender, it does not matter whether the imagined child is the son or daughter. Less morphologically transparent, the terms used for reference to males contain the cranberry element = *marna*. The expected non-future masculine direct object counterpart to the speech verb *mamnge* would be *mamna* 'he/she said/says to him'.[7] As the trirelational terms used for male referents are semantically analogous to those used for females, I presume *marna* to be derived historically from **mam-rna*, the trirelational term used by men for reference to a brother (Stanner 1937, p. 314), as exemplified by *yilamarna* in Box 3. As none of the described morphophonemic processes in modern Murrinhpatha prohibit the nasal cluster /mn/ (Street 1987; Walsh 1976), I presume these terms to have eroded prior to the modern morphophonology.[8]

Table 65: The eight attested Murrinhpatha trirelational terms.

Trirelational term	R	P1	$P_1 \rightarrow R$	$P_2 \rightarrow R$
kawumamnge	♀	♂	pipi (WiMo, MoMoBrDa)	kawu (MoMo)
mangkamamnge	♀	♀	pipi (HuMo, MoMoBrDa)	mangka (FaMo)
kangkurlmarna	♂	♀	kaka (HuFa)	Kangkurl (FaFa)
thamunymarna	♂	♂	kaka (WiFa)	thamuny (MoFa)
kalemamnge	♀	♀	munak (Zi)	kale (Mo, MoZi)
pipimamnge	♀	♂	munak (Zi)	pipi (FaZi)
kakamarna	♂	♀	ngathan (Br)	kaka (MoBr)
yilamarna	♂	♂	ngathan (Br)	yile (Fa, FaBr)

Source: Author's work.

> **Box 3: Transcript—incipient trirelational terms for 'sibling' formed with 'say'.**
>
> ```
> yilamarna < *yilemamna        (hypothesised surface form)
>             yile=mam  -rna (hypothesised underlying form)
>             Fa  =3SG.SB.8say/do.NFUT-3SG.M.IO
> "He/she calls him yile (Fa)"
> ```

Source: Author's work.

---

7 *Mam* is a very general non-future 'say/do' verb that is underspecified for aspectual viewpoint (Nordlinger & Caudal 2012). Therefore, while it usually means 'said', it can also mean 'says'.
8 A current morphophonemic process not mentioned in Street (1987) or Walsh (1976) is that the apical alveolar versus retroflex distinction is neutralised in nasal clusters.

In the next section, we investigate the place of trirelational terms within the larger collective of kinterms and how, from a pragmatic point of view, four of the terms plug functional holes in the paradigm of ordinary kinterms.

The Place of Trirelational Terms within the Larger Set of Kinterms

After only a few weeks of fieldwork in 1935, Stanner (1936) published the field report *Murinbata Kinship and Totemism*. In this report, he claimed the Murrinhpatha were in the process of transforming their kinship system from a simple Kariera type, with two lines of patrilineal descent, to a more complex Aranda type, with four lines of patrilineal descent (Berndt & Berndt 1999; Elkin 1968; Radcliffe-Brown 1930). He thought that this transformation was being driven by the Murrinhpatha's enthusiastic adoption of the Jaminjung subsections in the first decades of the twentieth century. Norwegian ethnographers Johannes and Aslaug Falkenberg, who had conducted six months of fieldwork at Port Keats in 1950, concurred with Stanner, and suggested that the process of transformation had advanced during the intervening 15 years (Falkenberg 1962, p. 206; Falkenberg & Falkenberg 1981, p. 142).

The passing decades revealed Stanner and the Falkenbergs to have been premature in drawing these conclusions. There is no linguistic evidence to support the borrowing of kinterms from Jaminjung.[9] Although there is no doubt that Murrinhpatha men, who ventured into the Victoria River district on account of the pastoral industry, borrowed the Jaminjung subsection terminology, the sociocentric system that each described (Falkenberg 1962, pp. 225–31; Stanner 1936, pp. 211–2) was a (four) section system with two (equivalent) names for each section. In the twenty-first century, this system is but a distant memory. For these

---

9   The three terms that Stanner (1936, p. 199) claimed to be borrowings from Jaminjung were *pugali* (MoBrCh and FaZiCh), *lambarra* ('[ZiSo]' whose daughter one marries') and *ngaguluk* (WiMoBr). *Lambarra* is a wanderwort, widely attested in Northern Australia, but seldom used by the Murrinhpatha. Stanner's own comparative chart of kinterms (AIATSIS MS3752 Series 5 Item 23[a]) attests *pugarli* in nearby Ngan'gi wumirri, Ngan'gikurungkurr, Marri Ngarr, Magati Ke and Wagiman, making the Jaminjung hypothesis difficult to sustain. Stanner claimed that the Murrinhpatha *ngaguluk* was a changed version of the Jaminjung *ngawuluk* (MoMoBrSo). If the term was diffused, linguistic evidence (which is weak at best) would suggest that the diffusion was in the opposite direction, given that lenition is more frequent than fortition in intervocalic environments (Butcher 2006).

ethnographers influenced by Radcliffe-Brown's structural-functional conceptual frame (Hinkson 2005), Murrinhpatha's 'dual augmented' kinship system (Keen 2013) appeared to be in flux. However, in the last 40 years, the kinship system has proven to be relatively stable, despite enormous population growth (Taylor 2010) and dramatic changes to many other aspects of social organisation (Furlan 2005; Ivory 2009; Mansfield 2013).

Using languages sampled from the AustKin database, Keen (2013) provided a modern classification of Australian kinship typologies that resembled the structuralist-functionalist models (Elkin 1938, 1939; Radcliffe-Brown 1930) because they were also based on lines of descent. Keen's 'dual' and 'quadruple' terminologies approximately subsume the Kariera and Aranda models respectively. He classified Murrinhpatha's terminology as 'dual augmented with separate cross-cousin terms' (Keen 2013, p. 15). However, he also noted that dual augmented was perhaps 'not a unitary type by a cover term for several distinct variants of Dual terminologies' (p. 28) that typologically 'move[d] closer to the Quadruple terminologies' (p. 18). Thus, the Murrinhpatha system is structurally intermediate between the earlier Kariera and Aranda types, but evidently not undergoing radical typological transformation.

Murrinhpatha's system of ordinary kinterms show a straightforward sibling merger for two of the four grandparent terms: *kangkurl* (FaFa = FaFaBr = FaFaZi) and *kawu* (MoMo = MoMoBr = MoMoZi). *Thamuny*, the term for MoFa, is merged not only for siblings (MoFa = MoFaBr = MoFaZi) but also with FaMoBr. A distinct term *mangka* exists for FaMo (showing merger only with FaMoZi) (see Figures 58 and 59). In ego's generation, cross-cousins *pugarli* (MoBrCh and FaZiCh) are distinguished from parallel cousins (FaBrCh and MoZiCh), which are considered equivalent to brothers (*ngathan*) and sisters (*munak*). Preferred marriage is to a matrilateral second cross-cousin (MoMoBrDaCh): *purrima* (♀) or *nangkun* (♂). *Purrima* is also a woman's husband and a man's sister-in-law, while *nangkun* is also a man's wife and a woman's brother-in-law.

13. GENESIS OF THE TRINITY

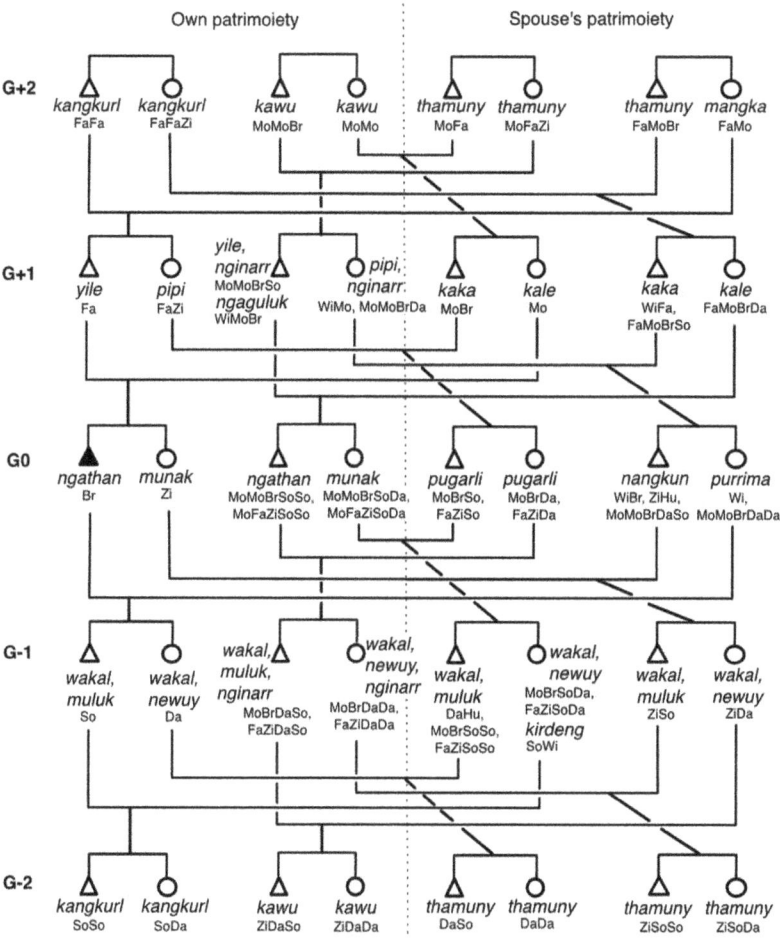

Figure 59: The Murrinhpatha kinchart for a male ego (trirelational kinterms are not included).
Source: Author's work.

The −1 generation is a typical Hawaiian pattern in distinguishing only males (*muluk*) from females (*newuy*). However, normally, all kin of this generation are referred to simply as *wakal* (literally, 'small'), without distinguishing gender. As avoided affines, children of a female *pugarli* (MoBrDaCh and FaZiDaCh) can also be referred to by the term *nginarr*.

SKIN, KIN AND CLAN

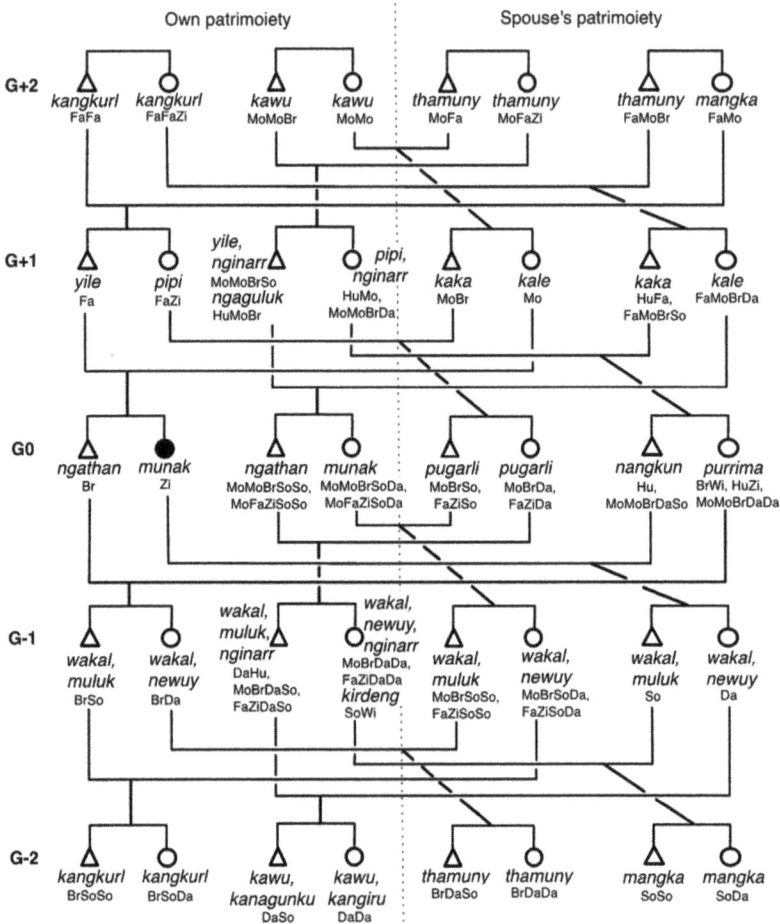

Figure 60: The Murrinhpatha kinchart for a female ego (trirelational kinterms are not included).
Source: Author's work.

The +1 generation makes terminological distinctions for gender and for ego's versus alter's patrimoiety. The four terms are *yile* (Fa, MoMoBrSo and MoFaZiSo), *kale* (Mo, FaMoBrDa and FaFaZiDa), *kaka* (MoBr, FaMoBrSo, FaFaZiSo and WiFa) and *pipi* (FaZi, MoMoBrDa and MoFaZiDa). Although terminologically equivalent, the affinal kin in either patrimoiety are by no means socially equivalent to the consanguineal kin. Stanner and the Falkenbergs thought the WiMo (*pipi*) could be was distinguished from FaZi (also *pipi*) using the phrasal expression *pipi nginarr* (Falkenberg 1962; Falkenberg & Falkenberg 1981; Stanner 1936, p. 199). Although Stanner was correct in realising that the term *nginarr* was also used for WiMo (Stanner 1936, p. 199), he did not appreciate the term's broader denotation of G±1 affine (male or female) in the MoMoBr's patriline (see Figures 58 and 59). The Falkenbergs presented WiMo/MoMoBrDa (as *pipi nginarr*, or *bip:i ŋinar* in their orthography) as being distinguished from FaZi (as *pipi ngutjngen*, or *bip:i ŋoitnan* in their orthography). Although the phrasal expressions *pipi nginarr* and *pipi ngutjngen* are grammatically acceptable in Murrinhpatha, a corpus-based examination failed to attest them. Rather, WiMo is referenced regularly either as *pipi* or as *nginarr*, but the combination has never been attested. The adjective *ngutjngen* means 'ordinary' and, in certain contexts, might contrast with a *pipi* in the MoMoBr's patriline. Thus, these phrasal expressions appear to be ad hoc descriptions of two functionally different types of 'aunt', probably produced under conditions of elicitation for explicating their social non-equivalence.[10]

These early ethnographers were right to expect that MoBrDa/WiMo should be terminologically distinguishable from FaZi, because the highly avoided affines demand very different kinship behaviour from that of a consanguineal 'aunt'. Although the conversational corpus revealed this ambiguity to be seldom problematic, it is reasonable to assume that an inability to *ever* make this distinction would indeed be problematic. However, the ad hoc solution provided for their benefit (no doubt produced by Murrinhpatha speakers when speaking predominantly in English) differs from the Indigenous solution—trirelational terms. *Kawumamnge* and *mangkamamnge* provide a means for specifying a *pipi* as being of the avoided *nginarr* variety (SpMo and MoMoBrDa) and not of the 'ordinary' variety (FaZi). In one's spouse's patrimoiety, *kangkurlmarna* and *thamunymarna* disambiguate the term *kaka*, effectively specifying a mildly avoidable SpFa, as opposed to a consanguineal MoBr. As such, these terms plug functional gaps in the paradigm of ordinary kinterms, giving the overall system the power to make functional distinctions when necessary.

---

10   Other such ad hoc phrasal descriptions in the Falkenberg monographs include *yile nginarr* (WiMoBr and MoMoBrSo) and *wakal nginarr* (MoBrDaCh), which have not surfaced in the conversational corpus. The former is either *yile* (and hence not distinguished from Fa using ordinary kinterms) or *nginarr* (and hence is not distinguished from any other G±1 affine in the MoMoBr patriline). MoBrDaCh is referenced either as *nginarr* or *wakal* (G–1), but never in combination, or as *muluk* (G–1 male) or *newuy* (G–1 female).

SKIN, KIN AND CLAN

A Structural Explanation for the Emergence of Trirelational Kinterms

Corpora of natural conversation provide valuable insights into how knowing individuals come to explain kin relationships to less informed individuals. If the person being spoken about is not well known to all present, then explaining that individual's place within a kinship network is more informative than merely providing the person's name. The most common device used by Murrinhpatha speakers to explain relationships is to combine a kinterm with a semantically general class 8 'say/do' verb,[11] as exemplified in Extract 1. In this extract, Mick, Rob and Dave talk about a woman named Janet who, until then, has only been mentioned by a nickname.[12]

Extract 1: Ngandimeli (20120715_JB_video_GYHM100_02).

```
1   Mick    janet janet murriny nuwunudhatjpirryu;
            janet janet murriny nigunu-dhatjpirr=yu
            ♀name ♀name speech  3SG.F -INTS      =DM
            Janet, Janet, that's her real name.

2           (0.1)
3   Rob     nuwunu yini damkardu mamkawadhadim yiniyu;
            nigunu nyini dam                  -ngkardu
            3SG.F  ANAPH 2SG.SB.13.NFUT-see/look
            mam             -ngkawadha=dim              =yu
            3SG.SB.8say/do.NFUT-say_name =3SG.SB.1sit.NFUT=DM
            That's her, you see, he is saying the right name.

4           (0.9)
5   Mick    Mhm.
6           (0.4)
7   Rob     nekika kaka mamnyewurran murnu,
            neki  =ka   kaka mam                   -nye
            1DU.INC=FOC MoBr 3SG.SB.8say/do.NFUT-1NS.INC.IO
            =wurran          murnu
            =3SG.SB.6go.NFUT bone [a nickname]
            Bone ((Dave)), [She] calls you and me "uncle".

8           (2.7)
9   Rob     Yu, kaleleka kurndjik aka nawa, kurndjik ngalla;
            yu  kale -RDP=ka  kurndjik nganaka  na  -wa
            yes mother-RDP=TOP stomach  you_know? TAG-EMPH
            kurndjik ngalla
            stomach  big
            yeah, her mother has the belly, you know,
            the fat belly.
```

Source: Author's work.

---

11 Murrinhpatha verbs are generally complex predicates comprised of an inflected classifier stem and an uninflected lexical stem (Nordlinger 2010). There are some 38 classifier paradigms (Blythe, Nordlinger & Reid 2007). Tentative semantic glosses can be provided for some of these, but not all (hence, they are given numeric labels).
12 All names here are pseudonyms.

Prior to this extract, Dave has enquired as to her identity. Mick provides her real name at line 1, which Rob confirms as being correct at line 3. At line 7, Rob explains to his classificatory brother Dave (addressing him with the nickname *murnu*, 'bone') how Janet relates to them. He does this with the kinterm *kaka* (MoBr/WiFa) plus the class 8 'say/do' verb *mamnyewurran*: '[She] says "*kaka*" to you and me' (effectively, 'she calls us "uncle" '). In doing so, one of the persons in the know associates the referent to himself and his interlocutor, and thus grounds his epistemic authority within a framework of kinship relations (Blythe 2010).

In this extract, and in many others besides, the 'saying' verbs used to explicate these relations are the same class 8 verbs from which the trirelational kinterms are composed. In the trirelational terms, these verbs, replete with bound indirect object pronouns, plus accompanying kinterms have become lexicalised as nouns. As we will see below, they are nouns imbued with a capacity to explicate thorny kinship relations.

In many dialects of Dutch, the term *neef* is ambiguous because it denotes both male cousins (PaSbSo) and nephews (SbSo). Likewise, *nicht* denotes both female cousins (PaSbDa) and nieces (SbDa). In some dialects of Dutch, the morphologically complex term *Oom* = *zegger* and '"uncle"* = sayer' specifies a nephew (or a niece), as distinct from a cousin. *Oomzegger* and related *tante* = *zegger* and '"aunt" = sayer' are comprised of embedded kinterms plus the explanatory 'saying' expression *zegger* (which is derivable from the speech verb *zeggen* 'to say').[13] The embedded terms focus on the phrasal terms' propositus (the uncle or aunt), thus disambiguating them from cousins (essentially because the 'cousin' sense of *neef* [or *nicht*] is a reciprocal relationship). These complex kinterms have a similar morphological structure to the Murrinhpatha terms, but, not being trirelational terms, are less semantically complex. Nevertheless, similar to the Murrinhpatha terms, they also deal with a structural ambiguity within the larger set of kinterms.

In the Murrinhpatha case, the specification problem is essentially that in G+1, within each patrimoiety, affines are not distinguished from consanguineal kin. This Kariera-type patterning fails to replicate descent lines that are (more or less) distinguished in G+2 by the somewhat lopsided Aranda-esque grandparent terminology (see Figures 59 and

---

13 I am grateful to Mark Dingemanse for alerting me to these terms.

60).[14] If Murrinhpatha speakers were to disambiguate an avoided *nginarr* type *pipi* from a consanguineal *pipi* (FaZi) by exactly employing the Dutch strategy, they would have to shoot for an expression meaning '"son-in-law"-sayer' or similar. The problem here is that although a woman's son-in-law can be referred to as *muluk* or *wakal*, the Hawaiian patterning in G–1 will not locate the son-in-law accurately within the MoMoBr's patriline. *Nginarr* does precisely this but does not specify the 'sayer' as male, nor specify him as G–1, as opposed to G+1. By taking the perspective of ego's son or daughter, the second propositus P_2, for practical purposes, is a downward-skewed version of P_1. If the propositus is skewed down a generation, the referent is effectively pushed up a generation into that part of the kinchart in which MoMoBr's patriline *is* distinguished terminologically from FaFa's patriline. *Kawumamnge* is able to specify WiMo/MoMoBrDa because *kawu* specifies *both* patriline and generation, whereas *wakal*, *muluk* and *nginarr* only specify either generation or patriline, but not both.

By taking the perspective of her children, a woman is able to use *mangkamamnge* to specify her HuMo/MoMoBrDa, as opposed to her FaZi. This becomes possible because P_2 is effectively a skewed-down version of P_1. By skewing down a generation, the referent is pushed up into G+2 as *mangka* (FaMo), which is the most distinctive of the grandparent terms. By the same mechanism, the two trirelational terms for fathers-in-law specify an affinal *kaka* (HuFa/FaMoBrSo), as opposed to a consanguineal *kaka* (MoBr). By skewing down the propositus as P_2, the term with a male P_1 (*thamunymarna*) targets a FaMo (*thamuny*), whereas the term with a female P_1 (*kangkurlmarna*) targets a FaFa (*kangkurl*).

The four trirelational terms for affines—*kawumamnge*, *mangkamamnge*, *kangkurlmarna* and *thamunymarna* (see Table 65)—solve the specification problems encountered by Stanner and the Falkenbergs. Although the phrasal expression *pipi nginarr* might be a perfectly acceptable way to distinguish WiMo/MoMoBrDa from FaZi, it appears not to be the actual solution. The Indigenous solution is to take the stock-standard kin-explaining expressions and use them in a way that takes the perspective of kinsmen (ego's children) who do not have problems specifying the same referents. The trirelational sibling terms have no such specification

---

14   Aranda systems have four distinct terms in G+2 (FaFa, MoMo, MoFa and FaMo)—each of which show sibling merger. The four terms demarcate distinct patrilineages (FaFa, MoMoBr, MoFa amd FaMoBr).

issues to resolve. *Kakamarna*, the special avoidance term used by women for reference to their brothers is, in practical terms, no more precise than the regular brother term *ngathan*.[15] Most likely, these sibling terms piggybacked on the affinal terms in also skewing down a second propositus (P_2). As all sibling names are avoided to some degree (at least in contexts of address), the addition of these trirelational terms to the regular sibling terms enriches the range of options for referring to (or addressing) siblings without resorting to their names. In this way, the sibling terms have sneaked through an avoidance window left ajar by the affinal terms.

The Utility-Driven Emergence of a Specialised Class of Words

Most Aboriginal languages of Australia are critically endangered or no longer spoken on a daily basis. The fact that trirelational kinterms are predominantly found in Australian languages makes them a highly endangered class of words. Findings show that semantically complex kinterms are acquired later than simpler terms (Haviland & Clark 1974),[16] leading to the prediction that highly complex lexical items that are difficult to acquire might be among the first items to fall into disuse, as minority languages become threatened by dominant languages. Research into the use of these words in naturalistic contexts is urgently required, particularly because their pragmatics can inform their diachronic development.

The Murrinhpatha trirelational kinterms have emerged as a result of usage-based constraints on person reference items. These constraints take the form of conversational preferences for 1) not using personal names under conditions of taboo (Blythe 2013; Garde 2008; Levinson 2007); 2) using recognitionals (reference forms that invite interlocutors to recognise who is being spoken about) (Sacks & Schegloff 1979; Schegloff, 1996, 2007); and 3) using forms that are not more verbose than necessary (Enfield 2013; Hacohen & Schegloff 2006; Levinson 1987). Trirelational terms satisfy these constraints by 1) not being names; 2) being highly specific and semantically dense reference forms—which makes them useful as recognitionals; and 3) being extremely compact.

---

15 Technically, it is more precise because the gender of P_1 is marked. However, when P_1 is the current speaker, this information is redundant because recipients are normally aware of the speaker's sex.
16 This accords with Garde's (2013, pp. 119–20) observation that Bininj Gunwok *Kun-derbi* terms are acquired by younger adults and teenagers (rather than children).

Yet, by no means are these terms the only available alternatives to names. Ordinary kinterms, nicknames, descriptions and even kin-based pronouns (Blythe 2009, 2013) are also used as devices for introducing new referents into conversation so that one's interlocutor can recognise who is being spoken about, as well as personal names. As previously discussed, the trirelational terms used for reference to affines are semantically more precise than their ordinary (binary) counterparts; however, this is not true of the sibling terms. If the trirelational sibling terms exist alongside their ordinary counterparts (*ngathan*, 'brother', and *munak*, 'sister') as alternatives to personal names, but are less frequently used than the binary terms, we can surmise that their usage will be pragmatically marked. This is probably true for all trirelational terms, as alternatives to the alternatives for names. At the time of writing, only one trirelational term has surfaced in the annotated (five-hour) corpus of conversation (*kalemamnge*, the term used for a sister, by a sister). An interactional analysis of the extract containing this term is included as a supplement to this chapter. The extract supports the notion of pragmatically marked referential usage—forms used for doing something special, over and above simple name avoidance.

Languages such as Bininj Gunwok, Mawng and Gurindji have larger collections of trirelational terms than Murrinhpatha, whereas for certain others (Watjarri and Yidiny), only one or two terms are reported (Dixon & Irvine 1991, p. 151; Douglas 1981, p. 251). The more expansive systems are possibly older than Murrinhpatha's.[17] The map in Figure 61 shows trirelational kinterms that have been attested in Australian in 23 languages belonging to seven distinct language families. That they are scattered in the north and the centre is probably testament to these languages being more vital and better described than those of the south and east of the continent, which was where the impact of European invasion was felt earlier. Thus, trirelational kinterms may have been even more widespread than the map would suggest.

---

17 In the case of Murrinhpatha, the relationship between P_1 and P_2 is presently fixed as 'parent of'. If this fixed relationship were to be unlocked such that P_1–P_2 could become variable, then we might expect a more expansive collection of terms to emerge—one that is less closely tied to avoidance contexts.

13. GENESIS OF THE TRINITY

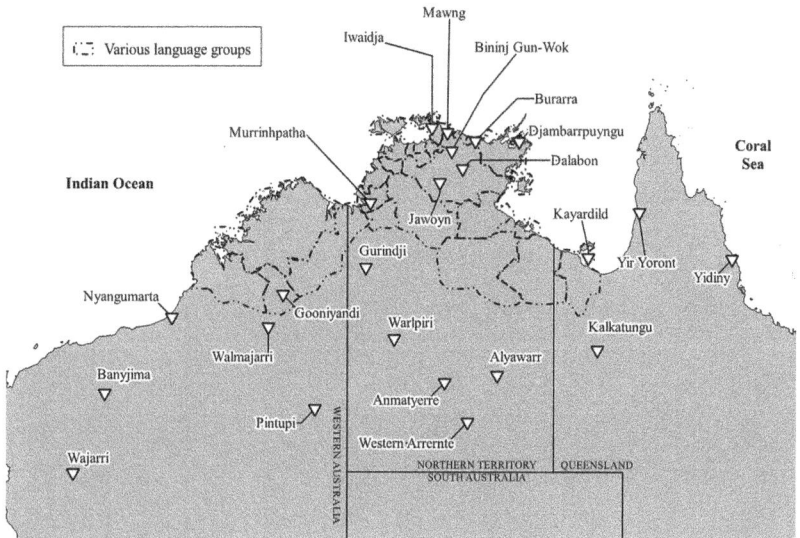

Figure 61: Australian languages for which trirelational kinterms have been attested.
Source: Author's work.

Murrinhpatha trirelational kinterms are used in all circumstances when producing the referent's name is inappropriate, which speaks to their evolutionary origins. A few researchers have specifically linked the use of these terms to avoidance contexts. For instance, McGregor (1996, p. 220) stated that the Gooniyandi terms 'are restricted to circumstances in which at least one of the persons, usually the referent, is in a strong in-law avoidance relationship with ego'. Of Mawng's *Kunteypi* trirelational terms, Singer et al. (in prep.) stated that 'nowadays only some terms are used, mainly those that refer to people for whom respect or avoidance is necessary such as opposite-sex siblings, mother-in-law and poison-cousin'.[18] For a number of languages,[19] it is evident that at least some of the trirelational terms are used when there is an avoidance relationship between two people in the implicated triad, or when one person in the triad is deceased (e.g. Walmajarri, Richards & Hudson 1990, p. 129). Thus, for 15 of the 23 languages in Figure 61, information

---

18   Cf. McConvell (1982, pp. 104–6) on Gurindji, and Green (1998, p. 41) on Alyawarr and eastern Anmatyerr.
19   Alyawarr and eastern Anmatyerr (Green 1998), Bininj Gunwok (Garde 2013), Dalabon (Evans & Garde 2013), Djambarrpuyŋu (Wilkinson & Zorc 2010), Gooniyandi (McGregor 1996), Gurindji (McConvell 1982), Jawoyn (Merlan 1989), Kayardild (Evans, Johnson & Kohler 1992), Mawng (Singer et al. in prep.), Pintupi (Hansen, Hansen & Tjapaltjarri 1974), western Arrernte (Strehlow 1907–15) and Yir-Yoront (Alpher 1991).

about their usage in avoidance contexts is consistent with the proposition that name avoidance lies behind their evolutionary emergence. The fact that the remaining languages are agnostic on this issue cannot be taken as evidence to the contrary. Either the researchers did not attest to usage in avoidance relationships because it was not their concern, or the vestigial documentary evidence on these systems did not inform a view of their historical pragmatics.[20] The Amazonian data also suggest a correlation between some trirelational kinterms and constrained relationships.[21]

Conversely, the relatively transparent morphosyntax of the Murrinhpatha trirelational terms plus the view of their position within the larger array of kinterms, along with information about their usage, illuminate a historical picture of the circumstances preceding their development. When Murrinhpatha speakers had specification issues to resolve, they did nothing extraordinary. They dealt with the G+1 ambiguity by taking the most ordinary relationship-explaining clauses, and configured them so as to indirectly target the affine whose name should be avoided, by using kinterms that located these affines within descent lines that were terminologically distinguished at G+2. To achieve this, indirect reference was made from the perspective of Ego's children. Although a brilliant technical solution, skewing the propositus down a generation was not a result of a teleological mechanism (Croft 2000, pp. 66–71). Rather, in order to have become lexicalised, it would have been the non-intended outcome of recurrent conversational practices (Blythe 2013; Keller 1994). Triangulating through Ego's children was a logical extension of the altercentric anchoring of kinterms that was characteristic of child-directed speech.[22] Thus, they might have originated as ad hoc descriptions of avoided kin produced in the company of Ego's children ('the one he/she calls X'), performed, in all likelihood, as multimodal utterances with accompanying points or glances towards the children in question. Through routinised use, these relationship-explaining clauses became lexically fused as nouns. In the case of the terms used for reference to males (whereby = *marna* < = *mam-rna*, 3SG.SB.say/do(8).NFUT-3SG.M.IO.), this was accompanied by loss of a segment, which could be construed as demorphologisation (Brinton & Traugott 2005, pp. 52–4). Although

---

20 Banyjima (Dench 1980), Burarra (Glasgow 1994), Nyangumarta (Geytenbeek & Geytenbeek 1982; O'Grady & Mooney 1973), Iwaidja (Bruce Birch, pers. comm.), Kalkatungu (Blake 1979), Warlpiri (Laughren 1982), Watjarri (Douglas 1981) and Yidiny (Dixon & Irvine 1991).
21 Lea (2004, p. 31) attested 24 Mẽbêngôkre trirelational kinterms associated with both consanguineal and affinal kin relationships, plus 17 associated with formal friendships.
22 I am indebted to Nick Enfield for suggesting this.

these male terms, morphologically, are only partially transparent, as lexical nouns they largely retain the explanatory semantics that have been previously attributed to the clausal domain, and can be parsed as such.[23]

Exactly how similar the mechanisms by which these semantic structures emerged in other Australian languages remains to be determined. Nevertheless, pan-continental classificatory kinship and practices of name avoidance suggest that the pragmatic motivations driving their development is similar. Conversationalists always need to make reference to others such that their recipients can recognise who they are talking about. Within Australian Aboriginal conversations, depending on who is present at the time, a reasonable proportion of individuals should not be mentioned by name—at least within certain contexts. There are many ways to bypass this problem. Many involve making circuitous reference to the 'nameless' individual by triangulating through another individual. Classificatory kinship systems provide a wide range of pathways along which these triangulations can be calculated. It can be done with a regular anchored kinterm; however, a pair of anchored kinterms will calculate the triangulation with greater precision.[24] Trirelational kinterms will calculate the triangulation with as much precision as a pair of kinterms— although more compactly. Conversational preference structure provides min–max design constraints that minimise lexical bulk while maximising referential precision. In circumstances in which there is a call for referencing that recipients will recognise but where particular personal names are dispreferred because of taboos, there is a strong motivation for selecting precise-yet-snappy referential expressions. While this motivation is observable within interactional timescales in face-to-face conversation, the fruit of these motivating pressures can also be observed within evolutionary timescales.

Within evolutionary biology, morphological adaptations can enter a population when genomic mutations are replicated vertically or horizontally through virally induced gene transfer. Useful mutations spread throughout a population because they afford the organism selective

---

23 A man's WiMoBr is an avoided affine that is normally referred to with the (binary) kinterm *ngaguluk*. I asked a consultant whether an acceptable way to refer to this man might be as *kawumarna* (a term that I thought up—potentially decomposable as 'the male person that one's son/daughter calls *kawu* [MoMoBr]'). The consultant had never heard the term but, after a moment's consideration, stated that it would be an acceptable way to talk about one's *ngaguluk* (Carmelita Perdjert, pers. comm.).

24 For example, 'The person who is my uncle and your cousin' is more precise than 'my uncle' and more precise than 'your cousin'.

advantage over members of the same population that lack the mutation. In convergent evolution, analogous ecological constraints drive the selection of similar morphological structures (phenotypes) in lineages that are either unrelated or distantly related. The resultant organisms share similar morphological adaptations that are purpose-built to suit the ecological conditions they inhabit.[25] If a population within one of these lineages then becomes separated and begins to diverge, the previously convergent feature becomes a feature shared by sister organisms within a subgroup of the previous lineage. If related yet disparate populations come into contact with each other, genetic material can recombine within a single hybrid population—sometimes giving the impression of a terminated lineage. The evolutionary pictures of an organism's prehistory are often complicated by the application of several evolutionary processes within the same lineage (King 2013).

As with biological evolution, the prehistoric picture of linguistic structures can be equally complicated. A convergent evolutionary account for the emergence of trirelational kinterms need not exclude shared inheritance, nor diffusion. These processes are clearly also implicated in the evolution of these semantic structures within the Australian context. Much work remains in unpacking how many of the related forms point to shared inheritance or borrowing—or both. However, the fact remains that the distribution of phenotypically similar trirelational structures within Australia is much more widespread than the distribution of trirelational terms displaying genetic relatedness. These distribution patterns clearly point to evolutionary convergence, as implicated in the prehistory of Australian kin-based linguistic structures. The ecological constraints driving the convergence take the form of interactional preferences pertaining to the selection of person reference items. The same sorts of structure emerge because they are recurrently good solutions to the constraining pressures that drive their emergence. Trirelational structures are only one type of kin-based phenomena to emerge in languages that

---

25 A dramatic example of convergent evolution in nature is that of hummingbirds and hummingbird hawk-moths that beat their wings in a similar fashion and at similar speeds. Both occupy the same ecological niche by sucking nectar from tubular flowers using a long proboscis (Bates 1863, pp. 180–92). Other examples include the independent development of echolocation in bats and toothed whales (Liu et al. 2010); thunniform body types in lamnid sharks, tunas, ichthyosaurs and whales (Donley et al. 2004); carrion and faecal scent mimicry in both angiosperm flowers and stinkhorn fungi (Johnson & Jürgens 2010); intermittent energy-reducing locomotory patterns in seals, sharks and migratory birds (Gleiss et al. 2011); and light-skin pigmentation in both European and East-Asian humans (Norton et al. 2007).

tend to emanate unusual kin-based lexical and morphological structures. From an evolutionary standpoint, the flowering of specialist kin-based/sociocentric lexicon and morphosyntax is absolutely what should be expected within an interactional ecology characterised by expansive networks of social relations and constraints on whether individuals can be referred to by name.

Supplement

Interactional uses of trirelational kinterms in conversation are hitherto undocumented. Extract 2 demonstrates the vocative use of a trirelational kinterm as an alternative to a name. Located within a generally humorous episode of conversation, the particular token is packaged as part of a turn designed to solicit laughter. In Extract 2, one of the conversationalists uses the term *kalemamnge* to address her classificatory sister, instead of a personal name, and instead of the ordinary 'sister' term *munak*. As such, the token is part of a lexically exaggerated tongue-in-cheek proposal that is understood to be non-serious.

Research within psychology, conversation analysis and interactional sociolinguistics on joking and teasing has revealed that conversationalists deploy a variety of playful off-record markers, so as to signal that the content of teasing turns should be interpreted non-literally. These markers include smiles and laughter particles, mock aggression, use of nicknames, marked pronoun usage and formulaic expressions, as well as prosodic exaggeration (e.g. amplitude and register shifts, vowel lengthening and singsong intonation) (Glenn 2003; Haugh 2010; Jefferson 1979; Keltner et al. 2001; Lytra 2007, 2010; Miller 1986; Straehle 1993). Relatedly, lexical selection can also be exaggerated (as with 'extreme case formulations': *all, always, the most, the best, every, never*) (Edwards 2000; Pomerantz 1986). In Extract 2, we see a variety of off-record markers employed to indicate that what is being proposed is not entirely serious.

In Figure 62, four women are sitting on a beach on the estate of the *Yek Nangu* Murrinhpatha patrilineal clan, watching the sun set into the sea. The sun is a totem of the *Yek Nangu* clan. Alice and Lily, classificatory sisters, are *Yek Nangu* clanswomen. Rita is Lily's daughter. Rita and Karen are both Marri Ngarr women of the *Rak Wakal Bengkuny* and *Rak Kungarlbarl* clans respectively. Like Rita, Karen's mother was a *Yek Nangu*

Murrinhpatha woman, which is why both Karen and Rita are visiting their *kangatji*—their 'mothers' country'. Alice's late father was a prolific composer of *djanba* songs, while Alice is a singer.

Figure 62: A video still corresponding to Lily's line 46 in Extract 2—*Bere, kalemamnge tepala murriny nartwardangu*, 'Right, deaf-one "sister", take it away!'
Source: Author.

Extract 2: Nanthak (20110828_JB_video_GYHM100_03_673560_737630).

```
01 Alice   kanyiya kale xxxxxxx ((singing))
           kanyi=ya kale
           PROX =DM mother
           this mother xxxxx
02 Alice   (kanyirdanimin [tjung] ngumangankartngime; (0.3) nyiniya.)
           kanyirda-nimin   tjung ngumanganka         -art -ngime
           PROX    -INTENS song  1SG.SB.9snatch.NFUT-sing-PC.FEM.NSIB
           nyini=ya
           ANAPH=DM
           this one/right here is what we sang, that one.
03 Karen                  [ Yu. ]
                            yu
                            yeah
                            yeah
03         (0.4)
04 Rita    tjung pana nardirelthaka ngarra ngay teleponyu.
           tjung pana nardi         -rel -tha -ka  ngarra
           song  RCG  2SG.SB.4be.PIMP-sing-PIMP-TOP LOC
           ngay telepon  =yu
           1SG.POSS telephone=DM
           That song you mob were singing is on my telephone (mobile).
05         (1.8)
06 Karen   kanyi ngawu (0.4)[kardu mere pumengewiyewiye nekiyu.] ((fortissimo)).
           kanyi ngawu kardu    mere
           PROX  hey   NC:HUMAN NEG
           pume            -nge      -wiye -wiye neki=yu
           1NS.INC.RR.SB.FUT-3SG.F.IO-be_bad-RDP  1PL =DM
           Hey look, we mustn't make fun of her/be disrespectful of her,
08                        [ ((pointing at Rita))             ]
09         (0.7)
```

```
10 Karen   kardu  kardu    yertpala i kardu   karnardurturt dininginthadha;
           kardu     kardu     yertpala  i    kardu     karnardurturt
           NC:HUMAN NC:HUMAN cycad    and NC:HUMAN crocodile
           dini            -ngintha    -dha
           1SG.SB.be(4).PIMP-3DU.FEM.NSIB-PIMP
           The cycad person and the crocodile person who are not sisters
           were sitting down (here).
11         (0.4)
12 Karen   manyenuwardapi [murriny tjung wardawa]
           ma            -nye          -nu -warda=pi
           3SG.SB.8make.FUT-1DU.INC.IO-FUT-TEMP =3SG.SB.8sit.FUT
           murriny tjung warda=wa
           NC:HUMAN song  TEMP =EMPH
           She has to make up a song for us two
13 Alice                [ha ha ha ha ha    mere] ngunyip(h)arlnukun;
                           mere ngu              -nyi  -parl-nukun
                           NEG  1SG.SB.23slash.FUT-2SG.IO-name-FUTIRR
                           ha ha ha ha ha    I won't make up a song for you
14 Karen   [punyiparllu. ]
           pu              -nyi  -parl-nu
           3SG.SB.23slash.FUT-2SG.IO-name-FUT
           She's gotta make up a song for us,
15 Lily    [(ngardathung)]
           ????
16 Unid    Mm.
17 Karen   ngarra kangatji peningintha puninkumardartjputjthanginthadini;
           ngarra kangatji         peningintha
           LOC    mother's_country 3DU.F.NSIB.POSS
           puni            -nku  -mardartjputj-tha-ngintha    =dini
           2SG.SB.23slash.PIMP-3DC.DO-relax         -PIMP-3DU.F.NSIB=3SB.SB.1sit.PIMP
           in which the two non-sisters were relaxing on their mothers'
           country...
18         (.)
19 Lily    ku[ngini damatha nyinika patha nyiniyu]
           kungini damatha nyini-ka   patha nyini=yu
           evening INTS    ANAPH-TOP good  ANAPH=DM
           In the evening, That's a good idea.
20 Karen   [nandji tina  dirranginthabatthadini ]
           nandji tina dirra            -ngintha    -bat-tha =dini
           NC:RES sun   3SG.SB.28watch.PIMP-3DU.F.NSIB-see-PIMP=3SG.SB.1sit.PIMP
           ...the two of them were looking at the sun
21 Alice   [(                                  )]
22         (0.6)
23 Karen   nandji tina dirranginthabatthadini.
           nandji tina dirra            -ngintha    -bat-tha =dini
           NC:RES sun   3SG.SB.28watch.PIMP-3DU.F.NSIB-see-PIMP=3SG.SB.1sit.PIMP
           ...the two of them were looking at the sun.
           ::              ::                  ::              ::
           ::              ::                  ::              ::
39 Alice   ngha ngha ha ha ha ha
40 Karen   kardu wakal bengku::ny kardu rak kungarlbarl;
           kardu    wakal_bengkuny kardu     rak kungarlbarl
           NC:HUMAN clan_name      NC:HUMAN clan clan_name
           A wakal bengkuny clanswoman and a rak kungarlbarl clanswoman
41         (1.1)
42 Karen   ?a?u? (.) panbunkumardatjputjnginthadim ngarra kangatji peningintha.
           ?a?u pan            -wunku -mardatjputj-ngintha    =dim
           INTJ 3SG.SB.23slash.NFUT-3DC.DO-relax         -DU.F.NSIB=3SG.SB.1sit.NFUT
           ngarra kangatji         peningintha
           LOC    mother's_country 3DU.F.NSIB.POSS
           poor things, the two non-sisters are being refreshed in their
           mothers' country.
43 Alice   yu[kuy.]
           yukuy
           that's right
           that's right
```

```
44 Lily     [yu:k]uy.
            yukuy
            that's right
            that's right
45          (0.6)
46 Lily     bere (0.3) kalemamnge tepala murriny nartwardangu.
            bere   kale    =mam                         -nge
            right  Mo/MoZi=3SG.SB.8say/do.NFUT-3SG.F.IO
            tepala murriny  na               -art      -warda-wangu
            deaf   NC:SPEECH 2SG.SB.9snatch.FUT-get/take-TEMP -away
            right deaf-one "sister", take it away.
47 Alice    he he he he he
48 Lily     (thu[rdunkuwerlarttu]ngintha.)
             thurdu         -nku   -werlart-nu -ngintha
             2SG.SB.29Shove-3DC.IO-??          -FUT-DU.F.NSIB
            (you grab and lead the two of them)
49 Karen       [yakay   kardu- ]
               yakay kardu
               INTJ  NC:HUM
               Oh dear, we-
50          (0.3)
51 Karen    kardu panguwathu nginginthakarrktukun,
            kardu  pangu-wathu ngi              -ngintha -karrk-nukun
            NC:HUM DIST -FOC   1SG.SB.1sit.FUTIRR-DU.F.NSIB-cry -FUTIRR
            we two non-sisters might cry.
52          (0.2)
```

Source: Blythe video recording and transcription (2012).

At line 1, Alice softly sings a line of a song, then explains (at line 2) that it was the song she and some others had sung (the previous night at church). At line 4, Rita recognises the song as one she has on her mobile phone. In a noticeably loud utterance, Karen teasingly admonishes Rita (at line 6, while pointing at her, line 8) for being flippant about *her*.[26] She then proposes (at lines 10 and 12) that Alice make up a song about Rita (a *Rak Wakal Bengkuny* 'cycad' woman) and herself (Karen, a *Rak Kungalbarl* 'crocodile' woman). Laughing at the suggestion, Alice refuses to comply (line 13). In an extended turn, Karen then embellishes her proposal by suggesting that the song should recount how she and Rita have been enjoying themselves in their respective mothers' country (lines 14 and 17), while watching the sun set (lines 20 and 23). The humorous proposal is further elaborated over several lines, which, for brevity's sake, have been removed.

Seemingly as content for this imaginary song, Karen then proposes (at lines 40 and 42) that Rita, as the *Rak Wakal Bengkuny* clanswoman, and she, as the *Rak Kungarlbarl* clanswoman, are being refreshed in their respective mothers' country. Alice and Lily's overlapped agreement tokens

---

26 In the mythical Dreamtime, the sun was a woman. I presume *kardu mere pumengewiyewiye nekiyu*, 'we mustn't be disrespectful of her', to be a reference to this sun-woman. Although the lexical content overtly labels the situation as serious, the loud and feigned aggression indexes the following proposal as non-serious (Lytra 2007, 2010; Miller 1986).

yukuy, 'that's right' (lines 43 and 44), seem to endorse this material as worthy of committing to song. At line 46, Lily instructs her sister to 'take it away' (that is, to start singing). The command is issued in the imperative with a second-person singular 'take' verb. Recipiency for the command is issued with double-barrelled avoidance address terms, *kalemamnge* and *tepala*. *Kalemamnge* is the trirelational term used by a woman for a sister, 'the female that "he/she" (my son/daughter) calls *kale* (Mo/MoZi)'.[27] Sisters normally address each other (not by name) with the nickname *tepala* ('deaf' < deaf-fellow). Alice laughs at the command (at line 47) and does not commence singing. The overlapped turns at lines 48 and 49 are difficult to discern. At line 51, Karen suggests that she and Rita might cry, which also prompts laughter from Alice (line 53). Presumably, Karen is suggesting that preserving this delightful scene in song would be so emotive that tears would well up in their eyes.

A single vocative expression is normally sufficient to solicit the attention of a targeted recipient. However, in this instance, *kalemamnge* co-occurs (at line 46) with another dedicated avoidance address term *tepala*, 'deaf-one'. As such, the use of two vocatives makes for a lexically exaggerated formulation of address that signals that the instruction to start singing should not be taken literally (as evidenced interactionally by the laughter and the non-compliance). Given that no song has been composed as yet, the instruction can only be interpreted non-literally.

This particular token surfaces when personal name avoidance is expected. Yet, when coupled with an additional name-avoidance vocative, the non-minimal vocative combination accomplishes something over and above regular name avoidance—namely, the solicitation of laughter. This lexical exaggeration (Edwards 2000; Pomerantz 1986) makes for pragmatically marked name avoidance that contributes to the generally jokey interactional frame.

---

27 Perhaps coincidentally, between the two sisters sits Lucy's daughter Rita, who ordinarily addresses Alice as *kale*, 'mother's sister'. Although I've been told that an actual son/daughter need not be present to use one of these trirelational kinterms, the presence of one clearly does not preclude their usage.

Acknowledgements

Many thanks to Aung Si, Jenny Green, Elena Mujkic, Ruth Singer, Lesley Stirling and the editors, Piers Kelly and Patrick McConvell, for commenting on prior versions of this manuscript. The research has also benefited from feedback following presentations given at the Max Planck Institute for Psycholinguistics in 2012, at the 2011 Australian Languages Workshop on Stradbroke Island and the 2012 Australian Linguistic Society Conference in Perth. I am indebted to Phyllis Bunduck, Lucy Tcherna, Gertrude Nemarlak, the late Elizabeth Cumaiyi, Carmelita Perdjert and Ernest Perdjert for advice on Murrinhpatha language and kinship, and to Mark Crocombe at the Kanamkek Yile Ngala Museum and Languages Centre in Wadeye for logistical support. The research was funded by the European Research Council (StG Project 240853) and the Australian Research Council (DP110100961 and DE130100399).

References

Alpher, B 1991, *Yir-Yoront lexicon: sketch and dictionary of an Australian language*, Walter de Gruyter. doi.org/10.1515/9783110872651.

Bates, HW 1863, *The naturalist on the River Amazons: a record of adventures, habits of animals, sketches of Brazilian and Indian life, and aspects of nature under the equator, during eleven years of travel. with a memoir of the author, by Edward Clodd*, London: John Murray.

Berndt, RM & Berndt, CH 1999, *The world of the First Australians: Aboriginal traditional life, past and present*, Canberra: Aboriginal Studies Press.

Blake, BJ 1979, *A Kalkatungu grammar*, Canberra: Pacific Linguistics.

Blythe, J n.d., *The language archive*, viewed 9 August 2017, corpus1.mpi.nl/ds/imdi_browser?openpath=MPI1469729%23.

Blythe, J 2009, *Doing referring in Murriny Patha conversation*, viewed 9 August 2017, hdl.handle.net/2123/5388.

Blythe, J 2010, 'Self-association in Murriny Patha talk-in-interaction', *Australian Journal of Linguistics*, 30(4), pp. 447–469. doi.org/10.1080/07268602.2010.518555.

Blythe, J 2013, 'Preference organization driving structuration: evidence from Australian Aboriginal interaction for pragmatically motivated grammaticalization', *Language*, 89, pp. 883–919. doi.org/10.1353/lan.2013.0057.

Blythe, J, Nordlinger, R & Reid, N 2007, Murriny Patha finite verb paradigms, Unpublished manuscript.

Brinton, LJ & Traugott, EC 2005, *Lexicalization and language change*, Cambridge University Press. doi.org/10.1017/CBO9780511615962.

Butcher, A 2006, 'Australian Aboriginal languages: consonant-salient phonologies and the "place-of-articulation imperative"', in J Harrington & M Tabain (eds), *Speech production: models, phonetic processes, and techniques*, New York: Psychology Press, pp. 187–210.

Croft, W 2000, *Explaining language change: an evolutionary approach*, Harlow: Pearson Education.

Dench, A 1980, 'Kin terms and pronouns of the Panyjima language of northwest Western Australia', *Anthropological Forum*, 5(1), pp. 105–20. doi.org/10.1080/00664677.1980.9967336.

Dixon, RMW & Irvine, T 1991, *Words of our country: stories, place names and vocabulary in Yidiny, the Aboriginal language of the Cairns-Yarrabah region*, St. Lucia, Qld: University of Queensland Press.

Donley, JM, Sepulveda, CA, Konstantinidis, P, Gemballa, S & Shadwick, RE 2004, 'Convergent evolution in mechanical design of lamnid sharks and tunas', *Nature*, 429, pp. 61–5. doi.org/10.1038/nature02435.

Douglas, WH 1981, 'Wadjarri', in RMW Dixon & BJ Blake (eds), *Handbook of Australian languages, volume 2*, Canberra: Australian National University Press.

Edwards, D 2000, 'Extreme case formulations: softeners, investment, and doing nonliteral', *Research on Language and Social Interaction*, 33(4), pp. 347–73. doi.org/10.1207/S15327973RLSI3304_01.

Elkin, AP 1938, 'Kinship in South Australia' *Oceania*, 8, pp. 419–52. doi.org/10.1002/j.1834-4461.1938.tb00434.x.

Elkin, AP 1939, 'Kinship in South Australia (continued)', *Oceania*, 10, pp. 196–234. doi.org/10.1002/j.1834-4461.1939.tb00276.x.

Elkin, AP 1968, *The Australian Aborigines: how to understand them*, Sydney: Angus & Robertson.

Enfield, NJ 2013, 'Reference in conversation', in J Sidnell & T Stivers (eds), *The handbook of conversation analysis*, John Wiley & Sons, Ltd, pp. 433–54.

Evans, N 2003, *An interesting couple: the semantic development of dyad morphemes*, Köln: Institut für Sprachwissenschaft der Universität zu Köln.

Evans, N & Garde, M 2013, *The stance triangle and Kunderbi trirelational terms*, presentation at the University of Queensland, 2012.

Evans, N, Golluscio, L & Mellico, F 2010, 'La construcción diádica en mapudungun y sus implicancias tipológicas', *Llames*, *10*, pp. 49–66.

Evans, N, Johnson, P & Kohler, M 1992, *Kayardild dictionary and thesaurus: a vocabulary of the language of the Bentinck Islanders, north-west Queensland*, University of Melbourne, Department of Linguistics and Language Studies.

Falkenberg, J 1962, *Kin and totem: group relations of Australian Aborigines in the Port Keats District*, Oslo: Oslo University Press.

Falkenberg, A & Falkenberg, J 1981, *The affinal relationship system: a new approach to kinship and marriage among the Australian Aborigines at Port Keats*, Oslo: Universitetsforlaget.

Furlan, A 2005, Songs of continuity and change: the reproduction of Aboriginal culture through traditional and popular music, PhD thesis, University of Sydney.

Garde, M 2002, Social deixis in Bininj Kun-wok conversation, PhD thesis, University of Queensland.

Garde, M 2008, 'Person reference, proper names and circumspection in Bininj Kunwok conversation', in I Mushin & B Baker (eds), *Discourse and grammar in Australian languages*, Amsterdam: John Benjamins. doi.org/10.1075/slcs.104.11gar.

Garde, M 2013, *Culture, interaction and person reference in an Australian Language*, Amsterdam; Philadelphia: John Benjamins. doi.org/10.1075/clu.11.

Garde, M 2014, 'Shifting relations: structure and agency in the language of Bininj Gunwok kinship', in RJ Pensalfini, M Turpin & D Guillemin (eds), *Language description informed by theory*, Amsterdam: John Benjamins, pp. 361–81. doi.org/10.1075/slcs.147.15gar.

Geytenbeek, J & Geytenbeek, H 1982, 'Nyangumarta kinship: a woman's viewpoint', in S Hargrave (ed.), *Language and culture work papers of the SIL-AAB*, Darwin: Summer Institute of Linguistics, pp. 19–31.

Glasgow, K 1994, *Burarra-Gun-nartpa dictionary with English finder list*, Summer Institute of Linguistics, Australian Aborigines and Islanders Branch Darwin.

Gleiss, AC, Jorgensen, SJ, Liebsch, N, Sala, JE, Norman, B, Hays, GC et al. 2011, 'Convergent evolution in locomotory patterns of flying and swimming animals', *Nature Communications*, 2, p. 352. doi.org/10.1038/ncomms1350.

Glenn, P 2003, *Laughter in interaction*, Cambridge: Cambridge University Press. doi.org/10.1017/CBO9780511519888.

Green, J 1998, Kin and country: aspects of the use of kinterms in Arandic languages, Master's research thesis, University of Melbourne.

Hacohen, G & Schegloff, EA 2006, 'On the preference for minimization in referring to persons: evidence from Hebrew conversation', *Journal of Pragmatics*, 38(8), pp. 1305–12. doi.org/10.1016/j.pragma.2006.04.004.

Hansen, KC, Hansen, LE & Tjapaltjarri, T 1974, *Pintupi kinship*, Institute for Aboriginal Development.

Haugh, M 2010, 'Jocular mockery, (dis)affiliation, and face', *Journal of Pragmatics*, 42, pp. 2106–19. doi.org/10.1016/j.pragma.2009.12.018.

Haviland, SE & Clark, EV 1974, '"This man's father is my father's son": a study of the acquisition of English kin terms', *Journal of Child Language*, 1, pp. 23–47. doi.org/10.1017/S0305000900000064.

Heath, J 1982, 'Introduction', in J Heath, F Merlan & A Rumsey (eds), *Languages of kinship in Aboriginal Australia*, Sydney: University of Sydney. doi.org/10.17953/aicr.06.1.r084676628205312.

Hinkson, M 2005, 'The intercultural challenge of Stanner's first fieldwork', *Oceania*, *75*, pp. 195–208. doi.org/10.1002/j.1834-4461.2005.tb02880.x.

Hull, DL 1990, *Science as a process: an evolutionary account of the social and conceptual development of science*, University of Chicago Press.

Ivory, B 2009, Kunmanggur, legend and leadership: a study of Indigenous leadership and succession focussing on the northwest region of the Northern Territory of Australia, PhD thesis, Charles Darwin University.

Jefferson, G 1979, 'A technique for inviting laughter and its subsequent acceptance-declination', in G Psathas (ed.), *Everyday language: studies in ethnomethodology*, New York: Irvington, pp. 79–95.

Johnson, SD & Jürgens, A 2010, 'Convergent evolution of carrion and faecal scent mimicry in fly-pollinated angiosperm flowers and a stinkhorn fungus', *South African Journal of Botany*, *76*(4), pp. 796–807. doi.org/10.1016/j.sajb.2010.07.012.

Keen, I 2013, 'The legacy of Radcliffe-Brown's typology of Australian Aboriginal kinship systems', *Structure and Dynamics*, *6*(1), viewed 25 June 2013, escholarship.org/uc/item/3xp687g1.

Keller, R 1994, *On language change: the invisible hand in language*, London: Routledge.

Keltner, D, Capps, L, Kring, AM, Young, RC & Heerey, AA 2001, 'Just teasing: a conceptual analysis and empirical review', *Psychological Bulletin*, *127*, pp. 229–48. doi.org/10.1037/0033-2909.127.2.229.

King, C 2013, 'The tangled tree of life: tangled roots and sexy shoots: tracing the genetic pathway from the last universal common ancestor to homo sapiens', *Genotype*, *1*.

Laughren, M 1982, 'Warlpiri kinship structure', in J Heath, F Merlan & A Rumsey (eds), *Languages of kinship in Aboriginal Australia*, Sydney: University of Sydney, pp. 72–85.

Lea, Vanessa. 2004, Aguçando o entendimento dos termos triádicos Mẽbêngôkre via os aborígenes australianos: dialogando com Merlan e outros. *Liames: Línguas Indígenas Americanas* 4, pp. 29–42.

Levinson, SC 1987, 'Minimization and conversational inference', in J Verschueren & M Bertuccelli-Papi (eds), *The pragmatic perspective: selected papers from the 1985 International Pragmatics Conference*, Amsterdam/Philadelphia: John Benjamins, pp. 61–129. doi.org/10.1075/pbcs.5.10lev.

Levinson, SC 2006, 'Introduction: the evolution of culture in a microcosm', in SC Levinson & P Jaisson (eds), *Evolution and culture: a Fyssen Foundation Symposium*, Cambridge, Mass.: MIT Press, pp. 1–41. doi.org/10.1093/acprof:oso/9780199206179.003.0001.

Levinson, SC 2007, 'Optimizing person reference—evidence from repair on Rossel Island', in NJ Enfield & T Stivers (eds), *Person reference in interaction: linguistic, cultural and social perspectives language culture and cognition*, Cambridge: Cambridge University Press, pp. 29–72.

Liu, Y, Cotton, JA, Shen, B, Han, X, Rossiter, SJ & Zhang, S 2010, 'Convergent sequence evolution between echolocating bats and dolphins', *Current Biology*, *20*, R53–R54. doi.org/10.1016/j.cub.2009.11.058.

Lytra, V 2007, 'Teasing in contact encounters: frames, participant positions and responses', *Multilingua*, *26*, pp. 381–408. doi.org/10.1515/MULTI.2007.018.

Lytra, V 2010, 'Constructing academic hierarchies: teasing and identity work among peers at school', *Pragmatics*, *19*, pp. 449–66. doi.org/10.1075/prag.19.3.09lyt.

Mansfield, J 2013, 'The social organisation of Wadeye's heavy metal mobs', *The Australian Journal of Anthropology*, *24*, pp. 148–65. doi.org/10.1111/taja.12035.

McConvell, P 1982, 'Neutralisation and degrees of respect in Gurindji', in J Heath, F Merlan & A Rumsey (eds), *Languages of kinship in Aboriginal Australia*, Oceanic linguistic monographs, Sydney: University of Sydney, pp. 86–106.

McConvell, P 1991, 'Long lost relations: Pama-Nyungan and northern kinship', in P McConvell & N Evans (eds), *Archaeology and Linguistics*, Oxford: Oxford University Press, pp. 207–35.

McGregor, W 1996, 'Dyadic and polyadic kin terms in Gooniyandi', *Anthropological Linguistics*, 38(2), pp. 216–47.

McGregor, W 2012, 'Kin terms and context among the Gooniyandi', *Anthropological Linguistics*, 54, pp. 161–86. doi.org/10.1353/anl.2012.0009.

Merlan, F 1989, 'Jawoyn relationship terms: interactional dimensions of Australian kin classification', *Anthropological Linguistics*, 31, pp. 227–63.

Merlan, F & Heath, J 1982, 'Dyadic kinship terms', in J Heath, F Merlan & A Rumsey (eds), *Languages of kinship in Aboriginal Australia*, Sydney: University of Sydney, pp. 107–24.

Miller, P 1986, 'Teasing as language socialization and verbal play in a white working-class community', in B Schieffelin & E Ochs (eds), *Language socialization across cultures*, Cambridge: Cambridge University Press, pp. 199–212.

Nordlinger, R 2010, 'Verbal morphology in Murrinh-Patha: evidence for templates', *Morphology*, 20, pp. 321–41. doi.org/10.1007/s11525-010-9184-z.

Nordlinger, R & Caudal, P 2012, 'The tense, aspect and modality system in Murrinh-Patha', *Australian Journal of Linguistics*, 32(1), pp. 32, 73–113. doi.org/10.1080/07268602.2012.657754.

Norton, HL, Kittles, RA, Parra, E, McKeigue, P, Mao, X, Cheng, K et al. 2007, 'Genetic evidence for the convergent evolution of light skin in Europeans and east Asians', *Molecular Biology and Evolution*, 24, pp. 710–22. doi.org/10.1093/molbev/msl203.

O'Grady, GN & Mooney, KA 1973, 'Nyangumarda kinship terminology', *Anthropological Linguistics*, 15, pp. 1–23. doi.org/10.2307/30029500.

Pomerantz, A 1986, 'Extreme case formulations: a way of legitimizing claims', *Human Studies*, 9, pp. 219–29. doi.org/10.1007/BF00148128.

Radcliffe-Brown, AR 1930, 'The social organization of Australian tribes', *Oceania*, 1, pp. 34–63, 206–46, 322–41, 426–56. doi.org/10.1002/j.1834-4461.1930.tb00003.x.

Richards, E & Hudson, J 1990, *Walmajarri-English dictionary*, Darwin: Summer Institute of Linguistics.

Sacks, H & Schegloff, EA 1979, 'Two preferences in the organization of reference to persons in conversation and their interaction', in G Psathas (ed.), *Everyday language: studies in ethnomethodology*, New York: Irvington, pp. 15–21.

Schegloff, EA 1996, 'Some practices for referring to persons in talk-in-interaction', in BA Fox (ed.), *Studies in Anaphora typological studies in language*, Amsterdam; Philadelphia: John Benjamins, pp. 437–85. doi.org/10.1075/tsl.33.14sch.

Schegloff, EA 2007, 'Conveying who you are: the presentation of self, strictly speaking', in NJ Enfield & T Stivers (eds), *Person reference in interaction: linguistic, cultural and social perspectives*, Cambridge: Cambridge University Press, pp. 123–48.

Singer, R, Garidjalalug, N, Hewett, H & Mirwuma, P in prep. *Mawng dictionary*.

Stanner, WEH 1936, 'Murinbata kinship and totemism', *Oceania*, 7, pp. 186–216. doi.org/10.1002/j.1834-4461.1936.tb00451.x.

Stanner, WEH 1937, 'Aboriginal modes of address and reference in the north-west of the northern Territory', *Oceania, VII*, pp. 300–15. doi.org/10.1002/j.1834-4461.1937.tb00385.x.

Straehle, CA 1993, '"Samuel?" "Yes, dear": Teasing in conversational rapport', in D Tannen (ed.), *Framing in discourse*, New York; Oxford: Oxford University Press, pp. 210–30.

Street, CS, 1987, *An introduction to the language and culture of the Murrinh-Patha*, Darwin: Summer Institute of Linguistics, Australian Aborigines Branch.

Strehlow, C 1907–15, *Die Aranda Und Loritja-Stämme in Zentral-Australien*, Frankfurt am Main: Joseph Baer & Co.

Taylor, J 2010, *Demography as destiny: schooling, work and Aboriginal population change at Wadeye*, Canberra: Centre for Aboriginal Economic Policy Research, The Australian National University.

Walsh, MJ 1976, The Murinypata language of north west Australia, PhD thesis, The Australian National University.

Wilkinson, M & Zorc, RD 2010, 'Djambarrpuyŋu Toolbox Import (2010-04-28)', *AUSTKIN*, viewed 7 July 2013, austkin.net.

Appendix 4: A Guide to Transcription Conventions

Abbreviations used in this paper: ANAPH = 'anaphoric' demonstrative, DC = 'daucal' (the morphological collapse of dual and paucal), DIST = distal demonstrative, DM = discourse marker, DO = direct object, DU = dual, EMPH = emphatic, F = feminine, FOC = focus, FUT = future tense, FUTIRR = Future irrealis, INC = inclusive of the addressee, INTJ = an interjection, INTS = intensifier, IO = indirect object, M = masculine, NC:ANM = nominal animate class, NC:HUM = nominal 'human' class (living Aboriginal people), NC:RES = nominal 'residue' class, NEG = negation, NFUT = non-future tense, NS = non-singular, NSIB = non-sibling, PC = paucal (several), PIMP = past imperfective, PL = plural, POSS = possessive, PROX = proximal demonstrative, RR = reflexive/reciprocal, SB = Subject, SG = singular, TEMP = temporal adverbial, TOP = topic, * (as in *word*) = reconstructed form or posited ancestral form. 1, 2, 3 = first, second, third person. Additional numbers between 1–38 convey verb class. For example, 3SG.SB.19Poke.PIMP expresses the fusion of: third singular subject, 19 'poke' verbal classifier, and past imperfective.

Kinterm abbreviations: Br = brother/brother's, Ch = child, Da = daughter/daughter's, Fa = father/father's, Hu = husband/husband's, m = man's [kin], Mo = mother/mother's, Pa = parent, Sb = sibling, So = son/son's, w = woman's [kin], Wi = wife/wife's, y = younger [kin], Zi = sister, sister's. For example: mZiDaCh = man's sister's daughter's child.

Symbols relating to the transcription of speech:

```
[ ]         Overlapping speech.
(0.9)       Silence (i.e., 0.9 seconds)
(.)         0.1 seconds of silence.
xxx xx      Indiscernible speech.
```

13. GENESIS OF THE TRINITY

(text)	Difficult to discern text. Bracketing indicates either a best guess at transcription or text alleged by consultants that I believe to be dubious
((text))	Transcriber's comments
?	Fully rising terminal intonation.
.	Fully falling terminal intonation.
;	Mid-low falling terminal intonation.
,	lightly rising terminal intonation.

Index

This index is subdivided into a 'General' section, for people, places and themes, and a 'Language group/subgroup/family' section for searching by linguistic areas.

General

Albany, WA 24
Alice Springs, NT 325, 326, 329, 346
Allen, Nicholas 6, 221, 261, 262
Alpine area/region 157, 158, 164, 166, 170
alternate generations 221, 228, 318, 382
Ambrym, Vanuatu 50
Annan River Tribe *see* Kuku Nyungkul in Language group/subgroup/family section below
Arabana 144, 367
Aranda kinship (structural type) 32, 391, 394, 404, 443, 444, 449, 450
Arnhem Land 6, 11, 12, 14, 34, 107, 274, 275, 286, 293, 294, 304, 306, 307, 308, 310, 311
Ashburton River district, WA 179–181, 183, 184
Austin, Peter 180, 186, 187, 189, 191, 193, 196, 197, 199, 217
AustKin 1, 3, 4, 5, 7, 8, 49, 70, 74, 77
avoidance 57, 114, 115, 367, 401, 438–441, 451–455, 461
see also taboo

Barker, Captain 24
Barkly Tableland 274, 288, 304, 311
Barranbinya 148, 149, 154
Barrow Creek (Telegraph Station) 329, 333
Barwick, Diane 329, 333
Bates, Daisy 170, 180, 183–190, 192–197
Beckett, Jeremy 152, 153, 154, 169, 171
Berndt, Ronald & Catherine 55, 65, 67, 108, 110, 111, 113–117, 119, 121, 123, 125, 142, 148, 163, 169, 183–185, 370, 371, 374
betrothal 16, 115, 116
Bickerton Island 379–381
Birdsell, Joseph 53, 63, 68
Blackburn, Kevin 47, 53
Blake, Barry 87, 147, 149, 154–156, 159, 160, 164, 167
Blythe, Joe 17, 448, 449, 451, 452, 454, 460
Boongarie, King 23
Bourdieu, Pierre 107, 133
Breen, Gavan J. 147, 249, 255, 346, 392–394, 397, 400, 402, 408–412
Bulmer, Reverend John 150

Cameron, A. L. P. 149, 150
Cape Conway 23
Cape York (Peninsula) 169, 189, 220, 224, 227–230, 232, 233, 234, 243, 245
Central Victoria 141, 151, 154, 162, 163
ceremonial exchange 66, 68
China 50
Chitchica 328, 372
chronological phases 342, 350
chronology
   absolute 353
   relative 323, 341, 347
circuitous reference/circumlocutory terms 439, 441
clan 1, 2, 8–13, 48, 50, 91, 93, 95, 97, 100, 232, 243–245, 250
   matriclans (*aka* matrilineal clans, matries) 17, 92, 93, 94, 97, 98
   patriclans (*aka* patrilineal clans) 11, 98, 179, 180, 186, 192, 196, 197, 198
Clark, Ian 149, 155, 159, 160, 167
classificatory relationship 4, 5, 21, 34, 369, 370, 372, 375, 383, 384
climate change 263
clusters, colour-coded 280–282, 307, 311, 312
coastal Wik 371–373
Cobourg Peninsula 14, 24, 286, 308, 310, 311
cockatoo 92–94, 96, 159–161, 166, 170
cognate 395, 396, 400, 406, 409, 411, 414, 416, 419–423
colexification 272, 273, 275–278, 280–282
   bee terms 219, 220, 229, 230, 233, 234, 236–240, 242, 245, 256, 257
   bird terms 219, 227, 232, 238, 239
   blood and shade 252
   body 271, 272, 278, 281–283, 285, 286, 289, 290, 297, 298, 299, 300
   country 278, 282, 293, 294, 296–297
   dermis 278, 281–283, 285–287, 299, 308, 309, 310, 311
   flavour 278, 282, 286, 288, 291, 299, 301
   hair 291, 292, 297, 299, 306, 308, 311
   head 278, 282, 283, 291, 292, 298, 306, 308, 311
   shadow 278, 282, 285, 293, 306
   smell 271, 278, 281, 286, 287, 307, 311
   sweat 271, 286, 287, 299, 311
   voice 283, 286, 299
'company' 124
compound names, development of 130, 131
Confalonieri 309
conflict, causes of 124, 126
connubium 220, 231, 304
convergent evolution 431, 432, 438, 456
conversation analysis 457
Cook, James 22, 23
Cooper Basin 141, 144, 146, 148, 151, 163, 167, 169
Cooper, Joe 309, 310
Cornally, James 184
cross-cousins 10, 34
   marriage, sister-exchange 34, 61
Crowley, Terry 243
cultural blocks 61
cultural contact 165, 166

Dampier, William 22, 23
Darling River 141, 148, 151, 161, 162, 164, 167, 168–170
Darwin, Charles 23
Davidson, Daniel 8, 33, 47, 48, 57, 61, 62, 66, 162, 224, 226

Dawson, James 85, 86, 87, 88, 89, 90, 91, 93, 95, 96, 99, 100, 101, 150, 151
deceased estate (landholding) 90, 99
Dharumbal 248, 254
disputation 107, 126, 127, 131, 133
distance
   genealogical 369, 375
   spatial 363, 369, 370–375, 378, 382
Dixon, R. M. W. 151, 163
Djamindjung (*aka* Jaminjung) 368, 370, 438, 443
Dorre Island 184, 196
Dousset, Laurent 4, 8, 16, 43, 49, 52, 59, 75, 261, 352, 375, 376, 378
Dravidian kinship 3, 6, 27, 30, 31, 35
dual classification systems 170, 171
Durkheim, Emile 32
Dutch 449, 450

ecology, adaptation to environment 63, 64
elicitation 433, 440, 441
Elkin, A. P. 15, 32, 33, 35, 58, 141, 142, 144–148, 163, 167, 169, 324, 366–368, 373, 375, 383, 384
empiricism 35
Engels, Friedrich 31
estate groups, merger and extinction 96, 100
ethnogenesis 260
etymology 10, 11, 140, 154, 157, 162
Evans, Nicholas 284, 289, 291, 302
exogamy 6, 62, 63, 72, 240, 241, 243, 245, 263
   family 89, 90, 96
extension (*also* extensionist theory) 221, 364, 386, 387

Falkenberg, Aslaug & Johannes 368, 370, 371, 380, 443, 446, 447, 450
Fison, Lorimer 1, 2, 3, 8, 25, 26, 27, 29, 30, 31, 32, 33, 47, 49, 59, 150, 364, 384
Fleck, David 221, 259, 260
François, Alex 272, 276, 277, 311

Garde, Murray 111, 112, 113, 117, 123, 431, 434, 451, 453
Gardner, Helen 26, 29, 30, 31
generalised exchange 34
generational levels/generational moieties 50–52, 58, 74, 319–321, 391, 393, 394, 398, 400, 409, 411, 420, 421, 424
German historical school 31
Gillen, Francis James 15, 32, 317, 319, 325, 326, 328, 329, 331, 333, 336, 338, 346, 349, 351, 352
see also Spencer, Walter Baldwin
Godelier, Maurice 4, 26, 261
Graebner, F. 56
Grampians 86, 87
Groote Eylandt 372, 378–381
Gulf of Carpentaria 274, 282, 285, 288, 291, 292, 299, 304, 306, 309, 391, 393, 394, 399, 406, 407, 409, 413, 420, 421, 423, 424
Gunbalanya 108, 109, 110, 113, 116, 118, 126, 131
Gunmogurrgurr names 108, 117, 118, 119, 120, 121, 122, 123, 124, 129, 130, 131
Gurindji 432, 437, 452, 453

harmonic/ disharmonic generation 117
see also generational levels/ generational moieties
Harts Range 326, 345

Henderson, John & Dobson, Veronica 319, 320, 326, 327, 345
Hermannsburg Mission 325–329
Hiatt, Les 34, 35, 369, 380, 381
historical linguistics 2, 10, 140, 263
historical particularism 32
Hockings, H. J. 233, 234, 238
homonymy 294–295
Hosokawa, Komei 183
Howitt, A. W. 1–3, 8, 9, 25–27, 29–33, 47, 48, 49, 55, 59, 85–91, 93, 94, 96, 98, 100, 141, 142, 145–162, 165, 169, 170, 232, 234–240, 261, 327, 333, 334, 364, 370, 384
  see also Fison, Lorimer

Ilpira (*aka* Ilpirra) 323, 324, 328–331, 336, 345, 350
indirect reference 440, 454
inheritance (linguistic) 165, 166, 225, 226, 263
initial K dropping 250
  see also truncation
initial K/P alternation 249, 250
initiation 48, 53
interactional analysis 436, 452
interactional preferences 421, 456

Jaminjung *see* Djamindjung
Jemmy, King 23

Kakadu (park area; *see also* Gaagudju language group in Language group/subgroup/family section below) 108, 109, 110, 127
Kariera (structural type) 5, 32, 61, 223, 443, 444, 449 *for the language see* Kariyarra *under* Language group/subgroup/family section below
Keen, Ian 183, 444
Kempe, Reverend H. 327

Kimberley district, WA 22, 274, 282, 288, 290, 291, 292, 303, 304, 305
king plates 23
kinship algebra 35
kinship terms 1, 3, 4, 5, 15–17, 108, 110, 112, 119, 221, 391–426
  altercentric 433, 454
  amalgamation 231, 256, 258, 260, 263
  asymmetry 391, 393, 394, 400, 402, 406, 407
  borrowing 111, 148, 153, 155, 156, 166, 335, 336, 339–348, 354, 393, 397, 411–415, 417, 418, 422, 443 *see also* loan(word)
  direction of spread 141, 144, 145, 354
  dyadic 436, 437
  egocentric 1, 71, 108, 110–112, 117, 132
  generic terms 271–275, 281, 297, 298, 299
  skewing 383, 450, 451, 454
  trirelational 17, 18, 431–451
kin types 3
Koch, Grace 343
Koch, Harold 317, 333, 342, 343, 345, 349
Kulturkreis 56, 57

Lake Eyre group 141
Lake Nash 332, 355
Lakes group 142
Lamarck, Jean-Baptiste 23
land tenure 3
  land claims 64, 127
  Land Rights Act see land claims
  native title 7, 8, 9, 59, 64
Lang, John Dunmore 23
language
  diversification 166, 171
  loss 96

names 108, 110, 119, 120, 121, 122, 128
Lévi-Strauss, Claude 4, 7, 34, 35, 49, 59, 364
levirate 99, 100
lexical strata 343
lexical/typological semantics 272
lexicalisation 17
linguistic stratigraphy 253
linguo-genetic classification 139, 140, 161, 163–166, 171
Lissarrague, Amanda 146, 148, 149, 151, 157, 165, 169, 251, 255
loan adaptation 317, 343, 347, 354
loan translation (*aka* calque) 13, 155, 166, 271
loan(word) 304, 306, 317, 339, 343, 344, 347, 353, 354
   see also kinship terms, borrowing
local descent group (*aka* local group) 1, 11, 13, 58, 59, 60, 61, 63, 232
   see also clan

macrolanguages 87, 95, 96
Maia 185, 188, 202–217
Malinowski, Bronisław 32, 35
malk/malng 271, 294, 295, 296, 297, 299
Mapoon 220, 232, 243, 244, 245
maps 8, 43, 44, 47, 48, 55, 64, 65, 67
marriage
   alliance 12, 16, 34, 219, 221, 223, 224, 227, 231, 232, 240, 243, 244, 249, 370, 371, 372, 373, 377, 379, 394
   class 89, 92, 219
   group marriage 27, 28, 29, 30
   kakkali 'spouse' 113, 116
   kanjok 'cousin' 113, 116
   legitimate /illegitimate 107, 112, 113, 114, 115
   preference 444
   prescription 374–377, 380, 383
   proscription 375, 383, 384

material culture 48, 57
Mathew, John 85, 91, 93, 161, 162, 170, 231, 256, 257
Mathews, R.H. 48, 53–56, 65, 85, 91, 93, 95, 142, 144, 146, 148, 154, 159, 161, 169, 326, 327, 334, 336, 345
matrifocal residence 95, 97, 102
matrilineal descent/inheritance (*aka* matrilineality) 9, 28, 48, 59, 85, 97, 98, 100, 102
matriphratry 275, 309, 310
McConnel, Ursula 369, 371, 372
McConvell, Patrick 3, 4, 6, 7, 12, 13, 26, 29, 30, 317, 324, 328, 338, 339, 342, 343, 345–347, 353, 397, 404, 412, 417, 418
McDonnell Ranges 328
McGregor, William 431, 433, 435–437, 453
Meggitt, Mervyn 322, 328, 329, 348, 353
Merlan, Francesca 436, 453
metonymy 284
Mirarr 119, 120, 122, 124, 131
moieties
   distribution of 139, 140, 142, 144, 149, 158, 161, 162, 163, 165, 166
   eaglehawk and crow 31, 150, 151, 155, 158, 166
   matrimoieties 50, 51, 72, 73, 86, 91, 95-98, 111, 112, 151, 163, 228, 229, 230, 233, 237, 255, 257, 258
   origin of 169
   patrimoieties 12, 50, 51, 72, 91, 163, 228, 229, 230, 233, 236, 237, 238, 240, 242, 249, 256, 258, 260, 319, 320, 449
Monaro 157, 158
Morgan, Lewis Henry 3, 25–32, 261, 364

mother-in-law
    bestowal 393, 402
    exchange 403, 420, 424
'mother's country' terms 123
Mulvaney, Derek John 65, 67, 68
Murray River 149, 155, 157
Mushin, Ilana 391, 393, 401, 402, 408,
Myers, Fred 373, 374, 377, 379

name 278, 292, 293
    absolute 52
    avoidance 432, 436, 437, 439, 440, 452, 454, 456, 461
    relative 52
namesakes 179, 180
Nash, David 338, 339
nations 9, 53, 54, 90, 91
Needham, Rodney 365, 375
New South Wales 26, 32, 225, 226, 245, 255, 258
Nicholson River 391, 409
Nind, Scott 24
non-Pama-Nyungan languages 287, 288, 290
Nordlinger, Rachel 402, 416, 418
Osborne, Charles 392–394, 397, 400, 402, 408, 409

Panoan languages (South America) 5, 13, 50, 221, 258, 259, 260, 262
parallel kin 4
Parker, Edward Stone 24, 25, 30
patriclan *see* clan
patricouple 319, 351
patrifilial 9, 179, 181, 182, 188, 198, 240
patrifilial local estate groups (*aka* patriclan) 85, 90, 93, 95, 96, 98, 99, 100, 179, 180, 182, 186, 187, 189, 191, 192, 196
    see also clan
patrifiliative inheritance of language and names 122

patrilineal 9, 380, 382, 383
patrimoiety 319–323
Pax Australiana 126
Pensalfini, R. 416
Peterson, Nicolas 58, 59
phonology 317, 324, 335, 341, 342, 354
phonotactics 343, 345
phratries 11, 24, 162, 180, 182, 183, 184, 186–190, 192, 195–197, 231, 232, 245
    matriphratries 92, 95, 98, 272, 275, 285, 301, 309, 310
    patriphratries, 13, 229, 231, 232, 243, 244, 245
phylogeny 3
Pilbara 8, 32, 33, 34
placenames 128, 129
polysemy 271, 275, 277, 285, 290, 296, 302, 306, 310, 311
population collapse 109, 110
Port Essington 308, 309
pragmatic equivalence 141, 222, 231, 232, 236, 240, 245
progressivism 23, 25, 31
propositus (*aka* anchor, pivot) 1, 17, 123, 434, 436, 437, 440, 449, 450, 451, 454
protolanguages (*aka* proto-languages) 6, 7, 10

Queensland 12, 13, 16, 25, 219, 220, 225, 227, 228, 229, 232, 233, 234, 236, 242

Radcliffe-Brown, Alfred 7, 8, 11, 26, 32, 33, 35, 58, 59, 60, 61, 63, 65, 149, 151–153, 163, 170, 184, 190, 191, 223, 261, 366, 369, 384
Rainforest languages 229, 230, 239, 242, 247–249, 252, 254, 257, 258
restricted exchange (alliance) 34

INDEX

Ridley, William 25, 26, 28, 29, 31, 261
Robinson, George A. 85, 91, 97
Roth, Walter 147, 148
Royal Geographical Society 24
Rumsey, Alan 379, 383–386

Sackett, Lee 374, 377
Schebeck, Bernhard 183
Scheffler, Harold 7, 35, 364, 384, 386
Schmidt, Wilhelm 48, 56
Schneider, David 35
Schulze, L. 325–327, 345, 352
Seccin, Roy Kamarrangi 391, 397
sections 1, 5, 6, 7, 10, 14, 26, 28, 29, 30, 33, 56, 59, 61, 70, 74, 184, 187, 190–198, 273, 274, 282, 291, 298, 317, 319, 320, 321, 324–329, 332, 346, 350–354, 443
    Queensland General section system 12, 220, 225,226, 237, 245, 246, 247, 254, 260, 263, 264
semantic mapping 14, 272, 276–278, 280, 281, 311
Shapiro, Warren 183, 386, 387
Sharp, R. Lauriston 229, 230, 236, 243, 244
sibling relationship 392, 411, 424
Simpson, Jane 333–337
Singer, Ruth 453
skin 1, 2, 5, 14, 221, 222, 271, 273, 286, 297, 298, 306–310
    back translations from Kriol 'skin' 297, 307
Smyth, R. B. 85
social categories 22–25, 27, 28, 31, 32, 55, 56, 89, 257, 261, 262
    see also progressivism
social change 48, 52, 61, 65, 71, 77
social evolutionism 22–25, 27, 28, 31, 32, 55, 56, 89, 257, 261, 262
    see also progressivism

social organisation 1–4, 6–9, 12, 21–27, 30, 32, 33, 43, 47, 48, 49, 50, 55
sociocentric 1, 4, 12, 108, 111, 112, 198, 273
sociology 31
song 286, 288, 292, 302
sound change 323–328, 339, 341–347, 353, 354
    *R>RT sound change in Maric 253
South America 219, 232, 258, 260
South Australia 10
south-west Queensland 10
Spencer, Walter Baldwin 15, 32, 309, 310, 319, 321, 333, 334, 326–340
    see also Gillen, Francis James
Stanner, William 17, 368, 370, 371, 438, 442, 443, 446, 447, 450
Stirling, E.C. 326, 327, 346
Strehlow, Carl 321, 326, 327
Strehlow, T.G.H. 330, 345, 352
structural functionalism 7, 8, 32, 60, 64, 76, 261
structuralism 35
subsections 1, 2, 4, 5, 6, 8, 12, 13, 14, 15, 33, 47, 51, 52, 54, 74, 108, 111, 112, 219, 220, 222, 223, 224, 227, 231, 271–355, 443
    junior subsection names 322, 333, 343, 347–349, 354
    Northern origin theory 354
    replacements 354
sub-totem 94
succession 99, 100
Sutton, Peter 369, 371, 372

taboo 116, 182, 402, 404, 432, 451, 455
    see also avoidance
Tahiti 22
technology 23, 27

SKIN, KIN AND CLAN

Telegraph Station *see* Barrow Creek
Tennant Creek, NT 333, 336, 338
territorial organisation 100
Testart, Alain 237, 258
Tetradic 6, 221, 261, 262
Thomas, William 31
Thomson, Donald 243, 244, 245
totemic centre 191, 2014, 208–211
totems 28, 58, 87, 92–94, 126, 157, 158, 160, 180, 182, 183, 186–193, 194, 196–198, 202, 227, 237, 248, 256, 260, 263, 272, 281, 282, 299–301
tribes 8, 9, 26, 29, 30, 32, 47, 53, 54, 55, 59, 63, 90, 91, 92, 95
truncation 335, 343, 347, 354
see also initial K dropping
Turner, David 364, 366, 368–370, 372, 373, 377–382
Turpin, Myf & A. Ross 322, 323, 334, 335, 348

unattested forms (hypothetical) 336, 342, 354
universal kinship 21, 221
University of Sydney 32, 33
updating (*aka* reborrowing, remodelling) 335, 340, 349

Victoria (state) 9, 10, 85, 86, 87, 88, 89, 95, 96, 97
Victoria River district, NT 13, 26, 30
viri-patrilocal residence 100
von Brandenstein, C. G. 224, 273, 298, 299, 300

Wadeye (*aka* Port Keats) 438, 452
Wafer, James 146, 148, 149, 151, 157, 165, 169, 251, 255
Warlmanpa 321, 325, 332, 335, 336, 338–340, 349, 353, 354
Warner, Lloyd 182, 183
Western Desert 286, 289, 290, 299, 304, 306, 368, 373–380

Whistler, Kenneth 4
wife
    bestowal 393–395, 398, 399, 401–404, 407, 420, 424
    exchange 393, 396, 402–404, 424
Wilkins, David 284, 289, 291, 302, 328, 345
Williams, Nancy 183
Wimmera (district, Victoria) 86, 87, 93, 98
Wirangu 142

Yallop, Colin 332
Yengoyan, Aram 5, 62, 63, 64
Yigurrumu exclamations 108, 118, 121, 122

Language group/ subgroup/family

Adnyamathanha 142, 144, 146, 166, 170, 171
Alawa 394, 396, 399, 402, 414, 419, 420–422
Alyawarr 320, 325, 329, 331, 332, 335, 336, 339, 340, 349, 353, 354
Anmatyerre 320, 322, 325, 329–333, 335, 340–351, 353, 354
Aranda *see* Arrernte
Arandic 282, 288, 306, 308, 311, 319, 321–325, 329, 331, 332, 333, 335, 339–343, 345–347, 353, 354, 405
Arrernte (*aka* Aranda, Arunta) 15, 32
    central 323, 327, 328, 341, 346, 352
    eastern 320, 327, 328
    lower 319, 325, 328, 329, 342, 345, 354
    north-eastern 320, 326
    southern 330, 352
    western 321, 326, 327, 329, 341, 345, 347, 352

INDEX

Baiungu *see* Payungu
Bangarang nation 154, 161
Banggala *see* Parnkalla
Banyjima 437, 454
Bardi 22
Barkly 391, 393–395, 402, 404, 413–419, 421–423
Bidawal (*aka* Bidwell) 158
Bidjara 152, 251
Bininj Gunwok 110–113, 115, 116, 121, 123, 126, 128, 434, 435, 451, 452
Bularnu 411–413, 422
Bunganditj (*aka* Buwandik, Booandik) 87, 159, 161
Bunganditjan 159, 160, 163, 164, 166
Bunuban 276, 293, 305
Burduna 185, 187, 190–192, 194, 195, 202–217

Central Victoria (*aka* East Kulin) 154, 155, 156, 157, 164, 165

Dadi Dadi (*aka* Tat-tati, Thartitharti) 149, 156
Dargari *see* Tharrgari
Dhirari (Dhirrari) 144
Diyari 144
Djabwurrung 159–161, 166
Djadjawurrung 154, 155, 157, 159, 164, 165

East Kulin *see* Central Victoria

Gaagudju 110, 111, 112, 118, 119, 120, 122, 127, 128, 129
Gajirrabeng (*aka* Gajerong) 290
Galali 146
Gamilaraay (*aka* Kamilaroi) 25, 26, 27, 28, 29, 30, 31, 32, 33
Garrwa 391–395, 397, 399, 401, 402, 408, 409–414, 416, 417–419, 421–423

Gidjingali 369, 380
Gooniyandi 435, 436, 453
Gournditch-Mara 160
Guli ('macrolanguage' grouping of languages; *also* Gulidjan, Colac) 87, 88, 89, 94, 159
Gundjeyhmi 122, 128, 129, 130, 131
Gundungerre *see* Omeo
Gunnai (*aka* Kurnai, Ganay) 158
Gunwinggu (*aka* Gunwinjgu, Kunwinjku) 116, 121, 370, 371
Guwa 147
Guwinmal (*aka* Kuinmurbera) 261

Iwaidja 285, 288, 301, 307, 308, 309, 310, 311

Jardwadjali 87, 159
Jarragan 288, 296, 304
Jaru 289, 290, 293, 304
Jawoyn 436, 453
Jingulu 276, 288, 306, 416–418, 422, 423
Jiwarli 187, 192, 195, 217

Kaiadilt of Bentinck Island (*aka* Kayardild) 372, 414, 415, 421
Kalkatungu 147, 148
Kamilaroi *see* Gamilaraay
Karangura 147
Kariyarra (*aka* Kariera) 33, 59, 60, 61
Karnic 140, 142, 144, 145, 146, 147, 148, 163, 162, 167
Karuwali 147
Kaurna 142, 144, 153, 166
Kaytetye 320, 322, 326, 329, 331–336, 339–343, 345, 347–351, 353, 354
Keramin (*aka* Kureinji, Kerinma) 149, 165
Kiabara 171
Kuinmurbera *see* Guwinmal
Kuku Nyungkul 232, 234, 236, 237, 239, 240, 241

Kuku Yalanji 229, 234, 236, 238, 239
Kulin 140, 149, 154, 157, 158, 160, 161–166, 170
Kumbaingeri (*aka* Gumbaynggirr) 366
Kunwinjku *see* Gunwinggu
Kurnai *see* Gunnai

Ladji Ladji (*aka* Letyi-letyi) 149, 151
Lardil 414, 415
Looritcha (*aka* Loritja, Luridja) 329
Lower Murray 149, 150, 151, 154, 164, 165

Maar *see* Warnambool
Madhi Madhi 149, 154, 155, 157
Malyangapa 146, 151, 152, 153, 154, 163, 169, 171
Marawara 148, 150
Maric 226, 229, 233, 245, 246, 247, 249, 250, 251, 252, 253, 254, 255, 256, 406, 414, 419
Marra 286, 393, 394, 396, 397, 399, 402, 406, 411, 414, 418, 419–421, 423, 424
Marulta (*aka* Marula, Mithaka) 148
Mawng (*aka* Maung) 452, 453
Mayi languages 147, 148
Mirndi 274, 276, 299, 305
Mogullum-bitch 158
Murngin *see* Yolngu
Murrinhpatha (*aka* Murinbata) 17, 18, 368, 370, 371, 380, 431–461
Muruwari 149

Narangga 142, 144
Nauo 142
Ngadjuri 142
Ngamini 142, 144
Ngarigu 157, 158
Ngarinyin (*aka* Ungarinyin) 379, 383, 384, 386
Ngawun 148
Ngerrikudi *see* Tjungundji

Ngulupulu 147, 148
Ngumpin 287, 288, 290
Nukunu 142
Nyangumarta 437

Omeo (*aka* Gundungerre, Ya-itma-thang) 157, 158

Paakantyi 149–151
Pallanganmiddang (*aka* Waywurru) 155, 156, 158, 166
Parnkalla (*aka* Banggala) 142, 161
Payungu (*aka* Baiungu) 187, 196, 217
Pintupi 374, 377
Pirladapa 146
Pitta-Pitta 147
Punthamara 146

Rembarrnga 296

Talaindji (*aka* Thalanyji) 187, 196, 202–217
Tangkic 292, 391, 394, 395, 398, 406, 408, 412, 414, 415, 418, 421–423
Tat-tati *see* Dadi Dadi
Tharrgari (*aka* Dargari) 187, 195
Tharti-tharti *see* Dadi Dadi
Thura-Yura 142–144, 163, 164, 166
Tjungundji (*aka* Ngerrikudi) 243, 244, 245

Ungarinyin *see* Ngarinyin

Waanyi 16, 391–424
Wadi Wadi 149, 155
Wadigali 146, 163
Wakaya 394, 409, 411–413, 417, 422
Wakka-Kabic (*aka* Waka-Kabic) 233–235, 248, 254, 256, 257
Walgalu 157, 158
Walmajarri 453
Wambaya 393, 416–418, 422, 423

Wangaaypuwan (*aka* Wongaibon) 148, 151–153, 170
Wangkamanha (*aka* Wonkamala) 142, 144
Wangkangurru 142, 144, 147
Wangka-Yutjuru 147
Wangkumarra 146, 171, 255
Warlpiri 3, 15, 16, 222, 223, 317, 321, 322, 324, 325, 328, 329, 333, 335–341, 343–354, 347–349, 351–355, 392, 394, 404–407, 414, 415, 419–421
Warluwarra 411
Warluwarric 391, 392, 396, 404, 411–415, 417, 418, 421–424
Warnungmanggala of Groote Eylandt 372
Warray 223, 225
Warrnambool (macrolanguage) 87, 88, 89, 94, 159–162, 164
Warumungu 321, 326, 332, 334–341, 349, 351, 352, 354, 355
Wathawurrung 154, 155, 164, 166
Waywurru *see* Pallanganmiddang
Weki-Weki 149
Wemba Wemba 159, 161, 165
Wergaia 155, 159, 161
Wik-Mungkan 371, 372
Wilyakali 367
Wolmalla (*aka* Wulmala) 339
Wotjobaluk 89, 94, 95
Wunamura 147

Ya-itma-thang *see* Omeo
Yabula Yabula 155
Yalarnnga 147
Yanda 147
Yandruwandha 144, 146
Yanyuwa (*aka* Yanyula) 286, 288, 292, 299, 301, 302, 393, 395, 408–415, 417–419, 422, 423
Yaralde 372, 373
Yardliyawarra 144, 163
Yari-Yari 149, 155

Yarli 144–146, 157, 163, 163, 164
Yawarrawarrka (*aka* Yowerawarrika nation) 144, 146
Yinjirlanji 409, 411–413, 422
Yitha Yitha 149, 155
Yolngu (*aka* Murngin) 6, 12, 34, 35, 182, 183
Yorta Yorta 154–158, 164, 166
Yotic 164
Yuin 157, 164
Yukulta 391, 398, 406, 414, 415, 422
Yuyu 149, 165

www.ingramcontent.com/pod-product-compliance
Lightning Source LLC
Chambersburg PA
CBHW041437300426
44114CB00026B/2916